This collection of essays presents the most recent work by sixteen scholars from Canada, Germany, Great Britain, and the United States on Germany's stormy and problematic encounter with mass politics from the time of Bismarck to the Nazi era. The history of elections, narrowly conceived, is abandoned in favor of a broader inquiry into the roots of German political loyalties and their relationship to the historic cleavages of class, gender, language, religion, generation, and locality.

PUBLICATIONS OF THE GERMAN HISTORICAL INSTITUTE
WASHINGTON, D.C.

Edited by Hartmut Lehmann
with the assistance of Kenneth F. Ledford

*Elections, Mass Politics, and Social Change
in Modern Germany*

THE GERMAN HISTORICAL INSTITUTE, WASHINGTON, D.C.

The German Historical Institute is a center for advanced study and research whose purpose is to provide a permanent basis for scholarly cooperation between historians from the Federal Republic of Germany and the United States. The Institute conducts, promotes, and supports research into both American and German political, social, economic, and cultural history, into transatlantic migration, especially in the nineteenth and twentieth centuries, and into the history of international relations, with special emphasis on the roles played by the United States and Germany.

Other books in the series

Hartmut Lehmann and James J. Sheehan, Editors, *An Interrupted Past: German-Speaking Refugee Historians in the United States after 1933*

Carol Fink, Axel Frohn, and Jürgen Heideking, Editors, *Genoa, Rapallo, and European Reconstruction in 1922*

David Large, Editor, *Contending with Hitler: Varieties of German Resistance in the Third Reich*

Elections, Mass Politics, and Social Change in Modern Germany

NEW PERSPECTIVES

Edited by
LARRY EUGENE JONES
and
JAMES RETALLACK

GERMAN HISTORICAL INSTITUTE
Washington, D.C.

CAMBRIDGE
UNIVERSITY PRESS

Published by the Press Syndicate of the University of Cambridge
The Pitt Building, Trumpington Street, Cambridge CB2 1RP
40 West 20th Street, New York, NY 10011-4211, USA
10 Stamford Road, Oakleigh, Victoria 3166, Australia

© German Historical Institute, 1992

First published 1992

Printed in the United States of America

Library of Congress Cataloging-in-Publication Data
Elections, mass politics, and social change in modern Germany / edited by Larry Eugene Jones and James Retallack.
p. cm. – (Publications of the German Historical Institute, Washington, D.C.)
Papers from a meeting of the German History Society, held in Toronto in Apr. 1990
Includes index.
ISBN 0-521-41846-10 – 0-521-42912-9 (pbk.)
1. Political participation – Germany – History – Congresses.
2. Elections – Germany – History – Congresses. 3. Political culture – Germany – History – Congresses. I. Jones, Larry Eugene.
II. Retallack, James N. III. German History Society (Great Britain)
IV. Series: Publications of the German Historical Institute.
JN3838.E44   1992
323'.42'0943 – dc20   91-33086
                                                                 CIP

A catalog record for this book is available from the British Library.

ISBN 0-521-41846-1 hardback
ISBN 0-521-42912-9 paperback

TO

Matthew Rosenbloom-Jones
Stuart Retallack
Hanna Retallack

Contents

Preface   *page* ix
Contributors   xi

Introduction: Political Mobilization and Collective Identities in Modern German History   *Larry Eugene Jones and James Retallack*   1

PART ONE
ELECTORAL POLITICS IN AN AUTHORITARIAN REGIME

1. Interpreting Wilhelmine Elections: National Issues, Fairness Issues, and Electoral Mobilization *Brett Fairbairn*   17
2. Antisocialism and Electoral Politics in Regional Perspective: The Kingdom of Saxony *James Retallack*   49
3. The Liberal Power Monopoly in the Cities of Imperial Germany *Hartmut Pogge von Strandmann*   93
4. Reichstag Elections in the Kaiserreich: The Prospects for Electoral Research in the Interdisciplinary Context *Peter Steinbach*   119

PART TWO
GENDER, IDENTITY, AND POLITICAL PARTICIPATION

5. Women, Gender, and the Limits of Political History in the Age of "Mass" Politics *Eve Rosenhaft*   149
6. Gender and the Culture of Work: Ideology and Identity in the World Behind the Mill Gate, 1890–1914 *Kathleen Canning*   175

7. Serving the Volk, Saving the Nation: Women in the Youth Movement and the Public Sphere in Weimar Germany   *Elizabeth Harvey*   201
8. Modernization, Emancipation, Mobilization: Nazi Society Reconsidered   *Jill Stephenson*   223

PART THREE
LOCAL DIMENSIONS OF POLITICAL CULTURE

9. Democracy or Reaction? The Political Implications of Localist Ideas in Wilhelmine and Weimar Germany   *Celia Applegate*   247
10. Communist Music in the Streets: Politics and Perceptions in Berlin at the End of the Weimar Republic   *Richard Bodek*   267
11. Weimar Populism and National Socialism in Local Perspective   *Peter Fritzsche*   287
12. Political Mobilization and Associational Life: Some Thoughts on the National Socialist German Workers' Club (e.V.)   *Roger Chickering*   307

PART FOUR
THE NATIONAL PERSPECTIVE: CONTINUITIES AND DISCONTINUITIES

13. 1918 and All That: Reassessing the Periodization of Recent German History   *Stuart T. Robson*   331
14. Generational Conflict and the Problem of Political Mobilization in the Weimar Republic   *Larry Eugene Jones*   347
15. The Social Bases of Political Cleavages in the Weimar Republic, 1919–1933   *Jürgen W. Falter*   371
16. The Formation and Dissolution of a German National Electorate: From Kaiserreich to Third Reich   *Richard Bessel*   399

Index   419

Preface

It is a particular pleasure for the editors to thank those individuals and institutions that helped make this volume and the conference out of which it developed possible. When the idea of a North American meeting of the German History Society was first floated in a London pub in October 1988, it received enthusiastic encouragement from Dick Bessel, Ian Kershaw, and Kathy Lerman. Roger Chickering, Tom Childers, Geoff Eley, Richard Evans, and Michael Kater provided important advice in organizing the conference that subsequently took place in Toronto in April 1990. The Toronto conference could not have been staged without substantial support from two major co-organizers: the German Historical Institute in Washington, D.C., and its director, Hartmut Lehmann; and the Goethe Institute in Toronto and its director, Rainer Lübbren. Other generous sponsors were the Social Sciences and Humanities Research Council of Canada, the Conference Group for Central European History, and both the former president of the University of Toronto, George Connell, and the former chairman of its history department, Michael Finlayson. For logistical support, special thanks are due to Doina Popescu of the Goethe Institute; Vicky Dingillo, Gayle Murray, Eileen Thomas, and Pat Yelle of the University of Toronto's history department; and four University of Toronto graduate students: Thomas Bredohl, Robin Brownlie, Michael Cavey, and Marven Krug. The task of editing the papers was made all the more pleasant by the conscientiousness of the individual contributors, who tolerated and finally acceded to our wish to see their revised essays appear in print as soon as possible. None of this would have been possible without the critical assistance of the series editor, Kenneth F. Ledford of the German Historical Institute in Washington, D.C. We are also grateful to Frank Smith of Cambridge University Press in New York for his early and continued interest in the project. Finally, we wish to thank our respective wives, Nancy Rosenbloom and Helen Graham, for their remarkable forebearance during the final stages of a project that all too often distracted us from the more important contributions they had just delivered to the world.

January 1991
Buffalo, New York
Toronto, Ontario

Larry Eugene Jones
James Retallack

Contributors

CELIA APPLEGATE is assistant professor of history at the University of Rochester in Rochester, New York. She is the author of *A Nation of Provincials: The German Idea of Heimat* (Berkeley, 1990), and is currently working on a study of music and German nationalism in the nineteenth century.

RICHARD BESSEL is senior lecturer in history at the Open University in Milton Keynes in the United Kingdom. He is the author of *Political Violence and the Rise of Nazism* (New Haven, Conn., and London, 1984) and editor of *Life in the Third Reich* (Oxford, 1987). He is completing a book on demobilization in Germany after the end of World War I for publication by Oxford University Press.

RICHARD BODEK is assistant professor of history at the College of Charleston in Charleston, South Carolina. He recently completed his doctorate at the University of Michigan with a dissertation entitled "We Are the Red Megaphone! Political Music, Agitprop Theater, Everyday Life and Communist Politics in Berlin during the Weimar Republic." He is currently working on a study of radical culture in Weimar Germany.

KATHLEEN CANNING is assistant professor of history at the University of Michigan in Ann Arbor, Michigan. She completed her doctorate at Johns Hopkins University in 1988 and is currently finishing a book tentatively entitled "Behind the Mill Gate: Gender, Class and the Politics of Work in the German Textile Industry, 1880–1930."

ROGER CHICKERING is professor of history at the University of Oregon in Eugene, Oregon. He is author of *Imperial Germany and a World without War: The Peace Movement and German Society, 1892–1914* (Princeton, N.J., 1975) and *We Men Who Feel Most German: A Cultural Study of the Pan-German League, 1886–1914* (Boston, 1984) and has recently completed a study of Karl Lamprecht. He is currently working on a history of Freiburg im Breisgau during World War I.

BRETT FAIRBAIRN is assistant professor of history at the University of Saskatchewan in Saskatoon, Saskatchewan. He received his Ph.D. in history from Oxford University in 1987 and is author of a dissertation entitled "The German

Elections of 1898 and 1903." He is currently involved in research on German elections and mass politics, as well as on the history of cooperative movements in Europe and North America.

JÜRGEN W. FALTER is professor of political science and comparative research on fascism at the Free University in Berlin. He is coauthor with Thomas Lindenberger and Siegfried Schumann of *Wahlen und Abstimmungen in der Weimarer Republik* (Munich, 1986) and author of *Politische Theorie in den USA* (Opladen, 1990). His most recent book is *Hitlers Wähler* (Munich, 1991).

PETER FRITZSCHE is assistant professor of history at the University of Illinois in Champaign-Urbana, Illinois. He is author of *Rehearsals for Fascism: Populism and Political Mobilization in Weimar Germany* (New York and Oxford, 1990), and *A Nation of Fliers: German Aviation and the Popular Imagination* (Cambridge, Mass., 1992). He is currently working on a study of boulevard newspapers and metropolitan life in Berlin.

ELIZABETH HARVEY is lecturer in German at the University of Salford in the United Kingdom. She has published extensively on youth, welfare, and youth unemployment in Weimar Germany and has coedited with Jennifer Birkett *Determined Women: Studies in the Construction of the Female Subject, 1900–1990* (London, 1991). Her current research is on young women in the Weimar Republic.

LARRY EUGENE JONES is professor of history at Canisius College in Buffalo, New York. He is author of *German Liberalism and the Dissolution of the Weimar Party System, 1918–1933* (Chapel Hill, N.C., 1988) and coeditor with Konrad H. Jarausch of *In Search of a Liberal Germany: Studies in the History of German Liberalism from 1789 to the Present* (Oxford, 1990). He is currently working on a historical monograph on the German right and the establishment of the Third Reich.

HARTMUT POGGE VON STRANDMANN is a fellow at University College, Oxford University. He is editor of *Walther Rathenau: Industrialist, Banker, Intellectual, and Politician. Notes and Diaries, 1907–1922* (Oxford, 1985) and has published extensively on various aspects of German economic and political history in the Wilhelmine and Weimar periods. He was coeditor of a recent book entitled *The Coming of the First World War*, 2nd ed. (Oxford, 1990).

JAMES RETALLACK is associate professor of history at the University of Toronto in Toronto, Ontario. He is author of *Notables of the Right: The Conservative Party and Political Mobilization in Germany, 1876–1918* (Boston, 1988). He is currently completing a study of political journalism in Germany from 1770 to 1920 and conducting research on electoral politics in the Kingdom of Saxony.

STUART T. ROBSON is professor of history at Trent University in Peterborough, Ontario. He received his doctorate from Oxford University in 1966 and is a specialist on the history of the two world wars. He is currently revising his dissertation on "Left-Wing Liberalism in Germany, 1900–1920" for publication.

Contributors

EVE ROSENHAFT is senior lecturer in German at the University of Liverpool in the United Kingdom. She is author of *Beating the Fascists? The German Communists and Political Violence* (Cambridge, 1983) and recently coedited with W.R. Lee *The State and Social Change in Germany, 1880–1980* (Oxford, 1990). She is currently preparing a history of German Communism, as well as a social history of modern Germany.

PETER STEINBACH is professor of political science at the Free University of Berlin. He has published extensively on German electoral history, regional history, and the anti-Nazi resistance in the Third Reich. His most recent books are *Die Politisierung der Region. Reichs- und Landtagswahlen im Fürstentum Lippe 1866–1881,* 2 vols. (Passau, 1989) and *Die Zähmung des politischen Massenmarktes. Wahlen und Wahlkämpfe im Bismarckreich im Spiegel der Hauptstadt- und Gesinnungspresse,* 3 vols. (Passau, 1990).

JILL STEPHENSON is senior lecturer in history at Edinburgh University in the United Kingdom. She is author of *Women in Nazi Society* (London and New York, 1975), *The Nazi Organisation of Women* (London and New York, 1981), and most recently "Women and the Professions in Germany, 1900–1945" in Geoffrey Cocks and Konrad Jarausch, eds., *German Professions, 1800–1950* (New York and Oxford, 1990).

Introduction:
Political Mobilization and Collective Identities in Modern German History

LARRY EUGENE JONES AND JAMES RETALLACK

One hundred years ago a Prussian diplomat named Count Carl von Dönhoff reported from Dresden on a Saxon election campaign. His observations reflected a deep concern felt about the rise of mass politics in Germany. "Those who support the parties of order," he wrote, "are apathetic and weary of elections." The Reichstag in Berlin was attracting the public's exclusive attention, he noted, whereas "interest politics" were intruding at the local and regional levels of German political life. "From this," he concluded, "arises the fear that men who represent only a narrow circle of interests and who have no understanding for the issues of state that bear on the general welfare of the people will enter the [Saxon] Landtag."[1]

For many Germans who lived through the historic events of 1989–90, the electoral "game" seemed as tiresome and unrewarding as it had to Count von Dönhoff a hundred years earlier. In March 1990 voters in the German Democratic Republic gave a resounding "yes" to unification, though apparently to little else. They appeared to do so again in the all-German elections of December 1990. Yet over this period the process of political mobilization became the subject of intense and contentious debate. Although it is true that apathy was hardly a prominent characteristic of either election in 1990, Germans still reacted as negatively to the same features of mass politics identified a century earlier: the political mobilization of special interests draped in the mantle of national consensus; the sudden intrusion of highly organized party machines into previously uncontested political terrain; the preference for immediate economic solutions over a broader reform agenda; the ascendance of a "managerial" style over

---

1. Count Carl von Dönhoff, Prussian envoy to the Kingdom of Saxony, to Chancellor Leo von Caprivi, report no. 122, 24 Sept. 1891, from the files of the Political Archive of the German Foreign Ministry, Bonn, I A Sachsen (Königreich), Nr. 60, Bd. 3.

true statesmanship; and the fracturing of a national vision between the hammer of social inequality and the anvil of regional particularism. Hence, even in the midst of postwar Germany's greatest achievement, the Germans remain "reluctant modernizers." Their accommodation to what one prominent historian has called "politics in a new key" appears to be as equivocal and problematic as ever.[2]

None of these events could have been forecast when preparations began for the first North American conference of the German History Society.[3] In early 1989 the fall of the Berlin Wall and the unification of the two German states were events that few, if any, observers could conceive, much less anticipate. However, by the time thirty-five specialists in modern German history had gathered at the University of Toronto in April 1990 for a conference on "Elections, Mass Politics, and Social Change in Modern Germany," all the participants were aware that the themes under discussion had both historical and contemporary relevance. In the eyes of its organizers, the purpose of the conference was threefold. First, it would bring together and encourage dialogue among those who represented different approaches and subdisciplines within the historical guild – for example, social historians and political historians. Second, it would foster an exchange of ideas and findings from scholars in Canada, the United States, Germany, and the United Kingdom. Third, it would bring younger scholars – some of whom had just entered the historical profession – together with more established scholars in the field. To achieve these ends, all papers were written and circulated before the conference, leaving ample time for discussion in each of the six sessions. Those sessions were introduced by commentaries on the papers and questions for further discussion prepared by David Blackbourn, Jane Caplan, Thomas Childers, Geoff Eley, Robert Moeller, and Peter Steinbach.[4]

Virtually all of the twenty-one papers discussed in April 1990 were written exclusively for the conference. Only fourteen of these papers, plus two others solicited after the conference, could be published here because of limitations of space, but each of the sixteen was revised in the light of the Toronto discussions and now represents the

---

2. The phrase was coined by Carl Schorske in his *Fin-de-Siècle Vienna: Politics and Culture* (New York, 1980), 126–80.
3. On the conference itself, see the detailed report by Elizabeth Harvey in *German History* 8 (1990): 325–33.
4. The editors wish to thank these colleagues for their special contribution; some of the points they raised at the time have been incorporated in the following remarks.

Introduction

author's latest thoughts on the themes of elections, mass politics, and social change.[5] In selecting the papers for publication, the editors sought to provide a fruitful mix of viewpoints by choosing (1) papers representing important theoretical contributions to an understanding of the themes around which the conference was organized; (2) papers offering new and promising methodological departures, particularly with respect to quantification; and (3) papers based on new and important empirical research. The editors meanwhile discovered a logical symmetry that argued for the organization of the papers into four parts. Although the sequence of papers provides a broad chronological progression through the volume from the *Kaiserreich* to the Third Reich, it is immediately apparent that most papers transcend at least one political caesura (i.e., 1914, 1918, 1933) and all of them address more than one theme identified in the title of the volume. The following comments are intended to illustrate this and, at the same time, to bring the papers into closer proximity with one another.

The four essays in Part One demonstrate the various ways by which the success or failure of political mobilization in an authoritarian regime may be measured. Although each contribution recognizes the importance of Bismarck's departure from office in 1890 as a watershed in German electoral history, each also reaches back to the 1870s and 1880s to identify early shocks to the traditional "politics of notables," or *Honoratiorenpolitik,* in Imperial Germany. The first and last essays do this by raising important methodological questions. In his essay on the Reichstag elections of 1898 and 1903, Brett Fairbairn argues that although elections in the *Kaiserreich* were about power, they also involved representation and issues. Through examples drawn from these two critical elections, Fairbairn shows that on the political right "fragmentation" went hand in hand with "coalition building," often with only minimal intervention from the government. The parties of the left, on the other hand, were better able to adapt to "politics in a new key." "Fairness issues" such as taxes, tariffs, and franchise laws provided them with stirring exam-

---

5. The other conference papers were David Crew, "*Alltagsgeschichte:* A New Social History 'From Below'?"; Robert Hopwood, "Casting a Local Polity: Kulmbach, 1880–1900"; Rudy Koshar, "Against the 'Frightful Leveler': Historic Environments and German Political Culture, 1890–1914"; Adelheid von Saldern, "The Old *Mittelstand* 1890–1939. How 'Backward' Were the Artisans?"; Jürgen Schmädeke, "Reichstag Elections in Wilhelmine Germany: 1890–1912"; Irmgard Steinisch, "Labor Relations in Imperial and Weimar Germany: The Case of the Steel Industry in the Ruhr Valley"; and Zdenek Zofka, "The Nazi Appeal in the Countryside (Bavaria)."

ples of the inequality and discrimination that were built into the social and political fabric of Imperial Germany, enabling them to hammer away at the privileged position of elites in one election after another. Over time, concludes Fairbairn, these parties accomplished far more in terms of changing the political culture of the *Kaiserreich* than historians have been willing to admit.

James Retallack takes up Fairbairn's point about the need for more research on regional elections by examining electoral politics in the Kingdom of Saxony. He makes use of unpublished diplomatic reports written by the Prussian envoy in Dresden to chronicle the way party leaders, government ministers, and grass-roots agitators helped determine the outcome of Landtag and Reichstag elections. In some special cases, these reports permit Retallack to focus on individual constituency races. Here he discovers a gap between the rhetoric and the reality of antisocialist unity that merits examination at the national level as well. Retallack also discusses anti-Semitism and the challenge it posed to the *Honoratiorenpolitik* of Saxony's traditional elites. Lastly, he documents the gradual emergence of a consensus among the nonsocialist parties that the Saxon Landtag franchise should be revised in order to prevent a socialist takeover of the legislature. Although that revision was apparently improvised and passed into law with unseemly haste in 1896, Retallack argues that it can be properly understood only in the context of a long-term mobilization of the Saxon electorate.

Hartmut Pogge von Strandmann shifts the focus to what he calls the "third tier" of German government: the cities. Here he demonstrates that German liberalism's alleged subordination to entrenched elites in the mid-nineteenth century stands in sharp contrast to the formidable power base that liberals were able to establish in thousands of town halls across the country. Bolstered by discriminatory voting regulations favoring the propertied and educated *Bürgertum*, the liberals were able to compensate for their loss of influence in the Reichstag, Prussian Landtag, and other state parliaments by retaining firm control of municipal and local politics. Yet liberal influence in municipal councils was already being challenged before 1900, not only by the Social Democrats but also by conservatives in Protestant Germany and the Catholic Center Party elsewhere. By 1914 the liberals had become so committed to preserving entrenched privilege and influence locally that they no longer recognized the extent to which this contradicted the ideals they had traditionally espoused.

Peter Steinbach's contribution offers a *tour d'horizon* of recent research in the field of electoral history and raises provocative new questions for future work. Steinbach notes that the integration of different methodologies and historical perspectives promises the greatest opportunity to fuse a quantitative analysis of election returns with a broader understanding of the role of electoral politics in German history. Such an understanding, he argues, in part requires an appreciation of the calculations that motivated Bismarck to risk a "revolution from above" through the introduction of the universal Reichstag franchise. It is also necessary to consider the larger social and economic developments in late-nineteenth-century Germany that conspired to frustrate Bismarck's political plans, particularly at the local and regional levels. For when one looks to the actual effects of the democratic franchise, argues Steinbach, the question arises: "Did it remain accessible to political manipulation, or did it instead develop an independence and momentum of its own as a consequence of autonomous political developments and aspirations?" To address this issue and to explore the evolution of Germany's electoral system under Bismarck's successors, Steinbach concludes that the historian must continue to search for the best mix of methodologies and interpretative models in order to avoid the limitations in any "purism" of methods.

The four papers in Part Two represent both a broad chronological sweep and a diversity of themes. Taken together they expand the repertoire of approaches available for studying how gender determined opportunities for political participation. They also remind us that class as a category is enormously complex, that women's participation in mass politics has reflected contradictory perceptions, and that the relationship of women to the political culture and the community demands much more historical investigation. The first and last essays in particular, by Eve Rosenhaft and Jill Stephenson, present fundamentally different approaches to an understanding of gender and its role in the political process.

Eve Rosenhaft begins provocatively by suggesting a new perspective on German women as "living, breathing" historical agents who are also part of a system of organizing social perception. These two roles are, of course, closely related; empirical bodies cannot be considered as entities that exist independently of, or outside, the body politic. Yet this is what much of German historical writing has tried to do, especially when it is concerned with electoral politics and party systems. The alternative, Rosenhaft suggests, is to expand our definition of how politics works and where it takes place, so that it includes familial, sexual, and other social relations that have heretofore been dismissed as nonpolitical. The traditional definitions of politics and political history have, as Rosenhaft argues, given privileged status to men and their forms of political interaction at the expense of women. To correct this limitation, Rosenhaft argues that one should not think of politics as something that is confined to male political parties or even to the exclusively male *Stammtisch* in the local pub. Instead, politics can be found on boarding house staircases and other "social places" populated principally by women. It was here, after all, that female consciousness in the broadest sense was generated – or not generated – and here that the networks of everyday life intersected with a larger political world.

Kathleen Canning considers the social history of the German working class, with special reference to the question of class formation in the textile industry. She argues that class consciousness in the *Kaiserreich* arose in ways that from the very outset were undercut and rendered problematic by gender. Solidarities were established at the same time that institutions and practices of exclusion became solidified. Appeals for unity stood in sharp contrast to the way in which political exclusivity was ordered along lines of gender. And collective identities were elaborated while contemporaries refused to acknowledge persisting dualisms. Moreover, just as Jill Stephenson and Eve Rosenhaft show for the later period, Canning demonstrates that in the nineteenth century those dualisms coded mass politics in gender-specific terms: They associated men with skilled work, with rationality, and with political control, and women with the home, with emotion, and with subordination. Because all this was inscribed in the language of class, Canning concludes that the culture of work – not to mention the larger processes of political mobilization – cannot properly be understood until historians have embraced the contradictory meanings of production, skill, politics, and class.

Elizabeth Harvey examines the development of political consciousness on the part of middle-class women as a result of their involvement in the *bündisch* movement. In exploring how women were politicized by their experiences in this movement, Harvey introduces the question of generational conflict and shows how it reinforced the sense of alienation that many young women felt toward the Weimar Republic. Because this attitude obliged these women to rethink their roles in the public sphere, Harvey seeks to determine the extent to which women in the *bündisch* movement were motivated by considerations of gender or of generation. Harvey's conclusion is that in the final years of the Weimar Republic "generational identity interacted with gender identity to shape the ideas that young women held about their political and public role." Still, Harvey cautions, a generational approach to the study of young women in the Weimar Republic is valid "only if it focuses on the way the depression polarized and fragmented any solidarity that might have existed among young women and produced responses that were diverse and not necessarily expressed in terms of generational consciousness."

Jill Stephenson examines the extent to which the history of German women can be placed within the context of a general theory of social, economic, and political mobilization. Modernization, she argues, has had a Janus face for German women. Going beyond the mere assertion that modernization has affected men and women differently, Stephenson illustrates how the "primacy of economics" and the "primacy of biology" have interacted with each other to determine women's status and their "freedom to act as responsible individuals in modern industrial society." By examining the way in which the Nazi regime sought to define women's economic and biological roles, she addresses herself to the long-standing debate about the extent to which the Nazis are to be regarded as modernizers or the opponents of modernization. Stephenson's conclusion is that although the Nazis made pragmatic use of economic modernization to employ women in jobs traditionally reserved for men, they were at best "partial modernizers" committed to an essentially patriarchal view of women's role in society and "determined to prevent the development of individual autonomy and a democratic polity." Thus, if modernization makes emancipation possible, it does not make it inevitable.

The four essays in Part Three underscore the importance of retaining a local perspective in a historical analysis of Germany's political culture. The first essay by Celia Applegate analyzes the political implications of localist ideas in the Wilhelmine and Weimar periods. Applegate regards the persistence of such ideas as a symptom of Germany's larger failure to integrate the separate spheres of German public life into a viable national political culture. In this respect, Applegate focuses on the intellectual legitimacy accorded to localist traditions by thinkers of such disparate political pedigrees as W. H.

Riehl, Eduard Bernstein, and Hugo Preuss. She also traces Preuss's efforts, as the architect of the Weimar Constitution, to revitalize the institutions of local and communal self-administration in an attempt to involve the individual more firmly in the fabric of national political life. But these efforts, Applegate concludes, were ultimately "of little moment" and had "neither the time nor the opportunity" in the crisis-ridden years of the Weimar Republic "to integrate themselves into the structure of everyday life."

Whereas Applegate's essay approaches the local dimension of Germany's political culture from a theoretical and essentially national perspective, Richard Bodek's study of Communist music offers a refreshing excursion into politics as a dimension of everyday life in the Berlin working class during the last years of the Weimar Republic. Bodek structures his analysis of the role that music played in the life of the German worker around a single incident: a demonstration in September 1930 against the dismissal of a Communist school teacher. Bodek not only examines the texts of the music the demonstrators sang and analyzes them as expressions of working-class hostility to the existing social and political order, but he also places these texts in the broader context of increased working-class militance in the Great Depression of the early 1930s. Music served the German left as an instrument of political mobilization that activists used to forge a greater degree of working-class solidarity in the face of the "ugly reality" in which the German worker was forced to live. But the net effect of all this, as Bodek shows, was not so much to unite the working class behind the banner of the German Communist Party as to exacerbate the political divisions separating Germany's working and middle classes.

The essays by Applegate and Bodek represent two poles from which the local dimension of Germany's political culture may be considered. In his essay on Weimar populism and National Socialism, Peter Fritzsche tries to bridge the gap between the essentially national perspective Applegate takes in her work on localist ideas and the detailed attention Bodek devotes to the everyday life of the Berlin working class. The focal point of Fritzsche's study is the city of Oldenburg. Through a careful analysis of local newspapers and other primary sources, Fritzsche discovers a remarkable resurgence of political activism on the part of the German burghers that in many ways anticipated the Nazi electoral success in the last years of the Weimar Republic. What happened in Oldenburg, therefore, was not unique but part of a much broader pattern of political protest and self-mobilization directed not only against the hated Weimar system but against established social and political elites as well. To stress the antielitist and antiestablishment character of this phenomenon, Fritzsche borrows the word "populism" from the vocabulary of American historiography and suggests that the populist insurrections of the German *Bürgertum* throughout the 1920s were not dissimilar to what happened in the United States at the end of the nineteenth century.

Whereas Fritzsche's essay draws attention to similarities and continuities between the rituals of bourgeois political mobilization in the 1920s and those employed by the Nazis in their bid for electoral support, the fourth essay in this part analyzes the success with which the Nazi Party was able to accommodate itself to the forms of associational life in the Weimar Republic. In a provocative essay on Nazi political mobilization and German associational life, Roger Chickering suggests that the invasive images historians have traditionally used to explain the Nazi Party's march to power obscure the extent to which this story might be more effectively "framed in metaphors of familiarity and growth from within." Chickering demonstrates that despite Hitler's tirades against the *Vereinsmeierei* of the German bourgeoisie, the Nazi Party "grew up within the culture of German club-life." The NSDAP's spectacular electoral successes in the early 1930s, therefore, were "conceivable only in the broader context of its gestation within institutions and rituals indigenous to German associational life." The novelty of Chickering's argument is that it draws attention to the way in which the Nazi Party was able to occupy – rather than invade – the associational milieu out of which it had originally emerged. Thus, the subtle irony of the essay's subtitle: "National Socialist German Workers' Club (e.V.)."

The essays in Part Four shift the focus of the volume from the local back to the national perspective. At the same time, they address themselves either directly or indirectly to the question of continuity in modern German history. In an essay with the tantalizing title "1918 and All That," Stuart Robson questions the conventional periodization of modern German history and suggests that, to the founders of the Weimar Republic, 1918 appeared much less a caesura than subsequent generations of German historians have been prone to think. As Robson argues, the establishment of the Weimar Republic represented the "culmination of an authentic tradition of reform reaching back at least as far as 1848." Moreover, the decisive rupture had occurred with the passage of the peace resolution in the summer of 1917 and the emergence of a parliamentary majority consisting of the Progressives, Center, and Majority Socialists. The majority first tried to reform the old imperial order through the chancellorship of Prince Max von Baden and then, following the collapse of the empire, founded the Weimar Republic. All of this leads Robson to suggest that it might be more fruitful to think of the entire period from 1916 to 1923 as a "German Time of Troubles" that began with the mobilization for total war and ended with the stabilization of the Weimar Republic on terms that were essentially similar to those that existed in other Western European democracies. It would be a mistake, therefore, to dismiss the Weimar Republic either as a historical aberration that was somehow thrust upon the German people in the wake of military defeat or as an improvisation destined to be tossed back on the "trash heap of history" once it became expedient to do so in the early 1930s.

If Robson suggests that one should not overemphasize the role of continuity in explaining the collapse of the Weimar Republic, Larry Jones turns his attention to one area in which there seemed to be a great degree of continuity from the Wilhemine to the Weimar periods, namely, the political apathy of the younger generation. Proceeding from the premise that generational cleavages were "every bit as important in shaping the general course of political development in the Weimar Republic as those of class, gender, and confession," Jones examines the efforts and eventual failure of the various nonsocialist parties in the Weimar Republic to mobilize the support of the so-called younger generation. Not only did this help "set the stage for the meteoric rise of National Socialism at the end of the 1920s and beginning of the 1930s," but the political alienation of the younger generation in the Weimar Republic represented the continuation, if not the culmination, of patterns of political behavior that had first manifested themselves in the last years of the Second Empire. The failure of Germany's republican parties to overcome the generational cleavages that Weimar had inherited from the Second Empire undermined the stability of the Weimar party system and contributed in no small measure to the electoral decline of all of Germany's more established bourgeois parties.

In his essay on the social bases of political cleavages in the Weimar Republic, Jürgen Falter underscores the extent to which the electoral behavior of the voting public in the Weimar Republic was shaped by socially and confessionally determined cleavages whose origins clearly antedated the political collapse of 1918. Falter proceeds from the premise that Weimar's political culture was characterized by cleavages between three political subcultures, or *Teilkulturen,* which he identifies as socialist, Catholic, and bourgeois-Protestant. Through the use of multivariate ecological regression analysis, Falter demonstrates that whereas the first two of these were relatively stable, the bourgeois-Protestant subculture was characterized by frequent and pronounced shifts in affiliation from one party to another within the subculture itself. Moreover, the bourgeois-Protestant subculture was also affected by greater net losses to the other subcultures than either the socialist or Catholic subcultures. If one includes the NSDAP – as Falter does for the purposes of analysis – within the bourgeois-Protestant subculture, then changes within the subculture were much more frequent than moves from it to either the socialist or Catholic subcultures. If, on the other hand, one excludes the NSDAP from the bourgeois-Protestant subculture, then it becomes clear that the two liberal parties – the German Democratic Party and the German People's Party – were almost totally decimated and the right-wing German National People's Party somewhat less so by defections to the NSDAP. Although the NSDAP also benefited from less significant defections from the other two subcultures, it was the instability of the bourgeois-Protestant subculture that accounted for the party's meteoric rise in the last years of the Weimar Republic.

Richard Bessel's essay on the formation and dissolution of a German national electorate takes a closer look at the reasons for the instability of Weimar voter allegiances. What Bessel has in mind when he uses the term "German national electorate," however, is by no means synonymous with Falter's concept of the bourgeois-Protestant subculture. Nor does it refer to the right-wing German National People's Party. By national electorate, Bessel means "an electorate which . . . was prepared to accept the value and legitimacy of voting and, on the whole, to vote in a manner constructive to the existing political system." One of the great paradoxes of modern German history is that "although the German electorate took shape within a political system that lent it very little power, it dissolved once it could vote for a real parliament." In the Weimar Republic, the tacit affirmation of the existing political system that had characterized voting in the Wilhelmine Empire gave way to a situation where "electioneering was largely decoupled from the politics of government, priorities, and policymaking." Bessel examines four areas in which the explanation for the collapse of a national electorate may be found: the general course of German economic development during the Weimar Republic, the changed relationship between parties and government after 1918, the broadening of the franchise in 1919, and the introduction of proportional representation to replace the system of single-member constituencies that had existed in Germany until 1918. The net effect of these developments was to increase the voter's sense of alienation from the existing political system, to fracture Germany's national electorate along lines of "sectional interest-group politics," and to encourage a politics of irresponsibility and demagoguery on the part of those who sought the favor of the masses.

In sum, these essays offer a broad array of conjectural hypotheses, innovative methodologies, provocative theories, and, in some cases, firm conclusions. Collectively, the contributors explore and explode historical paradigms with language that is intentionally familiar, inventive, and allusive all at once. They define and redefine class and periodization. They rethink genres, they juxtapose social upheaval and gender discrimination, and they explore the political manifestations of generational conflict. Some contributors speak of mass politics in almost seismic terms: They use words like "irruption," "intrusion," "fissures," "fracturing," "spectacle," and "frustrated expectations." Others remind us of the more familiar world of everyday life. Some point to the interdependence of local, regional, and national identities, whereas others study Germans who sought to celebrate both diversity and unity, both authority and authenticity. Some describe the processes of political mobilization and the increasing importance of national issues in elections; others concentrate on the splintering and dissolution of the electorate. Some emphasize the familiar turning points in German history and the discontinuities of social and political change associated with them; others argue for a fundamentally new periodization and emphasize the many continuities stretching through the entire period under debate. Some explore the complex ways in which one can aggregate and disaggregate voters statistically. Others pose the simple question: What were "elections" really all about?

Taken together, these essays reveal that historically Germans have searched for political consensus and social stability in many different ways. Whether those quests were fulfilled or ended in tragedy has been determined not by the outcome of elections narrowly conceived, but by the broadest imaginable set of "self-understandings." Through those self-understandings, some Germans sought to overcome divisions of class, generational cohort, gender, and locality. Others tried to accentuate such divisions or to deny their existence altogether. But whatever their particular goal may have been, the Germans examined in this volume rarely sought a form of "unpolitical politics," as has so often been claimed. Their reactions to mass politics and social change, whether measured at the ballot box or by another means, were far more uncertain, and opaque, than the term "unpolitical politics" would suggest. For that reason, in the years ahead, one can expect more research on the themes addressed in this volume – perhaps along the lines suggested here, perhaps along others not yet explored.

PART ONE

Electoral Politics in an Authoritarian Regime

1

Interpreting Wilhelmine Elections: National Issues, Fairness Issues, and Electoral Mobilization

BRETT FAIRBAIRN

What were elections *about* in Wilhelmine Germany? How did the parties fare? And what does this show about the German party system? Addressing these questions, even in a partial way, requires a combination of methodologies. These range from broad national-level comparisons, to more detailed analysis of specific campaigns, to the breakdown of results into social–economic categories. Almost invariably, each of these involves complex statistical analysis.

Elections can be interpreted as being about one of three things: power, issues, or representation. How a political party views an election affects its strategy – whether to aim for targeted seats and not to contest others, to aim for the maximum popular vote, or to aim to control specific issues in such a way as to capture particular social groupings. These decisions are conditioned by the political system within which they occur and tend to be interrelated, so that the resulting strategy is a mixture of these elements with some particular weighting. Equally, how a historian views an election determines how the results are measured and evaluated. Like the politician, the historian makes a decision that is conditioned by how he or she views the political system within which the election occurred. There is a different methodology to suit each view of what is important about an election.[1]

Some of the research on which this essay is based was supported by the Social Sciences and Humanities Research Council of Canada. The basic argument of this piece had the benefit of discussions at a number of conferences – though it was first presented in April 1990 in Toronto – and a different version of some of the material appears in *The Journal of the Canadian Historical Association*, N.S.1 (1990).

1. The classification of methodologies that follows is based roughly upon those used by Nils Diedrich, "Konzepte der Wahlforschung," in Otto Büsch, Wolfgang Wölk, and Monika Wölk, eds., *Wählerbewegung in der deutschen Geschichte. Analysen und Berichte zu den Reichstagswahlen 1871–1933* (Berlin, 1978); Peter Steinbach, "Stand und Methode der historischen Wahlforschung. Bemerkungen zur interdisziplinären Kooperation von moderner

If an election is viewed as a short-term, tactical struggle for power, then the results are measured by seats won and lost. Those concerned with the state as such, rather than with society at large, tend to see elections from the perspective of representation in the Reichstag. In 1898, *Schulthess' Europäischer Geschichtskalender,* a nationalist annual review of politics, observed that the Reichstag elections of that year, "which were carried out without particular excitement, produced no substantially different composition of the house."[2] Those elections saw a decisive breakthrough in the popular support won by the Social Democratic movement. They also saw bitter fights involving agrarian and anti-Semitic populists, an effort by nationalists to make the German battle fleet into a popular issue, and an attempt by the Catholic Center Party to clinch its "decisive position" in German politics.[3] Yet the Schulthess annual review concluded that these elections were unremarkable because the overall balance of deputies in the Reichstag did not change dramatically.

Those historians who are similarly concerned with the affairs of state tend to compare seats won or lost at the national level from one election to the next. This produces a kind of "trend study," the most general and basic variety of electoral analysis. Through comparisons with preceding and succeeding elections, trend studies highlight both the continuities and the variations represented in a particular election's overall results. For Imperial elections, there have been useful compilations of results that facilitate this kind of comparison at the national and regional levels.[4] By themselves, however, and especially on the national scale, trend studies of Wilhelmine Germany are of limited usefulness for two reasons. First, trends were gradual and – as noted previously – produced few dramatic changes, particularly in the popular vote. Second, the significance of election results, especially the tallies of seats won and lost, depended upon regional and tactical elements not always apparent in the global statistics. It is not

---

Sozialgeschichte und den politisch-historischen Sozialwissenschaften," in Hartmut Kaelble, Horst Matzerath, Hermann-Josef Rupieper, Peter Steinbach, and Heinrich Volkmann, *Probleme der Modernisierung in Deutschland. Sozialhistorische Studien zum 19. und 20. Jahrhundert* (Opladen, 1978); and Hermann Hiery, *Reichstagswahlen im Reichsland. Ein Beitrag zur Landesgeschichte von Elsass-Lothringen und zur Wahlgeschichte des Deutschen Reiches 1871–1918* (Düsseldorf, 1986), introduction.

2. *Schulthess' Europäischer Geschichtskalender,* N.F., 14 (1898): 388.
3. See Brett Fairbairn, "The German Elections of 1898 and 1903" (Ph.D. diss., Oxford University, 1987).
4. Gerhard A. Ritter and Merith Niehuss, *Wahlgeschichtliches Arbeitsbuch. Materialien zur Statistik des Kaiserreichs 1871–1918* (Munich, 1980); this study presents district (*Regierungsbezirk*) levels, as well as selected state election results.

always so simple to see whether a party did well or badly compared with previous elections. National-level results may disguise, for example, whether a decline in votes won by a party was due to tactical alliances that involved foregoing candidacies in some constituencies.[5] Trend studies become more meaningful when supplemented with in-depth analysis of the context of voting (the issues, strategies, and party alignments) and of the regional and social–economic environments in which voting occurred.

Elections in Imperial Germany revolved around particular issues: army bills, tariffs, taxation, political rights, or repression. Every party concerned itself with its own set of issues. Some, like Germany's agrarian parties, advanced a single exclusive issue and sought to make it the focal point of the electoral contest; they might run candidates to raise the profile of the issue, whether those candidates had a chance to win or not. Issues are a question of political context, and the traditional way to study them in depth is through the election monograph, which typically examines a single election campaign and its results. For the Wilhelmine period, such studies have been done for the last two prewar elections, those of 1907 and 1912.[6] Other elections of the period have not been studied in such depth, perhaps because sources are less abundant, perhaps because the campaigns of 1907 and 1912 were particularly dramatic (but hence also less representative of Wilhelmine elections as a whole). Election monographs also fit the trend away from national-level studies that emphasize the role of government and party leaders, and toward approaches that emphasize broader social perspectives.

The questions of broad context and social–historical perspective imply treating election results as representative of bigger, long-term forces in society. Some Wilhelmine observers, including many Social Democrats, saw elections as battles for representation – episodes in a long-term struggle to mobilize identifiable social–economic constituencies in order to retain, spread, and deepen popular support. The advance of the Social Democratic vote was taken to represent the

---

5. Carl H. E. Zangerl is one of the few to write about this point in "Courting the Catholic Vote: The Center Party in Baden, 1903–13," *Central European History* 10 (1977):221–2.
6. George Dunlop Crothers, *The German Elections of 1907* (New York, 1941); Jürgen Bertram, *Die Wahlen zum Deutschen Reichstage vom Jahre 1912* (Bonn, 1964). See also Dieter Fricke, "Der Regierungswahlkampf von 1907," in Büsch, Wölk, and Wölk, eds., *Wählerbewegung*, 485–504; and a number of American Ph.D. dissertations on these same two elections, notably Frank Joseph Ward, "The Center Party and the German Election of 1907" (University of California at Los Angeles, 1984), and Marvin William Falk, "The Reichstag Elections of 1912: A Statistical Study" (University of Iowa, 1976).

advance of industrialization and of the proletariat. In the long term, presumably, this approach, too, is concerned with power, whereas in the short term it involves concentration on particular issues that helped the parties mobilize their respective constituencies. But the resulting view of elections and of tactics differs from the preceding views. When Social Democrats won a great victory in 1903 they hailed it as their *Drei-Millionen-Sieg* (victory of three million), referring to the votes they had gained, not to the influence they would exercise on Reichstag legislation.

Historians concerned with how parties mobilized social–economic groups usually formulate long-term studies of populations with identifiable social–economic characteristics. They then attempt to explain party performances on the basis of the character of the population studies, rather than with reference to political tactics in the Reichstag. Some examine a historic region through changes in regime, in a German version of the French school of *géographie électorale*.[7] Others concentrate on the smallest possible unit of study, perhaps a single Reichstag constituency, over the *longue durée* – typically 1867 to 1933 or even to the present.[8] This approach has been applied in numerous local studies in West Germany, with the intention of gradually constructing a "party history from below" out of the accumulation of in-depth local and regional studies.[9] The main criticism to be leveled against this approach, however, especially from the viewpoint of the mainstream historian, is that it is too fragmented to allow one to grasp the general issues and developments in electoral politics within any one period.[10] Studies concentrating not on the smallest possible unit, but on state-sized regions and, in some cases, shorter time periods, seem to strike a more fruitful compromise between appreciation of local political culture, on the one hand, and broader historical changes on the other.[11]

7. For example, Rudolf Heberle, *From Democracy to Nazism. A Regional Case Study on Political Parties in Germany* (Baton Rouge, La., 1945), esp. chapter II. There is an excerpt in Büsch, Wölk, and Wölk, eds., *Wählerbewegung,* 73–84.
8. The chief advocate of this approach is Wolfgang Abendroth, as, for example, in "Aufgaben und Methoden einer deutschen historischen Wahlsoziologie," in Büsch, Wölk, and Wölk, eds., *Wählerbewegung,* 119–24.
9. Klaus Müller, "Das Rheinland als Gegenstand der historischen Wahlsoziologie," excerpt reprinted in Büsch, Wölk, and Wölk, eds., *Wählerbewegung,* 393–408. A series of dissertations on Rhineland politics was done at Bonn University between 1961 and 1969 under Max Braubach, including Müller's own, as well as those by Heinz-Jürgen Hombach, Hans Joachim Horn, Theo Monshausen, Horst Romeyk, Anni Roth, and Hans Willi Steil. See the bibliography by Ritter and Niehuss, *Wahlgeschichtliches Arbeitsbuch,* 200–3.
10. Hiery, *Reichstagswahlen,* 26, suggests that the units of study are simply too small.
11. Besides Heberle, consider Hiery, *Reichstagswahlen;* Günther Franz, *Die politische Wahlen in*

Still other historians have investigated long-term social–political relationships by applying statistical analysis techniques such as multivariate linear regression analysis. Such analysis sets up mathematical formulas that treat party votes as dependent variables, each determined by a linear function of multiple other variables; it is referred to in shorthand as "multilinear regression." However, some historians of German elections who have used multilinear regression have noted that the procedure is problematic because of peculiarities in the form of data from Imperial elections.[12] The best kind of statistical source is unavailable for pre-1914 Germany: interviews with individual voters. Without such information, it is impossible to be conclusive about how individuals' votes changed from election to election, or what factors motivated them to vote at all or in a certain way. To infer such individual behavior from aggregate results is to fall victim to the so-called ecological fallacy, although as one historian has commented, "the fruitless discussion of the ecological fallacy has largely . . . paralysed election research."[13] Ultimately, perhaps, the subject of election analysis is not individuals in any case – even when more differentiated data are available – but parties, groupings, and populations. The historian does not study "the voter," but rather the milieu and its associated behavior.

Each of these views of elections, and each of these methodologies, is by itself fragmentary. As a result, one researcher of German elections has called for an "electoral analysis in historical context," one that combines the rigor of long-term analysis and statistical techniques with trend analysis and the careful dissection of specific campaigns and their immediate issues. Another has noted the need for "supra-regional, 'cross-sectional' monographs of individual Reichstag elections" that "take the entire party system and electoral potential of the German Reich and its complete historical milieu, in their

---

Niedersachsen 1867 bis 1949, 3rd ed. (Bremen-Horn, 1957); Dietrich Thränhardt, *Wahlen und politische Strukturen in Bayern 1848–1953: Historisch-soziologische Untersuchungen zum Entstehen und zur Neuerrichtung eines Parteiensystems* (Düsseldorf, 1973); Karl Rohe, "Das Parteiensystem in den preussischen Westprovinzen und in Lippe-Detmold 1871–1933," in Ulrich von Alemann, ed., *Parteien und Wahlen in Nordrhein-Westfalen* (Cologne, 1986).

12. In particular, the diversity and regional nature of the parties means that most of the variables (party votes) are equal to zero in most cases (i.e., in most constituencies). See Stanley S. Suval, *Electoral Politics in Wilhelmine Germany* (Chapel Hill, N.C., 1985), 268, note 12; Falk, "Reichstag Elections of 1912," 251; and Wolfgang Schulte, "Die ökologische Korrelate der Parteien in den württembergischen Wahlen zur Zeit des Kaiserreichs," in Büsch, Wölk, and Wölk, eds., *Wählerbewegung*, 454–81, and, for this point, 454. As well, most of the social–economic statistics one can use – census data, confession, occupation, etc. – are imperfect.

13. Hiery, *Reichstagswahlen*, 27, note 20.

historical depth and with systematic breadth." A third has called for an "integration of methodologies" to study not just the election but also its ideological and sociopsychological functions.[14] The challenge is indeed to integrate such analyses; the key may be to identify patterns without losing sight of particularities.

"NATIONAL" ISSUES AND ELECTORAL MOBILIZATION IN GERMANY, 1871–1912

Reichstag elections took place against a background of issues, previous election battles, public opinion, and, broadly speaking, a political culture that influenced the way in which the elections were perceived by the voters and contested by the parties. There were two distinct kinds of Reichstag elections in Imperial Germany: "national" campaigns and all the rest. The "national" elections stand out as those in which the government set the tone of the campaign with a rousing patriotic or nationalistic appeal. The pattern was set in some respects with the *Kulturkampf*. This involved an assault on the Catholic minority in Germany and a powerful defensive response by political Catholicism; together these factors decisively colored the 1874 Reichstag campaign.

With the end of the *Kulturkampf* and changes in party alignments, the pattern of "national" elections became clearest in the period 1878–1907. In several cases during this period, the Reichstag was dissolved over the failure of a piece of legislation considered essential by the government, whose ministers then took the initiative in a campaign against the Reichstag majority. These were one-issue, government-led campaigns. In this category clearly belong the elections of 1878, based on the government's proposed antisocialist legislation; those of 1887 and 1893, both concerned with failed military bills; and those of 1907, which were occasioned by a dispute concerning colonial policy. In each case there was an increased turnout compared with the preceding election (with a drop in turnout in the following election, to create a kind of peak), together with increased

---

14. Karl Rohe, "Wahlanalyse im historischen Kontext. Zur Kontinuität und Wandel von Wahlverhalten," *Historische Zeitschrift* 234 (1982): 337–8; Büsch's introduction to Büsch, Wölk, and Wölk, ed., *Wählerbewegung*, 6; Steinbach, "Stand und Methode," 231–2. See also Peter Steinbach, ed., *Probleme politischer Partizipation im Modernisierungsprozess* (Stuttgart, 1982); David Blackbourn, *Class, Religion and Local Politics in Wilhelmine Germany: The Center Party in Württemberg before 1914* (New Haven, Conn., 1980), 11; and Hiery, *Reichstagswahlen*, 28.

seat totals for the right-wing parties. These right-wing gains were due both to increases in their combined percentage of votes and to firmer tactical alliances among them (see Table 1). The losers in such campaigns before 1907 were generally the left liberals. In 1907 it was the Social Democratic Party (SPD) that suffered, whereas the left liberals actually benefited in the final results. Each of these dramatic, polarized campaigns reinforced perennial issues and party alignments in German politics: attacks on "enemies of the Reich," militarism versus antimilitarism, imperialism versus anti-imperialism.

The cooperation among the right-wing (conservative and National Liberal) parties was formalized in the *Kartell* elections of 1887, which were the definitive "national" elections in Imperial Germany. In these elections Chancellor Bismarck achieved a combination of conservatives and right-wing liberals in a systematic first-ballot alliance, cemented in this case by a military bill and a war scare against France. He thereby created a configuration that persisted in electoral politics until 1907, long after the *Kartell* as a firm coalition within the Reichstag itself was dead. The *Kartell* parties saw their combined share of the vote increase from 39.6 percent in 1884 (already a good performance) to 47.0 percent and their seat total increase from 157 to 220, a firm Reichstag majority. The 1887 elections were the only ones between 1878 and 1918 in which the government's favored allies won a majority. This success provided an inspiration and a hope – as it turned out, a forlorn one – for those same governmental parties in subsequent elections.

These "national" elections were fundamental in the formation of German mass electoral culture. They ensured that great, abstract national-interest questions were reintroduced to the electorate periodically; this, in turn, affected the rhetorical style of the parties and the way in which they defined their causes. Elections were seen as "battles" between absolute and opposing systems, so that casting a vote took on an idealized character of loyalty to a historic cause. In this respect, some later campaigns were prefigured in the *Kulturkampf* era of the 1870s, when in Catholic parts of the Reich elections revolved around the conflict between church and state, religion and patriotism, freedom of conscience and secularization. The *Kulturkampf*, combined with the campaigns against particularists in eastern Prussia, Hanover, Schleswig, and Alsace-Lorraine and reinforced by "national" campaigns and antisocialism, created a systematic opposition of "German" and "anti-German" causes, of *Reichsfreunde* and

Table 1. "National" elections, 1871–1912

	1871	1874	1877	**1878**	1881	1884	**1887**	1890	**1893**	1898	1903	**1907**	1912
dissolutions		D		D			D		D			D	D
% turnout	51.0	61.2	60.6	**63.4**	56.3	60.6	**77.5**	71.6	**72.5**	68.1	76.1	**84.7**	84.9
change		+10.2	-0.6	+2.8	-7.1	+4.3	+16.9	-5.9	+0.9	-4.4	+8.0	+8.6	+0.2
"Kartell" seats	219	210	206	**215**	125	157	**220**	135	**153**	125	126	**138**	100
change		-9	-4	+9	-90	+32	+63	-85	+18	-28	+1	+13	-38
'Kartell' %	52.9	43.7	44.7	**49.6**	38.2	39.5	**47.0**	35.2	**32.1**	27.9	27.2	**28.0**	25.7
change		-9.2	+1.0	+4.9	-11.4	+1.3	+7.5	-11.8	-3.1	-4.2	-0.7	+0.8	-2.3

Comments: The elections of 1878, 1887, 1893, and 1907 share a number of features: all resulted from dissolutions, all involved some kind of nationalist or patriotic issue promoted by the government, all saw an increase in turnout followed by a decrease in the subsequent elections (except 1907), and all saw an increase in the number of seats won by the right-wing (Kartell) parties. Note that the dissolution of 1874, following the beginning of the Kulturkampf, went together with a similar increase in voter turnout. The election of 1884 also had some of the same characteristics, but without a dissolution.

Source: Calculated from figures given in G.A. Ritter and M.Niehuss, *Wahlgeschichtliches Arbeitsbuch: Materialien zur Statistik des Kaiserreichs 1871-1918* (Munich, 1980), pp. 38-42

Reichsfeinde. These various polarizations enhanced the sense of identity of the groups who suffered discrimination (Catholics, Poles, socialist workers), perhaps even more so than it enhanced the unity of the governmental parties in the regions affected.

In some respects, the great *Kartell* victory of 1887 and all the other "national" campaigns by the government carried within them the seeds of their own negation, for they whipped up voter participation to record levels. The 1887 election saw the turnout leap to 77.5 percent, compared with the previous high of 63.4 percent in 1878. Voter participation did not dip below 70 percent except in 1898, following a constitutional change that lengthened the period between the elections from three to five years. It appears that many new voters first mobilized by "national" campaigns remained mobilized even when the campaigns changed. This increasing overall level of mobilization helped provide the fertile ground for recruitment by Social Democrats, agrarians, and anti-Semites in the 1890s. One can echo Theodore Hamerow's comment that "by initiating the age of mass politics in Germany, Bismarck unwittingly strengthened those civic forces which in time undermined the system of authority he had spent his lifetime defending."[15]

There is also some evidence that these campaigns tended to "nationalize" German politics in the sense of introducing issues common to all regions, thus reducing regional disparities in electoral behavior. This is illustrated by Figure 1, which indicates that voter participation in the different German states varied widely in the 1870s – from less than 30 percent in the duchy of Oldenburg or the city of Lübeck to nearly 70 percent in the two Mecklenburg duchies and even more in Swabia. But participation in different regions converged toward the national average as it tended upward. The "national" campaigns of 1887, 1893, and 1907 stand out as peaks where participation curves from different regions pinched together. More rigorously and more precisely, this effect can be described as a decrease in both the standard deviation and the coefficient of variation of turnout in Reichstag elections (see Table 2).

It is probably clear enough to historians what "national" elections were about, since the issues German voters debated corresponded to

---

15. Theodore S. Hamerow, "The Origins of Mass Politics in Germany, 1866–1867," in Imanuel Geiss and Bernd–Juergen Wendt, eds., *Deutschland in der Weltpolitik des 19. und 20. Jahrhunderts. Fritz Fischer zum 65. Geburtstag* (Düsseldorf, 1973), 105–20 and, here, 120. Hamerow was referring to Bismarck's decision to include universal adult male suffrage in the constitution of the North German Confederation.

Source: Ritter and Niehuss, pp. 67-96

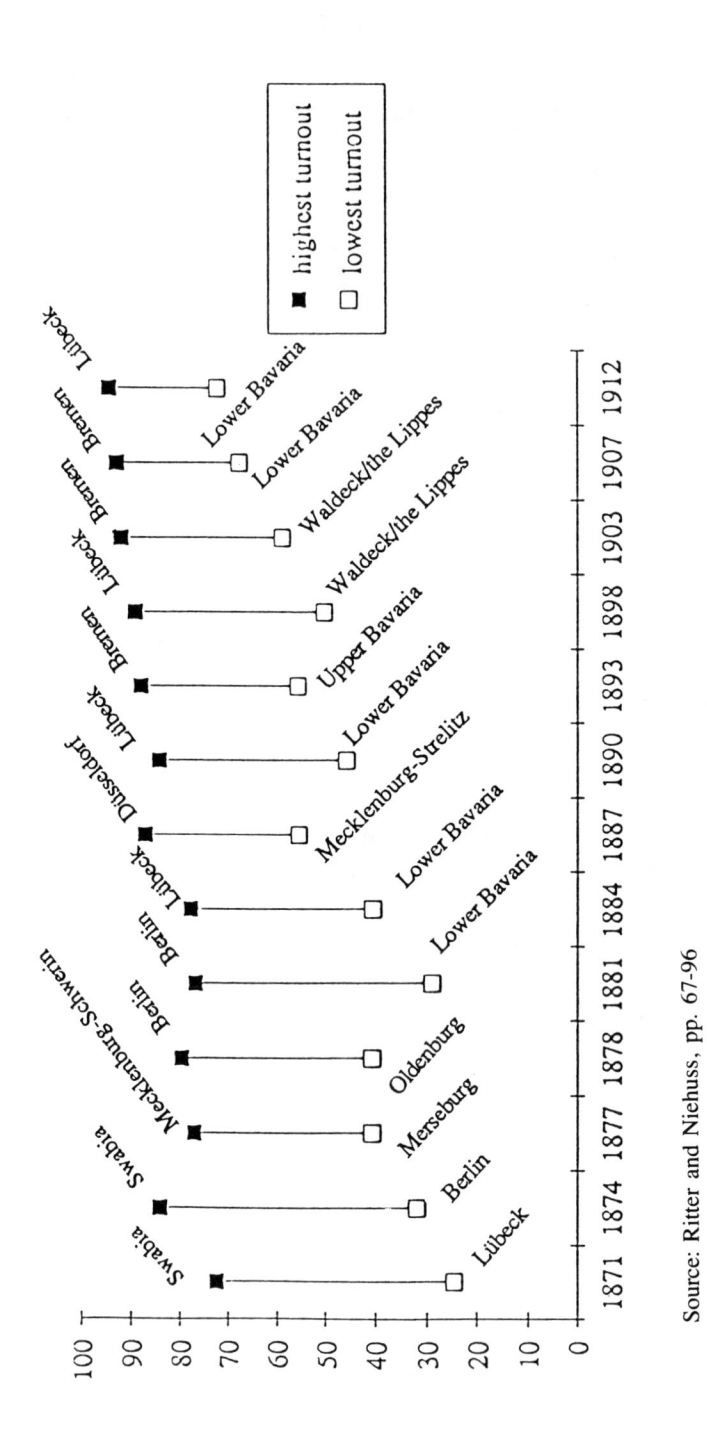

Figure 1. Highest and lowest turnouts in Reichstag elections, 1871–1912 (by region).

Table 2. *Statistics on variation in turnout in Reichstag elections, 1890–1912*

	1890	1893	1898	1903	1907	1912
Mean Turnout by Constituency (per cent)	71.0	71.9	67.4	75.5	84.7	84.6
Standard Deviation of Turnout by Constituency	10.9	8.4	10.5	8.32	5.72	5.46
Coefficient of Variation (Standard Dev. ÷ Mean)	0.153	0.117	0.156	0.110	0.0676	0.0645

Comments: While the mean turnout tended upward, the standard deviation of constituency turnouts decreased: turnouts were both higher and closer together between one constituency and another. Variation was less. Note the increased turnouts and decreased deviations in the "national" elections of 1893 and 1907.

Source: Author's constituency-level Reichstag election data.

the well-studied political, constitutional, and ideological themes of German history. Yet only four or five general elections of the thirteen that occurred in Imperial Germany fit this pattern. Not every campaign was plebiscitary. In "normal" elections, campaigns were more peaceful, or at any rate, controversy was more diffuse. Most of the elections in Imperial Germany came about through the natural expiry of a Reichstag, with the important issues of the dying session already resolved. The relative calm of these elections was reflected in lower voter participation, although this still increased from one "normal" election to the next. Given the lack of one specific issue dominating the campaign, the parties were more free to choose their own issues and concentrate on the sorts of campaigns that were advantageous in their respective regional and social environments. Each competed with the others to define what the election was about. One group of parties – particularly the conservatives and National Liberals – did well if the issues were "national" ones. But other parties – most notably the left liberals and Social Democrats – put forward quite a different political agenda.

This polarization was related to another polarization, this one a matter of style and structure. The SPD was the first modern, mass party in Germany. The left-liberal, agrarian, anti-Semitic, and Catholic Center parties borrowed from its "democratic" features. Among these borrowings were a permanent electoral organization, centralized campaigns, mass agitation and propaganda, and tight integration with particular social–economic groupings rather than appeals to the idealized patriotic "citizens" of the liberal model. The political terminology of turn-of-the-century Germany was laced with value-laden terms like *Demokratie* and *Demagogie*, *Volkspartei* (people's party) and *Volkstümlichkeit* (popularity), *Radikalismus* and *Agitation*. To traditional politicians and government leaders, all these words had universally negative connotations; but the populists who opposed the governmental parties (or who, within those parties, opposed the governmentalist leaders) were less disturbed by these terms, even proud to be associated with them.[16] During the 1890s, the emergence of mass politics exposed the weaknesses of the older *Honoratiorenpolitik* (politics of notables). To be successful, small cliques of notables and deputies now had to develop a more articulated party organization, in spite of their reluctance and their distaste for the new politics.[17]

The parties quicker to adopt mass agitation almost invariably beat the governmental parties to the punch in nominating candidates. For the non-"national" elections of June 1898 and June 1903, the SPD, Center, and agrarians were the first to begin their agitation in the Rhine province, often nominating their candidates before Christmas; the other parties, hindered by low morale and the illness of key people, had not yet decided on theirs in May.[18] Furthermore, under

16. Blackbourn, "The Politics of Demagogy in Imperial Germany," *Past and Present* 113 (1986): 152–84, examines the meaning of the term "demagogy" to contemporaries, as a characterization of how the radical nationalists and anti-Semites differed from moderates. James Retallack, *Notables of the Right: The Conservative Party and Political Mobilization in Germany, 1876–1918* (Boston, 1988), 2–5, makes a related point. Consider also Max Weber's argument that the new "professional politicians" of his time, in contrast to the old parties of notables, were "demagogues" whose party "machines" practiced a "plebiscitarian democracy"; "Politics as a Vocation," in *From Max Weber: Essays in Sociology*, ed. H. H. Gerth and C. Wright Mills (London, 1948).
17. The 1890s have been identified as a transitional period by virtually every historian who has examined popular politics. W. Wölk had referred to the period around 1890 as a "turning point in the development of the German Empire" ("Sozialstruktur, Parteienkorrelation und Wahlentscheidung im Kaiserreich am Beispiel der Reichstagswahl von 1907," in Büsch, Wölk, and Wölk, eds., *Wählerbewegung*, 546, note 35. See also, among others, Thomas Nipperdey, *Die Organisation der deutschen Parteien vor 1918* (Düsseldorf, 1961), 31–7; Blackbourn, *Class, Religion, and Local Politics*, 9–10 and 14–15; Geoff Eley, *Reshaping the German Right: Radical Nationalism and Political Change after Bismarck* (London, 1980). This said, more work is needed on antecedents in the 1870s and 1880s.
18. Hauptstaatsarchiv Düsseldorf (hereafter: HSA Düss), Reg Aachen Präs Paragraph 815,

Honoratiorenpolitik and its fluid idea of "party," protracted negotiations about the nomination of candidates were necessary at every election to reach a consensus among all the interested groups. As late as 24 May 1898, just three weeks before the voting, a liberal–conservative common front in Breslau collapsed when the Conservatives insisted on nominating a separate candidate. As late as 3 June the National Liberals in Hagen were still courting the support of the Conservative Party, offering the latter a Landtag seat if it would withdraw its Reichstag candidate. On 23 May 1903 a deal was reported whereby the Liberals were to drop their candidates in the constituencies of Meseritz-Bomst and Wirsitz-Schubin in exchange for the Conservatives giving them a Landtag seat in Birnbaum. On 12 June 1903 a former *Regierungspräsident* (district governor), von Arnstedt, campaigning in Wanzleben, announced that he was not, after all, a National Liberal and was really campaigning for the Conservatives. All of this meant that voters could not be sure until the last few days before the elections who the candidates would be or even what parties they would represent.[19]

Where *Honoratiorenpolitik* held together, it frequently did so because it adapted in some fashion to the changed circumstances and also because it managed to keep the attention of the electorate focused on the old issues. In many respects, "national" issues and "national" polarizations within the electorate remained the glue that held loosely organized parties together. Not only did these provide for internal cohesion, overcoming the impact of social and economic issues, which tended to fragment the consensus *within* the older liberal and conservative parties; "national" issues also provided for cohesion *between* parties to create effective coalitions within the overall party system.

The modern style of politics most clearly embodied in Social Democracy – "mass," agitational, interest-oriented politics – was not just an alternative structure; it was an alternative vision of what "party" was and how it related to society. The firmer organization of the agitational parties was in part based on firmer integrating principles:

nos. 110 and 158; Landrat (hereafter: LR) Aachen to Regierungspräsident (hereafter: RP) Aachen, 12 Nov. 1897 and 20 May 1898; HSA Düss Reg Düss Präs 587, no. 3, Oberpräsident Düss to RP Düss, 29 Jan. 1903 (and other reports in the same files).

19. *Berliner Tageblatt* (hereafter, *BT*), 24 May 1898 evening edition (hereafter: 24 May 1898 ev and "m" for morning edition, "n" for noon, "S" for Sunday, "m1" for first morning edition, etc.), 3; *Frankfurter Zeitung* (hereafter: *FZ*), 3 June 1898 ev, 2; *Kölnische Zeitung* (hereafter: *KöZ*), 3 June 1898 m, 2; *KöZ*, 23 May 1903 m1, 2; *BT*, 13 May 1903 m, 3, 10 June 1903 ev, 3, and 12 June 1903 ev, 3.

sectional economic interests, class, minority religion, or ethnicity. These proved far stronger than any mere community of sentiment. In this way, differences in structure and style were related to differences over issues. One way to explore these differences further (and in more concrete terms) is to turn once again to the non-"national" campaigns of 1898 and 1903.

"NATIONAL" ISSUES AND "FAIRNESS" ISSUES IN GERMAN ELECTIONS: 1898 AND 1903

The elections of 1898 and 1903 occurred as a result of the natural expiration of the respective Reichstags. The government did not mount strong public campaigns, nor did it appeal openly to the voters against the Reichstag majority. There was no sharp increase in participation, no rise in the proportion of the vote won by the governmental parties, no significant increase in their seat totals. These were not "national" elections.[20] This itself is significant, for these were the first two elections in the era of imperialist *Weltpolitik*, aggressive fleet building, and *Sammlungspolitik* (the politics of "rallying together" the governmental parties). For these reasons, these were the elections most likely to signal the implementation of the kind of "social imperialism" that has been attributed to Imperial Germany — by which historians mean the stabilization of the government's cause through manipulative elites and pressure-group activity.[21] Yet there

20. In his study of Oldenburg, Christoph Reinders concludes that the 1898 campaign was a national one, with the fleet being the main issue; "Sozialdemokratie und Immigration. Eine Untersuchung der Entwicklungsmöglichkeiten der SPD in einem überwiegend ländlich geprägten Reichstagswahlkreis auf der Grundlage der Wahlbewegung von 1893 bis 1912," in Wolfgang Günther, ed., *Parteien und Wahlen in Oldenburg: Beiträge zur Landesgeschichte im 19. und 20. Jahrhundert* (Oldenburg, 1983), 65–116, esp. 79–82 and 95–6. Because of local conditions, the fleet may have been emphasized more than elsewhere, but even here the overall turnout did not increase, the total National Liberal vote did not change significally from 1890 or 1893, and the main electoral shift was from the left liberals to the Social Democrats.
21. For advocacy of the social imperialism argument, see Hans-Ulrich Wehler, "Sozialimperialismus," in Wehler, ed., *Imperialismus* (Cologne, 1970), 83–96; Wehler, "Bismarcks Imperialismus und späte Russlandpolitik unter dem Primat der Innenpolitik," in Michael Stürmer, ed., *Das Kaiserliche Deutschland* (Düsseldorf, 1970), esp. 238; Wehler, *Das Deutsche Kaiserreich 1871–1914* (Göttingen, 1977), 166–7. Accepting or assuming this idea in the course of studies on other subjects are Paul Kennedy, "Tirpitz and the Second Navy Law of 1900: A Strategical Critique," *Militärgeschichtliche Mitteilungen* 2 (1970): 33–57, esp. 37; and John Röhl, *Germany without Bismarck: The Crisis of Government in the Second Reich, 1890–1900* (London, 1967), 241. A vague idea of "social imperialism" as the winning of mass support for the regime has found its way into such pocketbook histories as Eda Sagarra, *A Social History of Germany 1648–1914* (New York, 1977), 427; and Winfried Baumgart,

is little evidence of this in either of these Reichstag elections, despite their following so closely upon the *Sammlung* declaration of March 1898 and the fleet law of April 1898.[22]

Germany's noisy nationalist pressure groups were not in evidence during these campaigns. Of the Colonial Society nothing appears to have been heard, in spite of the fact that the seizure of the Chinese territory of Kiaochow, the Spanish-American War, and imperialist and naval matters in general were widely discussed in the press in the run-up to the 1898 elections. Even the more extreme and agitational Pan-German League seems to have missed the potential for publicizing its views in these campaigns. With 15,401 members in 1898, it would not have been a large agitational organization, but in any case it did not try to be. In its meetings in the midst of both the 1898 and 1903 Reichstag campaigns, it appears to have ignored the elections; far from undertaking agitation, those who attended a May 1903 meeting in Hanover actually decided to cancel a program of traveling speakers and did not discuss any domestic political questions.[23] Perhaps this lack of direct organizational involvement in election campaigns is explained by the fact that nationalist activists belonged to a separate cultural community of their own making, and that their taste for party and electoral politics was slight.[24] Even the Navy League, the only nationalist group in these years to attain a mass basis – from its founding in April 1898, it swelled to 200,000 members within eighteen months – made no attempt to challenge or supplant the established parties in 1898 or 1903 or to influence the public debate about the Reichstag elections. Instead, groups like the Navy

Deutschland im Zeitalter des Imperialismus (1890–1914) (Frankfurt a.M., 1972), 53–4. Dirk Stegmann mentions the intention of winning proletarian support without commenting on the reality: "Wirtschaft und Politik nach Bismarcks Sturz. Zur Genesis der Miquelschen Sammlungspolitik 1890–1897," in Geiss und Wendt, *Deutschland in der Weltpolitik*, 172, as does Volker Berghahn, *Der Tirpitz-Plan. Genesis und Verfall einer innenpolitischen Krisenstrategie unter Wilhelm II* (Düsseldorf, 1971), 139–57.

22. Geoff Eley is virtually alone among historians in having pointed out the failure of *Sammlung* and social imperialism in 1898; see his "'Sammlungspolitik', Social Imperialism and the Navy of 1898," originally published in *Militärgeschichtliche Mitteilungen* 15 (1974): 29–63 and reprinted in his anthology *From Unification to Nazism: Reinterpreting the German Past* (London, 1986). In 1974 Eley was flying in the face of a dominant interpretation. There is little indication that the theory of *Sammlungspolitik* was much revised in light of the points he rightly made.

23. Bundesarchiv, Abteilungen Potsdam (hereafter: BA Potsdam), 61 VE 1, Alldeutscher Verband, Nr. 504, Bl. 14 and 39.

24. See Roger Chickering, *We Men Who Feel Most German. A Cultural Study of the Pan-German League, 1886–1914* (Boston, 1984), 15–17 and 75–94, on the ideological environment of the League; 58–68 on its concerns and campaigns in 1897–1903 (Chickering does not mention elections).

League remained in the background, even though they drew support from much of the same nationalist milieu of middle-class notables upon which the National Liberal Party in particular was based.[25]

Indeed, the only nationalist, extraparliamentary groups in evidence during the 1898 and 1903 Reichstag campaigns were, first, anti-Polish activists of the Society for the Eastern Marches, whose hand can be seen in the intense campaigns to mobilize Germans against Poles in certain districts of eastern Prussia; and second, the veterans' associations (*Kriegervereine*), which in a few localities attempted to intimidate their members into voting against the Social Democrats. We know about these latter activities because they prompted a Reichstag committee to review the validity of election results in some constituencies.[26] The Navy League did presumably help make the battle fleet into an issue to be debated by the parties during the 1898 campaign, just as the right-wing Agrarian League made tariff protection an issue that the parties could not ignore during both the 1898 and 1903 campaigns (see the later discussion). But there is a clear difference between merely publicizing a cause – making it known – and popularizing a cause – making it broadly supported.

In 1903 one newspaper commented that "increased expenditures for the armaments of the Reich on water and on land are never popular and cannot be so."[27] The elections of 1898 and 1903 bear this out, for in each case the fleet's opponents attacked it with devastating effectiveness on the basis of its cost and the unfair tax base of Reich finances. The SPD and the bulk of the left liberals attacked both fleet and tariffs without fear or restraint, and in the SPD's case achieved two consecutive, decisive election breakthroughs by doing so. "One Billion Marks!" shouted an SPD pamphlet in 1903 in a frontal attack on all armed forces expenditures. "What will all the millions from tariffs and taxes be applied to? Are they perhaps to the benefit of the people? Oh, no! They serve primarily to *cover the costs* which the *army and fleet* require."[28]

25. See particularly Anthony Joseph O'Donnell, "National Liberalism and the Mass Politics of the German Right, 1890–1907" (Ph.D. diss., Princeton University, 1974), Chickering calls the National Liberals "the political arm of the German-national public." See Chickering, *We Men*, 204.
26. See Fairbairn, "Authority vs. Democracy: Prussian Officials and the German Elections of 1898–1903," *Historical Journal* 33 (1990):811–38.
27. *BT*, 23 May 19 ev, 1, "Centrum und Weltpolitik."
28. Leaflet in HSA Düss Reg. Aachen Präs 815, no. 194; "Volksfeinde und Volksfreunde," in Hessisches Staatsarchiv (hereafter: Hess SA) Marburg Bestand 180 Hersfeld Nr. 922. See also the FVP program in *BT* 6 May 1898 m, 1.

The parties that had voted for the fleet tried to shift the blame. The behavior of the Center, in particular, was potent testimony to the effectiveness of the SPD's criticism, for the Center took great pains to show itself not as the party instrumental in approving the fleet, but rather as the party that *limited* naval demands and forced the government to scale down its excessive projects. In 1898 the Center's national election platform claimed that it stood for "prudent thrift in all areas of the Reich budget, particularly with the army and navy." Among the party's achievements it listed the prevention of "new taxes, namely those which would have been a further burden to the broad masses of the people." The fleet was presented as a matter for the "practical politician" who "must reckon with the given circumstances" (that is, the fleet was inevitable); "the important principle" was that new taxes not rest "on the consumption of the broad masses . . . on the shoulders of the weak."[29] For their part, the two conservative parties avoided mentioning the fleet or treated it in the context of past army debates, as a patriotic duty for the good of the Fatherland. In the stock phrase, the fleet was just part of the program of "preserving and reinforcing the German Reich." "As burdensome as [the level of] armament is that the German people has to bear," the Imperial Party (*Reichspartei*)[30] consoled its voters, "it is nevertheless the precondition for the power, the influence, the health of the German empire."[31]

Of the major parties, only the National Liberals exhibited enthusiasm for the fleet. They declared in their 1898 national platform that they were filled with "joyous pride" at Germany's fleet and colonial policies. They claimed with eagerness the distinction of being "the first party which recognized unanimously and without reservation that the fleet law was a necessity for the preservation of peace, for the health and power position of Germany."[32] This solitary distinction brought the party no perceptible gains among the electorate: Compared with the 1893 results, the National Liberals won some 25,000 fewer votes and seven fewer seats. Their share of the popular vote, at 12.5 percent, was their lowest in the history of the empire (see Figure 2).[33]

29. *Kölnische Volkszeitung* (hereafter: *KöVZ*), 7 May 1898 ev, 1; *Niederrheinische Volkszeitung* 24 May 1898 m.
30. Known in Prussia as the Free Conservative Party.
31. "Wahlaufruf der freikonservativen Partei," *KöZ,* 7 May 1898 m, 1.
32. *Programmatische Kundgebungen der Nationalliberalen Partei 1866–1913* (Berlin, 1913), 64–8.
33. See the statistics in Ritter and Niehuss, *Wahlgeschichtliches Arbeitsbuch,* 38–42.

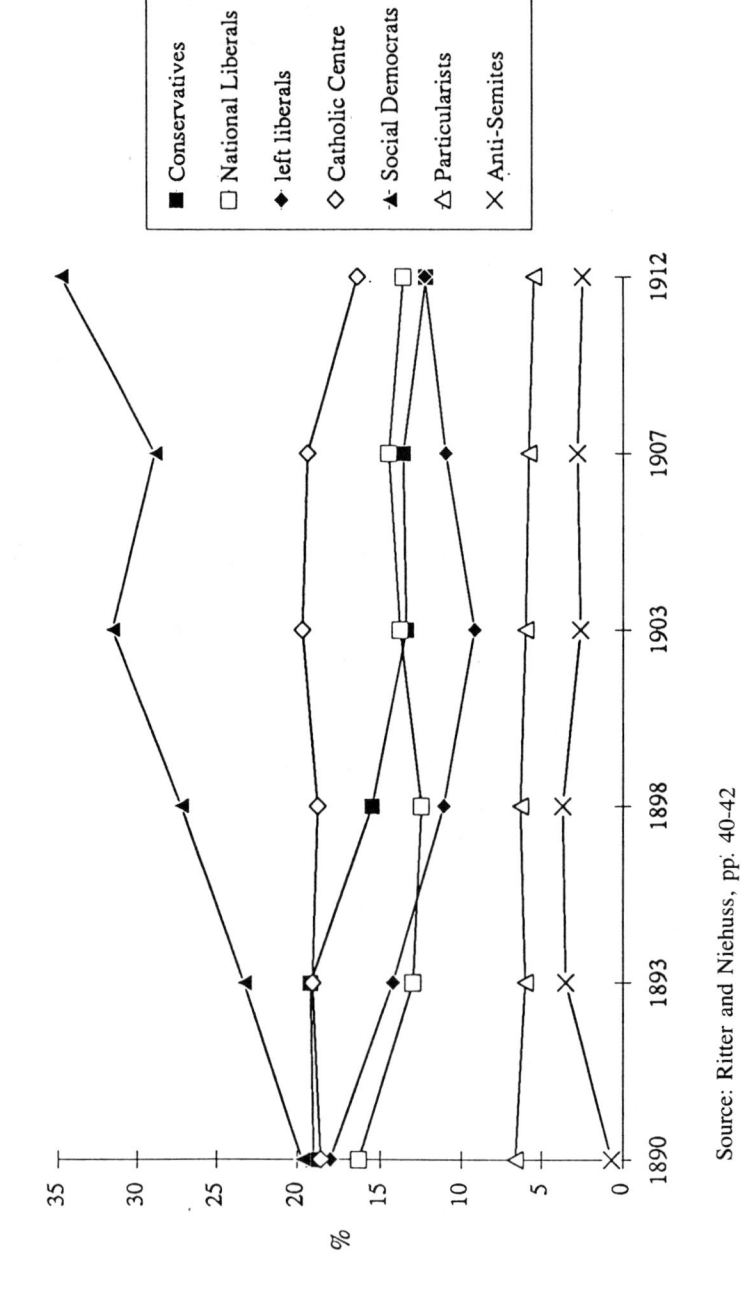

Figure 2. Percentage vote for parties in Reichstag elections, 1890–1912.

Source: Ritter and Niehuss, pp. 40-42

The positions taken by the parties in the 1898 and 1903 elections, when juxtaposed to the fate they suffered at the hands of the voters, must raise doubts about whether "social imperialism" exerted any perceptible effect on the political behavior of the masses in these years. The widest claims for social imperialism argue that it won "mass loyalty," "mass support," and "popularity" for the government. This was clearly not the case in non-"national" election campaigns. The fleet was controversial and fitted all too well into the opposition parties' critiques of the regime. "Mass support" in these elections went to the SPD, which opposed the fleet uniformly, and to the Center, whose deputies approved it but whose propaganda apologized for it. Even the effect on the Protestant middle classes has been exaggerated. The years 1896–1900 have been seen as the years in which liberal and power-political imperialism took over the entire liberal movement.[34] But this overestimates the proportion of liberals who were excited about the fleet. Eugen Richter's left-liberal Radical People's Party, engaged in sharp competition with the SPD for workers' votes and with agrarians for farmers' votes, was not enthusiastic about the fleet in 1898–1903. Richter's party was far stronger in electoral terms than the tiny "national" splinters around Theodor Barth and Friedrich Naumann, on whom historians have lavished disproportionate attention.

In the 1898 and 1903 campaigns, the most important effect of pressure groups was the accentuation of economic issues, and this posed special problems for those parties whose electoral support was not united on an economic basis. Parties that represented diverse economic bases could respond to the interest politics of the 1890s only by repudiating it, by stating their opposition to all exclusive interest demands, and by claiming a role as bargainers or brokers above the interests. The National Liberals advocated "Fatherland above party, the general good above special interests, independence from left and right and from government."[35] The People's Party emphasized that it was indeed "a people's party; it does not want to represent individual occupations or estates or confessions, but rather the whole people." In this context it criticized the way "special interests are pushing themselves forward and are seeking with mislead-

---

34. Wolfgang Mommsen, "Wandlungen der liberalen Idee im Zeitalter des Imperialismus," in Karl Holl and Günther List, eds., *Liberalismus und imperialistischer Staat: Der Imperialismus als Problem liberaler Parteien in Deutschland 1890–1914* (Göttingen, 1975), 109–47, esp. 122–5.
35. "Berliner Erklärung" of 1896, in *Programmatische Kundgebungen der NLP,* 60–3.

ing slogans of *Sammelpolitik* . . . to exploit the collectivity."[36] In similar terms, the Center Party in Westphalia proclaimed that its goal was "to serve the entire people, to further the compromise of all interests."[37] In each of these claims we can discern the attempts of the established parties to keep their heads above water as the tide of interest politics rose in the late 1890s.

The National Liberals' attempt, virtually alone, to extol the ideal-national virtues of the fleet to their voters in 1898, was in part an attempt to resurrect a "national" issue that would work to their advantage in election campaigns that otherwise centered on material or social issues. Conservatives emphasized to varying degrees "material-sectional *Sammlungspolitik*." Like *Flottenpolitik,* this had become a catch phrase only the year before. In 1897 Johannes von Miquel, the Prussian finance minister and vice-president of the Ministry of State, had selected an "Economic Committee" representing big industry and agriculture, together with members of (mainly) the conservative parties. Shortly before the 1898 elections the committee issued an "Economic Declaration," intended to rally the governmental parties to unite on the basis of tariff protectionism and anti-socialism. As envisioned by Miquel, this was to be an active governmental campaign to reconcile the divisions among the governmental parties engendered by the sectional interest debates of the preceding years. The government, however, was divided. Chancellor Chlodwig zu Hohenlohe-Schillingsfürst counseled caution lest the government put its prestige on the line and suffer defeat. As a result, there was no official sponsorship of *Sammlungspolitik* – a policy that in liberal eyes amounted to a surrender to agrarian tariff policy and, in the view of the Center, was indistinguishable from the restoration of the *Kartell*.[38]

The 1898 *Handbook for Social Democratic Voters* listed the rise of the agrarian movement as the most prominent new development since the last elections. This was echoed in local campaigns where socialists opened their assault with a discussion of tariffs. However, rather than treating the tariff issue narrowly, the SPD linked the agrarian movement to the government's turn to the right in the

36. G. W. C. Schmidt, *Die freisinnige Volkspartei. Wer sie ist und was sie will* (Dresden, 1895); FVP program as published in *BT,* 6 May 1898 m, 1.
37. *Germania* (hereafter: *Germ*), 4 June 1898 m,1. "Wahlaufruf der westfälischen Centrumspartei."
38. On the disagreement within the government, see Ministry of State, 19 April 1898 (II) in Bundesarchiv Koblenz (hereafter BA Koblenz), R43F, Nr. 1817, Bl. 9–11.

1890s, to "reactionary anti-worker and anti-popular endeavors."[39] This campaign had a profound impact. One worker, writing decades later, clearly remembered the impression it made on him. Nikolaus Osterroth, a clay miner, was eating lunch one April day in 1898 when an SPD election leaflet was thrown through his window.

> I began to read. Sentence by sentence there was an indictment against the government and the bourgeois parties, against armament expenditures that had been driven to unbearable heights, against the insanely increasing debt burden of the Empire, against the excess of the new naval appropriations that oppressed the people, and against the plundering of the masses by tariffs and indirect taxes. . . .
> Suddenly I saw the world from the other side, from a side that up to now had been dark for me. I was especially aroused by the criticism of the tariff system and the indirect taxes. I'd never heard a word about them before! In all the Center party speeches they kept completely quiet about them. And why? Wasn't their silence an admission . . . , a clear sign of a guilty conscience?[40]

The left-liberal press broadened the issue in a similar way. It launched a prolonged campaign in May and June 1898 featuring "the struggle against Junkers and reactionaries" as the primary issue. All liberals were to unite to fight the Junker, the "enemy of the peasant, the bourgeois, and the worker." Left-liberal slogans included such stock phrases as "Down with the Junkers" and "Rise up in the struggle against Junkerdom and reaction." Clearly, the agricultural issue was converted here by the opposition into a convenient opportunity to mount a much more comprehensive attack on privilege and repression.[41]

The left opposition's attempt to hang the albatross of agrarianism around the neck of the government was only one of the ways in which the new agrarian stridency created problems for governmental moderates. Separate Agrarian League and anti-Semitic candidates challenged moderate conservative and liberal candidates in many widely separated parts of the Reich. In 1893 and 1898 such candidates

---

39. *Handbuch für sozialdemokratische Wähler: Der Reichstag 1893–1898* (Berlin, 1898), 8. See Rolf Weidner, *Wahlen und soziale Strukturen in Ludwigshafen am Rhein 1871–1914: Unter besonderen Berücksichtigung der Reichstagswahlen* (Ludwigshafen, 1984), 417, on the opening of the SPD campaign in Ludwigshafen with an antitariff speech in February 1898.
40. From Alfred Kelly, ed., *The German Worker: Working-Class Autobiographies from the Age of Industrialization* (Berkeley, 1987), 170–1. Osterroth later became an SPD organizer and deputy; the autobiography from which this passage was taken was *Vom Beter zum Kämpfer* (Berlin 1920).
41. *BT*, 15 May 1898 S, 1; 16 May 1898 ev, 1; 24 May 1898 ev, 1; 26 May 1898 ev, 1; 1 June 1898 ev, 1; 21 June 1898 ev, 1; and 24 June 1898 ev, 1.

scored some remarkable victories. In northern and eastern Prussia, outside the zones of large estates and those of Polish population, there were numerous agrarian and anti-Semitic radicals with significant followings. In Hesse, rural anti-Semites challenged the National Liberals, the established governmental party in that region, and in adjacent Hanover the agrarians fought under the banner of the Agrarian League. These localized movements parallel rebellions among Catholic agrarians in southern and western Germany against the Center Party. Under such circumstances, *Sammlungspolitik* represented a desired, not a real, unity of interests, a damage-limitation policy to control agrarian defections from the government cause.

These same tensions and problems reappeared in a still more serious form in 1903. The tariff law debates of 1901–2 had dominated the Reichstag, consuming huge amounts of its time and provoking acrimonious disagreements both among and within the parties. The basic party positions and alignments had not altered greatly since 1898, but the level of tension had risen significantly. The SPD staged a filibuster to delay the measure as long as possible; as a result, the tariff law could not be passed until December 1902. This left the government barely six months before the constitutional expiry of the Reichstag in which to pass its essential measures, including the financial estimates. Given the bitter tariff debate, the lateness of the decisions, and the housekeeping nature of the remaining business, the parties could be in no doubt about the basis on which the election would be fought. The campaigns of the SPD and the Agrarian League in particular ensured that the question could not be forgotten.

Even more firmly than in 1898, the SPD wove together "the struggle against the agrarians," against privilege, against unfair taxes, and against wasteful armament spending into a single coherent campaign. Early in the campaign the leading SPD newspaper, *Vorwärts*, referred to the most important issues in the campaign as the fleet, the tariff, and the arms race; at the height of the battle it listed them as the tariff, militarism, and civil liberties.[42] Since closure had been invoked to silence the Social Democratic filibuster, the SPD was able to claim not only that it was the sole party to fight the tariff effectively, but also that the Reichstag majority had violated freedom of speech and the rights of the socialist deputies in forcing the measure through. "This new tariff is in our eyes a product of illegality and barbarism,"

---

42. *Vorwärts* [Berlin edition], 1 May 1903, 1; 3 June 1903, 1; and 16 June 1903, 1–2.

claimed the *Schwäbische Tageszeitung*.[43] In this way, the tariff debates enhanced the SPD's ability to portray itself as a party representing the people's interest. While campaigning against both a regressive financial burden on consumers and a restriction of political rights, it laid the blame for these policies on the parties that had voted for tariffs in December 1902.[44]

The inclusion of civil liberties as an election issue reflected the repressive antisocialism of the governmental parties. Debate revolved mainly around the suffrage question. The Reichstag suffrage, "universal, equal, secret, and direct," as it was described at the time, was the most democratic in Germany; but it conflicted with less progressive state suffrages, for example, with that of Saxony, which had been reformed in the opposite direction in 1896. By 1901 the new system had been phased in and all Saxon voters had experienced its extreme inequality. A powerful protest movement was growing in Saxony, but it could express its dissatisfaction effectively only in Reichstag elections. This contributed to the importance of the suffrage issue in the 1903 campaign. In Prussia, meanwhile, the conservatives and National Liberals were stubbornly resisting all reform to the three-class Landtag suffrage, prompting the SPD to contest Prussian Landtag elections for the first time (starting with the autumn elections of 1903) as a means to express protest. In southern Germany the suffrage reform movements were gathering momentum as the SPD and the Center grew in strength and as new party coalitions became viable. Baden, Bavaria, and Württemberg eventually saw suffrage reform enacted in 1905–6.[45]

The suffrage issue was another "fairness" issue that was woven into the Social Democrats' campaign against privilege, repression, regressive taxes and tariffs, and military spending. In pursuing this combination of issues, the SPD won two successive victories in the 1898 and 1903 elections. Equally, the Center Party made a great show of defending the Reichstag suffrage; even though it was less convincing in opposing repressive taxes and military spending because its

---

43. 2 May 1903; clipping in HSA Stuttgart, E130a, Nr. 1426.
44. Anni Roth, "Politische Strömungen in den rechtsrheinischen Kreisen Mühlheim, Wipperfürth, Gummersbach, Waldbröl und Sieg des Regierungsbezirkes Köln 1900–1919" (Ph.D. diss., University of Bonn, 1968), 146–7, provides a good example of how the tariff issue dominated the SPD campaign in 1903.
45. For state elections in Prussia, Bavaria, and Saxony, and concerning their suffrages, a convenient source is Ritter and Niehuss, *Wahlgeschichtliches Arbeitsbuch*, 132–89. Much more could be done concerning state suffrages.

deputies were instrumental in passing the offending bills, the party at least succeeded in deflecting enough of the blame to retain its popular support. This the other major party groupings could not do (see Figure 2).

Given these trends, the main question for the other parties was how to fight Social Democracy. The 1898 elections saw a crucial step in the coming together of the antisocialist cause. The 1898 runoffs compelled a kind of antisocialist coalition, for the SPD participated in ninety-four second-ballot contests that year, more than ever before and, in general, with better prospects in most of them. The governmental press that year abounded with calls for antisocialist unity in the elections, including a leaked letter from the Reich secretary of the interior, Count Arthur von Posadowsky-Wehner, suggesting that all nonsocialist parties band together.[46] As far as the government, the moderate liberals, and the conservatives were concerned, antisocialist unity was the single overriding issue; it took precedence over the existing divisions caused by the fleet, by tariffs, and by other issues. The challenge for them was to turn the antisocialist issue into an effective "national" issue that would rally together the governmental parties. By 1903 governmental politicians seeking ways to defeat Social Democracy were beginning to exhibit tinges of both fanaticism and despair. Letters, pamphlets, and newspaper clippings show that by 1903 more and more of the activists in the other parties were coming to believe that the time had come for a showdown. For them the unity of the nonsocialist parties and the need to halt SPD advances were the most important strategic considerations in the campaign. The conservatives, in particular, made the fight against Social Democracy the centerpiece of their campaign throughout Germany, proclaiming "a clear unambiguous slogan: Against Social Democracy!" Other parties were disparaged for not making this their chief task in the election campaign.[47] Government support behind the scenes for such efforts was greater than ever; Chancellor Bernhard von Bülow instructed one of his governors that SPD victories "must

---

46. See *Nationalzeitung,* 8 June 1898; *FZ,* 8 June 1898 m3; and Walther Peter Fuchs, ed., *Grossherzog Friedrich I. von Baden und die Reichspolitik 1871–1907* (Stuttgart, 1980), Nr. 1856 (Jagemann to Reck, 9 June 1898), for a discussion of the intention of the leak. Many clippings on the subject are collected in BA Potsdam, Reichslandbund Pressearchiv, Nr. 5076.

47. *KZ,* 19 April 1903 m, 1; 11 May 1903 ev, 1; 20 June 1903 ev, 1.

under all circumstances be prevented" and that this consideration should guide all tactical decisions.[48]

Yet antisocialist unity remained elusive. The Agrarian League and agrarian conservatives argued that further protectionist measures for agriculture were the highest priority and that the 1902 tariff law was insufficient. On this point they broke ranks with the government. Anticlericals in the National Liberal Party believed that the influence of the Center Party was more dangerous than that of the SPD. Liberals in general continued to emphasize that once the tariff law had been passed for agriculture, industry had to have its interests protected by ensuring long-term trade treaties and stable foreign markets. And the Center, although generally joining the campaign against the SPD, simultaneously continued its opposition to reactionary measures and "one-sided interest politics." Instead it offered a defense of the Reichstag suffrage and of trade union rights, renewed its rhetoric against nationalist *Kulturkämpfer,* and demanded parity for German Catholics. In short, although the desire to fight the SPD had increased generally among all the parties, the ability to do so had not. In 1907, Bülow did succeed in making one last national assault on the government's opponents, inflicting the only decline in Social Democracy's vote percentage between 1881 and 1912. But election campaigns like those of 1898 and 1903 show how difficult this kind of maneuver really was.

The issues in 1898 and 1903 were endemic issues of Wilhelmine politics: tariffs, suffrage, army, navy, taxes, socialism, nationalism. They were increasingly bound together into a polarized system of issues, pitting either fairness against privilege and reaction or, in the vocabulary of the other side, responsibility and loyalty against subversion. The parties that focused on "fairness" issues, appealed to specific social constituencies, and engaged in modern methods of agitation, emerged as the biggest winners in 1898 and 1903. The remaining parties were faced with crises of fragmentation or forced into defensive postures.

"FRAGMENTATION" AND COALITION BUILDING

Fragmentation is not always what it seems. The parties knew the difference between winning votes and winning seats, and over time

---

48. Bülow to Kaiserlicher Statthalter in Alsace-Lorraine, 17 May 1903, in BA Koblenz, R43F, Nr. 1792.

they made different collective decisions about which strategy they would follow. Like all majority systems (in contrast to proportional representation), the Imperial electoral system gave an important advantage to parties whose vote was concentrated regionally in a moderate way, rather than spread too thinly or concentrated too thickly. Parties essentially "wasted" the votes of their supporters if these were insufficient within a given constituency to carry that party's candidate to victory or if the votes were greatly in excess of what was required to win.

The parties that had cooperated in the so-called *Kartell* of 1887 – the German Conservatives, the Imperial Party, and the National Liberals – thereafter experienced declining shares of the vote. Particularly when challenged by rising socialist votes, they tended to withdraw to their regions of strength and make implicit or explicit deals not to compete with each other for first-ballot votes. Within many constituencies, these parties nominated only one strong "German" or "national" candidate. Naturally, the party affiliation of the joint candidate often differed from one election to the next. One way to examine this noncompetition among the *Kartell* parties is to do a multilinear regression, using the vote percentages for two *Kartell* parties to attempt to explain the voting strength of a third. This has been done in Table 3, which shows a very strong negative relationship between the German Conservative share of the vote and the Imperial Party and National Liberal Party shares up to 1912, when party alignments changed. Although we might expect *some* negative relationship between the vote shares for any two given parties, this very strong negative relationship is out of the ordinary. On the basis of these results, plus constituency by constituency analysis and anecdotal evidence, one could say that the *Kartell* remained an effective de facto electoral coalition until after 1907.[49]

Equally, one would have to conclude that the governmental coalition was less and less effective as time went on, in spite of "national" issues, *Sammlungspolitik,* and calls for antisocialist unity. Perhaps these various efforts mitigated the corrosive effects on the older parties of "fairness" issues and of increasingly well-organized mass socioeconomic constituencies, but they did not halt those effects. Even in 1907 there is no indication of a great improvement in the *Kartell*'s solidarity. Constituency-level results indicate that the increase in non-

49. Fairbairn, "German Elections," chaps. 2 and 3. The difference in 1907 was the more systematic inclusion of the left liberals in these arrangements.

Table 3. *Multilinear regression data on* Kartell *parties, 1890–1912*

DEPENDENT VARIABLE=% VOTE FOR DKP
REGRESSION COEFFICIENT ON TOP, T-RATIO BENEATH (390 DF)

	1890	1893	1898	1903	1907	1912
% Vote for RP	-.609	-.525	-.456	-.504	-.410	-.316
	-9.19	-7.20	-.608	-6.19	-5.07	-3.74
Vote for NLP	-.68214	-.539	-.500	-.533	-.407	not sig.
	-12.38	-9.37	-8.22	-8.67	-6.84	
adjusted r^2	.3144	.2191	.1760	.1864	.1277	.0295
F(from mean: 5, 391 DF)	91.813	56.559	43.299	46.368	29.991	7.011

Comments: There is a strong, statistically significant negative correlation between the votes won by the Reichspartei *(RP) and National Liberal Party (NLP) on one hand, and those won by the German Conservatives (DKP) on the other. This relationship persisted after the demise of the* Kartell *in 1890 but became weaker over time, as indicated by the declining magnitude of the coefficients and the r-squared.*

Source: Multilinear regression based on the author's constituency-level Reichstag election data. For simplicity in this table only the two dependent variables shown were used in the regression. The relationship shown remains strong and significant, however, even in larger regressions when other variables are included.

socialist seats that year was primarily due to increased cooperation between the left liberals, the government's longtime critics, and the governmental block.[50]

The coalition-type strategy of the *Kartell* parties took advantage of the benefits of concentration under the majority system in a way that was suited to a defensive policy rather than to a striving for one-party domination. On the whole, the *Kartell* parties, especially the Conservatives, were stronger than they appear in the vote totals, because their strategy was geared to maximizing seats rather than votes and because they functioned as a first-ballot electoral coalition in most areas. Nevertheless, they were still in retreat in most types of electoral environments, so their strategy tended more to slow their decline than to stimulate their growth.

Because the electoral law stipulated that the winning candidate had to receive an *absolute* majority of the votes cast, the consequent need for runoff elections in many constituencies also influenced these pat-

50. Ibid., 193–6.

terns and strategies. From 1893 on, close to one-half of all election contests required a second ballot. The runoff system provided little incentive for politicians to combine into two or three broad, formal major parties. In most circumstances, every party could run its own separate candidate on the first ballot: testing the waters, gaining what support it could, perhaps jockeying for position to gain concessions from larger parties needing its votes. Then, on the second ballot, the parties could combine according to their most urgent interests. If they strove for their maximum program on the first ballot, they reserved the opportunity on the second to be satisfied with their minimum. The second ballot therefore became the focus for the construction of party blocks. It was, for example, in runoff battles against Social Democrats, Poles, and other "undesirables" that a practical basis for the continuing cooperation of the *Kartell* parties was provided. Where such "un-German" enemies were strong, the left liberals and the Center Party were increasingly drawn into such second-ballot coalitions.

One therefore ought not to exaggerate the degree of fragmentation in electoral politics, as Wilhelmine liberals and conservatives – the parties that felt most divided and vulnerable – were wont to do. First, parties that would have been united in a simple majority setup were separate on the first ballot, united on the second. What in another system might have been a faction within a larger party was in Imperial Germany a party within a larger (second-ballot) coalition. Although this set of affairs created a *perception* of fragmentation, as well as genuine problems for the government in finding Reichstag majorities, it is not clear to what extent it reflected an actual fragmentation of local society. Perhaps the fragmentation so often referred to was less a fragmentation among parties and social groups within each region, and more a fragmentation among regions or types of electoral environments. The Reichstag presented a confusing array of more than a dozen significant parties, but there were no constituencies with equal twelve-way fights. Almost all constituencies had simple one-, two-, or three-way races, and several states and provinces displayed signs of emerging three-party systems.[51] In other words, the electoral system may have presented one face to the chancellor –

---

51. Franz, *Die politischen Wahlen in Niedersachsen,* 11 and 20 (the three parties in the province of Hanover were the National Liberals, Guelphs, and SPD); Hiery, *Reichstagswahlen,* 304, on Alsace-Lorraine (Center, liberals, SPD).

Table 4. *Explaining German party fragmentation: A model*

HYPOTHESIS: MOST CONSTITUENCIES HAD THREE-WAY (OR FEWER) RACES BETWEEN A LIBERAL OR CONSERVATIVE, A SOCIALIST, AND A CENTER OR PARTICULARIST CANDIDATE

PROCEDURE: FOR EACH CONSTITUENCY, THE VOTES WON BY THE LARGEST LIBERAL OR CONSERVATIVE, SOCIALIST, AND CENTER OR PARTICULARIST PARTY WERE SUMMED (THREE PARTIES ONLY)

	1890	1893	1898	1903	1907	1912
Proportion of votes accounted for by model (mean by constituency)	74.6%	74.4%	73.4%	77.6%	79.0%	76.4%
Proportion of constituencies in which model accounts for 2/3 or more of the votes cast	65.2%	69.0%	68.3%	74.8%	76.6%	72.3%

OBSERVATIONS: THE MODEL EXPLAINS ABOUT THREE-QUARTERS OF THE VOTES CAST; THREE PARTIES OF THE TYPE INDICATED ACCOUNT FOR TWO-THIRDS OR MORE OF THE VOTES IN 65-77% OF CONSTITUENCIES. FROM 1903 THIS PATTERN STRENGTHENED.

CONCLUSION: GERMAN PARTIES WERE NOT FRAGMENTED WITHIN REGIONS AND CONSTITUENCIES, BUT RATHER BETWEEN THEM.

and to historians who focus exclusively on the national level – but quite another face to individual voters and local organizations.

In a very broad way, one can say that most constituencies were contested by liberals or conservatives, by socialists, and by Catholics or particularists. Table 4 presents a test of this hypothesis. It shows that about three-quarters of the votes cast fit the model of a three-way race: between the largest liberal or conservative group in each constituency, the socialist, and the leading Center party or particularist candidate. Perhaps one can go so far as to speak of three loose party blocks.[52] The socialist candidates were certainly part of a single

52. Compare Suval, *Electoral Politics*, 62, where he recognizes the Center's Catholic constituency and the SPD's working-class as one of the three social groupings evident in Wilhelmine elections. The third category, "East Elbian rurals," is the only component of the liberal-conservative milieu which is substantiated in social–economic statistics.

national organization. The Center and many of the particularists, especially the less radical Poles and the Guelphs, made electoral deals and frequently voted together in the Reichstag. Although one cannot quite speak of a single liberal–conservative grouping, liberals rarely fought other liberals head to head, conservatives seldom fought other conservatives, and National Liberals did not frequently fight conservatives.[53] Certainly the government did what it could to promote liberal–conservative unity and reduce conflicts.[54]

The more agitational parties pursued a distinctive electoral strategy, based not on first-ballot coalitions but on the apparent nationwide unity of their movements. The Social Democrats, the Catholic Center, the anti-Semites, and to a lesser degree the left-liberal People's Party deliberately ran candidates wherever they could, no matter how hopeless the prospects. They did this in part to maximize their Reich-wide vote totals, which would in turn enhance the prestige and legitimize the abstract representational claims of their movements. Where no local candidate could be found, they resorted frequently to the device of *Zählkandidaturen* – multiple candidacies – whereby one individual stood for his party in many constituencies, often widely separated. For the SPD, these candidates gave local followers throughout Germany a chance to identify with the movement by casting a vote for it; they were also intended to reveal the true size of the party. Since the SPD's share of the vote was increasing, this served the purpose of creating a local presence and laying the basis for future growth. For a growing party like the SPD this strategy was opportune. The Center Party, on the other hand, was effectively limited to the Catholic electorate and was less likely to expand. Nonetheless the Center did mobilize its supporters for tactical purposes even where these were in a minority: Its aim was to barter with the other parties when the race between them was close, or to prop up other party groupings as dictated by regional and national strategies.

The net effect of these circumstances was that – at least up to 1912, when the Center Party's vote began to suffer – the SPD and the

53. The opposition of left liberals to conservatives, especially in eastern Prussia and especially in mixed rural–urban constituencies, is perhaps the chief reason why one cannot speak of a consistent pattern where only one strong Protestant-bourgeois candidate contested any given seat. At the editors' request and to save space, a lengthy analysis of different types and groupings of electoral environments was removed from this paper. Some of this analysis can be found in Fairbairn, "German Elections"; more will be presented in future work.
54. See Fairbairn, "Authority vs. Democracy."

Center were in a class by themselves as the perceived mass parties in the nation. Where other parties were strong in particular environments – like the Conservatives in the Baltic coast region, where large landholdings dominated the landscape, or the National Liberals in their regional pockets within middle Germany – the SPD and the Center were strong in environments that were numerous and widespread. The SPD was strongest in the very largest population centers, which swelled its vote totals, and was increasingly strong and winning seats in many different electoral environments. The Center Party, too, though in the main it did not go outside the bounds of the Catholic population, had a consistently strong, socially and economically integrated electoral base; it effectively tied together *all* Catholic areas, except for some Polish ones, over and above the regional identity of those areas. In the "fairness" elections of 1898 and 1903, when voters were mobilized around social and economic issues rather than around "national" issues, it was the SPD and the Center that maintained or increased their support, whereas all other parties declined and fell back into narrower geographic and social–political enclaves.[55]

To German nationalists and patriots, the picture was a discouraging one. The old enemies of the Reich (Poles, Catholics) could not be dislodged from their electoral strongholds on the eastern, southern, and western peripheries of the nation, and the new enemy, Social Democracy, not only resisted extermination but (except for 1907) advanced relentlessly. The "respectable" parties – the parties of order – were not doing well, and "respectable" politicians were understandably unenthusiastic about the whole exercise, least of all about the "extreme" and "agitational" methods that seemed to them to be the ruin of German political culture. They lacked the perspective to appreciate the social groupings that were being mobilized by new methods and by social–economic issues, even as those groupings were beginning to take over the political arena and demand the satisfaction of their own economic (bread-and-butter) or political (fairness) demands.

The judgment of German conservatives and nationalists that the elections of 1898 and 1903 are best ignored – that they are less worthy of attention then the dramatic "national" victories of 1887 or 1907 –

---

55. The Center and the SPD have been viewed as embodying "supra-local milieux" better suited to mobilization in a mass environment than the purely local milieux of the liberals and conservatives. See Rohe, "Wahlanalyse," 349.

ought not to be accepted. For the historian, each of these elections offers an unparalleled opportunity to observe the behavior of the voting public, the evolving bases of the political parties, and the social–cultural composition of the political nation. We can observe in these elections the efforts of German political parties to shape and adjust to the circumstances of a mass politics that was still emerging. Even if in the short term the campaigning and the voting were irrelevant to decisions of state – and it is not clear that they *were* irrelevant – they could not be ignored as reflections of German society. Germans looked at the popular vote and wondered about the balance of social forces and the direction of political change. The almost continuous growth of Social Democratic votes reinforced the optimism of that party and the disillusionment of the government and its allies, and the continuing strength of the Catholic Center until 1907 was a testimony to the power of its integrative force and its ability to adapt. As the campaign literature, press commentary, and party strategies reveal, these elections were fought not just for numerical ascendancy in the Reichstag but for moral ascendancy in a developing political nation. Whereas the waving of the flag by local notables became less effective, ascendancy appeared increasingly to be won by nationwide movements that appealed on the basis of "fairness" to the material interests and social–cultural identities of voters.

2

Antisocialism and Electoral Politics in Regional Perspective: The Kingdom of Saxony

JAMES RETALLACK

ANTISOCIALISM AND REGIONAL HISTORY

In this essay I explore the degree to which an alleged antisocialist consensus among Imperial Germany's elites was evident in the arena of electoral politics.[1] This is the first of three items on my agenda. I am interested only tangentially in rehearsing the strengths and weaknesses of a general perspective – dominant in the mid-1970s – that emphasized the coherence and durability of right-wing attempts to contain the threat of Social Democracy.[2] As this perspective came to dominate the field, it became de rigueur to argue that agrarian Junkers, heavy industrialists, and other elements of the educated or propertied *Bürgertum* enjoyed fundamental, long-lasting agreement about the dangers of revolution. In part because the authors who supported this view produced such a mountain of scholarship, most readers still believe that Imperial German elites practiced "unanimous

---

I am grateful to Brett Fairbairn, Roger Chickering, and Peter Steinbach for their thoughtful comments on early drafts of this essay; to Kenneth Mills and Greg Smith for research assistance; to the Social Sciences and Humanities Research Council of Canada for financial support; and to the librarians of Stanford University and the University of Toronto.

1. Among the most notable recent studies of elections in the *Kaiserreich* are Stanley Suval, *Electoral Politics in Wilhelmine Germany* (Chapel Hill, NC, 1985); Brett Fairbairn, "The German Elections of 1898 and 1903" (D. Phil. diss., Oxford University, 1987); see also the essay by Fairbairn in this volume; Karl Rohe, ed., *Elections, Parties and Political Traditions* (New York, 1990); Gerhard A. Ritter and Merith Niehuss, *Wahlgeschichtliches Arbeitsbuch* (Munich, 1980); G. A. Ritter, ed., *Der Aufstieg der deutschen Arbeiterbewegung* (Munich, 1990); Peter Steinbach, "Wahlrecht und Wahlbeteiligung im Fürstentum Lippe bis zum Ende des Kaiserreichs," *Lippische Mitteilungen aus Geschichte und Landeskunde* 58 (1989): 171–232; and P. Steinbach, *Die Zähmung des politischen Massenmarktes: Wahlen und Wahlkämpfe im Bismarckreich,* 3 vols. (Passau, 1990).
2. For the historiographical background see J. Retallack, "Social History with a Vengeance? Some Reactions to H.-U. Wehler's *Das Deutsche Kaiserreich,*" *German Studies Review* 7 (1984): 423–50; and Retallack, "Wilhelmine Germany," in Gordon Martel, ed., *Modern Germany Reconsidered* (London, 1991). Limits of space compel me to refer collectively to the work of Volker Berghahn, Fritz Fischer, Dieter Groh, Hans-Jürgen Puhle, Klaus Saul, Dirk Stegmann, and Hans-Ulrich Wehler.

discrimination" against socialists, both at the polls and when defending unfair franchise laws. However, a survey of electoral politics conducted with instruments of a finer calibration reveals quite another landscape. Here rhetorical flourishes about the "red specter" all too often evaporate under the impact of momentary crisis, cynical calculation, and personal ambition. Local elites choose to engage the enemy on one front and refuse on another. They pursue ill-defined goals with limited resources, and they break off the battle before they achieve their ultimate goal. All this can be seen only when the antisocialist *intentions* of Imperial elites are considered together with the actual *implementation* of their plans, particularly at the local and regional levels. James Sheehan seemed to understand this when he wrote that "a great deal of the political activity that goes on at the national level is designed to simplify issues, to clarify alignments, to reduce politics to a set of binary choices. . . . But . . . in the worlds of local politics, choices are frequently more fluid, alliances more uncertain, combinations more complex."[3] For this reason, the historian must make a special effort to view political choices as contemporaries saw them: not as clear alternatives but as confused options; not as national politics writ small but as reflections of autonomous rules and traditions. From this perspective, the antisocialist campaign in Imperial Germany emerges not as a kind of grand strategy drawn up before battle, but as tactical warfare constantly being adjusted to changing circumstances. Far from substantiating the view from "on high," the observer in the trenches sees confused armies advancing to exploit fleeting opportunities and retreating in the face of poor generalship and logistical constraints.

My second aim is to make this discussion specific and concrete by using the case-study approach. I focus on the Kingdom of Saxony: the empire's third largest state, dominated by small-scale industry and handicrafts, and effectively the cradle of both German Social Democracy and political anti-Semitism. Saxony deserves attention because of the political fireworks set off by conservatives, liberals, and socialists struggling to revise the Saxon Landtag franchise to their own advantage (two fundamentally different revisions were enacted in March 1896 and May 1909). But the case of Saxony also provides a unique opportunity to examine the texture of antisocialism in finer detail. The present essay concentrates on anti-

3. J. Sheehan, "What Is German History? Reflections on the Role of the *Nation* in German History and Historiography," *Journal of Modern History* 53 (1981): 21f.

socialism before 1900 as part of a larger research project that, when completed, will provide a comprehensive account of electoral politics in Saxony from 1866 to 1918. The following analysis examines the interplay among five mutually reinforcing processes: (1) qualitative and quantitative changes in the level of political mobilization in Saxony, especially after 1890 but also in the 1880s; (2) the increasing strength of Social Democracy; (3) the arrival of political anti-Semitism as a new and unwelcome player on the scene; (4) the effort of Conservatives and the government to preserve antisocialist unity at the polls; and (5) the campaign to revise the Landtag franchise in order to exclude the lower classes from political influence. Where appropriate, the interplay among local, state, and national politics is also sketched.

It bears emphasizing that my larger hypothesis about the relative disunity of antisocialist elites in both Saxony and the Reich is based in part on an examination of developments *after* 1900 that cannot be discussed here. For the Saxon case these developments included a bitter feud between liberals and Conservatives about a second franchise reform (and about many other issues besides); the repercussions of the Russian Revolution of 1905 and of reform movements elsewhere in the Reich; and the inability of right-wing forces to unite against the socialist threat during the Landtag elections of 1909 and the Reichstag elections of 1912. One aspect common to these investigations is nonetheless also found in the present study: the belief that antisocialism as displayed at the rhetorical and legislative levels is intimately connected with antisocialism as practiced at the ballot box. Alliances between parliamentary caucuses, appeals for governmental preferment, grass-roots agitation, franchise reform, the simple casting of a ballot – these were all struggles for power in one form or another. Because the act of restricting the franchise and the act of voting were both intimately bound up with issues of power and representation, considering these two political acts together makes each more meaningful.

Third, a study of Saxon politics provides a rare opportunity to launch a debate based on archival documents freely available to North American scholars. The copious materials published by the Saxon statistical office are available on microfilm,[4] as are most of the diplomatic reports sent to Berlin by one of the *Kaiserreich*'s most

---

4. The *Zeitschrift des K. Sächsischen Statistischen Bureaus* was used in or borrowed from the Stanford University library (MFilm N.S. 1529, reels 10–12).

insightful (but hitherto anonymous) political observers: the Prussian envoy to Saxony, Count Carl von Dönhoff.[5] Perhaps some readers will dig more deeply into these sources and suggest alternative readings of Saxon elections. But just as Richard Evans did with his study of franchise disturbances in Hamburg in January 1906, this essay also seeks to make a more comprehensive statement about the fruitfulness of combining quantitative history, local history, and social history.[6] There is currently much talk of using new kinds of sources – indeed, using events and facts themselves, including institutions and social relations of authority – as "texts" from which we can read the language of politics in imaginative ways. Might not the electoral records used in this study qualify as texts? If they do, one must also recognize that context becomes crucial when dealing with both local history and quantitative history. Numbers, like language, can be duplicitous and cryptic. Like spies, they have to be tortured and decoded before they reveal their secrets, and sometimes diplomatic communiqués from far-off lands provide the only means to understand such coded language. Therefore, like the lower classes who were excluded from representation in Saxony, election returns have to be listened to and considered in their full contemporary context. As Pierre Bourdieu has written: "The dominant language discredits and destroys the spontaneous political discourse of the dominated. It leaves them only silence or a borrowed language."[7] Although Saxon elites sought to silence the "little man" politically, the electoral record shows that they accomplished this only incompletely. By studying that record in a new way, we may be able to clarify important issues of agency in Imperial German politics and identify remaining gaps between the rhetoric and the reality of antisocialism.

RED KINGDOM OR AUTHORITARIAN PLAYGROUND?

Comparisons both implicit and explicit colored most descriptions of Saxony during the *Kaiserreich*. Often called the "model land of liber-

---

5. Found in the Political Archive of the German Foreign Ministry in Bonn (hereafter cited as PA Bonn); some files were consulted in Bonn, but most were acquired from the Center for Research Libraries, Chicago, which holds copies of films from the American Historical Association and University of Michigan projects (T 149, esp. reels 178–80). This essay was written before an extended visit to the Staatsarchiv Dresden and the Sächsische Landesbibliothek in the autumn of 1991. The same is true of a complementary essay, James Retallack, "'What Is to Be Done?' The Red Specter, Franchise Questions, and the Crisis of Conservative Hegemony in Saxony, 1896–1909," *Central European History* 23 (1990):271–312.
6. Richard J. Evans, "'Red Wednesday' in Hamburg: Social Democrats, Police and *Lumpenproletariat* in the Suffrage Disturbances of 17 January 1906," in idem, *Rethinking German History* (London, 1987), 248–90.
7. Cited in Bryan Palmer, *Descent into Discourse* (Philadelphia, 1990), 217.

alism," after 1903 it was also known as the "red kingdom of Saxony."⁸ Dresden, the state capital, was known as "Florence on the Elbe." Chemnitz was the "Manchester of Saxony." There were particularly good reasons for describing Saxony as the "workshop of the German Reich." Whereas the proportion of persons employed in industry, crafts, and mining averaged 42.8 percent for both Prussia and the Reich in 1907, the corresponding figure for Saxony was 59.3 percent – not only highest among all federal states, but exceeding even the Rhineland and Berlin.⁹ The 1907 census reported that all 23 of Saxony's Reichstag constituencies were included among those 197 constituencies in the Reich where the proportion of employees in industry and trade represented an absolute majority. Yet whereas large concerns and heavy industry predominated elsewhere, Saxony retained a great deal of household and craft industry. Thousands of family-owned firms, typically with just a handful of employees, also produced a wide variety of consumer goods. Of over 22,000 industrial enterprises in Dresden around the turn of the century, 86 percent had five or fewer workers.¹⁰ Meanwhile, between 1871 and 1895, the populations of Saxony's largest cities grew at astounding rates: Leipzig grew from 107,000 to 400,000 inhabitants; Dresden from 177,000 to 336,000; Chemnitz from 68,000 to 161,000; and Plauen from 23,000 to 55,000.¹¹

In the 1860s Saxony became the heartland of German socialism, providing the two most important socialist leaders after Ferdinand Lassalle's death, August Bebel and Wilhelm Liebknecht. By the time the Socialist Workers Party of Germany (*Sozialistische Arbeiterpartei Deutschlands*) was founded in 1875, the party's four local secretariats in Saxony included 18 percent ($N = 4,597$) of the national membership, even though Saxons represented just 6.7 percent of the population of the Reich.¹² In this period the socialists' share of the Reichstag vote was also growing rapidly: It virtually doubled – from

---

8. For much of the following see Rudolf Kötzschke and Hellmut Kretzschmar, *Sächsische Geschichte* (Frankfurt a.M., 1965), 371ff.; Donald Warren, Jr., *The Red Kingdom of Saxony: Lobbying Grounds for Gustav Stresemann, 1900–1909* (The Hague, 1964), 1ff.; Gerhard A. Ritter, "Das Wahlrecht und die Wählerschaft der Sozialdemokratie im Königreich Sachsen 1867–1914," in Ritter, ed., *Aufstieg*, 50ff.
9. Gerd Hohorst, Jürgen Kocka, and Gerhard A. Ritter, eds. *Sozialgeschichtliches Arbeitsbuch,* 2nd ed. (Munich, 1978), 2:73; Volker Hentschel, "Erwerbs- und Einkommensverhältnisse in Sachsen, Baden und Württemberg vor dem ersten Weltkrieg (1890–1914)," *Vierteljahresschrift für Sozial- und Wirtschaftsgeschichte* 66 (1979): 33, 38f.
10. Kurt Koszyk, *Gustav Stresemann. Der kaisertreue Democrat* (Cologne, 1989), 88.
11. Kötzschke and Kretzschmar, *Sächsische Geschichte,* 371.
12. Hartmut Zwahr, "Die deutsche Arbeiterbewegung im Länder- und Territorienvergleich 1875," *Geschichte und Gesellschaft* 13 (1978):466–8.

Table 1. *Reichstag elections in the kingdom of Saxony, 1871–1912*

Percentage of Vote Won, First Ballot	1871	1874	1877	1878	1881	1884	1887	1890	1893	1898	1903	1907	1912
Voter turn-out, percent	45.1	49.5	57.7	58.5	52.4	58.5	79.6	82.0	79.6	73.9	83.0	89.7	88.8
Conservative Party (K)	5.2	7.2	17.4	16.2	24.3	22.7	24.0	22.6	21.5	18.1	10.1	7.7	8.0
Imperial (Free Conservative) Party (R)	2.8	14.2	6.7	12.7	10.7	11.8	10.4	5.4	3.6	-	1.3	2.9	1.7
National Liberal Party (N)	22.4	27.1	22.8	19.9	14.0	17.7	31.1	19.7	8.4	14.7	12.5	26.1	21.9
Liberals (L), Liberal Union (LV), Radical Union	13.1	-	-	-	4.5	-	-	-	-	-	-	-	-
German Radical Party (DF)								9.2					
Ger. Progressives (F), Radical People's Party (FV)	27.0	14.0	14.3	12.8	17.9	12.2	5.7		5.1	2.5	4.0	4.4	
Progressive People's Party													8.7
Center Party (Z)	-	1.0	0.6	0.6	-	0.2	0.0	0.0	0.1	0.3	0.6	0.5	0.3
Social Democratic Party (S)	17.5	35.8	38.0	37.6	28.2	35.3	28.7	42.1	45.8	49.5	58.8	48.5	55.0
German Reform Party (Rp), other anti-Semitic (A)									15.8	12.1	9.8	6.9	4.0
Other (including BdL and Economic Union (WV))	12.0	0.7	0.2	0.2	0.4	0.1	0.1	1.0	0.1	2.8	2.6	2.2	0.4
Seats Won	5 L	1 K	4 K	4 K	5 K	8 K	8 K	10 K	5 K	5 K	22 S	2 K	1 K
	8 N	5 R	3 R	5 R	4 R	3 R	4 R	3 R	1 R	4 N	1 A	1 R	1 R
	8 F	7 N	7 N	5 N	5 N	3 N	10 N	3 N	2 N	11 S		6 N	1 N
	2 S	4 F	2 F	3 F	1 LV	4 DF	1 DF	1 DF	2 FV	3 Rp		2 FV	19 S
		6 S	7 S	6 S	4 F	5 S		6 S	7 S			8 S	1 Rp
					4 S				6 Rp			3 Rp	
												1 WV	

Source: Gerhard A. Ritter with Merith Niehuss, *Wahlgeschichtliches Arbeitsbuch* (Munich, 1980), 89; some figures calculated by the author.

18 to 35 percent – between the elections of 1871 and 1874 (see Table 1). At this time, one of every five votes for socialists in the Reich was cast by a Saxon. By the time of the Reichstag elections of 1898, the SPD was winning about 50 percent of the Reichstag vote in Saxony (see Figure 1), and the number of party members in the state had grown to about 25,000.[13]

Long before someone coined the label "red kingdom" for Saxony, another term might have been more appropriate: "playground of authoritarianism." The government's long record of discrimination against "outgroups" in Saxon society reveals that the Saxon polity was more highly charged, and the Saxon administration far more partisan, than contemporary observers liked to imagine. Official discrimination extended first and foremost to socialists. As early as November 1871, Saxony's government leader, Baron Richard von Friesen, warned publicly that the rise of socialism threatened the state. Consequently Bismarck's antisocialist laws were invoked with particular rigor in Saxony between 1878 and 1890. Of 647 legal actions taken against socialist *Vereine* (associations) and newspapers in the Reich, 156 occurred in Saxony, compared to 304 in all of Prussia and only 18 in Bavaria.[14] This discrimination also touched trade unionists and simple workers, the tiny minorities of Jews and Catholics in the state, and (most broadly of all) those members of the growing commercial and industrial classes who aspired to greater political influence and responsibility in government.

One advantage of focusing on a single region is that it allows us to define antisocialist elites more concretely than we can at the national level. In particular it provides an opportunity to consider when it is legitimate to ascribe an antisocialist consensus to "the right"; to a specific coalition of conservative, liberal, and anti-Semitic parties; or to members of local social and economic elites. Deciding when this ascription is valid in the case of Saxony is especially important for three reasons. First, a number of historians have stressed the need to distinguish between the German bourgeoisie's apparent lack of success in storming the bastions of political power on the one hand – indeed, their relative disinterest in "pure" politics at all – and their many successes in the social, economic, and cultural realms on the other.[15] A study of Saxony illustrates how closely social status, eco-

---

13. Cf. Dieter Fricke, *Handbuch zur Geschichte der deutschen Arbeiterbewegung 1869 bis 1917*, 2 vols. (Berlin, 1987), 1:314–16, 329ff.
14. Kötzschke and Kretzschmar, *Sächsische Geschichte*, 368–70.
15. See David Blackbourn and Richard J. Evans, eds., *The German Bourgeoisie* (London, 1991);

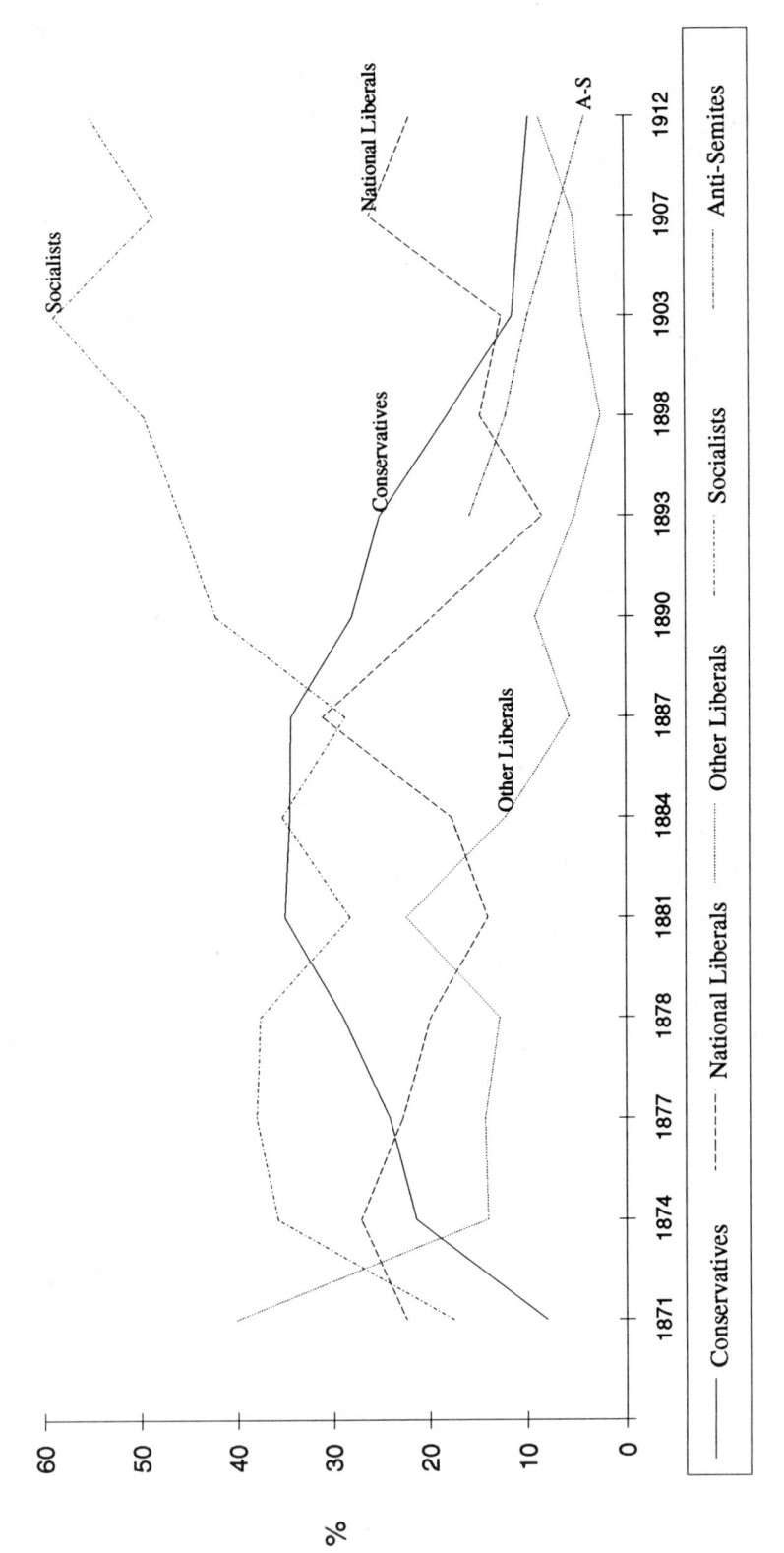

Figure 1. Reichstag elections in Saxony, 1871–1912. (Percentage of total vote.)

nomic influence, and political power were intertwined and thereby suggests why this distinction must not be overdrawn. Second, many historians have pointed to the way in which continued power in municipal councils largely compensated German liberals for their declining influence at the state and national levels.[16] Although this argument is convincing in the broad sense, the Saxon case illustrates that any such distinction becomes problematic when it suggests that municipal, state, and national politics were independent spheres of activity between which liberals had to choose. Third, Conservatives, National Liberals, and left liberals in Saxony tended to share common social origins, were closely connected in the business world, and held similar outlooks on the rise of Social Democracy. Therefore there is a real danger in equating the terms "liberal" and "bourgeois." Most members of the Saxon Conservative *Landesverein* (state association) were at the same time impeccably bourgeois and staunchly conservative. Yet it is difficult to imagine how most members of Saxony's National Liberal Party could be described as anything but conservative on a whole range of issues. Some of these issues were peculiar to Saxon politics; but many, including both antisocialism and franchise reform, were not, and some of these issues evoked a far less progressive response from liberals in Saxony than they did from liberals elsewhere in the Reich.

How, then, were left liberals, National Liberals, Conservatives, and anti-Semites oriented in the Saxon party constellation? From what social groups did each party recruit its supporters, and how did each party fare at the polls? Statistical overviews of Landtag elections are provided in Table 2 and Figures 2 and 3. To interpret these data, one must know that after 1869 only one-third of the Landtag's eighty seats were contested every two years, and deputies were elected for a term of six years. Hence what might appear to be mystifying fluctuations in the data from one election year to the next are explained by the fact that voters in the same twenty-six or twenty-seven constitu-

David Blackbourn and Geoff Eley, *The Peculiarities of German History* (Oxford, 1984); similar points were raised by Roger Chickering in his commentary on an earlier version of this essay.

16. James Sheehan, "Liberalism and the City in Nineteenth-Century Germany," *Past & Present* 51 (1971): 116–37; Helmuth Croon, "Das Vordringen der politischen Parteien im Bereich der kommunalen Selbstverwaltung," in Helmuth Croon, Wolfgang Hofmann, and Georg Christoph von Unruh, eds., *Kommunale Selbstverwaltung im Zeitalter der Industrialisierung* (Stuttgart, 1971), 15–58; Karlheinz Blaschke, "Entwicklungstendenzen im sächsischen Städtewesen während des 19. Jahrhunderts (1815–1914)," in Horst Matzerath, ed., *Städtewachstum und innerstädtische Strukturveränderungen* (Stuttgart, 1984), 56ff.; see also Hartmut Pogge von Strandmann's essay in this volume.

Table 2. Landtag elections in the kingdom of Saxony, 1869–1895

Year	No. of contested constit- uencies	No. of eligible voters	No. of votes cast	Voter turn- out	Conservatives Candi- dates	Conservatives No. of votes	Conservatives %	Conservatives Caucus	National Liberals Candi- dates	National Liberals No. of votes	National Liberals %	National Liberals Caucus	Saxon Progressives No. of votes	Saxon Progressives %	Saxon Progressives Caucus
1869	80	244,594	97,278	39.8%	66	40,610	41.7	41	37	21,896	22.5	30	7,828	8.0	8
1871	26	87,421	21,152	24.2%	33	10,296	48.7	37	0	0	0.0	20	0	0.0	5
1873	27	91,131	30,282	33.2%	31	17,028	56.2	38	13	5,443	18.0	17	2,459	8.1	5
1875	27	97,496	35,340	36.2%	20	12,939	36.6	35	15	9,426	26.7	15	10,089	28.5	14
1877	26	112,913	34,226	30.3%	26	14,386	42.0	37	11	8,395	24.5	19	6,618	19.3	20
1879	27	121,874	38,135	31.3%	30	17,801	46.7	36	14	7,899	20.7	20	4,125	10.8	19
1881	27	115,176	36,846	32.0%	35	21,083	57.2	45	10	4,637	12.6	14	7,219	19.6	15
1883	26	122,061	44,937	36.8%	26	22,144	49.3	47	3	3,461	7.7	11	8,395	18.7	15
1885	27	141,940	54,180	38.2%	24	23,303	43.0	47	10	11,526	21.3	11	4,699	8.7	14
1887	27	134,917	60,050	44.5%	25	34,385	57.3	47	2	2,888	4.8	12	6,481	10.8	13
1889	26	147,954	64,409	43.5%	17	24,649	38.3	48	6	10,031	15.6	12	8,715	13.5	11
1891	27	172,772	92,625	53.6%	22	33,004	35.6	45	9	12,338	13.3	10	4,604	5.0	11
1893	28	163,097	82,697	50.7%	27	38,636	46.7	43	5	7,217	8.7	14	4,376	5.3	8
1895	27	185,333	94,934	51.2%	20	35,313	37.2	44	6	9,762	10.3	16	4,719	5.0	6

Year	No. of contested constit- uencies	German Radicals and Other Liberals			Anti-Semites				Social Democrats				Other/ Spoiled No. of votes
		No. of votes	%	Caucus	Candi- dates	No. of votes	%	Caucus	Candi- dates	No. of votes	%	Caucus	
1869	80	2,192	2.3	1	4	247	0.3	0	0	0	0.0	0	163
1871	26	9,920	46.9	17	0	0	0.0	0	1	208	1.0	0	728
1873	27	4,445	14.7	20	0	0	0.0	0	0	0	0.0	0	907
1875	27	636	1.8	16	0	0	0.0	0	3	1,517	4.3	0	733
1877	26	0	0.0	3	0	0	0.0	0	7	4,078	11.9	1	749
1879	27	1,148	3.0	2	0	0	0.0	0	18	6,713	17.6	3	449
1881	27	1,078	2.9	2	0	0	0.0	0	7	2,472	6.7	4	357
1883	26	1,181	2.6	3	1	540	1.2	0	10	7,265	16.2	4	301
1885	27	1,660	3.1	3	0	0	0.0	0	17	12,560	23.2	5	432
1887	27	3,579	6.0	3	0	0	0.0	0	18	12,328	20.5	5	389
1889	26	3,280	5.1	2	0	0	0.0	0	17	17,269	26.8	7	465
1891	27	9,132	9.9	3	2	2,000	2.2	0	26	31,148	33.6	11	399
1893	28	1,795	2.2	1	5	4,053	4.9	2	29	26,210	31.7	14	410
1895	27	3,207	3.4	0	12	10,742	11.3	2	27	30,786	32.4	14	405

Notes: 1869 party vote totals indicate only votes cast for constituency winners.
"Anti-Semites" in 1893 includes 4 German Reform candidates and 1 German Social candidate.
"Anti-Semitic" caucuses of 1893 and 1895 include 1 German Reformer and 1 German Social.
Total Landtag seats = 80, except 1871 (79) and 1893-95 (82).
These totals do not include votes cast in by-elections and run-off elections.

Sources: Eugen Würzburger, "Die Wahlen für die Zweite Kammer der Ständeversammlung von 1869 bis 1896," Zeitschrift des K. Sächsischen Statistischen Landesamtes, Jg. 51, H. 1 (1905), 1-12.
Gerhard A. Ritter, "Das Wahlrecht und die Wählerschaft der Sozialdemokratie im Königreich Sachsen 1867-1914," in G. A. Ritter, ed., Der Aufstieg der deutschen Arbeiterbewegung (Munich, 1990), Tables 7 and 8.
Some figures calculated by the author.

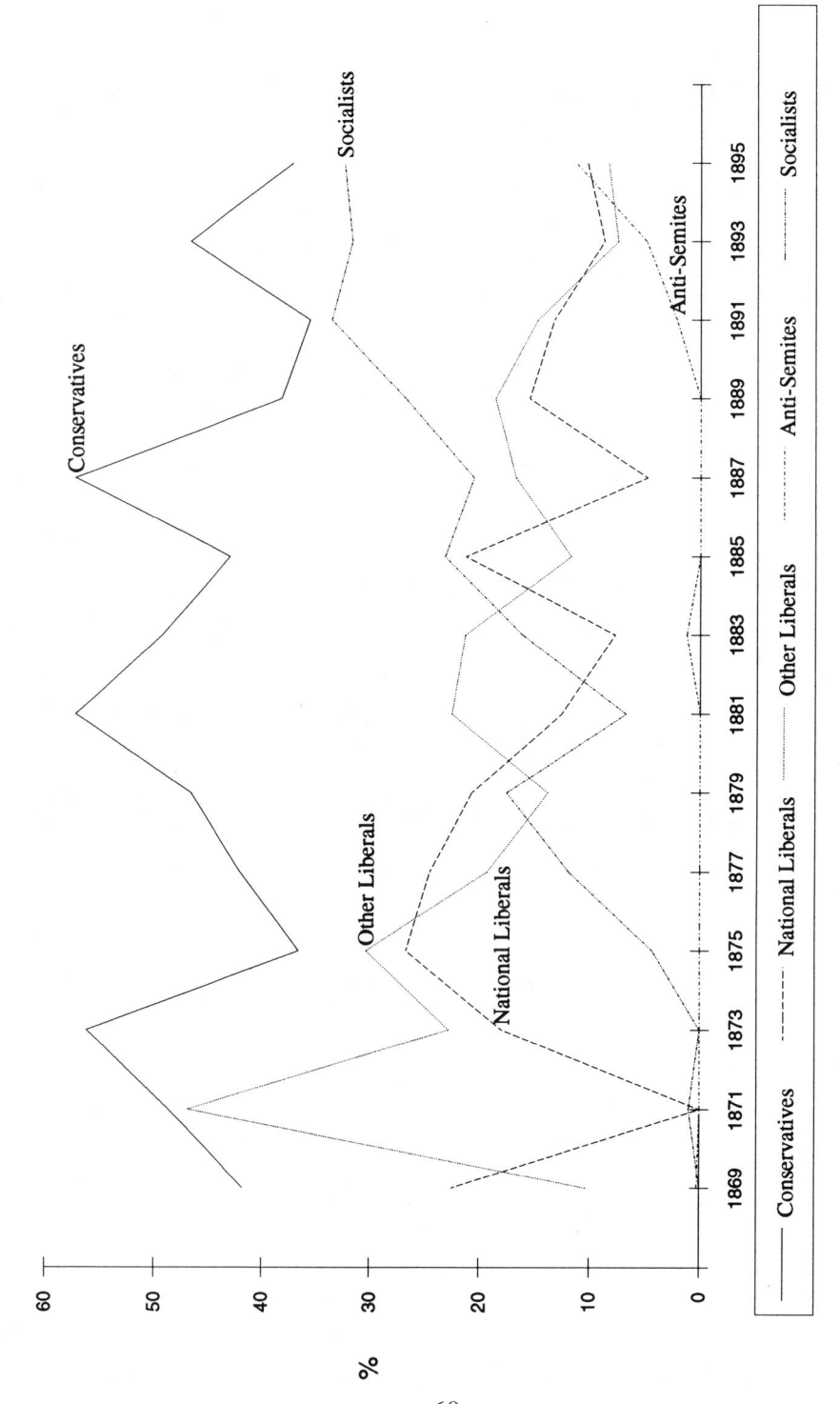

Figure 2. Landtag elections in Saxony, 1869–1895. (Percentage of total vote.)

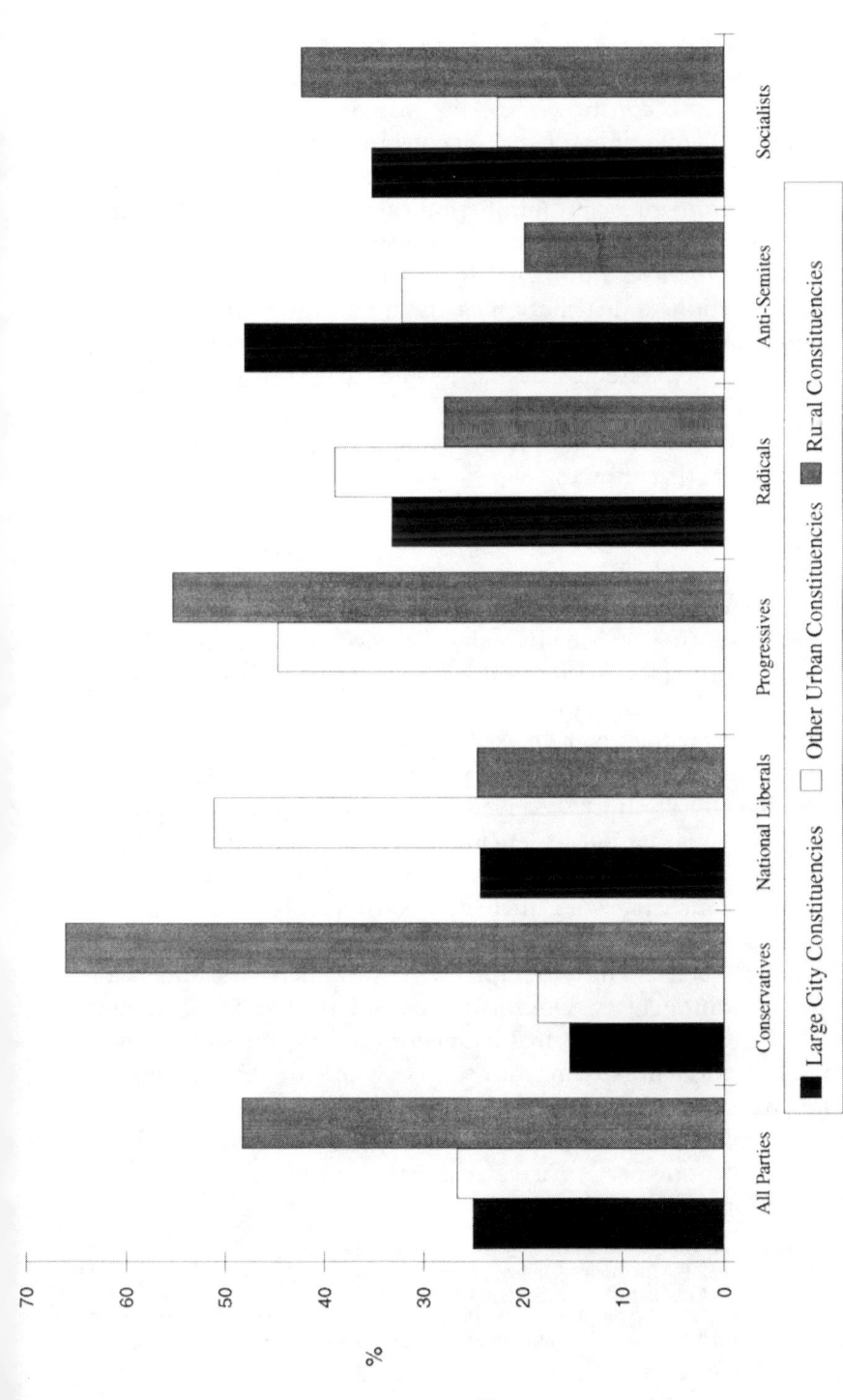

Figure 3. Saxon Landtag elections, 1891–95. (Percentage of party's vote won in each constituency type.)

encies cast ballots only in every third election, that is, every six years. It makes sense therefore to compare the results from successive elections in the same constituencies, for instance, in 1883, 1889, and 1895. As well, the eighty Landtag constituencies (two more were added in 1892) were divided into three categories. First came the "large-city" constituencies, numbering thirteen in 1895. The "other urban" constituencies numbered twenty-four in 1895, and the "rural" constituencies numbered forty-five. As Figure 3 illustrates, the disproportionate distribution of these constituencies resulted in 48.3 percent of all votes being cast in rural constituencies (which, of course, in Saxony were less classically rural than, for instance, in the eastern provinces of Prussia).

We know least about the various left-liberal party factions in the state. It appears that after a strong showing shortly after unification, a long-term decline was suffered by the most "principled" left-liberal faction, known in Saxony as the Radicals (*Freisinn*). This party was consistently described in disparaging tones by Count Dönhoff; he labeled its members "Radicals of Richter'ish persuasion," by which he meant that they ascribed to the "sterile" opposition and antimilitarism of the national Radical leader, Eugen Richter. The Radicals lost their last Landtag seat in the elections of October 1895, but long before then they had "ceased to be a serious opponent to the parties of order."[17] The Saxon Progressive Party (*Sächsische Fortschrittspartei*), by contrast, received conspicuous praise for its "undogmatic" representation of left-liberal views. Even after founding an independent *Verein* for Saxony in the mid-1870s, the Progressives' share of the Reichstag vote fluctuated considerably throughout the 1880s. This was due largely to a fluid demarcation between different factions of liberals. The biographies of these deputies underscore their social homogeneity. Dominant among left-liberal and National Liberal factions were municipal councilors and mayors, commercial and judicial councilors, bank directors, owners of various types of middle-sized manufacturing and business establishments, and members of chambers of commerce. This grouping also included a handful of small landowners, master artisans, and justices of the peace.

The National Liberal Party (*Nationalliberale Partei* or NLP) in Sax-

17. Count Carl von Dönhoff to Chancellor Chlodwig zu Hohenlohe-Schillingsfürst, 18 Oct. 1895, PA Bonn, I A Sachsen (Königreich) (hereafter cited as Sachsen) 60, Bd. 3. The following discussion is based on Dönhoff's reports; Fritz Specht and Paul Schwabe, *Die Reichstagswahlen 1867–1907*, 3rd ed. (Berlin, 1908), 218–34; Ritter and Niehuss, *Arbeitsbuch;* and the *Sächsischer Landtags-Almanach 1887* (Dresden, 1887).

ony was the party of choice for most successful and ambitious Saxon entrepreneurs. It won a large proportion of its votes in the urban constituencies outside Dresden and Leipzig (see Figure 3).[18] As the party most closely identified with Prussianism and unification, the Saxon NLP initially made little headway in a state where particularism remained strong. In the early 1870s it became standard practice for National Liberals to ally with Conservatives at election time, especially in Dresden. Although this cooperation paid dividends in the 1874 Reichstag elections, tensions erupted during the Reichstag campaign of 1877. By the Saxon Landtag elections of 1879, which were overshadowed by more stirring events in the Reichstag, the National Liberals had already grown "silent and apathetic."[19] A brief resurgence followed the implementation of Bismarck's *Kartell* with the Conservatives for the Reichstag elections of 1887. But in the early 1890s the National Liberals seemed to retreat into a policy of docility and indolence; they fielded candidates in only a few of the Landtag constituencies (see Table 2). Gustav Stresemann noted in the mid-1890s that the NLP was still ridiculed by influential Dresdeners, who equated it with "Prussianism."[20]

Of all the Saxon parties, it is the Conservative Party that emerges from the contemporary record in sharpest profile. A formal Conservative *Landesverein* was not established until May 1878. This statewide association, with which local Conservative clubs could not legally be affiliated, had fewer than 900 official members in the early 1880s and never attracted more than about 2,000. However, contemporaries estimated that about ten times that number belonged to local Conservative *Vereine*. These allegedly numbered about 50 in 1892 and over 100 in 1912. The largest were in Dresden, with about 2,000 members, and in Leipzig with about 1,500 members.[21] The Conservative *Landesverein* was led after 1883 by Baron Heinrich von Friesen-Rötha, a large landowner, a luminary in the German Society of Nobles, and a member of the national Conservative Party's Committee of Eleven. Friesen relinquished his chairmanship of the *Landesverein*

---

18. In 1907 45 local NLP *Vereine* existed in the kingdom, compared with 428 in Prussia and 819 in the Reich; *Organisationshandbuch der Nationalliberalen Partei des Deutschen Reiches*, 6th ed. (Berlin, 1914–15), 366–8.
19. H. B. Oppenheim to Eduard Lasker, 16 Aug. 1879, cited in Sheehan, *Liberalism*, 190.
20. Koszyk, *Stresemann*, 84.
21. Thomas Nipperdey, *Die Organisation der deutschen Parteien vor 1918* (Düsseldorf, 1961), 250; *Reichsbote*, 31 July 1892; Dönhoff to Hohenlohe, 15 May 1899, PA Bonn, Sachsen 48, Bd. 19; *Grossenhainer Tageblatt*, 12 Sept. 1905, no. 427; *Dresdner Nachrichten*, 10 Dec. 1912, no. 341.

in May 1894 after a heart attack and unwise investments had brought financial ruin. From that time on, the Saxon Conservatives had a de facto leader who epitomized what Friedrich Naumann called the "authoritarian type" (*Herrenmensch*) in Imperial Germany.[22] *Geheimer Hofrat* Dr. Paul Mehnert was dubbed "Paul I" and "the uncrowned king of Saxony" by those who envied or feared his power. Arguably he was Saxony's most well-connected party politician from the 1880s until World War I. Mehnert was an estate owner, a lawyer, and director of the State Agricultural Credit Association. He chaired Dresden's Conservative *Verein* after 1887 (when he was only thirty-five years old), the Conservative Landtag caucus from the mid-1890s, and the *Landesverein* after about 1908. He also served between 1899 and 1909 as president of the Saxon lower house, after which he was selected to the upper chamber. Mehnert's influence, however, reached far beyond Saxony, and even though he sat in the Reichstag only between 1890 and 1893, his reputation as a power broker of national importance was well deserved.[23] The list of organizations to which he had close ties, or on whose executive boards he sat, reads like a roll call of Imperial Germany's most powerful nationalist pressure groups and administrative bodies.

The typical Saxon Conservative was anything but a *Krautjunker*.[24] In the Saxon Landtag of 1887–9, fourteen of forty-seven Conservative deputies represented urban constituencies. Overall, the caucus was composed largely of bureaucrats and other state employees (including school administrators), army officers, mayors, lawyers, functionaries in agricultural associations, a few factory owners, a few artisans, and a number of estate owners. The same social origins were typical of those who belonged to the executive committee of the Saxon Conservative Party in 1909 and its representation on the national Conservative Party's Committee of Fifty in 1910. Thus Conservatives in Saxony were probably far closer in social background to

22. Friedrich Naumann, *Demokratie und Kaisertum* (Berlin, 1900), 92f.
23. Rudolf Martin, *Deutsche Machthaber* (Berlin, 1910). See also James Retallack, "Conservatives *contra* Chancellor: Official Responses to the Spectre of Conservative Demagoguery from Bismarck to Bülow," *Canadian Journal of History* 20 (1985): 228f.; and idem, "The Road to Philippi: The Conservative Party and Bethmann Hollweg's 'Politics of the Diagonal' 1909–1914," in Larry Eugene Jones and James Retallack, eds., *Between Reform, Reaction, and Resistance: Studies in the History of German Conservatism* (New York, Oxford, Munich, forthcoming 1993).
24. See K. von Langsdorff, ed., *Die Landwirtschaft im Königreich Sachsen* (Dresden, 1889), 100ff., 339ff.; for the following, see the *Sächsischer Landtags-Almanach 1887*, 63–81; *Deutsche Tageszeitung*, 21 Apr. 1909; and Charles Bacheller, "Class and Conservatism: The Changing Social Structure of the German Right, 1900–1928" (Ph.D. diss., University of Wisconsin–Madison, 1976).

their liberal and National Liberal colleagues than Conservatives anywhere else in the Reich; this allowed them to claim that they represented all social groups interested in combating the advance of Social Democracy. Even though political agitation in favor of the *Mittelstand* always stood at the center of Conservative politics in Saxony, by 1912 the *Landesverein* had established special working groups to address the interests of industrialists and officials. However, these innovations reflected less a genuine desire to broaden the party's constituency or represent a diversity of economic interests than an attempt to paper over a long-standing conflict between the urban-industrial and rural-agrarian wings of the party.[25]

This survey of the party constellation in Saxony suggests why both the old and the new *Mittelstand* provided fertile soil for every political faction in the state. With increasing frequency, all Saxon parties stressed their concern for the welfare of the *Mittelstand* and sought to make inroads in the political territory of their competitors with whatever means lay at their disposal. Figure 3 shows that in the Landtag elections of 1891–5 the anti-Semites were strongly represented in large cities and other rural constituencies, and the SPD was challenging the Conservatives for votes in the rural districts. Least advantaged in this struggle for *Mittelstand* votes were the left liberals, who were already in decline during the 1880s. Contemporaries and later historians agree that this decline was due principally to the defection of skilled workers, craftsmen, schoolteachers, small traders, small business owners, lower state officials, and other white-collar workers from Radical and Progressive ranks. These groups appear to have migrated principally to the Social Democrats and the anti-Semites, but they also defected in considerable numbers to the Conservatives. Thus in Reichstag elections the Conservatives,[26] allied with the National Liberals, did not suffer decline as early in Saxony as in the Reich as a whole – a point often overlooked in the literature. Between 1881 and 1890 the percentage of the vote won by these parties fluctuated little, beginning and ending just under 50 percent (see Table 1). Over the same period, however, voter turnout for Reichstag elections in Saxony rose sharply, so that the total number of votes won by these parties increased by over 75 percent. Moreover, together they won sixteen Saxon Reichstag seats in 1890

---

25. See, for example, *Reichsbote*, 6 Apr. 1904, no. 80.
26. Saxon contemporaries made no distinction between the German Conservative Party (*Deutschkonservative Partei* or DKP) and the Imperial Party (*Reichspartei* or RP), known in Prussia as the Free Conservative Party.

and held the socialists to six seats — a greater margin of victory than they had achieved in the late 1870s.

TROUBLED WATERS

One major political grouping remains to be located between the "forces of revolution" and the "parties of order" in Saxony: the anti-Semites. Before 1890 only a small number of Conservatives expressed concern about affinities between anti-Semitism and socialism. But Saxony's anti-Semites had challenged the traditional "politics of notables" (*Honoratiorenpolitik*) long before then. When Alexander Pinkert began to rally supporters in Dresden by founding the first anti-Semitic *Reformverein* there in November 1879, he prepared the way for the first International Anti-Jewish Congress, held in Dresden in 1882. Subsequently, *Reformvereine* sprang up quickly. By 1885 there were allegedly 52 such associations in Saxony; by 1890 there were 136.[27] A second Anti-Jewish Congress, held in Chemnitz in 1883, had meanwhile attracted more attention, not only internationally but from impoverished *Mittelständler* in the streets. Anti-Semitism also thrived in Leipzig. The anti-Semitic publicist Theodor Fritsch established a *Reformverein* there in the spring of 1886, and soon its membership grew to 1,500 (that is, equal to the membership of the Leipzig Conservative *Verein*).

It was in the state capital, however — where both municipal councilors and municipal senators jostled for influence with state legislators from both houses of the Landtag — that anti-Semitism had its greatest impact. Already in the late 1870s and early 1880s Conservatives and National Liberals in Dresden were refusing each other support when runoff ballots against socialists became necessary.[28] After one of August Bebel's victories in Dresden the Conservative *Dresdner Nachrichten* noted — only half regretfully — that "the results of the run-off ballot show only that Dresden's hatred of the National Liberals is stronger than its fear of Social Democracy." But soon the anti-Semitic Reformers and the Christian Social followers of Court Preacher Adolf Stöcker complicated matters further. In 1881 Stöcker faced a joint candidate nominated by the Conservatives and National

---

27. Peter Pulzer, *The Rise of Political Anti-Semitism in Germany and Austria* (New York, 1964), 104; Dieter Fricke, "Antisemitische Parteien," in D. Fricke et al., eds., *Lexikon zur Parteiengeschichte*, 4 vols. (Leipzig, 1983–6), 1:77–88, puts the 1890 figure at only eighty.
28. For the following, see Otto Richter, *Geschichte der Stadt Dresden in den Jahren 1871 bis 1902*, 2nd ed. (Dresden, 1904), 15ff., 36ff., 59ff.; Specht and Schwabe, *Reichstagswahlen*, 221.

Liberals: *Justizrat* Dr. Stübel, mayor of Dresden. In the runoff ballot between Bebel and Stübel, an extremely high voter turnout (82.4 percent) contributed to violent demonstrations in front of Dresden's city hall by crowds waiting to hear the results. This time the antisocialist candidate prevailed. But when Stübel entered the Reichstag he joined the National Liberal caucus, a move for which he was strongly criticized by a growing number of opposition deputies in Dresden's municipal council. Throughout 1882 and 1883 this criticism mounted, eventually taking the form of an opposition alliance among anti-Semites, property owners, and Conservatives. Having thoroughly disrupted the complacent and congenial world of municipal politics in Dresden – in both the lower and upper chambers – this faction ousted the last remaining Jewish representative in 1883. Soon thereafter it gained a majority in the lower house that proved to be remarkably durable. Leader of this disruptive "Conservative-Reformist" group was *Baumeister* (master builder) Gustav Hartwig, a member of the Saxon Conservative Party and a leading figure in Dresden's influential House-Owners Association. In 1884 the anti-Semites in Dresden rallied behind Hartwig, and although the Conservatives and National Liberals mounted a countercandidate, Hartwig entered the runoff ballot and defeated Bebel by some 2,700 votes. Hartwig joined the Conservative caucus in the Reichstag but was rewarded in November 1885 by being expelled from the Saxon Conservative Party. This paved the way for the victory of *Kartell* candidates in Dresden during the Reichstag elections of 1887 and 1890. Significantly, however, Saxon Conservatives refused a broader amalgamation of antisocialist forces in the state. In reaction to the idea of a "middle party" (*Mittelpartei*), to which both Chancellor Bismarck and the Saxon National Liberals aspired, Conservatives charged that such a "mish-mash party" would demand the surrender of their principles. The Prussian envoy and Bismarck, in turn, labeled the *Landesverein*'s chairman, Friesen, an "extreme Conservative, particularist and pugnacious," and one of the "hyperconservative elements" within the party.[29] Even Mehnert's enthusiasm for the *Kartell* had its limits; he fought a National Liberal incumbent for nomination as a *Kartell* candidate in 1890.

29. See Dönhoff to Otto von Bismarck, 5 Jan. 1881, 12 Feb. 1882, 24 Mar. 1883, 25 Feb. 1884, and [O. v. Bismarck] to Dönhoff, 7 Apr. 1883, in PA Bonn, Sachsen 50, Bd. 1; Dönhoff to [Herbert] v. Bismarck, 15 Nov. 1888, PA Bonn, I A Preussen Nr. 3, Bd. 1; *Reichsbote,* 31 July 1888, no. 182; and *Neue Preussische (Kreuz-) Zeitung* (hereafter *Kreuzzeitung*), 31 July 1888, no. 279.

These tensions were even more evident at the level of state politics after 1890.[30] In late September 1891, with Landtag elections just three weeks away, the right-wing parties in Saxony appeared headed for disaster. Their voters were more apathetic than ever, reported the Prussian envoy; bored with Landtag elections, they were focusing exclusively on events in the Reichstag. Hardly any Conservative or National Liberal election committees had been constituted, and this had two undesirable effects: Many constituencies were still without right-wing candidates, and in others the "parties of order" (*Ordnungsparteien*) were so hopelessly disunited that three, four, or five candidates were running against each other. In the meantime, the socialists had selected all their candidates in April. The agitation they had unleashed since then suggested that both Dresden constituencies would fall to the SPD – and others might too, Dönhoff wrote, unless the right-wing parties "soon join the election campaign with their *united* forces." Any victories the socialists scored would greatly increase their self-confidence, for they would allow their leaders to point to the "steadily growing successes of their party."

As Table 2 shows, the previous Landtag elections of 1889 had increased the SPD caucus to seven members (an eighth was added in a by-election in 1890). The balloting in 1889 had also shown a sharp decline in the Conservatives' share of the vote over 1887 and an increase for the SPD from 20.5 to 26.8 percent. These elections were governed by the electoral law of 3 December 1868, which provided for direct, equal, and (theoretically) secret balloting. Eligible to vote were all male citizens who had attained the age of twenty-five and who either owned landed property or paid direct state taxes of at least three marks.[31] In the early 1890s this 3-mark tax threshold for enfranchisement – known as the "electoral census" or *Wahlcensus* – corresponded to an income of roughly 600 marks. Rather like Benjamin Disraeli's second reform bill of 1867 in England, and under the influence of Bismarck's novel franchise for the North German Confederation, this had been set at a level in 1868 that would enfranchise the more prosperous and independent craftsmen in the state but

---

30. For the following, see Dönhoff to Caprivi, 18 and 24 Sept. 1891, PA Bonn, Sachsen 60, Bd. 3.
31. See Victor Camillo Diersch, *Die geschichtliche Entwicklung des Landtagswahlrechts im Königreich Sachsen* (Leipzig, 1918), 189f.; Eugen Würzburger, "Die Wahlen für die Zweite Kammer der Ständeversammlung von 1869 bis 1896," *Zeitschrift des K. Sächsischen Statistischen Landesamtes* (Dresden) 51, no. 1 (1905):1–11; Ritter and Niehuss, *Arbeitsbuch*, 164.

would exclude the mass of wage laborers.[32] Thus 9.9 percent of Saxons were enfranchised for Landtag elections in 1869. By 1895 this had risen to about 14.3 percent of the population (roughly 536,000 out of 3,755,000). Even then, about three of ten Saxon males who were eligible to vote in Reichstag elections were excluded from Landtag elections.

When the first results from the Landtag elections of 13 October 1891 were reported, the Prussian envoy met to discuss the outcome with his closest contact in the Saxon ministry: Interior Minister Count Georg von Metzsch-Reichenbach. Metzsch ascribed the fact that the SPD had almost doubled its vote (over 1889) to the lapse of the antisocialist laws in late September 1890.[33] As a consequence police action against socialist meetings was only intermittent, and the SPD press became "more free and more impudent [*freier und frecher*]" throughout 1891. Metzsch also blamed socialist gains on the defection of lower officials, who at the time received notoriously poor pay. Most important of all, he conceded, was the SPD's success in helping workers achieve the electoral census of three marks. Through savings and credit institutions, through a general increase in wages, living standards, and inflation, through encouraging in-migrants to apply for Saxon citizenship – but also through what Metzsch described as "sundry [and] often disreputable machinations" – the SPD had contributed to a sharp increase in the number of enfranchised voters, especially in the previous few years and especially in the large cities.[34] In 1891 22 percent more Saxons were eligible to vote than there had been in 1885, the last occasion elections had been held in the same Landtag constituencies. For this reason, Metzsch confided to the Prussian envoy that he thought the tax threshold of three marks was too low. He also believed that Saxony's repressive association law (dating from 1850) was now "more necessary than ever."

More revealing still is the bitterness with which both Metzsch and Dönhoff blamed the parties of order for the rise of the socialist vote. When Dönhoff drew up his survey of election results for Chancellor Leo von Caprivi on 14 October 1891, he could not have known that in the next fifteen years he would pen perhaps a dozen more such

---

32. As noted in Warren, *Red Kingdom*, 20.
33. Despite their Landtag majority the Saxon Conservatives had reluctantly followed the national trend and rescinded these laws; for this and the following, see Dönhoff to Caprivi, 14 and 16 Oct. 1891, PA Bonn, Sachsen 60, Bd. 3.
34. See Würzburger, "Wahlen," 2.

reports – or that most of them would capture his sense of disbelief and exasperation that the Saxon right was unable to unite in the face of the socialist threat. Although limits of space do not allow the lengthy citation necessary to convey the tone of this remarkable document, it touched on every theme that came to dominate the calculations of antisocialist forces in the years ahead. These included

1. the demographic inevitability of socialist gains at the polls unless association laws and voting regulations were rigidly enforced or revised;
2. the SPD's talent for recruitment, organization, discipline, propaganda, and rhetorical excess;
3. the moral victories scored by the SPD at the polls even though their caucus remained small;
4. the shame felt by Saxon burghers who were represented in parliament by SPD deputies with the most dubious background and character;
5. the unwillingness of the anti-Semites to join an antisocialist bloc and their preference for independent candidates (especially in the large cities);
6. the apathy and shortsightedness of right-wing voters;
7. the organizational incompetence of the parties of order and their inability to avoid competing candidacies in endangered constituencies;
8. the extremely slim margins by which right-wing candidates were either defeated or forced to contest what should have been unnecessary runoff ballots;
9. their belated discovery that they were largely agents of their own demise;
10. and the likelihood that the lessons learned in one election would be forgotten in the next.

THE TWIN FACES OF ANARCHY

Between the Saxon elections of late 1891 and late 1893, the challenge presented to the Conservatives by both socialists and anti-Semites gained in strength. Although the Conservatives were resolute in opposing the "party of revolution," they reacted in a much more ambiguous way to the sudden popularity of anti-Semitism as an election issue and to the anti-Semitic parties as potential allies. On the one hand, Saxon Conservatives displayed profound and genuine anti-

Jewish sentiments in both their propaganda and their suggested revisions to the Conservative program.[35] Thus the *Landesverein* stated proudly in one of its rare official publications that "not a single Jew is to be found in any Conservative *Verein* in Saxony."[36] Baron von Friesen called for the exclusion of Jews from all parliamentary bodies in Germany, and others claimed that there was no truth to charges that Saxon Conservatives liked Jews personally or did business with them. On the other hand, the Saxon Conservative leaders agreed with other moderates within the national Conservative Party that "rabble-rousing" anti-Semitism and Social Democracy were inherently similar and equally dangerous to state and society. They attempted whenever possible to state their opposition to the more extreme anti-Semites organized in the German *Reformvereine*, while at the same time calling repeatedly for a revision to the Reichstag franchise and for more repressive measures against Social Democracy. A long speech Friesen delivered at a Saxon party congress in June 1892 – which drew the scorn of anti-Semites everywhere – stated that some elements of the anti-Semitic movement lacked the "moral sobriety, the spiritual maturity, the historical learning [and] the calm circumspection" necessary for a proper consideration of the Jewish question. These deficiencies, Friesen continued, sprang from "quick tongues" and "strong lungs," from "dubious backgrounds [and] misspent lives." Whether they led men to seek sport or profit from anti-Semitism, they fostered a kind of demagoguery that in Saxony was splintering the forces of the right.[37]

The general policy of the Saxon Conservatives was therefore repudiated in three ways when the national Conservative Party revised its program at the Tivoli party congress on 8 December 1892. First, the rank-and-file party activists (including many anti-Semites from Saxony) who dominated the day's proceedings struck down a program plank condemning the excesses of radical anti-Semitism. Second, the congress endorsed a strongly antigovernmental and anti-*Kartell* orientation for future Conservative policy. Third, a proposal to add a new clause calling for more energetic state action

---

35. See Heinrich von Friesen-Rötha, "Gesichtspunkte für ein revidiertes konservatives Programm," copy in Bundesarchiv Koblenz (hereafter BA Koblenz), Sammlung Fechenbach, Bd. 19; H. von Friesen-Rötha, *Schwert und Pflug* (Berlin, 1907), esp. 524–6.
36. Konservativer Landesverein im Königreich Sachsen, ed., *Die Konservativen im Kampfe gegen die Uebermacht des Judentums und für die Erhaltung des Mittelstandes* (Leipzig, 1892), 1.
37. H. von Friesen-Rötha, *Conservativ! Ein Mahnruf in letzter Stunde* (Leipzig, 1892), 28; cf. *Reichsbote*, 17 June and 28 July 1892, nos. 139 and 182, respectively.

against Social Democracy was considerably watered down, so that all mention of the use of state force was deleted.[38] Thus Friesen, Mehnert, and others believed that the Tivoli congress had failed to support decisive action against the two greatest threats to society – the anti-Semites and the Social Democrats.

How did these developments at the national level affect legislative and electoral politics in Saxony? In the Landtag session of 1891–2 few ripples were felt. This situation changed in March 1892 when a Reichstag by-election in Saxony, at the height of anti-Semitic excitement in the Reich, resulted in the defeat of a Conservative incumbent.[39] It appeared that the anti-Semitic and Conservative candidates had split the nonsocialist vote, allowing the SPD to win on the first ballot with only 51 percent of the vote. This by-election generated considerable controversy because of feuding between National Liberal and Conservative activists at the constituency level and because Stöcker apparently supported the anti-Semitic candidate.[40] These developments, in turn, had been precipitated by the Conservative *Landesverein*'s sudden announcement the month before that the *Kartell* agreement with the National Liberals was terminated: Henceforth electoral committees in each constituency would decide what alliances were to be concluded.[41] This by-election showed immediately what the consequences of such a policy would be. Shortly thereafter, in the last days of the 1891–2 Landtag session, the parties of order reversed themselves and signed a new agreement (*Einigung*) to maintain their antisocialist posture in Saxony even during parliamentary recesses. This pact – soon known as the Saxon *"Kartell"* – included not only Conservatives and National Liberals drawn from both the upper and lower houses, but every parliamentary member of the Saxon Progressive Party as well. In all, 102 deputies signed it – a virtually unanimous alliance of the nonsocialist deputies in Saxony. The semiofficial and right-wing press was pleased that anti-socialist unity was now institutionalized, and Dönhoff personally hoped that such a *Kartell* would be inaugurated in the parliaments of Saxony's neighbors.

The story of political anti-Semitism's sudden breakthrough in the

---

38. Further details in James Retallack, *Notables of the Right. The Conservative Party and Political Mobilization in Germany, 1876–1918* (Boston and London, 1988), ch. 6; and idem, "Conservatives *contra* Chancellor," 210–15.
39. Dönhoff to Caprivi, 13 Nov. 1891, 4 and 5 Apr. 1892, PA Bonn, Sachsen 60, Bd. 3.
40. *Konservatives Wochenblatt*, 9 Apr. 1892, no. 177.
41. *Norddeutsche Allgemeine Zeitung*, 8 Feb. 1892, no. 64.

Reichstag elections of June 1893 is well known.[42] Neither of the two principal anti-Semitic groups, the German Socials and the German Reformers, had captured a significant number of Saxon votes in the Reichstag elections of 1890. In June 1893, however, anti-Semitic candidates in Saxony received over 93,000 votes (15.9 percent of the total). Each of the six anti-Semitic deputies elected in Saxony won seats that had previously belonged to Conservatives, including those held by Friesen and Mehnert, and both Dresden constituencies. The Conservative share of the popular vote declined only slightly, from 28.0 percent in 1890 to 25.1 percent in 1893. In fact the Conservatives out-polled the anti-Semites by a considerable margin. Yet the number of Conservative *seats* plummeted from thirteen to six, and the SPD increased its Saxon representation in the Reichstag from six to seven deputies (winning 45.8 percent of the popular vote). Not surprisingly, Friesen and other leaders of the Conservative *Landesverein* immediately escalated their criticism of the anti-Semites (and of the German Reform Party in particular). In August 1893 Mehnert referred to the German Reformers as "wild anarchists."[43] A few months later, an official Conservative declaration denounced the Reformers for their "selfish ambition," their "immoderate and impossible demands," and their preference for "noise and scandal."[44]

Did the government and the parties of order in Saxony unite more closely in the twin faces of anarchy? Hardly. Three factors disrupted antisocialist unity. First, in the winter of 1893–4 a serious conflict was raging between the Conservatives and the Saxon ministry. Interior Minister Metzsch actually condemned the Conservatives with the same charge of demagoguery that they were ascribing to the German Reformers, because they had leveled swinging attacks on the government for its alleged inaction against the Social Democrats and its refusal to invoke exceptional laws. In their official party organ, *Das Vaterland,* the Conservatives had warned Metzsch that their patience was exhausted: "The consciousness of power's plenitude is good, but its mere existence is not enough; it must also be palpable."[45] In the Landtag the Conservatives' repeated motions to invoke forceful measures against the SPD put the government in an acutely

---

42. Richard S. Levy, *The Downfall of the Anti-Semitic Political Parties in Imperial Germany* (New Haven, Conn., 1975), 85ff.; Pulzer, *Rise,* 123ff.
43. Mehnert to Stöcker, 5 Aug. 1893, cited in Fricke, "Antisemitische Parteien," 85.
44. *Dresdner Anzeiger,* 7 Dec. 1893.
45. Dönhoff to Caprivi, 9, 22, and 28 Dec. 1893, PA Bonn, Sachsen 48, Bd. 17, including the article, "Landgraf werde hart."

difficult position – no matter, Metzsch noted, whether it claimed that existing laws sufficed to combat the threat of subversion or whether it announced that new legislation was necessary. In either case only the SPD would profit from a public discussion of the issue, and Metzsch professed amazement that the Conservatives, of all people, would want to raise this troublesome question in parliament. In private too Conservatives were debating ways to force the government to abandon its "temporizing stance" toward Social Democracy. Though they never dared to do so publicly, in private party councils they used a word – "ruthless [*rücksichtslos*]" – to describe the way they expected the government to use the power of the state against the SPD. This conflict carried over into parliamentary debate on other issues. Finance Minister Werner von Watzdorf was heard to refer to "these so-called parties of order" and wondered aloud whether the Landtag was becoming a Reichstag in miniature, where government ministers would be forced to pass bills with ad hoc majorities that sometimes included the parties of opposition. But Count Dönhoff believed the explanation for Conservative intransigence lay in the electoral game itself. In Landtag and Reichstag campaigns, he observed, the Conservatives were forced into a "competitive struggle of promises" designed to win votes; this compelled Conservatives to adopt demands inconsistent with their character as a state-supporting party. It was all the more worrying, therefore, that the party was led at this time by a man (Friesen) "who operates by means of incitement" rather than moderation and whose "lust for battle" was directed mainly against the government.[46]

Second, the Landtag campaign leading to the elections of 19 October 1893 again found the parties of order in disarray.[47] Although the Saxon *Kartell* was still formally in place, Metzsch was gravely worried because each party was preparing its own election manifesto. The Conservatives feared a further defection to the ranks of the anti-Semites. They were therefore proclaiming their own determination to solve the Jewish question, for instance by seeking a ban on Jewish immigration into Saxony, even though many observers believed such a defection had already occurred during the Reichstag campaign six months earlier. The National Liberals were also stressing their own "separate demands," including a raising of direct taxes, guarantees of

46. Dönhoff to Caprivi, 28 Dec. 1893 and 9 Jan. 1894, PA Bonn, Sachsen 48, Bd. 17.
47. For the following, see Dönhoff to Caprivi, 29 Sept., 21 Oct., and 9 Dec. 1893, PA Bonn, Sachsen 48, Bd. 17; Dönhoff to Caprivi, 15 Nov. 1893, PA Bonn, Sachsen 60, Bd. 3.

political independence for state officials, the liberalization of Saxony's association laws, and an official repudiation of anti-Semitism. The National Liberals also declared that each party should contest whichever Landtag constituencies it believed it could win, whether in alliance with other nonsocialist parties or not. The Saxon interior minister reported that it would take all his energy to dissuade the Conservatives and National Liberals from publishing these separate manifestos; he was especially incensed that during the campaign he was forced to defend Saxony's association laws – which he continued to regard as essential to stem the tide of Social Democracy – in the face of attacks from both the right and the left. Meanwhile the anti-Semites were quarreling among themselves, and their campaign suffered accordingly. The German Reformers appeared unwilling to gamble for a victory in the Saxon Landtag elections because they did not want to diminish the euphoria lingering from their conquest of sixteen Reichstag seats. By contrast, the SPD's agitation was in full swing, this time focusing on one fairness issue that seemed to promise the greatest electoral rewards: the Saxon Landtag franchise. The SPD advocated the introduction of the Reichstag franchise for Saxony, not only for Landtag elections but for all local elections as well.

Third, when the polls closed on 19 October 1893, the anti-Semites had more than doubled their showing over 1891, winning 4,053 votes. True, the parties of order had averted the worst. Even though the SPD's caucus rose from eleven to fourteen members, its share of the vote fell off slightly, from the peak of 33.6 percent in 1891 to 31.7 percent. Yet the anti-Semites continued to pave the way for SPD victories in a number of constituencies, including the only one contested in Dresden. In one rural constituency the German Reformers mounted three separate candidates at the last minute, and in another urban constituency they achieved nothing other than to force the Conservative into a runoff ballot. "This demagogic party," Metzsch and the Conservatives agreed, was doing the work of the SPD by compromising antisocialist unity, by targeting Saxony's propertied classes as the enemies of the *Mittelstand,* and by conducting its agitation under the "mantle of loyalty." Worst of all, the Reformers seemed immune to the kinds of statesmanlike arguments that routinely pulled Conservatives and the more moderate German Socials back from the brink of formal opposition. When Metzsch dressed down Friesen for his party's recent attacks on the government, the Conservative chairman wrote an apologetic note and promised to put pressure on the editorial staff of *Das Vaterland*. When the German Socials took two seats from the National Liberals in the Landtag elections, they did so only after reaching an agreement beforehand that promised reciprocal support elsewhere. By contrast, when Metzsch summoned the prominent Dresden anti-Semite Gustav Hartwig for a personal audience and expressed his worries about the advance of the SPD, Hartwig's response was as ominous as it was cryptic: "Social Democracy," he declared, "is not yet the worst, by a long shot."

In the two Landtag sessions of 1893–4 and 1894–5 the parties of order appeared to consolidate their position. The Saxon *Kartell* was renewed after the first of these sessions in March 1894. At the same time, a new wrinkle was added by those determined to focus attention on the socialist threat. Mehnert took the lead in establishing a "Senior Assembly" (*Seniorenkonvent*) to foster antisocialist cooperation *outside* the Landtag. Consisting of four Conservatives, two National Liberals, and two Saxon Progressives, it was conceived as a kind of "appeals court" (*Schiedsgericht*) to which the right-wing parties could turn if they disagreed about how antisocialist unity was actually to be implemented.[48] But the balance of forces within this assembly revealed where the real power lay: the Conservatives dominated, and the National Liberals were grossly underrepresented.

Did electoral politics bear out this impression of right-wing solidarity? During Reichstag by-elections and the Landtag campaign of 1895, the answer must be no; later, when franchise reform suddenly became an issue in the winter of 1895–6, it is a qualified yes. There were a number of familiar factors that consistently hampered antisocialist unity. For one thing, the Berlin leadership of the Agrarian League (*Bund der Landwirte* or BdL) was notoriously unreliable in its endorsement of local pacts that Conservative *Vereine* made with National Liberals. For example, in a Reichstag by-election in May 1894 the Conservatives agreed to support the NLP candidate. However, the BdL leadership forced an unnecessary runoff ballot against a socialist when it refused to endorse this arrangement and called on its members to vote for an anti-Semitic candidate instead. This prompted Chancellor Caprivi to write "these asses!" in the margin to Dönhoff's report, and the latter complained about the arrogance of Berlin

---

48. Dönhoff to Caprivi, 18 Mar. 1894, PA Bonn, Sachsen 60, Bd. 3. Mehnert was the permanent *Geschäftsführer*.

politicians going over the heads of Saxon farmers and mixing in local election campaigns with which they were totally unfamiliar.[49]

The anti-Semitic Reformers also continued to lay roadblocks in the path of the parties of order. Again a Reichstag by-election was characteristic, this time in April 1895. In a constituency on the outskirts of Dresden a Conservative had narrowly defeated a socialist in 1890. In 1893 a Reform Party candidate overcame a Conservative rival and defeated a socialist in a close runoff ballot. But soon this anti-Semite had to resign his seat due to SPD "terrorism." His mother owned a large distillery in the area, and after the defeat of their candidate in 1893 the SPD had boycotted it. This boycott so reduced her income that she could no longer support her son while he attended Reichstag sessions in Berlin. The ensuing by-election campaign was extremely heated and closely observed: It pitted a compromise candidate of the Conservatives, National Liberals, and agrarians against a Reformer and a socialist. The SPD's confidence was considerably enhanced when the parties of order carelessly contravened Article 24 of Saxony's association law and issued a joint announcement of support for their candidate. In theory such "connections" between *Vereine* should have led the Saxon police to demand the immediate dissolution of the offending *Vereine*. In fact the police had recently done exactly that when SPD-affiliated gymnastic and choral societies had appeared together at a workers' festival. During the campaign, the Saxon government was therefore caught in the dilemma of finding a way to allow these state-supporting *Vereine* to continue their election campaigns in a critical constituency race while avoiding the charge that the government was already in effect invoking exceptional laws against the SPD. Some legal sophistry solved the government's dilemma, but it did not prevent an unhappy end to the campaign itself. By a margin of only 103 votes the SPD candidate won an absolute majority over the Conservative and the Reformer, who split the nonsocialist vote down the middle. Because the Social Democrats had not increased their vote at all over 1893, but also because they were not likely to relinquish the constituency in the future, their victory was all the more galling to the authorities and the Conservatives. If only the anti-Semitic candidate had withdrawn before the vote, Dönhoff observed, a runoff ballot would have pitted the Conservative against the socialist: In this case, those voters who stayed at home on

---

49. Report of 26 May 1894, PA Bonn, Deutschland 125, Nr. 3, Bd. 14.

the first ballot might have been more willing to do their patriotic duty and, in the runoff, tip the balance toward the Conservative. In the end, however, this fiasco showed yet again "that the intrusion of the anti-Semitic Reform Party in the election campaign only paves the way for Social Democracy."[50]

The blame for antisocialist disunity could not, however, be placed solely on the anti-Semites. Just two weeks before the elections the prospects for the parties of order were dismal, Dönhoff reported, "and indeed they are themselves to blame, for so far all sorts of petty squabbles and rivalries have not been conducive to a united campaign against the party of revolution."[51] The Saxon ministry expected that of the twenty-seven seats being contested, the SPD would retain its current five and would win four more. Hoping to avoid this, the government decided late in the campaign to offer concessions to the voters: Finance Minister Watzdorf cleverly announced that he would not invoke a 10 percent surtax on incomes that the Landtag had recently approved for the upcoming fiscal period. This deprived the SPD and the anti-Semites of one of their main campaign issues. The government's final call for right-wing unity also led some local Conservative and National Liberal election committees to abandon rival candidacies at the eleventh hour.

The Landtag election results in October 1895 surprised almost everyone (see Table 2). The SPD gained only one seat and lost another, leaving its caucus still at fourteen members. The anti-Semitic German Social Reform Party did not elect a single deputy, and the last Radical disappeared from the Landtag. However, the SPD polled over 13,000 more votes than in 1889.[52] Because the socialists appeared to have mobilized their supporters in many constituencies for the very first time, this upswing seemed certain to continue. And it was, of course, little comfort to the *Kartell* parties that, as in the Reichstag, the Social Democrats were winning a far greater proportion of the popular vote than they were Landtag seats. A degree of successful political mobilization was evident on the right too, but not in the middle. The Conservatives' total vote in the 1895 Landtag elections rose by about 10,600 votes over 1889, though its *share* of the vote compared poorly with its showing in 1889 and disastrously when compared to 1893. The total number of votes cast for National

50. Dönhoff to Hohenlohe, 15 and 27 Apr. 1895, PA Bonn, Deutschland 125, Nr. 3, Bd. 14.
51. For this and the following, see Dönhoff to Hohenlohe, 2, 15, and 18 Oct. 1895, 3 Nov. 1895, PA Bonn, Sachsen 60, Bd. 3.
52. Wurzbürger, "Wahlen," 1–11.

Liberals and Radicals declined slightly, and the Saxon Progressives lost almost half the votes they had gathered in 1889. The anti-Semites showed the greatest proportional increase: Having been completely unrepresented in these constituencies six years earlier, and having won about 4,000 votes in other constituencies in 1893, they now polled 10,742 votes or 11.3 percent of the total. More important, their showing in individual constituencies again split the *bürgerlich* vote and precipitated SPD victories. In one of the two Dresden constituencies contested, the SPD won with only 43.6 percent of the vote.[53] In two rural constituencies on the outskirts of Chemnitz, the SPD won with 46.7 percent of the vote in one and 51.7 percent in the other. In one urban constituency where the SPD polled fewer than 400 votes, a Reformer came within 21 votes of defeating a Conservative candidate. Another unhappy sign was that the Conservatives' increased vote total across the state revealed pockets where party agitation had obviously failed. Voter turnout in the two Dresden constituencies, for example, was less than 50 percent. "Certain" that the SPD and the anti-Semites had herded all their supporters to the polls, Dönhoff concluded that the overwhelming majority of nonvoters would have cast ballots for the parties of order. Therefore, he and other right-wing observers interpreted these results not only with "relief" but also as a "serious warning." The members of the Saxon *Kartell* had merely dodged another bullet – and they knew it.

THE CONTEXT OF FRANCHISE REFORM, 1894–6

Brief reference must be made to four final factors that, although not unrelated to those already discussed, had an important impact on the decision to revise the Saxon franchise. There is evidence, first, that some Saxon Conservatives believed a restricted Landtag franchise would debilitate the anti-Semites at the polls at least as much as it would the Social Democrats. This was because the radical anti-Semites allegedly drew the bulk of their support from the most impoverished and least sedentary elements of the *Mittelstand*. As well, in 1895 the anti-Semites were demanding that the Reichstag franchise be amended to introduce mandatory voting for all enfranchised citizens. They included this plank in their official Erfurt party program,

---

53. Under the Saxon system, a first-ballot victory was possible if a candidate won at least one-third of the votes cast.

when they also explicitly endorsed the preservation of the universal franchise for Reichstag elections.[54] That Conservatives would react allergically to the idea of mandatory voting is not as obvious as it might seem, for just such a proposal had already been considered in the Conservative press as a means to overcome the apathy of rightwing voters.[55] On balance, however, the Saxon Conservatives were strongly disinclined to consider a reform that would contribute further to the demagogic cultivation of the electorate.

The second factor influencing both the rationale and the *form* of franchise reform was a determination to stem the tide of Social Democrats entering the municipal councils of Saxony's largest cities. Although an examination of Saxon municipal politics must await a larger study,[56] Leipzig, Chemnitz, Dresden, and other cities contributed decisively to Saxony's growing reputation as "the classic land of disfranchisement." Although municipal councilors in these cities had already fine-tuned voting regulations before 1894, the introduction of class-based or occupational franchises for elections in Leipzig (1894), Chemnitz (1898), and Dresden (1905) cannot be underestimated. The Leipzig reform in particular set an important precedent for reformers in the Landtag and inspired similar action in countless smaller cities. It was not uncommon, for example, to find that when elections gave socialists a majority on a town council, antisocialist councilors would hastily pass restrictive franchise laws governing future elections before their mandate expired and before the new council was sworn in. Such legislation invariably received the immediate endorsement of the state ministry.[57]

Third, Saxon Conservatives played a large role in a turn to the right within the German Conservative Party in 1894–6. Before the Christian Social leaders were finally driven from the party, a debate raged on the general theme of "reform or revolution."[58] Some pro-reform Conservatives, especially those with anti-Semitic leanings, answered no to the question posed rhetorically in the title of one

---

54. Franz Stölting, "Wahlrecht und Wahlpflicht" (Ph.D. diss., University of Breslau, 1910), 28; Diersch, "Entwicklung," 191f.
55. For example, *Reichsbote,* 20 Oct. 1894, no. 246.
56. For the time being, see *Verein für Socialpolitik,* ed., *Verfassung und Verwaltungsorganisation der Städte,* 4/1 (*Königreich Sachsen*) = Schriften des Vereins für Socialpolitik 120 (Leipzig, 1905); Croon, "Vordringen," 32–4; Heinrich Heffter, *Die Deutsche Selbstverwaltung im 19. Jahrhundert* (Stuttgart, 1950), 565f., 613ff.; William H. Dawson, *Municipal Life and Government in Germany* (London and New York, 1914), 67–73.
57. Croon, "Vordringen," 34.
58. For further details and references, see Retallack, *Notables,* ch. 9.

popular pamphlet: "Should one drive the Social Democrats to acute revolution, to street battles?"[59] However, others agreed with the Saxon publicist Werner von Blumenthal, who had spoken up against radical anti-Semitism at the Tivoli congress and who wrote in 1894 that it was a "fatal mistake" to believe that one could disarm the SPD through social reform.[60] By 1896 most Conservatives felt that the government should regard the social question as a "pure question of power [*glatte Machtfrage*]." When the Conservatives dropped Stöcker in February 1896 – and with him the facade of being a people's party – they simultaneously injected a new stridency into their antisocialist rhetoric. This was revealed when a congress of party delegates deliberated social policy in November 1896. Whereas the DKP had explicitly rejected the use of force against socialists at Tivoli in December 1892, four years later Conservatives were just as resolute in the opposite direction – exactly as the Saxon Conservatives wished. The resolution agreed upon in November 1896 also explicitly warned against "party factionalism [*Parteizersplitterungen*]" in the face of the socialist threat.[61] It is therefore no accident that in the late 1890s the Saxon Conservative *Landesverein* had a particularly high profile within the national party. Dresden provided the venue in March 1897 for a DKP congress that aroused more than the usual press interest by virtue of its extreme antisocialist rhetoric: Among the policies advocated from the speaker' podium were a halt to social reform and the exclusion of SPD deputies from Reichstag committees. Although Mehnert was the ringleader, this "Bismarckian circus" offered what Dönhoff called a "great attraction" [sic]: Herbert von Bismarck. Because the younger Bismarck, like his father, symbolized a return to old-style *Kartellpolitik*, he immediately became the darling of the Saxon Conservatives. They subsequently tried to persuade him to run as a candidate in Dresden-Altstadt to prevent this constituency from going "red" in the next Reichstag election. Much to the relief of the Saxon government, Herbert declined the offer.[62]

The fourth factor – which, of course, partly determined the Con-

---

59. Karl von Fechenbach-Laudenbach, *Soll man die Sozialdemokratie zur akuten Revolution, zu Strassenkämpfen zwingen?* (Berlin and Leipzig, 1896).
60. Werner von Blumenthal, *Wer geht mit? Wider den Umsturz! Für den Mittelstand!* (Dresden, 1894), 8f.
61. "Beschlüsse des Delegiertentages der Deutschen Konservativen Partei vom 19. und 20. November 1896," in Felix Salomon, ed., *Die Deutschen Parteiprogramme,* 2nd ed. (Berlin and Leipzig, 1912), 2:97f.
62. Dönhoff to Hohenlohe, 23 Dec. 1897; PA Bonn, Deutschland 125, Nr. 3, Bd. 14.

servatives' move to the right – was a wave of antisocialist hysteria in national politics following the assassination of the French president in the summer of 1894. In September of that year Kaiser Wilhelm II tried to rally the Conservative Party for a campaign to protect "Religion, Morality, and Order." Though largely rhetorical, this campaign included the so-called Anti-Revolution Bill of 1894–5, which to the disgust of reactionary conservatives never achieved majority approval. It also included trials of socialist leaders alleged to have contravened Prussia's association laws in 1896–7 and the Hard-Labor Bill, which also failed to win approval in 1899. These bills themselves revealed the limits of the antisocialist consensus on the right,[63] but that, in turn, induced the Kaiser and others to try to bypass the Reichstag in order to implement reactionary measures in the individual federal states. As Wilhelm wrote to Chancellor Hohenlohe in August 1895: "This Reichstag can only be given thin gruel, like the budget. Something must be done in Prussia which the Empire can then copy. I believe that a short and severe association law would best solve the problems."[64] Wilhelm's observation was based in part on conversations with King Albert of Saxony, who also felt strongly that some legal curb on socialism was necessary and who had remarked to the Kaiser during maneuvers in 1894 that "things could not go on as they were."[65] By February 1895 King Albert and his ministers were hoping that Social Democratic violence in the streets might allow the federal princes to undertake a revision of the Reichstag franchise. We know that by the end of the decade the Saxon king and the other German princes thought better of such schemes. *Nevertheless,* the Saxons contributed decisively to the crisis of the mid-1890s. In 1895 they were still enthusiastic about a coup d'état against the socialists and the creation of a Reichstag consisting only of delegates from the various state Landtage. King Albert, Metzsch, and Dönhoff agreed that the federal states would have to have reasonably similar voting regulations for those Landtage. This might make

63. This view is supported by the work of Eleanor Turk: "An Examination of Civil Liberty in Wilhelmian Germany," *Central European History* 19 (1986): 327–8; and Turk, "Thwarting the Imperial Will: A Perspective on the Labor Regulation Bill and the Press of Wilhelmian Germany," in Jack Dukes and Joachim Remak, eds., *Another Germany. A Reconsideration of the Imperial Era* (Boulder, Colo., 1988), 115–38.
64. Letter of 31 Aug. 1895, cited in Turk, "Civil Liberty," 327.
65. Cited (n.d.) in Hellmut Kretzschmar, "Königreich und Land Sachsen," in Georg Wilhelm Sante and A. G. Ploetz Verlag, eds., *Geschichte der deutschen Länder. "Territorien-Ploetz"* (Würzburg, 1971), 2:548.

such a coup unworkable – but at least Saxony could lead the way.[66] The appropriate legislation was announced to the Landtag before the end of the year.

THE "ASSASSINATION" OF THE SAXON LANDTAG FRANCHISE

At the ceremonial opening of the 1895–6 Landtag session in mid-November 1895, storm signals were already flying. Within two days the SPD caucus introduced its familiar motion for the introduction of the universal franchise.[67] This time the parties of order departed from their usual response – silence – and went over to the offensive. Mehnert launched the counterattack when the SPD motion came up for debate on 10 December. In the course of a highly polemical speech, Mehnert presented his countermotion, signed by all members of the Conservative, National Liberal, and Saxon Progressive caucuses. This motion not only rejected the SPD proposal but gave the government guidelines for preparing its own legislation. Mehnert acknowledged that among themselves the nonsocialist deputies had diverse views about franchise reform. Some deputies favored raising the age of enfranchisement about twenty-five, others the electoral census above three marks. Some advocated mandatory voting, others plural voting. Some wanted proportional representation, others an estate-bound system. But all *bürgerlich* deputies agreed that the "wild agitation" evident during recent election campaigns was detrimental to the interests of the state. Thus Mehnert announced that the *Kartell* parties had agreed on the following principles upon which a future franchise reform bill should be based: (1) no one who currently possessed the Landtag franchise should lose it; (2) the distinction between urban and rural constituencies should be preserved; (3) no wholesale reelection of parliament should take place, but the system of partial renewal every two years should remain; and (4) in place of direct and unitary voting for deputies, a system of indirect multiclass voting should be introduced, along the lines of the Prussian model but designed to avoid its extreme plutocratic effects.

66. Dönhoff to Hohenlohe (copy), 12 Feb. 1895, in BA Koblenz, Nachlass Bernhard v. Bülow, Nr. 22, Bl. 61–8.
67. The following is based on paraphrased excerpts from speeches provided in Dönhoff's reports to Hohenlohe, 13 and 14 Nov. 1895; 4, 5, 12, 15, and 19 Dec. 1895; PA Bonn, Sachsen 60, Bd. 3; and in Diersch, "Entwicklung," 189ff.

Based so closely on the Prussian franchise, the advantages of such a system were obvious. Because the electoral census would be dropped and because the minimum voting age would not be raised, the nonsocialist parties could claim that they were actually broadening the franchise (later calculations estimated that about 150,000 Saxons would be newly enfranchised). Certainly no Saxon would be technically deprived of a constitutional privilege he had previously enjoyed. This point was of considerable importance to the two anti-Semites in the house and was obviously designed to undercut the immense propaganda value to socialist agitators if a more brutal act of disfranchisement were undertaken. In practice, of course, the three voting classes would give each voter in the first class disproportionate influence over those in the other two. As nonsocialist speakers made clear, they did not want Saxony to become another Hamburg, which was represented in the Reichstag by only the socialist deputies; instead Leipzig's recent franchise reform was invoked as exemplary. In this discussion not only the Conservatives and National Liberals, but also the Progressive and anti-Semitic speakers, joined the call for measures to protect Saxons from the "dictatorship of the proletariat."

The liberals had little to add to Mehnert's motion for one very good reason: Everything had been worked out beforehand by the members of Mehnert's Senior Assembly. At first, the *Kartell* parties had been unable to agree on what sort of restricted franchise could be implemented, so they called on Metzsch to mediate. They hoped that the government would go further and introduce the legislation itself, but Metzsch refused, insisting that the parties had to accept the odium of negative public opinion in first suggesting a franchise revision. The National Liberals and Progressives feared reprisals from their voters; although the Conservatives had fewer worries, they did not want to proceed alone either. Therefore it was decided that the Conservatives would introduce a joint motion on behalf of the *Kartell,* asking the government to draw up legislation, even though it was abundantly clear that the government would be happy to endorse virtually any franchise revision that had the prior approval of such a commanding majority. By day's end on 10 December, franchise reform had passed its first hurdle, and this unseemly haste continued throughout the entire legislative process. Within ten days, a technocrat from the Saxon administration was knocking on the door of his Prussian counterpart in Berlin to consult on the "extremely urgent" technical details. When these preparations were completed, the government introduced its bill to the lower house on 5 February 1896, which sent it to committee after only two days of debate. The revised bill was debated in plenum for another two days in early March and received final approval before the end of the month.

On the road to this amazing accomplishment, the parties of order displayed great discipline in sidestepping a number of divisive issues. For example, the National Liberals initially expressed their desire to redraw the balance between urban and rural constituencies. They also advocated a system whereby the entire Landtag would be elected at one time, and they were interested in a full-scale reform of the upper house. However, on 10 December the NLP speaker admitted that his party would not insist on any of these points if to do so endangered the success of the government's legislation. More important for the National Liberals was the issue of private versus public balloting. Whereas the Conservatives advocated the latter in accordance with the Prussian model, the National Liberals disagreed, and so did the Saxon government. Both believed that the SPD's "terrorism" at the polls would only be increased by public voting. The example of the anti-Semite's mother whose distillery was boycotted illustrates that these fears were not unfounded, although the National Liberals likely hoped that secret balloting would also disadvantage the Conservatives.

On the whole, Dönhoff and the Saxon ministry were impressed by the unanimity of the *bürgerlich* parties. Nonetheless, public reaction even among Saxony's middle classes was far from universally positive. Dönhoff reported on 15 December 1895 that it was entirely typical of the Saxon *Bürger* that he called for government protection against the socialists but became worried as soon as concrete measures were proposed. Uncomfortable with the obvious contrast between *Freiheit* and *Reaktion,* moderate liberals had already begun to snipe at the government. The left–liberal *Dresdner Zeitung* argued that the SPD should be combatted only with "spiritual weapons," which prompted other liberals to reply that one could not "enlighten" the man in the street as long as he stood under the influence of SPD agitation (*Verhetzung*) and as long as the growing SPD caucus prevented the Landtag from conducting its business "objectively." The left-liberal press struck a particularly responsive chord when it quoted Bismarck's criticism (in the 1860s) of the Prussian three-class franchise. When this tactic began to stir antireform sentiments among the Saxon *Bürgertum,* a conservative publisher sent a telegram to the former chancellor and received a prompt reply confirming his approval of the Saxon reform.

The anti-Semitic press also opposed the proposed reform. Labeling it an "assassination" of the Saxon franchise – a term also used by the socialists – the *Deutsche Wacht* called on Saxons to launch a "spiritual struggle" against plans to rob them of their right to vote. Predictably Dönhoff regarded this "demagogic bellowing" as further evidence that the anti-Semites identified themselves with the Social Democrats even though they continued to proclaim their national and monarchical sentiments at every opportunity. Significantly, both anti-Semitic deputies had quietly absented themselves from the house when the first vote on Mehnert's motion passed. When the bill was in final debate, an anti-Semitic speaker in the Landtag summed up his party's view fairly: Although he agreed with the antisocialist rationale for franchise reform, the current legislation overshot the mark.

The Social Democrats appeared to be in some disarray initially.[68] They had not expected Mehnert and his colleagues to switch so suddenly from the defensive to the offensive. Soon, however, their party press was calling for "a violent countermovement" against this repressive legislation. Over the Christmas recess the socialists launched this campaign, with large public rallies (some attracting over 5,000 listeners) and the distribution of thousands of leaflets. Two large rallies in Dresden on 15 January 1895 increased the scale of the protests, with about 9,000 in attendance. Yet, at the same time, the Saxon SPD leadership was becoming "nervous" that a successful revision of the Landtag franchise would pave the way for a revision of the Reichstag franchise (exactly as the Saxon king and his ministers hoped). Thus when Liebknecht declared at one large rally that without the universal franchise the German Reich was "not worth a trifle," he was not trying to stir up the crowd to more radical action; instead he was seeking to moderate the language proposed for a resolution against the government and at the same time bring the assembly to a peaceful conclusion. Of six large protest meetings held in Dresden on 7 February 1896, only one resulted in a dissolution by the police. Later, disagreement within the Saxon SPD arose over whether the party's Landtag deputies should resign their seats in

68. For the following, see Dönhoff to Hohenlohe, 9 and 18 Jan. 1896; 6, 10, 13, and 15 Feb. 1896; in PA Bonn, Sachsen 60, Bd. 4.

protest against passage of the government's bill. Although some socialists in Leipzig favored such a demonstrative move, others who dominated the Dresden and Chemnitz *Vereine* insisted that only a general state congress could decide the question. In the first week of April, immediately after franchise reform was enacted, such an assembly endorsed the policy of the moderates, thereby flying in the face of the Berlin SPD leadership.[69] Although it cannot be chronicled here, this *relative* passivity continued to characterize the Saxon party for some years. As one revisionist critic put it later, the Saxon people remained "quiet as a mouse" after their disfranchisement.[70]

The Conservative press was, of course, enthusiastic about the reform.[71] *Das Vaterland* heralded "the beginning of a new era of resolute struggle between order and revolution," which would bring Saxon citizens unprecedented "security and domestic peace." It hoped (as did Dönhoff and King Albert) that the rest of Germany might take heart from the "courage" Saxon parliamentarians had displayed. The *Dresdner Nachrichten* advised against compromise and "half-measures," and the National Liberal *Leipziger Tageblatt* argued that it had been only a question of time before the Landtag franchise required fundamental revision. But such statements cannot be taken at face value, as the Prussian envoy realized. After all, even right-wing voters in Saxony could reasonably say that the franchise of 1868 had served them well in preserving Conservative ascendance in the Landtag. Those parties that practiced "opposition at any price" had gained ground only slowly. Therefore Saxons might well ask: Why a franchise revision now? Exactly that question, in fact, had been put by Metzsch to the members of the Senior Assembly on 4 December. The relatively favorable results of the last Landtag elections, he was told in reply, had been "accidental." The SPD had launched a very active campaign, resulting in a considerable rise in its vote. The members of the Senior Assembly therefore argued that this trend could end only in the eventual domination of (first) elections and (then) Landtag legislation by the Social Democrats. Since time was short, something had to be done while the *bürgerlich* parties still had the Landtag majority necessary to invoke constitutional changes. In

---

69. Eduard Bernstein, "Die Sozialdemokratie und das neue Landtagswahlsystem in Sachsen," *Neue Zeit* 14, Bd. 2 (1896): 181–8; *Schulthess' Europäischer Geschichtskalender* (Munich, 1897), 55.
70. Cited in Warren, *Red Kingdom*, 23.
71. For the following, see Dönhoff to Hohenlohe, 10, 21, and 27 Feb. 1896; 3, 6, 8, 18, 20 and 28 Mar. 1896; and 24 Apr. 1896, in PA Bonn, Sachsen 60, Bd. 4.

an audience with Dönhoff, King Albert offered much the same rationale – with a slight twist. Noting that the SPD might eventually have to be admitted to Landtag committees, the king remarked tellingly (if perhaps also offhandedly) to Dönhoff that something had to be done before the "united Social Democrats and anti-Semites" won a majority in the house. King Albert nevertheless conceded that the existence of a viable socialist caucus had not been without its advantages. It had "brought the *bürgerlich* caucuses tightly together" and had thereby provided the government with "a strong majority which stands by it on all questions and makes united cause against Social Democratic attacks." For this reason, the king continued, it would be preferable to see a few (*einige*) Social Democrats elected to the house under a new franchise: "For if the *bürgerlich* parties were left to themselves, one must fear that they would become disunited and would make the government's lot a difficult one through quarrels [*Zerwürfnisse*] inside the chamber."

The government's bill, announced to the Landtag in outline on 5 February 1896 and debated on 12–13 February, accommodated all the wishes expressed by the house majority on 10 December, though the government sided with the liberals in proposing secret balloting. It apparently believed (like them) that this might mitigate the reactionary tenor of the legislation. As soon as the government's bill was published, however, divisions became more pronounced within both the left-liberal and National Liberal camps. The *Leipziger Tageblatt* acknowledged "profound differences of opinion" within the Saxon NLP, and both Metzsch and King Albert believed that these "might lead to a disintegration of the party or its splintering into two camps." Meanwhile a Landtag by-election in an urban constituency resulted in a socialist victory. In 1887 this seat had been won handily by a Conservative, and in 1893 the incumbent had narrowly defeated an SPD rival. This time the socialist beat the Conservative by only 317 votes, raising the SPD caucus from fourteen to fifteen members. Antisocialist deputies and the government attached a predictable spin to this election when they claimed that it illustrated the necessity of franchise reform. But the opposition argued with more insight that antireform protests had probably supplied the SPD candidate with his slim margin of victory. Another worrisome development intruded when socialist deputies began to attend committee meetings in which the final legislation was being hammered out. Although they had consistently been excluded from sitting on such committees, the socialist deputies could not legally be barred from attending their deliberations. Doing so, they provoked and embarrassed their *bürgerlich* colleagues with scrupulous note taking designed to give the impression that each deputy's remarks would appear the next day in the socialist press. Perhaps the gravest threat of all was posed by Hans Delbrück when he focused national attention on Saxony with his comments in the *Preussische Jahrbücher*.[72] Uncompromising in his criticism of the Saxon Conservatives, Delbrück called on the liberal man of principle to do what the liberal politician in Saxony could not: break with the Conservatives and follow his own conscience as a "politically enlightened and educated man." If this did not happen Delbrück predicted the worst, not only for Saxony but for the parties of order everywhere: "One will drive the Social Democrats out of the [Saxon] chamber – and double their influence in the land. In Saxony mammonism can celebrate its triumph – we in the Reich will have to face the music."

After encountering such rough sailing with a bill that was expected to experience exceptionally smooth passage, Metzsch avoided political shipwreck again when a minority report was issued by committee members responsible for the bill. When the committee presented its recommendation to a plenary session of the Landtag on 3 March 1896, only the most minor amendments had been made. However, two of the eight committee members – almost certainly National Liberals and/or Progressives – insisted that although the principal aim of the legislation was a worthy one, the institution of indirect voting was not. Therefore this minority report recommended rejection of the bill. By this late date such a protest was moot at best, and only two days were required to prove the point. The overfilled galleries of the Landtag were expecting fireworks, but they were thoroughly disappointed. The same pat phrases were used by all right-wing speakers, and even the SPD deputies failed to rise to the occasion; their speeches were marked by a spirit of resignation. The only flutter of controversy arose when one speaker raised the hackles of Saxon particularists by charging that this legislation reduced their state to a province of Prussia. When the crucial vote was taken on 6 March, the margin of victory was as one-sided as predicted: fifty-six votes in favor, twenty-two opposed, with a handful of deputies absent from the house. Of those deputies who voted against the bill, fifteen were socialists, four were National Liberals (mainly industrialists), one was a Conservative,

---

72. H. Delbrück, "Politische Korrespondenz," in *Preussische Jahrbücher* 83 (1896):592f.

and the remaining two were anti-Semites. Subsequently the brief deliberations of the upper chamber were a tiresome denouement. Metzsch's careful steersmanship was required one last time when some nobles advocated raising the age of enfranchisement and a return to the old system with an electoral census of ten marks. But eager not to rock a boat that was already safely in harbor, the members of the upper house passed the bill unanimously on 18 March, and on 28 March it became law. By then it had acquired a popular designation that was as pejorative as it was accurate. The new Landtag franchise was called simply "Mehnert's Law."

CONCLUSION

After franchise reform was enacted in 1896, voter turnout for Landtag elections dropped off sharply, for understandable reasons. Each successive election reduced the SPD caucus until in 1901 no socialists were left in the house. This story would require a considerable statistical apparatus to chronicle adequately. But the preceding analysis has tried to illustrate why numbers documenting such developments are insufficient (and in some ways inappropriate) yardsticks with which to measure the larger processes of political mobilization in Imperial Germany. By themselves statistics can make only a partial contribution to such an assessment, just as the myriad forms of antisocialist discrimination in Saxony cannot be read in a simple way from the electoral record. Instead a broader, wholistic approach is needed. Such an approach should seek to integrate the many "worlds" of politics inhabited by flesh-and-blood politicians in Germany's town halls, rural councils, state legislatures, and the Reichstag. It should explore the different understandings of what politics was all about by those who collectively mobilized the German polity: by voters trying to serve the "good cause" at the ballot box; by those who in the Anglo-American experience are known as "ward heelers," trying to maintain party discipline and conduct viable election campaigns in the individual constituencies; by party leaders in private counsels and in consultation with their comrades elsewhere in the Reich; by journalists addressing an unseen public and by party speakers performing before the multitudes; by deputies trying to influence the course of legislation in parliament; by state ministries hoping to preserve domestic peace; and even by heads of royal households. It should consider how grand strategies for political success often fail or fall short of their goal, how they mutate over time, and how they occasionally carry the day. Lastly, it should not only explore the uniqueness of a region or a locality, but also contribute to a rethinking of larger hypotheses about social and political change in modern Germany. Case studies that meet these desiderata could help shape challenging new research agendas for the future.

3

The Liberal Power Monopoly in the Cities of Imperial Germany

HARTMUT POGGE VON STRANDMANN

In the past historians have often started from the assumption that the decline of the liberal parties during the last decades of the nineteenth century indicated a lack of liberal sentiments and liberal commitment in German society.[1] According to this view political liberalism never really established itself in Germany. Consequently the so-called liberal era of the 1860s was followed by a return to conservative politics during the 1880s and 1890s. The resurgence of the conservative parties combined with a shift in Bismarckian policies to produce what some historians have called the second or conservative foundation of the German Empire.[2] Some historians have also argued that contemporary chauvinist, antisemitic, and conservative authors encouraged this supposed development with their attacks on economic and political liberalism.[3] However it is difficult to assess how extensive their influence really was. Other historians have pointed to the economic crisis after 1873 as another possible cause for the shift towards conservatism in the 1880s.[4] As a consequence economic and, in its wake,

---

This is a revised and extended version of an article which first appeared in Italian in Nicola Matteucci and Paolo Pombeni, eds., *L'Organizzazione della Politica, Cultura, Istittuzioni, Partii nell' Europa Liberale,* 2 vols. (Bologna, 1988).

1. For example, see Leonard Krieger, *The German Idea of Freedom* (Boston, 1957), 495–6; Ralf Dahrendorf, *Gesellschaft und Demokratie in Deutschland* (Munich, 1967), 69ff.; James J. Sheehan, *German Liberalism in the Nineteenth Century* (London, 1982), 273ff.; David Blackbourn and Geoff Eley, *The Peculiarities of German History: Bourgeois Society and Politics in Nineteenth-Century Germany* (Oxford, 1984), 45ff and 72ff.; and Günther Trautmann, "Die industriegeschichtliche Herausforderung des Liberalismus. Staatsintervention und Sozialreform in der Politikökonomie des 18./19. Jahrhunderts," in Karl Holl, Günther Trautmann, and Hans Vorländer, eds., *Sozialer Liberalismus* (Göttingen, 1986), 35.
2. Sheehan, *German Liberalism,* 181–8.
3. In this respect, see Fritz Stern, *The Politics of Cultural Despair* (Berkeley, 1961); George L. Mosse, *The Crisis of the German Ideology* (London, 1964); and Fritz Ringer, *The Decline of the German Mandarins* (Cambridge, Mass., 1969).
4. Hans Rosenberg, *Grosse Depression und Bismarckzeit. Wirtschaft, Gesellschaft und Politik in Mitteleuropa* (Berlin, 1967), 132–54, 189–91.

political liberalism were apparently weakened. Although a case can be made in favor of this rather deterministic view, it does not do justice to the complex relationship between economic and political liberalism and its place in Imperial Germany. Other historians have tended to emphasize a change in political style and political attitudes. According to them the constitutional practice of the new German Empire, Bismarck's manipulative and authoritarian style of politics and the continuation of Junker predominance in Prussia were responsible for a shift towards conservatism in the 1880s.[5] In addition, ostracism of the socialist party and of the trade union movement has been seen as a sign of a repressive regime which felt strong enough to withstand the gradually declining challenge of political and economic liberalism.

Nevertheless it is highly questionable whether the official antisocialist policy can be equated with a policy directed against the liberal parties. To be sure Bismarck was disenchanted with the National Liberals in the late 1870s and regarded the rise of the Left Liberals as a sign of stiffening opposition. After all, in the Chancellor's mind the Left Liberals were regarded as *Reichsfeinde,* or enemies of the Reich. The problem with an argument which stresses this new polarization in the Reichstag is that it cannot be automatically extended to all the liberal factions in the various regions and cities. Because of local diversity and inadequately developed party structures, the traditional view of centralized and consistent party lines is no longer tenable. It is based on the assumption that the parties in the Bismarckian period were clearly identifiable political groupings and that therefore the government was able to adopt a consistent policy towards them. The perception of the parties was, at least in the eyes of the Chancellor, based on leading personalities and the caucus of members around them. If we look at the supposed move to the Right in 1879–80, recent research has shown that this political shift was less dramatic than was hitherto supposed and that the Iron Chancellor continued to share many political interests with the Liberals. In fact neither the colonial acquisitions of 1884–5 nor the National Liberal–Conservative *Kartell* of 1887 would have been possible had Bismarck's repudiation of the National Liberals been as decisive as some historians have suggested.[6] Changing voting patterns within a

---

5. Michael Stürmer, *Das ruhelose Reich. Deutschland 1866–1918* (Berlin, 1983), 210–20.
6. For example, see Lothar Gall, *Bismarck: Der weisse Revolutionär* (Frankfurt, 1983), 587–91; Margaret L. Anderson, *Windthorst: A Political Biography* (Oxford, 1981), 217–34; Margaret

party system characterized by a high degree of regional diversity had a much stronger effect on elections at the national level than in municipal elections. As in late-nineteenth-century France, the formation of centralized party structures had only begun with the Social Democrats and would take other parties considerably longer. To be sure voting may have been influenced by factors of class, status and religion, but the predominance of economic interests in the towns made the municipal elections less responsive to changing social trends than at the national level. Together with the existing franchise this may help to explain why many towns were dominated by the liberal parties until 1918. The fact that the Liberals had fallen out of favor in Berlin in the late 1870s and that the Left Liberals were regarded as an oppositional party after 1880 seems to have had little effect on local elections. Even the flavor of dissent which characterized the liberal groupings before 1867 had disappeared in most cities a few years later. Yet even at the regional level the liberal parties had originally opposed the existing state governments. Whatever effect the process of unification, the creation of the German Empire, and the rise of the Center and Social Democratic parties may have had on the liberal parties on the national level, local liberal party groupings unfurled the banner of opposition in only a few incidents after 1870.

In addition to these well-known party political developments, it has been difficult to demonstrate the growing "illiberalism" in German society. It is no longer sufficient to cite particular political authors and their books as proof of an "illiberal" trend in German society. In addition historians have accused the *Bildungsbürgertum* of political apathy without establishing any systematic link between the decline of the liberal parties and the political indifference of the educated classes. Clearly it is not enough to state that the "hometownsmen were most notable in the politics of the Second Empire for their absence."[7] First, the period of the supposedly growing apathy does not overlap with the decline of the liberal parties. Second,

---

L. Anderson and Kenneth Barkin, "The Myth of the Puttkamer Purge and the Reality of the Kulturkampf: Some Reflections on the Historiography of Imperial Germany," *Journal of Modern History* 54 (1982): 664, 675ff. James Retallack has shown that Bismarck did not succeed in 1879 in bringing together the desired *Kartell* of Conservatives, Free Conservatives, and the "honorable part" of the National Liberals. See James N. Retallack, *Notables of the Right: The Conservative Party and Political Mobilization in Germany, 1876–1918* (London, 1988).

7. Mack Walker, *German Home Towns: Community, State and General Estate, 1649–1871* (Ithaca, NY, 1971), 425. See also Sheehan, *German Liberalism*, 233ff.

the increasing mobilization of the German electorate and the relatively high voter turnout belie any significant apathy on the part of the German voter. Contrary to the image of the "apolitical German," there appears to have been a level of political mobilization in Germany which exceeded that of France and Britain. In any case the often repeated reference to the apolitical German was typical of a certain political rhetoric which expressed forms of bourgeois domination and was part of the political culture of the educated classes. More work on the political culture of the Bismarckian and Wilhelmine eras will generate new insights into the political, social and economic behavior patterns of various groups.

In any comparative study of European politics in the prewar period, broadly similar patterns of development can be found, regardless of the different constitutions in each country. A number of countries were faced with similar problems even though they may have adopted different approaches to their solution. This can be seen in the rise and fall of liberal fortunes, the resentment which the nonsocialist groups felt towards the rise of working-class politics and the difficulties in the relationship between church and society. Clearly the disarray and the relatively early decline of the German liberal parties were not a specifically German phenomenon which was somehow linked to an ascending illiberalism, but were rather a consequence of the increasing political mobilization of social groups which made use of the universal franchise at the national level. Given that these developments were made possible only by massive urbanization and demographic change, as well as the rise of working-class politics, the German case appears to predate a European pattern of events at the end of the nineteenth and the beginning of the twentieth centuries.[8] Thus the argument that Bismarck's politics and the successful unification of Germany corrupted and crushed German liberalism appears oversimplified and may have to be replaced by an analysis which places the decline of the German liberal parties in a European context.

However, liberal party politics are not identical with liberal ideology or liberal political culture. In order to gain an insight into the latter, it may be necessary to reach beyond the national and regional levels of German political life to the level of local government. This

---

8. Gustav Schmidt, "Liberalismus and soziale Reform: Der deutsche und der britische Fall 1890–1914," *Tel Aviver Jahrbuch für deutsche Geschichte* 14 (1987): 212ff. See the various contributions in Karl Rohe, ed., *Englischer Liberalismus im 19. und frühen 20. Jahrhundert* (Bochum, 1987).

applies not only to Germany, but to other countries as well. Whatever the causal connections might have been between the decline of liberalism, increasing political mobilization, socioeconomic change and a constitutional but nonparliamentary governmental system in Berlin, the liberal parties were able to maintain their dominant position at the local level much longer than at the national and state levels – the other two tiers of German political life.[9]

As is well known, the liberal parties dominated the Reichstag, the Prussian Landtag and most other parliaments in the German states until the 1880s.[10] Thereafter support for the liberal parties began to drop in reaction to a resurgence of the Right, the growing Catholic vote and the rise of the Social Democrats. The steady liberal decline reached its nadir in the Reichstag elections between 1898 and 1903.[11] Whereas together the liberal parties managed to retain about one-fifth of the vote, the winners in 1903 and 1912 were the Social Democrats, who were supported by about one-third of the electorate. However between 1890, when the antisocialist legislation was lifted, and 1912, neither the Center Party nor the SPD managed to match the early successes of the liberals. In 1871 the liberals had won 47 percent of the vote, a figure which fell to 34 percent in 1890. The decline continued until liberal fortunes reached their nadir with 23 and 22 percent in 1898 and 1903, respectively. Because of the two-ballot system for Reichstag elections this low level of support endangered the liberal parties even more, but they were able to stage a moderate revival in 1907 and 1912, when they attracted 2 percent more than they had received in 1903.[12] Still their overall position was very different from what it had been during the 1870s. It is difficult to assess whether the liberals, especially the Progressive Party under the leadership of Friedrich Naumann, had any real prospect of an electoral comeback similar to the one the British Liberals managed to achieve for a number of years after 1906. The weakness of liberal party organizations, the regional character of German liberal politics

9. Sheehan, *German Liberalism*, 147–9, 221–9.
10. The loss of liberal seats in the Prussian Landtag was most dramatic. From 169 in 1876 they dropped to 66 in 1882. In the Reichstag their seats were reduced from 141 in 1877 to 47 in 1881. However, the decline in other state parliaments came later in the 1890s. In Saxony their fortunes rose after 1896, when the franchise was reformed along Prussian lines.
11. See Brett Fairbairn, "The German Elections of 1898 and 1903" (D. Phil. diss., Oxford University, 1987).
12. A modest upsurge of the Liberals can be detected in Saxony, Prussia, and Baden during the last years before 1914. The Left Liberals improved their performance in Hesse and Bavaria. Alastair Thompson, "Left Liberals in German State and Society" (Ph.D. diss., University of London, Birkbeck College, 1989).

and the lack of an appeal to a wider electorate may have prevented that from ever happening.

The reasons for the liberal decline at the Reichstag polls can be explained by the schism within the liberal camp between the National Liberal and the Left Liberal parties, by the lack of a popular program as well as a modern party structure and by the achievement of many liberal aims during the late 1860s and 1870s. Faced with demographic, social and economic changes, the liberal identification with the *Bürgertum* and the new state was not sufficient to sustain the level of support the liberals had once enjoyed among the Protestant "middle strata." By and large the liberals failed, with few exceptions, to attract the working-class voter, the Catholic voter and, in the east, the agrarian voter.[13]

Historians have not fully appreciated the fact that the liberal parties suffered a fate in the elections to the Prussian Landtag, with its three-class franchise, similar to the one they endured under universal suffrage for the Reichstag. Furthermore, between 1879 and 1913 the decline and modest rise in Prussia followed a pattern similar to the one in the Reich. However in the other German states the deterioration of the liberal position varied according to regional factors. In Saxony, for example, the liberals were able to reverse the downward trend from 1905 on and even managed after 1909 to displace the Conservatives as the largest party in the Landtag. In Baden the National Liberals never fell below 23 percent of the popular vote but were unable, before the war, to match their peak of 74 percent in 1889. In the other German states the National Liberal position experienced a decline similar to that in Prussia. The revitalized conservative and Catholic parties had ousted the liberals from their dominant position in Prussia, whereas in the other German states it was either the Catholics or the Social Democrats who had reduced the liberal appeal. However in Baden the Center had formed an electoral pact with the Social Democrats and Left Liberals in order to bring to an end the National Liberal predominance there. Later on the liberal

---

13. It is noteworthy that the limited rise of the liberals before 1914 coincided with the loss of some votes for the Center. See Sheehan, *German Liberalism*; Gerhard A. Ritter, *Die deutschen Parteien 1830–1914. Parteien und Gesellschaft im konstitutionellen Regierungssystem* (Göttingen, 1985); Fairbairn, "Elections"; Michael John, "Liberalism and Society in Germany, 1850–1880: The Case of Hanover," *English Historical Review* 102 (1987): 579–98; Karl Rohe, "German Elections and Party Systems in Historical and Regional Perspective: An Introduction," in Karl Rohe, ed., *Elections, Parties and Political Traditions: Social Foundations of German Parties and Party Systems, 1867–1987* (Oxford, 1990), 1–25.

vote survived in a few cases, but only with some assistance from the Social Democrats and the Center; the latter, despite its earlier feud with the liberal parties, had an interest in preserving a liberal balance there. In short regional differences were particularly strong in Imperial Germany. They were the result of economic and social differences, but it looks as if religious and political traditions had an even stronger effect.

There was one major political area in which the economic, religious and social differences were most strongly pronounced and in which the decline of the liberal parties was not as noticeable. At the level of local government, especially in the cities, liberal strength by and large persisted right up to the collapse of the Second Empire. Therefore it seems apt to call the city councils the last bastion of liberalism before the First World War.[14] The continuing strength of the liberal parties at the municipal level makes it much more difficult to equate the decline of liberalism generally with the loss of liberal influence. Conversely if the liberals were able to retain their position in the German towns, then it does not make sense to discuss without any reservation or qualification either the demise of the liberal parties or the supposedly growing illiberalism within German society. Whatever illiberalism might mean politically, it cannot be deduced directly from the decline of the liberal parties at the levels of the Reichstag or the Prussian Landtag when overall liberal strength persisted in local government.

For historians who study "high politics," the government or the process of central decision making, the neglect of local politics may be understandable. But if historians want to learn more about political parties, the electorate, the weight of certain political issues and political culture in general, then the local level could prove to be a more fruitful starting point for a political analysis than the other two tiers of politics. Moreover the functional autonomy of German local authorities seems to have been greater than that of their English counterparts, a factor which may explain why local politics played such an important role in rapidly growing towns.[15] But there is another factor which should give local politics even greater weight. From about 1900 on, local authorities maintained a higher level of

---
14. Sheehan, *German Liberalism*, 230.
15. William H. Dawson, *Municipal Life and Government in Germany* (London, 1914), vii–xi, 435ff.

budgetary expenditure than the Reich or the individual states.[16] Furthermore by 1910, in the towns which belonged to the Council of Cities, or *Städtetag,* over 93,000 people were regarded as necessary for administration.[17] Over one-third of these were in voluntary employment, which meant that this particular aspect of the world of the *Honoratioren* was still largely intact.

Did the liberals themselves regard local government as less relevant than the other two tiers in Germany's political life? Liberal politicians tended to consider local government important, and they tried to preserve their predominance in the cities as long as possible. For the defense of their position, they used all means available to prevent the advance of the Center and the Social Democrats in local government. Despite this exclusive attitude they regarded the municipalities as the "bearers of progress." To them local government represented the independent will of the community and its relationship to the state, without regard for national issues. The liberal members of local government conducted their politics as self-assured citizens and acted as if they had an inherent natural right to govern. It has often been said that the German *Bürgertum* was politically weak, but there is very little at the local level to support this assertion. It was there that the pulse of bourgeois politics was to be found.[18]

Before the First World War, local government enjoyed prestige because of the growing and visible achievements it was able to demonstrate.[19] After all, the infrastructure in the towns was highly developed, even if much remained to be done, especially in the area of housing. Thus Chancellor Theobald von Bethmann Hollweg told the leading industrialist, Walther Rathenau, that "we have the most perfect self-administration at local level," a judgment which Rathenau countered by remarking: "[But] only as far as the kitchen, not as far as the drawing-room."[20] Whereas Bethmann's judgment was shared by many contemporaries and accepted by many liberals, Rathenau's criticism referred less to local government and more to

16. Kurt G. A. Jeserich, Hans Pohl, and Georg Christoph von Unruh, eds., *Deutsche Verwaltungsgeschichte,* 6 vols. (Stuttgart, 1983–8), 3:583–7.
17. Heinrich Silbergleit, *Preussens Städte. Denkschrift zum 100jährigen Jubiläum der Städteordnung von 1808* (Berlin, 1908), 176–7, 182–3.
18. It is perhaps a weakness of the book edited by Jürgen Kocka, *Bürger und Bürgerlichkeit im 19. Jahrhundert* (Göttingen, 1987), that none of the contributions discusses bourgeois political culture in the cities.
19. Dawson, *Municipal Life,* chapters 6–8, 10, 11. See also Blackbourn and Eley, *Peculiarities of German History,* 148ff.
20. Hartmut Pogge von Strandmann, ed., *Walther Rathenau: Industrialist, Banker, Intellectual, and Politician. Notes and Diaries, 1907–1922* (Oxford, 1985), 164.

the central stage of imperial politics. To him parliamentary rule applied only to the city council, in this case the kitchen; since the legislative assemblies in Berlin did not have full parliamentary power, parliamentary rule did not reach the "drawing room." Without overinterpreting Rathenau's remarks, it is worth pointing out that he did not denigrate local government or its role in German political life. As an industrialist who had worked extensively with local authorities he knew more about their power than many political commentators.

In the volume published to commemorate the twenty-fifth anniversary of the reign of Wilhelm II, local government was praised by one of its practitioners, the mayor of Königsberg, who also complained about too much state supervision from Berlin – a problem which was more pronounced in northeastern Germany than in the south.[21] However strong local government in Germany may have been, its dependence on the governments of the individual states was still considerable. Yet a comparative study, encompassing Britain, France and Italy, would show that in certain respects the room for maneuver in Germany was sufficiently large for a high degree of economic and social development to be achieved.

Liberal domination of the majority of German cities and a number of German districts, or *Kreise,* in the countryside formed the basis for the emergence of the constitutional state in the middle of the nineteenth century. However, the reforms which Freiherr vom Stein had introduced in Prussia in 1807 and 1808 did not aim at creating a liberal state.[22] Stein had hoped to regenerate the moral fiber of the Germans in Prussia in the face of despotism and feudalism. According to him the character of the nation was to be developed by self-government and by a change in the relationship between state and citizen. Now the commune was to become the smallest unit of the state and, at one and the same time, a political organism of its own. It was to become the focus of the independent will of the community, whose relationship with the state was to be based on the freedom of

---

21. Siegfried Körte, "Die Selbstverwaltung," in Siegfried Körte, et al., *Deutschland unter Kaiser Wilhelm II,* 3 vols. (Berlin, 1914), 1:191–207. See also Herbert Jacob, *German Administration since Bismarck: Central Authority versus Local Autonomy* (New Haven, Conn., 1963), 64, as well as Celia Applegate's essay in this volume. However Dawson is convinced that the independence of local authorities from state supervision in Germany exceeded that of their British counterparts.
22. In this respect, see Heinrich Heffter, *Die deutsche Selbstverwaltung im 19. Jahrhundert. Geschichte der Ideen und Institutionen* (Stuttgart, 1950), 91–7; August Krebsbach, *Die preussische Städteordnung von 1808* (Stuttgart, 1957); and Thomas Nipperdey, *Deutsche Geschichte 1800–1866* (Munich, 1984), 34–40.

its citizens. Self-government was to create harmony between the spirit of the nation and the institutions of the state.

Stein's ideas took some time to take root, as the Prussian cities responded very slowly. Bearing in mind the opposition to the reforms and the restrictive legislation of 1831 it is remarkable that civic responsibility began to develop at all. A more democratic form of government was out of the question since it was a form of local government which barely existed. Instead the aspirations for bourgeois domination in the towns and for a liberal constitution merged under state supervision later in the nineteenth century with self-government of the German cities. At that time the city councils came closer to a parliamentary system than the representative institutions of the German states or, for that matter, the central government in Berlin. Neither the expansion of the cities nor the growing importance of urban politics nor the shift of emphasis in national political power from the various states to the metropolis of the Second Empire seem to have had much effect on the liberal domination of the cities. In fact, if anything, it was strengthened.

However the term "liberal" ought to be used with some caution, if for no other reason than the simple fact that the liberal parties emerged in local politics later than in the other two tiers of government. Even this generalization does not always hold. In Düsseldorf, for example, the liberals and the National Liberals in particular were better organized and more effective than was hitherto assumed despite the fact that after 1880 they were unable to break the predominant position of the Center.[23] *Honoratiorenpolitik,* or the politics of notables, had its firm roots in local politics and survived there much longer than at the national or state level. In fact local politics in the cities was the hub of *Honoratiorenpolitik*. It was here that the social and economic positions of the notables could be translated into visible influence. No wonder that the liberal parties made every effort to defend their power monopoly in the cities when the chips were down in the general elections. In this respect, the two liberal camps pursued the same aim, but whereas most National Liberals were unwilling to support a reform of the three-class franchise in Prussia, the Left Liberals were divided over this issue.[24] Like the conservatives, the National Liberals saw in the plutocratic three-class franchise a com-

---

23. Norbert Schlossmacher, *Düsseldorf im Bismarckreich. Politik und Wahlen, Parteien und Vereine* (Düsseldorf, 1985), 108–16.
24. Walter Gagel, *Die Wahlrechtsfrage in der Geschichte der deutschen liberalen Parteien 1848–1918* (Düsseldorf, 1985), 113–25, 163–7.

pensation for the losses they had suffered under the universal franchise in the Reichstag elections. Any substantial electoral reform for the Landtag would have reduced the power of the National Liberal notables in the cities.

Before the 1890s, local notables often gave the impression that they stood above the parties. Therefore, it may not be surprising to learn that with the exception of big cities like Berlin, Mannheim, and some Rhenish townships, party politics was not very prominent in council elections until the turn of the century.[25] But James Sheehan has gone too far when he coins the term "unpolitical politics" to describe the lack of party political polarization.[26] Certainly earlier on, class and social status seem to have mattered more than party affiliation. But even then, the local party organizations backed by political associations nominated the candidates and organized campaigns in one form or another to support them at the polls. Still, some voters did not know to which party the candidate for whom they were voting belonged. As late as 1910, the Catholic Center Party complained about the lack of political orientation in local elections. The party then went on to ask its members to support candidates of the Center Party, something it obviously could not automatically expect them to do.[27] In the Rhenish cities, the liberal *Honoratioren* exploited this situation to their own advantage by proclaiming that "politics and parties do not belong in the town hall."[28]

It is interesting to note that political associations were set up in several cities in order to put forward joint lists. One of the main purposes of this exercise was to fend off any advance of the Social Democrats. In this respect an all-bourgeois platform was thought to be an effective tool of class politics.[29] However there were exceptions to the all-bourgeois alignment. In a few instances electoral alliances with the SPD were concluded, but with the growth of the Social Democrats the bourgeois parties tended to defend any restrictive franchise. Political domination through electoral exclusiveness became the hallmark of the liberal government in most German cities.

---

25. Helmuth Croon, "Das Vordringen der politischen Parteien im Bereich der kommunalen Selbstverwaltung," in Helmuth Croon, Wolfgang Hofmann, and Georg Christoph von Unruh, eds., *Kommunale Selbstverwaltung im Zeitalter der Industrialisierung*, Schriftenreihe des Vereins für Kommunale Wissenschaft, no. 33 (Stuttgart, 1971), 32.
26. Sheehan, *German Liberalism*, 235–8. See also James J. Sheehan, "Liberalism and the City in Nineteenth-Century Germany," *Past and Present* 51 (1971): 135.
27. Croon, "Vordringen," 37.
28. Ibid.
29. Ibid., 38. See also Schlossmacher, *Düsseldorf im Bismarckreich*, 74–116.

The same applied to towns which were in the hands of the Center or the conservative parties.[30]

The liberals were not able to block reforms in all German states. In Baden the franchise was reformed against the will of the National Liberals there, but once they had become a minority party they were willing to form the *Grossblock,* a coalition of the entire Left, in order to prevent a Center majority.[31] Although the National Liberals in Baden could not hold out against a reform of the Landtag elections they managed to maintain a six-class franchise for the local elections. In any case the number of voters increased substantially in the lower classes. In Prussia the number of voters in the third class also grew substantially after Johannes Miquel's tax reform was introduced. Where the level of taxable income was lowest, most liberals were pleased that the political influence of the new voters could be contained. The plutocratic character of the Prussian franchise meant that in some cities 90 to 94 percent and in some cases even 98 percent of the electorate had to vote as members of the third class for the same number of deputies as the electors in the other two classes. Through the gradual reduction of the tax threshold the number of voters in the third class increased, so that in the Prussian cities between 50 and 65 percent of those who voted in the Reichstag elections could also vote in municipal elections. In some cases this figure moved up to between 70 and 80 percent, although this was rare. Of those who had the vote in the Prussian cities approximately 85 percent voted in the third class, 13 percent in the second class and 2 percent in the first class. However in the cities of Hannover, Schleswig-Holstein and certain parts of Pomerania an equal franchise was in operation, although restricted by a high tax threshold.[32]

In Prussia state citizenship and a residence qualification of one year were necessary to vote. In Hesse and Baden about the same number of Reichstag electors as in most Prussian cities was able to take part in municipal elections, although the voter did not have to be a citizen of these two states. In those states where citizenship was required for voting, participation rates were lowest. Thus in Rostock in Mecklenburg, only 8 percent of the Reichstag voters were allowed to vote for the town council. Acquiring citizenship was often an expensive procedure, as was the annual fee to retain it. To become a citizen an

30. Heffter, *Selbstverwaltung,* 749.
31. Beverly Heckart, *From Bassermann to Bebel: The Grand Bloc's Quest for Reform in the Kaiserreich* (New Haven, Conn., 1974), 91–121.
32. Croon, "Vordringen," 40–5.

application form had to be filled out, a procedure which deterred a number of potential voters from registering. Official encouragement was not given, as the right of citizenship was used exclusively.[33]

In Bavaria many cities used the condition of citizenship to exclude workers from the vote in local elections. A case in point was Nuremberg, where liberal Progressives dominated the city council until 1887. Between then and 1918 the Progressives formed a cartel with the National Liberals in order to exclude Social Democrats. Meanwhile the population grew between 1869 and 1887 from 80,000 to 120,000, while the number of admitted voters dropped from just over 6,000 to 5,500. By 1905 Nuremberg had an estimated 290,000 inhabitants, but only 16,000 were classified as citizens. The purpose behind this is clear from the remarks of the city mayor, who is on record as having said: "I don't like those people who harbor destructive tendencies; I object strongly to the Social Democrats who want to make the local representative body into a playground for their immature ideas."[34] Against such opposition it was impossible for the Social Democrats to make any headway at all. Since 1881 they had carried Nuremberg in one Reichstag election after another. In the 1905 Landtag elections the Social Democrats won an absolute majority in Nuremberg, although this was on the basis of an indirect franchise which allowed the coalition of liberal and conservative parties to manipulate this result into a majority for themselves by redrawing constituency boundaries. Of the hurdles the SPD had to overcome progressively, the most difficult was the fees which had to be paid in order to be a citizen and a resident. Together they represented ten weeks' earnings for a worker. In order to register workers for the local elections, the Social Democrats had to contribute funds from their own resources. Furthermore, the applicant had to prove that he was not a wage earner, but independent, to become a citizen.

In neighboring Fürth the situation was reversed. Fürth required no fees from its citizens, with the result that the SPD managed to gain its first seat in the city council in 1871. The party improved its performance and won ten seats in the local elections of 1908. The fact that Fürth was merged with Erlangen for the Reichstag elections prevented the SPD from winning; thus the seat was held by the Left Liberals until 1912, when it was finally won by the SPD.[35]

---

33. Ibid., 41.
34. Klaus-Dieter Schwarz, *Weltkrieg und Revolution in Nürnberg. Ein Beitrag zur Geschichte der Arbeiterbewegung* (Stuttgart, 1971), 30.
35. Ibid., 30–1. The SPD also won two places in the *Magistrat*.

The fees which had to be paid for the right to vote varied from city to city. In Bayreuth, for example, veterans of the 1866 and 1870–1 wars paid no fee, and workers who had stayed in single employment for at least fifteen years were relieved of any payment. But hardly anyone stayed in the same employment merely for the sake of gaining the right to vote. Nevertheless the number of those newly enfranchised increased dramatically throughout Upper Franconia between 1905 and 1911. By 1911 the percentage of the total population which was entitled to vote had grown to 5.5 percent in Bayreuth and to 7.5 percent in Kulmbach.[36] Due to the introduction of proportional elections in 1908 the SPD managed, three years later, to win about 19 percent of the seats in the representative bodies of fifteen communities through the region. Although the franchise had been reformed, the liberal *Honoratioren,* especially those who were also employers in that area, remained firmly in control of local politics. Consequently many programs for the improvement of the local infrastructure, which would have led to an increase in the costs of local industries, were rejected by the liberal majority at local elections.

In northern Germany the city state of Hamburg also operated a system of fees for the acquisition of citizenship. These were much lower than in Nuremberg, but in contrast to the Bavarian city only a few new inhabitants made the effort to acquire citizenship. So between 1875 and 1892 the number of citizens decreased from 33,000 to 26,000, whereas the number of inhabitants reached 600,000.[37] Eventually the city altered its franchise qualification. After 1896 a citizen had to declare an income of 1,200 marks for tax purposes over a period of five years.[38] But the attempt to involve more conservative-minded citizens backfired, as a number of artisans, dockers and shipyard workers had sufficient income to enroll as voters. The old patricians began to fear that the Social Democrats might gain a majority in the Hamburg city legislature, or *Bürgerschaft,* and rejigged the electoral law in 1906.[39] As a result a system

---

36. Robert Kandler, "The Effects of the Economic and Social Conditions on the Development of the Free Trade Unions in Upper Franconia, 1890–1914" (D.Phil. diss., Oxford University, 1987). See also the *Ostfränkische Volkszeitung,* 13 Nov. 1908. In 1907 the percentages for Bayreuth and Kulmbach were 3.08 and 5.78 percent, respectively.
37. The inequality of the franchise was emphasized by the fact that the notables (ca. 600) had three votes each. See Ernst Baasch, *Geschichte Hamburgs 1814–1918,* 2 vols. (Stuttgart and Gotha, 1925), 2:76, 96ff. See also Sheehan, "Liberalism and the City," 126, and Richard J. Evans, *Death in Hamburg: Society and Politics in the Cholera Years, 1830–1910* (Oxford, 1987), 48.
38. Croon, "Vordringen," 44. See also Evans, *Death in Hamburg,* 542ff.
39. Evans, *Death in Hamburg,* 542ff.

of proportional representation was introduced, but one which divided the voters into two classes whereby those with a higher income would elect forty-eight deputies and those with an annual income of less than 2,500 marks only twenty-four deputies. As in many other German cities, the liberals were able to hold on to their power in the Chamber even though they had lost the majority in the Reichstag elections some time ago. A comparison with other German cities has only limited value as Hamburg was also one of the federated states and is therefore comparable only to the other two Hanseatic city states, Bremen and Lübeck, or with other German states. Yet certain characteristics make Hamburg more akin to other large cities and their problems. Even then, such a political comparison cannot go beyond the demonstration of certain trends.

As the case of Hamburg so clearly illustrated, no other German state was willing to open the franchise during the last years before the outbreak of the First World War. Throughout the rest of Germany the liberals could easily see what effects the widening of the franchise had had in liberal-conservative Hamburg between 1896 and 1905. Moreover everyone was waiting for Prussia to set the example. If Prussia were to reform its franchise, the rest of Germany would follow. But in Prussia neither the government nor the nonsocialist parties were willing to reform the franchise in any substantial way. Although the National Liberal and conservative parties, as well as the Catholic Center, rejected demands for a reform of the franchise, the Left Liberals took a different line. When the Progressive People's Party was founded in 1910, the reform of the Prussian franchise was part of the program. But the Left Liberals aimed at an equal franchise, not necessarily a general one. Their program also stated that local elections were to be reformed, but restricted itself to repeal of the three-class franchise and the abolition of public voting. As the case of Schleswig-Holstein showed, this did not include the demand for a universal franchise. The Left Liberals held the Reichstag seats for Schleswig-Holstein and were strongly represented in the towns there, since an equal franchise had been in operation since 1869.[40] The National Liberals and Conservatives, on the other hand, were closely tied to the rural and official establishments and represented the two provinces in the Prussian Landtag. As a result the Left Liberals advocated a reform of the Landtag franchise along the lines of the

---

40. Oswald Hauser, *Staatliche Einheit und regionale Vielfalt in Preussen. Der Aufbau der Verwaltung in Schleswig-Holstein nach 1867* (Neumünster, 1967), 59–65.

local electoral law, whereas the National Liberals and Conservatives unsuccessfully demanded the introduction of the three-class franchise in municipal elections.

Whatever the chances of success may have been, the discussions of franchise reform in the various Landtage before 1914 had one important consequence. The parties became the focus of a wide-ranging political debate. Although, with a number of exceptions, the liberal parties still dominated the German city politically, the reforms which were introduced in the southern German states and even in Prussia in the last years before 1914 largely benefited the Center and the Social Democrats. The liberals, on the other hand, proved very reluctant to yield to any pressures emanating from below. The fact that *Honoratiorenpolitik* continued to work for them at the local level may help to explain why it was so difficult for the liberals to meet the challenge which the SPD and the Center posed with their mass-based party organizations. Through *Honoratiorenpolitik* it was possible for the National Liberals, the Conservatives and sections of the Center Party to cooperate with the governments, the church and the local establishment. For Social Democrats and some members of the Left Liberals this line of communication was either not available or was far more difficult to establish.

The number of elected Social Democratic representatives at the local level grew slowly but steadily before 1914. The party was kept from overturning the liberals by the existing franchise and other restrictive practices. Only in a few large cities did it break the liberal monopoly. One such place was Berlin, where the SPD was represented in the city council for the first time in 1883. Restricted by the anti-socialist legislation, the party won five seats. It had organized its campaign under the cover of the Committee for the Distribution of Bourgeois Culture. A few years later the party set up Associations for the Achievement of Popular Elections and won eleven of forty-two seats in the third class. In 1905 the SPD managed to win thirty-five out of forty-eight seats in the same class, and three years later it won its first seats in the second class. Before the outbreak of the war the liberals held ninety-eight seats in Berlin, whereas the SPD had increased its share to forty-four seats. Breaking out of the third class was a particular achievement, as only 32,000 citizens, that is, 8.3 percent of the total population, were allowed to vote in the second class.[41]

---

41. Hans Herzfeld, *Berlin und die Provinz Brandenburg im 19. und 20. Jahrhundert* (Berlin, 1968),

Liberal Power Monopoly in the Cities

The Social Democrats were further handicapped by the stipulation that a certain number of elected councillors had to be house owners. In Prussia and Saxony, for example, at least half of the councillors had to possess houses. In each city this number varied considerably. In Aachen 38 out of 39 councillors were house owners, whereas in Berlin the number was 92 out of 144.[42] As the German urban population did not often live in separate dwellings, but rather in apartment blocks, this restriction proved very effective in maintaining an exclusive clublike atmosphere. But the Social Democrats still managed to qualify for the city council. A wealthy member of the party had bought some land and, instead of building an apartment block, had built a row of smaller houses which were registered in the names of the socialist city council members.[43] In this way Paul Singer and Karl Liebknecht became house owners. Nonetheless house ownership proved to be a severe obstacle to socialist participation in local government. In Schönefeld near Berlin, for example, only 3 percent of the inhabitants were qualified by the terms of this rule to stand for half the number of seats available. In Prussia the government tried to abolish the house owners' privilege, but the amendment did not pass the Prussian Landtag.

The turnout for local elections varied enormously. Earlier in the century very few citizens went to vote. After the Revolution of 1848 this number grew substantially. In some cases the turnout for municipal elections was even higher than for the Landtag elections. In Weimar only 8.5 percent voted in the Landtag elections of 1888, whereas in the local elections about 30 percent turned out.[44] Only once in 1899 had voter turnout fallen to 19 percent; otherwise, the average figure was about 60 percent. In order to meet a strong socialist challenge, a staggering 80 percent went to the polls in 1909. A high turnout in local elections was not unusual when the outcome was uncertain. In many Rhenish towns participation figures were continuously high, as the Center began to reduce the former liberal predominance. In later years a three-cornered struggle among the Center, the Social Democrats and the liberals kept the turnout figures high. In Baden, on the other hand, a few localities occasionally mustered 95 percent in the second class of voters, but these high turnout

87–9. See also Annemarie Lange, *Das wilhelminische Berlin. Zwischen Jahrhundertwende und Novemberrevolution* ([East] Berlin, 1976), 383–7.
42. Dawson, *Municipal Life*, 71–3.
43. Lange, *Das wilhelminische Deutschland*, 386.
44. Gitta Günther and Lothar Wallraf, *Geschichte der Stadt Weimar* (Weimar, 1975), 466.

figures were leveled out throughout the whole of Germany by lower figures in the eastern area.[45] As a rule Reichstag elections and most Landtag elections attracted a greater number of voters than local elections. Berlin was a case in point. After the turn of the century barely 50 percent of the Berlin electorate went to the polls in local elections, whereas in adjoining Charlottenburg only about one-third of the citizens exercised their right to vote. In Prussia the number of citizens who were eligible to vote was substantially larger than in Bavaria, but in 1905 voter participation in local elections reached 77 percent in Munich, 84 percent in Nuremberg, 91 percent in Augsburg and 83 percent in Fürth.[46] To some extent these figures were comparable to the turnout of the first two classes in many Prussian towns. Thus the higher income groups took their right of exclusiveness seriously, whereas the third class of voters were often discouraged from making their mark in the struggle for more equal representation.

Were these high percentages – which would hardly find a parallel today – only the result of a challenge by one party to the local establishment? Or do they form a response to particular local issues? Obviously the old *Honoratioren* wanted to defend their position in the local social and economic hierarchies and continue to exercise their power. Apart from controlling the election process, they were able to mobilize a formidable array of practices to keep the many challenges at bay. These included the purchase of property for assessment purposes, the tax assessment itself and the declaration of income and occupation. All this had a direct influence on local elections. The haggling over constituency boundaries and the organization of the elections themselves provided further opportunities to stifle a serious challenge. In addition the liberals had other resources at their disposal which the SPD and the Center found it difficult to match. Control of the local press, for example, was largely in liberal hands. It was only in 1918 that the rule of the liberal oligarchies in the cities came to an end. It could be argued that as far as political representation was concerned, the revolution of 1918–19 had perhaps a greater effect on local politics than it did at the central level in Berlin.

---

45. In 1911 80 percent of the third class voted in municipal elections, a figure which dropped to 60 percent in the elections of 1914.
46. Between 6 and 12 percent of the inhabitants were classified as citizens. See Croon, "Vordringen," 43. However, in Fürth only 15 percent of the population was allowed to vote. See Jeserich, Pohl, and von Unruh, eds., *Deutsche Verwaltungsgeschichte,* 3:608.

Historians of local government agree that municipal elections are of vital importance for the understanding of local politics. But it would give a one-sided picture if city governments were to be considered only in terms of elections and the structural weaknesses of the liberal parties.[47] If the development of cities is to be analyzed, then local issues need to be investigated as well, as they strongly influenced the configuration of local politics. The construction of railway lines and stations, waterworks, power stations, sewage installations, the introduction of street lighting and local transport, as well as problems of land development and the entire area of social and educational questions influenced the outcome of local elections. Those who resented the power of the *Honoratioren* did not always have the question of electoral rights foremost in their minds. Although there were signs of a protest vote against the ruling local establishment, voters were also concerned with improving local provisions and services. Thus it was not only local issues and the bid for greater participation which posed a challenge to liberal predominance. The growth of the cities was accompanied by a process of social differentiation and economic diversification which helped to break up the old hierarchies and make room for what could be called new *Honoratioren*.

It has already been pointed out that local elections were increasingly fought along political rather than class lines. In the mainly Protestant cities of the north, liberal, conservative and socialist parties struggled for supremacy. In the west, the south and Silesia, the Catholic vote was an important factor, but in several constituencies Catholic voters did not follow the recommendations of the Center and opted instead for the liberal or conservative parties.[48] Moreover in some cities like Bonn and Trier, Catholic entrepreneurs belonged to the liberal parties, whereas judges, teachers and solicitors remained firm supporters of the Center. As the three-class franchise in Prussia favored the propertied classes and as Protestants in the Rhenish cities had been economically more active than their Catholic counterparts, the largely Catholic population was represented by liberals in the city councils. The liberals defended their position against the challenge of the Center by refusing to lower the tax threshold which determined one's eligibility to vote. As a result, they dominated the first and often the second class of voters, whereas in the

---

47. For this, see Sheehan, "Liberalism and the City."
48. Croon, "Vordringen," 24ff., 49.

third class they competed with workers. Consequently a number of civil servants, judges and teachers had to vote in the third class because they did not reach the income qualification of the other two classes. In cities with an overwhelmingly Catholic population, the Center gained strongly in the third class and sometimes even in the second. If this enabled the Center to win a majority, it then tended to defend its newly gained position against any Social Democratic challenge by maintaining restrictive practices similar to those employed earlier by the liberals.

Only in those towns with a traditional Catholic bourgeoisie did the city councillors tend to belong to the Center. This situation was, however, an exception. Until the turn of the century most German cities were dominated by the liberals; in the Rhineland these were largely National Liberals. Yet by the turn of the century the Center Party was able to record substantial gains. Earlier on, it had also been the *Kulturkampf* which prompted Catholic liberals to shift their allegiance to the Center. But in Trier, for example, it was not until 1911 that the Center gained the majority of the seats in the city council.

The conservative parties did not play as prominent a role in the cities as the liberal parties. Hence Conservatives tended to vote for the right-wing liberals, especially in areas where the Socialist vote was in the ascendancy. But in a number of cities the Conservatives were in the majority position, as for example in Breslau, Barmen, Würzburg and Dresden. Yet on the whole they were not of great importance in the cities, although they were able to compensate for this deficiency by dominating the *Landkreise,* especially in the east.

As there are no statistics to demonstrate the liberal predominance throughout Germany, some Social Democratic figures may give an indication of how large the numbers must have been if it is borne in mind that the SPD was a minority party in local government. By 1913 the Social Democrats were represented in 509 towns and nearly 3,000 rural communes. In the cities the Social Democratic councillors numbered only 2,753 and in the *Kreise* 8,928.[49] This gave the SPD a solid basis in local government, although before 1889 the party had not wanted to contest local elections. So far comparable

---

49. In this respect, see Dawson, *Municipal Life,* 79–81; Croon, "Vordringen," 30–5; and Jeserich, Pohl, and von Unruh, eds., *Deutsche Verwaltungsgeschichte,* 3: 612. Here slightly different figures are quoted. See also Dieter Rebentisch, "Die deutsche Sozialdemokratie und die kommunale Selbstverwaltung. Ein Überblick über Programmdiskussion und Organisationsproblematik 1890–1975," *Archiv für Sozialgeschichte* 75 (1985): 1–78.

figures for the Liberals and the Center were not available, but it is clear that they must have been much higher. Thus the Liberals were able to hold on to their hegemony in local government, although they had lost it in the Reichstag and in most of the Landtage.

The rapid pace of urbanization which Germany experienced between 1871 and 1914 is well documented and makes the study of the liberal party groupings within town hall-politics rewarding with reference to class, status, economic interest and religion. But what happened to the Liberals in the other unit of self-administration, the *Kreis,* or district? There were towns and *Landkreise,* and within the latter there were small rural communes and even estates or manors which retained their independence until 1927!

For the most part the *Kreise* represented a hybrid of self-administration and centralized administration by the state. The representative of the latter was the *Landrat,* who was appointed by the government and who wielded considerable administrative power and political influence. His function was, among other tasks, to supervise the communes and manorial estates in a given *Kreis.* The population of a *Kreis* was represented by the elected *Kreistag.* As a rule it consisted of twenty-five elected members. The more inhabitants who lived in a *Kreis,* the more representatives it had in the *Kreistag.* In addition the *Kreis* committee enjoyed the status of an executive committee and consisted of six members elected by the *Kreistag,* with the Landrat as its chairman. In Prussia the franchise was indirect and was based on the three-class franchise. The communes and town councils elected the representatives of the *Kreistag.* However election statistics and a detailed breakdown of the power distribution in the *Kreistage* have not been the subjects of extensive research. Much more information is needed before the role of the parties and the shift of power can be assessed.[50]

Whereas Freiherr vom Stein initiated the reforms for local government in the towns, the Prussian legislation for reforming the *Kreise* was influenced by Rudolf von Gneist. Gneist saw the *Kreis* as a substructure for state and society and hoped that self-administration

---

50. Apart from Unruh, few historians have recently worked on the *Kreise.* See Croon, "Vordringen," 91–105, and Jeserich, Pohl, and Unruh, eds., *Deutsche Verwaltungsgeschichte,* 3: 623–38. Yet, before the First World War the *Kreise* wielded substantial political influence. See, for example, Hein Hoebnik, "Entwicklung in Widerstreit: Die rheinischen und westfälischen Landkreise zwischen Stadt und Staat 1886–1986," in Landkreistag Nordrhein Westfalen, ed., *Hundert Jahre Kreisoidnung in Nordrhein Westfalen* (Düsseldorf, 1983), 25.

in the countryside could help to overcome the division between state and society. But as he did not plead for the introduction of a universal and equal franchise, it remains difficult to see how he thought this could be achieved. In contrast to the time when Stein suggested his reforms, the Prussian state was now in a stronger and more prestigious position, especially after 1871. The rejuvenation of a nation, as in 1808, was no longer on the agenda. The district government act, or *Kreisordnung,* of 1872 was therefore much closer to being simply an administrative reform through which the functions of the state were devolved to local institutions. It was a practical expedient which did not carry the same impetus as the introduction of self-administration in the cities. However in the Prussian Landtag it was argued that the *Kreisordnung* should represent the people's true sovereignty in a limited way. All that this demonstrated was that by this stage neither Bismarck nor the Liberals were keen to extend the Reichstag franchise to the *Kreistage.*

The political struggle to enact the new *Kreisordnung* showed that the supporters of the draft in the Prussian Landtag were the National Liberals and the Free Conservatives. The Conservatives and Left Liberals were against the new bill for opposite reasons. For the latter it did not go far enough, whereas the former feared for their predominant position in the eastern provinces. When the Conservatives succeeded in keeping the manorial districts as administrative entities, the passage of the bill became certain. In 1872 it passed by a majority of 195 but was defeated in the Prussian Upper House. As a consequence new members were appointed to the Upper House who later secured the passage of the bill. Bismarck had given up his earlier opposition to the bill and went so far as to support the Landtag against the opposition in the Upper House. But that was as far as he was prepared to go. A few years later when the National Liberals proposed the introduction of a secret ballot for local elections, along with a moderate reform of the three-class franchise and the establishment of municipal authority over the police, Bismarck torpedoed the proposal in the Ministry of State and in the Upper House and brought about the resignation of the Prussian Minister of the Interior, who had been responsible for the introduction of the *Kreisordnung.*[51]

Despite the modest scope of the reform proposals the National Liberals could still claim to be a party of reform, a posture they later

51. Ernst R. Huber, *Deutsche Verfassungsgeschichte seit 1789,* 4 vols. (Stuttgart, 1967–69), 4: 354ff.

abandoned. In the reform debates of 1875, Johannes Miquel, one of the leading National Liberals, had asked the government in the Landtag "to have confidence in the efficiency and the good will of the Prussian and German people. Look around; is the communal life in our cities not an example to other people despite the many legal obstacles?" But Bismarck would not hear of it.[52] For him and the Prussian Conservatives, the Liberals and their institutions were already too strong. Any further reforms would have strengthened the hand of the liberals in the *Kreise*. From Bismarck's point of view the strategy against reforms was successful, as the liberals never achieved the same level of domination in the *Kreise* as in the cities.

The functioning of the liberal power monopoly gave the foreign observer the impression, as the *New Encyclopedia of Social Research* stated, that "the municipality in Germany plans everything with a view to general harmony."[53] But given the intensifying political struggle after the turn of the century, nothing could have been further from the truth. In the previous edition of the same encyclopedia German local government was described as something "which belongs to the same paternal and therefore unsocialistic school" as the German social insurance system.[54] Thus the confusion about the power of German liberalism in the third tier of German politics has no limits.

In 1914 the former Chancellor, Prince Bernhard von Bülow, argued that "as much as Prussia could not be governed without the Conservatives, the Reich could not be ruled without the liberals."[55] This was true in the 1870s and for some years in the 1880s, but after 1890 the Center emerged as the biggest party in the Reichstag, as did the SPD after 1903. Although the liberals staged a modest recovery at the Reichstag polls of 1912 and the Prussian Landtag elections of 1913, it is still difficult to see how this could have led to the dawn of a new liberal era. Bülow had made no reference to the third tier of German politics, the cities. But it was here that the liberals were able to cling to their monopoly of power, although the signs of a decline in their position were clearly apparent. If the franchise had been widened, their monopoly of power would have collapsed even

---

52. Ibid.
53. William Dwight Porter Bliss, Rudolf Michael Binder, and Edward Page Gaston, eds., *The New Encyclopedia of Social Reform*, 2 vols. (London, 1908), 802–4.
54. William Dwight Porter Bliss, ed., *The New Encyclopedia of Social Reform* (New York, 1898), 656.
55. Körte et al., *Deutschland unter Kaiser Wilhelm II.*, 69.

though they would probably have remained in a prominent position in several towns. If they had been able to organize their parties as did the SPD and the Center, and if they had come out in favor of popular issues, then their chances might not have been too poor.

James Sheehan has called the city councils "the only representative bodies in which traces of the 'liberal era' remained more than the memory of a lost world."[56] This judgment seems to be colored by some form of nostalgia for the 1870s, when the National Liberals thrived with the universal franchise in the Reichstag. As they proceeded to lose their predominance in the Reichstag, so they would have lost their monopoly of power in the cities had the Reichstag franchise prevailed there as well. They also lost the majority in the Prussian Landtag, but not in the towns, where the three-class franchise was also valid. This may have given some party members the hope that a revival was possible. But the narrowly based power position in the cities contributed to an attitude of inflexibility which hampered the National Liberals in the Prussian Landtag, where over the years they had moved closer to the Conservatives. A chance to improve their performance at the national level could have arisen if they had been willing to integrate the three tiers of German politics more closely in their own election strategies. The election agreements between the Liberals and the Center Party in the Ruhr district showed the way. Thus the National Liberals were willing to offer the Center Party seats in the city councils in return for a pledge by the Center to ask its supporters to vote for the National Liberal candidate on the second ballot in the Reichstag elections.[57] This could have served as a model for similar agreements if the liberals had been determined to improve their showing at the Reichstag polls.

Regardless of this potential for survival, the persistence of the liberal's power in the cities gives substance to the conclusion that political liberalism remained a force in Germany after 1880 or even after 1890. Bülow claimed in 1914 that "liberalism is rooted as an intellectual characteristic with the German people."[58] This remark appears to be borne out by the existence of the power monopoly of the liberal parties in the German cities. The historian Heinrich Heffter supports this point by writing that "the liberal bourgeoisie . . . has remained a much stronger force in the intellectual

---

56. Sheehan, *German Liberalism*, 230.
57. Croon, "Vordringen," 54.
58. Körte et al., *Deutschland unter Kaiser Wilhelm II.*, 71.

and economic life [of the Empire] than the steady decline of its parliamentary position would make one believe."[59] In comparison with the "New Liberalism" which revitalized the parliamentary Liberal Party in England, the German liberalism had, apart from some Naumannite ideas, nothing new to offer. The liberal parties in both countries were not in favor of full democracy, but whereas in Britain social reforms proved to be a successful rallying cry, German liberals had nothing of this kind to offer. Even the rising popular appeal of the Left Liberals after 1912 was fueled more by votes of protest against the political and economic establishment than by new ideas. If liberal ideas were, however, still thriving among the German public, then the liberals, in order to retain their political credibility, would have had to come out in favor of reforming the local franchise, as Hans Delbrück and Friedrich Naumann demanded, even though this would have cost them their monopoly of power in the cities. But whether the majority of the Liberals would have sacrificed their position in order to fall into line with reformist liberal ideas is questionable.

59. Heffter, *Selbstverwaltung*, 661.

4

Reichstag Elections in the Kaiserreich: The Prospects for Electoral Research in the Interdisciplinary Context

PETER STEINBACH

"Even the vote is a rifle, and ballots are also bullets."[1] With this martial declaration, the democratic *Volkszeitung* joined the political campaign in the summer of 1867 preceding elections to the North German Reichstag. In the nineteenth century, election campaigns were evidently considered highly significant. This can be seen clearly in the fact that even election contests in other states were keenly observed and attracted detailed commentary.[2] Obviously the close inherent connection between "representation, political domination, and legitimation" was recognized at the time, to the point where general questions about political participation were broadly perceived as election issues by the contemporaries of Bismarck, Marx, and Nietzsche. Yet the present state of historical research on elections seems to stand in peculiar contrast to this observation.[3] It would be an exaggeration to claim that electoral research today stands at the *center* of current historical study. To be sure, such research continues to play an important role in debates about the foundations of political authority and the character of political systems in the nineteenth century. Rarely, however, are elections themselves the object of systematic historical research. For this reason, electoral research tends to be associated with the names of individual scholars, who frequently proceed independently of research trends and regularly attract the attention – if not even the admiration – of their colleagues. This was evident following the early death of an especially promising scholar interested in Wilhelmine elections, Stanley Suval.[4]

This essay was translated by Robin Brownlie and James Retallack.
1. *Volks-Zeitung*, 30 Aug. 1867, no. 202.
2. Cf. Elfi Bendikat, *Wahlkämpfe in Europa 1884–1889: Parteiensysteme und Politikstile in Deutschland, Frankreich und Grossbritannien* (Wiesbaden, 1988).
3. Cf. Peter Steinbach, *Die Politisierung der Region* (Passau, 1989), 35ff; Karl Rohe, "Wahlanalyse im historischen Kontext," *Historische Zeitschrift* 234 (1982):337ff.
4. See Stanley Suval, *Electoral Politics in Wilhelmine Germany* (Chapel Hill, NC, 1985).

It is incontestable that the connection between social change, democratization, and a transformation of political styles – from the politics of notables to a more fundamental politicization of the electorate based on parties – can be studied conclusively and in a comparative context only with the help of historical electoral research.[5] To this extent, this essay may be seen as a plea for the further development of older studies and research approaches.[6] Such a development could impel electoral research toward broadly based investigations of those systems of government that were confronted for the first time by social democratization or that had to overcome challenges resulting from the extensive mobilization, politicization, and polarization of the electorate. This broad focus suggests that one might regard as a historical unit the decades between the introduction of the universal franchise in 1867 and the abolition of regular democratic elections in 1933. For with the introduction of the universal franchise, the distance between state and society shrank. The institutions of the modern state could now influence social developments to a qualitatively new extent – steering change in a governmental direction or influencing and manipulating the interpretation of events through the press. At the same time, broadly based political countermovements had to be confronted: With universal suffrage they, too, had won a means to influence the setting of goals for society as a whole. Last and no less important, a new style of election campaigns intensified divisions and dissent within society. These struggles for mastery were often portrayed as contests for the best and fairest social order, but they were ultimately struggles about the exercise of power.

To a large extent, social scientists have lost a sense of the fundamental significance of the democratic franchise for the emergence of a modern political system – one no longer characterized by differentiation according to social estates (*Stände*). Investigations by social scientists have been mainly present-oriented:[7] Seeking to gauge the current mood of the population, they neglect the historical preconditions of a political culture that, after all, represents the outcome of a process rather than the sum of attitudes and values. To correct this

---

5. Cf. Horst Glück, "Politische Traditionen und Wählerverhalten," *Der Bürger im Staat* 40, no. 3 (1990):176ff.
6. Cf. Peter Steinbach, "Stand und Methode der historischen Wahlforschung," in Hartmut Kaelble et al., eds., *Probleme der Modernisierung in Deutschland* (Opladen, 1978), 170ff.
7. Cf. Max Kaase et al., *Wahlen und politisches System* (Opladen, 1983); Kaase, *Wahlen und politischer Prozess* (Opladen, 1986); Kaase, *Wahlen und Wähler* (Opladen, 1990).

imbalance, it is important not only to recall the historical dimensions of political expression and debate but, taking the interdisciplinary approach, to use the methodological tools of electoral research for the science of history. A presentist approach can be countered only by emphasizing historically–genetically oriented questions. This is crucial if electoral research – which sees itself as part of the larger investigation of political parties, associations, and constitutional life in the past – is to help reintegrate the fields of political and social history, which have been too sharply distinguished in discussions of historical methodology. Indeed, the science of history can and should be broadened by the adoption of research methods from social and cultural history *and* political science.

As it happens, the relative immaturity of electoral research as a field of study within German history is mitigated by several factors, among which can be included an increased perception of its relevance to current political debate. As long ago as the 1930s, scholars first became interested in determining which Germans had voted for National Socialism.[8] More recently, this interest prompted investigations into the proportion of workers among voters of the *Nationalsozialistische Deutsche Arbeiterpartei* or NSDAP).[9] This issue achieved a special resonance among the German public a few years ago when a vehement dispute broke out between the two largest political parties in the Federal Republic. This controversy was sparked by the assertion that Social Democrats and National Socialists alike had embraced collectivist values, and that it was therefore incorrect to describe social democracy as "generically" opposed to fascism. Claims by the Communist Party that it was the only true antifascist force in Germany and that it alone had been immune to the NSDAP also demanded in-depth investigation. In a larger context, the relevance of electoral sociology was demonstrated recently in a wide-ranging anthology of essays on the origins and rise of social democracy in the German Empire, which sprang from a conference at the Historisches Kolleg in Munich.[10] Here, too, questions about electoral politics related directly to the current political scene and to other features of Germany's political, constitutional, and social history. Since debates at this conference repeatedly touched on the political

---

8. Cf. Thomas Childers, *The Nazi Voter: The Social Foundations of Fascism in Germany 1919–1933* (Chapel Hill, NC, 1983).
9. Jürgen W. Falter, *Hitlers Wähler* (Munich, 1991).
10. Gerhard A. Ritter, ed., *Der Aufstieg der deutschen Arbeiterbewegung: Sozialdemokratie und Freie Gewerkschaften im Parteiensystem und Sozialmilieu des Kaiserreichs* (Munich, 1990).

factors affecting the development of social democracy in the nineteenth century, great significance was attached to the wider dimensions of the electoral struggle itself – including, for instance, efforts to implement franchise reform in the individual states of the German Empire such as Prussia and Saxony. These two examples illustrate that, even now, questions about workers' behavior in the *Kaiserreich*, in the late Weimar Republic, and in the early Nazi regime are considered significant far beyond specialist circles.

To avoid misunderstanding, it should be stressed that any assertion about electoral research as a relatively underdeveloped subfield of German history is not intended to justify this deficit. On the contrary, this essay seeks to argue that a reorientation along methodological lines preferred by electoral historians will provide an important stimulus to further research on political and constitutional history. The first section surveys international schools of electoral research and suggest ways in which this diversity of approaches may be more significant for historical methodology as a whole than electoral psychology, which aims to explain individual voter behavior.[11] The approaches favored by electoral historians permit the analysis of political factors affecting the outcome of elections in the broad sense – that is, those factors relating directly to the structure of power and the system of rule – and also facilitate the study of social change.

The second section discusses how electoral research provides fruitful guidelines for the investigation of political systems, using examples drawn from the empire of Bismarck and Wilhelm II. Proceeding from a detailed outline of Bismarck's political motivations for introducing a democratic franchise, this section also illuminates the politically autonomous way in which the universal, equal, secret, and direct manhood franchise for the German Reichstag functioned. Bismarck was, of course, unable to realize his intention of steering from above the social and political changes inaugurated by the introduction of the democratic franchise, and the consequences of his policy of internal struggle are well known: Internal contradictions divided German society, and they also burdened the political value system, the new style of politics, and finally the political culture of Germany as a whole. A long tradition of governmental influence in the political process was begun under Bismarck that encumbered

---

11. See the overview in Jürgen W. Falter, "Methodologische Probleme von Wahlforschung und Wahlprognose," *Aus Politik und Zeitgeschichte* 43 (1989):3ff.

German politics far beyond the end of the *Kaiserreich*. That tradition – among other factors – helps explain attempts in the final phase of the Weimar Republic to seek an authoritarian solution and, in the process, to rely on plebiscitarian alternatives as well.

The depiction of Bismarck's deliberations also offers an opportunity to address questions about the system of rule in Imperial Germany – specifically, about the intentions of political elites in introducing the universal franchise. At the same time, one can explore the political and social developments that changed or thwarted these calculations. For this reason, the third section sketches possible guidelines for further electoral research. Closely linked to the preceding section, this discussion also derives its essential stimulus from the political and tactical considerations that originally accompanied the introduction of the universal franchise. Such an approach juxtaposes, on the one hand, the granting of the vote as part of a government-initiated revolution from above and, on the other hand, the ways in which historical research can inquire into the actual consequences of this action. In this way, one contributes to discussions about political continuities within the *Kaiserreich* and between the nineteenth century and the twentieth. More concretely, one can suggest decisive political encumbrances in the history of German democracy between 1918 and 1933 that, although they cannot be investigated in this essay, are the object of other studies in this volume.

The concluding deliberations in the fourth section point to possible paths open to future historians of German elections. This research should continue to use methods and models derived from political science, especially those closely associated with Stein Rokkan, who suffered a tragically early death. By fusing history and political science in a unique way, Rokkan helped establish an historically informed social science that was eminently understandable and significant for historians as well. The deaths of Rokkan and Suval left breaches that to this day have not been filled – at least for the study of elections in the *Kaiserreich*. This is all the more regrettable since electoral historians like Thomas Childers and Jürgen W. Falter set methodological milestones for research on the Weimar Republic. In doing so, these two scholars more than held their own beside the presentist studies of research groups whose principal aim is to devise successful campaign strategies for Germany's current political parties. It remains to be seen whether in the future a new understanding will develop between historical and presentist electoral researchers – to the advantage of both disciplines and to the benefit of efficient research.

I

In the past decades, it has become clear that sophisticated electoral history can inquire into both the determinants of electoral behavior and the effect election outcomes have on the political system only through the integration of the most diverse methods and explanatory models. The contradiction between schools that preferred long-term studies on the basis of regional history, and those that attempted to analyze the most broadly conceived set of results in cross-sectional studies, was overcome at first by a combination of the two methods.[12] This was a prerequisite for the opening of electoral history to empirical and analytical questions from the social sciences, and hence also to methods of data processing and statistical analysis. The promoters of political electoral history adopted ever more precise ways of interpreting the psychological analysis of elections – often, however, without reflecting on their own approaches and source limitations. In the 1970s, therefore, previously integrated research approaches became more differentiated, and methodological discussions centered on pioneering electoral studies proved that many of the latter's conclusions were based on weak or problematic foundations. This insight was chiefly the result of studies and critical discussions initiated by Jürgen Falter, who set himself the task of researching the social bases of the Nazi Party and who developed a methodologically sophisticated research project through a critique of existing interpretations.[13]

Falter's procedure differed from that of another social scientist and historically minded researcher, Karl Rohe, who teaches in Essen.[14] Rohe, concentrating on the *Ruhrgebiet*, took as his starting point the

12. See, inter alia, Steinbach, "Stand und Methode"; Rainer-Olaf Schultze, "Funktion von Wahlen und Konstitutionsbedingungen von Wahlverhalten im deutschen Kaiserreich," in Otto Büsch, ed., *Wählerbewegung in der europäischen Geschichte* (Berlin, 1980); O. Büsch et al., eds., *Wählerbewegung in der deutschen Geschichte* (Berlin, 1978); O. Büsch and P. Steinbach, eds., *Vergleichende europäische Wahlgeschichte* (Berlin, 1983).
13. See Jürgen W. Falter et al., *Wahlen und Abstimmungen in der Weimarer Republik* (Munich, 1986), which includes important bibliographical references.
14. See Karl Rohe, *Vom Revier zum Ruhrgegiet: Wahlen, Parteien, Politische Kultur* (Essen, 1986); Rohe, ed., *Elections, Parties and Political Traditions* (New York, 1990). Rohe has announced a comprehensive study of German elections, likely to appear in 1992.

efforts of Rainer M. Lepsius to apprehend political-cultural milieux and to comprehend them as the expression of political "blocs" (*Lager*). For Lepsius, milieux became intertwined with party structures and represented a link between social relationships and political systems. Rohe analyzed Ruhr society in terms of its origins and its development since the period of intense industrialization in the nineteenth century. In its regional focus his approach resembled outdated historical research: Singularity and historicity determined his effort to describe specific regional milieux, whereas Falter was interested in testing a certain analytical method on a case of historic significance. But problems resulted both from attempts to generalize Rohe's results and from efforts to bring Falter's theses into harmony with individual case studies. In this respect, the difficulties of combining analytical methods and concepts from history and the social sciences were mirrored in both research trends.

Despite all the advances registered in the work of Rohe and Falter, there is evidence to suggest that another approach – built around analyses of election campaigns, electoral laws, and statistics and offering a consciously historical perspective – will continue to dominate the field. Gerhard A. Ritter is known as the chief representative of this school.[15] For Ritter, electoral research by historians is conceivable only on the basis of a diversity of sources and in-depth quantitative analysis, using the tools of both social and political history. In this view, electoral history does not constitute an end in itself; instead, it must contribute to the analysis of constitutional issues, social change and conflict, associational life, the party system, the genesis of political movements, and the institutions of authoritarian rule (*Herrschaft*).[16] This approach, like others, draws on a diversity of scholarly traditions.

The beginnings of election campaign description are generally identified with the British electoral studies of the Nuffield Group.[17] Originally a research technique used primarily by contemporary historians, these studies have become important historical sources in their own right. They aim to investigate the election process as precisely as possible, and therefore begin with an analysis of the legisla-

---

15. See Gerhard A. Ritter, *Die deutschen Parteien 1830–1914* (Göttingen, 1985).
16. Cf. G. A. Ritter, "Die Sozialdemokratie im Deutschen Kaiserreich in sozialgeschichtlicher Perspektive," *Historische Zeitschrift* 249 (1989):295ff.
17. See, for example, Uwe Webster Kitzinger, *German Electoral Politics: A Study of the 1957 Campaign* (Oxford, 1960); David Butler et al., *Political Change in Britain: Forces Shaping Electoral Choice* (Harmondsworth, 1971).

tive period immediately preceding the election in question, examining its significant political decisions and events. The depiction of the election campaign serves as the centerpiece of the analysis, and in some cases investigations of individual constituencies are carried out. Candidate profiles, press coverage of election activities, and later commentary on the outcome of the election are all studied in depth. An overall assessment of the election's outcome – often inadequately supported with statistics – usually concludes the analysis.

The organization of the Nuffield studies reflects the way liberal theory regards the act of voting. In this view, casting a ballot signifies both an "unburdening" (*Entlastung*) and a "committal" (*Festlegung*); therefore the assumptions and consequences of voting must be considered at some length. However, since voters do not act according to rational criteria alone, it is essential to investigate other influencing factors. These are traced chiefly through the political process – that is, in the interaction and structure of government, administration, parties, interest groups, and the media. They are also perceived through such social institutions as the church and associational life, and the transformation of social structures is frequently understood as a precondition for political change. For historians, the Nuffield studies are stimulating because they make more tangible the complex of events that culminate in the act of voting – the final stage of an organic development and the starting point of new political constellations. Elections also become an element of the system of rule: They are conditioned by the system and simultaneously influence its future. This is why it is so important to understand the way in which political institutions mold the process leading to the casting of a ballot. One limitation of the Nuffield approach becomes clear when factors influencing individual voting decisions are analyzed; such factors, part of the larger political system, can in general be combined analytically but not assigned relative weights. Nonetheless, electoral statistics are intended to supply the basis for a causal explanation of voter behavior. They are compiled on the assumption that elections represent comprehensive surveys of the electorate; that electorate then becomes visible as a differentiated collective in social, occupational, and economic statistics. Put another way, electoral statistics fulfill conditions for the analysis of context. In this sense, they represent a decisive link to electoral geography.

Electoral geography was developed mainly in France by André

Siegfried and his students.[18] The central concern for them is not the political system or the process shaping the outcome of elections, but the electorate itself. The electorate is seen as historically shaped by social and political factors. These include social structure, cultural and confessional profiles, the relationship between local or regional milieux and the external world, even climate, soil, and landscape. Adherents of this school consider such factors to be influential and long-lasting because they mold perceptions, attitudes, interest structures, and the willingness to regulate conflict. French electoral studies are thus oriented around the following schema: geographic requirements and conditions, production and market, and finally, the parameters of political life. Each of these aspects must first be described before the elections can be analyzed. Dependencies between the sociohistorical and regional foundations of an electorate and the act of voting are introduced interpretively or established through cartographic conversion of comparative data. Ultimately these efforts are directed toward a "total election history," a concept introduced by George Dupeux in the early 1960s.[19] Dupeux's study achieved an extraordinary intertwining of social, economic, and political factors, both nationally and regionally, thereby illuminating not only the transformation of a *departement* but also the secular transformation of the nineteenth century – economic, social, and political.

Comparing this method with that of the Nuffield school, it is noticeable that the two approaches need to be combined in order to encompass both the prerequisites of collective decision making and the consequences of the act of voting for the political system as a whole. French election research has always stressed the necessity of integrating social and political history while at the same time offering a thorough analysis of the social structure. The investigation of political processes, on the other hand, remained clearly dependent on the premises of political history, as was shown, for example, by the adoption of periodization from political history for the analysis of regional elections. Here it would be more meaningful to take as a starting point the well-differentiated election campaign studies of the British type in order to investigate the election process further.

18. André Siegfried, *Géographie électorale de l'Adèche sous la IIIe République* (Paris, 1949); more generally, see Pierre Barral, "La sociologie électorale et l'histoire," *Revue historique* 238 (1967):117ff.
19. George Dupeux, *Aspects de l'histoire sociale et politique du Loir-et-Cher 1848–1914* (Paris, 1962).

The research concept of political and social ecology assumes a close connection between social structures and election results. This concept was developed by Rudolf Heberle, relying on the work of Siegfried; it eventually became a key component of Heberle's political sociology.[20] The socioecological approach is at first glance difficult to distinguish from electoral geography. Heberle sees the purpose of the ecological approach in the "study of complexes of social phenomena in their geographical distribution and reciprocal effect" and defines it as a "technique of research into causality based on concrete, unique political events." Electoral ecology thus combines electoral statistics and electoral geography, but also the principle of singularity expressed in the campaign descriptions of the Nuffield school. The major characteristic of electoral ecology is the reconstruction of the environmental makeup of an electorate and the perception of electoral behavior as a collective act. The goal is not to explain the individual voter and his psychological disposition, but rather the behavior of voters in an entire constituency or electoral district. To be sure, the contribution of electoral ecology to election forecasting is meager, as is its value for those seeking to manage successful election campaigns. Nevertheless, its significance for historical investigations is equally uncontested. In contrast to research in electoral psychology, electoral ecology takes no interest in the formulation of "universally applicable laws of voter behavior." It is predicated instead on a constantly changing party system and takes into account the fact "that all political processes take place in 'historical' time." On the other hand, since the environmental relations of an investigated unit must be viewed not only from a temporal perspective but also from a spatial one, in electoral ecology long-term trends recede in the face of spatial history; thus, as a rule, electoral ecology researchers tend toward regional history. This means that primarily political influences on the system – parties, governments, the media – are less clearly illuminated than regionally specific factors. When this approach is pressed too rigorously, regional history actually begins to take the place of electoral analysis.[21]

This can be corrected only by an approach that frees itself from the

---

20. Rudolf Heberle, *Landbevölkerung und Nationalsozialismus* (Stuttgart, 1963); Heberle, *Hauptprobleme der politischen Soziologie* (Stuttgart, 1967). Cf. Steinbach, "Stand und Methode," 188ff.
21. Cf. the critical overview in Arno Mohr, "Politische Identität um jeden Preis? Zur Funktion der Landesgeschichtsschreibung in den Bundesländern," *Neue Politische Literatur* 35, no. 2 (1990):222ff.

goal of depicting regional social structures, confessional affiliations, or local political developments and instead sets the analysis of secular transformation processes as the task of electoral history. In this connection it may be useful to bring modernization theory into the discussion, especially as it has informed the work of Stein Rokkan.[22] According to Rokkan, developmental changes in political structures become visible through the medium of election contests. Elections and parties are perceived as a link between the social and political systems: Parties have to react to problems of development, and can maintain themselves only when they successfully address social change and its consequent problems in a way that impresses large sectors of the electorate and thereby attracts their votes. The most suggestive election analyses of the past years – those oriented equally to history and social science – have made reference to Heberle's and Rokkan's analyses. Thus, Lepsius introduced the generation concept, though not before he had succeeded in adapting the idea of the milieu for the analysis of the party system.[23] Max Kaase, the most important representative of empirical–analytical electoral research, emphasized the significance of following the process of opinion making over longer periods of time.[24] Meanwhile, in his still classic investigation of Landtag elections in the Saarland, Falter took the context model as the starting point of all analysis.[25] Although electoral research that is informed by the social sciences continued to focus on voter behavior – and is therefore closer to election psychology than to either socioecological research or election campaign history – there is no doubt that collective voter behavior, investigated on the basis of aggregate data, remains the primary object of electoral history.[26]

"The problem of the best combination" of methods was identified some years ago as the most important challenge in electoral history. Today, however, it seems to be more popular to place electoral studies in the context of power structures and processes of social change. This is particularly true for the German *Kaiserreich* and the Weimar

---

22. For an introduction, see Stein Rokkan, *Citizens, Elections, Parties: Approaches to the Comparative Study of the Process of Development* (Oslo, 1970).
23. Mario Rainer Lepsius, "Wahlverhalten, Parteien und Politische Spannungen," *Politische Vierteljahresschrift* 13 (1973):295ff.
24. Max Kaaase, *Wechsel von Parteipräferenzen* (Meisenheim, 1967).
25. Jürgen W. Falter, *Faktoren der Wahlentscheidung: eine wahlsoziologische Analyse am Beispiel der saarländischen Landtagswahl 1970* (Cologne, 1973).
26. Cf. Heinrich Best, ed., *Politik und Milieu: Wahl- und Elitenforschung im historischen und interkulturellen Vergleich* (St. Katharinen, 1989).

Republic. Neither political system could withstand crises of social and political change by raising its capacity for self-taxation, and neither fully exploited the democratic potential at hand to achieve its own political stabilization. This had serious consequences for the further course of German history, which oscillated between underparticipation and overparticipation and finally culminated in National Socialism.

It is difficult to draw convincing parallels between the founding of the German Empire in 1871 and the end of the Weimar Republic: In spite of all the negative developmental tendencies established during the *Kaiserreich,* many chances arose – and disappeared – for a stabilization of democratically legitimated reform. It is nevertheless beyond doubt that the introduction of the democratic franchise as the result of government initiative set the stage for a perversion of the democratic process. Not only the founding of the Second Reich, but also the granting of the vote first demanded and obtained in the revolutionary movement of 1848, was viewed by many clearsighted contemporaries – on the right as well as the left – as a revolution from above. If Theodor Schieder's hypothesis about the universal nightmare of revolution is valid,[27] and if (on the other hand) his assertion is correct that elections are an extraordinarily important link between state and society, the question arises: Why, during the decade between the constitutional conflict of 1861–6 and the founding of the Reich in 1871, was an effort made to block the fearsome prospect of political democratization through the introduction of the equally feared democratic franchise? Was this not like fighting the devil with Beelzebub?

Long ago, historians began to address these questions by inquiring into Bismarck's motives for introducing the universal franchise. By reviewing those motives in the following section, it is possible at the same time to reexamine continuities in the political expectations of ruling elites and to sharpen our awareness of the social developments that proved largely immune to governmental control. The mobilization of German society, accelerated by the universal franchise, by an expanding press, and by an increasingly dense network of *Vereine* and political parties, precipitated a rapid politicization that was perceived by ruling elites as a danger to state and society. Those elites de-

---

27. Theodor Schieder, "Die Krise des bürgerlichen Liberalismus: Ein Beitrag zum Verhältnis von politischer und gesellschaftlicher Verfassung," in Lothar Gall, ed., *Liberalismus* (Cologne, 1976), 192ff.

manded the mobilization of counterforces that, though they ultimately failed in the *Kaiserreich*, left deep traces in German political culture and were reactivated in the final phase of the Weimar Republic. Rejection of the party system and the control of free political expression through staged election campaigns – which appeared to some contemporaries as political "infernos" – reduced the stabilizing function of elections, which are ideally the consequence of a free interplay of political forces. Only by considering the different possible motives for introducing the democratic franchise, within the context of the political, social, and cultural consequences of that action, can we gain insight into the effects of political calculation and decision making.[28] For this reason, attention in the following section is devoted to Bismarck's deliberations, partly in order to satisfy a current biographical interest in the character of the first German chancellor but, more important, to explore the mechanisms of *Herrschaft* in nineteenth-century Germany and to make clear the need for a brand of electoral history that views the system of rule in a critical way. Here it is not sufficient to demonstrate the manipulation of election campaigns by the government, by the chancellor, or by the official press, as in the left-liberal tradition that even Michael Stürmer took as the foundation of his argument.[29] It is more important to document ways in which contemporary Germans successfully resisted governmental control and to investigate how German governments reacted to the expansion of the political arena. Despite important preparatory research, more work is needed on these official counterstrategies: how they were formulated, their effects, aftereffects, and failures. In this way, a heavy political mortgage in German history – the failure of democracy during the Weimar Republic – may also be traced back more precisely to its roots.

II

In the nineteenth century, the demand for the universal, equal, secret, and direct franchise constituted, quite simply, the program of political revolution. Even representatives of a moderate constitutionalism

---

28. I have attempted to address this question in Peter Steinbach, *Die Zähmung des politischen Massenmarktes: Wahlen und Wahlkämpfe im Bismarckreich im Spiegel der Hauptstadt- und Gesinnungspresse*, 3 vols. (Passau, 1990); see also Steinbach, "Nationalisierung, soziale Differenzierung und Urbanisierung als Bedingungsfaktoren des Wahlverhaltens im Kaiserreich," *Quantum–Historical Social Research* 15, no. 2 (1990):63ff.
29. Michael Stürmer, *Regierung und Reichstag im Bismarckstaat 1871–1890* (Düsseldorf, 1970).

who opposed the "monarchical principle" did not advocate the principle of popular sovereignty unconditionally or without reservation. The European revolutions of 1830 and 1848 had largely discredited the idea of democratically legitimated opinion making (*Willensbildung*): Revolutionary "extravagances," often labeled "excesses," had gradually made the bourgeoisie into a force of inertia. It was all the more surprising, therefore, that the introduction of the democratic and revolutionary, universal, equal, secret, and direct male franchise was realized in the North German Confederation. In this way a major political demand of the Revolution of 1848 was realized, as was a principal aim of European left-liberal and nascent democratic socialist movements. Above all, Bismarck, soon considered a "white revolutionary," obtained a highly favorable position for Prussia in the struggle to assume leadership in the process leading to German unification.[30] In the course of these developments Bismarck's attitude toward the revolutionary franchise was thoroughly transformed. Even though sources documenting Bismarck's change of heart are extraordinarily rare, this transformation can be studied by reference to the many warnings about the revolutionary franchise that emerged from his circle of associates.

At first Bismarck had vehemently opposed the introduction of the universal, democratic franchise. During the Revolution of 1848 he argued for an estate-based franchise, largely to facilitate a better representation of economic and social interests.[31] In the 1850s, he explicitly rejected "head-count elections" and "primary elections" (*Urwahlen*), while at the same time he opposed "indirect elections." In Bismarck's view, both the universal franchise and indirect voting procedures distorted the organic composition of society.[32] This argument reflected Bismarck's experience with an electoral law that had become an instrument for expressing the views of property owners. In the universal franchise, moreover, Bismarck saw a threat to crown

---

30. See the suggestive essays in Lothar Gall, ed., *Das Bismarck-Problem in der Geschichtsschreibung nach 1945* (Cologne and Berlin, 1971); see also the lengthy biographies by Lothar Gall, *Bismarck. The White Revolutionary*, 2 vols., trans. by J. A. Underwood (London and Boston, 1986); Ernst Engelberg, *Bismarck: Urpreusse und Reichsgründer* and *Bismarck: Das Reich in der Mitte Europas* (Berlin, 1985–90); and Otto Pflanze, *Bismarck and the Development of Germany*, 3 vols. (Princeton, NJ, 1990).
31. Otto von Bismarck, *Erinnerung und Gedanke*, Werke in Auswahl der Wissenschaftlichen Buchgesellschaft, vol. 8, pt. A (Darmstadt, 1975), 28ff.
32. Bernhard Studt, "Bismarck als Mitarbeiter der 'Kreuzzeitung' in den Jahren 1848 und 1849" (Ph.D. thesis, University of Bonn, 1903), 52.

and country; it signified for him a kind of political "lottery."[33] Bismarck considered election campaigns to be an inadmissible and fateful means to influence the populace, for the people were no longer free in their decisions after the election campaign was concluded.[34] During the period of reaction in the 1850s, however, Bismarck became convinced that elections need not always destabilize the political regime. Much more threatening, in his opinion, were plans for a coup d'état, such as those entertained by the more conservative Otto von Manteuffel.[35] Gradually, Bismarck came to believe that elections could be employed as a means of political domination. This is the sense in which one should interpret his statement in the 1850s that the constitution, because of the way it had recently evolved, had "ceased to impede government" and had become "more and more the vessel whose content is determined by the personalities who rule."[36] At the same time, and in peculiar contradiction to this thesis, Bismarck was convinced that the ruling statesman was not at all dependent on the support of the legislature.[37] Bismarck's attitude toward the franchise underwent further evolution during his diplomatic service in Paris. In this period he recognized "how easily a monarchical government can exploit liberal-national ideas and parliamentary institutions to enhance its power."[38] He also became convinced that the rural populace was disposed to be loyal to the king. For this reason, he increasingly regarded the universal franchise as an expedient that strengthened authority and the monarchical principle by means of the plebiscite. All in all, the evolution of Bismarck's thinking about the franchise revealed an early ambivalence: Reflecting both self-confidence and arrogance, Bismarck oscillated between the bonapartist and the monarchist understandings of electoral politics.

The question of Bismarck's motivation is of secondary importance to practitioners of electoral sociology. Yet the question of how far he realized his calculations can be answered only from the perspective of electoral history. Here it is clear that the rural population was not

---

33. Horst Kohl, ed., *Die politischen Reden des Fürsten Bismarck* (Stuttgart and Berlin, 1892), 1:89.
34. *Bismarck-Jahrbuch* 1 (1894):478f.
35. M. Stürmer, "Staatsstreichgedanken im Bismarckreich," *Historische Zeitschrift* 209 (1969):566ff.
36. Heinrich von Poschinger, *Preussen im Bundestage 1851–1859: Dokumente der Königl. Preuss. Bundestags-Gesandtschaft* (Leipzig, 1884), 4:39.
37. Horst Kohl, ed., *Bismarcks Briefe an den General Leopold von Gerlach* (Berlin, 1896), 263.
38. Richard Augst, *Bismarcks Stellung zum parlamentarischen Wahlrecht* (Leipzig, 1917), 25f.

constituted only of "dumb" and compliant subjects but, rather, might embody an oppositional potential that, in times of conflict with the monarch, could grow rapidly. For future developments, it was of decisive importance that in the mid-nineteenth century the Prussian three-class franchise was no longer merely a means of political defense; it had become a vehicle of potent political change. Thus the parliament elected under the three-class franchise offered determined resistance during the constitutional crisis over Prussian army increases in the early 1860s: That parliament even seemed to want to reorient itself within a British model of parliamentary monarchy.[39] As a consequence of this crisis, Bismarck attempted to deny civil servants the right to stand for election.

There is no doubt that the three-class franchise strengthened the influence of bourgeois elements within the political system. Hence it was natural that Bismarck sought to activate the pro-monarchist mood of the rural populace for his own purposes. Similarly, since Bismarck blamed the difficulties of the Prussian government on the right to vote,[40] it was natural to want to change the electoral system. Also relevant were plans to introduce by decree a franchise favoring the monarch and his policies. Bismarck studied such plans, and he was encouraged in this not least by conversations with Ferdinand Lassalle, in whom he saw the chief opponent of the bourgeoisie.[41] The French emperor, Napoleon III, is alleged to have recommended the introduction of the universal franchise in 1861 in order to end the Prussian constitutional conflict.[42] Bismarck's friend and close political associate, Hermann Wagener, also wanted to defeat the liberals at the polls with the help of the underclasses; he foresaw the introduction of the universal franchise diluted by vocational classifications.[43] We know that plans to decree an electoral franchise based on these schemes miscarried due to the attitude of the Prussian king, Wilhelm I. For Bismarck, experience gathered in the 1860s was nonetheless important for his assessment of the universal franchise in that, in a planned unification of Germany under Prussian domination, he intended to weaken the opposition liberals by activating the popular

---

39. See Adalbert Hess, *Das Parlament, das Bismarck widerstrebte* (Cologne and Opladen, 1964).
40. Augst, *Bismarcks Stellung*, 38.
41. Gustav Meyer, *Bismarck und Lassalle: Ihr Briefwechsel und ihre Gespräche* (Berlin, 1928).
42. Karl Ringhoffer, *Im Kampf um Preussens Ehre: Aus dem Nachlasse des Grafen Albrecht von Bernstorff* (Berlin, 1906), 456; cf. Augst, *Bismarcks Stellung*, 39.
43. Gerhard Ritter, *Die preussischen Konservativen und Bismarcks deutsche Politik 1858–1871* (Heidelberg, 1913).

masses with the help of such a franchise. Later, Bismarck expressed his intentions to ministerial councillor Baron von Völderndorff in the following terms:[44]

It would probably have appealed to people of anxious natures to narrow the franchise through all sorts of cautionary measures [Kautelen]; for this there are census thresholds, class-based elections, grading by electors, and other things. But I have never been of an anxious nature. To a people other than the Germans, though, even I might not have dared extend such a dangerous right. But the Germans are, in my opinion – at least in the north – in nine out of ten cases loyal to the king; the great mass of the population stand, in their hearts, by their government, even though they complain. The people know that they are ruled honestly and conscientiously, and in the decisive moment one can rely on them.

Bismarck, who wanted to create diplomatic problems for the multinational Habsburg empire, hoped in the mid-1860s to attract sympathy by introducing the universal franchise. His plan was then to implement his policies by means of an electorate that had been politically mobilized by this concession. Bismarck believed that both foreign and domestic difficulties could be reduced simultaneously in this way. He had first exploited such a dual strategy at the time of the London Conference in 1864, when he supported Napoleon III's suggestion to let the inhabitants of Schleswig-Holstein decide questions about annexation and the royal succession by means of a referendum (even though a friend warned Bismarck then "about bonapartism in nightgown and slippers").[45] The suggestion to introduce the revolutionary franchise, however, was primarily intended to overcome the political crisis inaugurated by the constitutional conflict. Bismarck wanted to weaken the liberals by avoiding a class-based franchise, which was for him an "artificial system" and therefore "much more dangerous" than any system that included the "fourth estate" in the process of forming and expressing the will of the people.[46] Bismarck wanted to implement a political system that permitted the "contact of the highest authority with the healthy elements" in the land, "which form the core and the mass of the people."

In a country with monarchical traditions and loyal disposition, the universal right to vote, by removing the influence of the liberal bourgeois classes, will

---

44. O. von Bismarck, *Werke* (Berlin, 1924–35) 3, no. 203. The conversation was held in the middle of May 1868, but an account was first published in 1902.
45. Gerhard Ritter, *Die preussischen Konservativen*, 112.
46. Heinrich von Sybel, *Die Begründung des Deutschen Reiches durch Wilhelm I.*, 3rd ed. (Munich, 1913), 4:318f. The letter from Bismarck to Count Bernstorff is dated 19 Apr. 1866; cf. Augst, *Bismarcks Stellung*, 91.

also lead to monarchical elections, just as it will lead to anarchical ones in countries where the masses feel revolutionary.[47]

Here the decisive theme of future election campaigns was introduced: the struggle between the forces of "inertia" and those of "movement." This conception conformed to a conservative theory of social change that had found its clearest expression in Wilhelm Heinrich Riehl's concept of "bourgeois society" as a status-bound system (*Standessystem*).[48] Bismarck's crucial mistake lay in believing in the viability and longevity of a pro- and antigovernment dichotomy within the electorate. In the process, he overlooked the internal fissures within the respective political blocs that made them capable of the most diverse coalitions, especially over time. For Bismarck, the granting of the right to vote was an expedient against the revolutionary transformation of German society and the parliamentarization of constitutional life. In order to avoid a "complete revolutionary pandemonium [*Zerrüttung*] . . . in the instability of present conditions" and to prevent "a catastrophe," he decided on the introduction of the revolutionary universal franchise as a "well-timed reform from above":

> It is not the mass of unjustified demands that lend strength to revolutionary movements, rather it is usually the meager portion of justified demands that offer the most effective pretexts for revolution and afford the movements lasting and dangerous force.[49]

With the help of the new franchise, "needs" – expressed through election campaigns and election results – were to be provided for "in orderly ways of reaching agreement," that is, through a balancing of interests. This "agreement" lay "in the interest of the monarchical principle," both for external political reasons and in the context of the movement for unification. This required sacrifice, not from individuals "but from everyone equally."[50]

Bismarck also wanted to integrate the political system by restricting the elected parliament to its representative functions. He clearly could not conceive that in the course of political and social change, forces would be awakened that no longer fit within the realm of his brand of constitutionalism and that strove for the parliamentarization of the system based on the prerequisite of fundamental democratiza-

---

47. Ibid.
48. Cf. Wilhelm Heinrich Riehl, *Die bürgerliche Gesellschaft*, ed. with an introduction by P. Steinbach (Frankfurt a.M., 1976).
49. Hermann Wagener, *Erlebtes. Meine Memoiren aus der Zeit von 1873 bis jetzt* (Berlin, 1884), 37f.
50. Ibid.

tion. Counting on the loyalty of the rural populace, Bismarck could neither imagine that public opinion would ultimately rise up in criticism of the government (and even the monarch) nor consider adequately the rise of the workers' movement. He believed that, should he come into conflict with the Reichstag, with firmness and skill he could personally withstand any threat to his position as minister. In this regard it seems deeply ironic that Bismarck was ultimately toppled by parliament: He had to resign in 1890 because he found no party constellation in the Reichstag to support him.

At the moment of the founding of the Reich, however, all doubts for Bismarck were outweighed by the advantages that the universal franchise offered in the face of attempts at foreign intervention. These advantages, based on a view of the franchise as the "principle of unity," included allusions to the political right of self-determination – or at least to the wishes of the majority of the German population. Misgivings of the conservatives he did not consider decisive, particularly because in the constituent North German Reichstag he found a favorable majority. Bismarck relied, moreover, on restrictive measures: The refusal to provide allowances for deputies, for example, was intended to permit only wealthy citizens to become Reichstag deputies. The inclusion of the secret ballot was not preordained, because for Bismarck, "un-German" secrecy was the expression of an absence of political courage.[51] The public designation of anti- and progovernment candidates was also considered, and the denial of the vote to active soldiers was intended to prevent the politicization of the army. Officials, too, were to be restricted in their right to vote, mainly because they had frequently spearheaded the opposition to Bismarck during the constitutional crisis. The fact that the government was unable to enact this restriction did not prevent Bismarck from denying them the passive franchise – the right to be elected – that he had conceded to members of the army.

The new franchise necessarily drew its explosive force from the principle of secret balloting. Bismarck, however, had not made this issue into a question of principle, perhaps because of time pressures resulting from his apprehension that the formation of the North German Confederation might be prevented or delayed by the danger of war, perhaps also due to internal political coalitions. Further deliberations about the franchise have been thoroughly analyzed elsewhere

51. Augst, *Bismarcks Stellung*, 156.

and need not be reiterated here.[52] It is indisputable that the North German Confederation, like the German Empire later, had one of the most democratic electoral laws of the time. In fact, however, its effects were mitigated not only by stipulations embedded in the constitution, but also by the three-class franchise in Prussia and other federal states. Attempts to change the electoral laws in the individual states – be it in the direction of greater equality or in order to defend the position of property owners – would thereafter shape franchise battles more prominently than the parrying of plans for a coup d'état that aimed at the elimination of the democratic Reichstag franchise. Regarded as a whole, the introduction of the universal franchise without further significant reservations – that is, with the simultaneous provision of electoral equality, the secret ballot, and the direct vote – was more than a risky political maneuver of Bismarck's in order to stabilize his leadership in the period of unification and within the Prusso-German constitution. Rather, this represented a watershed in German political history. Only with the universal franchise could a national political "mass market"[53] be formed in which government, parties, *Vereine,* and institutions like the churches vied for public support of their goals. The result of these contests was ambiguous. On the one hand, the government repeatedly succeeded in stabilizing its position in the political system. On the other hand, opposition currents increasingly found resonance and were able to mobilize broad support for their programs directed against the establishment. It is beyond doubt that Bismarck's self-confident calculations went awry: His personal political dominance was dependent on support from constantly shifting forces. That support sprang from politicians in the Reichstag's individual caucuses, to be sure, but it also had to be wrung from a political mass market that required direct manipulation in order to achieve the desired election results at the grass-roots level – within the electorate itself.

III

Bismarck's calculations in introducing the democratic franchise were inherently linked to his repeated attempts to manipulate public opin-

---

52. Walter Gagel, *Die Wahlrechtsfrage in der Geschichte der deutschen liberalen Parteien 1848–1918* (Düsseldorf, 1958).
53. See the conceptually pathbreaking work by Hans Rosenberg, *Grosse Depression und Bismarckzeit. Wirtschaftsablauf, Gesellschaft und Politik in Mitteleuropa* (Berlin, 1967).

ion after 1871. These included his willingness to sharpen internal social conflicts through the *Kulturkampf,* his persecution of socialists and his taming of liberalism during the "assassination elections" of 1878, and his use of the army *Septennat* and a right-wing *Kartell* to bolster his "anxiety campaign" of 1887. Focusing on these issues can help establish a framework for electoral research intended not only to explain individual or collective voter decisions in a sociological sense, but also to analyze the role of elections in the political system as a whole. In election contests, judgments were made about past political developments, but future political positions were anticipated as well. In addition, elections often terminated certain forms of political cooperation at the national level while partially or wholly establishing new means of cooperation at other levels. As yet, apart from a few pioneering studies, these aspects of German electoral history have not been systematically analyzed.[54]

Because Bismarck acquainted himself with the consequences of democratization largely under the influence of a bonapartist plebiscitary style of politics that remained governmentally influenced and controlled, the question arises as to the actual effects of the democratic franchise. Did it remain accessible to political manipulation, or did it instead develop an independence and a momentum of its own as a consequence of autonomous political developments and aspirations? Lively controversy has centered on this question, stemming from the observations of younger historians who, in part through regional studies, have refused to endorse the orthodox image of the *Kaiserreich* as an authoritarian state. Two British historians, Geoff Eley[55] and David Blackbourn,[56] have confirmed the existence of regional particularities that cannot be integrated into the Prussian-centered, bonapartist-caesarist model of constitutional and political authority. They have also used their studies of the party-political, cultural, and confessional profiles of Reich politics as the point of departure for more wide-ranging historical reflections and comparative interpretations. Future studies of elections must pursue these avenues further: first, to illuminate the way in which regionalism affected the course

---

54. Cf. the essays by Brett Fairbairn and James Retallack in this volume; also James Retallack, *Notables of the Right: The Conservative Party and Political Mobilization in Germany, 1876–1918* (London and Boston, 1988); Steinbach, *Die Zähmung des politischen Massenmarktes.*
55. Geoff Eley, *Reshaping the German Right: Radical Nationalism and Political Change after Bismarck* (New Haven, CT, 1980).
56. David Blackbourn, *Class, Religion and Local Politics in Wilhelmine Germany: The Centre Party in Württemberg before 1914* (Wiesbaden, 1980).

of democratization and political participation, and second, to qualify older views that stressed the semiautocratic, authoritarian nature of the *Kaiserreich.*

A new research emphasis could also facilitate a more realistic assessment of the historical linkages between democratization and constitutional change. Bismarck knew that the introduction of the democratic franchise would not inevitably lead to parliamentarization; rather, in situations of plebiscitary decision making that also happened to coincide with a liberal *Appelltheorie,* the government stood a good chance of sustaining its political legitimacy. For this reason, it is necessary to examine the conditions under which a gradual transformation of the German constitutional system took place and, in particular, what role the press, the political parties, and individual *Vereine* played in that process. It is clear that at the founding of the Reich, the option of parliamentarizing the constitutional system did not appear as the only alternative. The evolution toward an authoritarian caesarist system seemed equally conceivable as the consequence of a sharpening of political constellations initiated by the government. Future developments hinged on the newly instituted democratic franchise: Due to its ambiguity, only time would reveal whether it would become a plebiscitary instrument of control or a means for articulating and realizing democratic potentials. This outcome, in turn, depended, on the one hand, on the changing contours of the political mass market as it underwent fundamental democratization and, on the other, on the capacity of the political parties to assert themselves within the constitutional system. To increase their standing, the parties could rely on *Vereine,* newspapers, and the parliamentary caucuses. All of these subsidiary political institutions, however, gradually won new significance in their own right; they became at the same time powerful engines of further political change and the interpreters of political contingencies.

The actual accomplishments of those who wished to expand the opportunities for political expression under the universal, equal, secret, and direct franchise depended largely on the way the electorate itself viewed new political opportunities. The outlook of this electorate at first remained under the influence of traditional patterns of thought shaped by confessional or regional circumstances. German parties took their initial orientations not from the new and unfamiliar arena of Reich politics but from conflict structures and political experiences springing from their regional milieux. Only in the course of many decades did the regional contours of the German party system grow less distinct. It is noteworthy in this context that this process was intensified as constitutional controversies from the period of revolution and reaction came to form a less important component of the political self-image of Germans. In fact political battles from a former age had to be repeatedly revived and reinterpreted by the political press, the parties, and the politicians themselves in order to manipulate their followers. At the same time, however, the new national politics created its own systemic conflicts, which increasingly superseded regional conflicts, thus deregionalizing political discourse and gradually "nationalizing" it. Three developments were particularly important in this regard: (1) the experience of the *Kulturkampf* in the 1870s, which – ironically – served both to weaken the liberals and to integrate the representatives of political Catholicism into the *Kaiserreich*; (2) the attack on left liberalism as the "seedbed of social democracy" and the struggle against social democracy itself after 1878; and (3) anti-Semitic agitation from the late 1880s on. These stages in the governmental campaign to confront political opponents were milestones of national integration,[57] for their particular militance was largely the result of Bismarck's failure to integrate German society politically in the face of external threats – as became clear during the "war-in-sight" crisis of 1875.[58] Not until the 1890s was it possible to displace disputes between parties over economic and constitutional issues onto the plane of foreign, colonial, and military affairs. Thus the confrontational course was gradually shifted from internal to external enemies, although, as a rule, most debates about *Weltpolitik* reflected internal antagonisms as well.

It is not sufficient merely to affirm that regional lines of confrontation were superseded by political themes, preoccupations, and emphases generated at the political center. Every element of politicization at the national level had to be sustained by concrete developments at the regional and local levels as well, and every tactical maneuver in Reich politics was intensified or weakened, reinterpreted, and exploited by local elements as a means to revitalize outdated methods of political mobilization. For this reason, electoral studies have attempted to move beyond the reconstruction of time

---

57. Still valuable is the early essay by Wolfgang Sauer, "Das Problem des deutschen Nationalstaates," in Hans-Ulrich Wehler, ed., *Moderne deutsche Sozialgeschichte* (Cologne, 1966), 428ff.
58. See Andreas Hillgruber, "Die 'Krieg-in-Sicht-Krise' 1875," in Ernst Schulin, ed., *Gedenkschrift für Martin Göhring* (Wiesbaden, 1968), 239ff.

lines and the chronicling of party programs or election manifestos to investigate the deeper mechanisms of political opinion making. These studies have opened themselves to the history of everyday life by investigating how the electorate actually *responded* to election campaign strategies. They have also attempted to study how grass-roots politics and local election contests related to larger changes in the political power structure. In the process, these studies have revealed gaps between individual layers of political decision making that were frequently widened by confessional or regional peculiarities. Eley and Blackbourn in particular have directed attention to distortions arising, almost inevitably, from the fixation of historians on exclusively Prussian or Protestant aspects of the authoritarian state.

The conflict between various schools of interpretation – even those that focus exclusively on the *Kaiserreich* – cannot be traced here.[59] Certainly this conflict reflects more than an attempt to find the best means to explain the past through methodological innovation. In the final analysis, the debate is between those researchers who proceed on the basis of models and who wish primarily to test hypotheses, and those who endeavor to reconstruct a past reality without resorting to theoretical constructs. The ongoing controversy between representatives of political history and those of social history is also important in these debates. Nonetheless, the fact remains that electoral history offers one of the best opportunities to link empirical and theoretical analyses, to use the tools of both political and social history, and to integrate a number of other divergent approaches as well.

The two significant schools of German electoral research in the 1950s anticipated the rich dividends to be gained from this integration of methods. The Bonn school around Max Braubach[60] concentrated chiefly on Catholic constituencies in the Rhineland. However, it exposed itself to interpretive distortion in that the religious factor became artificially dominant. By contrast, the school around Wolfgang Abendroth[61] concentrated primarily on the analysis of socioeconomic determinants – that is, those factors that could

---

59. The debate can be followed in such historical journals as the *Historische Zeitschrift* and *Geschichte und Gesellschaft*; see also James Retallack, "Social History with a Vengeance? Some Reactions to H.-U. Wehler's *Das Deutsche Kaiserreich*," *German Studies Review* 7 (1984):423ff.
60. A good overview is provided in Klaus Müller, "Das Rheinland als Gegenstand der historischen Wahlsoziologie," in Büsch, ed., *Wählerbewegung in der deutschen Geschichte*, 393ff.
61. See Wolfgang Abendroth, "Aufgaben und Methoden einer deutschen historischen Wahlsoziologie," in ibid., 119ff.

be best studied through social history. Whereas the Braubach school emphasized the importance of institutions that interpreted the world and politics according to religious criteria, for the students of Abendroth, *Vereine,* political parties, and interest groups – as well as politicians active in these organizations – stood at the center of discussion, and their activities could only be understood against a background of socioeconomic interests. Unfortunately, despite contributing to the accumulation of intensive constituency studies, each approach ignored or isolated supraregional developments and structures.

A more fruitful perspective might concentrate on the relationship between political expression at the base of the political system – in the constituencies (*Wahlkreise*) and electoral districts (*Wahlbezirke*) – and the centers of political decision making at the state and national levels.[62] Historical analysis based on this perspective does not regard the act of voting as an autonomous political activity. The mobilization, activization, politicization, and polarization of the electorate depend less on local forces and circumstances than on impulses generated in decision-making centers within the political system. During the *Kaiserreich,* many key political actors influenced the climate of opinion through the information they provided or the way they stage-managed election campaigns: These included leaders of clubs, associations, and political parties; top government officials; journalists either intent on autonomy or dependent on financial backers; representatives of interest groups; heads of powerful economic enterprises; and even the monarch himself. Mass voluntary organizations like veterans' associations,[63] navy leagues, and mission clubs grew rapidly in size and number, often bringing together hundreds of thousands of members. As they increasingly influenced public opinion and promoted the politicization of daily life, they fostered a further deregionalization of politics and a nationalization of the electorate.

This description of politics in the *Kaiserreich* would seem to support the view that the formation of political will through elections

62. See the decisive contribution of Werner Conze, "Politische Willensbildung im deutschen Kaiserreich als Forschungsaufgabe historischer Wahlsoziologie," in Helmut Berding et al., eds., *Vom Staat des Ancien Régime zum modernen Parteienstaat: Festschrift für Theodor Schieder* (Munich and Vienna, 1978), 331ff.
63. See, most recently, Thomas Rohkrämer, *Der Militarismus der "kleinen Leute": Die Kriegervereine im Deutschen Kaiserreich 1871–1914* (Munich, 1990).

ultimately facilitated manipulation from above. However, this interpretation, too, has been challenged in recent years.[64] It is now clear that the shaping of political life under Bismarck and Wilhelm II was not determined solely by caucus leaders in the Reichstag, by the press in Berlin, or by a circle of top officials in the government. Rather, the political culture was shaped to a large extent by the resonance of political arguments at lower political levels and among a national electorate. It could hardly have been otherwise, for social, economic, religious, and constitutional developments had produced very different political cultures in the relatively democratic southwest and in the more authoritarian Prussian northeast. To be sure, such peculiarities often disappeared under the pressure of issues and personalities located in the capital. Yet even though regional disparities eroded over time, bygone or petrified political issues continued to influence national political debate. Thus, even in the period after 1890, when the Center Party became more or less a stabilizing factor in progovernment party constellations, representatives of political Catholicism recalled the experiences of the *Kulturkampf* in order to mobilize their adherents and revive familiar attitudes of defiance in the face of a collective threat. Similarly, although an intensive nationalization of electoral politics was dependent on a thorough politicization of the electorate, differences based on social structure, religion, and region operated contrary to this goal. Those differences explain the characteristic bastions of party strength (*Hochburgen*) that became visible in Germany's electoral geography. As yet we are not well informed about the political transformation that led to the weakening and eventual elimination of these bastions.[65] It is clear, however, that as German society became increasingly polarized politically, the differences between the proportion of votes received by individual parties were reduced even when they were involved in party coalitions.

IV

In recent years, historians have too rarely drawn explicit connections between the act of voting and the political system. The wave of

---

64. See especially Thomas Nipperdey's criticism of Hans-Ulrich Wehler's interpretation of the Kaiserreich; Nipperdey, *Nachdenken über die deutsche Geschichte* (Munich, 1986); cf. Retallack, "Social History with a Vengeance?"

65. Cf. Karl Rohe, "Die 'verspätete Region': Thesen und Hypothesen zur Wahlentwicklung im Ruhrgebiet vor 1914," in Peter Steinbach, ed., *Probleme politischer Partizipation im Modernisierungsprozess* (Stuttgart, 1982), 231ff.

electoral studies in the 1960s and early 1970s based on regional perspectives has now largely dried up. On the one hand, this has been the consequence of an excessive emphasis on methods derived from the social sciences, which reduced the historical interpretation of election results. On the other hand, the methods of modern electoral research also seem to deter historians, who are unable to interpret election results as a kind of public opinion survey drawn from the past, and instead focus only on those historic developments that can be linked to presentist dispositions and future-oriented expectations. However, analyses of the party system and of elections as a whole, when they are discussed in the context of constitutional change, do constitute a worthy ideal. To date they have been undertaken largely by non-German students of German history: The work of Stanley Suval is exemplary in this regard, for it combines detailed electoral analysis with an investigation into changes to the entire German political system and its constitutional structure.

One cause for the relatively underdeveloped state of electoral research might be the basic reorientation in the last ten years toward the history of everyday life.[66] Political factors, at least in Germany, have been researched less intensively as a consequence of this trend. Studies of political *Vereine* and parties have been pushed into the background, even though in the 1960s such questions had attracted great interest, particularly under the influence of Hans Rosenberg's inspiring study of the connection between the slowing of economic growth in the 1870s and the emergence of new forms of interest representation.[67] One might also cite the low repute of modernization theory and the receding interest in political development theory, again most marked since the 1960s;[68] for the crisis of modernization theory has not been without its impact on electoral research. The expansion of voting rights, accompanying and encouraging the process of politicization, made franchise questions central to discussions about the "crisis of participation" that shaped the nineteenth century and decisively influenced all other modernization crises. Franchise questions also touched on basic issues of political legitimacy and

---

66. See also Peter Steinbach, "Alltagsleben und Landesgeschichte," *Hessisches Jahrbuch für Landesgeschichte* 28 (1979):225f.; Steinbach, "Geschichte des Alltags – Alltagsgeschichte," *Neue Politische Literatur* 31 (1986):249ff.
67. Cf. Hans-Peter Ullmann, *Interessenverbände in Deutschland* (Frankfurt a.M., 1988).
68. Peter Steinbach, "Deutungsmuster der historischen Modernisierungstheorie für die Analyse westeuropäischer Wahlen," in Büsch und Steinbach, eds., *Vergleichende europäische Wahlgeschichte*, 158ff.

social stability. To be sure, modernization theory exposed itself to severe criticism in the 1960s due to its close association with the normative concept of westernization. However, there has been nothing to suggest the discrediting of this theory as an analytical concept that can be used to formulate important questions for an investigation of political development. Modernization theory is still relevant to electoral analysis, for it need not imply a normative interpretation of social and political change.

The abandonment of analytical conceptions of social change in favor of describing the experiences of those who were the "objects" of such change has undermined a sense of the contingent nature of social and political development. This has also influenced the way we try to explain political behavior, the effectiveness of political institutions, and participatory politics. Electoral research by historians, after all, has always been intended to analyze behavioral contexts from a diversity of perspectives: for example, to determine the dependence of voters' decisions on the social context of the electorate, on political impulses, or on traditional interpretations of politics. It has also sought to inquire into the importance of such factors as government propaganda, election platforms, campaign strategies, and images of the future state. Such research was initially oriented toward providing the most sophisticated models of political decision making possible. But the reorientation toward the history of everyday life frequently involved a loss of this political dimension and diminished analytical rigor. Only when the field of modern history sees a revival of interest in the political dimension of social history will electoral research regain its luster as an interdisciplinary effort and as a vital intersection point of political and social history. This will allow scholars to address more complex questions about the forces of social integration and authoritarian rule in German history.

PART TWO

Gender, Identity, and Political Participation

5

Women, Gender, and the Limits of Political History in the Age of "Mass" Politics

EVE ROSENHAFT

The problem discussed in this essay is this: It is still possible to write a general account of German history that excludes women. What happened in German "history," that is, can be quite effectively explained with reference to events or categories that may be expanded to include female actors but that lose nothing of their force when assumed to be masculine (or indeed neuter). This is most obviously because the events that make up "history" (or at any rate, the framework around which historical accounts are constructed) are *political* events. This is acutely obvious in the case of modern Germany, where much historical analysis is concerned directly or indirectly with the seizure and maintenance of state power by the Nazis. More broadly, history is by definition the story of events that manifest themselves publicly and are acknowledged to be relevant to society understood as a public body or polity. The territorial or national state itself (another issue of particular relevance in the construction of German history), which provides the apparently unproblematic field for the study of history, is itself a *Politikum* first and last. By extension, *class* relations are acknowledged as a historical force or a locus of historically relevant power insofar as production is seen to be allied with politics through their common habitation of a public sphere. This construction of "history" not only privileges public identities and public forms of power over those that function in or are assigned to the private sphere; it also prejudices the criteria by which the adequacy of explanations is measured.

Is it possible, then, to construct a general account of German *politics* in this crucial period that does not systematically and obtusely exclude women? I use the terms "systematically" and "obtusely" advisedly, because it seems clear to me that although there is still much to be discovered about the political activities of women, their inclusion in a general account cannot be accomplished by an empirical act of will. It may be that the best we can hope for from political history is an account that regretfully and self-consciously excludes women. This would constitute an acknowledgment that the historical study of politics within a particular national context is as much a special field as the history of medicine, military history, or indeed women's history. The definitive dethronement of political history, with its familiar borders and chronologies, would leave us without a basic or general history to which other historical studies might be subordinate or supplementary; and this would involve not only institutional confusion but also a radical challenge to the identity of the historical discipline and its practitioners. This must be one reason why the move continues to be resisted, in spite of the successive challenges of certain forms of social history, *Alltagsgeschichte*, and the radical pluralism of women's history. To abandon the *ideal* of historical synthesis, though, would be to leave (for example) women and politics more firmly separated than ever. It is not too early to look for ways to see and talk about the past that are selective without being exclusive.

The tendency of empirical research up to now has been to establish the role of women in politics as a positively charged absence; there was a women's politics, but it took place in spheres distinct from the one in which state power was directly assigned and exercised – in occupational and confessional organizations, the women's sections of political parties, the expanding field of public and private social work. Indeed, in order to find women in politics, historians have had to expand the definition of politics. The "separate sphere" of women's politics has been lovingly excavated, polished up, and placed on the mantelpiece. That it remains separate is a consequence not least of the intentions of its makers; what is peculiar about German history in this respect is both the firmness of its boundaries and the extent of organic development within them. Recent efforts to locate where the two spheres merge have proposed models of infiltration (the feminization of the public sector in the growth of the welfare state) and negative integration (the Nazi cooptation of the idea of female *Lebensraum*). The world of politics in which parties and other organized groups seek to translate perceived interests into power and to exercise power in pursuit of interest remains largely untouched by these approaches.

This is not peculiar to nineteenth- and twentieth-century Germany or its historiography. Whether in the discourses of historians or of politicians, whether the idiom is one of class politics or "high" politics, women's politics resists "fitting in" to the wider political scene. On the contrary, the appropriate metaphors all express not so much a mismatch as a nonmatch. In the words of a recent discussion of women's relationship to a socialist cultural politics in Britain, the position of women appears as "inescapably *appositional* rather than oppositional. . . . Denied the clarity of marginality, and the lucidity of its versions of exclusion, we kept experiencing ourselves as included – but on the wrong terms."[1]

An earlier metaphor, Joan Kelly's "doubled vision of feminist theory,"[2] now appears almost too neat. Being aware of the existence of "separate socio-sexual spheres" and at the same time determined to "understand the systematic connections between them," asserting that "women's place is not a separate sphere or domain of existence but a position within social existence generally" remains politically vital, just as it represents a meaningful program for empirical research on women. When we shift our attention to "social existence generally," or to those forms of generality that we talk about when we talk about "history," our vision becomes not so much doubled as distracted: Wherever one looks, women are simultaneously there and not there. I suspect that this state of simultaneous presence and absence, or of self-consciousness and self-oblivion, can be identified as a characteristic of women's self-perception, as articulated in their autobiographical and self-reflective writings. But the problem manifestly has more to do with history as constructed by historical actors and analysts than it does with women. Understood as the history of politics, or more broadly of public affairs, or still more broadly of politically relevant events and processes, it remains impenetrably masculine, in principle, in statistical terms, and not least as a function of legislative compulsion for significant parts of the period under review. What is curious is that this is rarely acknowledged by those of us who write about the epochal problems of modern German politics, and it is even more rarely problematized. What I want to do here is explore some issues, both empirical and interpretative, whose reconsideration appears to me to be unavoidable and that might

1. Julia Swindells and Lisa Jardine, *What's Left? Women and Culture in the Labour Movement* (London, 1990), xi.
2. Joan Kelly, "The doubled vision of feminist theory," in *Women, History and Theory* (Chicago, 1984), 51–64.

prove fruitful to the general discussion, if we accept that the masculinity of the public can no longer be taken for granted.

One approach to the limitations of existing political history is to try to achieve a fuller picture of women's actual role in national politics. We know that there were occasions when women mobilized around issues of national political concern or to influence major political decisions in the Wilhelmine and Weimar periods, but we know very little about how that happened. The making of the Civil Code (*Bürgerliches Gesetzbuch* or BGB) of 1896 is a case in point. The women's movement mobilized female opinion in protest against the intended retention of women's subordinate status in family law in two phases: first through the official submission to the drafting commission by the Federation of German Women's Associations (*Bund Deutscher Frauenvereine* or BDF) and in the final stages through a *"Frauenlandsturm"* consisting of mass meetings and petitions.[3] It is generally asserted that what reform the final Code did introduce (particularly in the property rights of working women) was the result of employer pressure; at the very least, it made a difference that one member of the relevant Reichstag commission was a major industrialist, Baron Karl Ferdinand von Stumm-Halberg, who did indeed have a distinctly liberal position on this question. There is a certain piquancy in the thought that in the enforced absence of real women from the parliamentary deliberations, their place was "held" by a coalition of Stumm and August Bebel. But their voice did not go unheard. Members of the Reichstag commission explicitly acknowledged this mobilization of female opinion in the background to their deliberations on marital property, and it was also cited in the commission's discussions about women's sense of honor and aptitude for political participation.[4] Neither the mainstream literature on the women's movement nor the most recent account of the making of the BGB in the context of Wilhelmine politics[5] offers any in-depth discussion of the activity of the women's movement on the issue of family law, although it is hardly surprising that organized women should have been involved in one of the hottest issues of a very heated public debate.

The year or so immediately following the end of the First World War is another interesting period, for which we have more informa-

3. Ute Gerhard, "Bis an die Wurzeln des Uebels. Rechtsgeschichte und Rechtskämpfe der Radikalen," *Feministische Studien* 3 (1984): 77–98.
4. Benno Mugdan, ed., *Die gesamten Materialien zum BGB* (1899–1900; reprint Aalen, 1979), 4: 1305–10.
5. Michael John, *Politics and the Law in Nineteenth-Century Germany* (Oxford, 1989).

tion about the economic demobilization of women than about their political mobilization. Women appear to have been participants in the general activation of that period, but within that context to have had their sentiments and energies engaged in gender-specific ways; this is suggested by their high rate of electoral participation, but also by the large numbers of women elected to the National Assembly and to office in the elections of 1920 – women who played a key role in the early family welfare measures of the Weimar Republic.[6] In a development that presages post–Second World War events, there were also calls for the formation of a women's party.[7] The same period reportedly witnessed a groundswell of protest against the abortion law, which remains less thoroughly explored and less clear in its structure than the remarkable campaign of 1931 that challenged abortion legislation (Paragraph 218 of the Criminal Code) as part of a perceived general attack on the rights of women.[8]

There is, then, plenty of room for new research on women's politics, but archaeology alone is not sufficient. For the harder we look at women's politics, the more apparent it becomes that it is different in character from men's. And this is hardly surprising, given the range of mechanisms by which women have been historically restricted to the sphere in which "politics" does not operate. Most of us are by now accustomed to responding to the undergraduate proposition that the Weimar Republic failed because the Germans were not used to democracy, with the reminder that Germany had universal (manhood) suffrage before Britain and that the prewar generation of Germans was already well practiced in election campaigns and mass politics. What we mean by this is that a recognizable and (in the literal sense) viable form of popular political self-consciousness was already in the making. But women pose a real problem before 1918 if we want to treat elections and political organizations as the motor and manifestation of political mobilization in this sense, since they did not have the national franchise and were largely excluded from

---

6. Cornelie Usborne, "Fertility control and population policy in Germany 1910–1928" (Ph.D. dissertation, Open University, 1989), 136ff. Cf. Christl Wickert, *Unsere Erwählten. Sozialdemokratische Frauen im Deutschen Reichstag und im Preussischen Landtag 1919 bis 1933* (Göttingen, 1986).
7. Irene Stoehr, *Emanzipation zum Staat? Der Allgemeine deutsche Frauenverein – Deutsche Staatsbürgerinnenverband (1893–1933)* (Pfaffenweiler, 1990), 93.
8. Usborne, *Fertility Control*, 368; Atina Grossmann, "Abortion and economic crisis: the 1931 campaign against Paragraph 218," in Renate Bridenthal, Atina Grossmann, and Marion Kaplan, eds., *When Biology Became Destiny. Women in Weimar and Nazi Germany* (New York, 1984), 66–86.

party-political activity until 1908. If mass politics is about elections, what place do women have in it when they do not have the vote? Perhaps it is sufficient to acknowledge the fact of disfranchisement and direct our attention to the size and vitality of the women's movement as a manifestation of extraparliamentary mobilization. And the women's movement regularly appears in the canon when we want to sketch the contours of an emerging grass-roots politics in the Wilhelmine era. This generates a paradox, though, when that politics is defined in light of the conditions for participatory democracy: "participation, but on whose terms?"[9] In the whole catalog of mass movements and pressure groups that characterized the prewar political scene, the women's movement stands out as the only one made up essentially and solely of people excluded by definition from participation in politics.

The 1931 mobilization against Paragraph 218 is a good example of the contradictions of women's politics. It is remarkable not least because it seems to have effectively cut across party barriers at a time when all accounts of the Weimar left tell us that progressive forces were hopelessly fragmented into separate camps (*Lager*). At the same time, the aftermath of that campaign confirms an apparently general pattern, namely, that issues of sexual or gender politics, even where they manifestly excite popular attention and lead to *large-scale, if sporadic,* mobilization of women, have not historically been successfully incorporated within party or electoral politics. Although there is every reason to insist on the importance of reproductive politics in the 1920s, for example, it remains the case that there is no historical parallel to the American elections of 1989, which were said to focus largely on the issue of abortion rights. This is the obverse of the proposition that organization within existing parties fragments and undercuts women's interests and causes. It cannot be explained simply in terms of the insensitivity of male-led and male-dominated parties, although everyday misogyny and programmatic masculinity were notorious features even (especially?) of those parties that expressed the most emancipatory intentions toward women. If it is true, it is so *in spite of* the good intentions of the progressive parties of the left and center.

There are grounds for taking seriously the proposition that the common concerns of women (which are social and material ones and hence *ought* to imply a politics of the public as well as of the private

---

9. James Retallack, *Notables of the Right* (Boston and London, 1988), 3.

sphere) and the forms of modern party politics are mutually confounding. It has been argued, for example, that the indisputable mobilization of German women that occurred after 1945, around a program that at last inserted women and their concerns into politics, foundered on the claims to exclusivity of the respective political parties once they were reestablished.[10] One apparent exception to this pattern is political Catholicism. Since the establishment of parliamentary democracy, the Center Party and its successors have made a politics of the reproductive sphere their own (family, marriage, sexual morality, education). During the deliberations on the Weimar Constitution and the *Grundgesetz*, in discussions about censorship, abortion, and divorce in the Wilhelmine and Weimar periods, the Catholic parties regularly used their key position in parliament and government to block or slow libertarian or secularizing reforms. At the same time, political Catholicism was notoriously successful in engaging women in its organizational efforts and mobilizing them in its campaigns. The strategy of political Catholicism *in extremis,* as embodied in the Catholic Action (*Katholische Aktion*) of 1928 and its attempt to replace party politics and *Vereinskatholizismus* with the "depoliticized *Sammlung* (rallying together) of a lay apostolic community"[11] that appealed equally to men, women, and the youth of both sexes, seems to illustrate that the essential conjunction of reproduction-based politics and a female constituency was perceived by the movement as a function of its own particular character. At the same time, it implies that effective mobilization behind these politics required a more thoroughgoing feminization of the movement itself, which in turn required the breakup of the male-dominated network of Catholic associations – confirming the contradiction between women and politics.

The problem is also apparent when we begin to examine our application of political categories and definitions to women. The role of women in political Catholicism, for example, raises with particular sharpness the questions of what mobilization is and how it happens. Studies of political mobilization focusing on both the popular politics of the Wilhelmine period and the mobilization of a Nazi constituency have emphasized the importance of locally based networks of com-

---

10. Annette Kuhn, "Frauen suchen neue Wege der Politik," in *Frauen in der deutschen Nachkriegszeit,* 2 vols. (Düsseldorf, 1986), 2:12–35.
11. Doris Kaufmann, "Vom Vaterland zum Mutterland. Frauen im katholischen Milieu der Weimarer Republik," in Karin Hausen, ed., *Frauen suchen ihre Geschichte* (Munich, 1987), 254–79, 258f.

munication and influence, informal public spheres, associational life, and "intermediate elites." A "milieu" implies just such structures; indeed, social historians have taken to using the term to denote a sphere in which politics emerges from the systematic overlapping of public and private. But what do these structures look like for women? Is there a female analogue to the *Kneipe* (pub), the *Stammtisch,* or the *Schützenverein* (shooting club)? The empirical search for parallels simply underlines the differences. We can, of course, identify a women's associational life, and some women's groups, like the housewives' associations of the 1920s, have been presented as performing the function of mediating between local class interest and state power (although the precise extent of their political influence and the processes of recruitment and mobilization at the grass-roots level remain unclear).[12] Among working-class women (in particular), gossip constitutes a kind of female public sphere with functions of both communication and social control. But are these forms genuinely analogous, or does the analogy not fail precisely at the point where men's networks give them access to economic and political power and influence, and where those networks, in turn, are informed by explicitly political concerns? The *Kneipengespräch* (pub conversation) is likely to be one about politics, the *Treppenhausgespräch* (staircase conversation) about people. Claudia Koonz has suggested that it was in the nature of National Socialism's radical denial of the divide between private and public that it could rely on the potency of women's neighborhood networks to enforce its socially and racially divisive politics.[13] Is such a radical redefinition of the functions and objects of state power on the part of the National Socialist regime in itself a sufficient basis for rethinking the structures of politics in preceding periods?

As has already been suggested, the difficulty of placing German women in politics is compounded by the irritating fact that the right of *political* participation was by no means the first demand of organized women. On the contrary, extensive research into the internal debates of the bourgeois women's movement has emphasized the resistance of its members to taking part in party and electoral politics. Where this resistance was not a matter of principled adherence to the separation of spheres, it reflected the fact that women faced the question of "participation, but on whose terms?" in a particular

---

12. Renate Bridenthal, " 'Professional' housewives: stepsisters of the women's movement," in Bridenthal, Grossmann, and Kaplan, eds., *Biology,* 153–73.
13. Claudia Koonz, *Mothers in the Fatherland* (London, 1987), 16f.

form: When the option of participation occurred, it meant adherence to political parties, and partisanship meant division.[14] Does the radical emphasis on unity in the bourgeois women's movement represent a special case of the wider phenomenon of popular indignation at the corrupt, self-serving, divisive character of the old parties, or of the persistence in German politics of attachment to the idea of a principle of moral authority "above parties"? Or should the movement's real, acknowledged, and felt presence within a general mobilization lead us to extend our search for common denominators in Wilhemine politics beyond those associated with the desire to exercise public power? This would be an alternative to the two predominant approaches to the history of the women's movement, which treat it either as a variant of the historical forms of masculine politics or in terms of a feminist tradition whose relationship with masculine politics is primarily defensive or reactive.[15] It is not yet clear where this search would lead; it suggests itself as a first step to thinking away the hermetic division between public and private – the distinction between things that make a difference to people and people who make a difference to things – that we all know to be artificial.

Reconsideration of the significance of reproductive politics might take us further in this direction. The policies of the Center Party on family and morality cannot be said to have created or attracted a constituency; they were rather a function of its rootedness in a particular milieu, serving to affirm and defend a predefined set of values, and were subject to negotiation only in their own terms (unlike questions of political strategy). This, at any rate, is how it looks from the vantage point of current "historical" knowledge. Recent developments suggest, at the very least, that reproductive politics has taken on a dynamic of its own and a capacity both to mobilize constituencies and to shake governments, and thus they might induce us to reread the significance of such issues to "politics" in the past as well. These developments include the politicization of abortion in Western Europe and the United States,[16] the centrality of the abortion issue to governmental negotiations on the unification of Germany, and the

14. Richard J. Evans, *The Feminist Movement in Germany 1894–1933* (London and Beverly Hills, Calif., 1976); Barbara Greven-Aschoff, *Die bürgerliche Frauenbewegung in Deutschland 1894–1933* (Göttingen, 1981).
15. The work of Richard Evans is characterized by the former approach, that of Elisabeth Meyer-Renschhausen and Claudia Koonz (inter alia) by the latter: see notes 13 and 14 and Elisabeth Meyer-Renschhausen, *Weibliche Kultur und soziale Arbeit* (Cologne and Vienna, 1989).
16. Cf. Joni Lovenduski and Joyce Outshoorn, eds., *The New Politics of Abortion* (London and Beverly Hills, Calif., 1986).

emergence in Eastern Europe of parties with no particular confessional profile, distinguished primarily by their differing stands on women's rights and family policy. What does it tell us about the character of German politics in the twentieth century if we consider the reproductive and family policies of the Center and the Christian Democrats not as a subsidiary function of their confessional orientation (which was, after all, growing progressively less pronounced from 1918 on), but rather as a characteristic feature of the parties' increasingly issue-based profile at the parliamentary and governmental levels?[17]

The next, and more difficult, step is to examine the "private" politics that is not only implicit in the familiar masculine forms of politics but constitutes its premise. It is not enough to note that the parties of the labor movement treasured the *Kneipengespräch* if we do not at the same time recognize that they devoted considerable attention to suppressing the *Treppenhausgespräch*. This means seeing not only the women (women's activities, women's interests) who are there, but also those who are not, and asking why not. It means, even where the evidence remains resolutely silent, taking the silence itself as evidence of a social or political process.[18] This is a step that has been taken most suggestively by scholars concerned with locating women within the central premises (in both senses) of labor history, by examining women's role in industrial production. Cynthia Cockburn's work on the British printing trade argues cogently for the emergence of a constructed association between skill and masculinity that underpinned craft identity and served male workers in a two-front negotiation: with female coworkers and with employers.[19] Kathleen Canning's work, too, demonstrates that women's apparent absence from the politically significant working class masks a process of deliberate exclusion of women workers and their experience from the general categories that define social and even individual agency (a process begun on the shop floor and perpetuated by mainstream labor historians).[20] One way to read women

17. For the post-1945 period, see Robert Moeller, "Reconstructing the family in reconstruction Germany: Women and social policy in the Federal Republic, 1949–1955," *Feminist Studies* 15 (1989): 137–69.
18. Cf. Judith Allen, "Evidence and silence: feminism and the limits of history," in Carole Pateman and Elizabeth Gross, eds., *Feminist Challenges. Social and Political Theory* (Sydney, London, and Boston, 1986), 173–89.
19. Cynthia Cockburn, "The material of male power," *Feminist Review* 9 (1981): 41–58; Cockburn, *Brothers. Male Dominance and Technological Change* (London, 1983).
20. See the essay by Kathleen Canning in this volume.

back into politics, then, is to identify the ways in which a particular politics involves measures of exclusion.

"Silence" and "exclusion" are perhaps misleading terms here, since they are meant to denote processes that work on the insider as well as the outsider. Political history can be "saved" for women's studies if the masculinity that is manifestly not only an affect but a premise of politics is itself problematized. Historians have begun to analyze individual political movements in terms of their emphasis on a problematic masculinity,[21] and this remains an important, although partial, project. The work of Cockburn and Canning on labor, like that of Leonore Davidoff and Catherine Hall on the English middle class,[22] points to an understanding of *class* identity as organically linked to gender identity. The task of deconstructing the masculinity of politics itself has until recently been left to political theorists, whose job may appear to us historians to have been made easier by the candor with which classical political philosophy dealt with the "woman question."[23] *Historical* work in this part of the field is only just beginning, but an example of what can be done is Dorinda Outram's study of the body in the French Revolution.[24] She delineates a critical historical experience through which modern ideas of the body politic and of the bourgeois individual as citizen came to be realized in social practice and internalized as part of a civic identity that was defined as essentially masculine.

At this point, we are talking about gender understood not as the qualities attributed to empirical individuals but as a system of organizing social perception in which sexual difference is pivotal. This is not the same as talking about women, but it seems to me to be vital to the project of seeing women in politics. Although I am sympathetic to the accusation, leveled at gender theorists like Joan Scott by social historians, that in focusing attention on such structural features of society we neglect or suppress the politically significant subjectivity or agency of women,[25] I think it misses its mark; as I

21. For example, Klaus Theweleit, *Männerphantasien*, 2 vols. (Frankfurt a.M., 1978); Luise White, "Separating the men from the boys: constructions of gender, sexuality and terrorism in Central Kenya, 1939–1959," *International Journal of African Historical Studies* 23 (1990): 1–25. (I am grateful to Pepe Roberts for drawing my attention to this article.)
22. Leonore Davidoff and Catherine Hall, *Family Fortunes: Men and Women of the English Middle Class, 1780–1850* (Chicago, 1987).
23. See, for example, Jean Bethke Elshtain, *Public Man, Private Woman* (Princeton, N.J., 1981); Susan Moller Okin, *Women in Western Political Thought* (Princeton, N.J., 1979).
24. Dorinda Outram, *The Body and the French Revolution. Sex, Class and Political Culture* (New Haven, Conn., and London, 1989).
25. See, for example, Joan Scott, "On language, gender and working-class history," *Interna-*

have suggested, women *are* invisible unless we are looking straight at them, and that has to be explained as well as overcome.

Having accepted the value of this kind of gender history, though, what is its relevance to modern Germany? Historians will want to raise the question of specificity of period and location. It may be that reconstructive deconstruction of the kind Outram is engaged in is possible only in places and periods where a particular crisis makes the stresses of gender visible. By definition, epochal change does not happen very often; modernity cannot be born more than once. This is not entirely separate from the methodological issue: Historians depend on sources, and not all events generate sources.

The simplest response to this lies in the by now well-established maxim of social historians that the relations of dominance and subordination in which social identities are implicated are subject to continuous negotiation. Historical studies of class are now almost universally premised on this view; the studies of class and gender cited previously tend to confirm it. The methodological problem is not thereby solved, but it can be further mitigated in the light of the necessity – also acknowledged in social-historical practice – of applying some inventiveness to identifying (sometimes redefining) historical sources. The study of gender poses perhaps the most radical challenge here, because the radical silence of one group, women's lack of access to the means to express identity, has been a constitutive element of that (subordinate) identity.

I have already suggested that an awareness of significant absences, an attentiveness to silence, is an important aspect of the study of women in history. The very centrality of that paradox to the construction of gender takes us beyond the programmatic open-mindedness of (say) *Alltagsgeschichte*. It demands the close inspection of discourses and ideologies, of our own as well as those of historical actors, and by extension calls not only for greater critical awareness, but for new ways of reading the past.

We might start with the ways in which the language we apply to politics is gendered. It is characteristic, for example, that when women appear in discussions of general (as distinct from women's) politics, their relationship to it is commonly construed as a negative or passive one. The idea of mobilization itself, for example, has taken

tional Labor and Working-Class History 31 (1987): 1–13, and Christine Stansell, "A Response to Joan Scott," ibid.: 24–9.

on a range of meanings, with slightly different emphases as applied to women. We might recall the passion with which nineteenth-century liberals and radicals insisted that the incorporation of women within the Catholic community was bad because it had a demobilizing (or depoliticizing) effect; what they meant was that it encouraged the wrong kind of politics. This insistence that mobilization equals demobilization when women do it is a recurrent theme, and I will return to it later. A more significant pattern among historians is to treat the mobilization of women within electoral politics in terms of the collective *response* to an appeal. In studies of the National Socialist constituency, for example, accounts of bourgeois mobilization emphasize the process of mobilization in and through the organizations and activities of the mobilized themselves,[26] whereas accounts of women's collective engagement with Nazism (even where they insist on the significance of women's associational life) continue to treat women as a mass of individuals responding either to the undifferentiated discontents of Weimar, or to aspects of Nazi policy that echoed their own ideological predispositions, or to Nazi propaganda directed at their material concerns.[27]

The gendering of the discourse of mass politics predates the linguistic lapses of historians, of course, and it invites attention as a specific feature of the period to which the present volume is devoted. On the face of it, there are good reasons why this account of women's mobilization is plausible. It points up a real tension in modern politics, namely, that between the manifestly structured character of daily life, in which political choices emerge out of the social shaping of interests, and the system of democratic elections, in which political actors register their choices as individuals and find themselves represented, through their choices, as a mass. *Historically,* women (and particularly German women) are peculiarly implicated in this tension because their admittance to political participation took the form characteristically of the extension of the franchise. If women

---

26. Richard Bessel, *Political Violence and the Rise of Nazism* (New Haven, Conn., and London, 1984); Rudy Koshar, "Contentious citadel: bourgeois crisis and Nazism in Marburg/Lahn, 1880–1933," in Thomas Childers, ed., *The Formation of the Nazi Constituency* (London, 1986), 11–36.
27. Koonz, *Mothers,* ch. 3; Thomas Childers, *The Nazi Voter* (Chapel Hill, N.C., 1983), 259f. This is not to discount detailed and illuminating accounts of women's activity within the Nazi movement, like Jill Stephenson's, which suggest an independent process of mobilization but tend to emphasize the attitudes and activities of individual leaders; cf. Jill Stephenson, *The Nazi Organisation of Women* (London, 1981).

were (and still are) perceived as a mass and addressed as such, this is not surprising; the entry of women into politics marks the beginning of mass politics.

I return to the idea of the "mass" with some misgivings. I think that most of us (historians), when we talk about mass politics, are thinking in terms of the *scale* of mobilization or participation. A generation's historical research and argument has been devoted to disaggregating the "mass" that, as the subject and object of politics, is the stuff of political myth and of naive and tendentious historiography. The idea of a particular politics of the mass is suspect not least because of its implicit irrationalism, which is easily refuted by the discovery of identifiable and perceived interests among political actors (class). What then are we to make of the fact that "mass politics," like "mass society" and "mass culture," was a characteristic preoccupation of German social and political thought in the period we are discussing? Identified in the 1880s and 1890s, though still in the form of an apprehended tendency, it appeared to be fully realized by the 1930s, and the Critical Theory of the 1940s saw Nazism as one of its logical consequences. There is some significance in the fact that political and cultural modernity were identified at their moment of coincidence with massification, rather than with (say) democracy *tout court*. The establishment of the Weimar Republic did, after all, represent a turning point in the formal conditions for political participation at both the popular and administrative levels; it fulfilled a radical democratic program (at the national level) precisely in the extension of the franchise to women and installed the "women's realm" (and women administrators) at the heart of the state apparatus in the machinery of the welfare state. This is how it looks (and looked) from the vantage point of women, at any rate; from male intellectuals of the 1920s we find a massive silence on this significant feminization of the political order. "Mass" appears almost as a deliberate circumlocution.

But at the same time, the mass was extensively identified as feminine. This gender tag has two referents. On the one hand, we find already in the nineteenth century the use of woman as metaphor for modernity: The anonymous woman (often a prostitute) sums up in her inscrutability the fascination and threat of urban life, the street, and the masses who people it. The metaphor approaches a statement of identity in the literature of crowd (Le Bon) or group (Freud) psychology, where the mass, made up of subjects who have abandoned their (masculine) individuality, takes on the features of irrationality and suggestibility, indeed, the status of patient – all characteristics of women in Freudian psychoanalysis.[28] This appears in vulgarized form in Hitler's own characterization of the masses as feminine. We have learned to read the association made in conservative and fascist literature between the mass and female immorality in terms of a compulsion to control the mass, the perception of the mass as a threatening "other" that expresses the crisis of (male) authority.[29]

On the other hand, contemporary observers were quick to note that the cultural forms that characterized the new mass society had a particular appeal or utility for women. Early empirical surveys of moviegoing established that women were being attracted in significant numbers, that women (and men) who had not previously been active theatergoers went to the movies, that working-class women preferred movies to political activities, and that women of all classes were remarkably homogeneous in their cinematic taste. Even before the First World War, filmmakers began to tailor their films to the presumed demands of a female audience, and in the 1920s movie critics routinely referred to the femininity of the audience, particularly when (like Siegfried Kracauer in his 1927 article, "Die kleinen Ladenmädchen gehen ins Kino") they wanted to emphasize the social and political dangers presented by "excessive" moviegoing (*Kinosucht*).[30] Radio, too, although not at first an object of mass private consumption (early radio broadcasts took place in auditoriums before large audiences), was rapidly identified as being of particular interest and utility to women. Here there was less occasion for moral reservations, and the establishment of a *Frauenfunk* (women's radio) was guided by the intention to educate women politically.[31]

The idea of the "mass" in politics, then, invites reconsideration in terms of its historical context as expressing awareness of an epochal change in the structures of participation and representation, in the cultural (or ideological) as well as the political sphere. As a term that simultaneously insists on the femininity of the new public and obscures the presence of women in it, "the mass" has the advantage of

28. Theodor Adorno, "Freudian theory and the pattern of Fascist propaganda" (1951), in Andrew Arato and Eike Gebhardt, eds., *The Essential Frankfurt School Reader* (New York, 1978), 118–37.
29. For example, the work of Klaus Theweleit.
30. Miriam Hansen, "Early silent cinema: whose public sphere?," *New German Critique* 29 (1983): 147–84.
31. Katharine Lacey, "Women and the emergence of the modern mass media in Germany" (Ph.D. dissertation, University of Liverpool, in progress).

directing us both to the operation of gender discourses in the definition of politics (and the political subject) and to the issue of how the development of new media of mass communication affects the ways in which political opinion and participation are shaped. Having acknowledged that "mass politics" and "mass culture" as concepts have a common historical trajectory in a period self-consciously preoccupied with the relationships between gender, culture, and politics, I am therefore interested in the ways in which students of mass culture (and those who have studied *them*) attempt to theorize those relationships. This involves crossing disciplinary boundaries that are still very tightly drawn.

The first step is relatively easy, and in some respects familiar. The study of popular culture, using the techniques of literary criticism, may help us both to identify new sources and to develop new ways of reading old ones. Analyses of mass or popular culture can contribute to our understanding of the structures of specifically political argumentation and response. One such contribution comes from the discussion of genre. Genre criticism, with its emphasis on the interplay between medium, audience, and the social context, has long been a preferred form of literary analysis for materialist cultural historians.[32] Indeed, its rootedness in a historicist and materialist ideology (its proponents cite Marx among its founders) means that it often invites a relatively naive approach to the character of that interplay. Its language has nevertheless been widely taken up by feminists, including both literary critics and social historians. The genre that has featured prominently in recent feminist studies is melodrama. Patrice Petro, for example, in a recent study of women in Weimar culture, identifies melodramatic features not only in the multiplicity of formal devices characteristic of the new cinema, but also in the forms of representation employed in other media of the period, namely, in illustrated magazines including the Communist *Arbeiter-Illustrierte-Zeitung*. Melodrama has recently come to be closely associated with women in many different kinds of writing. In the last few years, it has repeatedly been cited in historians' accounts of nineteenth-century gender politics as providing the "script" in whose terms women's rights and wrongs were argued; in these accounts, melodrama recommends itself both as a pervasive popular discourse and as

32. Cf. Fredric Jameson, *The Political Unconscious* (London, 1981), 105f.

one in which the (usually sexual) victimization of women was a common theme.[33] These accounts echo literary-historical studies that emphasize the ways in which fin-de-siècle "high" literature borrows structures and topoi from melodrama in its preoccupation with the "sexual circus."[34] I am inclined to be wary of the proposition that history consists of the acting out of scripts, but I would like to consider seriously how political discourses, arguments, and propaganda relate to the genres of popular culture, both in order to understand what is familiar and what is innovative in political discourse and in order to think in an organized way about the kinds of response it might elicit. To take a single example: The autobiography of the turn-of-the-century Austrian Social Democrat Adelheid Popp can be placed within a genre of accounts of political "conversion" that closely parallel those of religious conversion (and often involve a conversion from religious to political engagement). Read as an exemplar of political propaganda written by a woman for women, it displays the features of contemporary popular (women's) literature, of romance and particularly of melodrama. Drawn to politics (she says explicitly) through her fascination with accounts of lascivious Jews in the Catholic press, she sets out to win over the female reader with an extended narrative of her own industrial, medical, and sexual victimization.[35] None of this is meant to suggest that the story is not true. Truth and – above all – typicality are essential to the function of the narrative; the declared intention of this, as of most socialist autobiographies, is to show the reader that her situation is shared by other women, that hers is not a personal but a collective problem, not a private but a political one.[36] Making the invisible visible, laying bare the true workings of society, or, more dramatically, exposing and unmasking truths that by the nature of the terms promise to be *morally* significant – this is the stuff of modern political propaganda, and particularly of the propaganda of radically oppositional parties. It is a function

33. Patrice Petro, *Joyless Streets: Women and Melodramatic Representation in Weimar Germany* (Princeton, N.J., 1989); Ruth Harris, "Melodrama, hysteria and feminine crimes of passion in the fin-de-siècle," *History Workshop* 25 (1988): 31–63; Mary Poovey, "Covered but not bound: Caroline Norton and the 1857 Matrimonial Causes Act," *Feminist Studies* 14 (1988): 467–86; Judith Walkowitz, contribution to roundtable, "Patrolling the borders: feminist historiography and the new historicism," *Radical History Review* 43 (1989): 25–31.
34. Elizabeth Boa, *The Sexual Circus. Wedekind's Theatre of Subversion* (London, 1987).
35. Adelheid Popp, *Jugend einer Arbeiterin* (reprint ed., Berlin and Bonn, 1977), 70–2.
36. Cf. Mary Jo Maynes, "Gender and class in working-class women's autobiographies," in Ruth-Ellen B. Joeres and Mary Jo Maynes, eds., *German Women in the Eighteenth and Nineteenth Centuries* (Bloomington, Ind., 1986), 78–93.

that is central also to most definitions of melodrama: Melodrama "puts pressure on the representation of the real so as to heighten its meaning and give the unrepresented and repressed a material presence";[37] it allows us to "see not so much the working of individual fates but the underlying moral process of the world";[38] its "very existence is bound to the possibility, and necessity, of saying everything."[39]

In historical terms, melodrama has been identified as a form characteristic of postrevolutionary society; Peter Brooks has located its origins and heyday in France in the first third of the nineteenth century. This lends it a certain political ambivalence. On the one hand, its message is a confirmation of the moral rightness of the world as the conclusion of a struggle between the embodied principles of good and evil. Brooks sees melodrama as the secular affirmation of "truth and ethics" made necessary by the overthrow of the moral authority embodied in the sacred institutions of church and crown. On the other hand, the political order it addresses (and for which it speaks) is unavoidably a new one, its promise of justice available to a new popular public: "While its social implications may be variously revolutionary or conservative it is in all cases radically democratic, striving to make its representations clear and legible to everyone."[40] It has thus been argued that melodrama was (is) particularly attractive as a form to the lower classes and women. (It has also been suggested that women are particularly attracted to the multiplicity of subjects or protagonists in melodrama, which replicates their own divided subjectivity.[41]) Perhaps because of its appropriation by social groups who increasingly had reason to question the moral rightness of the world, melodrama itself was changing by the end of the nineteenth century; in France, it spawned a popular theater of pure sensationalism (*grand guignol*). In Germany its figures appear, on the one hand, in the fatalistic narratives of Naturalism and anti-Naturalism, and, on the other, in the optimistic literature of Social Democracy, in which the power of good is implicit in the process of exposing evil and its triumph projected into a near future.

37. Petro, *Joyless Streets*, 30.
38. John Cawelti, *Adventure, Mystery and Romance* (Chicago, 1976), 45.
39. Tania Modleski, *Loving with a Vengeance: Mass-produced Fantasies for Women* (New York, 1982), 107.
40. Peter Brooks, *The Melodramatic Imagination: Balzac, Henry James, Melodrama and the Mode of Excess* (London and New Haven, Conn., 1986), 15.
41. Modleski, *Loving*, 90–2.

As David Blackbourn has pointed out, there is another place where many of the features I have associated with melodrama are particularly apparent in Wilhelmine Germany, and that is in the realm of political debate itself. He has suggested that the theme of hidden enemies, of "men behind the scenes," was probably more prevalent in Germany than in other contemporary political systems, and has identified in the popular politics of the period "a powerful rhetoric dedicated to the idea of disclosing and unmasking."[42] His conclusion that the presence of this rhetoric was a function of the peculiarly "behind-the-scenes" nature of decision making and the institutionalized lack of responsibility of politicians under the Bismarckian constitution rests on a reading of the rhetorical forms as metaphorical or instrumental: Either they offer a description of perceived reality, or they are directed at winning support for an individual or a cause (which is, after all, what politicians are about). At any rate, their consequences are calculable and calculated in terms of a commonsense measure of credibility. Looked at from the standpoint of the genre, however, the argument might be turned inside out: The melodramatic idiom is expressive of a culture that bears all the features and anxieties of a well-established, secularized mass or popular or demotic (if not democratic) polity – *except* for effective popular sovereignty.

Although we find women as active in the public contest for influence as the men whose mobilization constituted a direct challenge to the frustration implicit in this political order, they stood, as secondhand citizens, outside the specifically constitutional contradiction. Arguably, this made the *figure* of woman all the more available for the representation of the anxieties and resentments it generated. A trade-off of this kind is suggested by Miriam Hansen in her study of American and German reactions to the early cinema. In America, the popular appeal and accessibility of the new medium was a cause for celebration; it was hailed as "democracy's theater" and mythologized as a force not for massification but for the education and integration of a disparate citizenry. German critics were unable to identify the prewar movie audience with any particular class or social group, and even observers on the political left took no note of the democratic possibilities of the new medium. Instead it was immediately addressed in terms of mass psychology, on the one hand, or claimed as an adjunct to literary culture, on the other. As soon as narrative films

---

42. David Blackbourn, "Politics as theatre: metaphors of the stage in German history 1848–1933," in Blackbourn, *Populists and Patricians* (London, 1987), 246–64, 252, 257.

established themselves as a popular form, film was approached as an object for reform in terms of "morality, hygiene and high culture." It was precisely the "comparative lack of a democratic mythology" in Germany, Hansen argues, that pushed concerns about the gender of the movie audience to the fore in German discussions.[43]

Film melodrama provides the basis for arguing that women themselves found in the new medium a locus for working out their side of the Weimar gender debate. But what is the relevance of the genre to specifically political discourse? Who uses the genre, and who sees themselves reflected in it? I have already suggested that as a political language melodrama belongs to the party of radical opposition. After the First World War, the melodramatic idiom passed from Social Democracy to the Communist Party and the Nazi Party. The propaganda of both parties combined a commitment to revealing truth (on the Communist side in the form of Marxist-Leninist science, on the Nazi side in that of petit bourgeois common sense) with the persistent appeal to sentiment and the techniques of repetition and visual or verbal exaggeration; politics became, like melodrama, "an expressionist genre"[44] that was satisfied with nothing less than the acting out of the speaker's state of mind. Both insisted on the victimization of those whose interest they championed (not least, of course, the German nation itself) and whose support they solicited, and both frequently invoked images of suffering women to epitomize that victimization. In the hands of the Communists, these techniques did not elicit a positive response from women. The Nazis were more successful in attracting female support within the social groups that formed their principal constituency. But again, the simple model of appeal and response may be misleading. Reconsideration of the form of the appeal ought to imply reconsideration of the response we anticipate. To expect women to be politically mobilized (in the conventional sense) simply because the form of political propaganda is calculated to engage their attention is to preempt the discussion of how people read rhetorical addresses or images – a discussion that is by no means settled but has already revealed a range of genuinely exciting possibilities. Petro's examples of "melodramatic representation" in the *Arbeiter-Illustrierte-Zeitung* illustrate neatly that women readers of the Communist press probably did not interpret the female images directed at them in the ways their authors intend-

43. Hansen, "Silent Cinema," 174.
44. Brooks, *Melodramatic Imagination*, 55.

ed. We might propose, for a start, that the prevalence of the melodramatic mode at critical places and moments in modern German politics reflects both the emergence of mass participatory politics and the particular ways in which participation was frustrated – absolutely for women, relatively for lower-class men.

"Reflects" is still a crude way of describing the relationship of a political discourse to the polity that produces it. But it opens up the possibility that women have a politically relevant position that is articulated throughout the system even when they themselves are unable to act. The politics of melodrama engaged its addressees – women and the lower classes – in politics; it involved them by the very nature of its address. If we (historians) want to go further in this theoretical direction, we can only benefit by engaging with critical practices that are less deferential to our concerns than traditional genre theory. Cultural theory and the application of literary-critical techniques to the study of ideology, even where they are cast as historical studies, challenge some of the most basic assumptions and epistemological premises of mainstream history. Historians occupied with the question of who did what to whom and with issues of evidence find disturbing leaps of faith in the extrapolation from a selection of texts to an ideology to social and political practices. The methods employed by literary and media studies, and particularly the genuine excitements of deconstruction, may appear to us, like their objects of study, arbitrarily selected and their conclusions unreliable, because they are not subject to the test of a clear causal nexus, of "what happened next." Like the related methodological issues discussed previously, many of the objections that historians have to literary theory (or would have if they engaged with it) have been aired in the *Alltagsgeschichte* debate. I suspect that the enthusiasm with which many of us have embraced the maxim that culture and ideology are as much matters of practice as of ideas – that statements, thought, and action are one – reflects less an acceptance of ideology as an object of historical study than a determination to rescue the vision of history as a series of political events (expanded to include moments in the class struggle) by assimilating new perceptions to it. Social history is political history – *really*.[45] But the claims of much

---

45. For a discussion of the relationship between *Alltagsgeschichte* and gender history (which does not, however, address the question of their respective relationship to political history), see Dorothee Wierling, "Alltagsgeschichte und Geschichte der Geschlechterbeziehungen," in Alf Lüdtke, ed., *Alltagsgeschichte* (New York and Frankfurt a.M., 1989), 169–90.

feminist literary theory are more radical than those of *Alltagsgeschichte*. Characteristically, such theory aims to give an account of a whole cultural formation, to elucidate the structure of a dominant ideology, albeit often in terms of the ways it operates to contain resistance. Although the texts studied are necessarily limited in number, they are selected for their authoritative or exemplary character; at best, they are treated not as a static reflection of conditions, but as the most accessible term in a dynamic interaction among individual, society, and text.[46]

This global vision implies a number of other features of cultural studies that make them at the very least a valuable antidote to a male-dominated canonical history, for they focus on a field of social activity in which the familiar dichotomies that construct significance in history are confounded; in which women's presence as producers has always been acknowledged (if grudgingly); in which the interdependence and moral equality of production and consumption are axiomatic; and in which the "private" and "public" realms intersect in the medium (or product) itself, as well as in its themes and the conditions of its production. But more: The explicit or implicit assertion that writing is a political act, in its most radical reading, turns the expectations of historians on their head, for what it proposes is less an expansion of "politics" (of the kind with which we are now familiar) than a redefinition of historically significant agency. If most historians are likely to be sympathetic to the global ambitions of this kind of literary theory, feminist historians looking for a history that encompasses women ought to be attracted by its insistence that things indeed happen even where the historian's instruments cannot register them as events.

The idea of the political potency of cultural production is embodied in the concept of the public sphere (*Öffentlichkeit*) itself.[47] To return to the theme of mass culture, it has been suggested that film, like the novel of the eighteenth and nineteenth centuries, represents a

---

46. A compelling exposition of the approach that combines historicism with deconstruction is offered by Mary Poovey, *Uneven Developments. The Ideological Work of Gender in Victorian England* (Chicago, 1987), ch. 1. For a recent discussion of the problem of how texts "work" on their readers, see Simon Dentith, *A Rhetoric of the Real: Studies in Post-Enlightenment Writing from 1790 to the Present* (Hemel Hempstead, 1990), Introduction. Judith Newton has commented on the convergence between feminist literary theory of the kind outlined here and feminist historiography of the kind represented by Davidoff and Hall: "*Family Fortunes:* 'New history' and 'New historicism,'" *Radical History Review* 43 (1989): 5–22.

47. Jürgen Habermas, *Strukturwandel der Öffentlichkeit* (Darmstadt, 1962).

mediation between the public and the private.[48] (As a venue, of course, the movie theater is significantly both public and private, the audience present but invisibly self- or screen-absorbed.) For women, who were in both cases the grudgingly acknowledged audience for the new medium, imaginative participation through fictional forms in the literate exchange that constituted classical bourgeois *Öffentlichkeit* may be read as a compensation for the nineteenth-century exclusion from politics. At least one critic has proposed that the emergence and popularization of the novel in England produced a feminization of culture, such that women readers and writers constituted the bourgeois public before an economically powerful (male) bourgeoisie existed.[49] In the case of film, given that women were no longer *formally* excluded, one is tempted to read its function as a distraction from politics or a locus for displacement of social and political reflection. In either case, there is the danger of overlooking women's early and continued participation, through writing, in specifically political and social debate. On the other hand, it seems reasonable to see the very breadth of women's reading as contributing to their politicization before the First World War, given the difficulties they faced in attending public meetings. Adelheid Popp, for example, in her account of her own politicization, cites as the moment of "conversion" her response to a Social Democratic speech, and in this she appears to be typical of nineteenth-century Social Democrats. Earlier passages in the account, however, make it clear that her interest in political questions arose from her casual reading of the right-wing press.[50]

We might wish instead, then, to emphasize the differences between a literary public sphere and the kind of public created by the mass media. In particular, the addressees of the mass media constituted a *Publikum* only in the sense of an audience, and no longer in the sense of a collectivity of reasoning individuals engaged in the interchange of opinions. Thus we might want to consider the implications of the fact that at the moment of fullest potential participation in political debate, and at the point where women enter the public as fully qualified citizens, the public is increasingly the object, the more or less passive receiver, of political argumentation rather than its sub-

48. Hansen, "Silent Cinema," 155.
49. Nancy Armstrong, *Desire and Domestic Fiction. A Political History of the Novel* (New York and Oxford, 1987).
50. Popp, *Jugend*, 72f., 78–80. Cf. Jochen Loreck, *Wie man früher Sozialdemokrat wurde* (Bonn, 1978).

ject. This approach slides easily into the characterization of fascism in terms of "politics as spectacle" or the "aestheticization of politics," and just as easily into Habermas's early dismissal of the politics of modern mass democracies as a process of generating and registering "non-public opinion."[51] Is there anything more to be said about it?

Weimar theorists of mass culture, Walter Benjamin and Siegfried Kracauer in particular, insisted on a congruence between cultural forms and forms of perception, and implied that the political consequences of media presentations depended on particular structures of perception in the audience; passivity was not the natural state of an audience as such, though it might be induced.[52] Recent feminist cultural theory has contributed extensively to the idea of spectatorship as a form of activity, moving on from an earlier position, informed by psychoanalytic theory, that postulated "a link between cultural forms of representation . . . and the acquisition of subject identity in social beings"[53] but treated the spectator as a passive receptor. Its consideration of the question of female spectatorship in mass culture is premised on the idea that meaning, and hence pleasure, is generated through the interaction of audience and image (or reader and text). The familiar association between women, passivity, and mass culture (like the familiar argument that whatever moves women demobilizes them) appears in this view as either itself an ideology tending toward demobilization or the result of a false assumption that women see in the same ways as men, with the same consequences. In her work on Weimar film, Patrice Petro insists on the difference between male and female ways of seeing.[54] She argues for identifying in the films of the period a characteristic *variety* of forms, an unsettledness that reflects precisely the social and political ambivalence of a new (largely and identifiably female) audience at the same time as it rehearses – whether in the expressionist nightmares of "modernism" or in the hackneyed form of the family drama – the possibilities of sexual ambiguity opened up by apparent changes in women's social position and the accompanying destabilization of masculinity. The implication of this approach is that the public sphere, even in its most apparently static form, may be characterized by a range of different ways of *seeing* (reading, hearing), as well as by

51. Habermas, *Strukturwandel*, 250–63.
52. Cf. Petro, *Joyless Streets*, 57–67.
53. E. Dierdre Pribram, "Introduction," in Pribram, ed., *Female Spectators. Looking at Film and Television* (London and New York, 1988), 2.
54. Petro, *Joyless Streets*, 145–59.

a multiplicity of visions (languages, arguments). This takes us beyond the "discourse" approach, which encourages the reading of politics as a contest of legible texts, and demands that we speculate on the reality not so much behind as before them. In fact it reflects a determination to rethink our understanding of subjectivity or agency and its historical determinants. This is manifestly a long-term project, but it is a concern that historians ought to share.

6

Gender and the Culture of Work: Ideology and Identity in the World behind the Mill Gate, 1890–1914

KATHLEEN CANNING

The transformation of the nineteenth-century German industrial landscape is usually described and studied in terms of structures in transition: workshop to factory, "community" to "society," estate to class. In its tendency to focus on newly-emerging modern structures such as factories, industrial towns, and workers' communities, mainstream German labor history has emphasized the social and economic origins of structural transformation. In doing so it has neglected the importance of ideology, politics, and culture as constitutive elements in the processes of industrialization and class formation.[1] This study of gender and the culture of work in western German textile mills explores the ways in which ideology shaped the structure of textile production, with special reference to ideologies that concerned male and female nature and productive or reproductive labor. It also discusses the significance of these ideological boundaries for the formation of work identities and work cultures. Lastly, it considers how gender divisions in the structures and cultures of work shaped the history of the organized labor movement and its politics of class.

Women and gender have remained peripheral in histories of the factory in Germany because historians have uncritically adopted the self-conceptions and class definitions of the late-nineteenth- and

---

I would like to thank Robert Moeller, David Crew, Geoff Eley, and James Retallack for their helpful comments on earlier drafts of this essay.
1. Such neglect can be attributed in part to the prevalence of modernization theory among social and labor historians. This approach has been criticized as well for its tendency to overlook alternative forms of production and alternative patterns of class formation, for instance, the persistence of peasant workers. See Charles F. Sabel and Jonathan Zeitlin, "Historical Alternatives to Mass Production: Politics, Markets and Technology in Nineteenth-Century Industrialization," *Past and Present* 108 (August 1985): 133–76; and Jean Quataert, "The Politics of Rural Industrialization: Class, Gender, and Collective Protest in the Saxon Oberlausitz of the Late Nineteenth Century," *Central European History* 20 (June 1987): 91–124.

early-twentieth-century labor movement itself. Thus most labor histories reproduce the ideal types of male and female workers that inhabit the pages of the union press and resound in the protocols of union congresses. Labor historians draw a sharp contrast between two ideal types by defining one in terms of what the other was not. Thus the Protestant male worker came to identify with his job or craft – a prerequisite for the development of class consciousness – based on skill acquired through formal apprenticeship training, relatively well-paid employment in an economically vital and highly productive industry, and long-term job stability. The typical female factory worker, by contrast, was unskilled – *"willig und billig"* (submissive and cheap) – and employed on a temporary or irregular basis; her experience at work was devoid of the ingredients necessary for the development of *Berufsinteresse* (job identification) and class consciousness.[2]

Underlying these images of male and female industrial workers are two implicit and contradictory assumptions in German labor historiography. The first of these suggests that the structure of production has a pivotal role in shaping the ways in which *male* workers view their work and form work identities. At the heart of this relationship between worker and work is the possession of skill (real or mythologized) and the claim to comprehend the labor process as a whole and to exercise some measure of control over that process. Political or class consciousness originates in the identities workers form in the workplace, in particular in their struggles at the point of production.[3] The second and contradictory assumption is that women's work identities, unlike men's, are *not* shaped primarily by their experience in production and their relationship to it. Marriage and motherhood, not the ten to twelve hours spent on the shop floor, are

2. Works in which these views of women workers are explicit or implicit include Brian Peterson, "The Politics of Working Class Women in the Weimar Republic," *Central European History* 9 (1977): 87–111; Gerhard A. Ritter and Klaus Tenfelde, "Der Durchbruch der Freien Gewerkschaften Deutschlands zur Massenbewegung im letzten Viertel des 19. Jahrhunderts," in Heinz O. Vetter, ed., *Vom Sozialistengesetz zur Mitbestimmung. Zum 100. Geburtstag von Hans Böckler* (Cologne, 1975), 61–120; Karl Ditt, *Industrialisierung, Arbeiterschaft und Arbeiterbewegung in Bielefeld, 1850–1914* (Dortmund, 1982).
3. "Work Identity" is not a term that the nineteenth- or twentieth-century labor movement actually employed. Rather, the relationship between *Berufsinteresse* or *Berufsidentität* and union membership is *implicit* in union rhetoric, as well as in more recent German labor historiography. The Christian textile union, for example, demanded better job training for women in order to solidify the relationship between *"Arbeiterin und Arbeit,"* which would, in turn, provide women with the experience and understanding necessary to become trade union leaders. See Zentralverband christlicher Textilarbeiter Deutschlands (hereafter ZCTD), "Warum braucht die Frau die Erziehung zur Gewerbetätigkeit?," *Textilarbeiterzeitung*, 22 January 1910, no. 12/3, 10.

viewed as constitutive of women's work identities and political behavior.[4] Moreover, this image of female labor implies that women's work for wages was something new: Severing female factory labor from its own traditions, it effectively erases the memory of home industry, where women had spent lifetimes working at looms or spindles.

The textile industry is the starting point for this attempt to deconstruct (and reconstruct) the image of the female factory worker. Not only was it the largest factory employer of women, but the two textile unions had the largest female contingents within the socialist and Christian union confederations. Furthermore, the history of the textile industry in the Rhineland and Westphalia during the period 1880–1930 shows that the steady expansion of the female work force was a conflictual process even where long-established traditions of female employment existed.[5] This analysis of the textile factory workplace has important implications for the history of mass politics among German workers, even if it cannot address them in detail in this essay. First, it points to the necessity of examining not only the ideological boundaries of the world behind the mill gate, but also the ways in which women and men transgressed those boundaries and contested dominant ideologies of gender on the shop floor and in the union halls. Thus, it proposes to expand the definition of "politics" beyond the level of unions and organized strikes to encompass the micropolitics of the shop floor. Furthermore, it places work at the center of a history that analyzes the political mobilization of German workers during the last quarter of the nineteenth century and the first three decades of the twentieth century. After 1890, as steadily increasing numbers of German workers joined the Social Democratic Party (SPD) and its affiliated trade unions, the social identity and vocabulary of "class" came to dominate mass politics within the

---

4. Leading German social historians such as Gerhard A. Ritter and Klaus Tenfelde claim that these attributes of female employment made the presence of large numbers of women in an industry *organisationserschwerend* (detrimental to unionization); see Ritter and Tenfelde, "Durchbruch," 101f. See also Ditt, *Industrialisierung,* 236, who claims: "It was not so much age or the degree of qualification, but rather female gender, that created a barrier for the organizational efforts of the free trade unions." Others argue that regardless of wages or skill, women's roles as mothers and wives banned them from the arena of working-class politics. Brian Peterson, for one, argues that working-class women were apolitical: This held for young women "because of the primacy of the personal" and for older women because of the "sheer weight of the double burden of maintaining a household and working." Peterson, "The Politics of Working-Class Women," 99. Until now, Peterson's claim has hardly been challenged.
5. See Kathleen Canning, "Class, Gender, and Working Class Politics: The Case of the German Textile Industry, 1890–1933" (Ph.D. diss., The Johns Hopkins University, 1988), esp. ch. 2, "Mechanization and the Making of a Modern Work Force."

German labor movement.[6] Despite its universalist claims, the identity of class was grounded in narrow conceptions of work and skill: It originated in the male experience of industrialization and signified *men's* relations to production. Indeed, class was constructed in terms of sexual difference, not only in the broad sense of *Geschlechtscharakter* (character of the sexes), but also in the specific terms of the sexual division of labor *at work*.[7]

IDEOLOGY AND PRODUCTION IN THE WORLD BEHIND THE MILL GATE

This analysis of the "structure" of textile work contests the prevalent assumption that production was a predominantly material or economic formation. Ideologies of gender – in particular, notions of proper work for men and women, of female dexterity and docility, of male skill and supervisory authority – were implicit in the design and implementation of textile technology. They also shaped divisions of labor, hierarchies of skill and wage, and the factory regime of discipline and punishment.

The social reformers, factory inspectors, entrepreneurs, and labor movement activists who participated in the intensive debates about female factory labor during the last quarter of the nineteenth century formulated new policies for the workplace as they sought to resolve the growing discrepancy between the continued expansion of the female work force and prevalent notions about proper work for men and women. Ideologies of gender took on a growing importance in shaping employers' policies, labor legislation, social reformers' investigations, and union campaigns during this period, especially as the pace of feminization intensified.[8] For example, legislators and factory inspectors resisted the call of many social reformers to ban married

---

6. This is not to suggest that non-Social Democratic workers' organizations were insignificant. Although Social Democratic visions of work and class may have set the terms of working-class politics in Germany, they were often contested and criticized, in particular by the Christian labor movement.
7. The term refers to Karin Hausen's article, "Family and Role-Division: The Polarisation of Sexual Stereotypes in the Nineteenth Century – An Aspect of the Dissociation of Work and Family Life," in Richard J. Evans and W. R. Lee, eds., *The German Family* (London, 1981), 51–83.
8. The ways in which ideology shaped production have been analyzed recently by Michael Burawoy, *The Politics of Production: Factor Regimes Under Capitalism and Socialism* (London, 1985); Patrick Joyce, ed., *The Historical Meanings of Work* (Cambridge, 1987); Sonya O. Rose, "Gender Segregation in the Transition to the Factory: The English Hosiery Industry, 1850–1910," *Feminist Studies* 13 (Spring 1987): 163–84, and "'Gender at Work': Sex, Class, and Industrial Capitalism," *History Workshop* 21 (Spring 1986): 113–31; and Wally Seccombe, "Patriarchy Stabilized: The Construction of the Male Breadwinner Wage Norm in 19th Century Britain," *Social History* 11 (January 1986): 53–75.

women's employment outside of the home during the 1890s. Instead, they legitimated women's factory employment while attempting to contain it within strict boundaries. Their efforts to uphold the delicate balance between women's work at home and in the mills – to regulate the work world in order to preserve the family – are also evident in the restrictions on women's work time. Such restrictions were imposed upon mill owners in 1891 and again in 1908, often in the face of vehement protest.[9]

Textile employers were able to implement the prevalent norms of women's work to create a female work force upon which their industry was dependent, even though that work force remained secondary in terms of wages and skill. Yet in doing so they challenged prevailing notions of sexual difference in a fundamental way. The intense debates between advocates and opponents of women's factory employment attested to this dilemma. Mill owners sought to deflect the widespread opposition to women's factory employment through their paternalist welfare activities, such as schools that offered courses in the skills of keeping house (*Haushaltsschulen*), cooking and sewing classes, and day-care centers.[10] The aim of these "charitable" institutions was to import the home into the factory; in a sense they represent the price employers had to pay in order to cultivate a stable, long-term supply of female workers (*Stammarbeiterschaft*).

Male labor leaders and workers, like middle-class social reformers, often equated female factory labor with social and sexual disorder and with decay of the family. These men inserted their own vision of domesticity into their campaigns for work-time reductions and wage increases, just as they did when they periodically protested against the hiring of women workers.[11] The normative and ideological components of gender-based wage scales, specifically the gendered wage categories of male breadwinner and female supplementary earners,

---

9. Paragraph 137 of the labor code of 1891 excluded women from night work, limited women's regular work day to eleven hours, and extended pregnancy protection to four weeks. It also curtailed their hours on Saturdays and allowed women with families to leave work one-half hour early at lunchtime in order to shop, cook, and clean. Hauptstaatsarchiv Düsseldorf, Jahresberichte der Königlich Preussischen Gewerberäte (hereafter HStAD, JBdKPG), 1892, 328–30. In 1908 the state again amended the industrial labor code, restricting women's work time to a maximum of ten hours during the first five days of the week and eight hours on Saturday. See HStAD, JBdKPG, 1910: Düsseldorf, 420.
10. Paul Mieck, *Die Arbeiter-Wohlfahrts-Einrichtungen* (Berlin, 1904), 194; see also Minna Wettstein-Adelt, *Drei-ein-halb Monate: Eine Practische Studie* (Berlin, 1893), 36.
11. The Social Democratic Textile Workers' Union, for example, formulated its arguments in favor of Saturday restrictions in terms of women's domestic responsibilities. Deutscher Textilarbeiter Verband, *Der Textilarbeiter*, 15 Aug. 1913, no. 25/34, 266f., "Wann werden wir den freien Sonnabendnachmittag haben?"

represent one point of consensus between employers and workers, even though the two parties were often at odds about every other aspect of wage negotiation. In the view of both employers and union leaders, wage scales did not primarily reflect differences in productivity (*Leistung*); rather, they were based on notions of the distinct and divergent needs (*Bedürfnisse*) of each sex. Conversely, many women workers defied the ideology of female nature that confined them to their homes, although most were forced to do so out of economic necessity. They often resisted the fusion of home and family – when it translated into lower wages, for example – and they fought to bring the home into the factory on their own terms, as with their demands for longer lunch breaks, shorter working days, and better health and safety protection.

The following discussion of two central aspects of the system of production – skill and the factory disciplinary regime – illustrates how normative prescriptions of gender roles shaped this system and its relations of production.

DIVISIONS OF LABOR AND DEFINITIONS OF SKILL

The distinct positions of men and women in the process of textile production had a direct bearing on the work identities they formed. The personnel records of textile companies indicate that a sexual division of labor prevailed in most sectors of production, including those where family members worked together. Preparatory and finishing tasks such as ring spinning, winding, reeling, piecing, napping, and darning tended to be exclusively female. The few jobs that required formal training, such as repairing and maintaining the machinery, and nearly all supervisory positions, were reserved for men, who constituted the elite of the textile work force: the so-called textile craftsmen (*Textilhandwerker*). The exercise of authority – in the sense of technical expertise and supervision of the shop floor – was the preserve of men. This meant that conflicts over the exercise of authority were infused with gender issues.

Most mule spinners, ribbon weavers, velvet weavers, dyers, and bleachers were male. Weaving represented contested terrain, especially in the Rhineland and Westphalia and most particularly in the branches of silk (Krefeld), cotton (Mönchengladbach), linen (Bielefeld), and woolen (Aachen) weaving. Employers sought to hire increasing numbers of women in these branches as factory production expanded during the last quarter of the nineteenth century. The entry of women into these sectors did not, however, signal a breakdown in the sexual division of labor. Rather, new hierarchies emerged that were still based on gender and age, and men retained a near monopoly over tasks of greater "skill." Men wove material with more complicated patterns or tended more looms than women did, and this division was often reinforced by segregating the sexes in separate weaving shops.

Definitions and divisions of skill are central to understanding the relations of power and authority on the shop floor. An examination of categories and hierarchies of skill in the textile industry show that they were defined less by the structure of production than by normative prescriptions of proper work for men and women. From the founding of the first mechanized textile mills in the mid-nineteenth century through the end of the Weimar Republic, the acquisition of skill was an informal process for most textile workers – both female and male – with the exception of the textile craftsmen. Only a small percentage of textile workers – in 1907, less than 1 percent – acquired their skills through traditional craft apprenticeships.[12] Most obtained their experience and dexterity on the shop floor, many under the tutelage of a parent, sibling, or neighbor. In the absence of a formal apprenticeship system, the meaning of such terms as "skilled" (*gelernt*) and "training" (*Lehre*) varied widely among textile regions, branches, and individual mills; so did the means by which they were acquired. According to reports by mayors of textile towns in the Rhineland in 1877 and factor inspectors' reports of 1912, apprenticeship contracts were customary only in the branches of ribbon weaving and dyeing.[13] Although both groups of observers acknowledged that the textile industry depended upon "a core of competent and *skilled* workers," comprising in most branches between 60 and 90 percent of the work force, they reported that most had acquired their skill in a few weeks and had become fully productive weavers or spinners within a year.[14]

12. Zentralstelle für Volkswohlfahrt, *Das Lehrlingswesen und die Berufserziehung des gewerblichen Nachwuchses*, Schriften der Zentralstelle für Volkswohlfahrt, 7 (Berlin, 1912):182. In 1907, there were 9,078 apprentices in the German textile industry. Among spinners, 1.4 percent were apprentices; among weavers, 2.5 percent; knitters, 3.3 percent; and among bleachers and dyers, 1.7 percent. See also Johannes Feig, "Deutschlands gewerbliche Entwicklung seit dem Jahre 1882," *Zeitschrift für die gesamte Staatswissenschaft* 56 (1900):684. According to Feig, textile workers comprised 1.5 percent of industrial apprentices in 1895.
13. HStAD, Regierung Düsseldorf, 33520.
14. Ibid.

In the language of the modern factory, as defined by factor inspectors, Reich statisticians, employers, and labor leaders, "skilled workers" (*gelernte Arbeiter*) and "specialized workers" (*Facharbeiter*) were those who had mastered specific manual tasks or could operate certain machines without assistance.[15] They had also completed some type of training (*Vorbildung*). By contrast, "unskilled workers" (*ungelernte Arbeiter*) generally had no training at all and could easily be replaced.[16] However, a factor inspector for the Düsseldorf district noted the fluid boundaries between the two categories, skilled and unskilled, as early as 1877:

> Even in factories that produce the same goods with the same machines, workers who perform the same function in different mills are called "skilled" in one mill and "common laborers" in another; in one mill they are trained to be fully productive workers within one year and in the other in a couple of months.[17]

In fact most textile workers of both sexes performed *angelernte Arbeit*, or semiskilled, specialized tasks, for which they received no formal apprenticeship training and that (unlike unskilled labor) required more than purely muscular strength.[18] Especially important in the performance of such semiskilled jobs as weaving, spinning, roving, and loom warping was the worker's role as a "thinking part" in a divided labor process.[19] Even less skilled tasks – such as reeling, winding, bobbin setting, threading, and throwing – required work-

---

15. Ibid., "Bericht des Fabrikeninspektors Dr. G. Wolff an die Königliche Regierung von 16.7.1877," 1. See also Gerhard Adelmann, "Die berufliche Ausbildung und Weiterbildung in der deutschen Wirtschaft, 1871–1918," *Berufliche Aus- und Weiterbildung in der deutschen Wirtschaft seit dem 19. Jahrhundert* = Beiheft 15, *Zeitschrift für Unternehmensgeschichte*, 21.
16. Marie Baum, "Die gewerbliche Ausbildung der Industriearbeiterin," *Kultur und Fortschritt* 107 (1907): 4; Bernard Jauch, "Das gewerbliche Lehrlingswesen in Deutschland seit dem Inkrafttreten des Handwerkergesetzes von 26.7.1897 mit besonderer Berücksichtigung Badens" (Ph.D. diss., University of Freiburg, 1911), 94–6; Hermann Schäfer, "Die Industriearbeiter. Lage und Lebenslauf im Bezugsfeld von Beruf und Betrieb," in Hans Pohl, ed., *Sozialgeschichtliche Probleme in der Zeit der Hochindustrialisierung* (Paderborn and Munich, 1979), 173.
17. HStAD, Regierung Düsseldorf 33520, "Bericht des Fabrikeninspektors Dr. G. Wolff," 1. See also Marie Baum, "Die Folgen ungelernter Arbeit für die Arbeiterin," *Kultur und Fortschritt* 282/283 (1910): 118. Baum points to a similar lack of distinction between skilled and unskilled work.
18. "Angelernt" was a category that the statistics of the German Reich did not incorporate until just before the First World War; see Schäfer, "Die Industriearbeiter," 173.
19. Baum, "Die gewerbliche Ausbildung," 4; Marie Bernays, "Berufsschicksale moderner Industriearbeiter," *Die Frau* 18 (December 1910): 132, and "Lehrwerkstätten und Fachschulen in der Textilindustrie," *Kultur und Fortschritt* 492/494 (1914): 14; Rosa Kempf, "Das Interesse der Industrie an der Ausbildung der weiblichen Arbeiterschaft," *Kultur und Fortschritt* 492/494 (1914): 12.

ers to be dexterous, attentive, perspicacious, and reliable. According to one observer, the textile industry employed almost no unskilled workers beyond the occasional cleaning ladies and janitors.[20] Despite the fact that men and women acquired their skills in the same way – again with the exception of the textile craftsmen, for which there was no female counterpart – men's work was endowed with higher status and rewarded with higher pay.

Gender was also an important factor in the advancement of workers within the mill. The best positions available to women – in terms of status based on wages and acquired skills – were those of weaver, loom warper, rover, or darner. Employers seldom promoted women to the supervisory positions of *Untermeister* or *Meister*, even in predominantly female mill divisions, because they lacked the necessary "skills," defined as years of accumulated experience in the mill, "personal qualities," and knowledge of the entire process of production.[21]

The difficulties in overcoming the ideological definition and restriction of female skill became apparent between 1908 and 1910, during a public discussion about whether young women should be compelled to attend a supplementary training school (such compulsory attendance was known as the *Fortbildungszwang*). Attendance at public *Fortbildungsschulen* had been obligatory for young men in many German states since 1891. Only in Baden, Württemberg, and Bavaria were young women also required to attend the schools.[22] Attendance was not obligatory for either sex in Prussia, and with the exception of female commercial employees, city or local governments could not require young women to attend the schools.[23] Thus,

---

20. Bernays, "Berufsschicksale," 132.
21. Adelmann, "Die berufliche Ausbildung," 20; Baum, "Die gewerbliche Ausbildung," 4–7, and "Die Folgen ungelernter Arbeit," 20; Bernays, "Lehrwerkstätten," 23; Zentralstelle für Volkswohlfahrt, *Das Lehrlingswesen*, 179f. I found only occasional references to female supervisors in all-female shops. The factory inspectors' summary report of 1899 on married women's work notes that some employers offered such posts to older married women because of their maturity, stability, and experience on the job. According to my reading of the sources, this constituted the exception. See Reichsamt des Innern, *Die Beschäftigung verheirateter Frauen in Fabriken, nach den Jahresberichten der Gewerbeaufsichtsbeamten für das Jahr 1899* (Berlin, 1901), 115, 246.
22. DTV, *Der Textilarbeiter*, 10 June 1910, nos. 22–23, 181: "Weibliche Arbeiterjugend, Fortbildungsschule und kapitalistische Interessen." The first *Fortbildungsschulen*, as noted earlier, were founded by employers. By 1891, most were run by the city or local (Kreis) governments.
23. ZCTD, *Textilarbeiterzeitung*, 7 Mar. 1914, no. 16/9, 67: "Gegen die Pflichtfortbildungsschule für Arbeiterinnen." The first obligatory school for women was founded for commercial employees by the Kaufmännischer Verband für weibliche Angestellte in Berlin. See Marie Lischnewska, "Die handwerksmässige und fachgewerbliche Ausbildung der Frau," *Kultur und Fortschritt* (1910): 14.

in 1910 the Prussian *Fortbildungsschulen* had only 14,241 female pupils in 150 schools for girls. By contrast, 340,748 male pupils – 47 percent of all male factory workers between the ages of fourteen and seventeen – attended 1,877 schools.[24]

The goal of the schools for boys was to provide young men with a broader understanding of their specific jobs, of the process of production in its entirety, and of the role of the textile industry in the German economy.[25] Young men usually received instruction a few hours weekly in general subjects such as reading, writing, arithmetic, and drawing, in addition to such specialized job-related subjects as basic mechanics or textile fabrics. Yet over half of the girls' *Fortbildungsschulen* in Prussia offered instruction only in household skills.[26] Most of the schools for girls "almost wholly disregard[ed] specialized job training for women and concentrate[d] on educating women workers for their future '*Frauenberuf*'" through courses in sewing, drawing, cooking, and household accounting.[27]

During the first decade of the twentieth century, social reformers and middle-class feminists initiated a campaign to improve job training for women, which was fueled by the pending revision of the industrial labor code. In 1908 Prussian legislators proposed revising the code to give local and city governments the legal option of extending compulsory attendance at training schools to young women.[28] Reformers' efforts to open the *Fortbildungsschulen* to women and to enhance their opportunities for upward mobility within factory hierarchies culminated in the founding of the Association for the Training of Women in Crafts and Specialized Skills (*Verband für handwerksmässige und fachgewerbliche Ausbildung der Frau*) in 1909.[29] This

---

24. Marie Elisabeth Lüders, *Die Fortbildung und Ausbildung der im Gewerbetätigen weiblichen Personen und deren rechtliche Grundlage* (Leipzig, 1912), 22–30, 44. According to Paragraph 120, Absatz 3 of the labor code of 1891, cities or district governments (with over 10,000 residents) could introduce a *Fortbildungszwang* for male workers. The obligatory attendance for young women in Baden, Bavaria, and Württemberg was decreed by state (*landesgesetzlich*) law.
25. Since relatively few workers attended specialized schools for specific branches of industry (*Fachsschulen*), the *Fortbildungsschulen* were the main institution of training for young industrial workers.
26. Kreisarchiv Viersen (KrA Viersen), Gemeindeamt (GA) Grefrath 1154, "Gewerbliche Fortbildungsschule, 1864–1912." See also Lüders, *Die Fortbildung*, 22f.
27. Erna Barschak, *Die Idee der Berufsbildung und ihre Einwirkung auf die Berufserziehung im Gewerbe* (Leipzig, 1929), 140f.
28. Ibid. See also Lischnewska, "Die handwerksmässige und fachgewerbliche Ausbildung," 27, and ZCTD, *Textilarbeiterzeitung,* 7 Mar. 1914, no. 16/9, 67: "Gegen die Pflichtfortbildungsschule."
29. Lischnewska, "Die handwerksmässige und fachgewerbliche Ausbildung," 14; Anne

association's attempts to expand the definitions of female skill and to prevent women from being confined to "the lowest and dullest rung of industrial labor" can be viewed as part of the continuing discourse about women's factory labor as a social problem.[30] The reformers recognized the importance of confronting the prevalent norms about women's work that prevented women from advancing to supervisory positions. According to factory inspector Marie Baum, the opposition of male workers to female competition and the resistance of employers to the obligatory instruction of women in the *Fortbildungsschulen* were the main obstacles to providing systematic job training for women.[31]

Despite the reformers' vigorous campaign, employers' organizations, again led by textile mill owners, succeeded in thwarting legislative efforts to extend compulsory training to young women in 1910.[32] The same organized employers who, in other instances, acclaimed textile work as a suitable "life's calling" for women and who sought to cultivate a core work force of older married women argued here against a long-term investment in the development of women's skill.[33] Their opposition made it clear that women were valuable workers only if they cost less to train and maintain than men. The opposition of the United German Silk Weaving Mills (*Vereinigten deutscher Seidenwebereien*) was particularly vehement:

... training schools have a completely different meaning and should fulfill a completely different function for male and female workers.... The schools fulfill the goal of adding to the practical knowledge men gain on the job and of providing them with the theoretical knowledge they need in their future careers. Thus, the training school is an important factor in their occupational lives. In the case of women, however, most of whom practice their occupation only temporarily until they marry, this goal is insignificant.

Schlüter, "Die Entwicklung weiblicher Lehrverhältnisse Anfang des 20. Jahrhunderts aufgezeigt am 'Verband für handwerksmässige und fachgewerbliche Ausbildung der Frau in Deutschland,'" *Die Ungeschriebene Geschichte: Historische Frauenforschung* (Dokumentation des 5. Historikerinnentreffens in Wien, April 1984) (Vienna, 1984), 259–67.
30. Kempf, "Das Interesse der Industrie," 9. See also Baum, "Die gewerbliche Ausbildung," 8f., and Lischnewska, "Die handwerksmässige und fachgewerbliche Ausbildung," 14, 29.
31. Baum, "Die gewerbliche Ausbildung," 6–9.
32. Ibid., 7f.; Barschak, *Die Idee der Berufsbildung,* 140f.
33. Hauptstaatsarchiv Detmold (HStADet), Regierung Minden M1IG 172, 273–300: "Eingabe des Arbeitgeberverbands der Deutschen Textilindustrie vom 28.10.1926 an die Reichsregierung." Here in the context of their debate with the unions about the dangers of textile work for pregnant women, the employers' association emphasized that because textile work was simple and presented no health dangers to women, it was the ideal female "*Lebensberuf.*"

For women there is no question of theoretical job training. For this reason it has been suggested – and emphasized in the Reichstag as well – that instruction in the *Fortbildungsschule* take the form of courses in house-keeping.[34] Members of the Chamber of Commerce in Elberfeld expressed similar views, suggesting that "at the most, one could consider instruction in house-keeping for women workers. Employers, however, cannot be expected to sacrifice work-time or money for this type of training, which serves a purely private purpose."[35]

After the First World War, a few of the largest textile employers in the Rhineland and Westphalia established training workshops (*Lehrwerkstätten*) in their mills, offering formal apprenticeship training to both young men and women.[36] Despite the avowed goal of training "efficient, conscious professionals (*Berufsmenschen*), good silkworkers," soon after beginning their apprenticeship most young women at the Delius silk mill still received instruction in household skills instead of factory skills (*Fabrikkunde*).[37] The goal of this kind of "job training" for women – even in the mills where hundreds of women worked – was "to create a satisfied workforce . . . for it is an undeniable fact that those workers whose wives know how to keep house are among the best workers in the factory."[38]

This discussion of categories of skill shows that an insignificant number of textile workers – only 7 percent of male and 2 percent of female members in 1929 – participated in the formal system of apprenticeship training.[39] It exposes the fictional dichotomy between

34. Rheinisch-Westfälisches Wirtschaftsarchiv (RWWA), 22:70, Industrie- und Handelskammer Wuppertal, "Gewerbliche Fortbildungsschule, männlicher und weiblicher Arbeiter 1864, 1908–1914: Denkschrift der vereinigten deutschen Seidenwebereien, Düsseldorf von 15.11.1910."
35. RWWA 22:70, "Schreiben der Handelskammer Elberfeld an den Hohen Reichstag zu Berlin von 1. April 1911."
36. Most of the *Lehrwerkstätten* were founded between 1926 and 1930. HStADet, Reg. Minden, Mi IG 172, 320, "Schreiben der Fa. C A Delius über ihre Lehrwerkstätten und Werkschulen, Oktober 1926."
37. DTV, *Arbeiterausbildung in der deutschen Textilindustrie* (Berlin, 1928), 45–9.
38. HStADet, Reg. Minden IG 172, "Schreiben der Firma C.A. Delius." In 1930 Delius employed 100 apprentices of both sexes in the *Lehrwerkstatt*. All held three-year contracts. The goal of the *Lehrwerkstatt* in the *Kammgarnspinnerei* in Delmenhorst was to educate young women as "housewife, mother, and responsible citizen." DTV, *Arbeiterausbildung*, 7, 10.
39. The numbers of textile workers who had received job training remained small at the end of the Weimar Republic: The Christian textile workers' union surveyed its members in 1929 and determined that 37 percent of men and 34 percent of women had received no training at all; 41 percent of male and 52 percent of female members had been trained for a period of two to six weeks on the shop floor; only 7 percent of male and 2 percent of female members had completed a two- or three-year apprenticeship. Zentralverband christlicher Textilarbeiter Deutschlands, *Jahrbuch*, 1929, 30f.

the "unskilled" female and the "skilled" male, and offers insight into the skills that female textile workers *did* acquire and possess. It also suggests that the category of skill is meaningful only in its historical specificity, for its usefulness depends upon clear distinctions among industries and between early and later periods of industrial development. Lastly, the tenacity of this fictional dichotomy is testimony to its rhetorical power: It shaped male cultures in the mills, it was upheld by union leaders, and it colored the analyses of labor historians long after the formal system of craft skill transmission was displaced by the modern and informal system of "*Anlernen*." A critical examination of skill as a social construction therefore challenges a fundamental assumption of German labor historiography about the relationship between skill and class consciousness. Dissociating skill from the teleology of "class consciousness" opens the way for a broader definition of politics.

GENDER IN THE FACTORY REGIME

Men and women shared many aspects of workplace culture: the physicality of mill work; the confinement behind high walls in the mill courtyards and the absence of sunlight; the "unbearable air," high temperatures, and excessive dampness in the spinning shops; the dust, dry air, and noise of the power looms in the weaving shops; and the long hours of standing at machines for both spinners and weavers.[40] The working lives of both male and female workers were governed by a factor regime of discipline and punishment, the two pillars of which were the work regulations (*Arbeitsordnungen*) and the system of penalties and fines for violations (*Strafsystem*). The objects of this regime were to ensure continuous production at a profitable pace and to teach workers of both sexes "to become more skilful, docile, efficient, prudent, in short, more useful and valuable" for the employer.[41]

40. See Bernays, "Berufsschicksale moderner Industriearbeiter," pt. 2, *Die Frau* 18/3 (December 1910): 212–15; Minna Wettstein-Adelt, *Drei-ein-halb Monate Fabrikarbeiterin* (Berlin, 1893). See also descriptions of the textile factory workplace in HStAD, Landratsamt Mönchengladbach 710; JBdKPG 1898: Minden, 254; 1899; Minden, 388; 1902: Düsseldorf, 338; 1904: Düsseldorf, 445; 1906: Münster, 333f.; 1908: Minden, 326; 1912: Minden, 393f.; 1913: Cologne, 540.
41. Lothar Machtan, "Zum Innenleben deutscher Fabriken im 19. Jahrhundert: Die formelle und die informelle Verfassung von Industriebetrieben anhand von Beispielen aus dem Bereich der Textil- und Maschinenbauindustrie," *Archiv für Sozialgeschichte* 21 (1981): 181f.

The factory regulations for C. A. Delius's silk-weaving mill in Bielefeld were typical of textile mills in the Rhineland and Westphalia during the 1890s.[42] They prescribed penalties for tardiness in the morning or ceasing work and washing up too early (thirty pfennigs); altering looms or other machines and adjusting the lights or heating system (fifty pfennigs); wandering around the mill and entering other shops (thirty pfennigs); and production of deficient materials (varied according to severity).[43] Workers were more severely punished for immoral behavior, "smoking, drinking alcoholic beverages, horseplay or noise on the job"; stealing materials; admitting strangers to workshops; or missing a day's work without permission.[44] But a study of union and police reports on workplace conflicts reveals the gendered subtext of the work regulations, including the ways in which they prescribed distinct norms of respectability and responsibility for men and women. Men were fined most often for rowdiness – drinking, smoking, or stealing – whereas female workers were penalized for behavior unbecoming to women – impudence, especially laughter or "sassing back" to masters or managers, and for the subversion of factory discipline through gossip and indecent horseplay in the secret realm of the bathroom.[45]

The concern of employers with workers' morality and virtue, as articulated in the factory disciplinary system, had little to do with profits and the place of production. Employers implemented the penalty system to enforce a code of moral conduct during work time, and they utilized their welfare and charitable activities (*Wohlfahrtstätigkeiten*) to gain custody over the private lives of workers, rewarding those who conformed to the code. Gender is central to understanding the efforts of employers and factory inspectors to impose a kind of moral tutelage upon workers, for they often singled out women as the source of both moral ruin and moral regeneration.

42. HStAD, Reg. Minden, MiIU 425, "Arbeitsordnung Mechanische Seidenweberei C.A. Delius & Söhne, Bielefeld, 1892," 93–5. The Delius company's regulations and fines were similar to regulations in mills in the Lower Rhine (the Schwartz velvet mill in Grefrath and the Deuss & Oetker silk mill in Schiefbahn). See also KrA Viersen, GA Schiefbahn 847, Deuss & Oetker, "Arbeitsordnungen 1892"; and the private archive of Herr Johannes Lipp, Oedt, Germany: "Arbeitsordnungen für die zu Grefrath gelegene mechanische Sammtfabrik der Firma Aktienweberei R. Schwartz & Co., Krefeld," April 1908.
43. HStADet, Reg. Minden, MiIU 425, "Arbeitsordnungen Mechanische Seidenweberei C.A. Delius & Söhne, Bielefeld, 1892," 93–5.
44. Ibid.
45. Ibid. On illegal breaks, horseplay, and gossip during work time, see Machtan, "Zum Innenleben," and Alf Lüdtke, "Organizational Order or *Eigensinn*? Workers' Privacy and Workers' Politics in Imperial Germany," in Sean Wilentz, ed., *Rites of Power. Symbolism, Ritual and Politics Since the Middle Ages* (Philadelphia, 1985), 303–33.

Gender and the Culture of Work 189

The labor code of 1891 recommended the segregation of the sexes at work, but it appears that in the Rhineland only a few Catholic textile employers put this policy into practice. Since separation of the sexes was not feasible in most shop divisions, owners often drew gendered boundaries through the factory's public space, forbidding the mingling of women and men, or of single workers with families, in cafeterias and courtyards.[46] One employer in Rheydt built a separate entrance for women workers to prevent socializing upon arrival at and departure from work.[47] Cotton industrialist Franz Brandts of Mönchengladbach included a section of "moral regulations" in his *Ordnungen,* drafted by a local priest in 1885. They prescribed the separation of the sexes at work, and more:

> ... all mutual dealings between [male and female workers] during their free time is forbidden. Violations, as well as all frivolous interaction, that breach Christian morality, even outside of the factory, between young people of both sexes, will be met with a warning from the workers' committee, and if this is ineffective, a notice of termination.[48]

Factory inspectors also sought to enforce a separation of the sexes in the nonproductive factory spheres – restrooms, dressing rooms, and cafeterias. Their goal was to prevent the erosion of women workers' "sense of shame, that powerful protector of morality."[49]

Behind the code of factor morality were visions of sexual licentiousness in the mills, often evoked by social reformers' reports on the conditions of industrial work. As early as the 1870s, before the abolition of night work for women, Alfons Thun and other social commentators accentuated the sexual undertones of everyday life in the textile mills of the Lower Rhine. Thun described male and female bodies, sweaty and scantily clad, working side by side in the factories, where "during the working day the way was paved for the excesses of the night."[50] According to Thun:

---

46. HStAD, JBdKPG 1907: Aachen, 500. The Wilhelm Peters and Co. woolen factor in Eupen had separate cafeterias for single men and single women, as well as "five small dining rooms for workers whose family members brought them their food, so they could take their meals together in peace."
47. The Düsseldorf factory inspector reported that the C. A. Bettmann Co. in Rheydt "established a special factory entrance for the women workers so that the principle of the separation of the sexes can be maintained whenever possible on the way to and from the workplace." HStAD, JBdKPG, 1893: Düsseldorf, 387.
48. *Die Fabrikordnung der Firma F. Brandts zu Mönchengladbach* (Mönchengladbach, 1885; reprinted with an introduction by Wolfgang Löhr, Mönchengladbach, 1974), xv, 5f., 14. Brandts employed no married women in his mill. Women were fired upon getting married, but they usually received a wedding gift from him.
49. HStAD, Landratsamt Mönchengladbach 710, 103: "Bericht des Gewerbeaufsichtsbeamten Mönchengladbach 14.12.1874."
50. Alfons Thun, *Die Industrie am Niederrhein und ihre Arbeiter,* 1 (Leipzig, 1879), 179.

In the early factory system and to some extent, still today, everyone works together without distinctions – children, half-grown boys and girls, men and women – in overheated shops, clothed only in blouses and skirts. Thus all modesty disappeared of necessity. The tone, like the dress, was crude and unrestrained. So at dusk . . . and also during the night, when they worked back to back or side by side, vulgar words became vulgar deeds.[51]

Minna Wettstein-Adelt, a social reformer who worked undercover in a textile mill for several weeks, was shocked by the sexual horseplay among women workers in the weaving mills:

The women workers outdid one another with disgraceful, truly beastly, raw jokes and stories like I have never heard in my life. . . . I found a moral depravity and vulgarity there that is indescribable. Most of these girls seem to lack any sense of shame.[52]

Although accounts like Wettstein-Adelt's implicitly laid the blame for moral excesses or out-of-wedlock pregnancies at the feet of the female workers, rape and other forms of sexual coercion were widespread in the mills, as union papers and factory inspectors' reports indicate.[53]

Firsthand observer Marie Bernays noted the differences between middle-class and working-class morality in her description of the sexual mores of women workers in the Gladbach spinning and weaving mill:

It is fair to say that female workers, at least those who do not live at home, are nearly as liberated in sexual relationships as male workers. In most cases, no social disdain was associated with unwed motherhood; among women workers in the vicinity it was regarded as something rather normal, a fact one inquires about when first getting to know a girl, as easily as we discuss our visits to the spa or the publication of a new book. . . .[54]

Figures compiled by the textile employers' association confirm Bernays's observations: In 1913, 38 percent of pregnant female textile workers were unmarried; in 1914 the figure was 46 percent.[55] In 1924–5 over half of the pregnant workers in Johann Scheidt's woolen mill were unmarried.[56] Many unwed pregnancies, however, were

51. Ibid.
52. Wettstein-Adelt, *Drei-ein-halb Monate*, 31.
53. Factory inspectors and union leaders acknowledged the severity of this problem in their persistent demands for female factory inspectors. They hoped that the presence of female inspectors would encourage women workers to report incidents of abuse. See HStAD, JBdKPG 1900: Düsseldorf, 303; 1903: Düsseldorf, 307; 1913: Düsseldorf, 526f. For union demands for female inspectors, see DTV, *Der Textilarbeiter*, 20 Aug. 1909, no. 21/34: 265; ZCTD, *Der christliche Textilarbeiter*, 12 Apr. 1902, no. 4/15; *Textilarbeiterzeitung*, 5 Dec. 1908, no. 10/49: 192.
54. Bernays, "Berufsschicksale," pt. 1, 132.
55. HStADet, Reg. Minden M1IG 172, "Eingabe des Arbeitergeberverbands," 27.

followed by belated marriages. Working-class men usually assumed responsibility for a girlfriend's pregnancy, and the young couple married as soon as it was financially viable.

Inspectors and reformers viewed the factory as the "site of moral ruin for nearly all of those young workers – male and female – who had to live away from home."[57] Although it was undoubtedly difficult, if not impossible, for inspectors or employers to infiltrate the arena of workers' libidinous liaisons or to reshape their morality through policies enforced in the workplace, they were able to assert some control over workers' free time and private lives. This was done through extensive networks of welfare activities that included housing, evening courses, recreational clubs, and child-care centers. For example, industrialists enforced a type of paternal custody over women's dormitories and endowed them with tasks that exceeded the provision of clean and respectable housing. Employers and state legislators entrusted the *Mädchenheime* (dormitories for young, single female workers) with a gender-specific moral mission, based on their view that crowded, unsupervised housing – like the "moral decay" in the factory itself – presented a greater threat to young women than to young men.[58]

This custodial claim meant that life in company housing was frequently governed by a disciplinary regime that resembled the factory *Strafsystem*. In one girls' dormitory in Aachen, for example, five factory *Meister* and their families lived dispersed among the mill girls in the dormitories, and each supervised one group of rooms and inhabitants.[59] Other dormitories, although financed by mill owners, were under the direction of Catholic or Protestant nuns.[60] The regulations in company housing were analogous to factory regulations. Time, for instance, was regimented nearly as strictly as in the factory itself. The rules for one mill's dormitory in the Cologne district were typical: The girls were awakened at 5:15 in the morning and had a

---

56. RWWA 60: 6/5 Bestand Scheidt, "Umfrage des Verbands der Arbeitgeber im bergischen Industriebezirk, 16 Nov. 1925."
57. HStAD, Landratsamt Mönchen–Gladbach 710, 108.
58. Kuno Frankenstein, "Die Lage der Arbeiterinnen in den deutschen Grossstädten," *Schmollers Jahrbuch* 12 (1888), 209.
59. HStAD, Reg. Aachen, 17793.
60. HStAD, JBdKPG 1898: Cologne, 386; 1899: Cologne, 584f.; 1903: Cologne, 415: The Mühlenthaler spinning mill in Dieringhausen housed mainly young women from East Prussia and was run by Protestant sisters, as was the boarding house at Krawinkel & Schnabel. The dormitory at C. A. Baldus & Sons near Gummersbach was run by Catholic nuns.

limited amount of time to wash, make their beds, and eat breakfast.[61] They were not allowed to use their rooms or beds during the day or early evening. In the evenings, the girls were to do their wash according to the housemaster's schedule and sew or darn their clothing under the watchful eye of his wife. Visitors were not allowed in the building. The residents were forbidden to go out without the housemaster's permission, and the dormitory was locked at 9:30 in the evening.[62] In the dormitory at Schoeller & Co., residents were prohibited from engaging in "indecent conversation or singing." In the event that they "violated propriety" during their leisure time, they were reported to the factory director and faced almost certain eviction from the home.[63]

Cooking and sewing courses for female employees, instituted by individual mill owners or by their philanthropic associations, also had a dual moral mission: Young women would be kept busy and prevented from immoral thoughts or illicit actions while they learned the values of their future calling (*Beruf*) of marriage and motherhood. One textile company near Cologne joined with a Protestant minister to transform a local home for wayward girls into a model educational institute (*Erziehungsanstalt*) that combined work in a spinning mill with instruction in domestic skills. The training it offered to its residents alternated between full-time work in the mill and full-time study in the *Heim,* both under the constant supervision of Protestant nuns.[64] In this case, employer and church concurred that factory work offered the young women a form of tutelage, a basis for the proficiency and perseverance they would later need as homemakers.[65]

61. HStAD, JBdKPG 1894: Cologne, 631–3, "Hausordnung für das Mädchenheim der Kammgarnspinnerei zu Eitdorf." These rules are very similar to those for the Mädchenheim at J. W. Scheidt's worsted spinning mill in Kettwig. RWWA, Bestand Scheidt 60, "Das Mädchenheim der Firma J. W. Scheidt, Kammgarnspinnerei und Tuchfabrik AG, Kettwig-Ruhr 1927."
62. Ibid., HStA, JBfKPG 1894: Cologne, 631–3.
63. RWWA, XIVe 295, *Die Fürsorge der Firma Schoeller.* The socialist textile union described similar conditions in company dormitories in Baden and in the dormitories of the Wülfing Kammgarnspinnerei in Lennep. See DTV, *Der Textilarbeiter,* 28 June 1907, no. 19/26, "Herr Trikotwarenfabrikant Jacques Schiesser in Radolfzell und sein gemeinnütziges Werk," and local report from Lennep, 22 Apr. 1910, no. 22/16: 127. See also Martha Hoppe's series on "Heime für Textilarbeiterinnen," *Der Textilarbeiter,* 30 July 1909, no. 21/31: 244; 6 Aug. 1909, no. 21/32: 250; and 13 Aug. 1909, no. 21/33: 259.
64. Subjects included mathematics, German, religion, hygiene, cooking, ironing, knitting, and sewing. HStAD, JBdKPG 1903: Cologne, 415.
65. Ibid. According to the factory inspector: "The purpose of factory work is that the girls become accustomed to perseverance, that they learn to be attentive, orderly, and neat and recognize that even the lowliest job is valuable in connection with the whole, that it is necessary and must be carried out with dedication, if the whole is not to suffer."

Mill owners and the state sought not only to prevent unwed pregnancies through tutelage and charity, but also to make women workers into better mothers. Although factory day-care centers facilitated women's employment by relieving them of the burdens of child care during working hours, their founders saw in them the opportunity to make factory work compatible with motherhood by instilling working women with the "responsibility of motherhood." For example, mothers whose children attended factory day-care centers were to bring their children personally to the center and to pick them up. Furthermore, as one social reformer observed:

... if the children appeared unwashed, uncombed, or in dirty clothing, the mothers were warned that if their children arrive at the center in this condition again, they will be turned away. In this manner the child-care centers function indirectly as an educational example for indolent and negligent mothers.[66]

Of the pillars of the system of production, the factory regime was the terrain on which ideologies of women's work and female nature were camouflaged *least*. This was true of both the restrictive, punitive aspects of that regime and its custodial, tutelary functions. The factory regime defined married women and mothers in their reproductive capacity, and it addressed young single girls as potential wives and mothers. Yet through such institutions of tutelage as cooking and sewing courses, day-care centers, and dormitories, that same regime constituted an arena of contradiction for working women. On the one hand, it recognized and even offered partial solutions to working women's double burden. On the other hand, the benefits it offered buttressed the authority of the individual employer and extended his dominance to the private lives and desires of his female employees. Female workers also responded to the factory regime in contradictory ways. They often utilized their jobs for their own purposes, attempting to maintain distance from the factory and trying to limit the control it exerted over their lives.[67]

This inquiry suggests that gender played a powerful role in the ideological construction of "production," including divisions of labor, hierarchies of skill, and the development of the factory regime. The experiences and meanings of work – in the realm of ideology

---

66. Mieck, *Die Arbeiter-Wohlfahrts-Einrichtungen*, 37.
67. See Susan Porter Benson, *Counter Cultures: Saleswomen, Managers, and Customers in American Department Stores, 1890–1940* (Urbana, IL, 1986), 228. Both Benson and Lüdtke view "distancing" as a central component of work culture. See Lüdtke, "The Historiography of Everyday Life: The Personal and the Political," in Raphael Samuel and Gareth Stedman Jones, eds., *Culture, Ideology, and Politics: Essays for Eric Hobsbawm* (London, 1982), 46.

and in everyday life on the shop floor – differed markedly for male and female workers. Their distinct experiences and meanings shaped the formation of work identities and the emergence of work cultures.

GENDER, WORK IDENTITIES, AND WORK CULTURES

The concepts of work identity and work culture represent new ways of thinking about the "politics of production." They open up the meaning of "politics" to encompass everyday work culture as a political "terrain where the abstract structures of domination and exploitation were directly encountered" and contested.[68] They also aim to dissolve the dichotomies between family and factory that permeate most German labor histories. The term "work identity" signifies the ways in which male and female textile workers viewed and utilized their jobs, the meanings they derived from and imparted to their work, and the ways in which it "got under the skin" of their lives.[69] Although the meanings of "work" encompassed the machines used by workers, the products of their labor, their ethics of work, the social networks that divided or united them on the shop floor, and even the physical spaces they shared in the mill, these meanings were not narrowly restricted to production. Rather, work identities were also embedded in family, neighborhood, and community.

Work identities are admittedly elusive historical subjects. They cannot be "reconstructed" in any definitive way, but instead are "read" and interpreted by comparing or contrasting a variety of sources, including textile company personnel records, factory inspectors' reports, police reports, and social reformers' observations of mill life. This task of reading and weaving together multiple aspects of women's work experience represents a consideration of possibilities that conventional labor historiography has ignored or dismissed. It allows for an exploration of the ways in which women workers developed and expressed pride in their work; the kinds of loyalties they manifested and the ways in which loyalties among coworkers, employers, families, and communities were fractured; the manner in which women traversed the boundaries between family

---

68. Geoff Eley, "Labor History, Social History, *Alltagsgeschichte:* Experience, Culture, and the Politics of the Everyday – A New Direction for German Social History?" *Journal of Modern History* 61 (June 1989): 324.
69. Patrick Joyce discusses the ways in which "work got under the skin of everyday life." See his *Work, Society, and Politics. The Culture of the Factory in Later Victorian England* (New Brunswick, NJ, 1984), 97.

and waged work; the needs and desires that propelled them into collective protest; and the counterideologies and countervisions that women themselves articulated.

As a starting point for a discussion of work identities, career patterns provide rare clues about how men and women organized their own working lives. A reconstruction of career patterns from eight textile mills in the Rhineland and Westfalia challenges the prevalent view of women in German labor history as temporary, uncommitted workers by documenting the presence of a core of female *Stammarbeiter*.[70] It indicates that job stability in the textile industry was not a preserve of male workers, nor was instability inherently female. Indeed, the yearly turnover rates for male textile workers were higher than or nearly identical to those for women, and men and women demonstrated similar job stability where they performed the same job. A study of career patterns also offers insight into the ways in which women workers, most of whom worked out of dire economic necessity, balanced their double burden, ultimately shaping the textile *Stammarbeiterschaft* according to their own visions of the convergence of family and work.

The records of the Diergardt foundation of Viersen in the Lower Rhine offer compelling evidence of comparable job commitment and stability on the part of male and female textile workers even where sharp gender divisions prevailed in the workplace.[71] Between 1904 and 1922, some 360 textile workers in Viersen received awards from the foundation: usually diplomas, golden pins, and cash. In order to be nominated for an award, employees had to have worked at least twenty-five years in one mill, and most had worked between twenty-five and forty years in the same factory. Most male recipients were masters, foremen, craftsmen, machinists, or mechanics – that is, workers who were atypical in that they had acquired skill through

---

70. The personnel records include payroll or wage books, and *Arbeiterstammrollen* – books in which employers registered vital information on each worker – from eight textile mills. The conditions of production and the location of each of the eight textile companies vary, ranging from a linen weaving mill in an industrial city to a velvet factory in a rural mill village. The eight mills were all large factories; most had 100 or more employees. Computer analysis was conducted on a data base of approximately 3,600 workers. See Canning, "Class, Gender, and Working-Class Politics," ch. 3, "The Textile Workforce: Career Patterns and Work Identities."
71. Stadtarchiv Viersen, Diergardt Stiftung III/056, 1904–1912: "Ehrungen und Belohnungen für Fabrikarbeiter aus der zu Mönchengladbach bestehenden Diergardt Stiftung, 1904–1912." Freiherr von Diergardt established his foundation in 1904 to reward workers for their loyalty to employers (as expressed in long tenures of employment) and to aid ailing or elderly workers.

traditional apprenticeship training. Female recipients, by contrast, had worked as spinners, winders, bobbin setters, or weavers – tasks that required no formal training. Despite this pronounced division, women comprised nearly half (45 percent) of this elite of the textile *Stammarbeiterschaft*. Their average overall length of employment (27.4 years) was only slightly lower than that of men (30.2 years).[72] Marital status could only be determined for a small percentage of the female recipients; nonetheless, over half of them were married.

The long tenure of many female workers in the textile mills is even more remarkable considering the fact that "family time" and family events – such as childbirth, illness, or death – were more likely to necessitate interruption of women's mill careers than men's.[73] In fact, married women and single mothers established their own rhythms of work, which many employers apparently sanctioned. Many women interrupted employment to give birth, returned to work for a few months, left the mill again to care for a sick child or relative, and returned once again when the family situation permitted. As early as 1874, the factory inspector in one textile town noted:

[W]omen who are responsible for a household come to work later and leave work earlier [than the others]. When someone in the family is ill, they do not come to work at all. There is a general, unspoken agreement by which married women are treated with leniency. Their situation is therefore a relatively favorable one.[74]

This analysis of career patterns suggests that the decisive difference between male and female work identities was not the *primacy* of the "private" or the family in women's identities, nor their experience of work through the filter of the family, but the *simultaneity* of the two realms in female identities, their continuous need to transgress the boundaries between family and work.[75]

Career patterns attest to the presence of women among the textile *Stammarbeiterschaft* and to the potential for women to develop a *Berufsinteresse* or *Berufsethos* (work ethic) based on their longevity in the mills. Those patterns offer far less conclusive evidence about the particular identities or consciousness female workers developed.

72. Ibid.
73. The term refers to Tamara Hareven, *Family Time and Industrial Time: The Relationship between the Family and Work in a New England Industrial Community* (Cambridge, 1982).
74. HStAD, Landratsamt Mönchen-Gladbach 710, Bericht des Gewerbeaufsichtsbeamten Mönchen-Gladbachs, 14 Dec. 1874, 104f.
75. A poignant portrayal of this constant transgression is offered in Deutscher Textilarbeiterverband, *Mein Arbeitstag – mein Wochenende* (Berlin, 1930). See the new edition with an introductory essay by Alf Lüdtke (Hamburg, 1991).

However, autobiographical testimony, factory inspectors' accounts, social reformers' observations, police reports on strikes, and occasional passages in the union press do offer fragmentary evidence about women's work identities. These sources suggest that women took pride in their machines and in the products of their labor. Such pride was expressed through the celebration of employment anniversaries, when workers often put their products on display and decorated their machines with colorful ribbons and trinkets. Dress codes also denoted self-definitions as spinner, weaver, or winder. Women workers identified themselves not only according to their place in production, but also as members of crews, cliques, and networks of solidarity on the shop floor. Camaraderie, gossip, and horseplay represented other important elements of the micropolitics of the shop floor, for they often formed the basis for militant walkouts or strikes.

The concept of work culture denotes the articulation of these individual and collective self-definitions, the defensive preservation of self, as well as the assertion of individual needs and desires. These aspirations originated in either the realm of waged work or the realm of household, family, and neighborhood – and sometimes in both.[76] Work culture encompasses the "expressive cultural practices" through which workers adapted to and subverted ordained positions within the factory regime and the dominant ideology of gender roles that underlay it.[77] The term implies the possibility of a "relatively autonomous sphere of action on the job" that workers created as they distanced themselves from the structure of production and the authority of the employers.[78]

The terrain of work culture, rooted in discrepant experiences of work, status, and power, was more likely to be divided – by gender, ethnicity, and age – than welded together by an abstract class identity.[79] Despite the many common experiences men and women shared

76. Although Alf Lüdtke does not formulate his concept of *Eigensinn* in terms of workplace culture, he emphasizes the importance of needs, anxieties, and desires in shaping workers' political behavior. See Lüdtke, "Organizational Order or *Eigensinn*?" 304.
77. See Douglas E. Foley, "Does the Working-Class Have a Culture in the Anthropological Sense?" *Cultural Anthropology* 4 (May 1989): 141.
78. Benson, *Counter-Cultures*, 228.
79. On the tendency of gender to divide class, see Kathleen Canning, "Gender and the Politics of Class Formation: Rethinking German Labor History," forthcoming in *American Historical Review* (June 1992). This argument challenges Patrick Joyce's contention in *Work, Society, and Politics*, 111: "As in so many respects, that which factory workers had in common is more important for an understanding of class relations than that which divided them."

in the workplace, men's work cultures in an industry such as textiles formed around male strategies to protect wage and skill privileges against the threat of "feminization." Similarly, unions were more likely to permeate and even set the tone of male work cultures, while female-dominated shops seemed to remain more insulated, not least because most union organizers were men.

Female work cultures often represented a kind of subculture or alternative culture within the culture of the factory: Here women voiced the desires that male workers and the organized labor movement disdained as peripheral. Women workers sought to establish and preserve a place for themselves, both on the shop floor and in the "inner face" of the labor movement.[80] Women's work cultures, like men's, were frequently formed in conflicts about control over the labor process. However, they were also – perhaps more often than men's – born of struggles over pride and honor, gossip and respectability, bodies and sexuality, charity and tutelage, because of the particular position women occupied in the system and in the ideology of textile production. Women's work cultures likely formed around attempts to contest, even dissolve, the fictitious distinctions between factory and family that many male workers upheld. Hence, those textile strikes in which women predominated sought to preserve the right of women to come late to work when burdened with sick children, to obtain longer lunch breaks in order to cook for their families, and to protest sexual intimidation or rape. In these ways women sought to insert "private" issues into the "politics of production."

CONCLUSION

An analysis of the gendered construction of production – of the fissures of gender in cultures and identities of work – offers a new and fruitful approach to the history of labor politics in Imperial and Weimar Germany. It calls for a history of labor that refrains from conflating the experiences of women and men, "skilled" and "unskilled" workers, Catholics and Social Democrats, urban and rural laborers. It offers a history of division as well as of cohesion, for it disaggregates these stories and explores their diversity, free of the compulsion "to put them back together again" as quickly as possible.[81]

80. The term "inner face" is Alf Lüdtke's. See Lüdtke, "Organizational Order."
81. Eley, "Labor History, Social History," 339.

Bringing gender into labor history also reveals the necessity of disengaging the history of the working class from the language of class and the teleology of class consciousness.[82] While it would be a mistake to overlook the ways in which the vocabulary of class set the tone of working-class politics in Imperial Germany, it is also important to recognize that work cultures and identities almost always formed around something more than "class" experiences. Indeed, the moments when the social identity of class overcame gender and regional or religious divisions should be weighed against those moments when gender fractured class, when women shunned this vocabulary or sought to transform it according to their own needs.

82. This is the main focus of my paper, "Gender and the Politics of Class Formation." Cf. David Crew, "Class and Community: Local Research on Working-Class History in Four Countries," in Klaus Tenfelde, ed., *Arbeiter und Arbeiterbewegung im Vergleich: Berichte zur internationalen historischen Forschung, Historische Zeitschrift* (Sonderheft 15) (Munich, 1986), 279–83.

7

Serving the Volk, Saving the Nation: Women in the Youth Movement and the Public Sphere in Weimar Germany

ELIZABETH HARVEY

I

In Weimar Germany the participation by both women and young people in the processes of mass politics was seen as problematic. Where the participation of women was concerned, perceptions of the problem were bound up with the general debate over women's emancipation in Weimar Germany. Feminists saw women's low level of participation in formal politics as the problem, and accordingly sought to make the emancipation of women proclaimed in the Weimar Constitution into a reality by educating the mass of women to take up and use their new political rights. In the eyes of antifeminists, who rejected the whole notion of women playing a role in the public sphere equal to that of men, the problem was women's political activity in any form. Meanwhile, the troubled relationship between successive generations of young people and the Weimar political system gave rise to concern about young people's political participation. The political parties of the republican camp sought to mobilize youthful support, whereas the republican authorities sought to combat youthful political activism where it threatened political stability and to channel it in the right direction.

Recent research on voting patterns, political parties, and organizations, as well as on youth organizations and the youth movement in

---

Research for this essay was funded by the Deutscher Akademischer Austauschdienst and the Salford University Research Committee, which I would like to thank for their support. I am also indebted to the staff of the Archiv der deutschen Jugendbewegung for their help and advice, and to Georgina Waylen, Christian Führer, Robert Moeller, and Larry Jones for their comments and suggestions.

Abbreviations used in this chapter: ADF = Allgemeimer Deutscher Frauenverein ADJB = Archiv der deutschen Jugendbewegung: Burg Ludwigstein, Witzenhausen, BA = Bundesarchiv Koblenz, BDF = Bund Deutscher Frauenvereine, DF = Deutsche Freischar, DMWB = Deutscher Mädchen-Wanderbund, DStV = Deutscher Staatsbürgerinnen-Verband, FjN = Freischar junger Nation, GDJ = Grossdeutscher Jugendbund, HLA = Helene Lange Archiv: Berlin, JNB = Jungnationaler Bund.

201

the Weimar Republic, has produced an increasingly differentiated picture of the political participation and political outlook of women and young people. Debates have focused in particular on the nature and extent of Nazism's appeal to women and to the young.[1] In view of the debates over the role of women and of youth in Weimar politics, analyzing the political participation and outlook of young women in Weimar Germany would clearly seem to be an important task for research. Until recently, however, relatively little work has focused on the political activity of young women.[2]

Young women's political participation in Weimar Germany could be examined in a number of ways. Starting from the contradictory impressions given by contemporary observers regarding young women's political activity and interest in politics, one could investigate, for instance, the extent to which young women made use of their newly granted citizenship rights, as measured in terms of voting turnout. One might also look at changing levels of membership in party organizations and ask to what extent young women were radicalized and mobilized, along with young men, in the crisis of the Republic. These are just two areas that require further investigation. This essay, however, focuses on a different issue that is equally vital to an understanding of young women's political behavior, namely, young women's attitudes toward politics and political participation.

This essay examines how young women in the *bündische Jugend*

1. On the "youth factor" in voting patterns, see Jürgen W. Falter, "The National Socialist Mobilization of New Voters: 1928–1933," in Thomas Childers, ed., *The Formation of the Nazi Constituency 1919–1933* (London, 1986), 202–31. On women's voting patterns, see Helen Boak, "'Our Last Hope': Women Voters for Hitler – A Reappraisal," *ASGP Journal* [ASGP = Association for the Study of German Politics], no. 15 (Spring 1988): 1–22. On the appeal of the NSDAP to young women voters see p. 12, as well as Jill Stephenson, *The Nazi Organisation of Women* (London, 1981), 80. For a survey of women in relation to the political parties of the Weimar Republic, see Jill Stephenson, *Women in Nazi Society* (London, 1975), 16–21, and Renate Bridenthal and Claudia Koonz, "Beyond *Kinder, Küche, Kirche*: Weimar Women in Politics and at Work," in Renate Bridenthal, Atina Grossmann, and Marion Kaplan, eds., *When Biology Became Destiny: Women in Weimar and Nazi Germany* (New York, 1984), 33–65. On the relationship of the youth movement and confessional youth organizations to National Socialism, see Irmtraud Götz von Olenhusen, *Jugendreich, Gottesreich, Deutsches Reich: Junge Generation, Religion und Politik 1928–33* (Cologne, 1987), and Matthias von Hellfeld, *Bündische Jugend und Hitlerjugend: Zur Geschichte von Anpassung und Widerstand 1930–39* (Cologne, 1987).
2. On women in the youth movement, see Rosemarie McWhorter-Schade, "The Leading Edge: Women in the German Youth Movement 1905–1933" (Ph.D. diss., University of York, 1985) and Marion E. P. de Ras, *Körper, Eros und weibliche Kultur: Mädchen im Wandervogel und in der Bündischen Jugend 1900–1933* (Pfaffenweiler, 1988). On the pre-1933 development of the *Bund Deutscher Mädel*, see Martin Klaus, *Mädchenerziehung zur Zeit der faschistischen Herrschaft in Deutschland* (Cologne, 1983), 220–30, 322–40.

Serving the Volk, Saving the Nation

viewed their role in the public sphere and in formal politics. The *Bünde* (leagues) were tightly structured organizations that came to dominate the youth movement as it evolved after 1918 away from the freer *Wandervogel* traditions associated with the hiking groups of the pre-war period.[3] I would justify the focus on the *Bünde* on several grounds. First, the dynamics within the *Bünde* and the ideological stance of their activists (and, where this can be identified, by their rank-and-file members) are of intrinsic interest in that they shed light on the responses of particular groups of young middle-class women to social and political change.[4] Second, the young women in the *bündische Jugend* tended to see themselves and were seen, for instance by bourgeois feminists, as opinion leaders whose ideas had influence in youthful circles outside the *Bünde*. Third, women in the *Bünde* are significant in this context because they explicitly addressed the question of their political and public role as women and as members of the youth movement, and were prepared to enter into public debate on the issue.

Focusing on young women in the *Bünde*[5] also has its problems. Generalizing about attitudes within even a single *Bund* is difficult given the resistance of the *bündische Jugend* to clear programs. Identifying trends in the *bündische Jugend* overall is even more difficult. Moreover, focusing on the *Bünde* is clearly problematic in the context of a volume that seeks to shed light on mass politics. The *Bünde* were highly elitist: Far from seeking to mobilize the youthful masses, they recruited selectively. The membership of the *Bünde* was socially and educationally privileged. Rosemarie McWhorter-Schade's study of women in the *Bünde* found them to be "overwhelmingly middle-class" in social origin and with educational qualifications well above average. Of her sample, only 5 percent had no qualifications beyond elementary school (*Volksschule*), whereas over 35 percent had qualifi-

---

3. On the history of the youth movement in its *bündisch* phase, see Walter Laqueur, *Young Germany: A History of the German Youth Movement*, 2nd ed. (New Brunswick, N.J., 1984), 133–87.
4. The principle in the *bündische Jugend* of youth being led by youth means that the sources such as the journals, even if they do reflect the views of leaders and activists more than those of the grass-roots membership, still at least express the views of predominantly young women (to a greater extent, for instance, than journals produced by the confessional girls' organizations).
5. The present essay focuses on three *Bünde* or groups of *Bünde*: the *Deutscher Mädchen-Wanderbund*, the *Deutsche Freischar*, and the *Freischar junger Nation* together with its forerunners, the *Grossdeutscher Jugendbund* and the *Jungnationaler Bund*.

cations at the level of university entrance (*Abitur*) or above.[6] The size of the *Bünde* reflected their exclusivity. The number of girls in organizations identifiable as groups of the *bündische Jugend* was estimated in 1927 to be 11,700 out of a total of 40,150 members of both sexes. By early 1933 this had risen to 17,000 out of a total of 77,000 members of both sexes.[7] The latter figure was equivalent to 0.3 percent of the total number of young women between the ages of fourteen and twenty-five in 1933 (5.58 million) and 0.6 percent of the young women in that age group who were members of youth or sports organizations (2.5 million).[8] Compared, for instance, with the 760,000 members of the Central Federation of Catholic Young Women's Associations (*Zentralverband der katholischen Jungfrauenvereinigungen Deutschlands*) at the end of 1932 and the 213,000 young women who at that time belonged to the largest Protestant girls' organization, the Protestant National Federation of Female Youth (*Evangelischer Reichsverband weiblicher Jugend*), the membership of the *Bünde* shrank into insignificance.[9] Given the size of the *Bünde* and their atypical social and educational composition, the relevance of developments in the *bündisch* milieu for young women generally, or even for young middle-class women, is an obvious problem, to which one keeps returning.

This essay seeks to explain, first, the extent to which young women in the various *Bünde* under investigation underwent a process of politicization, defined broadly as the acquisition of a basic level of political awareness. I ask how far these young women could be regarded as "political," not in the narrower sense of being politically mobilized, but in the broader sense of being actively concerned with

---

6. McWhorter-Schade, "Leading Edge," 29–31. Such levels of educational qualification have to be seen in a context of girls' low rates of participation in full-time schooling over the age of fourteen: In 1931, taking the Reich as a whole, only 13 percent of girls aged fourteen to sixteen were in school full-time; of these, 3 percent were in middle schools (*Mittelschulen*) and 9 percent were in the upper schools (*höhere Schulen*) that prepared pupils for the university entrance qualification. Participation rates fell again sharply at sixteen: Of the girls aged sixteen to nineteen in 1931, only 2 percent were attending upper schools (compared to 6.9 percent of the boys). See Peter Lundgreen, *Sozialgeschichte der deutschen Schule im Überblick: Teil II: 1918–1980* (Göttingen, 1981), 118–19.
7. These figures included the members of the scouting (*Pfadfinder*) organizations. For 1927 figures, see "Die Mädchen in den Jugendverbänden," in Emmy Wolff, ed., *11. Jahrbuch des BDF 1929 (1927–8)* (Mannheim, 1928), 81. For 1933 figures, see Josepha Fischer, *Die Mädchen in den deutschen Jugendverbänden: Stand, Ziele und Aufgaben* (Leipzig, 1933), 10.
8. For census figures of June 1933, see Hertha Siemering, *Deutschlands Jugend in Bevölkerung und Wirtschaft* (Berlin, 1933), 122–3; for figures on organized female youth, see Fischer, *Mädchen*, 4.
9. Fischer, *Mädchen*, 5, 7.

their role in relation to the nation, the state, the system of government, and the public sphere. In examining the process of politicization, this essay explores the way in which a growth in political awareness was linked to a readiness to enter into debates with bourgeois feminism.

Second, the essay examines how those young women in the *Bünde* who *were* political in the sense just outlined envisaged their role in relation to politics and the public sphere, particularly during the final years of the Weimar Republic. In this respect, it is important to determine how these women were shaped by factors that were gender- and generation-specific. This is partly a question about the ways in which young women's perceptions of their political or public role may have been formed by their experiences as women and as young people growing up in Weimar Germany. But it is also partly a question about how far young women's definitions of their political role expressed a conscious identification of themselves as female and/or youthful political actors: in other words, how far they saw themselves as having a special role to play in politics by virtue of being female and belonging to the young generation.

The essay ends with some observations on the usefulness of a generational perspective for a study of young women's political outlook and behavior in Weimar Germany. Historians have seen signs of generational differences in women's voting patterns toward the end of the Weimar Republic[10] and have noted the existence of a gap dividing the bourgeois feminist movement in the Weimar period from a younger generation of women.[11] Atina Grossmann has portrayed a generational divide in social as well as political terms, arguing that young women in Weimar Germany sought to escape the drudgery in which their mothers had been trapped and to grasp opportunities to play a wider role in society. Grossmann suggests that fascism may have appealed to young women "because in fact it also celebrated their competence, their ability to manage in a new and modern world, and indeed offered mass political activity and mobilization as an escape from the restrictions of both wage labour and

---

10. See note 1.
11. Stephenson, *Women in Nazi Society*, 26–7; Irene Stoehr, "Neue Frau und alte Bewegung? Zum Generationskonflikt in der Frauenbewegung der Weimarer Republik," in Jutta Dalhoff, Uschi Frey, and Ingrid Schöll, eds., *Frauenmacht in der Geschichte* (Düsseldorf, 1986), 390–400.

domesticity."[12] In this, she shares the view of other historians who have argued that National Socialism sought to mobilize young women not simply through a revaluation of women's traditional domestic role, but also through its promise of a wider role extending into the public sphere and providing an outlet for young women's activism.[13]

II

Political issues generally – and specifically the question of youth's role in the political order – were matters of great concern to the youth movement in its *bündisch* phase and contributed to the deep rifts between and within the *Bünde*. Research on young women in the *Bünde* has suggested that they were generally less politically minded than the men, but it has also stressed the varying levels of political interest in the different *Bünde* and has suggested that the interest shown by women in the youth movement in political and public affairs increased over the course of the Weimar period.[14]

One indicator of the level of awareness on the part of young women in the *Bünde* of their political and public role as women was, I would argue, the extent of their readiness to engage with the ideas of the bourgeois feminist movement. The feminist movement promoted a distinct set of ideas regarding women's role in public life, and young women who saw gender as relevant to women's role in public and the public sphere sooner or later had to engage with that set of ideas.

Rosemarie McWhorter-Schade, evaluating the replies by former members of the *bündische Jugend* to her questionnaire, has shown that the level of interest in feminism that respondents recalled having had in their youth was fairly high.[15] However, she argues that the interest in feminism shown by young women in the youth movement declined after 1919.[16] This seems a paradox worth exploring: One would expect that if there was indeed a generally increased level of

12. Atina Grossmann, "'Girlkultur' or Thoroughly Rationalized Female: A New Woman in Weimar Germany," in Judith Friedlander, Blanche Wiesen Cook, Alice Kessler-Harris, and Carroll Smith-Rosenberg, eds., *Women in Culture and Politics: A Century of Change* (Bloomington, Ind., 1986), 76–7.
13. See, for example, Klaus, *Mädchenerziehung*, 332–3. Koonz also stresses the idea that the Nazis appealed to women's activism as opposed to their desire for a traditional domestic role, though she does not see this idea as being particularly targeted at or attractive to young as opposed to older women. See Claudia Koonz, *Mothers in the Fatherland: Women, the Family and Nazi Politics* (London, 1987), 122–3.
14. McWhorter-Schade, "Leading Edge," 108.
15. Ibid., 50, 232.   16. Ibid., 50, 232, 240.

awareness of and interest in political issues and in women's political role, there would also have been a growing readiness to engage with (if not necessarily to adopt) feminist ideas regarding women's place in politics and the public sphere.

One *Bund* can be cited as evidence that there was a link between political and social change, politicization and the growth of interest in feminism: the German Girls' Hiking League (*Deutscher Mädchen-Wanderbund* or DMWB).[17] The journal of the DMWB from the end of 1918 on carried debates on politics and on the feminist movement in which not only the leaders of the DMWB but also ordinary members participated. The debates were triggered by the 1918 revolution and the granting of the vote to women. "At a stroke we are faced with tasks which until now we have shied away from," wrote the DMWB's leader in December 1918.[18] The lively political discussions in local DMWB groups that ensued in the following months were not welcomed on all sides. Tensions arose as the DMWB moved from the social conservatism and political abstentionism that had characterized it since 1914 toward a more active engagement with politics. One critic of this trend warned that political debate would "take from us those qualities of quietness, gentleness and goodness which we need absolutely if we are to be the fitting complement to manhood [*Mannestum*]."[19] The divisive consequences of increased political debate were soon clear: The DMWB split in 1922 over the issue of whether to admit Jewish members (the majority of members left rather than drop the commitment to a *völkisch* position). The split gave the leaders of the DMWB in 1923 the opportunity to move away from classic youth movement concerns to forge links with the women's movement and with young feminist circles.[20] In a new constitution adopted in 1923, the League declared that it intended to "seek

---

17. On the DMWB, see de Ras, *Körper*, 116–48, and McWhorter-Schade, "Leading Edge," 17. The DMWB was unusual in being an all-female *Bund*. The average age of its membership was between sixteen and twenty-eight years: de Ras, *Körper*, 116. Its membership grew as follows: 1916: 100, 1918: 400, 1920: 600, 1921: 732, 1922: 1,400 members. After the 1922 split, membership fell to circa 300. For membership figures, see Sigrid Bias-Engels, "Der Deutsche Mädchen-Wanderbund im Umbruch der Zeit 1914–1923" (unpublished Staatsexamensarbeit, University of Bonn, 1981), 24.
18. L. Walbrodt, "Zeitenwende," *Der Landfahrer* 4, no. 8 (Dec. 1918): 12.
19. Erna Mayer, untitled comment, *Der Landfahrer* 5, no. 4 (April 1919): 8.
20. On the DMWB's turn toward the women's movement and the split with the *völkisch* faction, see "Zum Bundestag," *Der Mädchen-Rundbrief* 1, no. 2 (June 1923): 1–3. On the young feminist circles, see Emmy Wolff, "Die sozialen Jugendgemeinschaften, ihr Werden und ihr Ziel," *Die Frau* 28 (1920): 65–70; idem., "Erste Ansätze und Erfahrungen in den Jugendkreisen für Frauenfragen," *Die Frau* 29 (1921–2): 139–42.

out and tread the paths which women must follow together in order to fulfil their special role in the culture of the nation and of mankind as a whole." Subsequent issues of its journal were devoted to discussion of the place of women in public life, the significance of voting, the legal position and rights of women, and girls' education.[21] The DMWB, however, failed to recruit new members on the basis of its new commitment to feminism and went into decline.

The case of the DMWB shows that the ideas of the bourgeois feminist movement did have some impact on a section of young women in the youth movement in the early Weimar period. However, the DMWB was not typical of the youth movement at that time. In the early 1920s, feminist leaders lamented young women's mistrust of the feminist movement and apparent indifference to public affairs.[22] Feminists were particularly worried by such attitudes when encountered in young women from the youth movement.[23] This was because the *Bünde* were seen as an opinion-forming force; their members potentially mobilizable for social goals congruent with those of the feminist movement; their activists, like the activists of the feminist movement, educated and middle-class. Accordingly, feminist organizations, in particular the Federation of German Women's Associations (*Bund Deutscher Frauenvereine* or BDF) and one of its affiliated organizations, the German Women Citizens' League (*Deutscher Staatsbürgerinnen-Verband* or DStV), sought to promote a dialogue with young women in the *Bünde*.[24]

In the later 1920s, feminist efforts to promote the exchange of ideas with the *Bünde* intensified and met with more positive interest in dialogue and debate than ever before. In 1929 both the BDF and the DStV staged large public events that dealt with questions of women's political participation and citizenship and were aimed at young women, particularly those from the *Bünde*. The DStV, hosting the elev-

---

21. On the new constitution of 1923, see L. Walbrodt, "Rückblick und Ausblick," *Der Mädchen-Rundbrief* 1, no. 2 (June 1923): 5. For articles on issues relating to women's position in society and politics, see *Der Mädchen-Rundbrief* 1, no. 3 (July 1923) and no. 4 (April 1924).
22. Stoehr, "Neue Frau," 393–5.
23. Gertrud Bäumer, "Die Bundestage in Köln," *Die Frau* 29 (1921–2): 48; "Jugend und Frauenbewegung," in Else Ulich-Beil, ed., *10. Jahrbuch des BDF 1927 (1921–7)* (Mannheim, 1927), 80; Agathe Schmidt, "Die Mädchen in den Jugendverbänden und ihre Stellung zur Frauenbewegung," *Die Frau* 36 (1928–9): 543–51.
24. "Bericht über die 31. Generalversammlung des ADF in Hannover," *BDF Nachrichtenblatt* 1 (1921): 4; Protokoll der Generalversammlung des BDF in Köln, 8 Oct. 1921, Helene Lange Archiv (hereafter cited as HLA): Bestand BDF 65-279/2.

enth congress of the International Alliance of Women for Suffrage and Equal Citizenship in June 1929 in Berlin, arranged as part of the conference a public meeting on the subject of "The Youth Movement and the Women's Movement," addressed by a representative of the youth movement and attended by an estimated 1,500 young women. Three months later, as part of the program of the Königsberg general assembly of the BDF, Else Ulich-Beil addressed an audience of around 1,000 at a public meeting on "Youth, Women and the State." A discussion on "Questions of Female Citizenship" brought representatives of the BDF together with speakers from youth movement organizations, a white-collar union, and student organizations.[25] Following up and trying to capitalize on the interest shown at these meetings, feminist organizations after 1929 continued in their efforts to promote intergenerational dialogue. Such efforts appeared all the more urgent in view of the need to mobilize young women against growing attempts to discriminate against women at work and to exclude them from public life.[26]

What is not entirely clear from the sources is how far the positive response to feminist initiatives came from members of the *Bünde* as opposed to non-*bündisch* young women. However, it was significant that a major journal of the youth movement (*Der Zwiespruch*) carried reports on the feminists' "youth events" of 1929,[27] and there are other signs of an increased interest in the bourgeois women's movement among members of several important *Bünde* in the late Weimar years. Such signs were evident from the late 1920s on in the Youth League for a Greater Germany (*Grossdeutscher Jugendbund* or GDJ) and the Young National League (*Jungnationaler Bund* or JNB), two explicitly nationalist *Bünde* that merged in 1930 to form the Young Nation Corps (*Freischar junger Nation* or FjN).[28] Articles on person-

---

25. On the DStV event, see "Jugendliche, nehmt teil an dem Frauen-Weltkongress!," *ADF-Mitteilungen* 1 (1928–9): 18. See also Irene Stoehr, *Emanzipation zum Staat? Der Allgemeine Deutsche Frauenverein – Deutscher Staatsbürgerinnenverband (1893–1933)* (Pfaffenweiler, 1990), 130–1. On the BDF event, see *Nachrichtenblatt des BDF* 9 (1929): 70.
26. Else Brökelschen-Kemper, "Politik, Frauenbewegung und junge Generation," *Die Frau* 39 (1931–2): 236–9; Margarete Kurlbaum-Siebert, "Grundlagen zur Mitarbeit der Frau am Staat," *Nachrichtenblatt des BDF* 12 (1932): 114–18.
27. Elly Schüler, "Jugend- und Frauenbewegung," *Der Zwiespruch* 11 (1929): 315–16; idem., "Jugend, Frauen und Staat," *Der Zwiespruch* 11 (1929): 439–4.
28. The *Grossdeutscher Jugendbund*, known until 1924 as the *Deutsch-Nationaler Jugendbund*, was founded in 1919. In 1930 it was said to have 10,000 members, of whom a third were girls. "Grossdeutscher Jugendbund," in Hertha Siemering, ed., *Die deutschen Jugendverbände* (Berlin, 1931), 79. The *Jungnationaler Bund* was formed in 1921 as a breakaway group from

alities and events associated with the women's movement began to appear in the journals of these organizations,[29] and there was more frequent mention of meetings where topics such as women's rights, the history of the women's movement, and women and politics were discussed.[30] Among young women in the German Corps (*Deutsche Freischar* or DF),[31] there was a similar growth of interest, particularly on the part of leaders and older members, in current affairs and in problems relating to women's position in society, public life, and politics.[32] A meeting of older girls and women in the DF at Whitsun 1930 took as its theme "Women in Public Life."[33] In the winter of 1930–1, student members of the DF in Leipzig were discussing current political developments and "all sorts of educational and women's issues,"[34] and a DF seminar (*Arbeitswoche*) in September 1932 opened with an address that explored the place of women in public life and the DF's relationship to the bourgeois feminist movement.[35]

With respect to the *Bünde* under scrutiny here, the interest taken by their women members in feminist ideas was clearly not in decline after 1919. On the contrary, the growing eagerness evident in the later years of the Weimar Republic on the part of both leaders and members of the *Bünde* to concern themselves with politics and the role of women went hand in hand with an increased interest in the ideas of the bourgeois feminist movement.

the *Deutsch-Nationaler Jugendbund*. The number of girls in the *Jungnationaler Bund* was given in 1928 as 1,800. See "Mädchenerziehung in den Jugendverbänden: Wandlungen, Zustände, Ziele," *Das junge Deutschland* 24 (1930): 392. The number of girls in the *Freischar junger Nation* was given in 1933 as 3,496. See Fischer, *Mädchen*, 9. On the history of girls in the *Jungnationaler Bund* and in the *Freischar junger Nation*, see de Ras, *Körper*, 216–36.

29. For an enthusiastic report on an exhibition mounted by the women's movement on the feminist press, see T. Herfeld and H. Brunkhorst, "Die deutsche Frauentagung in Köln," *Das deutsche Mädel* 3 (1928): 107–9.
30. C. Bennett, "Der Berliner Aelterenring," *Das deutsche Mädel* 3 (1928): 41–3; Magdalene Strathmann, "Dienstpflichtigenlager 1931," *Mädel im Bunde* 6 (1930–1): 276–7.
31. The DF was formed in 1927 as the result of a merger of several youth movement groups belonging to the *Wandervogel* tradition and saw itself in the late Weimar years as the standard bearer of the youth movement tradition. Membership figures for girls in the DF: 1928: 1,550, 1933: 500. For the 1928 figure, see "Mädchenerziehung in den Jugendverbänden: Wandlungen, Zustände, Ziele," *Das junge Deutschland* 24 (1930): 392. For the 1933 figure, see Fischer, *Mädchen*, 9.
32. De Ras, *Körper*, 210–11.
33. "Bericht über die Pfingsttagung 1930 der Frauen und Mädchen auf dem Ludwigstein," *Deutsche Freischar* 3 (1930–1): 33–72.
34. Studentinnenrundbrief, Feb. 1931, Archiv der deutschen Jugendbewegung (hereafter cited as ADJB): A2-22/3.
35. "Aus der Einleitung unserer Arbeitswoche auf dem Roderberg, September 1932," *Mädchen* 1933, no. 1 (Feb. 1933): 11–13.

III

Toward the end of the Weimar Republic, *bündisch* women were increasingly ready to discuss and define women's political and public roles and to engage with the ideas of the women's movement. However, this did not necessarily bring an ideological rapprochement with bourgeois feminists.

In one respect there was a consensus shared by bourgeois feminists and by the young women in the *Bünde* examined here. All downplayed or denied an egalitarian feminist concept of citizenship according to which there should be no fundamental differences in the roles played by women and men in the public sphere.[36] Instead, bourgeois feminists and the young women from the *Bünde* alike insisted on the centrality of gender for defining women's role in relation to politics and public life. Female citizenship, in their eyes, was to be defined in terms of the specific contribution women might make to the body politic on the basis of their feminine expertise, experience, or "nature."

There were, nevertheless, considerable differences between feminists and young women in the *Bünde* over the form women's participation in politics should take. One source of disagreement stemmed from different attitudes to the Weimar Republic and parliamentary democracy. The mainstream bourgeois feminist position, true to feminism's origins in liberalism, was to uphold the system of parliamentary democracy and to advocate participation in party politics. Although critical of existing political practices and the male-dominated culture of party life, feminists called on women, whom they saw as having the potential to exert a superior moral force in the public sphere, to use their political rights and work within existing institutions to bring their influence to bear on all aspects of public affairs.[37] Among the *Bünde* examined here, it was only within the

---

36. On the tensions between the "egalitarian" and "dualistic" concepts of women's emancipation in the bourgeois feminist movement up to the founding of the Weimar Republic, see Bärbel Clemens, *Menschenrechte haben kein Geschlecht: Zum Politikverständnis der bürgerlichen Frauenbewegung* (Pfaffenweiler, 1988). On the conservatism of the bourgeois feminist movement in the Weimar period and its growing emphasis on a women's sphere in politics, see Richard J. Evans, *The Feminist Movement in Germany 1894–1933* (London, 1976), and idem., *Comrades and Sisters: Feminism, Socialism and Pacifism in Europe 1870–1945* (Brighton, 1987), 169–76.
37. For the feminist argument that women should concern themselves with *all* areas of politics, not just women's issues, see Frances Magnus-Hausen, *Zehn Jahre deutsche Staatsbürgerin* (Berlin, 1930), 7–8.

German Girls' Hiking League that a similar position with regard to participation in Weimar politics was advocated. In the journal of the Hiking League, members' contributions combined a critique of political life with an acceptance of party politics as a mechanism for regulating and mediating conflicts of interest in society.[38] The women in the other *Bünde* under examination here, however, tended to reject the idea of participation in politics as it was currently constituted. This hostility to Weimar democracy and to party politics might be interpreted as a case of women simply following the lead of their male comrades. For all the political differences that divided *bündisch* youth, there was across the spectrum of the *bündisch* milieu a common suspicion of party politics as divisive and antagonistic to national interests. But the rejection of party political involvement by young women in the *Bünde* was amplified by their specific rejection of *women*'s involvement in party strife as something alien to women's nature.[39] A position of political abstentionism based on *bündisch* ideology thus became fused with a conception of femininity embodying the principles of harmony and reconciliation, and moreover, so Gertrud Bäumer suspected, with an inferiority complex on the part of young women regarding their marginality to and ignorance about politics.[40] The refusal by young women in the *Bünde* to conceive of politics in terms of the representation of conflicting interests led them to reject not only party politics but also campaigns for women's rights. Campaigns for women's rights were rejected on the grounds of generational solidarity with male comrades in the *bündische Jugend*. Although this sense of solidarity can be taken at face value, it may also be interpreted more negatively as young women's fear of challenging or confronting their male peers and of exacerbating tensions that already existed between the sexes in the *Bünde*. However it is interpreted, young women's insistence on solidarity with their male peers was a central point of conflict between the young women in the *Bünde* and bourgeois feminists.[41]

The disagreements between young women from the *Bünde* and bourgeois feminists can be seen at one level in terms of a conflict between a liberal position and a right-wing antidemocratic position

38. Käte Burchard, "Wir und die Parteien," *Der Landfahrer* 5 (1919): 5–7; "Politische Fragen, politische Stellungen," *Der Mädchen-Rundbrief* 1, no. 4 (1924): 3–5.
39. Liesa Riehm, "Frau und Politik," *Jungnationale Stimmen* 1 (1926–7): 69–70.
40. Gertrud Bäumer, "Die Stellung der weiblichen Jugend zum politischen Leben," *Die Frau* 37 (1929–30): 638–45.
41. Stoehr, "Neue Frau," 392–3.

prescribing abstention from party politics for women as well as men. However, this picture is not complete, since the actual rejection of participation in Weimar politics did not necessarily imply an absolute denial in principle of a public or political role for women. Young women in the *Bünde* also outlined women's role in relation to the public sphere and to politics in schemes that abstracted from the political context of the Weimar Republic and were blueprints, however hazy, for an alternative political system.

One variant of a future polity that was current within the *bündisch* milieu featured the exclusion of women from politics and the public sphere altogether. The young women proposing this solution to the problem of women's political participation were arguing from a paradoxical position. They belonged to organizations that by definition took their members out of the narrow scope of the domestic sphere. They took part in debates within the public sphere and were politicized in the sense that they defined their role in relation to a political framework. However, the end result of their political thinking was to define woman's sphere as entirely separate from public affairs and politics. They presented this as restoring women to the place where the *Volk* needed them most: Women were to serve the nation and the community simply by fulfilling their duties in the domestic sphere. Although this view was to be found as a strand of thinking in Nazi girls' organizations,[42] it was also advanced in the more right-wing nationalist *Bünde* looked at here. "Men make history, they steer with an iron grip the destiny of the nation and the state. The inner values, and with them true culture, rest in the hands of women," stated a programmatic article in the opening number of the girls' journal of the Young National League in 1925.[43] A similar view was expressed in 1932 by a leader of the Young Nation Corps who warned against a tendency to try to mobilize girls as an active, militant, collective entity: "Girls are not intended to be a troop or a front but to exert their influence as individuals, as a source of strength and goodness for others."[44]

Rosemarie McWhorter-Schade sees the spread of this highly reactionary view of women's role in politics as the most significant and characteristic development among young women in the *Bünde* during

---

42. Raba Stahlberg, "Die Haltung der weiblichen Jugend in der NSDAP," *Die Frau* 38 (1930–1): 46–7.
43. "Deutsches Frauentum," *Mädel im Bund* 1 (1925): 3.
44. Freischar junger Nation, Landesführerinnen und Dienstpflichtigen-Führerinnen-Rundbrief, signed: Irmgard (= Irmgard Doctor), 13 Oct. 1932, ADJB: A2-55/3.

the final years of the Weimar Republic.[45] Feminists were alarmed at what they saw as a tendency among young women in some of the *Bünde* to adopt arguments peddled in the antifeminist backlash triggered by the Depression and to propagate a version of women's role that – regardless of its being dressed up in *völkisch* ideology – represented from a feminist standpoint a relapse into blinkered pettybourgeois attitudes (*Spiessbürgertum*).[46] But, as the feminists commented with some relief, this trend was not the only one to be found among young women in the *Bünde*. Alongside the more reactionary and limited versions of women's role that became increasingly widespread during the last years of the Weimar Republic, there existed a broader vision of women's special mission extending from the domestic into the public sphere. In the words of a DF leader reporting on a meeting on "Women in Public Life" and stressing the need for women's aspirations to evolve in line with changing times: "It can no longer suffice for us to be, in however noble a sense, the 'guardian of hearth and home.' Our task must also lie in sharing the task of shaping public life."[47]

The question of what form this broader public role for women might take gave rise to a number of proposals, some more clearly defined than others. Of the *Bünde* looked at here, the women in the Youth League for a Greater Germany were most prone to speculation about the role of women in a possible future order. In the corporatist order they envisaged, the public sphere would be divided into a masculine and a feminine domain, though how this division was to work in practice is hard to deduce from the way such plans were outlined. The feminine domain would be that in which women's "motherly qualities can and must unfold."[48] Women's tasks, it was argued, should extend

beyond the living community of the family into which we are born, to the communities of endeavor, the school, church and the *Bund,* and beyond them to the communities of productive work and action: labor and the state. All these communities are given life through the organic principle of organization [*das organische Prinzip der Gliederung*], the disciplined integration and subordination of all the forces whose variety and particular charac-

---

45. McWhorter-Schade, "Leading Edge," 242, 254, 277, 309.
46. Else Brökelschen-Kemper, "Politik, Frauenbewegung und junge Generation," *Die Frau* 39 (1931–2): 236–9; Gertrud Bäumer, "Die politische Krisis und die Frauen," *Die Frau* 40 (1932–3): 164–6.
47. Josi Grabert-von Maydell, "Die Grossdeutschen und wir," *Deutsche Freischar* 3 (1930–1): 68.
48. "Erpel," *Das deutsche Mädel* 2 (1929): 71.

teristics enrich and give life to the community. They become frozen and lifeless if the principle of equality is applied mechanically. As they need the creative force of man, so too do they need the conserving strength of women.[49]

In other *Bünde* the idea of special womanly tasks extending beyond the confines of the home served as the basis for slightly more concrete concepts of how women might participate in the public and political spheres. A corporatist plan for a women's chamber (*Frauenkammer*) was promoted from the late 1920s by the Young German Sisterhood (*Jungdeutsche Schwesternschaft*), the women's section of the Young German Order (*Jungdeutscher Orden*), as a framework for women to play a political role that would correspond to their allegedly different nature and interests.[50] Although the visions of the Youth League for a Greater Germany and the Young German Sisterhood overlapped with the ideas of the bourgeois feminists to the extent that woman's special qualities and expertise were seen as the basis for her role in the public sphere, they were in conflict with the bourgeois feminist movement insofar as the latter sought to bring specifically "feminine" values and female influence to bear on *all* areas of public life and politics. However, these *bündisch* blueprints did at least suggest, despite the incoherence of their formulation, some scope for public action on the part of women in a future political order.

The common denominator in *bündisch* definitions of women's public role was the idea of service to the community and to the nation. This might take the form of voluntary or professional social work, which the *Bünde*, like bourgeois feminists, saw as an extension of the maternal role into the community. However, women in the *Bünde* also saw their role in terms of larger, vaguer forms of womanly public engagement that were more specifically *bündisch* and that focused on serving and preserving the nation and its cultural heritage. Weeks spent in the countryside helping with the harvest and living with the peasants were conceived of as a way to help overcome the crisis in agriculture and to prop up the struggling population of Germany's eastern regions. Camping expeditions to East Prussia, or to areas beyond the borders of the Reich where German minorities

---

49. Hannah Brandt, "Das deutsche Mädel und der Ruf des Staates," *Das deutsche Mädel* 4 (1929): 62–3.
50. On the idea of the *Frauenkammer*, see Hanna Klostermüller, "Der Jungdeutsche Staatsvorschlag und seine Frauenkammer," *Die Frau* 37 (1929–30): 295–7; Annemarie Doherr, "Frauen und Wahlreform," *Die Frau* 37 (1929–30): 674–6.

lived, were given a political gloss, the aim being to boost the morale and stiffen the national resolve of the Germans living in areas of ethnic tension. Such activities had the advantage of being distinctively *bündisch,* whereas myriad organizations and public authorities were already involved in social work in the cities. They also fitted in better with the youth movement's tradition of exploring and reclaiming the *Heimat* and with the priorities of young men in the *Bünde.* Moreover, they probably appealed to the ethos among young women in the *Bünde* of comradeship with men: Women's participation in such activities involved a greater symmetry, though not identity, between the types of service to the nation (*Dienst am Volk*) performed by women and by men than if women concentrated on more traditionally "feminine" charitable work. But the idea of a truly feminine warrior (*Kämpferin*) entailed contradictions. The effort to express ways in which women might engage in the national struggle alongside men while cultivating their feminine identity (*weibliche Eigenart*) involved a difficult balancing act, as the following passage shows:

The border region needs strong, brave and capable people, regardless of whether they are boys or girls. What it needs are not soft and sentimental types, but people who are clear in pursuit of their goals, who know where and how they can actively intervene in situations where it is within our power to aid the Fatherland. Here, girls have the great and satisfying task of ensuring, while preserving absolute discipline and strictness in their outlook and their actions as a *Bund,* that the German spirit and the gentle soul of woman prevails.[51]

The idea of women's special mission in the public sphere almost certainly exercised a particular attraction for young women in the *Bünde* in the midst of depression and political crisis. Not only did the increasing mobilization of youth in the crisis help politicize the members of the *Bünde,* it also caused the *Bünde* to lose members of both sexes to the youth organizations of the radical political parties. The leaders of the girls' sections of the DF and the FjN watched in dismay as some of their most active members deserted them for the youth organizations of all parties, above all for that of the NSDAP.[52] In the face of this competition, the *Bünde* saw themselves becoming, despite

51. S. Scheuffele, "Meine Ostlandfahrt und Eindrücke aus der dortigen nationalen Jugendarbeit," *Das deutsche Mädel* 2 (1927): 21–4.
52. Deutsche Freischar, Mädchenführung, 2. Rundbrief 1932, September 1932, ADJB: A2-22/3; Freischar junger Nation, Land Berlin, Bericht, 15 May 1932, ADJB: A2-55/6.

their identification with the national cause, increasingly irrelevant and marginal to the new national politics. Accordingly, the *Bünde* sought a new focus for generation-based action that would enable them, as youthful pioneers, to become more closely involved in the work of national redemption.[53] One girls' leader maintained bravely that the political crisis and the crisis of the welfare state was in fact an opportunity:

The state no longer relieves us of the task of caring for ourselves and our neighbors. We can join in and lend a hand once again [*Wir dürfen wieder zupacken*]. Let us not miss this opportunity! Perhaps a great era lies ahead for our *Bund*.[54]

Women joined with men in the youth movement in expressing exaggerated hopes that the *Bünde* would provide models on which to build a new national community. Projects such as the work camp movement (*Arbeitslagerbewegung*) and the state-sponsored voluntary labor service for the unemployed (*Freiwilliger Arbeitsdienst*) were seen as means to educate German youth outside the *Bünde* to become active members of the *Volksgemeinschaft*.[55] Such hopes may have masked fears that, despite the ambitions of the *Bünde* to act as the youthful vanguard of the nation, the national mobilization was taking place without them.

Young women in the *Bünde* declared that women had a vital role in the formation of new *bündisch* forms of community life.[56] The wish to participate alongside their male comrades in public service to the nation can be interpreted in a number of different ways. At one level it can be read as a sign that they, like their male peers, were defining their public role in terms of their generational identity. Their demand for participation in the generational "front" was consistent with the view held in the mixed *Bünde* such as the DF and the FjN that, as a model for the future *Volksgemeinschaft*, the *Bund* had to incorporate both sexes. But the demand may also be interpreted as an attempt to assert specifically for women a role in the public sphere that was perceived as both vital and under threat. The ethos of service to

---

53. Helmuth Kittel, "Politische Kolonne auf der Leuchtenburg, 17. bis 24. Oktober 1931," *Deutsche Freischar* 4 (1931): 110–11.
54. 6. Rundbrief der Deutschen Freischar, Mädchenführung, December 1931, ADJB: A2-22/3.
55. Anneliese Hohberg, "Von der Schulungswoche im Boberhaus," *Mädchen* 1933, no. 2 (Spring 1933): 30. See also "Einsatzmöglichkeiten," *Mädchen* 1932, no. 5 (November 1932): 73.
56. Deutsche Freischar, Mädchenführung, 1. Rundbrief 1932, 16 Mar. 1932, ADJB: A2-22/3.

others, which was embedded in the socialization of middle-class girls[57] and writ large within the *Bünde* as service to the nation, was activated by a sense of national emergency during the crisis of the Weimar Republic. The idea, much propagated in the *Bünde,* of serving others in one of the "caring" professions open to educated middle-class girls – such as social work and teaching – was hard to pursue in an overcrowded labor market. The option of service through some other channel of public activity may thus have appeared all the more attractive. At the same time, the assertion of the importance of women's contribution may be seen as a reaction to antifeminism both within the *Bünde* and in society and politics generally. Young women in the DF were, for instance, aware of the marginalization of girls in state youth policy. They realized that the attempts by the last governments of the Weimar Republic to integrate youth into the national community focused primarily on young men.[58] Writing about the difficulties they experienced in getting involved in the voluntary labor service, they commented on the problem of obtaining the cooperation of the public authorities who "like the National Council for Youth Fitness [*Reichskuratorium für Jugendertüchtigung*] are probably of the view that 'Germany's *youth* must be made into *men* fit to fight!' "[59]

From this one can only conclude that those young women in the *Bünde* who asserted their right to a role in the public sphere did so all the more vehemently in the face of their double marginalization, first as *bündische Jugend* in relation to mass politics and then as women in relation to patriarchal structures both within the youth movement and in society as a whole.

The contrast between the "activist" and "reactionary" models of women's roles put forward within the *bündisch* milieu in the final phase of the Weimar Republic is clear. Nevertheless, it is possible to

57. On the propagation in the 1920s of psychological theories of a female *Pflegetrieb* (nurturing instinct) and on the inculcation into middle-class girls via school curricula of an ethos of serving and caring for others, see Susanne Zeller, *Volksmütter: Frauen im Wohlfahrtswesen der zwanziger Jahre* (Düsseldorf, 1987), 53–64.
58. The expansion by the Papen government of the Voluntary Labor Service from July 1932 on and the launching of the National Council for Youth Fitness (*Reichskuratorium für Jugendertüchtigung*) in September 1932 were measures pushed by von Schleicher as part of an ambitious policy to educate and mobilize (male) youth in the interests of the state. Schleicher to Papen, 17 Oct. 1932, Bundesarchiv Koblenz: R43II, 519. See also Heinrich A. Winkler, *Der Weg in die Katastrophe: Arbeiter und Arbeiterbewegung in der Weimarer Republik 1930 bis 1933* (Berlin/Bonn, 1987), 736–7.
59. "Ein 'politischer' Brief und einige Randbemerkungen," *Mädchen* 1933, no. 1 (February 1933): 13.

see a connection between them. The ideology of the *Bünde,* coupled with the conditions of the dual crisis of the Republic in its final years, discouraged young women in the *Bünde* from tackling political issues in concrete terms and encouraged them to conceive of their role in relation to politics and the public sphere in terms that were either very passive or overly ambitious. The consequence of this was to see women either firmly rooted in the domestic sphere as guardians of the national soul, building the "inner Reich," or in the public sphere, alongside their male comrades, as saviors of the nation.

IV

The final years of the Weimar Republic witnessed not merely a resurgence of reactionary ideas on women's role within the *bündisch* milieu, but a stronger polarization of views, with each camp elaborating its own ideas more fully in the process. Although some young women supported the complete withdrawal of women from the public sphere, others continued to press for an active role in the public sphere that adequately expressed their identity *as* women and *as* youth. In the latter case, generational identity interacted with gender identity to shape the ideas that young women held about their political and public roles. This raises the question of just how useful a generational perspective can be when one is looking more generally at the political views and behavior of young women in the final phase of the Weimar Republic. Can it be useful, for instance, as a way of highlighting common experiences affecting young women in the Depression? Is it fruitful to see young women's responses to the crisis as expressions of a collective "generational consciousness"?

A generational perspective may help in focusing on common experiences shared by the female members of the same age cohort. This approach was adopted by contemporary observers seeking to construct typologies of successive generations of young women growing up during the First World War and afterward. Such analyses have a clear appeal where they assess the common impact of major events and epochs, such as the First World War or the Depression, on a defined age cohort. However, the concept of generation has to be defined more precisely; on closer examination, such typologies often turn out to fit only limited portions of a cohort, defined by class. Thus, when Gertrud Staewen-Ordemann stressed the effects on a generation of young women of being caught up in the national mobilization of 1914,[60] or when Gertrud Bäumer looked at the way the Depression dampened and frustrated young women's career hopes and plans,[61] both were referring primarily to the mentality and expectations of generations of educated middle-class young women.

Identifying common experiences shared by an age cohort or a portion of an age cohort may be useful, but relating them to common responses is difficult where the Depression is concerned. Political divides among young people were becoming more fixed and insuperable during the final years of the Weimar Republic. The ideological fragmentation and polarization of youth appear to have taken particular forms in the case of young women. One expert on youth organizations across the political spectrum commented on "organized" young men that, although they might engage in political and ideological battles with each other, they were at least united by common types of activity, a common style of organization, and common ideas of masculinity. By contrast, she pointed out, "organized" young women were much more fundamentally disunited because of the vast disagreements among them regarding women's role: These conflicts added to the existing political and ideological cleavages dividing socialist from conservative, internationalist from *völkisch* young women.[62]

The problems of using a generational perspective become all the greater if one is trying to identify young women's responses to the crisis as the specific expression of a generational consciousness. To be sure, a sense of social and political marginalization as young people may have strengthened the desire on the part of some young *bündisch* women for a role in the public sphere where they could act in their specific capacity as youth alongside their male peers. However, although the experience of social and political marginalization may have extended to much wider groups of young women, a response in terms of their mission to combat the crisis as *young* women was probably less common, being specifically a product of the *bündisch* milieu and its long-standing cult of youth and youthfulness.

A generational perspective may shed light on young women's political outlook and political participation in the final years of the

60. Gertrud Staewen-Ordemann, ed., *Kameradin. Junge Frauen im deutschen Schicksal 1910–1930* (Berlin, 1936), 7–26.
61. Gertrud Bäumer, "Die Zukunft der weiblichen Jugend im deutschen Schicksal," in Emmy Wolff, ed., *12. Jahrbuch des BDF 1932 (1928–31)* (Mannheim, 1932), 66–76.
62. Josepha Fischer, "Probleme der heutigen weiblichen Jugendführung," *Das junge Deutschland* 26 (1932): 403–11.

Weimar Republic, but only if it focuses on the way the Depression polarized and fragmented any solidarity that might have existed among young women and produced responses that were diverse and not necessarily expressed in terms of generational consciousness. The women in the *Bünde* who demanded an active role in the public sphere alongside men can be seen as responding to their situation as young women in the crisis. That response may have been shared by wider circles of young women outside the *Bünde* who were frustrated by the narrowing of options open to them. However, it was only one of a range of possible responses to the crisis, and the *bündisch* rhetoric about the integration of women into a common generational front could neither disguise the disunity among women and between the sexes within the *Bünde* nor politically mobilize young women en masse.

8

Modernization, Emancipation, Mobilization: Nazi Society Reconsidered

JILL STEPHENSON

I

Elections and mass politics are features of a modern polity, even where that polity may also retain characteristics of a more archaic political form. Imperial Germany was such a hybrid, with universal manhood [sic] suffrage uneasily in tandem with authoritarian monarchical government. The exclusion of women from national political life before 1919 reflected the backward-looking cast of mind of the ruling elites, which was well illustrated in the patriarchal family law provisions of the new all-German civil code of 1900. Yet by that time, the forces of social and political change consequent on far-reaching economic and technological development, especially from the 1870s, included features that would radically alter women's role – actual and perceived – and would remove some of the practical disabilities that had, since time immemorial, been used to justify the relegation of women to subject status, subordinate to a husband or a male relative. Above all, increasing control of their own fertility permitted women to respond to new opportunities. As women became better able to compete with men, however, particularly in the employment market, artificial restraints were increasingly demanded and sometimes imposed to protect the privileged position of men in society, especially in economic and professional life.

Modernization, therefore, provided the preconditions for emancipation but did not make it inevitable. Certainly, full political modernization in Germany at the end of the First World War made the electoral mobilization of women an issue that political activists could

I should like to thank Robert Moeller and James Retallack for their helpful comments on the version of this essay discussed at the conference of the German History Society held in Toronto on 20–22 April 1990.

not afford to ignore, especially given the larger numbers of women than men eligible to vote. Even in Hitler's Germany, the political leadership's desire for active support from the population as a whole meant that women, like men, had to be courted and won over to National Socialist points of view so that they would cooperate in policies that might – or, more often, might not – benefit them. Individuals' interests were to be willingly subordinated to the regime's demands and priorities. This meant that individual measures that perhaps *appeared* to give women greater opportunity did not amount to emancipation at all, because they were enacted for short-term motives and might be reversed when circumstances changed. And in other respects, of course, women's fortunes were arbitrarily controlled by a branch of the state's or the party's apparatus, with an at least partially successful assault on women's freedom of maneuver by a dictatorial masculine political elite.

Individual countries have experienced the modernization process at different times, and within countries some regions have experienced it earlier than others. Modernization has also had at times contrasting emphases in its effects on men and women; it has also had a varying impact on rural and urban inhabitants. Where modernization is seen as "progressive," areas touched by it little or late are regarded as "backward," and those people who oppose the disruption it occasions are dismissed as "reactionary." As far as women are concerned, the two aspects of modernized society that particularly determine their place within it have been employment opportunity and fertility control – production and reproduction. It is no coincidence that the two major areas of Nazi policy that particularly affected women as women were the Nazis' fundamental fixation with population policy and the regime's response to the economic problems and possibilities of the 1930s and early 1940s. It was not alone among governments of the time in facing these problems and seeking to solve them by resort to a combination of old-fashioned and new policies. In the Soviet Union, France, and Austria, for example, there were clear instances of both the kinds of issue that confronted German governments in the interwar years and the solutions to which they resorted.[1]

1. Urie Bronfenbrenner, "The Changing Soviet Family," in Donald R. Brown, ed., *The Role and Status of Women in the Soviet Union* (New York, 1968), 99–106; Susan Bridger, *Women in the Soviet Countryside* (Cambridge, 1987), 9–17; James F. McMillan, *Housewife or Harlot: The Place of Women in French Society, 1870–1940* (Brighton, 1981), 163–92; Maité Albistur and Daniel Armogathe, *Histoire du Feminisme Français du moyen âge à nos jours* (Paris, 1977), 392–7; Edith Rigler, *Frauenleitbild und Frauenarbeit in Österreich vom ausgehenden 19. Jahrhun-*

There has been much debate about whether the Nazi regime was reactionary and backward-looking or – even if perhaps unwittingly – a modernizing force. This has normally been viewed as a class issue, with proponents of the "reactionary" interpretation arguing that Hitler was more than content to maintain the existing social structure while cynically trying to persuade Germans (especially in the urban manual working class) that the old class-based society was being superseded by a *Volksgemeinschaft* in which old status barriers were irrelevant. On the other hand, authors from Ralf Dahrendorf and David Schoenbaum onward have argued, for example, that by disregarding traditional class or caste grounds for preferment in a variety of areas, the National Socialists were effecting revolutionary social change – a view that Hitler himself came to favor.[2] But as Detlev Peukert recognized, this modernizing aspect and the unparalleled horrors occasioned by the industrialization of racial persecution and genocide are indivisible; the linkage between "normality and modernity in a society, and fascist barbarism" calls into question the idea of modernization as "progressive."[3] The development of National Socialism before 1933 as a political force can be seen as a direct result of modernization and as a reaction against some of its effects, even though the Nazis were relentless in utilizing its facilities for their own heinous and often bizarre purposes. This apparent contradiction has led Jeffrey Herf to coin the term "reactionary modernism" to try to explain the relationship between tradition and technology in Nazism.[4]

Modernization has, in the nineteenth and twentieth centuries, meant the breakdown of the old land-based feudal order in economic, social, and political terms. This has occurred under pressure from newer forces – capitalism, liberalism, rationalism, secularism – and the development of urban, industrial society based on market economics, waged labor, mechanized transport, mass production

---

dert bis zum Zweiten Weltkrieg (Munich, 1976), 132–53; Josef Ehmer, "Frauenarbeit und Arbeiterfamilie in Wien vom Vormärz bis 1934," *Geschichte und Gesellschaft* 7 (1981): 422–3, 453–7, 464–73.

2. Ralf Dahrendorf, *Society and Democracy in Germany* (London, 1968), 402–18; David Schoenbaum, *Hitler's Social Revolution. Class and Status in Nazi Germany, 1933–39* (London, 1967), 245–301. On the last point, see Rainer Zitelmann, *Hitler. Selbstverständnis eines Revolutionärs*, 2nd ed. (Stuttgart, 1987), 457, 486, 488.
3. Detlev J. K. Peukert, *Inside Nazi Germany. Conformity, Opposition and Racism in Everyday Life*, trans. Richard Deveson (London, 1987), 16.
4. Jeffrey Herf, *Reactionary Modernism. Technology, Culture and Politics in Weimar and the Third Reich* (Cambridge, 1984), 1–2, and passim.

and consumption, and increasing state regulation. Industrial and technological progress has brought far-reaching social changes, including the creation of new urban structures and, often, the destruction of traditional communities and culture, with the disorientation of those uprooted from traditional village society and thrust into the expanding urban melting pots of the pre– and post–First World War periods. The processes of modernization in Germany – especially rapid industrialization and urbanization – were a long-term development that had, by the 1930s, "transformed [Germany] from an agrarian and newly industrializing nation at the time of Unification to a fully industrialized nation."[5] The major transition in German economic and social conditions was effected before the First World War, even if substantial areas – especially in the south and east – essentially retained their traditional styles and structures. That this transition took place without fundamental political change, specifically democratization, is at the heart of the *Sonderweg* debate that dominated much of German historical scholarship in the 1970s and 1980s.[6] It is now clear, though, that industrialization can occur within virtually any kind of polity and that its effects do not necessarily include liberalizing political change, at least in the short term (consider Soviet Russia). The immediate areas of change consequent on industrialization and urbanization are not necessarily political but rather socioeconomic and demographic – the very areas that strongly exercised the Nazi leadership and that governed much of their policy toward women. This has ensured that although modernization is indeed a class issue, it is also a gender issue.

John E. Knodel is of the view that the "emancipation of women" is a customary concomitant of modernization.[7] Certainly, *in the long term,* modernization has tended to improve women's position, in absolute terms and vis-à-vis men. As industrial society developed, women's literacy rates and educational opportunities improved – although generally to a lesser extent than men's – enabling them eventually to compete with men for better-paid posts in the civil service and the professions and to make certain areas of clerical and other white-collar work their own preserve. It was a sure sign of women's increasing fitness for, and aspirations to, such posts that

5. John E. Knodel, *The Decline of Fertility in Germany, 1871–1939* (Princeton, N.J., 1974), 225.
6. Charles S. Maier, *The Unmasterable Past. History, Holocaust, and German National Identity* (Cambridge, Mass., and London, 1988), 102ff, gives a brief and cogent critique of *Sonderweg* theory.
7. Knodel, *Fertility,* 229.

their male competitors did their best to undermine their chances of appointment. This was particularly evident in the legal and medical professions and in higher education, but it applied also in other nonmanual areas.[8] This, then, is one reason why modernization is a gender issue, although it would perhaps be extravagant to see it entirely as a "battle of the sexes."

The corollary of this is that women living and working in rural areas were not emancipated, that they had fewer rights and less freedom of action than women in modern urban society. Part of rural tradition was that a farmer's wife, daughters, and other female adherents worked on the family farm without receiving formal remuneration. This put them in the census category of "assisting family members," which well reflected their dependent status and function, one that persisted at least into the Second World War.[9] I have argued elsewhere that in some sections of society, especially in the *Mittelstand*, the work and responsibilities that devolved onto women in small business and agriculture during the Second World War were generally experienced as burdensome and as the antithesis of emancipation.[10] Not surprisingly, then, one of the major characteristics of modernization is migration from the countryside to the towns; even though there was plenty of urban squalor and hardship, the brutal drudgery of life on the land made the gamble of uprooting oneself and seeking some fortune in an unfamiliar environment one that seemed to many to promise favorable odds, for women as well as men.

In some respects, modernization affected men and women differently. Particularly in the manual working class, women were left to shoulder the double burden of paid work and housework, based on a reluctance to turn down the opportunity of paid employment and instead remain at home to look after the house and family. On the

---

8. Michael H. Kater, *Doctors under Hitler* (Chapel Hill, N.C., and London, 1989), 89–90; Jill Stephenson, "Women and the Professions in Germany, 1900–1945," in Geoffrey Cocks and Konrad Jarausch, eds., *German Professions, 1800–1950* (New York and Oxford, 1990), 273–9; Carole Elizabeth Adams, *Women Clerks in Wilhelmine Germany. Issues of Class and Gender* (Cambridge, 1988), 12–15, 26–30, 35, 37–8; Ute Frevert, "Traditionale Weiblichkeit und moderne Interessenorganisation: Frauen im Angestelltenberuf 1918–1933," *Geschichte und Gesellschaft* 7 (1981): 510–33.
9. See tables based on censuses in *Statistisches Jahrbuch für das Deutsche Reich* (St.J.), published annually by the Statistisches Reichsamt, Berlin. The term was still in use in *Statistisches Jahrbuch für die Bundesrepublik Deutschland* (Berlin, 1959), 115, giving the results of the 1957 census.
10. Jill Stephenson, "'Emancipation' and Its Problems: War and Society in Württemberg 1939–45," *European History Quarterly* 17 (1987): 345–65.

land, there was increasingly demanding farm work for women, as well as household chores. Before the days of consumer durables, convenience foods, and supermarkets, ordinary household duties like shopping, cleaning, and cooking – to say nothing of providing care for children – were extraordinarily time-consuming. Carrying this double burden of paid work and housework was indeed onerous. Arthur E. Imhof has attributed to it the persistence of high rates of mortality in the younger, childbearing cohorts of women in the nineteenth century, although from the early twentieth century on, German women's life expectancy began to outstrip men's in all age groups as industrialization and modernization affected a majority of Germans.[11] This is one of the greatest advantages over men that modernization has brought women in the twentieth century.

Nevertheless, the critical factor that helps to make modernization a gender issue is that the processes of modernization over which man [sic] has had control have been determined by men. In the later nineteenth century, work in heavy industry was circumscribed by what male strength and stamina could tolerate. Conditions and hours of work took little account of family or household demands because male employees were deemed to have either a mother or a wife to attend to these things at home.[12] In the professions, whose size and significance grew rapidly from the later nineteenth century, entrance qualifications were explicitly determined by middle-class male educational standards. Especially before women were admitted to German universities (beginning in Baden in 1900), this meant that overwhelming male dominance was assured; in some cases, as in the legal profession, a male monopoly prevailed.[13] Women thus have had to meet male standards of achievement in order to have a chance of competing with men in arenas where skill, intelligence, training, and stamina are prerequisites for access, appointment, or promotion. Where there has been a clear division of labor between "men's work"

---

11. Gabrielle Wellner, "Industriearbeiterinnen in der Weimarer Republik: Arbeitsmarkt, Arbeit und Privatleben 1919–1933," *Geschichte und Gesellschaft* 7 (1981): 550–3; Arthur E. Imhof, "Women, Family and Death: Excess Mortality of Women in Child-bearing Age in Four Communities in Nineteenth-century Germany," in Richard J. Evans and W. R. Lee, eds., *The German Family. Essays on the Social History of the Family in Nineteenth- and Twentieth-Century Germany* (London, 1981), 149–55, 172. See also Hartmut Kaelble, *Industrialization and Social Inequality in 19th-century Europe* (Leamington Spa, 1986), 133–7.
12. The first factory social workers were, however, appointed before 1914. See Carola Sachse, *Industrial Housewives. Women's Social Work in the Factories of Nazi Germany* (New York and London, 1987), 15–16.
13. Stephenson, "Professions," 274–5; Kater, *Doctors,* 89–90.

and "women's work," the latter has been explicitly lower in status and generally significantly less well paid. This was the case particularly in the expanding area of clerical work, where women were generally admitted only to the lower grades, while the more prestigious and better-paid positions remained the preserve of men.[14] None of this, of course, was peculiar to Germany.

During the twentieth century, the industrialization of warfare has helped to define the varying (and sometimes contradictory) set of roles that women are called upon to fulfill in modern society. Above all, particularly in times of job shortage, attitudes toward women's employment are at best ambivalent and often hostile, among some women as well as men.[15] It is then that the true extent of women's opportunities is revealed, and is revealed to be conditional in a way that opportunities for men are not. If job vacancies consistently exist in the economy as a whole, or even in only some sectors of it, women are welcomed as employees; especially in wartime, they are expected or actually required to make good the labor deficit. If the opposite is the case – that is, if there are not enough jobs for available men – then women are expected to make way for them. The "primacy of economics," therefore, powerfully determines women's opportunities, at least in the short term, in modernized societies, whatever the political complexion of government. This is true not merely of employment but also of education and training: When work requiring recognizable skills is undersubscribed by men, women have to be turned into capable recruits, whereas when there are sufficient skilled men, the preparation of women for skilled work has a low priority.

In short, methods of production and conditions in the employment market, whether it operates freely or under government control, have done much to determine the extent to which women are permitted, or even required, to work outside the home and, ultimately, to seek a place alongside men in the public service and in public life. But perhaps even more fundamental to women's capability and availability for work is their ability to control their own fertility. Without this, women's capacity for exercising rights and responsibilities both within and beyond the home and family is ar-

---

14. Adams, *Women Clerks*, 7–19.
15. Helen R. Boak, "The State as an Employer of Women in the Weimar Republic," in W. R. Lee and Eve Rosenhaft, eds., *The State and Social Change in Germany, 1880–1980* (New York, Oxford, and Munich, 1990), 68–90, 96–7; Stephenson, "Professions," 276, 279–80.

bitrarily circumscribed, whether the absence of reliable methods of birth control is due to technological underdevelopment or to political (or religio-political) obscurantism. The more primitive a society, the greater the resort to abortion, or even infanticide, as means of family limitation. By contrast, successful contraception prevents not only births but also the start of pregnancies that may not come to term, whether through spontaneous or contrived abortion. Modernization has also brought advances in nutrition, public health, and hygiene, all of which have helped to reduce dramatically the levels of miscarriage, perinatal mortality, and infant mortality.[16] Thus, where heirs are desired, fewer conceptions and births have sufficed to secure an inheritance. The impact of these developments on women's health and strength, and therefore on their ability to develop aspirations and skills, can hardly be exaggerated. Together, the "primacy of biology" and the "primacy of economics" are the chief determinants of women's status and women's freedom to act as responsible individuals in modern industrial society.

In the Third Reich, official attitudes to these determinants seemed at first compatible in a time of deep economic depression; but from about 1936 they came increasingly into conflict with each other. The Nazis' programmatic desire to raise the birthrate and to maintain the allegedly traditional role and status of German "Aryan" women as primarily that of housewife and mother – with its corollary of compulsory abortion and sterilization for "less valuable" women[17] – was at odds with their drive to exploit modern technology in industry, in business, and ultimately in waging war. It also conflicted with the effort to mobilize all available reserves of labor, female labor included. The creation of hundreds of thousands of new jobs between 1933 and 1939 dictated the need for extra labor at a time when the declining birthrate cohorts of the First World War years and after were producing fewer new recruits for the job market.[18] At the same

16. There was, e.g., a dramatic reduction in the level of infant mortality in Germany: per 100 live births, the following number died in infancy: 1905, 20.5; 1910, 16.2; 1915, 14.8; 1920, 13.1; 1925, 10.5; 1930, 8.6; Figures from *St.J.*, 1933, 46. See also Kaelble, *Industrialization and Social Inequality*, 143–7.
17. Gisela Bock, "Racism and Sexism in Nazi Germany: Motherhood, Compulsory Sterilization, and the State," in Renate Bridenthal, Atina Grossmann, and Marion Kaplan, eds., *When Biology Became Destiny. Women in Weimar and Nazi Germany* (New York, 1984), 271–96. See also Gisela Bock, *Zwangssterilisation im Nationalsozialismus. Untersuchungen zur Rassenpolitik und Frauenpolitik* (Opladen, 1986).
18. The birth rate (number of live births per 1,000 inhabitants) was as follows: 1850s, 35; 1860s, 37; 1870s, 39; 1880s, 37; 1890s, 36; 1900s, 33; 1915, 20; 1916, 15; 1917, 14; 1918, 14; 1919, 20. From *St.J.*, 1921–2, 37.

time, extra demands were being made of school leavers and students, with compulsory service schemes, including the Labor Service, as well as compulsory military service for young men. Thus women were called on to fill vacancies in virtually all sectors of the economy in the late 1930s and during the war. There is nothing particularly unusual about this. Women had taken over jobs vacated by conscripted men during the First World War, in Germany and in other belligerent countries, and would do so again in the Second. But this attempt in the Third Reich at a *mobilization* of female resources (even before the war) has been seen by some as providing, at least in practice, the long overdue *emancipation* of women in industry, white-collar work, education, the professions – that is, across class barriers.[19]

In the Third Reich, mobilization was to mean more than simply recruiting women to fill vacancies in both the employment market and party-sponsored service schemes. A "politicization" of German women was to be effected – by the Nazi Party and its women's organizations – so that they would respond to government requirements automatically, with the unthinking willingness of a hypnotic. Women were to accept the desperate need for more "racially valuable" (and fewer "racially worthless") children and to cooperate with Nazi population policies. They were to encourage their children to accept indoctrination at school and through the Nazi youth organizations. They were to be prepared primarily to work in areas designated as "women's work," for example, in kindergartens or girls' schools, or as nurses or social workers. Otherwise, they were to withdraw from paid employment when there were substantial numbers of men out of work and to return to work when there was a shortage of male labor. They were to sacrifice their own career aspirations to family duties and to the higher priority given to German men. Put another way, they were to pursue a career when they were needed and only for as long as they were needed. Like men, they were to accept the overriding will of the Nazi establishment, but to a much greater extent than men, they were to adapt to changing condi-

---

19. See the discussion in Ute Frevert, *Women in German History. From Bourgeois Emancipation to Sexual Liberation* (Oxford, Hamburg, and New York, 1989), 240–52. Jacques R. Pauwels, *Women, Nazis and Universities. Female University Students in the Third Reich, 1933–1945* (Westport, Conn., 1984), 132–4, writes of an "academic emancipation of women" taking place during the Second World War as a means of sustaining the war effort. Joan Campbell, *Joy in Work, German Work* (Princeton, N.J., 1989), 367, emphasizes women's "new opportunities for relatively skilled and interesting employment outside the home."

tions regardless of the pattern of their own personal and employment development. Women were to function as a "reserve army" of conscripts, for deployment wherever personnel shortages appeared, from engineering to farm work. It is now well known that Nazi policies toward women were not only discriminatory and damaging but also in some respects unsuccessful, especially as far as mobilizing women in the urban middle classes was concerned.[20] That does not minimize the extent to which some women were damaged, whether in terms of being denied career opportunities or physically, through either abortion and sterilization or unwanted pregnancy.

II

How, then, can any of this be termed "emancipation"? It all depends, of course, on one's definition of emancipation. Yet, even by the most elastic interpretation, it would be difficult to argue that the subordinate role assigned to women's interests in Nazi society served to extend women's rights or horizons. It is true that some women enjoyed enhanced opportunities, but that was incidental, merely a byproduct of circumstances that the regime either could not or would not control. There was no emancipation by any liberal definition embracing formal equality and the removal of artificial barriers to advancement based on gender. In fact, quite the reverse happened: New barriers were erected to curtail existing opportunities for women. First and foremost, women were excluded from all genuine positions of responsibility in both party and state in the Third Reich. If it is true that few women had held high office in the Weimar Republic, and that most men were excluded from political responsibility in Nazi Germany, the fact remains that the only people wielding real power and authority were, as a matter of deliberate principle, men. And in Hitler's intrusive dictatorship, these men claimed comprehensive rights of control, even (or perhaps *especially*) over the most intimate aspects of a woman's life, particularly those concerned with reproduction.

Before the Third Reich, the extent to which women had enjoyed opportunities, responsibilities, and choice was seriously limited, al-

---

20. Dörte Winkler, *Frauenarbeit im "Dritten Reich"* (Hamburg, 1977), 107–12, 121, 141–4; Leila J. Rupp, *Mobilizing Women for War. German and American Propaganda, 1939–1945* (Princeton, N.J., 1978), 107, 110–11, 172; Jill Stephenson, *The Nazi Organization of Women* (London, 1981), 180–8.

though the Weimar years generally saw an improvement over their position in Wilhelmine Germany. But the term "emancipation" can be justifiably applied to Weimar Germany as long as it is restricted to the removal of disabilities that restrained women before 1918 and as long as it is not confused with the complete liberation of women from every kind of discrimination and exclusion on grounds of gender. Gaining the vote at the national level in 1918 is the most obvious example of the removal of an artificial constraint. Similarly, women were at last admitted to the legal profession in 1922 and were to have equality of opportunity in the civil service – in theory. But continuing institutional or statutory barriers to equal treatment through terms of appointment, pay, and promotion – to say nothing of informal but deep-rooted prejudice, such as the fact that being married was regarded as a disability for women but not for men – meant that women's emancipation, even by this restricted liberal definition, was piecemeal and limited even before the Depression and the Nazi takeover of power.[21]

The liberation of women, or absolute emancipation, is concisely defined by Ute Frevert:

equal legal and material participation by men and women in social life, in the exercise of power and in decision-making in the economic, social, cultural and political system . . . requir[ing] equal access to the resources of action, and an end to gender-specific ascription of spheres of action.[22]

In the 1920s, this was hardly a viable proposition. Only a few radical feminists and the Communist Party called for complete equality of men and women in all aspects of life, and some radical feminists demanded the abolition of labor protection measures for women on the grounds that these were used as an excuse for discriminating against women in employment opportunities.[23] The conditions for absolute emancipation would have included free access to all means of birth control, including legal abortion; substantial paid maternity leave; the provision of state- or employer-funded nurseries; fully coeducational schooling at all levels; equal access to every kind of paid employment; equal pay for equal work; and a thorough reform of the civil code's provisions that gave a husband or a father far-reaching authority in the home. Virtually none of this had been implemented

21. This is the well-illustrated argument in Boak, "The State as Employer of Women," 61–98. See also Kater, *Doctors*, 89–90, 92; Stephenson, "Professions," 275–80.
22. Frevert, *Women in German History*, 4.
23. Jill Stephenson, *Women in Nazi Society* (London, 1975), 9, 77–8.

by 1933, and few liberals (let alone conservatives) would have supported such an agenda.

The trajectory of modernization in Germany, as elsewhere, was determined by men, and it imposed conditions that favored the retention of a modified form of patriarchal society, with priority and authority in all sectors of life, both inside and outside the home, residing decisively with men. Perhaps this was inevitable in a highly developed capitalist economy that strongly accentuated the private ownership of property and its transmission by male-oriented inheritance laws. In the 1920s, conservatism on the "woman question" prevailed among both men and women and across the political spectrum from the churches, the DNVP and the Center Party to the Social Democratic Party and its trade union grouping, the ADGB. This meant that even moderate liberal emancipatory measures were widely unpopular and therefore neglected. At the same time, some of the gains made for women in the early years of the Republic – such as equality for women, including married women, in the public service – either were revoked or came increasingly under threat.[24]

Above all, conservatism informed attitudes toward Germany's demographic development. The mounting concern about the size and quality of the population that was visible before 1914 became obsessive in the 1930s, and not only in Nazi and Nationalist circles: in 1920, the Social Democratic Reich minister of the interior, Carl Severing, appointed a committee to investigate the extent of and reasons for Germany's declining birthrate, which was higher than that of France but significantly lower than the birthrates of Germany's eastern Slavic neighbors. It was not understood that the same process of modernization that had, in a few decades, produced large-scale industry and urbanization had also brought irreversible changing patterns of fertility, resulting in what the Nazis castigated as "the one- and two-child Weimar system," especially in the towns.[25] In the 1920s and 1930s, conservatives saw the decline in the birthrate as evidence of postwar decadence, of the spread of information about and assistance with birth control, whose entire ethos they condemned.

This attitude was shared by both the Roman Catholic and Evan-

---

24. Boak, "The State as Employer of Women," 68–90, 96–7.
25. Paul Weindling, *Health, Race and German Politics Between National Unification and Nazism, 1870–1945* (Cambridge, 1989), 446–8; Knodel, *Fertility*, 206–11. The number of live births per 1,000 women of childbearing age was: 1910–11, 128; 1922, 90; 1926, 71; 1929, 69; 1930, 67; 1931, 62; 1932, 60; 1933, 59; 1934, 73; 1935, 77; 1936, 78; 1937, 77; 1938, 81; 1939, 85; 1940, 84. Figures from *St.J.*: 1938, 47; 1941–2, 77.

gelical churches and the National Socialist leadership, especially in view of the extremely low birthrates in the Depression years.[26] Birth control, they said, was used to enable women to take paid work as a long-term occupation, in the expectation that an unplanned pregnancy would not occur to disrupt it. This accusation, leveled by the pronatalists, was self-evidently true and described an eminently rational course of action. Of course, birth control of one kind or another – including abortion and infanticide, as well as contraception – had been utilized long before the twentieth century. And freedom from arbitrary pregnancy was by no means complete in Germany circa 1930, as an annual rate of abortions estimated at between half a million and a million testified. But the plummeting birthrate during the Depression was a clear demonstration that voluntary control of fertility was widely possible and practiced. Groups providing cheap contraceptive advice and devices – groups often associated with the political parties of the left – offered a service particularly to overburdened working-class wives.[27]

The Depression was a major reason for Hitler's accession to power in 1933, but it was also the environment in which particular hostility intensified toward women in paid work, whether manual, clerical, or professional, and in higher education. There was a shrinking market in all sectors of employment, exacerbated by the fact that women were at times preferred to men as employees because they were cheaper and more docile. Clearly, this had little to do with opening up opportunities for women and much to do with "the laws of the market" and employer opportunism. Against this background, it seemed in the initial years of the Third Reich as if the "primacy of economics" and the "primacy of biology" could be reconciled, conveniently achieving congruence between conservative and Nazi objectives. If possible, women were to be removed from paid employment to make way for unemployed men, and were to be encouraged to be not only full-time housewives but also mothers of large families: so far, so traditional. The reinforcing of measures taken or proposed in the later Weimar years, such as restrictions on women's employment in the public service and a quota imposed – but never fully enforced – on women's admission to higher education,[28]

26. Weindling, *Health, Race*, 459; Stephenson, *Women*, 57, 60–1.
27. Atina Grossmann, "Abortion and Economic Crisis: The 1931 Campaign Against Paragraph 218," in Bridenthal et al., eds., *Biology*, 66–86; Stephenson, *Women*, 58–60.
28. Stephenson, *Women*, 85–9, 133–4, 155–9; Pauwels, *Nazis, Women*, 21, 29, 36, 39.

reassured conservatives that the days of actual or threatened emancipation for women were over.

But the Nazi leadership desired much more than the relegation of women to domestic concerns of "women's work" and the raising of the birthrate: These backward-looking aims formed only one strand of their socioeconomic objectives. Beyond these, they attempted a colossal and perverted exercise in social engineering to realize their racial and imperial fantasies. In population policy, they wanted not merely *more* children but specifically more "racially and hereditarily valuable" children born to families who had not demonstrated "asocial behavior patterns." The grotesque corollary of this policy – that "undesirable" persons were to be prevented from procreating – posed an additional arithmetical problem, since it implied fewer births in some sections of the population. Thus the "valuable" families would have to compensate for that shortfall *as well as* contribute extra children to raise the total birthrate quantitatively. This self-imposed problem helps to explain the manic nature of large-scale Nazi campaigns to try to persuade the "racially valuable" to procreate.[29]

Ideas about managing population growth not merely quantitatively but also qualitatively predated the First World War. Eugenics was a new science whose theories about the eradication of genetic disorders through selective procreation were first given official sanction in the 1920s, and were then utterly distorted and abused by the National Socialists in their quest for "racial purity," as defined in their own perverted way.[30] This aspect of the "primacy of biology" had a direct impact on women in the Third Reich. As Gisela Bock has shown, compulsory sterilization of those judged to be less than "valuable" was inflicted on women as well as on men. The idea of "genetic disorders" was criminally and brutally distorted to embrace new Nazi definitions of racial or hereditary "disease," as well as a loosely defined illness like "schizophrenia" and nonspecific, nonmedical criteria like "asociality." A virtual industry was constructed on the basis of Nazi criteria to seek out and compel unwilling victims to undergo

---

29. Bock, "Racism and Sexism," 273, 276, 284–5; Jill Stephenson, "'Reichsbund der Kinderreichen': The League of Large Families in the Population Policy of Nazi Germany," *European Studies Review* 9 (1979): 350–75.
30. For contrasting recent views of the theory and practice of eugenics before 1933, see Ann Taylor Allen, "German Radical Feminism and Eugenics, 1900–1906," *German Studies Review* 11 (1988): 32–5, 44–5; Paul Weindling, "Eugenics and the Welfare State during the Weimar Republic," in Lee and Rosenhaft, eds., *State and Social Change*, 131–60.

sterilization; doctors and lawyers, among others, were deeply implicated in the procedure.[31]

Nazi government attempts from 1933 to close down birth control clinics and to reduce abortion by introducing swingeing penalties certainly made life more difficult for women; yet Himmler lamented in 1940 that there were still as many as 600,000 abortions annually.[32] And tireless pronatalist propaganda campaigns had little success in persuading "valuable" Germans that a large family could be anything other than a serious financial burden. It is true that various benefits were paid to parents of large families, largely financed by taxing the childless. But these amounts – paid to the father, not the mother[33] – even when they were recurrent, were insufficient to compensate for an extra mouth to feed and for prolongation of the period when the full-time mother could not contribute to the family income. This was perceived particularly in urban areas, where overcrowding could occur, whereas in rural areas, especially where the influence of the Catholic Church was strong, there continued to be larger families – even if they were mostly not as large as the Nazis would have liked.[34] On a farm, the mother's labor would be only partly and temporarily foregone during late pregnancy and the birth and infancy of the child. For a woman factory or clerical worker, by contrast, the imminence and arrival of a baby could mean the final loss of a job whose remuneration was vital to the family's income. The help of a female member of an extended family in looking after the child was much less likely in a town than in the countryside, because many urban workers were first-generation townspeople, remote from their families, and because accommodation problems in towns made it less likely that different generations would live at close quarters.

III

The precondition of complete emancipation is a policy by which individual autonomy and self-determination are sacrosanct. In the Third Reich, this was patently not the case, as the clear order of priorities demonstrated. First came "the common good before self-

---

31. Bock, "Racism and Sexism," 272–82, 286–7; Kater, *Doctors,* 118–19, 143–4.
32. Stephenson, *Women,* 68. Bock, "Racism and Sexism," 278–9, reports that in 1937 Himmler gave estimates of between 400,000 and 800,000 abortions per year.
33. Bock, "Racism and Sexism," 284–5.
34. Stephenson, "'Reichsbund'," 363–4, 367–9.

interest," as defined by the Nazi leadership; then came the needs of "racially desirable," nondeviant male members of society, whether they simply needed a paying job or had study or career aspirations. Women came a poor third, providing a convenient floating resource to be tapped in varying quantities, as necessary, for whatever sector was understaffed, whether in factories, in agriculture, or ultimately, even in the armed forces. Even before 1933, in the Depression – the major crisis of the modernized economy – it seemed as if the basic aim of increasing the birthrate would be compatible with this policy, since jobs were scarce: Women could concentrate on the production of factory and cannon fodder. The "primacy of economics" demanded that women either sacrifice job opportunities in favor of men or else replace men at lower rates of pay to favor an employer. This climate enhanced traditional prejudices and brought discriminatory, if pragmatic, responses, ranging from the pope's encyclical of 1931, *Quadragesimo Anno,* to legislation in the Reichstag in May 1932 that permitted the dismissal of a married woman from the public service if her husband was employed.[35]

However, with the remarkable economic recovery of 1933–9, the National Socialist government suffered increasingly from the problems of success. It experienced actual and imminent shortages of personnel in key areas of the modernized economy, not only in heavy and light industry but also in skilled white-collar and professional areas and in the plethora of organizations associated with the Nazi Party where female doctors especially were in demand.[36] Women formed the only substantial reserve of potential employees and students, and many were therefore able to find employment or a place in a university or college. With men called up in 1939 and afterward, women had to be persuaded to make good the shortages. It cannot be denied that this provided unprecedented opportunities for women, but these always lay within the lines of demarcation arbitrarily drawn by Hitler's periodic dogmatic pronouncements. For example, when asked by Hess in 1936 to give a ruling on whether female lawyers should continue to be permitted to participate in the work of a court of law – which Hess opposed – Hitler decided that they should not.[37]

The career opportunities that opened up for women from about 1936 certainly benefited those able to take advantage of them. For

35. Stephenson, *Women,* 19, 151–3; Boak, "State as Employer," 82–9.
36. Kater, *Doctors,* 107–9.
37. Stephenson, *Women,* 170–3.

example, there was a significant and steady increase in the number of qualified female doctors during the Third Reich, even if they continued to figure disproportionately highly in the lower and generalist sectors of the profession.[38] But this could hardly be called emancipation because it was merely short-term pragmatism and was not based on the principle of equality of opportunity for men and women: There could be no guarantee that this development would not be reversed in the future, and there is every reason to believe that it would have been had a shortage of jobs occurred again. It just so happened that, for a time, as a result of the Nazis' own policies, the "primacy of economics" worked in favor of women with career ambitions. For those women who, for financial reasons, had no choice but to take paid employment, at least they were now able to suffer the tedium or drudgery of work without also being castigated for depriving a man of a job. For those women who neither wished nor were required to take employment, who had been pleased to be able to remain full-time housewives when that was what Nazi propaganda preached, there was now the irritation and the threat of being put under pressure to go out to work "in the national interest."

Thus, once again, it was the demands of the "primacy of economics" that determined these opportunities. One proof of this is the way in which the "compulsory year of service" scheme, introduced in February 1938, was to apply specifically to teenage girls who were neither taking a job in industry nor embarking on higher education. Those voluntarily following a career path that would promote the government's policies were exempted from this unpopular conscription into either farm work or domestic service, whereas those settling for low-priority jobs – in the tobacco industry or in clerical work, for example – were at least temporarily to serve the government's purpose in areas designated by it as being in particular need of extra staff.[39] To try to generate extra recruits for both the armed forces and occupations that were short of labor, senior schooling was reduced by a year in 1938, although Bernhard Rust, the education minister, also referred to "important reasons of population policy" that lay behind this measure. In this case, the interests of "economics" and "biology" coincided, but the character of the new education structures for girls, which were markedly different from those for boys, showed that "biology" was paramount. The intention clearly

38. Kater, *Doctors*, 89–91.
39. Stephenson, *Women*, 104–5.

remained to educate men and women in different disciplines, separately, to accord with the roles that they were (it was said) most likely to assume in adult life. Accordingly, girls were to be diverted from most scientific subjects and the classics in favor of modern languages and homecraft.[40] The fact that within a few years, in wartime, this proved to be inadequate preparation for the increased numbers of female students now required in all disciplines does not alter the way in which it reflected the regime's long-term aims.

IV

Most of these developments were more applicable to the urban than to the rural population. The gap between the aspirations and rewards enjoyed by the two groups therefore widened in the last few years of peace as the modernized economy expanded and became geared for war. By 1939, the available *and willing* reserves of female labor had been absorbed into the employment market.[41] A new flexibility was built into the system through promotion of the idea of half-day factory work for women with families, although fewer women took up this option than the Nazis had hoped. Also, as Carola Sachse has shown, there was continuity from the Second Empire to the Third Reich in the idea of employing factory social workers to minister to the needs of working women at their workplace – helping them to manage their domestic responsibilities while in full-time work – and, at the same time, to instill in them attitudes acceptable to the prevailing regime.[42]

These facilities were peculiar to industrialized society and contrasted markedly with the harshness of life on the land for many, especially peasant families on smallholdings. One indicator of the contrast between town and country was a rate of infant mortality in rural areas that was markedly higher than that in urban areas, suggesting that even in the inner-city areas of modern society, the environment was more conducive to healthy childbearing and rearing.[43] When some rural women were, for the first time, brought into

40. Ibid., 121–3.
41. Winkler, *Frauenarbeit,* 102–3; Stephenson, *Women,* 101–3.
42. Sachse, *Industrial Housewives,* 33, 39–40, 44–54.
43. As a very rough indicator, rates of infant mortality per 100 live births were consistently lower in Berlin and Saxony than in Pomerania and Bavaria in the years 1913 and 1928–37. See *St.J.*: 1933, 46; 1938, 66.

close contact with urban women who had been evacuated to rural areas during the war, they could hardly believe their assertiveness in complaining about the deprivation that they had to endure in the countryside as evacuees and their extravagant (by rural standards) expectations. The townswomen, for their part, despised the peasants for apparently tolerating squalor and hardship as their inevitable lot.[44] Being brought face-to-face with the products of modernized society in this way, or receiving some assistance from Labor Service recruits with an urban background, at last opened up new vistas for some women, usually younger ones. They then could hardly wait to escape to a town where they expected to find greater freedom and a wage-earning job.[45]

The attractiveness to young female country dwellers of life in the towns, the centers of the modernized economy, compared with the drudgery of rural life, suggests that even in a repressive polity, modernization can bring an emancipation of women in at least one sense: liberation from virtually forced labor on the family farm without the reward of a regular rate-for-the-job wage. Throughout the Third Reich, women's role on the land continued to be the traditional dual one of worker as well as wife and mother. This would be reinforced by the renewed flight from the land during the 1930s as the economic upturns strengthened and the shortage of farm labor became acute. During the war, the conscription of farmers and male farm laborers led to even greater hardship for rural women.[46] Whether before or after 1933, it is clear that even limited emancipation was not an option for women as long as they remained on the land.

Further, "primacy of biology" considerations burdened both rural and urban women and undermined any potential for more than limited emancipation for the latter. If traditionalists had felt defensive in matters connected with sexual activity and reproduction in the 1920s, the Third Reich promoted a reassertion of conservative views about women held by broad sections of German society, with the effects of the Depression seeming to justify their prejudices. Yet, as Robert Moeller has pointed out, the eugenics side of the Nazis' biological equation was *modern,* a new development dating from the turn of the

44. Stephenson, "'Emancipation'," 358–9.
45. Jill Stephenson, "Women's Labor Service in Nazi Germany," *Central European History* 15 (1982): 259.
46. John E. Farquharson, *The Plough and the Swastika. The NSDAP and Agriculture in Germany 1928–45* (London, 1976), 188–92, 196–202, 232–8; Stephenson, "'Emancipation'," 354–5, 357–60.

century.[47] In the Third Reich, it was harnessed to a pronatalist policy that looks antimodern because it flew in the face of conventional population development in modernized societies, where the nuclear family is the norm. This combination was effective in appealing to a wide range of prejudices, even if Germans did not respond in the manner encouraged by Nazi propaganda – by having large families. Whatever nostalgia there was for a time when order rather than chaos seemed to reign, before 1914, the nation's response showed that, as far as population development was concerned, there would be no return to the prewar order, notwithstanding attempts to prevent effective contraception and abortion, which had helped to emancipate many women from unwanted pregnancy.

"Eugenics" policies, then, would combine with increased emphasis on antenatal protection and mother-care skills to ensure that those "racially and hereditarily valuable" babies that were conceived reached and survived birth and infancy. As a consolation, there would be a higher yield of "desirable" children from a relatively small number of conceptions. This mitigation of the failure of Nazi population policy in quantitative terms was never regarded as other than unsatisfactory, and the manic attempts to achieve higher rates of procreation continued to the end, even as the wartime birthrate plumbed the disastrous levels of 1914–18.[48] In population policy, therefore, the Nazis were, by intention, both traditionalists and modernizers – the latter with a vengeance, as far as the "racially and hereditarily unfit" were concerned. Both modes operated in a dictatorial way that aimed to leave little room for maneuver to individuals, male and female. In both, however, women, as childbearers, were the particular focus of the regime's policies. Even if they benefited from the improved perinatal and maternity care that modern scientific and medical techniques afforded, they were denied the element of individual choice that emancipates an individual from either paternalist or collectivist supervision.

In terms of employment, it was Hitler's regime that had less room for maneuver, first because of the economic crisis in which it came to power and second because of the dictates of its own economic and imperial policies, which were based on modernized economic and technological developments that it largely inherited. At first, the

---

47. Robert Moeller made this point in his comments at the session of the German History Society conference in Toronto at which the earlier version of this essay was discussed.
48. For the 1914–18 birthrate, see note 18. On Nazi policy and its results, see Bock, *Zwangssterilisation*, 142–6; Stephenson, "'Reichsbund'," 363–8.

crisis of the modernized economy suggested that restricting women to their "traditional" roles was necessary in order to try to ensure that each family had one (male) breadwinner, whatever his occupation might be: "Jobs first for the fathers of families" was the slogan. But soon, especially from 1936, a new surge of modernization, with the buildup of a war-related economy, provided opportunities for some urban women to win a degree of economic independence, even if the problem of the double burden persisted. There were attempts to mitigate that burden through various service schemes, including the "compulsory year" introduced in 1938, which used young people as a cheap source of domestic and farm labor. But these piecemeal projects did not begin to address the extent of the problem.[49]

Although there had been a cruel logic about the Nazi hierarchy's expressed policies toward, and expectations of, women in the Depression years, thereafter the leadership gave contradictory signals, extolling traditional ways while appealing for more women – including mothers – to staff expanding industries and offices, burgeoning administration, and indispensable professions. This apparent contradiction is a good example of the Nazis' "reactionary modernism." They made pragmatic use of the advantages of the modernized economy – where often enough women were perfectly able to perform what had traditionally been viewed as "men's jobs" – while at the same time looking "forward" to a better past, where male breadwinners and large families would be the rule. The promotion of industry, which was essential to their power-political aims, took them in the opposite direction from their ultimate goal, making them perhaps reluctant modernizers. As such, they were only partial modernizers, determined to prevent the development of individual autonomy and a democratic polity that, however imperfectly, characterized modern political and social systems elsewhere – in Britain, the United States, and France, for example. Whether complete emancipation of women is possible in modern capitalist society, "where the inferior status of women not only has a long tradition but is embedded in the social framework itself,"[50] remains an open question. It is, however, clear that although modernization provides the necessary conditions for emancipation, as for democratization, it makes neither inevitable; the former remains conditional upon the achievement of the latter.

49. Farquharson, *Plough and Swastika*, 199–200; Jill Stephenson, "Nationalsozialistischer Dienstgedanke, bürgerliche Frauen und Frauenorganisationen im Dritten Reich," *Geschichte und Gesellschaft* 7 (1981): 559–61.
50. Marilyn Rueschemeyer and Hanna Schissler, "Women in the Two Germanys," *German Studies Review*, DAAD Special Issue (1990), 81.

PART THREE
Local Dimensions of Political Culture

9

Democracy or Reaction?
The Political Implications of Localist Ideas
in Wilhelmine and Weimar Germany

CELIA APPLEGATE

The search for usable traditions in Germany's political development has lost much of its attraction since the 1950s, when a number of historical studies attempted to create for Germans of the Bonn Republic a collective memory of constitutionalism and responsible reform.[1] In the concluding lines of his massive volume on German local government in the nineteenth century, Heinrich Heffter suggested that – "tender plant" though it was – Germany democracy in the form of self-administration and communal autonomy was a far more authentic foundation for the political future than imported English or American institutions.[2] Fifteen years later, such essentially hopeful sentiments about the legacy of the past had become uncommon, or at the very least, discredited by association with a conservative establishment. With the work of Fritz Fischer and Ralf Dahrendorf, the focus of German political archaeology became instead the finding, indeed the rooting out, of *un*usable traditions. The scholarly act shifted from one of affirmation to one of criticism. Fritz Fischer, for instance, believed that "it is by facing the obscure forces within us and the unpleasant truths about ourselves that nations, like individuals, can cope with the world around them and face the future."[3] And although the triumph of this therapeutic mode of historical inquiry was and remains more decisive outside Germany than

---

1. Gerhard Ritter's political biography, *Stein*, 3rd ed. (Stuttgart, 1958), may be taken as exemplary. I wonder if we do not hold a mildly exaggerated view of the failings of pre-Fischerite (and postwar) historiography. For instance, Roger Fletcher's otherwise excellent introduction to his translation of Fischer's *Bündnis der Eliten* is subtle and thorough in its treatment of post-Fischerite historiography but summary and dismissive of pre-Fischerite work for its alleged high-political conventionality and conservative complacency. See Roger Fletcher, "Introduction," in Fritz Fischer, *From Kaiserreich to Third Reich*, trans. Roger Fletcher (London, 1986), 12–13.
2. Heinrich Heffter, *Die deutsche Selbstverwaltung im 19. Jahrhundert* (Stuttgart, 1950), 790–1.
3. Cited in Fletcher, "Introduction," in Fischer, *Kaiserreich to Third Reich*, 20.

247

inside it, the pursuit of history-as-expurgation has proven stunningly productive. The German past would seem easily to provide more material for discard than for retention. Authoritarianism has not been a tender plant, nor have its victories over democracy and self-government been all that difficult to achieve.

Nevertheless, our attention to German democracy should not be confined to examining the forces arrayed against it. In search not of rehabilitation but of illumination, I would like to return to Heffter's preoccupation – the cluster of ideas associated with local self-rule and, in turn, their contribution to democracy in Germany – and see whether or not forty prolific years of German historical scholarship do not enable us to take a fresh look at localism in terms of both its limitations and its more subtle strengths. The subject seems almost quaint in the context of a volume devoted to such thoroughly modern themes as mass politics and social change, but the uneasy juxtaposition is precisely the point. For, as we shall see, despite numerous efforts of German thinkers to articulate a link between the local and the national, between an "old" politics of community and a "new" politics of party and state, German public life failed in important ways to integrate these separate spheres and thus remained fragmented by geography – by "place" – well into the Weimar period. The implications of such fragmentation for political transformation in general, and for democratization in particular, will be addressed throughout this chapter.

That anyone even attempted to mount a progressive defense of local politics is itself an anomaly worth pondering. The first self-consciously progressive politics, that of liberal nationalism, had from its beginnings in the French Revolution been characterized by an uncompromising opposition to things local. The Jacobins' virtual invention of the concept "*ancien régime*" in the course of the Revolution associated local attachments with "privilege" and therefore consigned them to the dark side of the polarized world they created.[4] The Jacobins' image of a nation one and indivisible, with priority over older corps, communities, universities, and orders – indeed, eventually over the revolutionary individual himself – was impressed upon their admirers in Central Europe.

But such a nation had been the outcome, not the starting point, of

---

4. On the term *ancien regime*, see Diego Venturino, "La formation de l'idée d'ancien régime," in Colin Lucas, ed., *The French Revolution and the Creation of Modern Political Culture*, vol. 2, *The Political Culture of the French Revolution* (Oxford, 1988).

the French revolutionaries; its priority over the concept of rights emerged out of revolutionary practice, out of the practical logic of liberty, equality, fraternity, and war. For the German national movement, the late acquisition of this advanced technology of national ideology – and in a political context where "nation" meant an unachieved unity, not the democratization of an already existent one – made it immediately tempting to subordinate the original agenda of citizens' rights to the Jacobin worship of secular unity. Thus it was that particularism, not privilege, became the watchword of opposition to the old regime in Germany. And long after the radical origins of nationalism had been buried in Germany, self-consciously progressive intellectuals still held on to the revolutionaries' original critique of localism: A politically progressive program could still be achieved, they seemed to think, even in the dubiously parliamentary regime of the Second Empire, by asserting the superiority of a centralized nation-state over the particularistic regions and localities. Looking back on the 1870s, Gustav Schmoller wrote approvingly of "new legislation" that would "enlighten" and "pave the way for justified practical reforms" for Germans "still hounded by the narrow-minded, individualistic provincial prejudices and traditions of times past."[5] In Max Weber's famous disparagement of the political capacities of the German bourgeoisie, one can find elements of this reflexive antilocalism.[6] For Weber, particularism lived on not so much in Bavaria's special rights as in the inability of many Germans to grasp the possibilities of great power and the concept of national interests.

But out of harmony with the centralism of a Weber or a Schmoller there existed in the German "public mind" a strain of decentralist – sometimes federalist, sometimes not – thought, to which we need also listen. Particularism had its admirers even after the founding of the Reich, and nationalism had its own localist aspects.[7] Indeed,

---

5. Gustav Schmoller, *Zwanzig Jahre deutscher Politik 1897–1917* (Berlin, 1920), 23–5.
6. See Rudy Koshar's comments on Weber's analysis of local politics in his *Social Life, Local Politics, and Nazism: Marburg, 1880–1935* (Chapel Hill, N.C., 1986), 5–7.
7. In 1979, Martin Walser found this nationalism of the homelands a potential source of resistance to the centralism of the Bonn Republic. See his "Händedruck mit Gespenstern," in Jürgen Habermas, ed., *Stichworte zur 'Geistigen Situation der Zeit'*, 2 vols. (Frankfurt, 1979), 1:39–50. Habermas also believes that in Germany the "concept of the nation preserves ties to regionally rooted folk culture more strongly than is the case with older nation states." See Habermas, "Introduction," in Jürgen Habermas, ed., *Observations on 'The Spiritual Situation of the Age'*, trans. Andrew Buchwalter (Cambridge, 1984), 17. See also my own *A Nation of Provincials: The German Idea of Heimat* (Berkeley, Calif., 1990).

intrinsic to the German national experience are the tensions between centripetal and centrifugal tendencies, between the forces of aggregation and those of disaggregation or particularism, between the alternating celebration of diversity and of unity, between the desire for strength and the longing for authenticity. That these tensions were as often as not detrimental to the flourishing of public life is a point that the whole course of German history reveals.[8] But, as James Sheehan has written, we ought to be concerned not only with "apparent necessities" – in this case, the likely ill effects of an uneven national integration – but also with "latent possibilities."[9] And here one must surely include the possibility that the legacy of German particularism would be a respect for diversity, an appreciation of individuality, and a desire for self-governance.

The quirky and original Wilhelm Heinrich Riehl was among the first German intellectuals to propose a solution to the antipathy between communal life and the then only theoretical national state. Riehl's *Naturgeschichte des deutschen Volkes,* written in the 1850s "under the influence of the seething, struggling, but also youthfully idealistic time" of the 1848 revolution, sought in three slender volumes to create the basis for an entirely new statecraft, what he called *soziale Politik.* Riehl was disturbed by the lack of attention among state-obsessed German politicians to the nature of German society. Given that in Germany society was "a many-armed giant" compared to which the state was but a "dwarf," Riehl felt that a truly German politics ought to take as its subject and inspiration communal life, which Riehl intended to reveal in all its complexity and diversity in the *Naturgeschichte.* Communal life would form the basis of German citizenship, and the political potential of Germans could unfold within what Mack Walker later called the "web of community relations." Riehl believed the constitutions the French had imposed on local communities had in fact *de*politicized the German people by taking away the only politics – a social politics – that they understood. He also drew a firm line of development from such soulless, centralized constitutions to the bureaucratic states of the 1850s and urged the

---

8. The concluding chapter of Mack Walker's *German Home Towns: Community, State, and General Estate* (Ithaca, N.Y., 1971) contains a stimulating discussion of the possible links between nostalgia for home town and "wholeness" and National Socialist successes with the Weimar electorate.
9. James J. Sheehan, *German History 1770–1866* (Oxford, 1990), 914.

Democracy or Reaction?

eager nation builders of his time not to "go against the spirit of the true German community" by building a uniform, centralized, and ultimately inauthentic state.[10]

Riehl is important to a fuller understanding of German political thought because he refused to accept that national unification, which on the whole he favored, would inevitably come into conflict with the rich variety of German society. He refused, in other words, to accept the necessity of a dualism between state and society, between public and private spheres, between locality and nation. The escape from a "roman" model of politics would in fact come, he thought, from a firmer appreciation of the locality. Riehl's notion of a social politics found more sophisticated enunciation several decades later in the legal scholarship of Otto von Gierke.[11] Gierke was the key figure in the late-nineteenth-century revival of the old controversy between "Germanists" and "Romanists" in the study of law – a revival inspired in part by the debates over the writing of an all-German Civil Code.[12] The leader of the Germanists, he based an elaborate interpretation of German legal development on what critics considered the medieval fantasy of *Genossenschaftsrecht,* or the traditional legal foundations and claims of certain kinds of groups in German society. Gierke discerned two principles operating in German history: One, the principle of *Genossenschaft,* was the embodiment of "freedom"; the other, the principle of *Herrschaft,* or mastery, was the embodiment of its opposite, unfreedom, which he, revealingly, described as "unity." All forms of social existence fell along the spectrum defined by these two and combined them in various proportions: The modern state, he believed, could yet become the ideal reconciliation of the *Genossenschaftsidee* with the *Herrschaftsidee.*[13] Alarmed by what he called the "hegemonial federalism" of the Bismarckian Reich, he asserted the fundamental rights of the self-administering local commune, the legal and political recognition of which could be the basis

---

10. W. H. Riehl, *Naturgeschichte des deutschen Volkes,* ed. Gunther Ipsen (Leipzig, 1935), 9–10, 16, 21, 116–17.
11. Compare, for instance, the sheer bulk of Gierke's four massive volumes on *Deutsche Genossenschaftsrecht* (Berlin, 1868, 1873) to the succinct, pithy style of Riehl's little *Naturgeschichte.*
12. Michael John's *Politics and the Law in Late Nineteenth-Century Germany: The Origins of the Civil Code* (Oxford, 1989) includes a detailed discussion of Gierke's criticism of the Code (pp. 244–6 and passim).
13. Ernst-Wolfgang Böckenförde, *Die deutsche Verfassungsgeschichtliche Forschung im 19. Jahrhundert* (Berlin, 1961), 147–58.

of a new "constructive federalism."[14] Gierke believed that such intermediary bodies as municipalities and associations represented Germany's "unique and crowning contribution to the theory and practice of liberty." The small communities, he wrote, "alone offer the opportunity of combining the large, inclusive, unified state with active civil freedom and self-government."[15]

Like Riehl's, Gierke's political attitudes, especially his attitudes concerning the virtues of land ownership, have usually been seen as reactionary.[16] But the reactionary label does not do justice to Riehl's or Gierke's fears about the modern state as it was then taking shape. Gierke's arguments about the special nature of land ownership were, indeed, anticipated in John Stuart Mill's concerns about the decline of peasant proprietorship in England. His understanding of the importance of associations in the social and legal fabric of the nation was in turn absorbed by F. W. Maitland, for whom it came as a kind of revelation about the nature of modern society and an inspiration to develop a socially pluralistic version of liberalism.[17] Michael John rightly recognized that Gierke's criticism of the Civil Code embodied a vision of national integration quite different from that of the Code's supporters, but this vision was not so much antiliberal in inspiration as antiunitary, or at least anticentralist.[18] Mack Walker's characterization of such localism as romantic is perhaps more accurate, as long as one acknowledges the possibility of what Nancy Rosenblum has called "another liberalism," one able to bring together romantic and liberal concerns in a renewed communitarianism and an expressive pluralism.[19] Gierke represented both a liberal resistance to the narrowness of a political sphere defined by competing economic interest groups and a liberal insistence on the social complexity that centralizing bureaucracy sought to homogenize.

Riehl and Gierke may have articulated a recognizably localist ideology, but neither showed much sympathy for the democratic poten-

---

14. Gerhard Schulz, *Zwischen Demokratie und Diktatur: Verfassungspolitik und Reichsreform in der Weimarer Republik* (Berlin, 1963), 11.
15. Cited in Antony Black, *Guilds and Civil Society in European Political Thought from the Twelfth Century to the Present* (Ithaca, N.Y., 1984), 211.
16. John, *Politics and the Law*, 110–15.
17. John Burrow, *Whigs and Liberals: Continuity and Change in English Political Thought* (Oxford, 1988), 135–50; see also Maitland's famous introduction to his own translation of Gierke, *Political Theories of the Middle Ages* (Cambridge, 1900).
18. John, *Politics and the Law*, 244–6.
19. Nancy L. Rosenblum, *Another Liberalism: Romanticism and the Reconstruction of Liberal Thought* (Cambridge, Mass., 1987).

tial of such a perspective. Gierke's student, Hugo Preuss, developed the democratic implications of Gierke's thought, and it is through him, not through a host of antimodernist reactionaries, that we may trace the lineage of localism into the twentieth century. Almost exclusively known for his contributions to the Weimar Constitution, Preuss was an eloquent public writer and politician, as well as a sometime historian and jurist. Before the First World War, he mounted arguments in the liberal press and other public forums for, among other reformist causes, a responsible executive and the abolition of the Prussian three-class voting system. But the vision that informed his political positions gave a distinctly German complexion to these familiar left liberal reforms. It emerges clearly from his scholarly work, in particular from his dissertation on the differing organizational nature of commune, small state, and empire and from his four-volume account of the development of German cities, in which he tried to prove the existence in Germany of a democratic tradition of self-administration and self-government.[20]

According to Preuss, the state was only "one link in the chain of human communal life [*Gemeinwesen*]," whose original form was the small community and whose "highest form" would be a future "all-embracing organism of a community of peoples."[21] A follower of Gierke, Preuss recognized a fundamental distinction between a people's state, or *Volksstaat,* based on associations and individuals, and an authoritarian state, or *Obrigkeitsstaat,* based on the principle of hegemony. He sought in the German past a principle for democratic development in the German present and found one in the ideal of communal equality (*genossenschaftliches Gemeinwesen*).[22] This ideal had been first undermined by the rising power of the princes, who had abrogated communal constitutions to aggrandize their own power. It had been revived by a princely state in the process of transcending its narrow, particularistic origins, in the form of Stein's municipal ordinance of 1808. It had suffered setbacks and struggles in the course of the nineteenth century, flourishing in the 1870s under the auspices of a briefly united *Bürgertum.* And it again faced a possibly terminal crisis in the socially polarized, rapidly expanding cities at the turn of the century. Preuss noted that the growth of an urban

20. The relevant titles are *Gemeinde, Staat, Reich als Gebietskörperschaften: Versuch einer deutschen Staatskonstruktion auf Grundlage der Genossenschaftstheorie* (Berlin, 1889) and *Entwicklung des deutschen Städtewesens* (Leipzig, 1906).
21. Hugo Preuss, *Gemeinde, Staat, Reich als Gebietskörperschaften,* Forward.
22. Hugo Preuss, *Die Entwicklung des deutschen Städtewesens,* Vol. I (Leipzig, 1906), Forward.

working class had produced a backlash in the form of increasingly exclusive forms of local government, which sought to deny workers the rights accruing to community membership; even more alarming was the gradual withdrawal of important economic and political functions from the cities themselves.[23] Both tendencies threatened the principle that communal rights and responsibilities were the basis of a healthy state existence. At the same time, the increasing complexity of urban life – the need for streetcars, gas and electrical works, water and sewage facilities – meant that cities more than ever needed strong and consensually based government. Appalled by the growing chaos of Greater Berlin, Preuss was concerned lest public works should become private undertakings, lest local affairs should become national functions. He advocated instead a communalization of governmental functions, the return to the local level of important state activities – policing and taxation, for instance.[24] Against the usual assumptions about the course of modernization, he insisted that the proper response to urbanization, industrialization, and class formation was decentralization: "City self-administration," he wrote, was the "solution to modern problems"; through urban reform, one might build a nation.[25]

Preuss was not alone in his hopes for local politics in general and the city in particular in Imperial Germany. Eduard Bernstein's *Evolutionary Socialism* can be read, albeit cautiously, as a vindication of local initiative in the socialist movement and a defense of local organization, particularly in what he called the "giant towns" of Europe.[26] Bernstein's affinities with the localist vision are implicit in his sympathetic discussion of the cooperative movement, but they become clear in his discussion of the meaning of democracy for socialism. He denies, characteristically, that the phrase "dictatorship of the proletariat" has any but a negative relevance to contemporary socialism and seeks instead to associate socialism with liberalism, with constitutional practice, and above all with the language of citizenship. Social democracy, if it "is not to exceed centralised absolutism in the

23. Ibid., 373–4.
24. A typical statement of the need for decentralization of administration was his 1915 article, "Burgfriedliche Kriegsgedanken zur Verwaltungsreform," reprinted in Hugo Preuss, *Staat, Recht und Freiheit: Aus 40 Jahren Deutscher Politik und Geschichte*, ed. Theodor Heuss (Hildesheim, 1964), 102–9.
25. Preuss, *Staat, Recht, und Freiheit*, 378–9. See also Peter Gilg, *Die Erneuerung des demokratischen Denkens im Wilhelminischen Deutschland* (Wiesbaden, 1965), 92–100.
26. Eduard Bernstein, *Evolutionary Socialism*, trans. Edith C. Harvey (New York, 1961), 154. See also Schulz, *Zwischen Demokratie und Diktatur*, 12.

breeding of bureaucracies," must "be built upon an elaborately organised self-government with a corresponding economic, personal responsibility of all the units of administration as well as of the adult citizens of the state." "Nothing," he continues, "is more injurious to its healthy development than enforced uniformity."[27] Bernstein, like Preuss, was no advocate of complete decentralization – a goal he saw as unrealistic, given the complexity of economic and social ties within and among nations. But he did hold to an ideal of a national state, built "from the bottom upwards," with the greatest possible degree of self-government retained at each level as one moved upward and outward toward "the central assemblies."[28] In an argument Preuss developed only during the war, Bernstein laid great emphasis on the process of education inherent in democratic self-government at the local level. Workers would become citizens through slow and gradual – evolutionary? – experience in self-governing bodies.

Conciliatory as such ideas sounded, they had to be cast in the future tense of hope, rather than – all Preuss's efforts at democratic archaeology notwithstanding – in the past tense of recovery. By 1900, the feudal tradition of local, especially rural, governance had succumbed to a series of laws on county and municipal reform. But a perplexing variety of local arrangements persisted, baffling efforts to turn cities into bastions of democratic politics and ultimately hindering the emergence of a local democracy that might nourish a national one. Plutocratic electoral arrangements and the bureaucratic-absolutist tradition of local control both undermined the democratic promise of local self-government. Unlike the situation in Great Britain or the United States, where local self-government and national self-government were all of a piece, advocates of democratic localism like Preuss had to contend with both centralist illiberalism and a strongly reactionary heritage at the local level – the heritage of self-administration as a negative "particularism" rather than a positive "grass-roots democracy."[29] In 1910, for instance, Clemens von Delbrück wrote in considerable frustration, "How is it possible to have a liberal government? For the past fifty years no *Landrat,* no *Regierungsrat,* nor District Officer, almost no Provincial Governor either, no

27. Bernstein, *Evolutionary Socialism,* 155.
28. Ibid., 160.
29. See the useful discussion of the limits of reform before 1918 in Arthur B. Gunlicks, *Local Government in the German Federal System* (Durham, N.C., 1986), 1–31.

Political Magistrate, almost no village mayor east of the Elbe was appointed who was not conservative to the bones."[30] The growth of national political parties, although certainly one token of democratization, often had the consequence for local politics of exacerbating conflict to the point where paralysis set in over even mundane issues like street names or, as Rudy Koshar has shown (and Preuss himself observed), of encouraging the growth of an antiparty politics of bourgeois reaction. Given such a depressing reality, Preuss's and Bernstein's case for the benefits of local action seems, for all its surface practicality, utopian; it makes sense only as the natural reaction to the abuses of a powerful central state and the shortcomings of nationally organized opposition. Bernstein's colleagues did not share his localist interests. Bebel's attention to local affairs was purely administrative, and Kautsky could see no difference between localism and yokelism, the famed idiocy of rural life.[31]

It is possible to conceive of the dilemma faced by democratic reformers like Preuss and Bernstein as a crisis of constituency, not unlike that faced by liberals of all sorts in the Second Empire. Preuss and Bernstein confronted a paralyzing paradox that undermined any constructive program of localist reform. On the one hand, the very diversity of Germany's regional political traditions seemed to justify, even encourage, a faith in locally rooted democratic reform. After all, a good number of local communes and provinces, particularly in western Germany, *were* democratically inclined and had in the course of the nineteenth century asserted democratic claims in the context of movements for local autonomy (the Palatinate against Bavaria, the Rhineland against Prussia). Fixated as he was upon the example of Stein, Preuss saw hope for another age of German liberation, again based on applying the lessons of the western provinces to all of Germany. The paradox lies, though, in the nature of that democratic heritage, which was French revolutionary and thus committed to local action only as an expedient, not as a principle. Those who would have made local political life democratic often did not believe

---

30. Cited in Herbert Jacob, *German Administration since Bismarck: Central Authority versus Local Autonomy* (New Haven, Conn., 1963), 64.
31. See Bebel's *Die Frau und der Sozialismus*, 9th ed. (Stuttgart, 1891). Kautsky wrote that "the rights and duties of the individual communities [will be] determined by the interests of all the states or the nation, not by the individual communities," and further that "communal political life has no intrinsic value," and indeed that "in peaceful times the politics of the village and the small town amount to nothing more than quaffing in the local pub" (cited in Gilg, *Erneuerung*, 77).

in its importance; those who believed in the importance of local political life did not practice it democratically. Thus, although it is far too simple to associate decentralism exclusively with particularistic reaction, Preuss saw his political allies fade into the woodwork on the issue of the devolution of power to local authority.

The solution to this dilemma was education, the universal magic of liberal reform and, in its intended effects, an acceptable form of violence against Riehl's social realm. Education was, indeed, a centralist solution masquerading as one attentive to local particularity – the same masquerade that had been performed by Stein's municipal ordinance. Preuss's recourse to political education became apparent in his wartime writings and later emerged in his contributions to the Weimar constitution. During the war, he publicly aired his doubts about the political capacities of the Germans and hence about any easy transition to democratic government. *Das deutsche Volk und die Politik*, written in 1915, linked Germany's uncomfortable international isolation to the "otherness" (*Anderssein*) of its authoritarian regime.[32] As a first step toward a just peace, Preuss advocated administrative decentralization, which would infuse the state with the energy of the people, and constitutional reform, which would make Germany's political system compatible with those of the allied powers.[33] By 1917, he was writing that only drastic changes in German politics could save the nation from its desperate isolation and decline. In the face of virtual military dictatorship, he refused to blame Germany's problems on the iniquities of a ruling caste. Instead, he argued that the authoritarian state had developed only in default of an "active and purposeful common political will" in the people themselves; the shaping (*Bildung*) of such a common will (*Gemeinwillen*) through a "profound transformation of the political spirit of the people" should be the goal of the state.[34]

Such admirable but ineffectual sentiments hardly seem worth repeating, except that Preuss, unlike most German reformers, was improbably given the chance to translate his constitutional notions into political practice.[35] In November 1918, the revolutionary council of

32. Hugo Preuss, *Das deutsche Volk und die Politik* (Jena, 1915), passim. See also "Deutsche Demokratisierung," in Preuss, *Staat, Recht und Freiheit*, 335.
33. See "Burgfriedliche Kriegsgedanken zur Verwaltungsreform" and "Vorschläge zur Abänderung der Reichsverfassung und der Preussische Verfassung, nebst Begründung," in Preuss, *Staat, Recht und Freiheit*.
34. Preuss, "Deutsche Demokratisierung," 337.
35. On Preuss and the constitution, see Schulz, *Zwischen Demokratie und Diktatur*, 12–17.

the people's deputies in Berlin commissioned him to prepare a "Draft of a Future Constitution of the Reich," to be published in conjunction with the proposed elections to a National Assembly, scheduled for January 1919.[36] Preuss's original draft was revised once by the council itself, then again by a constitutional committee of the new National Assembly after being bitterly attacked by representatives of the states. The final draft that went into effect on 11 August 1919 was thus very far from being Preuss's work, but perhaps not so far as to render pointless a closer look at his original conception of a German constitution. Two issues in particular have direct bearing on the problem of localist democracy: the first, territorial organization and sovereignty; the second, responsible citizenship. Taken separately, as many historians have done, they yield fragmented insights: The first has been seen to be at the heart of constitutional controversies, the second a democratic truism; the first has seemed resonant with the ages, the second a recent product of modern liberal preoccupations; the first a profoundly German issue, central to the question of continuity, the second a superficial importation from other political cultures. But taken together, as Preuss almost certainly took them, they reveal a single preoccupation with the meaning of German traditions of local self-government, and they represent a composite effort to build a democratic political culture that embraced both community and nation. For Preuss, the settlement of territorial issues was essential to solving the dilemma of political citizenship in Germany. Territory, constructed along certain lines, would be the cradle of the responsible democratic citizenry. Territory and citizenship were thus touchstones of the Preussian conception of German democracy, which he tried, with only limited success, to carry through into the final version of the constitution.

Before its successive revisions by the people's council and the states, Preuss's constitutional draft laid out a plan for a decentralized unitary state, that is to say, a state with only one center of authority

36. Ebert's choice of Preuss was perhaps surprising, especially given Preuss's past quarrels with the Social Democrats, but he had the knowledge, the democratic sensibilities, and the civil courage to prepare a constitution for the new Republic. Besides that, he was on hand in Berlin and was widely rumored to have a draft already in his pocket. More luminous German jurists, like Max Weber, became involved shortly thereafter. See Elmar M. Hucko, "Introduction," *The Democratic Tradition: Four German Constitutions* (Oxford, 1987), 46–9; Preuss, "Vorschläge für Abänderung der Reichsverfassung," in *Staat, Recht, und Freiheit;* and Wolfgang Mommsen, *Max Weber and German Politics,* trans. Michael Steinberg (Chicago, 1984), 303, 333–6.

but in which the basic functions of the state – the means by which the state made itself felt by its citizens – were returned to the local level. The draft addressed itself to two problems in the structure of the German polity; Preuss's insight lay not in identifying the problems – everyone knew they would be what they were – but in showing that the solution to both was the same. The first was, predictably, the problem of Prussia – its dominant size, its dominant economy, its dominant political power. The second, equally predictably, was the problem of the states – their peculiarly privileged place in the distribution of power and their often arbitrary mediation between the modern state and its citizenry. The German polity was, as Pufendorf had observed centuries before, a kind of monstrosity, neither unitary nor entirely federalist, neither centralized nor entirely particularistic. For Bismarck, the monstrosity of the German state was precisely what made it so stable, so relatively immune to popular disruption; the smaller and medium-sized states, he thought, were essential to the preservation of Prussian monarchism in its authoritarian form. For Preuss, the smaller states were what stood in the way of the democratization he imagined emerging from a local politics unmediated in its relation to the nation-state. Preuss aimed to transform the monster into a rational creature. His failure left the way open to a more violent resolution of the issue a decade and a half later.

As is fairly well known, the Preussian solution to the Prussian problem was to get rid of it entirely.[37] He envisioned a German polity consisting of eleven more or less equal states: Prussia would be dissolved into several parts and the smaller states consolidated into medium-sized ones; Austria would be added as a further balance, and Berlin and Vienna would exist as independent capital cities. The state, however, would be unitary, albeit with federalist overtones. Many of its administrative and self-governing powers would fall not to these eleven states but to even smaller units – municipalities, communes, districts. Here was decentralization plus unitarism, home town plus nation-state, the first German Empire without the chaos, the second German Empire without the Iron Chancellor. Preuss's was a solution that built on the particularism of persistent local loy-

---

37. A still useful summary of this and related issues is Arnold Brecht, *Federalism and Regionalism in Germany: The Division of Prussia* (Oxford, 1945). For a detailed examination of Prussia's place in the republican Reich, as well as important insights into Preuss's career, see Horst Möller, *Parlamentarismus in Preussen 1919–1932* (Düsseldorf, 1985).

alties and provincial identities in Germany but not the particularism of Metternichian and Bismarckian reaction, not the particularism of divide and conquer.

It did not survive, however, even the first revisionary assault on Preuss's constitutional draft. The German states, the *Länder,* were not prepared to cede their traditional powers either to the central state or to the smaller districts and blocked significant changes in the *Reich–Länder* relationship.[38] The division of Prussia also came to nothing. Already by the summer of 1919, an ironic truth was becoming evident: Prussia, once the embodiment of reaction, was now the stronghold of left liberalism and social democracy, and thus the bulwark of the Republic in a hostile political environment. To divide Prussia might have been desirable in the long term, but in the short term, so reasoned the republican parties, it would have meant the end of German democracy. Thus reform of Germany's federal structure was shelved for the time being, though in effect made a permanent part of the political landscape by provisions in the final form of the constitution that allowed for changes in the boundaries of the *Länder.*

The form of the Weimar constitution adopted in the summer of 1919 tended more toward the incoherent form of federalism that Germany had had since 1870 than toward Preussian unitarism. Prussia's predominance was somewhat attenuated in the second assembly, the *Reichsrat,* where a voting procedure divided Prussia into its constituent regional parts. Preuss's vision of local autonomy also remained unfulfilled, at first because of bureaucratic resistance, especially from the states, and later because of national financial reforms that undercut local financial independence. In 1928, a renewed movement for reform of the territorial arrangements of the Reich seemed for a time to be making headway. An alliance of many groups, including the German Council of Cities (*Deutscher Städtetag*), the oldest and most important organization of communes and districts, agreed on what they called the "principle of differentiation," thus linking – in the spirit of Gierke – the concepts of communalism, freedom, and diversity. Although Preuss had died in 1925, the principle of differentiation owed much to the lingering influence of his ideas. It called essentially for a strengthening of the central authority *and* for a strengthening of the local authorities – in other words, *Reichsaufbau* and *Selbstverwaltung.* It also called for an end to the

---

38. Kurt Eisner, as head of the revolutionary Bavarian government, proved the most recalcitrant of the resurgent federalists, leading a rebellion of the southwestern German states.

dualism between Prussia and the Reich, for the redrawing and rationalization of certain borders, and in general for a weakening of small-state particularism. Its timing, however, was unfortunate. By 1929 the disastrous political consequences of the worldwide Depression were already being felt. By 1930, the Weimar Republic had entered into its final stage of political crisis, from which there would be no salvation by means of territorial redirection.

Why did these territorial issues, these issues of political units, so preoccupy interwar Germans? They quickly become tedious to the outsider – perhaps that is a clue right there. René Brunet, a French political scientist who wrote one of the first books available to Americans on the subject of the Weimar constitution, expressed his impatience with the endless debates over federalism or unitarism, centralism or decentralism, over whether to call the states "states," "republics," "member states," "free states," or "lands." Brunet wrote in 1921 that the territorial issue "has not progressed one step in three generations; one studies it but does nothing about it, for there is no reality in it."[39] The reality in it, which Brunet missed, was that the issue of intra-German boundary lines suggested the answer to the troubled question of German citizenship. Who was the citizen? What were the citizen's rights, duties, obligations? How were the right kind of citizens to be produced? For Preuss and many other Germans from all parties, these questions all somehow began and ended in the geographical question: *Where* was the citizen to be made, to live, to act, to flourish? And given that the question was posed in such a way, the answer was simple: in the locality, at home, in the *Heimat*.

This communitarian understanding of citizenship helps to explain the tempered individualism of the Weimar constitution's articles on "the fundamental rights and duties of Germans." Its makers saw it as a set of maxims that would furnish an intellectual background to the Republic, a "solid foundation for the juridical culture of the German people," as well as "the basis for the civic and political education of the people."[40] Every "negative" liberty – freedom of speech, of assembly, of conscience, right to hold property, and so on – was matched by a duty: Article 153 stated that "property rights imply property duties"; articles on education construed it first as an individual's right and then (once educated) as an individual's duty to "cooperate in the most effective fashion in the well-being of the

39. René Brunet, *The New German Constitution*, trans. Joseph Gollomb (New York, 1921), 71.
40. Ibid., 196.

community." The idea of the social function of man dominated the Weimar constitution; individual liberties no longer formed an end in themselves or an independent good.

The well-known paragraphs of Article 163 delineated the interdependent right and duty to work: "Every German has, without prejudice to his personal liberty, the moral duty to use his intellectual and physical powers as the good of the whole demands." It further stated: "Every German shall have the opportunity to earn his living by economic labor." For many contemporary observers, such paragraphs simply represented the influence of socialism on the constitution. Charles Beard, for example, fancied that the new constitution "vibrate[d] with the tramp of the proletariat." For Brunet, Article 163, with its repudiation of economic egoism, represented "a real transition from the old world to the new."[41] But it is also possible to find in Article 163 evidence of an anti-industrialism inspired both by a future socialist order and a past communalist one. Perhaps for the heirs of Kautsky and Bebel, Article 163 was a declaration of their revolution. For the democratic liberals like Preuss and for some Social Democrats, on the other hand, Article 163 declared the restoration of a proper balance within civil society, a balance encompassing all in a network of moral obligations and duties. Thus Article 163 represented less the victory of socialism than the communitarian attenuation of liberalism. It was the constitutional culmination of a characteristically German discourse that combined economics and ethics in an idealization of the community and the self-determining freedom of the ancient Germans and the guild towns – a discourse that, in Antony Black's terms, made solidarity and exchange, *Gemeinschaft* and *Gesellschaft,* not opposite principles but complementary poles "around which the values of the guild and civil society, respectively, rotate."[42]

The image of a self-regulating economic and political community, one necessarily limited in size, power, and potential for growth, thus reentered German political culture by way of the Weimar constitution's definition of republican citizenship. The citizen was not the *citoyen* but the *Bürger,* an embedded, determined, limited social being. To be sure, the Weimar declaration of rights and duties democratized this *Bürger,* gave the right of suffrage to both men and women, destroyed differences based upon property ownership, and

41. Ibid., 204.
42. Black, *Guilds and Civil Society,* 237.

tried to ensure a level of civil and religious toleration that had been notably absent in the old walled communities. But self-control (*Selbstbeherrschung*) and communal control remained essential to the maintenance of this community; the pursuit of a common good, not individual happiness, was the citizen's primary assignment.

The ethical locality served not just as origin and inspiration but as means and as end. For Preuss, the building of the new state could only be contemplated as an all-embracing, radical process (in the literal sense of the word). This process would start at the bottom, in the communes themselves, and move in widening circles of influence until all of national political life was affected and changed. Preuss's emphasis on the devolution of powers to the local level and the reinvigoration of communal autonomy came from a vision that operated in the opposite direction. For Preuss, this was not a process by which a powerful center granted powers downward to the periphery, but one by which a new German state would be built upward, from the self-regulating communes. Such a state was not an "organized national community [*Volksgemeinschaft*]" but – and here is the subtle, yet for him important, difference – an "incorporated popular state [*körperschaftlicher Volksstaat*]."[43] Such a political order would provide a "political education for an unpoliticized people." It would bring about the "awakening of the common spirit through the participation of the people in public life, the ruled in the ruling," and serve as "a universal national-pedagogical system of education, bringing the participating citizens out of the narrow circle of their communal experience, step by step into the great matter of national politics."[44]

The constitution's statement of rights and duties, in turn, attempted to set the terms of this participation, providing the foundation for the juridical, the civic, and the political education of the German people on the model of the local community. Indeed, the first and most important official agency established for the propagation of information on the constitution and the Republic was called, cryptically, the Reich Center for Homeland Services (*Reichszentrale für Heimatdienst*).[45] It operated especially in the occupied areas on Germany's borders, encouraging loyalty to the Republic against the blandishments of the French or other national groups. But its appeal

---
43. Schulz, *Zwischen Demokratie und Diktatur*, 126.
44. Ibid., 128.
45. Gotthard Jasper mentions it in conjunction with "constructive" steps toward the protection of the Republic. See his *Der Schutz der Republik: Studien zur staatlichen Sicherung der Demokratie in der Weimarer Republik* (Tübingen, 1963), 228, 241–50.

was not simply to German patriotism. Its directors decided, after initially poor results in the Rhineland, that the only effective means of securing loyalty to the Republic would be through the vehicle of local loyalties, local political and culture identities. "The thoughts and the warm-hearted feelings that we must care for and strengthen in the Rhineland," wrote one "Heimat service" official, "are consciousness of the distinctive character of this land and of its interconnectedness with the entire organism of the German people."[46] Here, in a slightly different context, was Preuss's notion of building upward from the locality. Here, to stretch the point a little further, was Gierke's association of freedom, community, and diversity.

These themes reverberated throughout the decade of the 1920s in a number of different contexts. The diverse and decentralized movement for adult education, or *freie Volksbildung,* put particular emphasis on political, civic education through the lessons of the "things of the earth and the homeland" (*Bodenständige und Heimatliche*). The goal of adult education was not only to create good citizens of the Republic but, just as important, "to develop individuals into full personalities and into valuable members of the community of people [*Volksgemeinschaft*]."[47] The head of adult education in the Palatinate thought that Germans could become passionate about the Republic if only it were made directly relevant to their everyday lives and not understood as a far-off national state.

Such movements were ultimately of little moment. In the crisis-ridden years of the Weimar Republic, they had neither the time nor the opportunity to integrate themselves into the structure of everyday life. Similarly, the constitution's statement of the fundamental rights and duties of Germans never acquired legislative form. It fell victim to party conflicts and remained little more than a blueprint for a political edifice that was never built. Perhaps most important, its conception of citizenship depended on a fundamental alteration of the balance of power among locality, state, and nation – an alteration that never happened. The political education of Germans, if one accepts the logic of this vision, thus suffered accordingly.

There is a further dimension to the problem, and that is the incompatibility of political culture and political economy in Weimar Ger-

---

46. Ministerium für Wissenschaft, Kunst, und Volksbildung, "Kulturpflege im besetzten Rheinland," 18 Nov. 1920, Bayerische Hauptstaatsarchiv Munich, MK 15557.
47. H. Fitz, "Was will der Pfälzische Verband für freie Volksbildung," *Heimatkalendar 1922* (Neustadt/Pfalz, 1921), 71.

many. Local self-rule and self-administration were democratic ideals that proved dangerously ineffectual in the face of the concentration and centralization of economic power in the 1920s and 1930s. To devolve political responsibilities on the cities without comparable economic empowerment was to promote political irresponsibility and corruption. City mayors like Ludwig Landmann of Frankfurt spoke bravely of revitalizing city life – in much the same spirit as Preuss – but the political-cultural benefits that were to flow from that revitalization foundered on deep indebtedness and eventually near-total bankruptcy. As Harold James has shown, the communal level in Weimar Germany was marked by grand schemes and meager finances – too much independence in undertaking expensive projects and too little independence in raising the money to pay for them.[48] As a consequence, local political life was widely discredited, and many a National Socialist rode to fame by denouncing local corruption and incompetence. "Communal administration," writes James, "had been the most obvious and most disliked form of government intervention in the 1920s. It disappeared as a result of the tensions produced by the economic crisis." In the end, it was the Nazis who solved the communal debt crisis by simply eradicating communal independence.[49] More generally, it was the Nazis who decisively broke with the localist tradition in Germany, subordinating the many and competing claims of province, city, and association to the absolutely prior claim of nation and leader.

Despite these clear signs of Nazi disrespect for the particularist, localist tradition in Germany, many Weimar voters nevertheless accepted Nazi promises to restore the lost wholeness of political life and create a synthesis of old community and new nation.[50] We cannot easily separate a pathological, centralist tradition in German political development from a healthy, pluralistic, and decentralist one.[51] Both traditions met and mingled in a variety of incompatible political figures. The answer to the question of what German localism contributed to the initial triumph of Nazism is both ambiguous and contradictory. Localism both helped and hindered the rise of political extremism, both exacerbated and healed the divisions in German political culture. Nostalgia for a simpler, more intimate life, that

48. Harold James, *The German Slump: Politics and Economics 1924–1936* (Oxford, 1986), 87–8.
49. Ibid., 108.
50. Walker, *Home Towns*, 427–8.
51. It should be noted that Fritz Fischer tries to do just that in his *Kaiserreich to Third Reich* (see note 1).

most malleable of quasi-political sentiments, informed the outlook of committed democrats, republicans, liberals, and socialists just as surely as it led others to make the fateful commitment to National Socialism. In retrospect, Preuss's hopes for a grass-roots democratization of Germany were not so much misguided as incomplete, and at the very least woefully inadequate to the challenges of the 1920s.

10

Communist Music in the Streets: Politics and Perceptions in Berlin at the End of the Weimar Republic

RICHARD BODEK

THE INCIDENT

At 6:20 P.M. on 29 September 1930, a group of 130 to 150 people – 60 to 70 of whom were children – gathered at the Reuterplatz in Berlin's working-class borough of Neukölln. Their subsequent march through the streets was ostensibly to protest the firing of Fritz Beyes, a Communist teacher in one of Neukölln's schools.[1] This protest, sponsored by some Communist parents and students from Neukölln, wound its way through the borough, ending at Richardplatz at 7:35 P.M. The column was led by members of the Young Spartacus League (*Jung Spartakusbund* or JS), an organization for ten- to fourteen-year-old children affiliated with the Communist Party of Germany (*Kommunistische Partei Deutschlands* or KPD). Wearing uniforms consisting of a smock, neckerchief, and insignia, these children bore a striking similarity to the American Cub Scouts. One of them carried a red flag that read "From the Lenin Youth League of Charkow to the Communist Children of Berlin!"[2] Members of the Commu-

---

I would like to thank Professor Geoff Eley, Professor Kevin Boyle, and Ms. Amy Shore for their close reading of this essay.

1. The story of the demonstration is based on the following sources: Polizeipräsident, Abteilung IA, File Nr. 1313 IA.3a.30, dated Berlin, 23 Oct. 1930, in the Institut für Marxismus-Leninismus der Zentralkomitee der SED in Berlin (hereafter IML), St22/169 (all files in this note are from this same collection); Officer Friedrich Werviel [sic?], official report, 30 Sept. 1930; anon., "'Heraus auf die Barrikaden!' Pflichtvergessene Polizei," *Berliner Börsen-Zeitung*, 30 Sept. 1930; anon., "'Heraus auf die Barrikaden – zum blutig roten Sieg!' Bürgerkriegspropaganda unterm Schutz und mit Hilfe der Schutzpolizei," *Der Reichsbote*, 1 Oct. 1930; (illegible signature), Krim. Sekr. Abt.I.A. III.G.St. report, 9 Oct. 1930; (illegible signature), letter from the police president (Abt.I.A., Tgb. Nr. 1313, IA.3a.30), 23 Oct. 1930.
2. This is the slogan according to the two newspaper reports. An internal police document reported it as "From the Leningrad Youth of Charkow to the Communist Children of Berlin." Polizeipräsident, Abteilung IA, File Nr. 1313 IA.3a.30, dated Berlin, 23 Oct. 1930, in IML, St22/169.

nist Youth League of Germany (*Kommunistischer Jugendverband Deutschlands* or KJVD) and a number of local working-class parents also took part. Some of the adults carried four other banners, all bearing the motto "Struggle Against the School Fascism." In addition to the banners and flag, participants shouted the slogans "We are protecting the red teacher" and "Where are the free school books?" The marchers sang a number of Communist songs.

The march ended with a demonstration at the Richardplatz, at which Fritz Beyes and another man spoke. The unnamed speaker's remarks included the phrase "The proletariat will lead the revolutionary struggle to bring about the downfall of the decadent bourgeoisie, even in schools." In addition, he called for "the destruction of the present order" and claimed that "the bourgeoisie sees that it is in for it now (*das es ihm um Kopf und Kragen gehe*)." Beyes repeated these sentiments; for example, he urged the construction of a Soviet Germany. He also spoke more specifically about issues of immediate concern to the audience, most notably the epidemics then afflicting schoolchildren in Neukölln and Lichtenberg. After this speech the demonstration ended with a mass singing of the "Internationale."

Two of Berlin's most conservative newspapers, the *Berliner Börsen-Zeitung* and the *Reichsbote,* found this event significant enough to devote long articles to it. Although the ostensible purpose of the march was to protest the firing of Beyes, other reasons also underlay the gathering. Disease was rampant among the district's children; parents doubted the quality of their children's education; and the living standard of the district's poorer citizens was abhorrent. On the face of it, this was a rather ordinary Communist demonstration. The only unusual incident reported by the policeman assigned to it was a confrontation he had with a newspaper reporter; the officer contended that the reporter complained about a song that was not performed.[3] Otherwise, the march confined itself to a proletarian district of the city where the KPD had strong support. It was relatively small, unaccompanied by violence, and seemed nonthreatening. Like many such incidents, however, it cannot be dismissed so lightly; for these marchers invoked a number of symbols that, recalling other places and events, fixed the protest of that September evening within a much broader framework of working-class politics.

The interwar Communist Party occupied a distinct place in Ger-

---

3. Officer Friedrich Werviel [sic?], official report of 30 Sept. 1930, in IML St22/169.

man society, finding its popular support principally in the poorer districts of working-class areas. This support waxed and waned with the fortunes of the German and world economies, as specific historical conjunctures dictated how the working class viewed the Communist Party, what they expected from it, and whether they heeded its advice. This essay tries to locate the KPD in a specific time, place, and social milieu. This is in itself an unusual enterprise, as historians have tended to treat the party either as the physical embodiment and expression of the political ideas of a few leading cadres who worked in the Karl Liebknecht House (the KPD's headquarters) or as a disembodied presence that somehow represented, expressed, channeled, or thwarted the dreams and aspirations of Germany's working class.

In an attempt to unite the new social history, which has made such strides in understanding the everyday life of the German working class, with more traditional narrative history, this essay studies one political incident that aligned the KPD's overall revolutionary goals with the more limited goals of the inhabitants of one specific working-class neighborhood. It takes as its "texts" the music sung, the banners carried, even the neighborhood itself. As will be shown, this approach differs from most work on German working-class music. Additionally, this essay treats the Communist Party as an integral part of the working-class world; it investigates the interaction of party, working class, state, and civil society. It details the course of what should have been a minor political incident. This incident, however, seems to have catalyzed a series of measures that contributed to the growth of political repression at the end of the Weimar Republic and furthered the alienation of the poorest fraction of Berlin's working class from the Social Democratic Party (*Sozialdemokratische Partei Deutschlands* or SPD) at a time when class unity was most necessary.

To explain these developments, this essay first describes the neighborhood in which the Beyes incident took place. It then examines the particular political background of the incident, the texts invoked by the protesters, the reactions these texts provoked in segments of the bourgeois press, how these reactions influenced future police conduct, and how the incident affected relations between Communists and Social Democrats in the final critical years of the Republic. Common to all these investigations is a careful attention to language. To receive Communist sponsorship, the demonstrators had to employ Communist language and symbols. For them, the use of cataclysmic language – language that did not bear directly on the issues at hand – was not problematic, since its invocation won the support of the party with the largest vote tally in the city.[4] Yet winning the KPD's support practically guaranteed the hostility of the rest of society. The language of revolution was probably incidental to the marchers' purposes. It was precisely this language, however, on which the press focused. By concentrating on the lyrics of the songs the protesters sang, the slogans they shouted, the banners they carried, and the clothing they wore, conservative reporters presented a very different impression of the show. This misapprehension had wide-ranging political consequences.

Like contemporary observers, historians of German working-class culture also err in decontextualizing music. Befitting its centrality to the working-class movement, proletarian music has received considerable attention, principally from historians of the former German Democratic Republic. This research, like that done in the west, has concentrated on a narrow set of issues, including lyrics and music's organizational milieu. Typical questions posed in such work include: Which sections of the movement were revolutionary? Which were reformist? What do the texts of the songs say about the ideology of the choruses? Were the pieces sung by the choruses truly folk music?[5] Among western German historians, Werner Fuhr has differentiated between proletarian and critical bourgeois songs (*Vortragslieder*). The former, he believes, moved beyond explications of the contradictions between bourgeois ideals (individualism) and the reality of bourgeois society (mass poverty) and developed a positive, concrete socialist alternative. In addition, the singer of such lyrics no longer acted as a mere individual but rather as a megaphone for his or her class.[6] Gert Hagelweide is another who analyzes the imagery of Communist songs sung during the Weimar and postwar periods. However, be-

---

4. In the Reichstag elections of 14 Sept. 1930, fifteen days before the protest march took place, the KPD received 27.3 percent of Berlin's vote, 0.1 percent greater than that of the SPD, the second largest party. For the complete figures, see Table 4, "Reichstags-, Landtags-, Stadt- und Bezirksverordnetenwahlen 1920–1933 in Berlin (Gesamtergebnisse)," in Otto Büsch and Wolfgang Haus, *Berliner Demokratie 1919–1985*, vol. 1, *Berlin als Hauptstadt der Weimarer Republik 1919–1933* (Berlin/New York, 1987), 323.
5. One of the most important scholars who studies this issue is Wolfgang Steinitz. His major work is *Deutsche Volkslieder demokratischen Characters aus sechs Jahrhunderten*, 2 vols. (East Berlin, 1954–62). See also Kurt Thomas, "Arbeiterlied-Volkslied-Arbeitervolkslied: Eine Studie zur Problematik des folklorisierten Arbeiterliedes," *Beiträge zur Musikwissenschaft* 13 (1971): 83–8 (photo reprint by Verlag Neue Musik, Berlin, 1979).
6. Werner Fuhr, *Proletarische Musik in Deutschland 1928–1933* (Göttingen, 1977), 201.

cause of limited access to the sources, he presents only a sketchy picture of how they were performed and by whom.[7]

One of the most significant western historians of German working-class music is Vernon Lidtke. Yet even his valuable work on both working-class music during the Weimar Republic and Nazi music is based largely upon textual analysis.[8] Lidtke differentiates among three functions of Communist and Social Democratic songs: social polarization, social integration, and communication.[9] In his discussion of the songs' integrative functions, he does not discuss performance venue, audiences, who is being integrated, or into what; rather, he bases his assertions on a study of the choral books used by the Social Democratic movement.[10] Unfortunately, this approach leaves no room for studying working-class music in its full context. The present essay therefore attempts to unite the study of lyrics with the larger social reality within which they operated.

NEUKÖLLN

In 1926 the Communist Party's flagship newspaper, the *Rote Fahne*, described the district where the Beyes incident took place as follows:

Long gray streets. Apartment buildings squeezed narrowly together. Rental barracks, narrow courtyards, rear buildings four stories tall. In between factories and then more apartment buildings. The rumble of wagons on poorly-made streets, the honking of horns, the ringing of street cars, the whistles of the factories and locomotives mix with the cries of the street traders, who call out their wares in the courtyards. The noise of the big city.[11]

Two years later, the *Rote Fahne* published a portrayal of what it called Neukölln's "Zille House."[12] Although the newspaper subtitled the

---

7. Gert Hagelweide, *Das publizistische Erscheinungsbild des Menschen im kommunistischen Lied. Eine Untersuchung der Liedpublizistik der KPD (1919–1933) und der SED (1945–1960)* (Bremen, 1968). His brief discussion of performers and performance appears on pp. 29–34.
8. Vernon Lidtke, "Songs and Politics: An Exploratory Essay on Arbeiterlieder in the Weimar Republic," *Archiv für Sozialgeschichte* 14 (1974): 253–73; Lidtke, "Songs and Nazis: Political Music and Social Change in Twentieth-Century Germany," in Gary D. Stark and Bede Karl Lackner, eds., *Essays on Culture and Society in Modern Germany* (College Station, Texas, 1982), 167–200.
9. Lidtke, "Songs and Politics," 257–9.
10. Ibid., 257f.
11. Anon., "Neukölln," *Die Rote Fahne*, 3 July 1926.
12. Anon., "Das 'Zille-Haus' in Neukölln: ein charakteristisches Bild Wohnverhältnisse," *Die Rote Fahne*, 15 Aug. 1928. This name was derived from Heinrich Zille, an artist whose

article a "characteristic picture," the sanitary conditions of this apartment building were much worse than those in which most workers lived. The description, however, indicates the living conditions of Berlin's poorer working class. Located on Richardstrasse 35 (a street that ran from Richardplatz, where the Beyes demonstration ended), the "Zille House" was an architecturally typical Berlin tenement. The complex, which housed approximately 400 people in 130 apartments, had a building facing the street and five buildings rowed behind it. The *Rote Fahne* chose to concentrate its description on two of the buildings, Numbers Three and Five. Building Number Three contained twenty-five apartments, twenty of which were six square meters in size (these dimensions included the apartments' one room and kitchen). The building's eighty-eight residents shared nine toilets. The ground floors of these buildings were extremely unsanitary. There, the ratio of residents to toilets was 17:1 in building Number Three and 14:1 in building Number Five. It was not unusual for the floors to be covered with human waste, as the building's pipes were frequently broken or backed up. (Of Neukölln's 5,412 parcels of built-up land, only 3,912 were connected to sewers in 1928.)[13] For these apartments on Richardstrasse, tenants paid between twenty-five and thirty marks per month – close to the average rent for a one-room apartment in Berlin at the time.[14] These conditions were not "mere" Communist propaganda. Neukölln's housing department reported a housing shortage, especially during the 1920s, when lodgings – those with one or two rooms – that fell within the affordable range for the borough's poor residents were in particularly short supply. It was not unusual for a family with ten members to inhabit such a residence. Although the borough's housing department also singled out Richardstrasse 35 as an especially noxious example, it added that there were many other equally unhealthy apartments in the area.[15]

work concentrated on the lives of Berlin's working class. For a compilation of autobiographical information by Heinrich Zille, see *Heinrich Zille in Selbstzeugnissen und Bilddokumenten*, dargestellt von Lothar Fischer (Reinbek bei Hamburg, 1979). For a representative sample of his work, which shows Berlin's proletariat at work and play, see Herbert Reinoss, *Das neue Zille-Buch* (Hannover, 1981).
13. Paul Körner, "Neukölln – Rixdorf," *Die Rote Fahne*, 5 Dec. 1928.
14. See the chart listing the legal rent rates for Berlin in Statistischen Amt der Stadt Berlin, ed., *Statistisches Jahrbuch der Stadt Berlin, 1930* (Berlin, 1930), 49.
15. Neukölln's housing department's report is reprinted in Bruno Schwan, *Die Wohnungsnot und das Wohnungselend in Deutschland*, vol. 7 in a series published by the Deutsche Verein für Wohnungsreform (Berlin, 1929), 128f.

Communist Music in the Streets 273

These dangerous conditions were reflected in the disease rate for the district. In 1928 Neukölln's tuberculosis station examined a total of 18,539 possible cases of tuberculosis. This number was approximately 7,100 more than in the second worst district, Lichtenberg, also a proletarian quarter.[16] The health of the district's inhabitants was certainly not helped by the fact that Neukölln had only six physicians for every 10,000 residents; this was proportionally six times fewer than the number of doctors who served the wealthy district of Charlottenburg.[17]

If this were not enough to generate widespread bitterness among the district's population, growing unemployment and a police massacre of workers on 1 May 1929 added to the brew. By 1933 the district's unemployment rate would reach 33.6 percent, a total of 56,952 people.[18] The story of "Bloody May" has been told elsewhere in great detail.[19] It is enough to note here that the Communist Party's peaceful May First celebrations of 1929 were interrupted by police shots in which a number of innocent people were killed. In the wake of these events, residents of the boroughs of Wedding and Neukölln built barricades. As the police tore down these barricades, even more people were killed. This action certainly spawned a great deal of bitterness against the SPD-controlled police department and, by extension, against the SPD. In the state elections of 20 May 1928, the SPD received 40.3 percent of Neukölln's vote, against the KPD's 30.9 percent. Following this election, the parties' positions slowly began to shift. In the Reichstag elections of 14 September 1930 the KPD received 34.9 percent of the district's vote, against 32.6 percent for the SPD.[20]

---

16. See chart 291, "Städtische Tuberkulosefürsorge 1928," in *Statistisches Jahrbuch der Stadt Berlin, 1930,* 221.
17. See ibid., 214, for chart 285, "Ärtzte, Heilpersonal und Apotheken Ende 1928."
18. See the table "Arbeitslose" in Büsch and Haus, *Berlin als Hauptstadt,* 443. Unfortunately, I have no unemployment statistics for Neukölln in 1930.
19. The only book-length study of these events is Thomas Kurz, *"Blutmai." Sozialdemokraten und Kommunisten im Brennpunkt der Berliner Ereignisse von 1929* (Berlin/Bonn, 1988). See also Chris Bowlby, "Blutmai 1929: Police, Parties and Proletarians in a Berlin Confrontation," *Historical Journal* 29 (1986): 137–58; and Eve Rosenhaft, "Working-class Life and Working-class Politics: Communists, Nazis and the Battle for the Streets, Berlin 1928–1932," in Richard Bessel and Edgar Feuchtwanger, eds., *Social Change and Political Development in Weimar Germany* (Totowa, N.J., 1981), 207–40.
20. These figures come from the election chart in Büsch and Haus, *Berlin als Hauptstadt,* 444.

THE RESPONSE OF THE COMMUNIST PARTY

On 29 March 1930 the KPD's Central Committee sent the secretaries of the party's various district leaderships strategy guidelines for the upcoming elections to parents' committees in the schools.[21] In addition to a directive to expand the struggle against the school authorities' measures to save money, the Central Committee stressed the need to link this issue to broader ones: the lack of money for health and welfare and the fight against rent increases, as well as issues related directly to schools, such as free school materials for the students. The enclosure referred to a school strike in Neukölln the previous October – organized to protest the deaths of three children from diphtheria – as a possible example to follow.[22]

On 23 September 1930 the *Rote Fahne* ran an article asserting that a new diphtheria epidemic was sweeping through a number of Neukölln's schools. The newspaper claimed further that sanitary conditions in the district's schools were catastrophic. Unfortunately, the closest year to 1930 for which pertinent health information exists is 1928. In that year Neukölln reported 424 cases of diphtheria; this figure was the sixth highest among Berlin's twenty districts and more than four times the number reported in the wealthy district of Zehlendorf.[23] In response to these conditions, revolutionary socialist (probably Communist) students had already launched a protest. Furthermore, some parents of girls enrolled in the Käthe Kollwitz school, which was near the six schools affected, held a protest meeting at 8 P.M. on 23 September 1930 in the auditorium of the Karl Marx School on Kaiser-Friedrich-Strasse.[24]

On the same day that the *Rote Fahne* reported the diphtheria outbreak, it also reported a protest held by a group of what it described as "Christian" parents against the firing of the teacher, Fritz Beyes,

---

21. Hektographiertes Anweisungen des Sekretariats, Bundesarchiv (hereafter BA) Koblenz, R 134/60/174–214, and BA Koblenz R 451V/24/238, reprinted in Hermann Weber and Johann Wachtler, eds., *Die Generallinie. Rundschreiben des Zentralkomitees der KPD an die Bezirke 1929–1933*, Quellen zur Geschichte des Parlamentarismus und der politischen Parteien, Dritte Reihe: Die Weimarer Republik, vol. 6 (Düsseldorf, 1981). The enclosure, "Anweisungen der Agitpropabteilung zu den Elternbeiratswahlen," was signed by the Zentralkomitee Agitprop; 139–42.
22. Ibid., 140.
23. See Table 39, "Gemeldete übertragbare Krankheiten 1928," in *Statistisches Jahrbuch der Stadt Berlin, 1930*, 36.
24. Anon., "Diphtherieepidemie in Neukölln: Kampf um ein neues Schulgebäude," *Die Rote Fahne*, 23 Sept. 1930.

"who enjoys the respect and love of the whole school." The newspaper asserted that these parents were certain to appear at future protest meetings as well.[25] The following day, the newspaper printed a description of a school in Lichtenberg that had also suffered a diphtheria epidemic. Between October 1929 and Easter 1930, seventeen children had contracted diphtheria, of whom four died. Since then nothing had been done to disinfect the building, and two more children had contracted the disease.[26] Four days later, the *Rote Fahne* reported on a meeting that had taken place on 23 September 1930 to protest what it called the Prussian government's belief that by firing Beyes it had removed the proletarian parents' influence on their children's education. The newspaper exhorted parents and civil servants to attend that evening's demonstration to protest the firing of Beyes – this is the demonstration described at the outset of this essay.[27] The Communist Party used these disparate elements to construct one story, asserting that it was up to proletarian parents to take matters into their own hands, as the government did not care about either the health or the education of working-class children.

THE TEXTS

As is true of all forms of expression, songs have both strengths and weaknesses as means of communication. Songs last longer than slogans. Moreover, music underscores the explicit meaning of the phrases, providing them with a rhythm and verve that they would otherwise lack. But the very brevity of songs restricts their impact. Songs can tell stories and advocate resistance or attack, but they cannot develop a strategy or provide serious tactical advice. The more complex their structure, the more difficult they are to perform. If they are too complex and difficult, they are inappropriate for street demonstrations. The most that can seriously be expected of songs sung at demonstrations is that they provide a self-representation of the performers – who they are and what they hope to accomplish.

25. Anon., "Elternprotest bei SPD.-Minister Grimme. Besucht die Elternversammlungen und beschliesst Kampfmassnahmen!" *Die Rote Fahne*, 23 Sept. 1930.
26. Anon., "Seuchenschule in Lichtenberg. Innerhalb eines Jahres fünf Todesopfer – Die Auswirkung der Spardiktatur des SPD. Magistrats," *Die Rote Fahne*, 24 Sept. 1930. It is odd that the body of the article claims four deaths, whereas the headline claims five.
27. Anon., "Gegen den Schanderlass der preussischen Regierung. Solidarität mit F. Beyes. Ein Aufruf der Reinickendorfer Arbeitereltern," *Die Rote Fahne*, 28 Sept. 1930.

The following analysis of the material sung by those street protesters who wished to reinstate Fritz Beyes is divided into six categories (see the Appendix):[28]

1. The singer's "voice."
2. The song's subject.
3. Tactics advocated in the lyrics.
4. Attitudes toward state and society.
5. Goals expressed in the songs.
6. Symbols used or referred to in the songs' texts.

The songs under consideration were written either in the first person – expressing the hopes, actions, or appearance of the performers – or in a combination of the first and third persons.[29] The first-person narrative lends the songs an immediacy and an urgency that might be lacking in a different format. This urgency is especially important in the light of the songs' subjects. They are all songs of struggle, either recalling the struggles of the January 1919 revolution or urging an attack against an indeterminate enemy, against businessmen and fascists, against Carl Severing's prohibition of Communist paramilitary organizations, or against Hitler and his storm troopers. The singing of these songs during a protest march would have had a visceral effect on the participants and the observers. Although the songs are spirited, and some refer to rifles and shotguns, they are quite vague in the tactics they advocate. They express hostility to the state and society as it was constituted, for example, equating both with Severing's prohibition. One song, the "Buxensteinlied," refers to the armed forces – in the context of the 1919 revolution – as "Noske's Hounds," recalling how the Free Corps, under the orders of Social Democrat Gustav Noske, had crushed left-wing resistance

---

28. The parade participants sang the RFB's version of "Wir sind die erste Reihe" (this is probably what the reporter referred to as the "Barricade Song") and the "Büxensteinlied." The song that the police identified as the "Antifa-lied" was probably the "Antifaschistenlied" written by the agitprop troupe, Curve Left, Berlin, for the Antifascist Young Guard, the successor organization to the outlawed Red Young Front. In addition, what the *Berliner Börsen-Zeitung*'s reporter referred to as the "Trutzlied" of the illegal Antifascist Young Guard may have been the song, "Trotz Verbot," written by the agitprop troupe named Red Blouses, Berlin, to protest the prohibition of the Red Young Front. The song titles, listed in order and in English translation, are: "We are the First Row," reprinted in Inge Lammel and Elfriede Berger, eds., *Das Lied im Kampf Geboren,* Lieder des Roten Frontkämpferbundes, vol. 8 (Leipzig, 1961), 65f.; "Büxenstein Song," in ibid., 109f.; "In Spite of Prohibition," in ibid., 94f.; and the "Antifascist Song," in ibid., 96f.
29. In a variation of this first-person perspective, the "Antifaschistenlied" was a call to arms, providing reasons to join the struggle.

to the creation of the Weimar Republic.[30] This reference would have had special resonance in Neukölln, where only sixteen months earlier, SPD-controlled police had once again massacred workers.

The lyrical symbols are militant; they include the Spartacists, the Soviet Union, Rosa Luxemburg, and Karl Liebknecht. In addition, the lyrics refer to significant colors. In the song "Trotz Verbot," the gray shirts of the working class are coupled with the red fist, red flag, red army, red Berlin, and red front. The intended contrast is between mundane existence and the excitement of revolution. The songs' goals are fairly uniform. They include defeating Hitler, building a new world, protecting the Soviet Union, and planting the Soviet flag.

Like the lyrics themselves, the march and the accompanying speeches were also texts. This march was a small local affair. The circumstances leading up to it – the firing of a popular teacher, diphtheria in the schools – were of direct local concern. Certainly it lacked the mass character of a huge party-sponsored demonstration, an event that was typically accompanied by the speeches of famous Communist leaders. To the participants, however, this march had an immediacy that was reinforced by the fact that they were, in effect, protesting the ugly concrete reality surrounding them. Such a meeting strengthened solidarity, as the conditions under protest were obvious. Normally, the advantages of immediacy were overshadowed by the lack of resonance that such a small-scale action would have elsewhere, especially in the very well-to-do districts located only a few miles to the west of Neukölln. In other words, solidarity and immediacy were achieved at the expense of effectiveness. However, for reasons only tangentially related to the march itself, this protest action did resonate, even though the consequences of the resonance were completely different from what the protesters wanted or expected.

It is important to note the language with which the marchers aired their concerns. Beyes and the other speakers expressed the concerns of the local citizens in Communist Party terms. Thus they invoked

---

30. For a brief history of the events of January 1919, see Anthony J. Nicholls, *Weimar and the Rise of Hitler* (New York, 1968), 23f. Nicholls rightly underscores the unnecessary brutality of the action. In his book, *Von Kiel bis Kapp*, Gustav Noske repeated his infamous statement, "Einer muss der Bluthund werden, ich scheue die Verantwortung nicht!" (One must be the bloodhound, and I will not shirk the responsibility!) This statement is reprinted in Gerhard A. Ritter and Susanne Miller, eds., *Die Deutsche Revolution 1918–1919. Dokumente* (Frankfurt a.M., 1983), 181.

the language of cataclysm, a language that in the contemporary political situation might be therapeutic, ascribing an ultimate power to the proletariat that present reality denied. The rhetoric of violence and civil war, coupled with praise for the Soviet Union, could not, of course, improve the lot of Neukölln's poor. Such language could only console the listeners with promises of retribution and a golden future or conjure up the appearance of international support for their cause. But consolation and unfounded hope were *not* what bourgeois journalists reported as hallmarks of the march.

THE BOURGEOIS PRESS

Although the lyrics sung by the marchers were merely one in a series of texts partially dictated by circumstance, two newspapers did not find them innocuous. Police warned the marchers to desist each time they attempted to sing either the "Antifaschistenlied" or the "Barrikadenlied." Because the marchers heeded the warning, the police saw no need to end the protest.[31] Two representatives of the conservative bourgeois press, however, took a much more literal, less sanguine view of the event. They chose to concentrate on what would have been seen as the more inflammatory aspects of the march: the songs, slogans, speeches, and uniforms.

The same day that the officer charged with controlling the march filed his report, the *Berliner Börsen-Zeitung* published an outraged article about the event, entitled, "To the Barricades! Police who have Forgotten their Duty."[32] The author described the event as a scandal taking place under the eyes of the police. The parade was led by a "blood red" flag on which were inscribed the Russian words "From the Lenin Youth Group of Charkow to the Communist Children of Berlin!" It was accompanied by songs whose lyrics included the phrase "striding toward a blood red victory." The reporter took the songs' lyrics literally, relating them to an article he had recently read in the *Junge Garde,* which had advocated military training for the imminent civil war. The *Berliner Börsen-Zeitung*'s reporter contended that a number of the songs sung by the marchers had been legally prohibited and that surely the police had heard them. The author

---

31. Polizeipräsident, Abteilung IA., File Nr. 1313 IA.3a.30, dated Berlin, 23 Oct. 1930; in IML, St22/169.
32. Anon., "'Heraus auf die Barrikaden!' Pflichtvergessene Polizei," *Berliner Börsen-Zeitung,* 30 Sept. 1930, in IML, St22/169.

concluded the piece by asking how Berlin's police president and Prussia's police minister[33] planned to deal with the KPD's preparations for civil war.

The following day, the conservative *Reichsbote* printed a description of the event that, if anything, was even more hysterical in tone.[34] This article was entitled "'Out to the Barricades – To Bloody Red Victory!' Civil War Propaganda under the Protection and with the Help of the Police Force." It offered a more detailed description of the procession than had appeared in the *Börsen-Zeitung*. It claimed that most of the participants were members of what it referred to as the "infamous" Young Spartacus League and the Communist Youth League of Germany. The *Reichsbote*'s reporter described the Soviet banner as a flag of civil war and claimed that the police had been duplicitous in what was perhaps the most blatant civil war propaganda Berlin had experienced since the Spartacus uprising. Even greater outrage was expressed over "such an unimaginably heavy damaging of the state's authority and security." Accordingly, duty demanded that the Prussian minister of the interior and the Berlin police president report how they were going to stop the Communists' preparations for civil war. After announcing that the bourgeoisie's patience must end, the reporter concluded the article with the dubious assertion: "Everybody knows quite well that if a politically right-wing organization were to sing even one song of 'bloody victory on the barricades' they could expect the sharpest interference of the police and the heaviest punishment. It would be broken up without delay and charged with high treason."[35] An editorial comment attached to the article added that every non-Bolshevik reading the piece must

---

33. Such a ministry did not exist; the author was probably referring to the minister of the interior.
34. Anon., "'Heraus auf die Barrikaden – zum blutig roten Sieg!' Bürgerkriegspropaganda unterm Schutz und mit Hilfe der Schutzpolizei," *Der Reichsbote*, 1 Oct. 1930, in IML, St22/169.
35. In fact, in political cases the left was always treated with greater severity than the right. The most infamous example of this was, of course, Adolf Hitler's minimal sentence for his involvement in the Munich Putsch. According to Istvan Deak, "in the first four years of the republic German courts convicted 38 Leftist offenders accused of 22 political murders. Ten of these defendants were executed, the rest were given an average of fifteen years in prison. In the same period, there were 354 rightist political murders but the courts convicted only 24 rightists. Not one of these defendants was executed and those convicted received an average of four months in prison. Twenty-three of the confessed rightist murderers were acquitted." These figures come from Emil J. Gumbel, *Von Fememord zur Reichskanzlei* (Heidelberg, 1962), 46, and are reprinted in Istvan Deak, *Weimar Germany's Left-Wing Intellectuals. A Political History of the Weltbühne and Its Circle* (Berkeley, 1968), 123.

conclude that Germany was at the same stage as France during the Great Terror, when the armed sections of the Parisian proletariat gathered together to rape the parliament.

There were a number of important discrepancies between the accounts presented by the officer on duty and by the newspaper reporters. For example, the officer said that the march never became uncontrollable. Yet, stripped of the hyperbole, even the newspaper reports do not relate a horrible tale. The reporters infused a sense of danger into the event that neither the participants nor the police seemed to see. The references to children and teenagers as "notorious" and the description of an innocuous banner as a "flag of civil war" are, on the face of it, gross overreactions. In context, however, it is possible to see how such interpretations were reached. The reporters heard references to the January 1919 revolution, which many middle-class Germans remembered with horror. The fact that these references were made in one of the "barricade districts" where police had clashed with workers in May 1929, coupled with the presence of what could be construed as military uniforms and "dangerous" banners, make this overreaction more understandable still. Most unfortunate of all was the fact that the police authorities were ready to act upon these complaints rather than trust the judgment of their officers in the field.

THE POLICE

Although a second police report reiterated points made in the first, stating that the protesters obeyed police directions, the newspaper articles created a storm within the Berlin police hierarchy.[36] Two weeks after the second report, the police department sent yet another report to the Prussian ministry of the interior. This memorandum seems to have been based primarily upon the police reports and newspaper articles discussed earlier. It concluded with the policy statement that in the future police would disperse parades and demonstrations as soon as the participants began to sing prohibited songs.[37] This conclusion was allegedly based on past experience indicating that as soon as police left the scene, demonstrators sang unacceptable material.[38]

36. Illegible signature, report dated 9 Oct. 1930, Krim. Sekr. Abt.I.A. III.G.St., in IML, St22/169.
37. Illegible signature, letter from the Police President, 23 Oct. 1930, Abteilung IA, Tgb.Nr. 1313 IA.3a.30, in IML, St22/169.
38. Ibid.; this report seems to accept the newspaper accounts of what was sung but does not refer directly to Werviel's report.

After the Berlin police reported to the Prussian minister of the interior, the crackdown on agitational music intensified. On 21 November 1930 the *Rote Fahne* reported that the police dissolved a protest march due to the singing of prohibited music. The newspaper advised its readers to report future incidents to Arthur Golke.[39] Golke, one of the KPD's delegates in the Prussian parliament,[40] had written a letter to the Berlin police on 10 October 1930, complaining that the police dissolved many Communist demonstrations because prohibited songs were sung.[41] Stating that the police used the performance of such labor classics as the "Internationale" and "Brüder zur Sonne, zur Freiheit" to end demonstrations, Golke requested a list of the prohibited pieces.

According to the *Rote Fahne,* as late as 18 November 1930 – that is, thirty-nine days after he first wrote to the police – Arthur Golke had not yet received a reply to his query.[42] Because the police failed to respond to Golke, a reporter from the *Rote Fahne* approached the police press office (which was set up at a demonstration in the Lustgarten) to inquire as to which songs could not be sung. The officer in charge of the office was not present; however, an officer from Division IA (the political police) was available to answer questions. This man stated that there was no list of forbidden songs. Rather, the prohibition was to be left to the discretion of the officer in charge. The *Rote Fahne*'s reporter used this answer to launch a diatribe against "social fascism." By this he meant the "reactionary" SPD, which was the largest party in the Berlin city parliament, and which controlled the state of Prussia and therefore the Berlin police.[43]

---

39. Anon., "Durchkreuzt die Provokationen, 'Verbotene Lieder' Demonstrationsauflösungen sind sofort an den Genossen Golke zu melden," *Die Rote Fahne,* 21 Nov. 1930.
40. Arthur Golke (1886–1937?) belonged to the KPD's left wing and entered into a marriage of convenience with Ruth Fischer to allow her to obtain German citizenship. He was a deputy in the Prussian parliament from 1924 to 1933 and was a member of the party's central committee from 1927. After 1933 he emigrated first to Paris, then to the Soviet Union, where he disappeared in 1937. This biographical sketch is taken from Hermann Weber, *Die Wandlung des deutschen Kommunismus: Die Stalinisierung der KPD in der Weimarer Republik,* 2 vols. (Frankfurt a.M., 1969), 2:140.
41. Arthur Golke to the commander of Berlin's Schutzpolizei, 10 Oct. 1930, in IML, St22/169.
42. Anon., "Weshalb Zörgiebel, Grzesinski, Severing Arbeiterlieder verbieten. Der Provokationsplan der Berliner Polizei. In einer Woche 25 Demonstrationszüge wegen Singens 'verbotener' Arbeiterlieder aufgelöst," *Die Rote Fahne,* 18 Nov. 1930.
43. In the city parliament elections of November 1929 the SPD received 28.4 percent of the vote; the second largest delegation was the KPD, with 24.6 percent, followed by the German National People's Party (DNVP), with 20.8 percent. These figures are from Büsch and Haus, *Berlin als Hauptstadt,* 63. For the SPD's communal politics in Berlin, see Edward Gough, "Die SPD in der Berliner Kommunalpolitik 1925–1933" (Ph.D. diss.,

As the Communist Party protested this vague prohibition, the police department drew up a response to Golke. The first draft claimed that the police would interfere in a demonstration only when words were used that specifically broke criminal law.[44] It provided two examples. The first of these was the lyric "My son was murdered by the police (*Schupo*)," which was alleged to slander police officers. The second was the lyric "We are the Red Front Fighters League." This allegedly broke Articles 4 and 11 of the Law for the Protection of the Republic, since the Red Front Fighters League (*Rote Frontkämpferbund* or RFB) was an outlawed organization. An addendum of sorts to this letter noted that if the overwhelming majority of persons in a procession were to sing outlawed songs, the demonstration could no longer be considered legally peaceful; in this case, in addition to the prosecution of the individual singers, police would disperse the parade. This letter was apparently never sent. Between the time the first letter was drafted and a second was sent, police attitudes seem to have hardened.

An internal memorandum dated 3 November 1930 took a number of police officers to task for failing to deal harshly enough with those who sang prohibited songs during demonstrations and marches. Henceforth, the singing of such songs would prompt the immediate dispersal of the demonstration and, if possible, the arrest of the singers, who were to be turned over to Division IA. Included in this memorandum was a list of examples of lyrics and songs that were legally unacceptable, as well as the promise that a complete list of unacceptable Communist – and National Socialist – songs was being prepared.[45] In the wake of this memorandum the police sent Golke a

---

Free University of Berlin, 1984). For Prussia's government during this period, see Hans-Peter Ehni, *Bollwerk Preussen? Preussen-Regierung, Reich-Länder-Problem und Sozialdemokratie 1928–1932* (Bonn, 1975), and Horst Möller, *Parlamentarismus in Preussen 1919–1932* (Düsseldorf, 1985). On the police see H.-L. Liang, *The Berlin Police Force in the Weimar Republic* (Berkeley, 1970). Berlin's police president for much of this period, Albert Grzesinski, published his memoirs under the title *Inside Germany* (New York, 1939).

44. Letter from the police president (Division IA) to Arthur Golke, written in October 1930 (no specific day), in IML, St22/169.

45. Internal police memorandum, 3 Nov. 1930, signed Heimannsberg. Reprinted in Inge Lammel, ed., *Arbeitermusikkultur in Deutschland 1844–1945* (Leipzig, 1984), 87. By July 1931 there was a list of prohibited material, where the "Antifaschistenlied" and "Wir sind die erste Reihe," both sung at the Beyes protest, were cited. For the complete list as of 1 July 1931, see "Verzeichnis der nach einer Mitteilung des Landeskriminalpolizeiamts Berlin vom 1.7.1931 verbotenen kommunistischen Lieder," reprinted in Hagelweide, *Erscheinungsbild*, 323.

letter that consisted of little more than the following remarkable passage:[46]

In response to your letter of 10-10-1930, the singing of songs at demonstrations which you mentioned depends solely upon the lyrics. It is well known that they change, so that the texts of the "same songs" often differ. When the wording of the songs breaks criminal law, it is the duty of the police to intercede. *It is left to the singers to consider in advance and carefully whether they are breaking the law* [italics added].

On 2 December 1930, three weeks after the police responded to Golke's request for information, Fritz Löwenthal, a Communist Reichstag deputy, wrote a letter of protest to Berlin's police president.[47] Here he complained about police brutality in ending demonstrations at which the "forbidden songs" were sung. In addition, he expressed his unhappiness that, although the Nazis had a list of material that they knew was impermissible to sing, Communists never knew what would be allowed in any given situation. Löwenthal added:

The police cannot base their actions on the claims that the songs are sung in differing versions. I know of a number of cases in which the police, upon hearing preparations to begin singing a song (the standard version of which is perfectly allowable), began swinging their rubber truncheons in their usual brutal manner. In other words, they did not wait to see whether the song would be sung in a manner which could be legally prohibited.

On this basis, Löwenthal made the quite understandable demand that the police either inform the KPD which songs would break the law – and which law was being broken – or at the very least explain the rules they used to determine whether a song was acceptable.

Unfortunately, the archives hold no evidence that Löwenthal's letter was ever answered. However, a court case that was decided two weeks after Löwenthal's letter was sent gives some indication of the lack of sympathy with which the authorities viewed his position.[48] The KPD-affiliated Worker's Sport Club Köpenick held a march on 24 August 1930. Attached to, but separate from, this march was a group of ten youths preceded by a flag bearer. During this march this group sang the "Propellerlied," which on the occa-

---

46. Letter from the police president (Division IA) to Arthur Golke, 11 Nov. 1930, in IML, St22/169.
47. Löwenthal to the police president of Berlin, 2 Dec. 1930, in IML, St22/169.
48. The following is based upon Mitteilungen des P.P. Landeskriminalpolizeiamts IA Berlin, 1 Mar. 1931, and Enclosure L 4, both in IML, St10/59/1.

sion of this "performance" included the lyric "We soar in spite of Severing's prohibition! Red Front!" This lyric replaced the standard refrain "We soar in spite of hate and scorn!" Lieutenant Lange, the police officer in charge of the detachment that accompanied the march, forbade the singing of this lyric. At that point the group replaced it with the line "We soar in spite of hate and prohibition!" The police saw this as support for the outlawed RFB. Thus it constituted, first, an open meeting in support of an illegal organization and, second, a public call to ignore legally constituted authority. The police charged the singers with violation of Article 4 Z.1 of the Law for the Protection of the Republic.

In court, seven of the defendants admitted that they sang this lyric. In their defense, however, they claimed that when Lieutenant Lange forbade them to sing the first line, they stopped. They had then asked Lange if it was legal for them to sing the last line in combination with "Red Front!" As Lange did not answer, they had assumed that it was legal. However, the court found that the silence of the lieutenant was an inadmissible defense: "The defendants could not use the witness's [Lieutenant Lange's] silence as an assent. He was correct in refusing to answer, as he had clearly expressed his prohibition and explained the consequences. Also, it was not his job to instruct the questioners."[49] The three other defendants had a different strategy. They based their claims to innocence on the assertion that they could not sing; in any event, they added, they did not know the text. The court rejected this defense too, explaining that their membership in the KJVD proved explicit support for the singers: purely outside factors prevented them from joining the singing. The final defendant was declared innocent, as he claimed that his attachment to the group was accidental. In the end, the court sentenced six of the defendants to three months' incarceration each. Three of the others were sentenced to two weeks' incarceration each. The final two were set free.[50]

CONCLUSION

These minor incidents must be considered in the broader context of working-class politics. The overreaction of the police to the essen-

---

49. Enclosure L 4, in IML, St10/59/1.
50. The police report to which the enclosure was attached concluded with the following remark: "The sentence is not final. All of the convicted have appealed the decision [Das Urteil ist nicht rechtskräftig. Sämtliche Verurteilte haben Revision eingelegt]."

tially juvenile pranks of some young Communists was merely one indicator of the poisoned relationship between the SPD and the KPD. It was just one of many obstacles to a rapprochement between the two major left-wing parties. The poorest fraction of the working class and the state deepened their mutual distrust. These same proletarians, not surprisingly, identified the SPD with the state and withheld their votes accordingly, whereas the KPD saw and responded to their concerns. Communist Party support radicalized their language, but it did nothing to make proletarian politics more effective. Indeed, the apparently radicalized working class seems to have lost middle-class sympathy and thus any hope for political effectiveness. This is because the KPD's infusion into this reality merely resulted in more noise, not more action to solve the problems of the working class. As the conditions of the poorest elements of the working class worsened, their increasingly radical protests merely served to intensify bourgeois hostility and police action. This was a further step in the disintegration of the working-class movement into two warring factions. One faction retreated into the politics of rhetoric, which further frightened the dominant elements of society. The other found itself forced into the uncomfortable role of favoring right-wing opinions and policies diametrically opposed to the interests of its "natural" constituency. Thus Weimar Prussia found itself in the unenviable position of acting to repress and therefore alienate a large section of the population while never doing enough to satisfy the extreme right wing. In the end, having lost its working-class support but having failed to win any conservative support to replace it, Weimar Prussia, and later the entire Republic, died an almost unmourned death.

Appendix.

Song	Voice(s)	Subjects	Tactics	Relationship to State and Society	Symbols Employed	Goals
1. Trotz Verbot	-Alternates between the first and the third persons plural -"We" hold the red flag -R.J. Marches	-RJ will not be prohibited -We fight the SA, Hitler cannot destroy Red Berlin -After the battle is won, we will build in shafts and factories	-Unclear, however there is a reference to shotguns	-Severing's prohibition of the RJ	-Gray shirts (work shirts) -Red fist, red flag, red army, red Berlin, red front.	-To defeat Hitler -To build a new world
2. Wir sind die erste Reihe	-First person plural -Hands full of soot and callouses -Hands grasping rifles -Empty Stomachs -foreheads bathed in sweat	-one of identity, e.g. who the singers are and what they want	-To attack (mention of rifles) -To prepare for class struggle -To march -To "storm in the sign of the people's revolution" -"Jump on the barricades" -"Out to civil war"	-There is mention of the lack of fear for the weapons of the police	-The Soviet Union -Rosa Luxemburg -Karl Liebknecht	-Plant the Soviet Flag -To achieve a blood red victory
3. Buxensteinlied	-Alternating first and third person plural	-Revolutionary battle of January 1919	-Street fighting	-Reference to Noske's hounds	-The Sparticists	-All men will be brothers -Nobody will starve
4. Anti-faschistenlied	-The song is a call to workers	-Businessmen and Fascists are preparing for battle -They will attack the USSR -The Young Plan, reparations and rationalization rob bread from the workers as capital becomes stronger	-Unclear	-None is directly stated	-The USSR	-The protection of the USSR

11

Weimar Populism and National Socialism in Local Perspective

PETER FRITZSCHE

Historians agree that National Socialism should not be regarded as an unfortunate accident, or *Betriebsunfall,* marring German history but troubling the sweep of German tradition only very little.[1] It is misguided to understand the Nazis in terms of accidents or emergencies. Yet metaphors and images that draw attention to the chaos and breakability of Weimar continue to circulate widely. These seem to be indispensable components of an explanation of 1933. The mind's eye of the historian imagines economic crisis and political extremism pushing burghers farther and farther to the political periphery until they hit Nazism. Hans Fallada's *Little Man, What Now?* (1931), the chronicle of one young German who becomes a social castaway in Depression-era Berlin, is only the most literary example of this dominant historiographical trope.

Demolition is the most useful and orthodox strategy used to narrate twentieth-century German history. To get to Nazism, historians usually wreck all sorts of things in the 1920s: They undermine cherished assumptions about national identity, upend long-standing political loyalties to liberal and conservative parties, and destroy worlds of economic security and social intimacy. The German *Bürgertum,* in particular, is disassembled. The plot is familiar: Military defeat in 1918 comes as a shock to most Germans; the November Revolution realizes the worst nightmares of burghers, who are natural counterrevolutionaries; inflation and the "cold" stabilization that followed are equally traumatic; and finally, the traditional middle-class parties

---

1. I appreciate the comments of the Social History Group at the University of Illinois, particularly those of Carol Leff. Larry Eugene Jones and James Retallack have also been very helpful. I should add that this essay and the important contribution of Richard Bessel in this volume neatly represent two sides of a debate. This coincidence is helpful and nourishing, but I have not rewritten my paper as a direct response to his.

fall apart. As disaster follows disaster, narratives edge toward Nazism, which is comprehended as the final and most extreme register of Weimar's disorder. These metaphors of disintegration and disarray suggest that National Socialism is a tragic "worst case," an unlikely destination.

There is much in this view that is defensible. The economic hardships suffered by German burghers and the widespread political uncertainty that accompanied the rapid-fire creation of a new order in 1918 and 1919 leave historians dizzy even two generations later. The inflation, its resolution, and especially the Great Depression composed difficult and extraordinary years for all Germans. Yet the concentrated emphasis on crisis empties Nazism of any abiding popular appeal. Was National Socialism so improbable that it can only be made explicable in terms of turmoil and contingency? Is the rhetoric of consternation the most suitable to apprehend fascism?

In explaining National Socialism and the rough politics of interwar Europe more generally, pride of place is conventionally given to notions of "crisis" rather than "political appeal." In the economy of explanation, social and economic circumstances that act on historical subjects in ways that are rationally sensible are privileged over the distinctive self-understandings and aspirations that guide the interventions of social groups in ways that are not necessary. I want to explore this ontology more critically and, specifically, probe the extent to which the Nazis represented a welcome political formula to Protestant German burghers and even appeared to address basic expectations of political reform and enfranchisement. To focus on the continuities between middle-class politics in the 1920s and National Socialist success after 1930 and to draw attention to the basic familiarity rather than the novel singularity of the Nazi brownshirts, I have recirculated the concept of "populism," which is intended to evoke the robust style and reformist politics that bourgeois contenders shared in the Weimar period without erasing the important distinctions that remained.

A local perspective is particularly useful to identify popular assumptions and public dispositions about Weimar politics. To enter the political world of the provinces is to become aware of how peripheral the issues of the history books such as the stability of parliamentary government or the fate of Weimar democracy had become. It is on market squares and small-town streets, not in the Berlin offices of lobbyists and parliamentarians, that the confident style and insurgent substance of bourgeois politics in the 1920s emerges most clearly. However, local history, whose proper charge is to apprehend the fullness of political life, can mislead because it often makes general claims on the basis of particular evidence. The two pairs of examples that I provide from Oldenburg, a north German provincial capital in a largely agricultural state, are illustrative of dramatic shifts in the political culture of postwar Protestant communities, particularly in northern Germany, but should be treated with caution nonetheless. Fewer than 100,000 people lived in Oldenburg, mostly civil servants and the artisans and retailers typical of any *Residenzstadt*, but, thanks to Oldenburg's network of canals and railways, also a growing number of small manufacturers and blue-collar workers.[2] Oldenburg, like other German towns, saw repeated confrontations between socialists and nonsocialists. At the same time, however, middle-class constituents grew increasingly belligerent in their attempts to attain the political voice that they had been largely denied in the *Kaiserreich*.

Shortly after the beginning of the new year of 1919, on January 6, Oldenburg's prosperous merchants and shop owners met for the first time since the outbreak of the November Revolution. Speakers who addressed the Business and Trade Association of 1840 (*Gewerbe- und Handelsverein von 1840*), Oldenburg's most prominent commercial organization, surveyed the challenges posed by the new democratic era. The power socialists had assembled and the plans for socialization and municipalization they proposed plainly troubled business owners. Postwar demobilization and shortages of basic raw materials and foodstuffs added unwelcome burdens to the economy. At the same time, however, speakers urged merchants to make their voices heard in the political arena. However turbulent the process of revolutionary change was, Germany's venture into democratic politics offered Oldenburg's middle classes an unprecedented opportunity to secure political power. "The era of party bosses and kingmakers has passed," the chairman of the association announced. To work within the established bourgeois parties and take part in the horse trading and compromises of party politics was admittedly distasteful, he

---

2. On Oldenburg, see Oldenburgischer Landeslehrerverein, *Heimatkunde des Herzogtums Oldenburg* (Bremen, 1913); Hugo Ephraim, "Die Stadt Oldenburg in sozialstatistischer Beleuchtung," *Zeitschrift für die gesamte Staatswissenschaft* 34 (1910): Ergänzungsheft 1–126.

conceded, but the necessity of wielding parliamentary influence was also undeniable.[3]

The harsh lessons of democratic politics were learned by Oldenburg's artisans as well. For too long, explained one critic, artisans had been trailed along helplessly by indifferent patrons like the "fifth wheel on the wagon." The task ahead was to learn self-reliance and establish interest groups to lobby the major parties. Accordingly, in January 1919, bakers, carpenters, electricians, and other handicraftsmen formed a local branch of the Northwest German League of Artisans, the most influential handicraft group in northern Germany. The League of Artisans represented a declaration of independence: Artisans would now go the political course alone.[4]

For both merchants and artisans the traditional bourgeois parties, namely, the republican German Democratic Party (*Deutsche Demokratische Partei* or DDP), the liberal German People's Party (*Deutsche Volkspartei* or DVP), the conservative German National People's Party (*Deutschnationale Volkspartei* or DNVP), and, in Catholic areas, the Center Party, were the unquestioned sites of interest articulation in the first years after the revolution; single-interest parties, such as the fledging Business Party (*Wirtschaftspartei des deutschen Mittelstandes*), founded in 1921, prompted the angry denunciations of interest-group spokesmen who argued that only the established parties secured middle-class constituents parliamentary influence.[5]

The political ambitions of the Business and Trade Association of 1840 and the League of Artisans testified to the increasingly prominent role that middle-class interest groups played in parliamentary politics after the war. Even before 1914, interest groups had exerted considerable influence. The eminent sociologist Emil Lederer, for example, surveyed contemporary developments and forecast a contentious German future in which parochial economic interests would come to replace embrasive political principles entirely.[6] But in Wilhelmine Germany, it was mainly agricultural and industrial in-

3. *Nachrichten für Stadt und Land* (Oldenburg), 7 Jan. 1919, no. 6; 24 Jan. 1919, no. 23; 30 Jan. 1919, no. 29; and 16 June 1919, no. 161.
4. *Nachrichten für Stadt und Land* (Oldenburg), 7 Jan. 1919, no. 6; 24 Jan. 1919, no. 23; and 16 Apr. 1919, no. 161. See also Heinrich August Winkler, *Mittelstand, Demokratie und Nationalsozialismus: Die politische Entwicklung von Handwerk und Kleinhandel in der Weimarer Republik* (Cologne, 1972).
5. *Nachrichten für Stadt und Land* (Oldenburg), 19 Aug. 1922, no. 224; *Die Schutzwehr* (Braunschweig), no. 11 (Nov. 1919); Winkler, *Mittelstand, Demokratie und Nationalsozialismus*, 128.
6. Cited in James Sheehan, *German Liberalism in the Nineteenth Century* (Chicago, 1978), 250.

terest groups, rather than their numerous middle-class counterparts, that attained power in the bourgeois parties.[7] Difficult years of war and revolution ended this reticence on the part of artisans, shopkeepers, farmers, civil servants, and white-collar employees.[8] No longer dominated exclusively by municipal notables or powerful capitalist elites and now contested by many more middling interest groups, Weimar politics was pursued in a much more crowded arena.

This mobilization of interest deployed the democratic idiom of the November Revolution. No matter how unsettling the revolution's socialist aspect turned out to be, the notion that ordinary middle-class constituents had a right to a greater political voice found broad appeal. Parliamentary leaders understood the new requirements of democratic politics, as the ubiquitous references to the people's community, or *Volksgemeinschaft,* and the people's party, or *Volkspartei,* which saturated political language during the Weimar years, attested. Political drama in the liberal and conservative parties after 1918 revolved largely around the struggle to accommodate the contentious middle-class interests that war and revolution had brought to life.[9]

Nine years later, Oldenburg witnessed political events of a very different kind. Three weeks of localized protests culminated in a massive public demonstration on the Horse Market, in the center of Oldenburg, on 26 January 1928. From across the wintry countryside, small-town farmers tramped into the provincial capital, joining angry artisans and shopkeepers from the city itself. By the end of the

---

7. Dirk Stegmann Deutschlands., *Die Erben Bismarcks: Parteien und Verbände in der Spätphase des Wilhelminischen Sammlungspolitik 1897–1918* (Cologne, 1970), 22–8, 44–6, 143–7. See also Anthony O'Donnell, "National Liberalism and the Mass Politics of the German Right" (Ph.D. dissertation, Princeton University, 1973); Charles Robert Bacheller, "Class and Conservatism: The Changing Social Structure of the German Right, 1890–1928" (Ph.D. dissertation, University of Wisconsin, 1977); and Thomas Childers, *The Nazi Voter: The Social Foundations of Fascism in Germany, 1919–1933* (Chapel Hill, N.C., 1983).
8. See, for example, Winkler, *Mittelstand, Demokratie, und Nationalsozialismus;* Robert G. Moeller, *German Peasants and Agrarian Politics, 1914–1924: The Rhineland and Westphalia* (Chapel Hill, N.C., 1986); Andreas Kunz, *Civil Servants and the Politics of Inflation in Germany, 1914–1924* (Berlin, 1986); and Michael Prinz, *Vom neuen Mittelstand zum Volksgenossen: Die Entwicklung des sozialen Status der Angestellten von der Weimarer Republik bis zum Ende der NS-Zeit* (Munich, 1986).
9. See Lothar Albertin, *Liberalismus und Demokratie am Anfang der Weimarer Republik: Eine vergleichende Analyse der Deutschen Demokratischen Partei und der Deutschen Volkspartei* (Düsseldorf, 1972); Larry Eugene Jones, *German Liberalism and the Dissolution of the Weimar Party System 1918–1933* (Chapel Hill, N.C., 1988); Lothar Döhn, *Politik und Interesse: Die Interessenstruktur der Deutschen Volkspartei* (Meisenheim am Glan, 1972); and Annelise Schulze, "Die Stellungnahme der deutschnationalen Volkspartei zu den Problemen der Sozialpolitik" (Ph.D. dissertation, University of Rostock, 1927).

day, over 40,000 protesters had assembled in one of the largest political demonstrations ever seen in Lower Saxony.

By 1927, rural impoverishment had become prevalent. A credit squeeze withdrew the margin of security that farmers had enjoyed during the inflation. A depressed livestock market was made worse by heavy winter floods. But economic tribulations themselves, unhappy as they were, do not explain the scope and temper of the protests that eventually filled market squares across northern Germany. Speakers who addressed the angry assemblies repeatedly indicted the "Weimar system" and the right-of-center *Bürgerblock* coalition governing in Berlin since January 1925. In their view, the coalition partners, particularly the German People's Party and the German National People's Party, had betrayed their long-standing commitment to a healthy *Mittelstand*. They had allegedly pursued a "socialistic economic policy" and, at the same time, had pandered to industrialists and financiers, neglecting in any case the needs and aspirations of the middle classes. German Nationalist politicians who tried to soothe electoral discontent were loudly heckled and abused.[10] It was not only mainstream politicians who lost credibility. Spokesmen for the dominant middle-class interest groups, whose clout depended on the continuing electoral success of the established parties, found their memberships increasingly impatient. The proliferation of grass-roots protests in Oldenburg and elsewhere across northern Germany was one more sign that the authority of Berlin-based peak organizations, or *Spitzenverbände,* had declined precipitously; beginning around 1924, groups of homeowners, artisans, farmers, and civil servants fielded dozens of breakaway lists in local and regional elections, bypassing the leaderships of the traditional parties and ignoring the furious protests of established interest brokers. The mutual arrangements between interest groups and parties that had regulated middle-class politics since the revolution threatened to come completely undone just ten years later.

Landvolk protests dramatically evoked the explosion of middle-class interest group politics at the end of the 1920s. In addition to the angry protests of farmers and artisans, creditors demanded restitution for losses suffered during the inflation, employees called for

---

10. On the *Landvolk,* see Rudolf Heberle, *From Democracy to Nazism: A Regional Case Study on Political Parties in Germany* (Baton Rouge, La., 1945); Gerhard Stoltenberg, *Politische Strömungen im schleswig-holsteinischen Landvolk 1918–1933* (Düsseldorf, 1962); and Michelle Le Bars, *Le Mouvement Paysan dans le Schleswig-Holstein 1928–1932* (Bern, 1986).

more complete social welfare schemes, and homeowners and shopkeepers demanded relief from heavy taxes. These sharp-edged economic resentments seemed to dissolve anything but the most self-serving political loyalties. Single-issue voting became increasingly prevalent, and splinter parties prospered. The established parties found it more and more difficult to assemble broad-based electoral combinations.[11]

Contemporary observers were keenly aware of this middle-class political volatility. More than anyone else, Theodor Geiger, a sociologist at the technical university in Braunschweig, cast the metaphors and images by which scholars have made sense of Weimar's social reality. "Panik im Mittelstand," perhaps Geiger's most well-known piece, posed desperate middle-class occupational groups precariously between two great blocks, labor and capital. Over time, he argued, the *Mittelstand*'s distinctive social and corporate identities would erode, by virtue either of real impoverishment and proletarianization or of ideological alignment with the working class, but in the meantime, the short-term consequence was political radicalism (notably *Landvolk* protest and National Socialism) or simply confusion.[12] Historians have recirculated Geiger's imagery. Indeed, the political cries and economic tribulations of particular interest groups add up to the most well-documented aspect of modern German social history.

The political commotion of occupational constituencies and special interest groups was noisy. *Landvolk* marches, breakaway single-interest lists, and dissident middle-class parties all composed a dramatic politics in the mid-1920s. What is not clear, however, is whether Geiger's imagery of despair and disintegration is particularly helpful in understanding this noise. To be sure, from the perspective of the established liberal and conservative parties, the consequence of middle-class panic was fragmentation. Party leaders such as Count Kuno von Westarp, Alfred Hugenberg, Gustav Stresemann, and Erich Koch-Weser all bemoaned the growing incoherence of parliamentary politics and pointed to what they took to be the political immaturity and economic narrow-mindedness of voters. Taken together, the collapse of the traditional parties, including that of the

---

11. This story is best told by Larry Eugene Jones, *German Liberalism*.
12. Theodor Geiger, "Panik im Mittelstand," *Die Arbeit* 7 (Oct. 1931), 638–53. See also his *Die soziale Schichtung des deutschen Volkes: Soziographischer Versuch auf statistischer Grundlage* (Stuttgart, 1932).

unmistakably antirepublican German National People's Party, registers the disorder of the Weimar Republic in most textbook narratives. The graphic contains the explanation. The vote totals of the traditional parties fall off at a steady rate, whereas those of the National Socialists ascend, the two lines – one falling, the other rising – crossing each other in 1930.[13] The assumption seems to be that the established bourgeois parties preserved at least a measure of republican stability.

There is no doubt that the largely middle-class electorates of the older liberal and conservative parties eventually reassembled under the banner of National Socialism. And as the foundations of Koch-Weser's or Stresemann's or Westarp's party were kicked out from under the feet of astonished parliamentary leaders, the republic lost that much stability. What I find frustrating with this narrative, however, is that it places the fate of the Weimar Republic at the center of deliberations about Nazism; Weimar becomes the plot. Yet this view looks past middle-class groups themselves, for whom the "plot" of the 1920s may have been very different. As long as the politics of the 1920s are conceived in terms of the survival of the party system or the Weimar Republic, the vocabulary of disintegration will probably endure. The question is: How serviceable is this vocabulary in reconstructing the political ambit of middle-class groups or comprehending their aspirations? Did political fragmentation necessarily imply the social and cultural disarray of the *Bürgertum,* as some have suggested?[14] Is Nazism comprehensible only against the scarred and unfamiliar landscape of economic catastrophe?

Before turning to these questions, I want to offer a final pair of vignettes, again from Oldenburg.

Walther Rathenau's assassination on Berlin's Königsallee on 24 June 1922 deprived the republic of one of its most able ministers. The murder was also an audacious act undertaken by an increasingly intransigent right-wing opposition. Chancellor Wirth, speaking in the Reichstag after the Rathenau murder, concluded with the angry

---

13. See the graphs in Hagen Schulze, *Weimar: Deutschland 1917–1933* (Berlin, 1982), 183, 288, 290, 303, 382, and endsheets.
14. See, for example, Walter D. Burnham, "Political Immunization and Political Confessionalism: The United States and Weimar Germany," *Journal of Interdisciplinary History* 3 (1972), 1–30; Peter Steinbach, "Politische Kultur in der Krise: Neuere Beiträge zur Bestimmung der politischen Kultur in der Weimarer Republik," *PVS-Literatur* 22 (1981), 123–57; and the essay by Richard Bessel in this volume.

indictment: "The enemy stands on the right." It is unlikely, however, that German burghers saw the assassination and the events that followed as comforting (or disconcerting) examples of a resurgent right.

Three days after the assassination, Oldenburg's Democratic premier, Theodor Tantzen, spoke at a large memorial service in front of the Landtag. Hundreds of trade unionists and Social Democrats made their way to the city center. Socialist notables were also represented on the dais, alongside Tantzen and other government officials. City and state employees, released from work, joined teachers, who, following a ministerial directive, came with their classes in tow. Tantzen intended to make the Rathenau commemoration part of a sturdy civic repertoire of Constitution Days, state funerals, and inaugurations that would provide the young republic with the public symbols of popular legitimacy. But far from creating republican consensus, the memorial service revealed the depth of political antagonisms. Civil servants resented being forced to participate in what they regarded as an explicitly political affair. Even more strident were the protests of parents, whose children had been forced to attend the service. "It proceeded like any political assembly: demonstrations, marches, a representative conveying the demands of workers," wrote one pastor to Oldenburg school authorities. Another angry father worried about the "confusing" impression his child had gotten after seeing loud catcalls interrupt a figure of authority.[15]

There is more going on in these protests than simply objections to the political flavor of Tantzen's exercise in civics. They are laced with the fear of the working-class crowd. The aftermath of the affair leaves the lingering impression that burghers considered the socialists' appropriation of streets and other public sites dangerous and threatening. Rathenau's death was only one in a series of incidents after 1918 – food riots, general strikes, May Day rallies – when workers seemed to take over public places. On these occasions, burghers invariably retreated to private sanctuaries. "Remain Quiet and Discreet," one small-town newspaper urged in the tense aftermath of Matthais Erzberger's August 1921 murder; "the street is not the place to carry out political and economic conflicts."[16] When the Law for the De-

15. Schütte to *Evangelisches Oberschulkollegium*, Oldenburg, 30 June 1922; Friedrichs to Schütte, 19 June 1922, Niedersächsisches Staatsarchiv Oldenburg, 132/112; and letters and commentary in *Nachrichten für Stadt und Land* (Oldenburg), 28 June 1922, no. 178; 29 June 1922, no. 179; 30 June 1922, no. 180; and 1 July 1922, no. 181.
16. *Goslarsche Zeitung*, 31 Aug. 1921, no. 203. See also the issue for 26 Aug. 1920, no. 197.

fense of the Republic was promulgated in July 1922, in response to the Rathenau assassination, burghers considered the lurking threat from the street constitutionally validated. The law closely regulated patriotic festivity and associational life, banned outdoor events altogether in some states such as Oldenburg, and left burghers feeling increasingly embattled and vulnerable. Invoking the "fear that makes the heart of many a respectable burgher pound when the radical masses walk the streets," one correspondent explained his opposition to republican legislation: That is what we "understand from the constant emphasis on protecting the constitution, which we all curse from top to bottom, namely – fear!"[17] At least in the early 1920s, burghers considered public demonstrations foreign, vaguely frightening, and distinctively proletarian events.

However, Oldenburg seemed to belong to an entirely different political universe in 1925. On 1 October, the eve of the seventy-eighth birthday of the newly elected president of the republic, Paul von Hindenburg, Oldenburg's streets filled with patriotic revelers. The provincial capital's largest newspaper, the liberal *Nachrichten für Stadt und Land,* gleefully reported the revival of "the wonderful, old custom" of the *Zapfenstreich* or torchlight parade. The evening march, which was organized by the patriotic veterans' association, the Stahlhelm, wound its away along the city streets to general applause. Editors welcomed the new military style – "Just a few short, terse commands . . . and the army of torchbearers assembled in glorious formation" – and reported a rekindled sense of familiarity ("wonderful, old custom") with patriotic events in public places.[18] Burghers reasserted their claims to the streets with regularity in the years that followed, celebrating Hindenburg Day, Front Soldiers Day, and other nationalist occasions with boisterous demonstrations in 1926 and 1927.[19]

Hindenburg festivity in 1925 stands in sharp contrast to the public reactions in the aftermath of Oldenburg's Rathenau commemoration three years earlier. I do not want to draw an overly schematic distinction between prior intimidation and subsequent public confidence;

17. Hepp to Stresemann, n.d. [1922], Politisches Archiv des Auswärtigen Amts, Bonn (hereafter cited as PA Bonn), Nachlass Stresemann, 3109/231/141460. The laws are discussed in Gotthard Jasper, *Der Schutz der Republik: Studien zur staatlichen Sicherung der Demokratie in der Weimarer Republik 1922–1930* (Tübingen, 1963).
18. *Nachrichten für Stadt und Land* (Oldenburg), 2 Oct. 1925, no. 268.
19. See Peter Fritzsche, "Presidential Victory and Popular Festivity in Weimar Germany: Hindenburg's 1925 Election," *Central European History* 23 (1990): 205–24.

many burghers remained shy of the streets and of loud proletarian enthusiasms throughout the Weimar period, just as many also repudiated the political color to the Rathenau memorial service but unhesitatingly joined public demonstrations – to protest the Franco–Belgian occupation of the Ruhr in winter 1923, for example. These caveats expressed, it is still striking how politically agile and assertive burghers had become by the late 1920s. One aging member of the Pan-German League, in its time among the most influential patriotic organizations, contrasted the sedentary round of lectures and indoor meetings that had encompassed political agitation before the war with the street tactics and public poise of nationalists after 1918.[20] The veterans' group, the Stahlhelm, in particular, was a prominent element in this novel repertoire, providing burghers with important organizational resources and a sense of common purpose. Oldenburgers flocked to the group; the membership of the local branch swelled from 672 to 1,394 in 1924.[21] Throughout Germany, the Stahlhelm emerged as the largest and most active patriotic association in the 1920s.

What does all this Hindenburg festivity and Stahlhelm activity add up to? Did not streetcorner nationalists, like *Landvolk* protesters, rob the republic of its fragile stability as the nation slipped into depression? Do not the recollected images of economic hard times come with a sound track of boots marching along cobblestoned streets? Weimar's foreign minister, Gustav Stresemann, for example, dismissed Hindenburg's election as another example of political immaturity: Germans simply "wanted a man in uniform . . . with lots of decorations."[22] As for the Stahlhelm, Stresemann grew increasingly intolerant of the nationalist group and its strident opposition to his foreign policies. In his view, the Stahlhelm was typical of the mindless *Stammtisch* patriotism so prevalent in postwar Germany.[23] Again, the question is: How should historians interpret political noise in the late 1920s?

20. Franz Sontag, quoted in Roger Chickering, *We Men Who Feel Most German: A Cultural Study of the Pan-German League, 1886–1914* (Boston, 1984), 301. See also James Diehl, *Paramilitary Politics in Weimar Germany* (Bloomington, Ind., 1977).
21. *Nachrichten für Stadt und Land* (Oldenburg), 9 Jan. 1924, no. 8; 6 Nov. 1924, no. 304; 10 Jan. 1925, no. 9; and Hans Brenning, *10 Jahre Stahlhelm: Kreisgruppe Oldenburg* (Oldenburg, 1930).
22. Quoted in Erich Eyck, *Geschichte der Weimarer Republik* (Zurich, 1954), 1:447–51.
23. See Henry Ashby Turner, Jr., *Stresemann and the Politics of the Weimar Republic* (Princeton, N.J., 1963), 251. See also Stresemann to Scholz, 26 Sept. 1928, PA Bonn, Nachlass Stresemann, 3163/292/151191.

Seen from the perspective of German neighborhoods, the Stahlhelm appears as a confident and aggressive political organization. Although originally founded as a veterans' group, the Stahlhelm did not gather uprooted political desperados but instead played a central role in provincial life, wrestling from the bourgeois parties the management of local patriotic occasions such as Sedan Day and Founding Day and including in its ranks established and respected citizens – shopkeepers, artisans, and professionals – most of them family men in their thirties when, after 1924, the Stahlhelm was at its height. Far from being clannish and contemptuous of bourgeois society, like Freikorps units immediately after the war, for instance, the Stahlhelm maintained frequent contacts with the social clubs – choral societies, business groups, *Schützenvereine* – that made up the fabric of civic life.[24] Stahlhelmers were active at the very center of bourgeois sociability.

With thousands of branches in rural hamlets and metropolitan neighborhoods, the Stahlhelm disclosed the increasingly close-knit organization of the *Bürgertum*. As Rudy Koshar has pointed out, the strains of the First World War had already impelled provincial burghers to organize at a furious pace. As the war ground on, towns and villages saw the formation of a wide range of patriotic groups, economic self-help organizations, and war relief efforts.[25] This trend was amended by the revolution. It is difficult to exaggerate the tumult of political campaigning that swept over Germany after November 1918. Many fair-sized towns, in which as many as 15,000 or 20,000 people lived, saw party bureaus established and permanent political staffs organized for the first time. By the time Prussia's 1924 municipal elections took place, the prewar convention of a single unity list had given way almost completely to a half-dozen or more strident political contenders. Youth groups, recreational clubs, and nationalist associations mushroomed during this period as well. Mobilization for war in 1914, war bond rallies, and, in the years after 1918, the trauma of territorial loss, open revolt on Germany's eastern borders, and the occupation of the Ruhr all gave a sturdy nationalist frame to the invigoration of civic life.

24. Peter Fritzsche, *Rehearsals for Fascism: Populism and Political Mobilization in Weimar Germany* (New York, 1990), 164–89.
25. Rudy Koshar, *Social Life, Local Politics and Nazism: Marburg, 1880–1935* (Chapel Hill, N.C., 1986), 127–50; Geoff Eley, *Reshaping the German Right: Radical Nationalism and Political Change after Bismarck* (New Haven, Conn., 1980), 336.

The growth of clubs and associations points to the widespread mobilization of interest and inclination. In bourgeois neighborhoods, civic life became more dense, more socially embrasive, and more resourceful. As club members, arrayed in dozens of choirs, gymnastic societies, patriotic associations, and business groups, burghers participated in the public routines of the community. They commemorated patriotic holidays, celebrated Hindenburg's election, and organized the annual *Schützenfest*. A similar trend, beginning in the 1890s and proceeding apace with the growth of Social Democracy, can, of course, be identified in working-class communities. Since recreational clubs and service organizations came in pairs in most German towns, one recruiting mostly workers, the other burghers (a typical community had two canoe clubs, two mens' choral societies, and two social welfare societies; Goslar even had two voluntary fire companies), club life also upheld the fractured community. Clubs gave definition and a sense of unity to the *Bürgertum,* even as burghers divided on a variety of difficult social and economic issues.

Led by the Stahlhelm, burghers reclaimed for themselves provincial streets and market squares. After the "hot" summers of the early 1920s, when burghers had retreated into their homes in the wake of strikes against the Kapp Putsch and the Rathenau murder and during proletarian food riots, burghers now stepped into the public arena with greater confidence and poise. Stahlhelm nationalism, for all its chauvinism and unthinking hurrah patriotism, described a fundamental political mobilization.

If the Stahlhelm provided an important measure of cohesion to the bourgeois community, it would seem that economic interest groups and endemic breakaway lists in local elections continuously dismantled the unity achieved. The quotidian business of civic life seemed to perpetuate an endless process of combination and division. After all, what happened to the camaraderie of Hindenburg's election in Oldenburg? At first, the enthusiasm of victory led to strenuous efforts to maintain the Hindenburg coalition. The major nationalist parties, the German People's Party and the German National People's Party, combined in a *Landesblock* and won a major victory in Oldenburg's June 1925 state elections; they would never do so well again. After a few years, however, bourgeois unity crumbled as middle-class interest groups fielded their own parties, first in Oldenburg's

November 1927 municipal elections and then in May 1928 state elections.[26]

Given these conditions, the question arises: How sturdy or politically consequential was the political unity laboriously assembled and displayed by the Stahlhelm? Were not the motions of demobilization at least as strong as those of mobilization? Yet it is misleading to oppose special-interest politics to grass-roots nationalism, the one dismantling, the other reconstructing, the bourgeois community. To do so ignores the social context in which interest groups operated and distorts their political role and appeal. Occupational interest groups and single-issue parties, adversarial as their protests were, did not lead resentful constituents out of civic unions and resettle them on the political periphery. Political allegiances during the Weimar period were never so exclusive; if club officers demanded *Verbandspatriotismus* from members, they were rarely successful in getting it. Artisans, shopkeepers, farmers, and employees, for example, may well have been active members in their respective occupational groups, but they were also members of church congregations, gymnastic societies, and veterans' groups. An understanding of Weimar politics would be incomplete without admitting the multiple identities that ordinary burghers assumed.

If interest groups did not play Hameln's Pied Piper, leading desperate and politically unchurched constituents beyond the town square, they remained influential civic players and helped shape the political expectations of provincial burghers. Like the Stahlhelm, economic interest groups and business associations were embedded in the rhythms of civic life, joining patriotic festivals such as Stahlhelm Day or Hindenburg celebrations and accepting the hospitality (the *Schützenhaus* was a frequent site for meetings) and services (the Stahlhelm band often played at trade conventions) of other clubs. Local associations all shared members, circumstances that continuously stitched together a mutual sociability.

More important, civic groups also shared basic dispositions about public activism. That local artisans' leagues or employees' unions had been founded with such alacrity after the war, and had learned to organize demonstrations and field electoral slates over the course of

---

26. The best introductions to Oldenburg politics are Klaus Schaap, *Die Endphase der Weimarer Republik im Freistaat Oldenburg, 1928–1933* (Düsseldorf, 1978), and Wolfgang Günther, "Parlament und Regierung im Freistaat Oldenburg 1920–1932," *Oldenburger Jahrbuch* 83 (1983): 187–207.

the 1920s, reflected a long-term mobilization of political capacity. The startled editors of Holzminden's *Täglicher Anzeiger* reported the unprecedented gestures of this mobilization: "Farmers must really be suffering if they are determined to employ the weapons of political revolutionaries."[27] Alongside workers, more and more burghers emerged as self-reliant and assertive "political revolutionaries," able to utilize a variety of civic resources and willing not only to pressure policymakers but also to untie themselves from established municipal patrons and long-standing parliamentary allies.

To listen only to the self-absorbed rhetoric of a single interest group, to read only the angry protests of its spokesmen and the strident language of its trade publications, one might easily come to regard Weimar's interest groups as "small republics," each sovereign and self-contained.[28] Indeed, Frank Domurad argues that artisans in the late 1920s contested the very jurisdiction of the German state and sought to stake out the boundaries of their own guarded sovereignty.[29] But, on the local level, there is little evidence that constituents considered their associational loyalties absolute or that interest groups endeavored to secede from a wider civic life. Rather, the tremulous activism of interest groups reflected a broad commitment to give political voice to a wide range of middle-class constituents, including the artisans, employees, and small tradespeople who, by and large, had been ignored by the traditional parties before the war. Again and again, the demands for inclusion in the political order and for the construction of a more accessible, less deferential social order resounded in the public rhetoric of Weimar's splinter parties and interest groups. As Thomas Childers has pointed out, economic claims commingled with broader conceptions of the good society, self-interest with ideology.[30]

The years since the 1918 revolution traced an insurgent process of mobilization. By the end of the 1920s, patriotic associations and economic interest groups, both the Stahlhelm and the *Landvolk,* had developed an insistent repertoire of public activism similar to the one

27. *Täglicher Anzeiger* (Holzminden), no. 65, 16 Mar. 1928.
28. The metaphor is from Hans Staudinger, *Individuum und Gemeinschaft in der Kulturorganisation des Vereins* (Jena, 1913), 3.
29. Frank Domurad, "The Politics of Corporatism: Hamburg Handicraft in the later Weimar Republic, 1927–1933," in Richard Bessel and E. J. Feuchtwanger, eds., *Social Change and Political Development in Weimar Germany* (Totowa, N.J., 1981), 174–206.
30. Thomas Childers, "Interest and Ideology: Anti-System Politics in the Era of Stabilization," in Gerald D. Feldman, ed., *Die Nachwirkungen der Inflation auf die deutsche Geschichte 1924–1933* (Munich, 1985), 1–20.

that Social Democrats had honed for over thirty years. Boisterous street marches and loud public assemblies, long regarded as the rowdy gestures of the working classes, were now among the most useful tactics of nationalists. Burghers emerged as increasingly self-reliant political contenders, resolved to reorder the national community on a more egalitarian basis but also to challenge the socialist left in a more assertive manner. Weimar's "burgher dissidents" agreed that the time had finally come to find a place for the "little man" in Germany's political structure. The notion of *Volkssouveränität*, or people's sovereignty, captures the sense of genuine enfranchisement for which small-town burghers believed they were struggling. And yet, they did not speak with a single voice. Interest groups and patriotic associations disagreed loudly about political aims and tactics. Relations among nationalist groups were impossibly bad. The hyperactive search for bourgeois unity at the end of the 1920s constituted an acknowledgment of the depth of political differences; attempts to construct common fronts, build bourgeois blocs, and establish new people's parties all ended disastrously.[31]

How, then, do we describe the process of mobilization that seems to have enlisted broad elements of the bourgeois community and yet remain faithful to the prevailing picture of disharmony and discord? Elsewhere I have used the term "populism," which other German historians have found useful as well.[32] Lawrence Goodwyn's description of American populism as "more than a passing creed" but "less than a fundamental social theory" also applies to middle-class dissidence in Germany.[33] Political insurgency in the 1920s was not simply a rash of protests in economic hard times, but was sustained by deeply held convictions about what constituted the good society. On the other hand, Weimar populism was not an identifiable political entity with party offices, a partisan press, and activists at the grassroots level. Populism draws attention to common dispositions and shared assumptions. It brings to mind popular protests against political privilege and economic concentration in industrial society without conjuring up the more sweeping critique of socialism; it evokes

---

31. Larry Eugene Jones, "Sammlung oder Zersplitterung? Die Bestrebungen zur Bildung einer neuen Mittelpartei in der Endphase der Weimarer Republik 1930–1933," *Vierteljahrshefte für Zeitgeschichte* 25 (1977): 265–304.
32. Fritzsche, *Rehearsals for Fascism*; Eley, *Reshaping the German Right*; and David Blackbourn, *Populists and Patricians: Essays in Modern German History* (London, 1987).
33. Lawrence Goodwyn, *Democratic Promise: The Populist Movement in America* (New York, 1976), xi.

the moral righteousness and political self-reliance so typical of Weimar's middle-class dissidents without suggesting specific political aims; and, most important, populism underscores the belligerent style of political contenders. Historians agree that nineteenth-century American populists never attained significant legislative representation. It was a more nebulous movement that elected only a handful of eccentric congressmen and state representatives but generated countless courthouse rallies, parades, and church picnics. Practicing the routines of public action and learning the scale of political possibility in the 1880s and 1890s was, in many respects, to become an American populist. German burghers learned similar lessons in the 1920s; they discovered the possibilities of political action, reveled in the vitality of community protests, and applauded the contributions of the "little people."

Much of the appeal of National Socialists and their affinities with Weimar's middle-class insurgents in the 1920s is comprehensible in terms of populism. The Nazis were successful insofar as they adhered strictly to the changing requirements of bourgeois politics. They were particularly adept at finding the right balance between attacks on privilege and attacks on the "Weimar system." On the one hand, the Nazis accommodated the advancing democratization of the bourgeois polity. Precisely because the National Socialists advertised themselves as populists – honoring the postwar icons of worker and soldier, lending an attentive ear to the resentments of occupational groups, organizing ceaselessly in neighborhoods – they succeeded where earlier *völkisch* groups such as the German–Racist Protective and Resistance League (*Deutschvölkischer Schutz- und Trutzbund*) or the elitist Freikorps or even the excessively mainstream Stahlhelm had failed. More successfully than most political contenders, the Nazis broke down social barriers and persuaded sympathizers of their commitment to construct a *Volksgemeinschaft,* the ideal by which so many postwar Germans took their political bearings. On the other hand, Nazis willingly confronted the socialist left, risking immediate violence and disorder to eventually furnish a semblance of nonsocialist order.[34] Burghers recognized in the Nazis what they believed to be the strategic advantages of the socialists, namely, organization, determination, and fanaticism, without having to purchase proletarian economics.

34. On this theme, see Richard Bessel, *Political Violence and the Rise of Nazism: The Storm Troopers in Eastern Germany, 1925–1934* (New Haven, Conn., 1984).

The success of the Nazis, then, should be placed in the context of the advancing democratization and the growing sense of political confidence that distinguished burghers during the Weimar years. If Hitler's party had not adhered to this formula, it would not have found popular support. The Nazi seizure of power in 1933 was a product of crisis and immediate opportunity, but also of long-term social mobilization, a political continuity in twentieth-century German history that has been neglected. From the perspective of German burghers, the Nazis were as much the congenial, though hardly the only, endpoint of long-term aspirations for political enfranchisement and political authority as they were a final, desperate alternative after seasons of economic dislocation and parliamentary disarray.

Perhaps historians should be less astonished at the success of the Nazis at the end of the 1920s than surprised that populist mobilization did not take place sooner. To be sure, German anti-Semites and agrarian populists unsettled traditional ways and means of political management before the turn of the century. Geoff Eley, for example, identifies the composition of radical nationalism around 1900. Notions of the people's community, the people's state, and the people's party, which were so prevalent after 1918, had infiltrated political rhetoric before 1914. But the scale of this populism remained limited. The public activism of the Navy League or the Pan-German League was also tentative and by the onset of the war had returned to conventional political channels.[35] To explain the timing of Germany's populist upheaval, the frank acknowledgment of political precedents before 1914 is necessary but not sufficient: Historians have to turn to total war in 1914 and democratic revolution in 1918, events that gave prewar aspirations greater focus and a more workable vocabulary of political sovereignty.

August 1914 offered German patriots a credible vision of a more emotionally satisfying political community. The August days created durable patriotic images and themes around "the people" and "the nation" and eroded hierarchical allegiances to state and dynasty. The ideas of 1914 continued to inform popular expectations for fundamental change in November 1918, when both socialists and burghers embraced various eclectic visions of a democratic *Volksstaat*. Notions of community were vague and easily manipulable; it was easy to stick

---

35. Eley, *Reshaping the German Right*, 356–7.

all sorts of partisan agendas behind the happy ideal of the *Volksgemeinschaft,* and yet this ideal exerted enormous emotional appeal that cut across conventional political camps. Fraternity, the third imperative of the French Revolution, is as powerful a political promise as it is elusive.

Revolution in 1918 also retooled the means of political mobilization. The occasional raucous American-style election before the war became the norm after the war. Weimar interest groups carefully brokered the votes of constituents, candidates worked with more or less well-equipped political machines, and open-air meetings and street demonstrations lost their exclusively proletarian connotations. By the mid-1920s, patriotic associations and occupational interest groups had disengaged themselves from the parties altogether. Their public acts added up to a self-reliant "movement culture," Goodwyn's term characterizing the autonomy of American populists that distinguishes Weimar's insurgents as well. The idea of movement culture is particularly important because populism was more than a blast of political temper against big labor and big capital or a plea for the enfranchisement of the plain people but it was also always a robust collective practice. Local perspective confirms just how dramatic and strident was the political activism that war and revolution enabled. Even the smallest towns generated patriotic festivity and marketplace demonstrations, and observed the daily contests between nationalists and socialists. Although there is no straight line that connects 1914 and 1933, the years marked a volatile process of civic invigoration, popular mobilization, and political self-assertion that was played out in the market squares, tavern rooms, and athletic fields of bourgeois neighborhoods and that fashioned the virtues of self-reliance and community on which Nazi appeal would rest.

To fold National Socialists back into the political engagements of the 1920s is not to argue that Nazism was the only or even the most natural expression of German populism. It was not. By the same token, the decline of National Socialism as a popular movement, arguably a possibility at the end of 1932, would probably not have brought Weimar's populist insurrections to an end or restored political stability to the old parties in the Reichstag. What I think needs emphasizing, however, is the suitable ideological fit between National Socialism and basic dispositions and insurgencies among German burghers. To understand the appeal of National Socialism is less a matter of underscoring the disarray of economic crisis or the fragility of political order than one of reconstructing what seemed to nonsocialists to be Nazism's modern, vigorous, and "reformist" message, and also an unhappy one of remembering that liberalism and democracy have not been modernity's only destinations.

12

Political Mobilization and Associational Life: Some Thoughts on the National Socialist German Workers' Club (e.V.)

ROGER CHICKERING

The rise of the Nazis to power conjures up spectacular images. The monster rallies in the beer halls of Munich, the annual gathering of thousands of party loyalists in Nuremberg, the parades and demonstrations of the storm troopers, and the violent assaults of these men on their political opponents all suggest a style of politics that was successful by virtue of its dramatic impact. These images are also invasive. The Nazis' success at mobilizing support seems best understood in terms of irruption and innovation; the novelty of the NSDAP's (Nationalsozialistische Deutsche Arbeiterpartei) politics enabled the party to break into the political realm in Germany with revolutionary force. The rise of the Nazis thus featured the penetration and takeover of traditional institutions and rituals of politics by a new style and ethos, whose challenge and danger the party's opponents, tired and conventional in their approach to politics, were too slow to grasp.

This analytical perspective on the rise of National Socialism has been pervasive and compelling. It has found powerful metaphorical expression in Hermann Broch's novel, *The Spell*.[1] Like Broch, historians have written as if the Nazis appeared as an alien element with strange new powers of persuasion to take over the realm of German politics after the First World War. In his seminal study of Nazi mobilization at the local level, William Sheridan Allen introduces his protagonists in a chapter entitled "Enter the Nazis."[2] Peter Merkl's study of the essays in the Abel Collection includes a chapter whose subtitle

---

1. Hermann Broch, *Die Verzauberung* (Frankfurt a.M., 1976); in English, *The Spell* (New York, 1987).
2. William Sheridan Allen, *The Nazi Seizure of Power: The Experience of a Single German Town, 1930–1935*, rev. ed., (New York, 1984), 23.

is "The Brownshirts Come to Town."[3] Rudy Koshar's analysis of Nazism and local associations in Marburg is likewise couched in terms of penetration and takeover,[4] and Geoff Eley has written of a "general invasion of the cultural sphere."[5] A variety of this analytical tradition comprises those studies that emphasize the force of Hitler's charisma or the infectious power of the party's ideology and propaganda. In this case, the argument dwells on dynamic new elements in an agitational repertoire that the Nazis imported into German politics in order to transform participants into fervent believers.[6]

The object of this essay is not so much to challenge the validity of this interpretive tradition as to suggest that the perspective it offers is incomplete. The success of the National Socialists is, of course, unintelligible without reference to the innovation and energy they brought to German politics. It deserves emphasis, however, that a majority of the party's membership, to say nothing of the masses of its voters, never participated in street riots or attended the Nuremberg rallies or marched in parades or, for that matter, took part in a rally at which Hitler spoke.[7] The success of the National Socialists is thus no less unintelligible without examination of another side of their agitation. This one was rooted in the institutions and rituals that constituted the mundane, traditional framework of German political culture. Invasive images are misleading to the extent that they ob-

---

3. Peter H. Merkl, *Political Violence under the Swastika: 581 Early Nazis* (Princeton, N.J., 1975), 555–80. See also Ulrich Mayer, *Das Eindringen des Nationalsozialismus in die Stadt Wetzlar* (Wetzlar, 1970).
4. Rudy Koshar, *Social Life, Local Politics, and Nazism: Marburg, 1880–1935* (Chapel Hill, N.C., and London, 1986). See also Koshar, "From *Stammtisch* to Party: Nazi Joiners and the Contradictions of Grass Roots Fascism in Weimar Germany," *Journal of Modern History* 58 (1987): 4; Koshar, "Contentious Citadel: Bourgeois Crisis and Nazism in Marburg/Lahn, 1880–1935," in Thomas Childers, ed., *The Formation of the Nazi Constituency, 1919–1933* (Totowa, N.J., 1986), 23.
5. Geoff Eley, "What Produces Fascism: Preindustrial Traditions or a Crisis of the Capitalist State?", most recently in Michael N. Dobkowski and Isidor Wallimann, eds., *Radical Perspectives on the Rise of Fascism in Germany, 1919–1945* (New York, 1989), 87.
6. For example, James M. Rhodes, *The Hitler Movement: A Modern Millenarian Movement* (Stanford, Conn., 1980); Joseph Nyomarkay, *Charisma and Factionalism in the Nazi Party* (Minneapolis, 1967); Karl Dietrich Bracher, *Die Auflösung der Weimarer Republik: Eine Studie zum Problem des Machtverfalls in der Demokratie*, 4th ed. (Villingen, 1964), esp. 125–6. For an interesting discussion of this problem, see Richard Bessel, "The Rise of the NSDAP and the Myth of Nazi Propaganda," *Wiener Library Bulletin* 33 (1980): 20–9; and the rejoinder from Ian Kershaw, "Ideology, Propaganda, and the Rise of the Nazi Party," in Peter D. Stachura, ed., *The Nazi Machtergreifung* (London, 1983), 173–6.
7. On the limited character of Nazi violence, see Richard Bessel, "Violence as Propaganda: The Role of the Storm Troopers in the Rise of National Socialism," in Childers, ed., *Formation*, 131–46.

scure this other dimension of the story, which is better framed in metaphors of familiarity and growth from within.

Hitler, who, as an Austrian, was admittedly a political invader, was the loudest exponent of the view that National Socialism represented a revolutionary intrusion into the traditional institutions and practices of German politics. *Mein Kampf* contains a rambling assault on the institution that seemed in Hitler's eyes to embody the worst features of political culture in Germany. "Terrible, terrible!" he wrote of his first encounter with the German Workers' Party. "This was club-life [*Vereinsmeierei*] of the worst manner and sort." "This absurd little organization," he continued, typified "the complete helplessness and total despair of all existing parties, their programs, their purposes, and their activity."[8] Hitler's diatribe made clear that the source of the problem was the very institution of the *Verein* – the whole range of those "clubs and clublets [*Verbände und Verbändchen*], groups and grouplets" whose principal function was to encourage in their members a mindless obsession with rules, debates, votes, committees, and procedures.[9] Meetings of these groups, he complained several years later in a different context, were calculated only to produce "petty conflicts, jealousies, and squabbles [*Streitigkeiten, Eifersüchteleien und Stänkereien*]."[10] Effective political action, he explained in *Mein Kampf,* was impossible within the confines of a "respectable" organization of this sort, which operated like a "gossip society [*Träträklub*]," or, as he remarked in another passage, like a "literary tea-club or a shopkeepers' bowling society [*spiessbürgerliche Kegelgesellschaft*]."[11]

The root of the problem, in Hitler's view, was that these political clubs embodied in microcosm the principles of parliamentarism.[12] In their organization and rituals, *Vereine* typified the whole system of politics that the National Socialists aspired to destroy and replace with an authoritarian system modeled on military principles. But the

---

8. Adolf Hitler, *Mein Kampf,* trans. Ralph Mannheim (Boston, 1943), 222–3. The German terms have been taken from the German edition of the same year (Munich, 1943), 241. See also Georg Franz-Willing, *Die Hitlerbewegung: Der Ursprung 1919–1922* (Hamburg and Berlin, 1962), 68.
9. Hitler, *Mein Kampf,* 461; German ed., 515.
10. Cited in Albrecht Tyrell, ed., *Führer befiehl . . . . : Selbstzeugnisse aus der "Kampfzeit" der NSDAP* (Düsseldorf, 1969), 241–2.
11. Hitler, *Mein Kampf,* 343, 357; German ed., 387, 392.
12. Hitler, *Mein Kampf,* 587.

comfortable inefficacy of Germany's political clubs had an additional dimension, to which Hitler alluded in an account of a patriotic meeting he once attended in Munich. This meeting displayed classic afflictions of club life. "On the platform sat the committee," Hitler recalled. "To the left a monocle, to the right a monocle, and in between one without a monocle. All three in frock coats." The speech, by a "dignified old gentleman," quickly had the whole audience "dozing along in a state of trance, which was interrupted only by the departure of individual men and women, the clattering of the waitresses, and the yawning of more and more numerous listeners."[13] Hitler's account betrayed his conviction that *Vereinsmeierei* was also a social problem. The "muffled respectability," the timidity and pedantic concern for procedures that paralyzed the political clubs – particularly, Hitler suggested, the patriotic associations – reflected the prominence of staid, well-educated burghers in these organizations.[14] In its rituals, its principles of organization, and its social composition, the traditional *Verein* represented, in Hitler's eyes, the bedrock of a moribund political culture. *Mein Kampf* was a call for a radical alternative, which was to be based on blind discipline in the service of an uncompromising ideology and populated by a new, militant breed of patriots.[15]

Hitler's strictures against *Vereinsleben* (club life) are to be read with some skepticism. They grew out of his personal frustrations in the German Workers' Party and were designed to justify his own seizure of power in that organization in the summer of 1921. Albrecht Tyrell's research suggests, however, that the feature of club life that Hitler found objectionable was not so much its observance of parliamentary rituals as the demands that routine committee work placed on his time and freedom of action.[16] Hitler's complaints in *Mein Kampf* rehearsed, in all events, a popular litany of stereotypes, in which the *Verein* was ridiculed as the lair of the *Spiessbürger,* that peculiarly German philistine whose mark was an obsession with orderly procedure and a penchant for patriotic bombast that required only the encouragement of large quantities of alcoholic spirits.

13. Ibid., 481.
14. Ibid., 101–9.
15. See Wolfgang Schäfer, *NSDAP: Entwicklung und Struktur der Staatspartei des Dritten Reiches* (Hannover and Frankfurt a.M., 1957), 6.
16. Albrecht Tyrell, *Vom "Trommler" zum "Führer": Der Wandel von Hitlers Selbstverständnis zwischen 1919 und 1924 und die Entwicklung der NSDAP* (Munich, 1975), esp. 31–41, 133–46.

These stereotypes were too current not to have reflected real characteristics of German associational life, where activity on behalf of a political cause could blend comfortably with narrow organizational patriotism and the cultivation of sociability. The difficulty for Hitler was that the *Verein* was also an omnipresent feature of German political culture. Every political party was organized on a foundation of local associations, or *Ortsvereine,* which coexisted with myriad other such groups, some overtly political, others not.[17] Clubs of every conceivable description had long been the basic units of political mobilization in Germany, and they tended to coalesce on the strength of the multiple affiliations and social contacts of their members.[18] The rituals of club life were consequently a matter that no aspiring politician in Germany could afford to disdain.[19]

Hitler not only familiarized himself with these rituals in his early activity on behalf of the party, he became their virtuoso. At the time he joined it, the German Workers' Party was in form and practice like countless other political clubs.[20] Upon its foundation, it had drawn up an elaborate set of by-laws, which regulated all phases of its governance and proceedings in accordance with the law of associations.[21] These by-laws the party's leaders then submitted, along with a membership list, to the police, who enrolled the little organization as a "registered association" (or *eingetragener Verein,* e.V.); thereafter the leadership dutifully informed the police of successive changes in the by-laws.[22] The minutes of the early meetings confirm Hitler's recollections that the organization met in side rooms in Munich's taverns to hear patriotic declamations and debates among its mem-

17. Thomas Nipperdey, *Die Organisation der deutschen Parteien vor 1918* (Düsseldorf, 1961).
18. See Anthony Oberschall, *Social Conflicts and Social Movements* (Engelwood Cliffs, N.J., 1973), 102–203. Rudy Koshar's research confirms the truth of this proposition in the case of Marburg: Koshar, *Social Life,* esp. 209–44.
19. See Thomas Nipperdey, "Verein als soziale Struktur in Deutschland im späten 18. Jahrhundert und frühen 19. Jahrhundert," in Hartmut Boockmann et al., *Geschichtswissenschaft und Vereinswesen im 19. Jahrhundert: Beiträge zur Geschichte historischer Forschung in Deutschland* (Göttingen, 1972), 1–44; Otto Dann, ed., *Vereinswesen und bürgerliche Gesellschaft in Deutschland* (Munich, 1984); Hermann Bausinger, "Vereine als Gegenstand volkskundlicher Forschung," *Zeitschrift für Volkskunde* 55 (1959): 98–104; Roger Chickering, *We Men Who Feel Most German: A Cultural Study of the Pan-German League* (London, 1984), 161–7, 183–5.
20. Franz-Willing, *Hitlerbewegung,* 62–6; Reginald H. Phelps, "Hitler and the Deutsche Arbeiterpartei," *American Historical Review* 68 (1963): 974–86; Dietrich Orlow, *The History of the Nazi Party: 1919–1933* (Pittsburgh, 1969), 11–20.
21. Satzungen des Nationalsozialistischen Deutschen Arbeitervereins, e.V., in Bundesarchiv (BA) Koblenz, Bestand NS26 (hereafter NSDAP Hauptarchiv), folder no. 76.
22. For example: Amtsgericht München to Polizeidirektion München, Munich, 12 Oct. 1920, NSDAP Hauptarchiv, folder no. 79.

bers, but that it also devoted much of its time to approving minutes, reports, and changes in the by-laws or the executive committee.[23]

How Hitler changed the party's fortunes is a well-known story. His success was not, however, due principally to changes he made in the structure or procedures of what became known in the spring of 1920 as the National Socialist German Workers' Club. Hitler's assumption of dictatorial powers – a change in the statutes that was also duly registered with the police – made little difference in the format of the organization's day-to-day activities. Hitler's contribution was instead to bring these activities to ritualistic perfection. His ability to give long speeches represented only part of the story; he was also a masterful leader of public meetings. He dispatched business matters with as much skill as he did the hecklers, whose interventions were standard parts of the speeches and the discussions that followed.[24] Above all, this *Rednerkanone,* as he quickly became known, knew how to make meetings entertaining, exciting, and hence attractive to many people whose only motive for attending was curiosity. He thus became a great asset, which the party's leaders were quick to exploit. "Because Herr Hitler is a brilliant speaker," read one of their posters, which appeared on kiosks in Stuttgart in May 1920, "we can promise a most exciting evening."[25]

The spectacular success of the Nazi Party in Munich in the early 1920s thus represented less the importation of new forms of politics than the realization of the potential of the old ones. Meetings of the NSDAP broke out of Munich's small taverns and into the city's largest watering holes, where the flow of beer contributed to the excitement, as did the brawls that became a ritual element in these meetings once the hecklers began to organize.

Because the fortunes of the NSDAP were not as spectacular elsewhere in the early 1920s, it was easier to recognize the extent to which the party comported with the traditions of Germany's associational culture. The branches of the party were hardly distinguishable, in either their membership or the character of their activities, from veterans' associations, local anti-Semitic political parties, the Ger-

23. Ordentliche Mitgliederversammlung der NSDAV, München, 21 Jan. 1921, NSDAP Hauptarchiv, folder no. 79; Hitler, 221–2. See also Ernst Deuerlein, ed., *Der Aufstieg der NSDAP in Augenzeugenberichten* (Düsseldorf, 1968), 100–2.
24. Protokoll der ordentlichen Generalmitgliederversammlung des NSDAV München, e.V., 30 Jan. 1922, NSDAP Hauptarchiv, folder no. 79. See also Reginald H. Phelps, "Hitler als Parteiredner im Jahre 1920," *Vierteljahrshefte für Zeitgeschichte* 11 (1963): 274–330.
25. Franz-Willing, *Hitlerbewegung,* 71.

man-Racist Protective and Resistance League (*Deutschvölkischer Schutz- und Trutzbund*), and numerous other associations that traced their roots back to the Empire and made up what one might call the patriotic milieu in Germany's cities and towns.[26] Many of the NSDAP's local groups, like the one in Marburg, were best described as a "paramilitary *Stammtisch*."[27]

"Paramilitary *Stammtisch*" is perhaps an oxymoron. But it well describes the tensions, if not the contradictions, in the first phase of the NSDAP's history. During the early 1920s the party not only adapted to the demands of German associational life, it prepared for a violent assault on the seats of power. As the party's strategy increasingly emphasized the mobilization of fighters rather than voters, the paramilitary formations, which had originally been formed to protect the huge *Stammtische* that assembled in Munich, took on a new, increasingly autonomous role.[28] The culmination of this strategy came in the November putsch, whose collapse marked the end of the first phase of the party's development. The putsch represented, to be sure, a dramatic act of political invasion, but its failure documented the unsuitability of the *Stammtisch* as a medium of revolutionary violence, as the Nazis found it impossible to generate sufficient military power within a traditional associational framework.

Earlier successes in the beer halls figured large in Hitler's thinking in the aftermath of the putsch, as he reverted to a strategy better geared to the realities of German associational life. The local club, the *Ortsgruppe,* was henceforth to be the "fundamental unit [*Urzelle*]" in the National Socialist movement, and the function of this group was

26. See Uwe Lohalm, *Völkischer Radikalismus: Die Geschichte des Deutschvölkischen Schutz- und Trutz-Bundes 1919–1923* (Hamburg, 1970); Albert Krebs, *Tendenzen und Gestalten der NSDAP: Erinnerungen an die Frühzeit der Partei* (Stuttgart, 1959), 41; Johnpeter Horst Grill, *The Nazi Movement in Baden, 1920–1945* (Chapel Hill, N.C., 1983), 55–70. On the rituals of the *Kriegervereine*, see especially Thomas Rohkrämer, "Der Militarismus der 'kleinen Leute': Die Kriegervereine im Deutschen Kaiserreich (1871–1914)" (Ph.D. diss., Freiburg i. Br., 1989), 47–70. See also Dieter Düding, "Die Kriegervereine im wilhelminischen Reich und ihr Beitrag zur Militarisierung der deutschen Gesellschaft," in Jost Dülffer and Karl Holl, eds., *Bereit zum Krieg: Kriegsmentalität im wilhelminischen Deutschland 1890–1914* (Göttingen, 1986), 99–121.
27. Koshar, "Stammtisch," 4–6. Minutes of early meetings of *Ortsgruppen* in Ansbach, Berchtesgaden, and Weida are in NSDAP Hauptarchiv, folder nos. 216–17, 220.
28. Andreas Werner, "SA: 'Wehrverband,' 'Parteitruppe' oder 'Revolutionsarmee'? Studien zur Geschichte der SA und der NSDAP 1920–1933" (Diss. phil., Erlangen-Nuremberg, 1964), 19–174.

to be the mobilization of masses of voters through the medium of the local meeting or *Versammlung,* which was designed to be, as one historian has described it, "nothing less than a constituent element in National Socialism."[29] As passages in *Mein Kampf* made clear, Hitler envisaged a revolution in German associational life, for these meetings were to feature a fundamentally new kind of political association, organized along military lines and driven by a revolutionary dynamism. But Hitler was by now also experienced enough to realize that the established practices of club life were so inveterate and pervasive that any campaign to mobilize opinion could do so only within their constraints.

"Organization will be carried out, in accordance with the conditions and regulations of the law of associations, on the basis of the old statutes; alterations of the statutes and program can only take place at a general meeting of the membership."[30] With these gestures to prescribed practices, Hitler announced the refounding of the NSDAP in February 1925. During the next five years the party managed to find a comfortable place in local associational networks throughout the country.[31] The only invasion this process involved was the appearance in a locality of the *Wanderredner,* the itinerant organizer sent out from national or district headquarters.[32] The employment of these organizers was common among political organizations in Germany, however; and like other organizations, the Nazis quickly learned that taking root in a locality required adaptation to the demands of local associational life.

The prominence in the membership of young people from the Protestant artisanal, commercial, and clerical lower middle classes reflected the manner in which the party now adapted to these demands.[33] In many localities it became a focus for a milieu not otherwise tightly bound by associational ties of class or confession. The pattern was well illustrated in the Bavarian town of Dillingen, where the local NSDAP group grew up around a core of people who were members of the local gymnastic society, an organization known as

29. Rainer Hambrecht, *Der Aufstieg der NSDAP in Mittel- und Oberfranken (1925–1933)* (Nuremberg, 1976), 196; Tyrell, *Führer befiehl,* 230–2.
30. Ibid., 105–7.
31. Wolfgang Horn, *Führerideologie und Parteiorganisation in der NSDAP (1919–1933)* (Düsseldorf, 1972), 209–327; Orlow, *Nazi Party,* 76–127.
32. Jeremy Noakes, *The Nazi Party in Lower Saxony, 1921–1933* (Oxford, 1971), 99.
33. Michael H. Kater, *The Nazi Party: A Social Profile of Members and Leaders 1919–1945* (Cambridge, Mass., 1983), 32–50.

the "Club of the Clubless [*Verein der Vereinslosen*]," the preserve of the "village nobodies" who could not join the "better" clubs.[34] In many places, the principal affiliations of these kinds of people were with the veterans' association, which provided fertile recruiting grounds for the NSDAP local group.[35] In all events, recruiting was primarily a question of exploiting personal networks within this milieu. The technique was known in party circles as *Kleinarbeit* or "mouth-to-mouth propaganda," and it was ritually invoked in exhortations to members personally "to invite friends and supporters of the movement" to local party meetings.[36]

The success of this technique required that the local meetings be interesting and attractive. This principle, in turn, placed heavy burdens on the local leader, who had not only to be familiar with local conditions and the concerns that weighed on prospective members, but to possess skills of organization, persuasion, and entertainment. As innumerable disappointments demonstrated, the most essential skills were oratorical. When Heinrich Himmler spoke before the local group in Ingolstadt late in 1927, the meeting was a failure. His talk was "animated," a sympathetic policeman reported, but he spoke so fast that he was scarcely comprehensible. "The handful of listeners in the large room could warm up neither to the speaker's well-crafted lecture nor to the powerful exclamations [*Kraftsprüche*] of the moderator." Many of the participants left before the meeting was over.[37] To say that meetings like this failed for want of charisma on the part of the speaker obscures the point: Effective speaking at club meetings meant addressing, in a coherent and forceful manner, the specific issues of local concern that usually stood atop the agenda.[38] The rapport between speaker and audience was critical, and it followed a dynamic of its own. The effectiveness of one leader in Hamburg rested on his ability to shock his auditors and to "express his

---

34. Wolfgang Kaschuba and Carola Lipp, "Kein Volk steht auf, kein Sturm bricht los," in Johannes Beck et al., eds., *Terror und Hoffnung in Deutschland 1933–1945: Leben im Faschismus* (Reinbeck, 1980), 131. See also Allen, *Seizure of Power*, 26–7.
35. Martin Broszat and Elke Fröhlich, *Alltag und Widerstand: Bayern im Nationalsozialismus* (Munich and Zurich, 1987), 112–13.
36. Ortsgruppe Weida, Zusammenkunft, 29 Nov. 1925, NSDAP Hauptarchiv, folder no. 221; Zdenek Zofka, *Die Ausbreitung des Nationalsozialismus auf dem Lande: Eine regionale Fallstudie zur politischen Einstellung der Landbevölkerung in der Zeit des Aufstiegs und der Machtergreifung der NSDAP 1928–1936* (Munich, 1979), 92; Noakes, *Lower Saxony*, 206.
37. Öffentliche Versammlung der Naz. Soz. Arbeiter Partei, Ortsgruppe Ingolstadt am 30. Nov. 1927 im Schäfferbräukeller Ingolstadt, NSDAP Hauptarchiv, folder no. 169.
38. Wilfrid Böhnke, *Die NSDAP im Ruhrgebiet 1920–1933* (Bonn, 1974), 109–10; Deuerlein, *Aufstieg*, 310.

opinions without inhibitions."[39] But in the rituals of German club life, audiences were not passive; and the speaker who shocked or offended his listeners had to contend with formal rebuttals, as well as with spontaneous interventions from the floor. Both forms of response, if not parried with what a police official in Offenbach described as "quick-witted aplomb [*schlagfertiges Auftreten*]," could be devastating; and both did turn many a meeting into a virtual battle of speeches, or *Redeschlacht*.[40] Not all local leaders were as adroit as the one who in 1929 addressed a meeting in Hoechstenbach, a village in the Westerwald, where he so effectively parried the objections of the local pastor that the poor man "left the hall amidst the laughter of all present, never to be seen again."[41]

Many of the party's national leaders owed their prominence to their mastery of these arts; and these men were immense attractions at local meetings, for their presence guaranteed the foundation or revivification of an *Ortsgruppe*. Goebbels and Gregor Strasser were constantly in demand. Julius Streicher was a "star" in Franconia, where the meetings over which he presided were known in the socialist press as the "*Variété* Streicher."[42] Hitler set the standard, of course, and the *Führerbesuch,* his appearance at a meeting, was the highlight in the history of any local club.[43] When he graced the chapter in Ingolstadt with a visit in 1928, the police report commented that he "was greeted with an uproar and was received most humbly [*untertänigst*] by the local leaders, in the manner once reserved for a prince."[44]

Most meetings of local groups could not offer this kind of spectacle. So clubs had to rely on other means to hold the interest of their

---

39. Helga Anschütz, "Die Nationalsozialistische Deutsche Arbeiterpartei in Hamburg: Ihre Anfänge bis zur Reichstagswahl vom 14. September 1930" (Ph.D. diss., University of Hamburg, 1955), 121.
40. Bernd Klemm, ed., ". . . *durch polizeiliche Einschreiten wurde dem Unfug ein Ende gemacht"*: *Geheime Berichte der politischen Polizei Hessens über Linke und Rechte in Offenbach 1923–1930* (Frankfurt and New York, 1982), 256.
41. Kampferlebnisse des Pg. Hammer, Altenkirchen/Westerwald, 3 Mar. 1937, NSDAP Hauptarchiv, folder no. 142.
42. Robin Lenman, "Julius Streicher and the Origins of the NSDAP in Nuremberg," in Anthony Nicholls and Erich Matthias, eds., *German Democracy and the Triumph of Hitler: Essays in Recent German History* (London, 1971), 143; Hambrecht, *Mittel- und Oberfranken,* 197.
43. Horn, *Führerideologie,* 222, 225; Geoffrey Pridham, *Hitler's Rise to Power: The Nazi Movement in Bavaria, 1923–1933* (New York, 1973), 51.
44. Öffentliche Versammlung der Nationalsoz. Arbeiterpartei, Ortsgruppe Ingolstadt, 30 Mar. 1928, NSDAP Hauptarchiv, folder no. 169.

members while the agenda, which was identical in form to what governed practice in other *Vereine,* occupied the evening with routine announcements, committee reports, elections, lectures, discussions, and the conscientious taking of minutes. The methods that the Nazis employed to generate interest also resembled practices in other *Vereine,* for the Nazis were no less rooted in an associational culture whose central locus was the tavern. The *Lokal* provided more than a place to hold meetings; to the club associated with it, it offered a sense of identity that was both institutional and territorial, so that failure to find a regular tavern posed a serious obstacle to the survival of the *Ortsgruppe*.[45] In localities of all sizes, the Nazis' club was "known" by its tavern. In Ingolstadt their place was the *Schäfferbräukeller;* in Wetzlar it was the *Deutsches Haus;* and in the Thuringian town of Weida the *Parteilokal* was the "*Feldschlösschen.*" Many of the local party's activities, particularly the smaller membership meetings called *Sprechabende,* took place around the *Stammtisch* at one of these places.

Even at the less intimate meetings, the spatial arrangements normally accommodated participants who wished to sample the liquid refreshments that the tavern made available. Drinking continued throughout the course of the meetings, during the portions devoted to business as well as those reserved for light, patriotic entertainment and socializing, often to musical accompaniment. Common consumption of alcohol signified collective bonds; and those who, like Albert Krebs in Hamburg, refused to partake had to contend with suspicion, if not ostracism (a principle that did not apply to Hitler).[46] The flow of spirits also nurtured a festive atmosphere, which relieved the tedium of the reports, made marathon speeches bearable, and lent merriment to the debates that followed. The unfortunate pastor who was laughed out of the meeting in Hoechstenbach was one of scores who fell victim to these rituals. Admittedly, many of the victims were complicit in their own fate. One such was the socialist in In-

---

45. Adolf Gimbel, "Entwicklung der NSDAP in Hessen-Nassau 1920 bis 1927" (1939), 6, NSDAP Hauptarchiv, folder no. 142; "Chronik der Ortsgruppe Trier-Mitte," in Franz-Josef Heyen, *Nationalsozialismus im Alltag: Quellen zur Geschichte des Nationalsozialismus vornehmlich im Raum Mainz-Koblenz-Trier* (Boppard, 1967), 77–81. See also Eve Rosenhaft's analysis of the problem of territoriality, *Beating the Fascists? The German Communists and Political Violence, 1929–1933* (Cambridge, 1983), as well as Richard Bessel, *Political Violence and the Rise of Nazism: The Storm Troopers in Eastern Germany, 1925–1934* (New Haven, Conn., and London, 1984), esp. 46–7.
46. Anschütz, "Hamburg," 99.

golstadt who tried in September 1925 to distract the speaker with "several silly interruptions" and was then escorted, half drunk, out of the tavern.[47]

This atmosphere, which raised the level of emotions at the same time as it lowered inhibitions, contributed as well to the violence that attended these meetings. Most of the violence grew – one is tempted to say organically – out of the meetings. Its occasion was the attempt of SA toughs to silence opponents who sought to invade the meeting or, conversely, the attempt of the same toughs to break into the taverns in which their opponents congregated. The instruments of violence included beer glasses, knives and forks, chairs and stools, and other traditional props in the tavern, which now lent themselves to a new kind of employment. It bears emphasis, however, that between 1925 and 1929 the incidence and level of political violence in the taverns were low – a fact obscured by the frequency of bloodletting in the capital, where terror became the custom once Goebbels arrived in 1926 with a strategy of invading taverns in Communist neighborhoods.[48] Elsewhere, meetings ran as a rule in a more orderly fashion; and in some localities, notably in the Ruhr, the debates between the Nazis and their opponents on the left were remarkable for their civility.[49]

During the years of rebuilding after 1925, the NSDAP constructed a network of some 1,400 local clubs, which claimed a membership of a little over 100,000.[50] The size of these groups varied significantly. Some of the larger cities boasted organizations of several hundred members, whereas in other places, like Northeim or Witten in the Ruhr, the handful of local Nazis could only be generously described as a *Verein* at all.[51] Because the cultivation of sociability seemed to recommend a measure of intimacy, the party's leaders encouraged the subdivision of the larger groups into *Bezirksvereine,* or neighborhood clubs, of thirty to forty members – a figure governed by the need to fill the local tavern. "People sat pleasantly warm and close together," Krebs recalled of his experience in Hamburg; "people got

---

47. Bericht über die öffentliche Versammlung der NSDAP und des Völkischen Blocks, Ortsgruppe Ingolstadt, 2 Sept. 1925, NSDAP Hauptarchiv, folder no. 169.
48. Martin Broszat, "Die Anfänge der Berliner NSDAP 1926/27," *Vierteljahrshefte für Zeitgeschichte* 8 (1960): 85–117.
49. Böhnke, *Ruhrgebiet,* 122.
50. Schäfer, *NSDAP,* 11–12.
51. Böhnke, *Ruhrgebiet,* 121; Allen, *Seizure of Power,* 25.

to know one another well and had no need of new faces." Krebs also noted that the practice of subdividing the organizations had the additional virtue of involving members in the busy work of newly spawned subcommittees.[52]

In this and most other respects, the local Nazi *Vereine* were difficult to distinguish in their practices from the countless other clubs that provided the organizational framework for both recreation and political engagement in Germany.[53] The Nazi clubs resembled the others in one other respect. The high rate of turnover in their membership revealed that they were no less immune than others to the squabbles and rivalries connoted by the term *Vereinsmeierei*.[54] Hitler's lament in 1927 about "petty conflicts, jealousies, and squabbles" spoke to a general problem, which was fueled in an atmosphere of suspicion by conflicts over finances, personalities, and turf – particularly, in the last instance, between the officers of the club and those of the local SA unit.[55] In the Hamburg group, the "sectarians," "cranks," and members who refused to pay their dues made life so miserable for Krebs that he eventually resigned his office.[56] In Frankfurt a local leader complained of the "ambitious climbers [*Streber*]," "false prophets, and enemy informers" whose "selfish endeavors" sowed discord in the club as it attempted to start over in 1925.[57] These kinds of members were to be found everywhere – even in Berlin, where one local militant wrote in 1926 of meetings filled with "passionate debates whose contents consisted at least 75% of personal arguments."[58]

However often these conditions in the local organizations led their leaders to lament, the similarities between the Nazi clubs and other local *Vereine* represented the party's most enduring success in the period of its reconstruction. In cities and towns throughout the land, the NSDAP had set down roots. Nazi clubs had become visible and

52. Krebs, *Tendenzen*, 54.
53. This principle applies to the manner in which these activities were represented in the party press. Here, like the accounts of meetings of other so-called national associations, reports told of members united in patriotic commitment and seriousness of purpose: see, for example, *Völkischer Beobachter* (Bayernausgabe), 11 Feb. 1927, 4. On the significance of the language of this kind of reportage, see Chickering, *We Men*, 152–5, 185–7.
54. Böhnke, *Ruhrgebiet*, 102, 121; Allen, *Seizure of Power*, 27–8; Klemm, *Hessen*, 131; Ingrid Buchloh, *Die nationalsozialistische Machtergreifung in Duisburg: Eine Fallstudie* (Duisburg, 1980), 46.
55. Bessel, *Political Violence*, 57.
56. Krebs, *Tendenzen*, 54. See also Anschütz, "Hamburg," 123.
57. Gimbel, "Entwicklung der NSDAP," 10–11, NSDAP Hauptarchiv, folder no. 142.
58. Broszat, "Anfänge," 103.

familiar, if not entirely respectable, fixtures in local associational cultures, where they were distinguished from other *Vereine* primarily in the constituencies with which they were associated and in the uncompromising way they invoked national symbols in opposition to the reigning political system. Only after 1928 did they begin to evolve into something fundamentally different; and they did so only in response to a dramatic shift in the dynamics of associational life in the movement.

In their rituals and practices, as well as in their afflictions, most of the local groups that grew up after the refoundation of the NSDAP bore little resemblance to the image of the militant, disciplined, revolutionary association that Hitler had announced in *Mein Kampf*. The discrepancy between image and reality occupied Hitler and the national leadership, and much of the reorganization of the party they undertook in the late 1920s was directed at the associational basis. The challenge was formidable, for the local practices that the leadership regarded as obstacles to militant action were not tangential features of club life. The distractions of *Vereinsleben* were difficult to disentangle from its attractions.

The basic difficulty was that active involvement, disagreement, and debate were essential aspects of associational life. As Klaus Tenfelde has argued, *Vereine* had served historically as instruments of "emancipation, democratization, and participation" in Germany; and they provided a public arena in which to practice "the orderly articulation of will and regulation of conflict."[59] The degree to which this emancipatory impulse continued to operate in the 1920s is too broad an issue to confront here, but as long as voluntary associations remained voluntary, they presented inherent obstacles to authoritarian control. Leaders could not afford to disregard the wishes of members, who could demonstrate their resistance simply by resigning in numbers large enough to threaten the association's survival.

The effects of what was known in the National Socialist movement as the *"Berliner Geist"* – the spirit of the "vilest parliamentarianism," of "intrigues and insults," "cow-trading and petty maneuvering [*Ellenbogenfreiheit*]" – quickly registered in countless requests for Hitler's personal intervention in local factional disputes.[60] That the

---

59. Klaus Tenfelde, "Die Entfaltung des Vereinswesens während der industriellen Revolution in Deutschland (1850–1873)," in Dann, ed., *Vereinswesen*, 111.
60. Bruno Wenzel, "Zur Frühgeschichte der NSDAP in Niedersachsen," 23, NSDAP Hauptarchiv, folder no. 141. See also Nyomarkay, *Charisma and Factionalism*, 35–47.

situation was in need of repair soon became evident in Munich. "I must urgently request that you spare Herr Hitler this kind of trifling [*Kleinkram*]," wrote the beleaguered Rudolf Hess in the summer of 1925 to a local leader who was quarreling with his comrades. "Where is it all to lead, if every local group calls on the *Führer* to decide every spat that breaks out?"[61]

The party leadership's principal response to the problem was to invoke the *Führerprinzip* (leadership principle), which was supposed to dissolve both lethargy and local factionalism in an ethos of commitment and obedience to a hierarchy of command. The practical implications of this principle for the locals became clear in a series of administrative reforms that were undertaken after 1925 in order to buttress the power of the national leadership in Munich and to establish the *Gauleiter* as the intermediaries between Munich and the *Ortsgruppen*.[62] The local clubs were henceforth required to register their members in Munich, to submit detailed reports of their activities, and to render precise accounts of their finances; the *Gauleiter* were to confirm all local leaders in office.

An assault of this kind on the autonomy of the local clubs was both risky and difficult to enforce. The party bureaucrats in Munich were compelled to ignore many of the local factional disputes elsewhere in the hope that the survivors would provide the ablest leadership.[63] Hitler also made a significant concession to traditional local practices when, in *Mein Kampf*, he sanctioned the principle of "Germanic democracy."[64] The authority of the *Ortsgruppenführer* was to be absolute, he explained, and all the committees were to be subordinate to this figure; but the membership retained the power to elect the local leader by acclamation.[65] Many of the locals were not content with this concession. They continued to operate in defiance of the *Gauleiter's* control, and they otherwise resisted the bureaucratization of the party.[66] The amount of time reserved in meetings for the formal expulsion of members who had failed to pay dues or to attend meetings attested to the vigor of other forms of local resistance.

61. Hess to Hartmann, Munich, 31 July 1925, NSDAP Hauptarchiv, folder no. 86.
62. Horn, *Führerideologie*, 226, 278–9; Pridham, *Bavaria*, 49–50; Orlow, *Nazi Party*, 71–5.
63. See Krebs, *Tendenzen*, 66.
64. Hitler, *Mein Kampf*, 344.
65. Horn, *Führerideologie*, 279–80; Tyrell, *Führer befiehl*, 230–2.
66. Horn, *Führerideologie*, 280–3; Detlef Mühlberger, "Central Control versus Regional Autonomy: A Case Study of Nazi Propaganda in Westphalia, 1925–1932," in Childers, ed., *Formation*, 67–8. See also Joachim C. Fest, *Hitler* (New York, 1974), 246–7, who overestimates the ease with which Munich imposed central control.

The administrative centralization of power over the local groups culminated only later, in radically different circumstances. In the meantime, the campaign against *Vereinsmeierei* inspired several other proposals. In 1926 Hitler officially forbade members to belong to other local political clubs or paramilitary organizations in the belief that simultaneous memberships would undermine discipline and breed factionalism or divided loyalties. He was enough aware of the sources of the local associations' recruiting grounds, though, to exempt veterans' associations from this prohibition.[67] The institution known in party circles as the USchlA was likewise introduced in 1926 to minimize the internal friction that plagued the local clubs. These "Committees of Investigation and Mediation" (*Untersuchungs- und Schlichtungsausschüsse*) were attached to the locals in order to "reconcile differences of opinion among individual *Parteigenossen* in an amicable fashion," as well as to remove "unworthy members" from the party.[68] The danger was that the selection, composition, and competence of these committees could themselves become sources of contention.

The establishment of a national propaganda office in 1926 had more far-reaching implications for life in the local groups, for it signaled a design to orchestrate the local meetings from Munich. As long as Gregor Strasser led this office, however, its intrusion into the affairs of the locals remained modest, confined to an attempt to draw up a common set of guidelines for propaganda and to establish a national register of accomplished speakers on whom the local groups might draw.[69]

The effort to manage the local meetings took much more remarkable form in the establishment in 1928 of a party speakers' school.[70] This undertaking rested on an acute appreciation of the dynamics of life in the clubs and on the belief that the impact of associational rituals could be enhanced by scripting them. "It is necessary to train party-comrades who have the aptitude to become National Socialist

67. Tyrell, *Führer befiehl*, 141, 165.
68. Richtlinien für die Untersuchungs- und Schlichtungsausschüsse der NSDAP (USchlA), n.d., NSDAP Hauptarchiv, folder no. 79. See also Horn, *Führerideologie*, 308–9; Tyrell, *Führer befiehl*, 230–2; Pridham, *Bavaria*, 96.
69. Mühlberger, "Westphalia," 81–2; Pridham, *Bavaria*, 53. See also Peter Stachura, *Gregor Strasser and the Rise of Nazism* (London, 1983), 60–6.
70. Thomas Wiles Arafe, Jr., "The Development and Character of the Nazi Political Machine, 1928–1930, and the NSDAP Electoral Breakthrough" (Ph.D. diss., Louisiana State University, 1976), 115–37.

speakers," wrote Fritz Reinhardt.[71] Reinhardt, one of the Bavarian *Gauleiter,* thereupon became the moving spirit behind a far-flung correspondence school, whose object was to train party members in the arts of effective oratory, particularly for meetings in the smaller localities. Members who participated in the course were rehearsed in a variety of roles demanded in the meetings. They learned not only to present by rote the party's position on a wide range of issues; they were taught to parry the heckles these positions commonly provoked, for the script required, as Reinhardt explained, an "immediate and quick-witted response" to all interruptions from the floor.[72] The same sense of dramatic necessity underlay Reinhardt's insistence that his students be themselves practiced in the role of heckler – in the use of, as he put it, the "intellectual weapons with which we can embarrass the speaker in the meetings of our opponents."[73]

The thousands of party members who passed by mail through Reinhardt's course attested to his sense of the dynamics of club life, as well as to his organizational talents. But the man was blind to the implications of his own success. "You are not actors," he wrote emphatically (and with no sense of irony) in one circular to his pupils:

the course is *not* designed to teach you how you should move your *mouth* or your whole *body* when you speak, or the extent to which you should use your *arms* and *fists,* or which *facial expressions* you should put on, or when you should speak *softly* and when *loudly,* etc.[74]

The point was, of course, that despite all these concessions to the spontaneity of their gestures, the Nazi speakers *were* supposed to be actors, whose confident performance of their roles was to be the surest guarantee of their success at the local meetings in which they starred. When Himmler announced in 1929 that Reinhardt's course had been officially designated a party institution, he inadvertently alluded to the same principle. The purpose of the course, he pointed out, was to produce speakers "who from the start have no stagefright [*Lampenfieber*]."[75]

71. Quoted in Tyrell, *Führer befiehl*, 257–60.
72. Ibid.
73. Ibid.
74. Reinhardt Circular, n.d., NSDAP Hauptarchiv, folder no. 274.
75. Himmler Memorandum, Munich, 6 May 1929, quoted in Tyrell, *Führer befiehl*, 261–3.

The speakers' school was a facet of a broad effort to mold traditional institutions and rituals of German associational life into a more effective and coordinated machinery of political mobilization. The effort required depriving the local Nazi clubs of most of their autonomy and spontaneity, and thus turning them into something unlike the other clubs (outside those of the Communist Party, KPD) with which they had coexisted in localities throughout the country. That the Nazis would succeed in breaking down traditional practices that served as barriers to this kind of coordination was by no means self-evident before 1929. The success of the party's leadership was due in the end to the transformation of German politics that came in the wake of economic collapse.

In the elections to the Reichstag in September 1930 the National Socialists attracted well over 6 million votes – roughly eight times as many as they had polled in 1928. By the time of the 1930 elections, party membership had nearly trebled since the end of 1928; and at the end of 1930 it stood, according to an official count, at nearly 400,000.[76] Electoral success, the upswing in the party's membership, and the changing character of club life in the movement were interrelated phenomena, and the relationship was complex. The brief remarks that conclude this essay are designed only to introduce the problem.

The NSDAP's breakthrough at the polls began in local and regional elections in 1929. It thus preceded the dramatic expansion of party membership and suggested that the "push" factors born of the economic downturn initially weighed more heavily than the "pull" factors of agitation and propaganda conducted within the framework of the clubs.[77] The clubs were by no means insignificant factors in the initial electoral success, but their significance lay primarily in their very presence. The party's great achievement at the onset of the crisis was to have established a system of local *Vereine* known to represent a radical but "national" alternative to a political system that was beginning to display ever more persuasive symptoms of its own bankruptcy.[78]

The transformation of the Nazi clubs was less the cause than the consequence of the electoral breakthrough. Success at the polls pro-

---

76. Schäfer, *NSDAP*, 17. See also Horn, *Führerideologie*, 379, on the difficulty of interpreting these figures.
77. See Mühlberger, "Westphalia," 78.
78. Bessel, "Rise of the NSDAP," 23. See also Kershaw, "Ideology," 173.

duced a fundamental change in the dynamic of associational life in the Nazi movement and turned the local groups into political instruments whose effectiveness in mobilizing support, both in the meeting halls and at the polls, made them unique among local political associations.

Electoral success made the Nazis interesting. It also produced a massive influx of party members. Nazi clubs were now beseiged with more members than they could accommodate. Although the rate of turnover in the clubs remained high, the members who remained tended to be enthusiastic and dedicated, and there were plenty of them. Consequently, the threat that large-scale resignations could bring a club's collapse disappeared. The availability of an enormous pool of members removed the major obstacle to centralizing and coordinating the party's organization on a national scale, as it led to an intensified assault on the initiative and autonomy of the *Ortsgruppen* and to the imposition of demands on their members' time and resources that other clubs were unable to contemplate. As one official pondered the reasons for the party's stunning growth in his district in 1931, he emphasized the play of these circumstances. "The membership dues are very high in comparison to those of other parties," he noted, "and strong dedication and active agitation on behalf of the party are demanded of those who join."[79]

In these circumstances, plans that the national leadership had been pursuing with difficulty came to fruition. The third edition of *Mein Kampf,* which appeared in 1930, omitted all reference to "Germanic democracy" and specified instead that all local leaders were to be "installed from above" by the *Gauleiter.*[80] Hitler's pronouncement reflected the new realities of the party's organization. All aspects of the locals' business now became targets of bureaucratic regimentation from Munich.[81] The replacement of Strasser by Goebbels at the head of the national propaganda office in 1929 signaled the beginning of a determined campaign to remove the last traces of spontaneity from the local meetings. Local propaganda committees, responsible to Goebbels's office, were to serve as conduits, not only to distribute speakers and propaganda materials to the locals, but to provide the clubs with instructions on themes, procedures, and frequency of

---

79. Heyen, *Alltag,* 50. See also Schäfer, *NSDAP,* 20.
80. Horn, *Führerideologie,* 278–9.
81. NSDAP Reichsleitung, *Dienstanweisung für Ortsgruppen und Stützpunkte der Nationalsozialistischen Deutschen Arbeiterpartei über den Geschäftsverkehr* (Munich, 1931).

meetings.[82] The script left nothing to chance. "Precise reports of the meetings with a thorough evaluation of the speaker must be submitted without fail," read the instructions from a subbranch of Goebbels's office. "By this means," the instructions went on,

> unqualified speakers can be removed from the lists [*ausgeschaltet*] in the shortest order. Meetings must always be led in a manner worthy of our movement. Appropriate instructions for all local officers on this subject will come from the district officials.[83]

The "unofficial" parts of the meetings remained, of course, but instructions now directed that these were to "serve the purposes of sociable conversation [*Aussprüche*] among guests and party members."[84] Even the violence took on a measure of regulation, as its increasing prominence in Nazi party life after 1929 registered the polarization of German politics. The emergence of a set of standard group tactics for the tavern brawl, or *Saalschlacht,* was not the only sign of the regimentation of this aspect of the rituals; the party also set up an insurance fund, to which all locals were required to subscribe.[85] Its purpose was to provide for the orderly repair of property damage sustained in the meeting hall whenever the final section of the script called for chaos.

The centralization of the party's organization and the growing coordination of all aspects of its political strategy made possible an extraordinary campaign, which compensated in vigor and cohesion for what it sacrificed in initiative and spontaneity at the local level. The building blocks in this campaign remained the local meetings, but these were now orchestrated to exploit the talents of the growing cadre of speakers and to maximize the sense of entertainment without which no party could hope to succeed. National Socialism seemed at last to have transcended *Vereinsmeierei.* The Nazis created, as Richard Bessel has suggested, a convincing if contradictory image of both roughness and respectability.[86] The virtuosity with which

---

82. Horn, *Führerideologie,* 380–1; Orlow, *Nazi Party,* 204–5.
83. Hartmann to Alle Kreisleiter, Ortsgruppen- und Stützpunktleiter, Propagandaleiter des Gaues München-Oberbayern, Munich, 9 Dec. 1932, NSDAP Hauptarchiv, folder no. 178.
84. NSDAP Bezirk München-Nord, Propagandaleitung to Ortsgruppen-Leiter und Propagandawarte des Bezirkes München-Nord, Munich, 5 Jun. 1931, NSDAP Hauptarchiv, folder no. 171.
85. Die Sachschädenkasse der Nationalsozialistischen Deutschen Arbeiterpartei, Memorandum, Munich, 2 Apr. 1931, NSDAP Hauptarchiv, folder no. 176. See also NSDAP *Dienstanweisung,* 10–11.
86. Bessel, *Political Violence,* 75.

they conducted their meetings documented their familiarity with the staple practices of middle-class tavern culture and enabled them to appeal to the many burghers who, as Sigmund Neumann noted at the time, looked to the party as a respectable alternative, as a "radical DNVP."[87] At the same time, however, the small-scale wars that periodically erupted within the meeting halls emphasized the party's energy and determination, just as they enhanced the atmosphere of excitement at the meetings.

The images of invasion, irruption, and spectacle acquired more validity after the electoral breakthrough, as the party itself attempted, by means of massive rallies, marches, and other demonstrations, to emphasize just these aspects of its campaign and to carry this campaign into broader milieus. The extension of the network of *Ortsgruppen* now took place primarily into small towns and villages. The agitation that accompanied this campaign was not only coordinated to convey the impression of sovereign control in an atmosphere of political crisis; it was orchestrated to seem like an invasion. Its principal form was the arrival, in trucks and often to the accompaniment of a band, of uniformed SA contingents in the town square; here they staged parades and rallies for the benefit of local residents, many of whom had never before heard of the NSDAP.[88] As important as these loud intrusions were in the last years before the Nazi seizure of power, the party owed its success no less to its invasion of another sphere. After 1929 the party began to win the support of local notables and to penetrate the associational milieus of the propertied and educated Protestant middle classes.[89] These people had hitherto disdained the Nazis in favor of the traditional patriotic associations, where they earned Hitler's derision for their pedantry, caution, and obsession with respectability. Their gravitation toward the NSDAP represented a significant broadening of the social coalition that supported the party; and not the least of its causes was the party's success in establishing its own respectable position within the network of German associations.

87. Sigmund Neumann, *Die Parteien der Weimarer Republik,* 2d ed. (Stuttgart, 1970), 84. See also Kershaw, "Ideology," 174.
88. Hambrecht, *Mittel- und Oberfranken,* 206; Zofka, *Ausbreitung,* 81; Broszat and Fröhlich, *Bayern,* 112–13; Fest, *Hitler,* 276.
89. Elke Fröhlich, "Die Partei auf lokaler Ebene: Zwischen gesellschaftlicher Assimilation und Veränderungsdynamik," in Gerhard Hirschfeld and Lothar Kettenacker, eds., *Der "Führerstaat": Mythos und Realität* (Stuttgart, 1981), 261–3; Kaschuba and Lipp, "Kein Volk," 133; Kater, *Nazi Party,* 62–71; Koshar, *Social Life,* 197–205. See also Richard F. Hamilton, *Who Voted for Hitler?* (Princeton, N.J., 1982).

Even in the last stages in the NSDAP's march to power, the spectacular images, which emphasized innovative propaganda techniques and the invasion of powerful new forces into German political culture, must be interpreted with some care. These images inhered in the party's self-representation and informed its propaganda. But the invasion came from a redoubtable, familiar source. The effectiveness of the party's propaganda techniques had a long prehistory, during which the NSDAP grew up within the culture of German club life. In the course of the party's growth, the leadership modified certain of the practices prescribed by this culture in the name of centralized control. The party's spectacular mobilization of support in the early 1930s was nevertheless conceivable only in the broader context of its gestation within institutions and rituals indigenous to German associational life.

PART FOUR

The National Perspective: Continuities and Discontinuities

13

1918 and All That: Reassessing the Periodization of Recent German History

STUART T. ROBSON

It flatters the egos of historians to repeat Kierkegaard: Life must be lived forward but can only be understood backward. Yet in understanding history backward, the hardest part may be recapturing the sense of what it was like to live life forward without knowing what came next. Hindsight is the only sight historians have; abusing it is all too easy. Forcing the past into neat periods does not help. Now that British historians, with a comic shove from Sellar and Yeatman, have discarded periodizing by reigns, German history is a prime candidate for a revision of its eras. Arguing that "the way we divide history up, the events we select for emphasis, and the dates we pick out as turning points are important because they reflect our whole view of the past," Geoffrey Barraclough called for "a new chronological frame" to replace both the liberal and conservative interpretations of German history.[1] Yet for all the new approaches that have been tried since he wrote in 1972, the old historical divisions have remained more or less intact. *Vormärz*, Revolution, Restoration, Bismarck, *Kaiserreich*, Weimar, Nazism, Postwar and now Post-Wall: Hook the wagons together and drive them along the *Sonderweg*. The Procrustean effect of imposing retroactive caesuras on the past is heightened when the juncture between periods coincides with a moment of fear and bewilderment. This is certainly the case with the year 1918. No one on either side of the Western Front expected what finally came to pass.

In trying to recapture how Germans experienced the end of the Great War, I concentrate in this essay on a small group that has been the focus of my research, the left liberals in the Reichstag, and also on

---

1. Geoffrey Barraclough, "A New View of German History; Part III: Mandarins and Nazis," *New York Review of Books*, 16 Nov. 1972.

their colleagues in the Center and Majority Socialist parties.[2] What matters in history is not just what happens but what people think is happening or about to happen. From that perspective, the first thing to note about the attitude of the politicians is their frequent surprise and confusion. We may see them as living in the last days of one period or the first of another, and may be critical of them for failing to realize that history has turned a page. They did not necessarily share our view. Like shocked victims of a traffic accident, they found it difficult to assimilate what was happening, and for a while they tried to carry on as they had before things came unstuck. Their view of the times they were trying to survive has been slighted, perhaps because of the difficulty historians have in appreciating the importance of accident, confusion, and contingency. Given our professional bias toward finding pattern and design, we do not like the way history often behaves like a cat, refusing to go in straight lines.

Defeat as such did not come entirely as a surprise to the politicians of the moderate left. Ever since Erich Ludendorff's all-or-nothing decision to unleash the submarine as an ultimate weapon in early 1917, the Progressives, the Majority Socialists, and, by July 1917, the Center Party feared a catastrophic outcome. Indeed, the remarkable revival of the so-called Zabern Coalition in mid-1917 arose out of the expectation that unless Germany put its house in order and made the first move toward a compromise peace, it would lose the war. To support the apparent shift of Chancellor Theobald von Bethmann Hollweg to constitutional reform in Prussia and to support an impending peace proposal from the Vatican, the three parties formed an Inter-Party Coordinating Committee and passed a peace resolution in early July.[3]

2. I have drawn upon my unpublished doctoral thesis, "Left-Liberalism in Germany, 1900–1919" (Oxford University, 1966). Its archival sources include the Conrad Haussmann papers (Hauptstaatsarchiv Baden-Württemberg, Stuttgart, hereafter cited as HStA Stuttgart); the papers of Georg Gothein, Erich Koch-Weser, Friedrich von Payer, Hartman von Richthofen and August Weber, all in the Bundesarchiv Koblenz, hereafter cited as BA Koblenz; and the party records of the German Democratic Party and the German People's Party, also in the BA Koblenz. Published documentary sources include Erich Matthias and Rudolf Morsey, eds., *Der Interfraktionelle Ausschuss* (Düsseldorf, 1959), hereafter cited as *IFA;* and Matthias and Morsey, eds., *Die Regierung des Prinzen Max* (Düsseldorf, 1962), hereafter cited as *Reg. Max.*
3. For the origins of the Inter-Party Committee and the Peace Resolution, see Johann Bredt, *Der Deutsche Reichstag im Weltkrieg* (Berlin, 1926), 73–81, 166–8; Klaus Epstein, *Matthias Erzberger and the Dilemma of German Democracy* (Princeton, N.J., 1959), 182–90; Georg Gothein, "Aus meiner politischen Arbeit," BA Koblenz: Nachlass Gothein, 12/115–18; Conrad Haussmann, *Schlaglichter, Reichstagsbriefe und Aufzeichnungen* (Frankfurt a.M, 1924),

At first, Gustav Stresemann of the National Liberals and Matthias Erzberger of the Center did not share the wider view about reform, nor did Stresemann accept Erzberger's view that a compromise peace was necessary. They did agree that Bethmann Hollweg must go, and so joined the conspiracy of the High Command to force the Kaiser to change chancellors.[4] When the new chancellor turned out to be the obscure Prussian bureaucrat Georg Michaelis, and when Michaelis, in turn, eviscerated the Peace Resolution Erzberger had steered through the Main Committee of the Reichstag by saying that he supported it "as I understand it," the scales did not immediately fall from Erzberger's eyes. He claimed that the equivocal reply of the new government to the Papal Peace Note was fully in harmony with the Peace Resolution and tried to cooperate with Michaelis.[5] But at the same time he became a pillar of the new Reichstag majority, which consisted of the Majority Socialists, the Center, the Progressives, and, when reform alone was at issue rather than a compromise peace as well, the National Liberals, and had as its center of coordination the Inter-Party Committee.[6]

The first crisis the majority faced was the question of replacing the hapless Michaelis in October 1917.[7] Conrad Haussmann and Friedrich von Payer of the Progressives had been aghast that Bethmann Hollweg had been sacked without a replacement in hand at least as acceptable to the majority.[8] Haussmann was soon in touch

---

95–115; *IFA* 1: Introduction, "Die Entstehung des Interfraktionellen Ausschusses", XI–XXXV; Friedrich Payer, *Von Bethmann Hollweg zu Ebert, Erinnerungen und Bilder* (Frankfurt a.M, 1923), 28–31. The allusion to the "Zabern Majority," the cooperation of left liberals, socialists, and Centrists that had censured the government in 1913, was made explicitly by Conrad Haussmann in a letter to the editor of the *Berliner Tageblatt*, Theodor Wolff, on 14 Apr. 1917. HStA Stuttgart, Nachlass Haussmann, 117. The letter is reprinted in *IFA* 1:XIX, but without the important footnote in which Haussmann called for a continuation "of the tone of 1913."

4. For Erzberger and the fall of Bethmann Hollweg, see Epstein, *Erzberger*, 193–202; for Stresemann, see Hartwig Thieme, *Nationaler Liberalismus in der Krise: Die nationalliberale Fraktion des preussischen Abgeordnetenhauses 1914–1918* (Boppard, 1963), 99–107; Marvin Edwards, *Stresemann and the Greater Germany* (New York, 1963) 143–6; *IFA* 1: XIX–XXI. For Bethmann Hollweg himself, see Konrad Jarausch, *The Enigmatic Chancellor: Bethmann Hollweg and the Hubris of Germany* (New Haven, Conn., and London, 1973), 373–80.
5. Epstein, *Erzberger*, 214–22.
6. The best introduction to the Inter-Party Committee remains the one Matthias and Morsey provide (*IFA*, 1). See also Epstein, *Erzberger*, chapters VIII–XI.
7. For the "October Crisis," see *IFA* 1:213–599; Haussmann, "Die Kanzlerkrise vom 9.10. zum 9.11.1917," HStA Stuttgart, Nachlass Haussmann, 26.
8. Payer, *Erinnerungen*, 31–3; Haussmann to Rauscher, 26 July 1917, HStA Stuttgart, Nachlass Haussmann, 114; Haussmann's summary "über die innenpolitische Entwicklung seit Juli 1917," dated November 1917, ibid., 137 (also in *IFA* 1:596–9). For Haussmann and Prince

with Kurt Hahn, secretary to Prince Max of Baden, a notable whose liberal bona fides consisted mainly of work with the Red Cross on behalf of prisoners of war. When the secretary of the navy, Admiral von Capelle, made a clumsy attempt to blame a naval mutiny on the Independent Socialists and threatened to suspend their parliamentary immunity, the two socialist parties moved a motion of nonconfidence in Michaelis. The Center and the National Liberals hung back, and Haussmann worked behind the scenes to replace Michaelis with Prince Max and Vice-Chancellor Helfferich with Payer.[9]

In the end, Erzberger sorted out the crisis. He persuaded the Inter-Party Committee to tell the Kaiser that Michaelis must go.[10] Although the majority deferred to the Imperial prerogative of selecting the head of government, it insisted that before taking office the new chancellor must meet the majority and accept its program. The majority program called for the formal acceptance of the reply of the German government on 19 September to the Peace Note of the Pope (i.e., regarding concessions over Belgium), equal suffrage in Prussia, an end to political censorship and the meddling of the army in politics, the introduction of labor–management councils, and repeal of the prohibition of boycotts. This remained the minimum program of the majority for the following twelve months. Erzberger's pressure carried the majority's demands to the attention of the Kaiser, and by the end of October, he let it be known that his choice to succeed Michaelis was Count Hertling, an elderly Bavarian from the conservative wing of the Center. Hertling accepted the majority program but bluntly rejected any move toward responsible parliamentary government. This angered the Majority Socialists and Progressives, but each politician had a different candidate for the chancellorship in mind, and in the end the majority accepted Hertling, hoping that Payer, as vice-chancellor, would keep the government honest.[11] Meanwhile, Haussmann, who was absent from Berlin at the height of the affair, drew up a detailed program for peace and reform that would have pledged the new government to restore Belgium unconditionally, to make the unification of a liberal central Europe a goal of policy, to discuss a League of Nations at the postwar peace conference, to reform the Prussian franchise, and to resist military and

---

Max, see Prince Max of Baden, *Memoirs*, 1:129–30; Haussmann to Kurt Hahn, 27 July 1917, HStA Stuttgart, Nachlass Haussmann, 115.
9. *Reg. Max.*, XVI–XXIX.
10. *IFA* 1:248–50; Epstein, *Erzberger*, 223.
11. *IFA* 1:322–599.

annexationist interference in affairs of state. Whether Haussmann subsequently presented his program to the majority and was ignored, or whether he remained silent when he returned to face a fait accompli, is unknown, but his program was, word for word, the one the majority adopted in September 1918.[12]

Before the final crisis of the Empire in September 1918, the majority almost fell apart over the Treaty of Brest-Litovsk.[13] From the start of negotiations in December 1917 to the signing of the punitive treaty in March 1918, Ludendorff's annexationist ambitions in the east were patently clear, and moved even the German foreign office and Austrian delegates to protest. But with a peace of conquest once again in sight, the right wing of the majority forgot about the Peace Resolution and once again began to dream in color. Haussmann managed to keep the Progressive Reichstag caucus pledged to the Resolution, and henceforth he and Georg Gothein controlled the party's caucus and central organization, but the Center and the National Liberals behaved as if 1917 had never happened.[14] With the Majority Socialists forced to move to the left to head off the general strike of munition workers in January, the majority seemed to have fractured itself beyond repair. Ludendorff was home free. All he had to do was win on the western front. But forcing a breakout on a grand scale was beyond the technology available in 1918, so that even Ludendorff's breakthrough against the British Fifth Army was pyrrhic, consuming the best of the manpower that was packed into the elite storm units and testing the worn-down German war economy beyond its limits. In effect, Ludendorff won his way to defeat.[15]

To the Social Democrats and to Progressives like Haussmann and Gothein, the tragedy Germany faced was clear from the outset of Ludendorff's offensive. They might not have been as well connected as Erzberger – who was? – but they could read neutral newspapers

12. For Haussmann's draft program, see *IFA* 1:417, n. 25.
13. For the Majority and Brest-Litovsk, see *IFA* 2: Section V.
14. For the struggle that Haussmann, despite an acute attack of erysipelas, an inflammation of the skin, and Gothein waged against revived annexationists (especially Ernst Müller-Meiningen and Otto Fischbeck), see Haussmann, *Schlaglichter*, 187–8; *IFA* 2: 353–66.
15. For the spring offensive of 1918, see Martin Middlebrook, *The Kaiser's Battle: 21 March 1918* (London, 1978), especially chapter 2; Hubert Essame, *The Battle for Europe, 1918* (New York, 1972); John Terraine, *To Win a War* (London, 1978), chapters 1–4; General Sir Herbert Gough, *The March Retreat* (London, 1934); Roger Parkinson, *Tormented Warrior: Ludendorff and the Supreme Command* (London, 1978); Barrie Pitt, *1918: the Last Act* (London, 1962), chapters 1–7; John Toland, *No Man's Land* (New York, 1980), part 1; Bruce Gudmundsson, *Stormtroop Tactics: Innovation in the German Army, 1914–1918* (New York, 1989), chapter 10.

and correspond with neutral experts. Haussmann, for example, was in touch with the Swiss military writer Hermann Stegewald and closely followed the withering of the German offensive in the west.[16] After the one-two punch of Allied victories at Villers-Cotterets in late July and at Amiens on 8 August, the leaders of the majority were at least as well informed as the government and the foreign office. But this is only to say that no one outside Ludendorff's inner circle at the High Command knew about the real turning point that was looming, Ludendorff's nervous crisis.[17]

Outsiders knew that a peace of conquest was no longer likely after 8 August, but they believed that the combination of a determined defense along the Siegfried Line with careful overtures and diplomatic concessions could still secure a compromise peace. Such guarded hopes might seem unrealistic in retrospect, but their rational basis, the defensive strength of the German position, and the novelty of Allied success in attacking meant that almost all the Allied leaders took the same view and did not expect a German collapse in 1918. Field Marshal Haig was the one exception, but predicting victory after one more push had become a fixed idea his colleagues did not necessarily share.[18]

With these reasonable if tenuous hopes of a negotiated peace in mind, around the end of August the Inter-Party Committee met to consider replacing Hertling's government with one controlled by the Reichstag majority and dedicated unequivocally to peace and reform. Led by Erzberger and Haussmann, whose program of a year earlier now became the program of the majority, the majority asked Payer to tell Hertling to resign.[19] But the initiative of the majority coincided almost exactly with Ludendorff's nervous breakdown.[20] The attacks of the Canadian Corps on the northern end of the Siegfried Line and those of the British in Flanders had caught Ludendorff in a classic military bind, without reserves to cover both mortal threats in the area of the front in which he had packed the most divisions.

16. For Haussmann and Stegemann, see Haussmann, *Schlaglichter,* 171; Prince Max, *Memoirs,* 1:248–9.
17. Ludendorff's collapse, touched on by Martin Kitchen, *The Silent Dictatorship* (London, 1976), Barrie Pitt in *1918: The Last Act* (London, 1962), and Correlli Barnett in *The Swordbearers* (London, 1963), has been best documented by Siegfried Kaehler in *Studien zur deutschen Geschichte des 19. und 20. Jahrhunderts* (Göttingen, 1961).
18. For Haig, see Terraine, *To Win a Victory,* 126.
19. *IFA* 2:469–748.
20. The importance of the coincidence between the initiatives of the majority and the High Command is stressed in *Reg. Max,* XI–XVI.

Raging at the failures of everyone else, he broke down on the afternoon of 28 September, and when he recovered his poise, he persuaded Hindenburg to agree that a new government must appeal to President Wilson for a cease-fire.[21]

Hertling arrived at the High Command at Spa thinking that he was responding to the initiative of the Reichstag, only to be blind-sided by an identical demand from the generals.[22] For a few days after the Imperial decree announcing Hertling's resignation, no one in Berlin realized that a military initiative had been involved, and when the role of the High Command did become clear, with the briefing Major von dem Bussche gave the Reichstag leaders on 2 October, both the new government of Prince Max and the politicians wrongly but reasonably concluded that a general catastrophe on the western front must have led to the self-defeating appeal for an armistice.[23] When it became clear that the front remained intact and that Ludendorff was in effect looking for civilian scapegoats to take the blame for defeat, it was too late to undo what had been done.

Nevertheless, Prince Max, who became chancellor primarily because of Haussmann's machinations behind the scenes, led a government that embodied all the goals of the majority, including parliamentary control of domestic, foreign, and military policy.[24] When President Wilson seemed to make the Kaiser's abdication the prerequisite to peace, war weariness turned into republicanism and republicanism into an apparent revolution.

Defeat was not unexpected; it had loomed as a possible consequence of Ludendorff's conquer-or-perish gambling since the start of 1917. It was the manner in which defeat came that was utterly unexpected and confusing: victory in the east, astounding advances in the west – and then, seemingly out of the blue, at least for the uninitiated, catastrophe. The leaders of the majority always seemed to be one step behind the pace of events, but then, so was everyone else in Germany and elsewhere. What is worth noticing is that they nevertheless persisted in trying to reform the Empire in ways they thought

---

21. See Kitchen, *The Silent Dictatorship*, 252–7.
22. See the note Count von Galen prepared in October, reprinted in *IFA*, 2:789–96.
23. For Major von dem Bussche's briefing, see *A Preliminary History of the Armistice* (New York, 1924), 43–6; Prince Max, *Memoirs,* 2:11. Matthias and Morsey document the cross-purposes afflicting the soldiers at headquarters in Spa and the politicians in Berlin (*Reg. Max.*, part I, "Vor der Regierungsbildung").
24. See Georg Gothein, "Aus meiner politischen Arbeit," BA Koblenz, Nachlass Gothein, 12/80; note by Haussmann on the government of Prince Max, *Reg. Max.*, 631–3.

were fundamental, ways moreover that embodied the ideas of reform they had espoused before the war. Despite the chaos of events, they tried to maintain the *continuity* of their work. Before we conclude that their effort was vain and deluded, given the entrenched power of illiberal and authoritarian structures, we should pay attention to the sense they had until the final days of the government of Prince Max that they had succeeded. This sense of achievement, in turn, seems to have guided Friedrich Ebert through the bewildering "revolution" of November and December.

The determination of Ebert and the Majority Socialists to avoid social revolution "like sin" and make the revolutionary drama of Russia in 1917 turn out differently in Germany is well known.[25] But did Ebert have a positive aim in mind as he balanced his conservative legitimacy as chancellor with his revolutionary legitimacy as one of six people's commissars? When one considers what he had done in the year before November, the answer would seem to be that his positive aim was to restore the reformist coalition that had controlled the government of Prince Max. According to both Haussmann and Payer, Ebert at first asked Haussmann and the other Progressives to remain in the government.[26] Moreover, he remained wedded to the program of the coalition: parliamentary democracy at home, and abroad a peace of reconciliation based on President Wilson's Fourteen Points.

The domestic side of this program led directly to the Weimar Coalition of February 1919, to the constitution of the new republic, and to the coalition that dominated Prussia throughout the 1920s. The failure of this coalition of the moderate left was essentially a result of the swing of the middle classes from the Democratic Party to Stresemann's German People's Party in the national election of 1920 and the split of Bavarian Catholics away from the Center Party. But even in federal politics, much of the original agenda of the Weimar Coalition remained intact.

The foreign policy of the Weimar Coalition was flawed by its

25. See, for example, A. J. Ryder, *The German Revolution of 1918* (Cambridge, 1967), 151–4, 261–4, and *Twentieth-Century Germany* (New York, 1973), 190–1; David Morgan, *The Socialist Left and the German Revolution* (Ithaca, N.Y., and London, 1975), 128–30; William Maehl, *The German Socialist Party* (Philadelphia, 1986), 1–9; Richard Hunt, *German Social Democracy 1918–1933* (New Haven, Conn., and London, 1964), 27–32.
26. Haussmann, *Schlaglichter*, 270–2; Payer, *Erinnergungen*, 165. See also Prince Max, *Memoirs*, 2:354, where Prince Max quotes Ebert on 9 November as having "nothing against" the inclusion of the bourgeois parties, as long as Majority Socialists had a "decisive majority."

assumption that the enemy shared the liberal desire for reconciliation, an assumption that events in Paris were to shatter. Yet before we treat this as yet another sign of naiveté, we ought to ask if the foreign policy of, say, David Lloyd George or Woodrow Wilson was noticeably more realistic than that of the German republicans. Ten years later, Lloyd George told Harold Nicolson that he and Georges Clemenceau had regarded the Treaty of Versailles as little more than a "temporary measure of a nature to satisfy public opinion in the belligerent countries".[27] Everyone was scrambling at the peace conference. Yet before we condemn the victors for shortsightedness or the German government for encouraging unrealistic hopes that negotiations would be evenhanded, we should ask if the peace settlement in its final form was as punitive or premeditated as this criticism implies. The actual terms of the Treaty of Versailles were the occasion of German disbelief and anger; but the underlying cause of German resentment, surely, was defeat itself. Given the widely shared German assumption that the armistice was a contract arising out of military stalemate and promising a peace of justice, *any* likely terms the victors presented would have seemed unfair.

In short, the people who built the Weimar Republic believed in the continuity of their work and thought they had steered the cause of democracy to a safe harbor.[28] To them, the collapse of 1918 was the direct result of military countergovernment, and the revolution was a completely gratuitous upheaval, coming about mainly because the people desperately wanted peace and neither they nor President Wilson recognized the real shift in power that had taken place in the last six weeks of the Empire. Ebert's primary aim after 9 November was thus to return Germany to the position it had been in just before misunderstanding and confusion threatened all that had been gained. With the decision on 19 December of the Congress of Councils to support elections for a Constituent National Assembly and the subsequent elections for the Assembly, Ebert had reason to think he had won. The anathema of Bolshevism seemed to have been defeat-

---

27. Harold Nicolson, *Diaries and Letters, 1930–1939* (London, 1966), 82.
28. British historians in the 1920s stressed this sense of democratic tradition more than did later historians. See, for example, Hugh Quigley and R. T. Clark, *Republican Germany* (New York, 1968; first published 1928), chapter 2; G. P. Gooch, *Germany* (London, 1926), cited in J. W. Hiden, *The Weimar Republic* (London, 1974), 3. For a recent view of the Republic as a culmination rather than an aberration, see Larry Eugene Jones, *German Liberalism and the Dissolution of the Weimar Party System, 1918–1933* (Chapel Hill, N.C., 1988), 12.

ed with the suppression of the Spartacist uprising. Ebert was once again working with the people he had come to trust, bourgeois allies who shared his goals and proved their devotion to a reformed Germany.

From the point of view of the founders of the Republic, was 1918 a caesura? The left wings of both socialism and liberalism certainly took it to be the dawn of a bright new age, whereas the right saw only bad things coming. But the extremes of left and right were not in charge; to those moderates who were, 1918 seemed no more or less pregnant with change than 1917 had been. War may bring change or, as Arthur Marwick stresses, at least the sense of change, but the very mood of crisis it engenders also tends, as he says, to affirm the search for continuity and stability.[29] People in all warring nations look for new means to achieve old dreams or preserve traditional institutions. Even reform becomes a way of changing less essential things to keep what appears, in the terrible light of collective sacrifice, to be all-important. To be sure, stopping the killing makes a difference, but when peace breaks out, the forces war sets in motion do not vanish. German Social Democracy, for example, had been split asunder by the issue of war aims, and its internal feud could not be put aside just because the war was over.[30] Nor could the liberals make a fresh start and unify themselves; Stresemann's annexationism had been too flagrant for the Progressives to forget. Yet it was not just wartime grudges that carried over into peace. Older dreams and ideals also persisted. Those who created the Republic had to present it as something new, unburdened with the sins of the old regime, if only to impress the victors. Conservative nationalists accepted the claim of novelty and turned it into a criticism, arguing that liberal democracy was alien and artificial.

Looking back on the Republic, historians have tended to agree.[31] In doing so, they have overlooked the degree to which the Republic

29. Arthur Marwick, "Problems and Consequences of Organizing Society for Total War," in N. F. Dreisziger, ed., *Mobilization for Total War: The Canadian, American and British Experience, 1914–1918, 1939–1945* (Waterloo, Ont., 1981), 1–21.
30. See Morgan, *The Socialist Left*.
31. For example, among others, Hans-Ulrich Wehler, *The German Empire* (Leamington Spa, 1985), chapter 8, section 4, especially 219–20 (where he disputes Matthias and Morsey about the importance of the majority's initiative); Karl Dietrich Bracher, *Die Auflösung der Weimarer Republik* (Villingen/Schwarzwald, 1960), 3–27; S. William Halperin, *Germany Tried Democracy* (New York, 1965); Walter Laqueur, *Weimar: A Cultural History* (New York, 1974), chapter 1; Ralf Dahrendorf, *Society and Democracy in Germany* (New York, 1979), chapter 24; Eberhard Jäckel, "The Predicament of the Weimar Republic," in Michael Laffan, ed., *The Burden of German History 1919–45* (London, 1988), 48–55.

was in part the culmination of an authentic German tradition of reform reaching back at least as far as 1848. Instead of seeing the Republic exclusively as a new and distinct era, beginning and perhaps even ending in 1918–19, we should try to see it as the people involved in its creation saw it, as a reformed, parliamentary version of the *Kaiserreich* or, in crudely Hegelian terms, a synthesis arising out of the dialectical clash between the Bismarckian Reich and its military antithesis. As advertisers would say, it was not supposed to be "All New" but "New and Improved."

If the sense of continuity in 1918 was as powerful as the sense of change, at least in terms of the expectations of the political leaders of Germany, what becomes of the conventional periodization of German history? In proposing a new view of German history, Barraclough suggested that the years between 1917 and 1923 formed a distinct era. It began with the usurpation of power by the High Command and the virtual demolition of the Bismarckian constitution; it ended with the stabilization of the mark, the affirmation of civilian supremacy, and the reintroduction of Germany into the concert of nations. The main *political* issue in the period was military countergovernment, most obviously with Ludendorff's "silent dictatorship" but also with the Freikorps between 1918 and 1920, the Kapp Putsch, the Black Reichswehr, and General Hans von Seeckt's exercise of exceptional powers in 1923. The main rivals the generals faced were the civilian democrats, yet it should be remembered that the bureaucracy and educated elites were also unhappy at the power of sword over scepter. That is, the civilian elites took military countergovernment to be the exception rather than the rule. They did not see their own history the way foreign liberals did, and considered Prussian militarism, whether in the case of Zabern in 1913 or Ludendorff's dictatorship, to be either a momentary aberration or a perversion of the actual military traditions of Prussia and Germany. Moreover, the period ended with the scepter ruling the sword. Seeckt used his emergency powers to suppress uprisings on the left and right and then stepped back behind the curtains. When he got out of line in 1926, he was sacked, as was the minister of defense, Otto Gessler, when he misbehaved. Hindenburg swore an oath as president to uphold the constitution, and if anything he stuck too close to the letter of the law in the *Dauerkrise* after 1930, when his reluctance to use the emergency powers at his disposal helped to undermine the three chancellors before Hitler.

The main *economic* issue Germany faced between 1916 and 1925, apart from war production and the conversion to peacetime production, was inflation.[32] It was not just the product of the debacle after 1918, but had been built into the shortsighted way the *Kaiserreich* had financed its prewar arms buildup after the failure of tax reform in 1909 and then mismanaged its war effort on the complacent understanding, to quote Helfferich, that the losers would pay. Indeed they did. Inflation crippled the organizations of the smaller bourgeois parties and thwarted their efforts to mobilize public opinion for continued reform. Then as now, inflation bred conservatism.

It remains to sum up the period between 1916 and 1923, the German Time of Troubles. For aims that were initially only marginally more utopian and aggressive than those of the Entente, Germany boxed itself into a total war that Bethmann Hollweg and Falkenhayn, the civilian and military leaders of the early war, realized could not be won by conventional methods. To escape the box, Falkenhayn conceived of the attack toward Verdun as a way of achieving an unlimited result through limited attacks. He got unlimited war instead. He gave way to Hindenburg and Ludendorff. Their dictatorship brought in expedients of total war: the (literally) concrete form of the Siegfried Line in the west, the Hindenburg program of war socialism, the effective destruction of the Bismarckian constitution without a clear substitute, and unlimited submarine warfare, all justified by the most extreme sorts of imperialist war aims. For two years, the radical means and ends interacted, the means requiring breathtaking ends, the ends requiring even more desperate means. Not even Ludendorff intended to turn Germany upside down and inside out, but the situation of total war renders intentions irrelevant. Results alone matter. Between the spring of 1917 and mid-1918, it appeared that Ludendorff's improvised dictatorship had gained the success that alone would keep it going. Britain seemed close to defeat in the Atlantic and in Flanders, the French were succumbing to defeatist politics and mutiny, and American belligerency remained more a nuisance to Germany than an immediate threat. Hoping to nail down a peace of conquest, Ludendorff staked everything on the mammoth offensive in the west. He lost. To escape blame, he devised the grotesque fiction of the "stab in the back," offering the first version of it to his

---

32. It is significant that one of the few works in English that transcends the dividing line of 1918 is Gerald Feldman's study *Iron and Steel in the German Inflation, 1916–1923* (Princeton, N.J., 1977).

staff on the evening of 29 September, when he informed it of his decision to seek an armistice.[33] His alibi succeeded better than he could have anticipated, because his demand for a scapegoat happened to coincide with the demand of the Reichstag majority for a share of power. Then and now, the outside world saw only the hand of Ludendorff behind the government of Prince Max; the civilian politicians were credited with power only in the perverted myth of the *Dolchstosslegende*.

With the Kiel naval mutiny and the collapse of the dynasties in the face of street demonstrations for peace, the poisoned cup of power passed to Ebert. He set himself to return the country to the status quo ante 9 November and to what he regarded as the fruitful partnership of the Majority Socialists, Center, and Progressives. Voter support for the Weimar Coalition in the elections of 1919 proved to be tissue thin, resting as it did on hopes of appeasing the Allies and taking the breeze out of the sails of the radical left. That the new Republic survived the shock of the Treaty of Versailles is remarkable; that it somehow coped with the troubles that followed is almost miraculous: paramilitary violence, hyperinflation, separatism, and pariah status abroad. Yet after almost a decade of shocking surprises, something like a functioning parliamentary democracy remained in place, admittedly more conservative and bureaucratic than the founders of the Republic had hoped, at least federally, but certainly more resilient and popularly accepted than the regimes of the successor states of central Europe. The radical intelligentsia predictably was not amused or impressed with the Republic, but given its occupational disease of self-induced alienation and its chronic aversion to pragmatic politics, the mythology of cultural pessimism it preferred need detain only those who still cling to tie-died shirts and the Grateful Dead. As the Time of Troubles finally receded into oblivion, the German Republic behaved much like the other functioning pluralistic democracies of the Atlantic rim: Interest groups were conniving, old elites conspiring, industrialists plotting to do in the unions, unions marching to throttle the industrialists, generals dreaming of the good old days, intellectuals dreaming of the brave new world, and ordinary people keeping on keeping on, relieved to have escaped from "history." Few other than Oswald Spengler or the Nazis were willing to predict the future, which was not what it had been. That being so,

---

33. See Albrecht von Thaer, *Generalstabsdienst an der Front und in der OHL* (Göttingen, 1958), 234–7.

historians should be careful not to predict the past. The eventual demise of parliamentary democracy in Germany was not inevitable. Rather, it was a *necessary* consequence of the traditionalism of a majority of Germans. But traditional ways of thinking are not immune to sudden change, as a glance at Europe now shows us.

The key to understanding the Time of Troubles, apart from putting the continuity from war to peace in 1918 in context, is to take each wave of events seriously. Total war did not break out in 1914 but arrived as a consequence of the failure of limited war to stay limited in 1916; defeat was not written in the stars after the Marne, Verdun, or even unlimited submarine warfare, however much it may appear inescapable to retrospective experts, but arrived suddenly in September 1918; revolution was not a losing cause until it actually lost; and parliamentary democracy was not tossed on the trash heap of history until the long crisis, induced primarily by the Depression, of 1930 to 1933. Just like good show horses, historians should not jump their fences too early.

Robert Darnton suggests that most people can grasp the idea of "a fundamental change in the tenor of everyday life," but few can assimilate it. Without the prodding of a traumatic shock, people tend to take things as they come.

Such shocks often dislodge individual lives, but they rarely traumatize societies. In 1789 the French had to confront the collapse of a whole social order – the world that they defined retrospectively as the Ancien Regime – and to find some new order in the chaos surrounding them. They experienced reality as something that could be destroyed and reconstructed, and they faced seemingly limitless possibilities, both for good and for evil, for raising a utopia and for falling back into tyranny.[34]

The Time of Troubles can be seen as having a similarly traumatic impact on the Germans. The accumulation of shocking surprises gave them a sense that reality could be changed radically. Unlike the French in 1789, they did not welcome the discovery, not because they were Germans, afraid of making revolution because it meant walking on the grass, but because they had not wanted radical change in the first place but only a better version of what they already had. Between 1916 and 1925, Germany went through an approximation of what France endured between 1791 and 1795, and by the end of the Troubles, what the German middle classes in particular wanted was

---

34. Robert Darnton, *The Kiss of Lamourette: Reflections in Cultural History* (New York, 1990), 4.

not more change but a change *from* change, a shelter from history. The conservative, bureaucratic Republic that had emerged by 1925 may have been more a lean-to than a mighty fortress, although critical judgments about its flaws ought to compare it to liberal-conservative democracies elsewhere. But it did hold out the minimal promise of tranquility. Then Wall Street laid an egg.

14

Generational Conflict and the Problem of Political Mobilization in the Weimar Republic

LARRY EUGENE JONES

The literature on generational conflict and its role in the rise of National Socialism is indeed extensive.[1] With few exceptions, the principal thrust of this literature has been to trace a direct line of continuity from the rebellion of the German youth movement in the Wilhelmine period to the alienation of the younger generation and the rise of National Socialism in the Weimar Republic.[2] Yet for all the interest that the problem of generational conflict in the Weimar Republic has attracted, little attention has been devoted to the efforts of the more established bourgeois parties to overcome the alienation of the younger generation and – at least in the case of the German Democratic Party (*Deutsche Demokratische Partei* or DDP) and German Center Party (*Deutsche Zentrumspartei*) – to win it over to the

1. For a survey of this literature, see Peter Stachura, "Deutsche Jugendbewegung und Nationalsozialismus," *Jahrbuch des Archivs der Deutschen Jugendbewegung* 12 (1980): 35–52. Of the more recent contributions to this discussion, see Michael Kater, "Generationskonflikt als Entwicklungsfaktor in der NS-Bewegung vor 1933," *Geschichte und Gesellschaft* 11 (1985): 217–43; Hans Mommsen, "Generationskonflikt und Jugendrevolte in der Weimarer Republik," in Thomas Koebner, Rolf-Peter Janz, and Frank Trommler, eds., *"Mit uns zieht die neue Zeit." Der Mythos Jugend* (Frankfurt a.M., 1985), 50–67; and Elisabeth Domansky, "Politische Dimensionen von Jugendprotest und Generationenkonflikt in der Zwischenkriegszeit in Deutschland," in Dieter Dowe, ed., *Jugendprotest und Generationenkonflikt in Europa im 20. Jahrhundert. Deutschland, England, Frankreich und Italien im Vergleich* (Brunswick and Bonn, 1986), 113–37. See also the provocative essay by Peter Loewenberg, "The Psychological Origins of the Nazi Youth Cohort," *American Historical Review* 76 (1971): 1457–1502.
2. For example, see Michael Kater, "Bürgerliche Jugendbewegung und Hitlerjugend in Deutschland 1925 bis 1939," *Archiv für Sozialgeschichte* 17 (1977): 127–74, and Irmtraud Götz von Olenhusen, "Die Krise der jungen Generation und der Aufstieg des Nationalsozialismus. Eine Analyse der Jugendorganisationen der Weimarer Zeit," *Jahrbuch des Archivs der Deutschen Jugendbewegung* 12 (1980): 53–82. See also the interesting observation by Richard Bessel on generational factors and their role in the breakdown of a national electorate in his essay in this volume.

support of the Weimar Republic.[3] These parties, after all, were acutely aware of the extent to which their own political effectiveness, as well as the survival of the political order with which they were so closely identified, depended upon the outcome of their efforts to win the support of those young men and women who had reached political maturity since the last years of the Second Empire. The purpose of this essay, therefore, is to trace the general outlines of the relationship that developed between Germany's nonsocialist parties and the younger generation in the Weimar Republic and to suggest why by the beginning of the 1930s these parties, with the notable exception of the Center, had failed to attract and retain the support of Germany's younger voters. At the same time, this essay offers at least a partial explanation of why Weimar's younger generation proved so susceptible to the appeal of Nazism.

Generational cleavages were every bit as important in shaping the general course of political development in the Weimar Republic as those of class, gender, and confession. A generational breakdown of Weimar political culture reveals the existence of at least four distinct cohort groups separated by fundamentally different life experiences. At the top of the gerontological ladder stood two generations, one that had been born before the founding of the Second Empire and the other in the first decade or so after German unification. By the end of World War I virtually all of the key positions in German political, economic, and intellectual life were held by representatives of these two generations. The third generation consisted of those who had been born in the 1880s and 1890s, and whose social and political values had been shaped first by their involvement in the prewar German youth movement and then by their experiences at the front in World War I. In Weimar political parlance, this was the so-called front generation that had received its baptism by fire in the trenches of World War I, only to return home at the end of the war to find the nation it had gone off to defend in a state of complete collapse. The term "youth," on the other hand, was generally reserved for those who had been born since the turn of the century and whose formative life experience had been the deprivation of the war and the immediate postwar period. In many respects, this was a superfluous

---

3. For a partial corrective to this deficiency, see Larry Eugene Jones, "German Liberalism and the Alienation of the Younger Generation in the Weimar Republic," in Konrad H. Jarausch and Larry Eugene Jones, eds., *In Search of a Liberal Germany: Studies in the History of German Liberalism from 1789 to the Present* (Oxford and New York, 1990), 287–321.

Generational Conflict and Political Mobilization 349

generation whose access to economic opportunity and political power was blocked by a gerontocracy that had survived the collapse of 1918 with most of its prerogatives intact.[4] The term "younger generation," on the other hand, was characteristically vague, and in the Weimar Republic generally referred to the last two cohort groups without a careful distinction between them.

The political alienation of the younger generation in the Weimar Republic represented the culmination of a process that had had its roots in the last years of the Second Empire. One of the more striking features of Wilhelmine political culture was the emergence of a youth movement that both rejected the social and moral conventions of Wilhelmine Germany and sought to invest life with a deeper meaning through fellowship and communion with nature. Though avowedly apolitical, the German youth movement was profoundly alienated from the way in which Germany had developed since the founding of the Second Empire and espoused a disdain for modern political life that drew much of its inspiration from the revolutionary conservatism of thinkers such as Paul de Lagarde and Julius Langbehn. Although the movement became increasingly politicized with the approach of war, efforts to unite the older members of the youth movement under the aegis of the Free German Youth (*Freideutsche Jugend*) in an attempt to bring about the reformation of German public life lacked clear ideological direction and foundered on the antipathy of the rank and file of the German youth movement toward the very idea of partisan political activity. For the most part, however, the German youth movement remained fervently nationalistic and went off to the front in 1914 with an enthusiasm that was to prove suicidal.[5]

Following the collapse of 1918, the various nonsocialist parties that emerged from the November Revolution made a concerted effort to

---

4. The foregoing analysis is deeply indebted to Detlev J. K. Peukert, *Die Weimarer Republik. Krisenjahre der klassischen Moderne* (Frankfurt a.M., 1987), 25–31. The limitation of such an approach lies in its failure to incorporate a social or class dimension into the analysis of generational behavior. It is, for example, naive to assume, as Peter Loewenberg has done in his article on the psychological origins of the Nazi youth cohort (see note 1), that middle-class and working-class youth experienced the deprivations of the war and the postwar period in precisely the same ways. To correct such an oversight, it is necessary to supplement cohort analysis with careful attention to the way in which the life experience of a given cohort group differs according to social class.
5. On the history of the German youth movement during the last years of the Second Empire, see Walter Laqueur, *Young Germany. A History of the German Youth Movement* (New York, 1962), 3–98, and Peter Stachura, *The German Youth Movement 1900–1945. An Interpretative and Documentary History* (New York, 1981), 13–37.

overcome the alienation of the younger generation and to mobilize it in support of their own partisan causes.[6] Of the bourgeois parties that dotted Weimar's political landscape, only the German Center Party had existed before the war and could rely upon the support of a youth organization with roots in the Wilhelmine era. In 1895 the Center had taken the initial step toward integrating Germany's Catholic youth more firmly into its own organizational structure by founding the first in a series of Windthorst Leagues (*Windthorstbünde*) at a special demonstration in Essen. By 1914 the Windthorst Leagues numbered approximately 20,000 members with an estimated 300 chapters throughout the country. After the end of the war, when the number and form of Catholic youth organizations began to proliferate with the creation of the Young Center Clubs (*Jungzentrumsvereine*) and the Ketteler Leagues (*Kettelerbünde*), the Center Party's leadership moved to coordinate this activity under the umbrella of a single organization and to integrate it more firmly into its own organizational structure. This led to the founding of the National League of German Windthorst Leagues (*Reichsverband der deutschen Windthorstbünde*) at a demonstration of young party activists in Fulda in May 1921.[7]

Although the Windthorst Leagues defined themselves as a "living community," or *Lebensgemeinschaft,* in language reminiscent of the prewar German youth movement, their primary purpose was to serve as a liaison between the Center and the more than 1 million men and women who were active outside the party in a variety of church-affiliated Catholic youth organizations. Of these, the most important were the Catholic Young Men's Association of Germany (*Katholischer Jungmännerverband Deutschlands*), with close ties to the Christian labor movement;[8] the Central League of Catholic Youth Women's Associations of Germany (*Zentralverband der katholischen*

---

6. For a general overview of political youth organizations in the first years of the Weimar Republic, see Normann Körber, *Die deutsche Jugendbewegung. Versuch eines systematischen Abrisses* (Berlin, 1920), 5–9.
7. For further details, see the organizational report by Katzenberger in Deutsche Zentrumspartei, Reichsgeneralsekretariat, ed., *Offizieller Bericht des Zweiten Reichsparteitages der Deutschen Zentrumspartei. Tagung zu Berlin vom 15. bis 17. Januar 1922* (Berlin, n.d. [1922]), 39–42, as well as the report by Bockel, "Jugend und Partei," at an expanded meeting of the National League of German Windthorst Leagues, 16 Jan. 1922, ibid., 119–22. For further information on the ideological and organizational development of the Windhorst Leagues, see Erwin Niffka, "Werden und Wirken," in *Um Volk und Staat. Der Weg der deutschen Windthorstbunde,* special issue of *Das Junge Zentrum. Monatsschrift des Reichsverbandes der Deutschen Windthorstbunde* 3, nos. 6–7 (June–July 1927): 11–36.
8. In this connection, see Georg Wagner, "Katholischer Jungmännerverband Deutschlands," in Hertha Siemering, ed., *Die deutschen Jugendverbände. Ihre Ziele, ihre Organisation sowie ihre neuere Entwicklung und Tätigkeit* (Berlin, 1931), 184–95.

Jungfrauenvereinigung Deutschlands), with over 750,000 members;[9] and the newly founded Coalition of Catholic German Student Associations (*Arbeitsgemeinschaft der katholischen deutschen Studentenverbände*).[10] The Center and the Windthorst Leagues were thus able to tap into a rich Catholic infrastructure that was not available to Weimar's other nonsocialist parties. Within the Center, the Windthorst Leagues stood on the party's extreme left wing and were among the party's most ardent defenders of Germany's new republican order. At its Hildesheim and Glatz congresses in 1923 and 1924, respectively, the National League of German Windthorst Leagues issued unequivocal statements in support of Germany's fledgling republican system. At the same time, the Windthorst Leagues espoused a progressive social policy and called for the creation of a social *Volksgemeinschaft* on the basis of the republican form of government.[11]

The Center Party's unique confessional character gave it an advantage in recruiting the support of the younger generation that none of Weimar's other bourgeois parties enjoyed. The leaders of the newly founded DDP tried to compensate for this by appealing to the idealism of those who had been involved in the prewar German youth movement in the hope that they might be enlisted in the establishment of a democratic Germany.[12] In this respect, they were aided by the defection of the National Association of National Liberal Youth (*Reichsverband der nationalliberalen Jugend*), the youth cadre of the prewar National Liberal Party (*Nationalliberale Partei* or NLP), at the height of the November Revolution.[13] Following the elections to the National Assembly, the leaders of the DDP proceeded to found

---

9. For further information, see H. Klens, "Zentralverband der katholischen Jungfrauenvereinigung Deutschlands," in Siemering, ed., *Jugendverbände*, 199–203.
10. Hermann Hagen, "Die katholischen Studentenverbände," in Siemering, ed., *Jugendverbände*, 221–7. On the politics of the German student movement during the Weimar Republic, see Wolfgang Zorn, "Die politische Entwicklung des deutschen Studentums 1918–1931," in Kurt Stephenson, Alexander Scharff, and Wolfgang Klötzer, eds., *Darstellungen und Quellen zur Geschichte der deutschen Einheitsbewegungen im neunzehnten und zwanzigsten Jahrhundert* (Heidelberg, 1965), 5: 223–307. On the early years of the Weimar Republic, see the detailed study by Jürgen Schwarz, *Studenten in der Weimarer Republik. Die deutsche Studentenschaft in der Zeit von 1918 bis 1923 und ihre Stellung zur Politik* (Berlin, 1971).
11. Heinrich Krone, "Die junge katholische Generation in der deutschen Politik," in Karl Anton Schulte, ed., *Nationale Arbeit. Das Zentrum und sein Wirken in der deutschen Republik* (Berlin and Leizpig, n.d. [1929]), 458–69.
12. For example, see Eduard Staedel, *Die Pflicht der Jugend. Ansprache gehalten im Auftrag der Demokratischen Partei am 5. Januar 1919 in Darmstadt* (Darmstadt, n.d. [1919]).
13. Bruno Marwitz, *Deutsche Demokratie und nationaler Liberalismus*. Deutsche Demokratische Ziele, no. 6 (Berlin, 1919).

the National League of German Democratic Youth Clubs (*Reichsbund Deutscher Demokratischer Jugendvereine*) under the leadership of Max Weissner in an attempt to consolidate their party's position within the younger generation.[14] This organization, which held its first national congress in April 1919, called upon German youth to defend the Weimar Constitution, to struggle for the creation of economic democracy, and to reject "racial hatred and the whipping up [*Aufpeitschung*] of all lower instincts."[15] A sister organization known as the National League of German Democratic Students (*Reichsbund Deutscher Demokratischer Studenten*) was subsequently founded with similar goals for university matriculants throughout the country.[16]

Whereas the Democrats moved quickly to establish a foothold within German youth and student movements, the leaders of the other liberal party – the German People's Party (*Deutsche Volkspartei* or DVP) – found their overtures to the younger generation severely hampered by the defection of the National Liberal youth cadre to the rival DDP. The leaders of the DVP hoped to compensate for their lack of a youth organization by working within the German National Youth League (*Deutschnationaler Jugendbund* or DNJ), an ostensibly nonpartisan youth organization in which all those who were committed to the reconstruction of the Fatherland on the basis of Germany's Christian culture could unite,[17] but withdrew from the DNJ in the fall of 1919 when the right-wing German National People's Party (*Deutschnationale Volkspartei* or DNVP) tried to politicize it for its own partisan purposes.[18] The DVP's national leadership then proceeded to establish its own youth organization – the Youth Cadre of the German People's Party (*Jugendgruppen der Deutschen Volkspartei*) –

14. On the history of the Young Democratic movement, see Ernst Schein, "Die demokratische Jugendbewegung," in Richard Thurnwald, ed., *Die neue Jugend*, Forschungen zur Völkerpsychologie und Soziologie, no. 4 (Leipzig, 1927), 239–51, and Richard Winners, "Reichsbund der Deutschen Jungdemokraten E. V.," in Siemering, ed., *Jugendverbände*, 264–74.
15. Deutscher demokratischer Jugendverein Gross-Berlin, "Jugend heraus!" *Mitteilungen für die Mitglieder der Deutschen Demokratischen Partei* 2, no. 5 (May 1920): 180–1.
16. For further details, see Wolfram Müllerburg, "Reichsbund Deutscher Demokratischer Studenten," in Siemering, ed., *Jugendverbände*, 274–6, as well as the following articles by Wilhelm Mommsen, "Studentenschaft und Demokratie," *Die demokratische Jugend* 1, no. 1 (10 Oct. 1919): 11–15; "Studentschaft und demokratischer Staat," *Die Hilfe* 26, no. 25 (17 June 1920): 376–8; and "Demokratische Arbeit an den Hochschulen. Zum Jenaer Studententag am 6. und 7. Oktober," *Der Demokrat* 2, no. 40 (6 Oct. 1921): 769–71.
17. On the founding and program of the DNJ, see Wilhelm Foellmer, *Der deutschnationale Jugendbund. Vorschläge und Anregungen* (Berlin, 1919).
18. *Deutsche Jugend — Deutsche Volkspartei*, Jugend-Schriften der Deutschen Volkspartei, no. 3 (Berlin, 1924), 10–15. See also Waldemar Reichardt, "Ein Rückblick auf die Geschichte der Jugendbewegung," *Schaffende Jugend* 3, no. 15 (1 Aug. 1926): 231–5.

under the honorary chairmanship of pastor Hans Luther.[19] Shortly thereafter the party also created a sister organization for university students known as the National Student Committee (*Reichsstudentenausschuss*) of the DVP from the time of its founding in 1922 until the beginning of 1925, when it was named the National Committee of University Groups of the German People's Party (*Reichsausschuss der Hochschulgruppen der Deutschen Volkspartei*).[20]

Throughout all of this, the leaders of the right-wing DNVP continued to eschew the creation of a special organization for youth and students on the assumption that they would be able to develop a foothold within the postwar German youth movement. In this respect, they could only have been deeply frustrated by developments within the DNJ. In the first year of its existence, the DNJ had over 90,000 members and seemed well on its way to establishing itself as a mass organization for the more nationalistic elements of Germany's bourgeois youth. At its Nuremberg congress in August 1921, however, the DNJ splintered into three separate factions: the Young German League (*Jungdeutscher Bund*), the Young National League (*Jungnationaler Bund*), and what still remained of the badly decimated DNJ. The first of these organizations, the Young German League, had been founded in August 1919 by Frank Glatzel, Wilhelm Stapel, and a small group of young conservative intellectuals with close ties to the German National Union of Commercial Employees (*Deutschnationaler Handlungsgehilfen-Verband* or DHV). Regarding itself as a direct descendant of the prewar German youth movement, the Young German League sought to rebaptize the DNJ in the spirit of the prewar German youth movement at the same time that it hoped to unite on a *völkisch*-national basis all those who had been left homeless by the demise of the Free German Youth.[21] Although its ideological objectives were essentially the same as those of the Young German League, the Young National League was much more rigid in its basic organizational concept and demanded the complete subordination of the individual to the welfare of the group. In this respect,

---

19. In this respect, see "Der Hindenburgbund, Jugendgruppen der Deutschen Volkspartei," in Siemering, ed., *Jugendverbände*, 258–61.
20. Kurt Goebel, "Reichsausschuss der Hochschulgruppen der Deutschen Volkspartei," in Michael Doeberl et al., eds., *Das akademische Deutschland*, 4 vols. (Berlin, 1931), 2: 603–4.
21. Frank Glatzel, "Der Jungdeutsche Bund," in Bundesamt des Jungdeutschen Bundes, ed., *Jungdeutsches Wollen. Vorträge gehalten auf der Gründungstagung des Jungdeutschen Bundes auf Burg Lauenstein vom 9.–12. August 1919* (Hamburg, 1920), 11–32. See also Glatzel, "Die Jungdeutschen," in Thurnwald, ed., *Die neue Jugend*, 191–7.

the founders of the Young National League hoped to translate the experiences of those who had served at the front during the Great War into a new way of life that would, in its own way, serve as a model for the rebirth of the entire German nation.[22]

The fragmentation and subsequent demise of the DNJ in the first years of the Weimar Republic left the leaders of the DNVP with no alternative but to found their own youth organization. At the beginning of 1922 the party's youth leaders met in Hannover to found the DNVP's National League of Youth Groups (*Reichsverband der Jugendgruppen der Deutschnationalen Volkspartei*), an organization that in the following fall was named Bismarck Youth of the German National People's Party (*Bismarckjugend der Deutschnationalen Volkspartei*). Unlike the Windthorst Leagues or the Young Democratic movement, the Bismarck Youth was completely subordinated to the party organization and had no autonomous existence of its own. Nevertheless, the Bismarck Youth proved relatively successful during the first year or so of its existence in recruiting new party members from the ranks of the younger generation. By the middle of 1923, however, these efforts began to stagnate, and it was not until the end of the decade that the Bismarck Youth was able to recover any sort of momentum.[23] Whereas the Center and the Windthorst Leagues had proven remarkably successful in using the infrastructure of the Catholic church as a way of recruiting new party members, the Bismarck Youth was singularly ineffective in its efforts to secure a similar foothold among influential Lutheran youth organizations such as the National League of Lutheran Young Men's Associations of Germany (*Reichsverband der evangelischen Jungmännerbünde Deutschlands*). Here the general antipathy within the younger generation toward the existing party system was even too strong for an opposition party like the DNVP to overcome.[24]

The stagnation and decline of party youth organizations was a

---

22. In this respect, see Heinz Dähnhardt, "Die jungnationale Bewegung," in Thurnwald, ed., *Die neue Jugend*, 46–56. For a more thorough examination of this phenomenon, see Felix Raabe, *Die bündische Jugend. Ein Beitrag zur Geschichte der Weimarer Republik* (Stuttgart, 1961).
23. For further details, see "Der Bismarckbund der Deutschnationalen Volkspartei," in Siemering, ed., *Jugendverbände*, 255–8. See also Konrad Meyer, *Organisationsfragen. Vortrag, gehalten am 23. September 1925 auf der deutschnationalen Schulungswoche*, Deutschnationale Flugschrift, no. 226 (Berlin, 1925), 12–14.
24. For an overview of these organizations, see Philipps, "Der Reichsverband der evangelischen Jungmännerbünde Deutschlands und verwandter Bestrebungen," in Siemering, ed., *Jugendverbände*, 125–33.

general feature of Weimar political culture in the second half of the 1920s. Of the various party youth organizations that had been established in the aftermath of the November Revolution, only those that were affiliated with the Center were able to sustain respectable membership levels throughout the second half of the 1920s. In the DDP, on the other hand, membership in the National League of German Democratic Youth Clubs declined from an estimated 20,000 at the beginning of the Weimar Republic to less than 2,300 by the end of 1926, and the National League of German Democratic Students was decimated by the social, economic, and political crises of the early 1920s.[25] Although much of the lethargy of political youth organizations in the second half of the 1920s can be explained as a consequence of the runaway inflation of the early 1920s and the disappearance of funds for the maintenance of political organizations of all sorts, a factor of even greater significance was the increasing appeal of paramilitary organizations like the Stahlhelm and the Young German Order (*Jungdeutscher Orden*).[26] Though essentially vehicles by which the so-called front generation sought to organize itself for political action, the paramilitary *Bünde* also sought to reach across the generational cleavage that divided those who had served at the front from those who had reached political maturity after the end of the war. It was in this spirit that the Young Stahlhelm (*Jungstahlhelm*) and the Young German Youth (*Jungdeutsche Jugend*) were established by their parent organizations in 1924 and 1925, respectively, for those between the ages of sixteen and twenty-two.[27] By the second half of the 1920s, organizations of this nature came to offer an increasingly attractive alternative to the political youth organizations that the various nonsocialist parties had created for their own partisan purposes.

Even though many of the *Bünde* remained self-consciously elitist and never sought to attract a mass or popular following, their presence on the Weimar political scene severely hampered Germany's traditional bourgeois parties in their efforts to attract the support of the younger generation. There was, as no less a pundit than Theodor Heuss pointed out, a fundamental incompatibility between *Bund* and

25. Werner Stephan, *Die Deutsche Demokratische Partei im Berichtsjahr 1926. Jahresbericht der Reichsparteileitung* (n.p., n.d. [1927]), 24–6.
26. On the emergence and early development of paramilitary organizations in the Weimar Republic, see James H. Diehl, *Paramilitary Politics in Weimar Germany* (Bloomington, Ind., 1977).
27. In this respect, see B. Bartels, "Jungstahlhelm," and v. Salzenberg, "Die jungdeutsche Jugend," in Siemering, ed., *Jugendverbände*, 38–41.

party that militated against the younger generation's integration into the institutional fabric of German political life.[28] With few exceptions, the *Bünde* that became politically active during the Weimar Republic professed little sympathy for the symbols and institutions of Germany's new republican order. To the contrary, the leaders of the *bündisch* movement held parliamentary democracy responsible for having exacerbated the social, confessional, and regional antagonisms that divided the German people and dismissed political parties as concrete manifestations of the national divisiveness that had accompanied the introduction of parliamentary government. By the same token, the *Bünde* lamented the triumph of economic egoism and longed for a return to some sort of precapitalist order inspired by the concept of the *Volksgemeinschaft* and based upon the "front experience" and the "socialism of the trenches."[29] By invoking the myth of the front experience, the leaders of the front generation hoped to reach across the generational divide that separated them from those who had reached political maturity since the end of the war and to mobilize them in the struggle against the hated "Weimar system."[30]

At the same time that the leaders of Germany's paramilitary right tried to mobilize the younger generation for a full-scale assault on the existing political system, the leaders of the German Lords' Club (*Deutscher Herrenklub*) hoped to enlist young academics and university students in the conservative cause by establishing a series of young conservative clubs throughout the country.[31] Founded in December 1924, the Lords' Club was an unabashedly elitist organization that sought to bring young conservative intellectuals together with representatives of Germany's traditional conservative elites in the hope of inspiring the former to assume a more active role in the

28. Theodor Heuss, "Parteien und Bünde," *Wille und Weg. Eine politische Halbmonatsschrift* 4, no. 2 (15 Apr. 1928): 40–6.
29. Raabe, *Jugend,* 115–30. See also Georg Schroeder, "Der Sozialismus der nationalen Jugend," *Der Arbeitgeber. Zeitschrift der Vereinigung der Deutschen Arbeitgeberverbände* 20, no. 8 (15 Apr. 1930): 218–20, and Josef Winschuh, "Bündische Bewegung und Sozialpolitik," *Soziale Praxis. Zentralblatt für Sozialpolitik und Wohlfahrtspflege* 39, no. 24 (12 June 1930): 561–5.
30. This, for example, was the clear purpose of the trilogy of war novels that the founder and leader of the Stahlhelm, Franz Seldte, published between 1929 and 1931. For example, see the preface to the first of these novels in Franz Seldte, *M.G.K.,* (Leipzig, 1929), 7–8. See also Otto Schmidt-Hannover, *Kriegsgeneration und Jugend im Freiheitskampf gegen den Marxismus. Rede, gehalten auf dem 9. Reichs-Partei-Tage der D.N.V.P. in Kassel am 23. November 1929,* Deutschnationale Flugschriften, no. 340 (Berlin, 1929).
31. In this respect, see *Der Jungkonservative Klub* (n.p., n.d. [1927]).

struggle for the overthrow of the Weimar Republic.[32] A key figure in these efforts was Edgar Jung, an ambitious and intellectually precocious young conservative who enjoyed close ties to the paramilitary right in Bavaria and other parts of the Reich.[33] A proud and self-conscious member of the front generation, Jung deplored the fact that the idealism and selflessness of those who had chosen to risk their lives at the front had no place in a society where egoism and self-aggrandizement had become the order of the day.[34] In an attempt to infuse young intellectuals with the spirit of the front experience and to convert them to his own brand of revolutionary conservatism, Jung founded a Young Academic Club (*Jungakademiker Klub*) in Munich in February 1926 as the first in a series of such clubs that he was to establish over the course of the next half decade. In outlining the new organization's ideological objectives, Jung implored the younger generation to become more directly involved in the struggle for Germany's political future and to take the lead in forging a new sense of national unity sufficiently powerful to override the social, political, and confessional cleavages that had become so deeply embedded in Germany's parliamentary system.[35] By the end of 1932, Jung would claim either the direct or indirect paternity of nearly a dozen such clubs throughout the country.[36]

The emergence of young conservative clubs in Berlin, Munich, and other parts of the country went hand in hand with the increased politicization of Germany's paramilitary right. Both of these developments represented a stinging indictment of the way in which the German party system had developed since the founding of the Weimar Republic and constituted a frontal assault on the role that

32. On the history and ideological orientation of the German Lords' Club, see Manfred Schoeps, "Der Deutsche Herrenklub. Ein Beitrag zur Geschichte des Jungkonservatimus in der Weimarer Republik" (Ph.D. diss., University of Erlangen-Nuremberg, 1974), as well as the more recent contribution by Yuji Ishida, *Jungkonservative in der Weimarer Republik. Der Ring-Kreis 1928–1933* (Frankfurt a.M., 1988).
33. Jung to Pechel, 4 and 8 May 1926, in the unpublished Nachlass of Fritz Klein (hereafter cited as Nachlass Klein), in the possession of his son, Fritz Klein, Jr.
34. In this respect, see Edgar Jung, "Die Tragik der Kriegsgeneration," *Süddeutsche Monatshefte* 27, no. 5 (May 1930): 511–34. On Jung's political career, see Larry Eugene Jones, "Edgar Jung: The Conservative Revolution in Theory and Practice," *Central European History* 21 (1988): 142–74.
35. Edgar Jung, *Die geistige Krise des jungen Deutschland. Rede vor der Studentenschaft der Universität München* (Berlin, n.d. [1926]). See also Jung, "Vom werdenden Deutschland," *Schweizersche Monatshefte* 7, no. 1 (Apr. 1927): 11–22, and no. 2 (May 1927): 76–88.
36. Jung to Pechel, 29 Oct. 1932, Nachlass Klein. See also the enclosure to Pechel's letter to Humann, 2 Nov. 1932, ibid.

conservative economic interests had played in the economic and political stabilization of the Weimar Republic after 1924.[37] At no point were the effects of these developments more apparent than in the May 1928 Reichstag elections, when all of Germany's established bourgeois parties sustained moderate to heavy losses. The DDP and the DVP, for example, lost 21.7 and 12.1 percent, respectively, of their popular vote in the December 1924 Reichstag elections, and the Center lost 9.9 percent of what it had polled four years earlier. The heaviest losses, however, were sustained by the right-wing DNVP, which lost nearly 2 million votes – or 31 percent of what it had received in the last national elections four years earlier. To be sure, a variety of factors, not the least of which was the success of middle-class splinter parties, accounted for the poor electoral performance of the various nonsocialist parties. To many political observers, however, the most important lesson of the election was the fact that more than 10 million eligible voters had stayed away from the polls. Although it is statistically impossible to determine just how many of these voters had become eligible only since the last national election, contemporary political analysts were quick to see a clear correlation between the apathy of the younger generation and the decline of the more established bourgeois parties.[38]

The outcome of the 1928 Reichstag elections bore dramatic testimony to the political alienation of Germany's younger generation and marked the beginning of a determined effort on the part of Germany's nonsocialist parties to reintegrate it into the organizational fabric of German political life. In November 1928 Stresemann launched a reform of the DVP's national organization that sought, among other things, to enhance its recruitment of those who belonged to the younger generation.[39] At the same time, the DDP tried to rejuvenate their party organization by electing Young Democratic leader Ernst Lemmer to the co-chairmanship of the DDP managing

37. In this respect, see Larry Eugene Jones, "In the Shadow of Stabilization: German Liberalism and the Legitimacy Crisis of the Weimar Party System, 1924–30," in Gerald D. Feldman, ed., *Die Nachwirkungen der Inflation auf die deutsche Geschichte* (Munich, 1986), 21–41.
38. For example, see Wilhelm Ziegler, "Die übersprungene Generation," *Deutsche Stimmen* 40, no. 12 (20 June 1928): 357–62, and Werner Stephan, "Die 'Führerkrise' oder der Generationswechsel in der Politik," *Wille und Weg* 4, no. 16 (15 Nov. 1928): 378–81, as well as Richard Wolff, *Ideenkrisis – Parteienwirrwarr. Eine historisch-politische Betrachtung* (Berlin, 1931), 66–78, and Arthur Dix, *Die deutschen Reichstagswahlen 1871–1930 und die Wandlungen der Volksgliederung* (Tübingen, 1930), 32–7.
39. In this respect, see Stresemann, "An die Jugend," *Nationalliberale Correspondenz*, 29 Dec. 1928, no. 235. For further details, see Jones, *German Liberalism*, 325–6.

committee and by creating fifteen positions on the party's executive committee for representatives of the Young Democratic movement.[40] Within the DNVP, on the other hand, generational cleavages played a major role in the bitter internal crises that ripped through the party from 1928 to 1930. In the summer of 1928 Walther Lambach, a member of the DNVP Reichstag delegation and a trade union secretary with close ties to the young conservative movement, ignited a major controversy when he had the temerity to suggest that the DNVP might abandon its commitment to the restoration of the monarchy in order to make itself more attractive to the younger generation.[41] In the struggle for control of the party that ensued, young conservatives' hopes that the DNVP might some day recapture the support of those who had reached political maturity since the end of the Great War suffered a devastating setback when Alfred Hugenberg, the epitome of social and political reaction, was elected to the party's national chairmanship in October 1928.[42]

In the meantime, a marked revival of political interest on the part of Germany's liberal youth could be seen in the emergence of young liberal clubs in one part of the country after another. The most important of these were the February Club, which young liberals in Cologne with close ties to the local DVP organization established in February 1928, and the "Front 1929," which Stresemann's personal friend and biographer, Rochus von Rheinbaben, founded in Berlin in March 1929.[43] At Stresemann's urging, Rheinbaben established contact not only with the Young German Order and the various young liberal clubs that had surfaced throughout the country since the beginning of the preceding year but also with the young conservatives in the DNVP. Rheinbaben's ultimate objective – and in this respect, he had the full support of the DVP party chairman – was to bring

40. Minutes of the DDP executive committee, 23 Mar. 1929, in Lothar Albertin, ed., *Linksliberalismus in der Weimarer Republik. Die Führungsgremien der Deutschen Demokratischen Partei und der Deutschen Staatspartei 1918–1933* (Düsseldorf, 1980), 486–7.
41. Walther Lambach, "Monarchismus," *Politische Wochenschrift* 4, no. 24 (14 June 1928): 495–8.
42. For examples of the young conservative response to Hugenberg's election, see Jungnationaler Ring, ed., *Der Niedergang der nationalen Opposition. Ein Warnruf aus den Reihen der Jugend* (n.p., n.d. [1929]), and Hermann Ullmann, *Die Rechte stirbt – es lebe die Rechte* (Berlin, 1929), esp. 20–37.
43. In this respect, see Kurt Goepel, "Entwicklung und Stand der politischen Reformbestrebungen der jungen Generation," *Hochschulblätter der Deutschen Volkspartei*, no. 30 (May 1929): 1–4, in the unpublished records of the DVP, Bundesarchiv Koblenz, Bestand R 45 II (hereafter cited as BA Koblenz: R 45 II), 6/11–14. For further details, see Jones, *Liberalism*, 326–9.

about the creation of a united middle party that would provide the younger generation with the political home it so desperately needed.[44] Rheinbaben's most enthusiastic support came from Mahraun and the leaders of the Young German Order. Though deeply critical of parliamentary democracy for the way in which it had surrendered the welfare of the nation as a whole to special economic interests, the Young German Order had disentangled itself from the antirepublican right in the second half of the 1920s and was now committed to the peaceful evolution of the Weimar Republic to a higher and more perfect form of democracy called the *Volksstaat*. An essential prerequisite for accomplishing this goal was the consolidation of the German middle into a solid phalanx capable of sustaining itself against the twin dangers of big business and organized labor.[45] In this respect, Rheinbaben and Mahraun found themselves in total agreement with the DVP's party chairman.

In the spring of 1929 Mahraun and his associates initiated a "People's National Action" aimed at overcoming the fragmentation of the German middle.[46] Mahraun's agitation for the consolidation of the German *Staatsbürgertum* into a "people's national front" free from the domination of special economic interests injected a distinctly populist note into the efforts to mobilize the younger generation in support of the existing system of government.[47] The People's National Action drew to a climax with three mass demonstrations in Dortmund, Danzig, and Dresden in the summer and early fall of 1929 and clearly raised the specter of a new political party.[48]

44. On Rheinbaben's negotiations in the spring of 1929, see his letter to Stresemann, 23 Mar. 1929, in the unpublished Nachlass of Gustav Stresemann, Politisches Archiv des Auswärtigen Amts, Bonn (hereafter cited as PA Bonn, Nachlass Stresemann), 3176/78/169430–5. For Stresemann's own hopes for "Front 1929," see the memorandum of his remarks during a conversation with Rheinbaben and Stein, 26 Apr. 1929, ibid., 3164/105/174987–8.
45. For the most comprehensive statement of the Young German ideology, see Artur Mahraun, *Parole 1929* (Berlin, 1929), 3–34. For further details, see Diehl, *Paramilitary Politics*, 222–7, as well as the monographs by Klaus Hornung, *Der jungdeutsche Orden* (Düsseldorf, 1958), 51–86, and Alexander Kessler, *Der jungdeutsche Orden in den Jahren der Entscheidung I (1928–1930)* (Munich, 1975), 7–29.
46. Protocol of the 19th High Chapter of the Young German Order, 26–27 Jan. 1929, in the unpublished records of the Young German Order, Bundesarchiv Koblenz, Bestand R 161 (hereafter cited as BA: R 161), 12/45–53. See also Mahraun, "Volksnationale Aktion," *Der Meister. Jungdeutsche Monatsschrift für Führer und denkende Brüder* 4, no. 6 (March 1929): 243–54.
47. For a fuller treatment of the populist impulse in right-wing Weimar politics, see Peter Fritzsche, *Rehearsals for Fascism: Populism and Political Mobilization in Weimar Germany* (New York and Oxford, 1990).
48. Kessler, *Der jungdeutsche Orden*, 46–61.

Throughout all of this, the Young German leadership was hoped to attract the support of those elements within the DNVP that were on the verge of rebelling against Hugenberg's leadership of the party. Not only did the leaders of the anti-Hugenberg fronde belong to the so-called front generation, but more important there was, in Mahraun's own eyes at least, a greater ideological affinity between the ideas of his followers and those of the dissident Nationalists than with those of other political groups.[49]

As Mahraun and his associates intensified their campaign for a reform and rejuvenation of the German party system, the leaders of the established bourgeois parties became increasingly apprehensive that this might lead to the founding of a new political party. In an attempt to forestall such a development, a group of young DVP activists under the leadership of Frank Glatzel and Josef Hardt founded the Reich Association of Young Populists (*Reichsgemeinschaft junger Volksparteiler* or RjV) at a special demonstration in Weimar in May 1929. Designed specifically for party members between the ages of twenty-five and forty, the RjV sought, as Glatzel explained in his keynote address at its founding ceremonies in Weimar, to infuse the DVP with the spirit of the younger generation and to free it from the domination of outside economic interests so that it might serve as the crystallization point around which a progressive and socially heterogeneous middle party could form.[50] In this respect, Glatzel and his associates hoped not only to dissuade the Young Germans from founding a new party of their own but also to establish closer political ties with the young conservative wing of the DNVP.[51] Neither of these hopes, however, ever materialized. With the introduction of Hugenberg's campaign against the Young Plan in the summer of 1929 and Stresemann's untimely death the following October, Mahraun and his associates felt that they could ill afford to wait any longer and decided to go ahead with the founding of a new middle party at a confidential meeting of the High Chapter of the Young German

---

49. For an indication of Mahraun's interest in the young conservatives, see Mahraun, "Gedanken über die Politik des Jungdeutschen Ordens," *Der Meister* 4, no. 4 (January 1929): 145–66, as well as the list of honorary guests invited to the Young German Order's Dortmund demonstration in July 1929, appended to Mahraun to Stresemann, 4 June 1929, PA Bonn, Nachlass Stresemann, 3177/81/170107–10.
50. On the founding of the RjV, see Reichsgemeinschaft junger Volksparteiler, *Aufmarsch und Ziel* (Lobau, n.d. [1929]). For Glatzel's goals, see his letter to Winschuh, 25 Mar. 1929, BA: R 45 II/69/417–19.
51. In this respect, see Glatzel to the members of the DVP executive committee, 11 Dec. 1929, in the unpublished Nachlass of Karl Jarres, Bundesarchiv Koblenz, vol. 40.

Order on 12–13 October.[52] For his own part, Mahraun continued to hope that the young conservative faction from the DNVP could be persuaded to join him in his crusade for the creation of a comprehensive and socially progressive middle party committed to a reform and rejuvenation of the existing system of government. But whatever excitement he may have felt when twelve members of the DNVP Reichstag delegation seceded from the party in December 1929 turned to immediate disappointment when the young conservatives decided to found their own organization, known as the People's Conservative Association (*Volkskonservative Vereinigung* or VKV).[53] In defining their political objectives, G. R. Treviranus and the founders of the VKV employed the language of generational conflict and appealed for the support of precisely those groups that Mahraun and his associates had identified as their primary constituency.[54]

Although the leaders of the Young German Order were clearly disappointed by the lack of interest the DNVP secessionists had taken in their plans for a reform and rejuvenation of the German party system,[55] they did not let this deter them from their plans to found a new party. In early April 1930 Mahraun and his associates officially reconstituted the People's National Action as the People's National Reich Association (*Volksnationale Reichsvereinigung* or VNR).[56] Despite disclaimers to the contrary, the founding of the VNR raised the specter of still another political party and marked the beginning of an intensified struggle on the part of Germany's nonsocialist parties for the loyalties of the younger generation. The situation was particularly critical within the DVP, where Ernst Scholz, Stresemann's successor as the party's national chairman, had tried to stave off a revolt by the leaders of his party's youth wing by issuing an appeal at the Mannheim party congress in March 1930 for the

52. Protocol of the 23rd High Chapter of the Young German Order, 12–13 Oct. 1929, BA: R 161/12/77–81.
53. For further details, see Erasmus Jonas, *Die Volkskonservativen 1928–1933. Entwicklung, Struktur, Standort und staatspolitische Zielsetzung* (Düsseldorf, 1965), 57–60.
54. In this respect, see Hans-Erdmann v. Lindeiner-Wildau, *Erneuerung des politisches Lebens. Reichstagsrede gehalten am 13. Dezember 1929*, Schriften der Deutschnationalen Arbeitsgemeinschaft, no. 1 (Berlin-Charlottenburg, 1929), and G. R. Treviranus, *Auf neuen Wegen*, Volkskonservative Flugschriften, no. 2 (Berlin, 1930).
55. Bornemann, "Persönlicher Brief an alle Grossmeister," n.d., reproduced in an internal communique from the Jungdeutscher Orden, Grossballei Westdeutschland, 31 Jan. 1930, BA: R 161/59.
56. For the VNR's ideological orientation, see Artur Mahraun, *Der Aufbruch. Sinn und Zweck der Volksnationalen Reichsvereinigung* (Berlin, 1929), 53–77, as well as Mahraun's speech in Volksnationale Reichsvereinigung, *Der erste Reichsvertretertag am 5. und 6. April 1930* (Berlin, 1930), 14–59.

consolidation of the "state-supporting bourgeoisie."[57] In the last week of April, the leaders of the DVP tried to shore up their party's precarious position vis-à-vis the younger generation by holding a special leadership conference for the members of the newly renamed Hindenburg League – Youth Group of the German People's Party (*Hindenburgbund – Jugendgruppen der Deutschen Volkspartei*).[58] None of this, however, proved to much avail, for in early May the VNR announced that it would take part in the Saxon state elections that had been scheduled for the third week in June.[59] This announcement confirmed the worst fears of the established party leaders and prompted bitter charges by the leaders of the DVP's young liberal movement that Scholz and the party's national leadership were indifferent to the aspirations of the younger generation.[60] Whether or not under these circumstances the DVP – or, for that matter, any of Germany's nonsocialist parties – could retain the support of their younger followers remained to be seen.

Efforts to mobilize the younger generation drew to a dramatic climax following the dissolution of the Reichstag on 18 July 1930. For their own part, the leaders of the younger generation could not have been more profoundly disappointed by the response of the existing political parties to their demands for a realignment and rejuvenation of the German party system. At the heart of their disillusionment lay the continued fragmentation of the German bourgeoisie and the failure of the established nonsocialist parties to set aside their own political differences for the sake of a common national agenda. To be sure, the leaders of the younger generation should have been able to derive a measure of consolation from the fact that both the Conservative People's Party (*Konservative Volkspartei* or KVP), which had been founded under young conservative auspices on 25 July 1930, and the German State Party (*Deutsche Staatspartei* or DStP), whose founding was announced three days later by the leaders of the DDP and VNR, took great pains to portray themselves as parties of

57. Speech by Scholz in Deutsche Volkspartei, Reichsgeschäftsstelle, ed., *8. Reichsparteitag der Deutschen Volkspartei in Mannheim vom 21. bis 23. März 1930* (Berlin, 1930), 3–6.
58. For further details, see Hindenburgbund – Jugendgruppen der Deutschen Volkspartei, *Staatsbürgerliche Jugend. Unsere Reichsschulungswoche in Braunlage/Harz vom 22. bis 27. April 1930* (Berlin, n.d. [1930]).
59. On the VNR's decision to enter the Saxon elections, see Mahraun to the VNR's local chapters, 21 May 1930, in the records of the NSDAP Hauptarchiv, Bundesarchiv Koblenz, vol. 875.
60. Croon, Rodens, and Sieling to Scholz, 22 May 1930, in the unpublished records of the Cologne February Club, Bundesarchiv Koblenz, Kleine Erwerbung 484, vol. 2.

the younger generation. This, however, did little to dispel the fact that the younger generation was more fragmented than ever and the cleavage between *Bund* and party greater than ever.

The fate of the DStP is particularly illustrative. The party was founded on 28 July 1930 as part of a concerted attempt by the DDP leadership to secure a breakthrough into the ranks of the younger generation and to overcome that cleavage between *Bund* and party that had become such a prominent feature of Weimar's political culture. Not only were the Democrats hopeful that the Young German Order and its allies in the VNR would provide the German bourgeoisie with the spiritual cement it so sorely needed,[61] but the "Manifesto of the German State Party" that the founders of the new party issued on 22 August[62] was essentially a reformulation of traditional Democratic objectives in the vocabulary of the German youth movement. Although the founders of the DStP received immediate declarations of support from the leaders of the "Front 1919," the West German February Club, and other young liberal organizations,[63] their hope that the DStP would establish itself as the party of the younger generation was undercut by two ominous developments. First, the left wing of the Young Democratic movement regarded the DDP's alliance with the paramilitary Young German Order as a betrayal of the pacifist principles for which it had always stood and proceeded to reconstitute itself as the Union of Independent Democrats (*Vereinigung Unabhängiger Demokraten*).[64] Second, Glatzel and the RjV refused to support the new party and summarily expelled those members of the RjV who either belonged to the Young German Order or had joined the DStP.[65] The net effect of all this was to tarnish seriously the DStP's image as a party of the

61. Remarks by Bäumer before the DDP executive committee, 25 July 1930, in Albertin, ed., *Linksliberalismus,* 561.
62. Artur Mahraun, *Die Deutsche Staatspartei. Eine Selbsthilfeorganisation deutschen Staatsbürgertums* (Berlin, 1930), 41–8.
63. Press release from the founders of the DStP, 28 July 1930, in the unpublished Nachlass of Erich Koch-Weser, Bundesarchiv Koblenz (hereafter cited as BA: NL Koch-Weser), 105/47. See also Theodor Eschenburg, "Die Deutsche Staatspartei," *Berliner Börsen-Courier,* 29 July 1930, no. 347, and Josef Winschuh, "Junge Generation vor die Front!," *Kasseler Tageblatt,* 3 Aug. 1930, no. 212.
64. In this respect, see Erich Lüth, "Vortrupp der neuen Linken," *Das Tagebuch* 11, no. 32 (16 Aug. 1930): 1295–7, and Otto Stündt, "Die alte Fahne treu! Von Gründung, Zweck und Ziel der Vereinigung unabhängiger Demokraten," *Das Echo der jungen Demokratie* 12, nos. 8–9 (August–September 1930): 111–17.
65. In this respect, see Glatzel and Kruspi to Scholz, 12 Aug. 1930, BA: R 45 II/5/41–9, as well as the reports in the *Kölnische Zeitung,* 4 Aug. 1930, no. 421, and the *Berliner Börsen-Courier,* 5 Aug. 1930, no. 359.

younger generation and to compromise its ability to reach out across the generational divide to those who had become so profoundly alienated from the existing party system.

All told, the need to reach across generational lines to those who had just begun to exercise their political rights played a far more important role in the strategy for the 1930 elections than in any previous election. The KVP, for example, was every bit as determined as the DStP to achieve a breakthrough into the ranks of the younger generation and set the task of freeing German youth from the hypnotic spell of National Socialism as one of its major campaign goals.[66] By the same token, the leaders of the DVP were desperate to contain the damage that the founding of the DStP and the KVP had done to their party's own youth organizations and made a more concerted bid for the support of the younger generation than they had done in any previous campaign.[67] But, as the outcome of the elections so poignantly revealed, the principal beneficiary of the generational cleavages that had become so deeply embedded in the fabric of Weimar electoral politics was neither the more traditional bourgeois parties nor any of the myriad middle-class splinter parties that had appeared on the German political landscape since the middle of the 1920s but the National Social German Workers' Party (*Nationalsozialistische Deutsche Arbeiterpartei* or NSDAP) under the leadership of Adolf Hitler.[68] At the very least, it was clear that the efforts to build a bridge between the younger generation and the existing party system had ended in failure. The DStP, for example, went down to a devastating defeat in which it lost approximately a fifth of the votes the DDP had received just two years earlier. The DVP, in the meantime, had lost more than a third of its 1928 vote. Nor had it been possible, as the KVP's fate so stunningly demonstrated, to rally the younger generation to the support of the more moderate elements on the German right. For when the votes were

---

66. For example, see Ludwig Grauert, *Worum geht es am 14. September 1930?* (n.p., n.d. [1930]), 5–7.
67. Among other things, the DVP party leadership offered Glatzel a secure place on the party's national slate as a way of assuring themselves of the RjV's loyalty in the campaign. See Kruspi to the RjV local chapters, 8 Aug. 1930, BA: R 45 II/6/221–3.
68. Although statistical evidence on the political affiliations of those who were voting for the first time is far from complete, Jürgen Falter has suggested that "for the more urbanised counties the NSDAP share of the vote in both [the September 1930 and July 1932 Reichstag] elections grew faster where the percentage of young voters was high and that it tended to grow more slowly where the (relative) number of young voters was small." See Jürgen Falter, "The National-Socialist Mobilization of New Voters: 1928–1933," in Thomas Childers, ed., *The Formation of the Nazi Constituency, 1919–1933* (London, 1986), 226.

finally tallied, the KVP had polled fewer than 300,000 votes and managed to elect only four deputies to the Reichstag.[69]

The outcome of the 1930 Reichstag elections dealt a devastating psychological blow to those who had pinned their hopes on overcoming the generational cleavages that had become so deeply embedded in Weimar's political culture. Following its defeat at the polls, the tenuous alliance upon which the DStP had been founded began to unravel, and in the first week of October 1930 the Young Germans announced their secession from the DStP.[70] The Young Germans had been severely chastened by the way in which their venture into the realm of German party politics had ended, and they moved quickly to put their ill-fated alliance with the DStP behind them in the hope of repairing the damage their role in the founding of that party had done to their credibility as a spokesman for the front generation.[71] In the meantime, the Young Democratic movement had become irreparably divided between those who supported the DStP and those who joined the Association of Independent Democrats to found the Radical Democratic Party (*Radikaldemokratische Partei*) in November 1930.[72] Nor was the situation any more promising within the DVP. For although the party's younger leaders could rejoice at the election of Eduard Dingeldey to the DVP party chairmanship in November 1930,[73] the party's effectiveness in recruiting new members from the ranks of the younger generation was hampered by an ongoing conflict between the Hindenburg League and the Reich Association of Young Populists over their respective func-

69. For the best analyses of the electoral transformations between 1928 and 1930, see Jerzy Holzer, *Parteien und Massen. Die politische Krise in Deutschland 1928–1930* (Wiesbaden, 1975), 64–103, and Thomas Childers, *The Nazi Voter: The Social Foundations of Fascism in Germany, 1919–1933* (Chapel Hill, N.C., 1983), 119–91. Unfortunately, neither of these two studies nor any other study of Weimar electoral behavior has successfully isolated the extent to which the generational variable played a role in the defeat of the nonsocialist parties and the Nazi breakthrough.
70. For further details, see Jones, *German Liberalism*, 388–91.
71. On the effects of the Order's role in the founding of the DStP on its national organization, see Alexander Kessler, *Der Jungdeutsche Orden in den Jahren der Entscheidung (II) 1931–1933* (Munich, 1976), 7–29.
72. In this respect, see Otto Stündt, "Die neue Linke greift an! Zum Gründungsparteitag der Radikaldemokratischen Partei in Kassel," *Das Echo der jungen Demokratie* 12, nos. 11–12 (Nov.–Dec. 1930): 161–4. See also Radikaldemokratische Partei, Reichsgeschäftsstelle, ed., *Radikale Demokratie!* (Berlin, n.d. [ca. 1930–31]).
73. For example, see Glatzel to Dingeldey, 12 Dec. 1930, in the unpublished Nachlass of Eduard Dingeldey, Bundesarchiv Koblenz (hereafter cited as BA: Nachlass Dingeldey), 53/46–7. Dingeldey had a long history of supporting the younger generation in its efforts to gain a more influential voice in party affairs. For example, see Dingeldey, "Jugend und Partei," *Frankfurter Nachrichten*, 31 Mar. 1929, no. 90.

tions within the party.[74] By the same token, whatever hopes the KVP might have had of recovering from its demoralizing defeat at the polls in September 1930 were shattered by a bitter dispute in the winter and spring of 1931 between the party's parliamentary leaders and the conservative revolutionaries around Edgar Jung. This, in turn, destroyed what little credibility the KVP still possessed in the eyes of Germany's young conservative intelligentsia and hastened its departure from the German political stage.[75]

By the summer of 1932 virtually all of Germany's political youth organizations, with the exception of the Windthorst Leagues and the rapidly growing Hitler Youth (*Hitler-Jugend*), were on the verge of complete collapse. The National League of State Party Youth (*Reichsbund staatsparteilicher Jugend*), which the leaders of the DStP had founded after the Young German secession in October 1930, met with a cold response from former Young Democrats and never succeeded in legitimizing itself as a viable contender for the loyalties of the younger generation.[76] Within the DVP, on the other hand, the conflict between the Hindenburg League and the Reich Association of Young Populists continued to rage as the two organizations feuded over whether the DVP should continue or terminate its support of the Brüning government.[77] As the feud continued, the leaders of the two organizations – Ernst Hintzmann of the Hindenburg League and Glatzel from the RjV – became so disillusioned with their party's lack of direction that they resigned in protest and went their own separate ways, Hintzmann to the right-wing DNVP and Glatzel into premature political retirement.[78] Within the DNVP, Hintzmann was quickly enlisted to help the Nationalist party leadership develop the German Youth League (*Deutscher Jugendbund*) in an attempt to attract those members of the younger generation who had been left home-

---

74. In this respect, see Hindenburgbund, Führer-Brief no. 4, 26 Jan. 1931, BA: Nachlass Dingeldey, 54/9, as well as the protocol of the meeting of the national leadership of the Hindenburg League, Berlin, 19 Apr. 1931, in the unpublished Nachlass of Hermann Klingspor, Hauptstaatsarchiv Düsseldorf (hereafter cited as HStA Düsseldorf, Nachlass Klingspor), 5/232–3.
75. In this respect, see Jung to Treviranus, 7 Oct. 1930, in the unpublished Nachlass of Edgar Jung in the possession of Karl-Martin Grass, vol. IXa, and Jung to Treviranus, 5 Jan. 1931, in the unpublished Nachlass of Rudolf Pechel, Bundesarchiv Koblenz, vol. 102. For further details, see Jones, "Jung," 152–4, and Jonas, *Volkskonservativen,* 100–4.
76. On its difficulties, see Kluthe to Jaeger, 4 Dec. 1930, in the unpublished Nachlass of Hans Albert Kluthe, Bundesarchiv Koblenz, 11/14.
77. In this respect, see Klingspor to Dingeldey, 20 Nov. 1931, HStA Düsseldorf, Nachlass Klingspor, 6-I/173–4.
78. For further details, see Hintzmann to Dingeldey, 21 Apr. 1932, BA: Nachlass Dingeldey, 122/39–43, and Glatzel to Dingeldey, 6 July 1932, ibid., 53/199–201.

less by the demise of the other nonsocialist parties.[79] These efforts, however, were doomed to failure by the legacy of neoconservative animosity toward Hugenberg and by the way in which he had been stigmatized by Jung and other young conservatives as the architect of social and political reaction. The net effect of these developments was to leave the younger generation, insofar as it was politically active, with little alternative but to turn to the NSDAP and the various student and youth organizations it had created as part of its own crusade for popular support.[80]

The failure of the more established bourgeois parties to attract and retain the support of the younger generation played a major role in their electoral decline and helped set the stage for the meteoric rise of National Socialism at the end of the 1920s and the beginning of the 1930s. Of the various nonsocialist parties that existed in Germany at the beginning of the Weimar Republic, only the Center experienced any notable success in retaining the support of its younger voters, although even here the Windthorst Leagues underwent a major ideological reorientation in the last years of the republic's existence and beat a cautious retreat from the aggressive stand they had taken in favor of the republican form of government in the early 1920s. The political alienation of the younger generation resulted from a variety of factors, not the least of which were the profound changes that had taken place in its material situation as a result of the general course of German economic development during the Weimar Republic.[81] Still, economic factors would not have had such a profound effect upon the political loyalties of the younger generation were it not also for the fact that all of Germany's more established political parties had become so closely identified with special economic interests that they

79. On the German Youth League, see Deutscher Jugendbund Westfalen-Süd, circular no. 1, 23 Mar. 1932, HStA Düsseldorf, Nachlass Klingspor, 6-I/48, as well as Klingspor, "Sinn und Ziel nationalpolitischer Jugendarbeit," n.d. [Apr. 1932], ibid., 6-I/18–20.
80. For further details, see Hans Waldemar Koch, *The Hitler Youth: Origins and Development, 1922–1945* (New York, 1975), 57–83, and Peter Stachura, *Nazi Youth in the Weimar Republic* (Santa Barbara, Calif., and Oxford, 1975), 21–42, as well as Michael Steinberg, *Sabers and Brown Shirts: The German Students' Path to National Socialism, 1918–1935* (Chicago, 1973), 72–130, and Geoffrey Giles, *Students and National Socialism in Germany* (Cambridge, 1985), 44–100.
81. Götz von Olenhusen, "Krise und Aufstieg," 61–5. On the high rate of unemployment among the younger generation during the Great Depression, see Peter D. Stachura, "The Social and Welfare Implications of Youth Unemployment in Weimar Germany, 1929–1933," in Peter D. Stachura, ed., *Unemployment and the Great Depression in Weimar Germany* (New York, 1986), 121–47.

were no longer acceptable to the vast majority of those who had either served at the front or had reached political maturity since the end of the Great War. When the younger generation began to lend its voice to the cacaphony of protest against the way in which the existing political parties had betrayed the welfare of the nation to special economic interests, it was challenging the legitimacy of a system whose increasing fragmentation along lines of economic self-interest had severely undermined its ability to define and articulate Germany's national interest. In this respect, the younger generation was seeking to reassert the primacy of the national and political moment in German political life over the purely economic.

This impulse became increasingly powerful during the last years of the Weimar Republic and found an echo in the "new nationalism" of patriotic associations like the Stahlhelm and the Young German Order. The invocation of the front experience, with its juxtaposition of the selfless heroism and brotherhood of the trenches to the discord and flabbiness of the home front, represented part of a concerted attempt by the self-appointed leaders of the front generation to redefine the polis on essentially male terms and to exclude those whom they held responsible for the collapse of 1918 from any sort of meaningful role in determining Germany's political future. The susceptibility of the younger generation to this sort of rhetoric was greatly enhanced not only by the strong sense of nationalism to which defeat and the humiliation of Versailles had given rise but, more important, by its profound disaffection from the older generation of political leaders who had led the ship of state into the troubled waters of interest politics. In their efforts to free German public life from the tyranny of economic self-interest, however, the leaders of the younger generation unwittingly fertilized the soil in which the seeds of Nazism could take root and flourish. For as the fate of the German State Party and the People's Conservative movement so clearly revealed, the crusade to rebaptize the German party system in the spirit of the front generation did little to reconcile the generational cleavages that had become such a prominent feature of Weimar political culture. On the contrary, the net effect of this crusade was only to accelerate the drift of Germany's younger voters into the ranks of those who sought the nation's salvation not in the reform but in the destruction of the existing political system.

15

The Social Bases of Political Cleavages in the Weimar Republic, 1919–1933

JÜRGEN W. FALTER

The research project that constitutes the basis of this essay proceeds from the assumption that because of distinct handicaps in Germany's political development there was "neither a homogeneous nor a dominant political culture" in the Weimar Republic[1] but rather – and this is particularly true for the period after 1928 – an extraordinarily "fateful fragmentation [of the political system] into a multiplicity of political subcultures."[2] The inability of these subcultures either to interact with each other or to establish social and political hegemony, in turn, contributed in no small measure to the rise of National Socialism. This essay uses the methodologies of historical electoral research to investigate the electoral strength of the most important of these political subcultures and to determine the changes that took place in their composition between 1919 and 1933.

It is first necessary to clarify certain assumptions regarding use of the term "political subculture." In terms of the project as a whole, this concept has been used rather loosely. Together with the conceptually related, though not necessarily coterminous, notions of "political milieu" and "political camp," the concept of "political subculture" is replete with variations and nuances. For the purposes of this investigation, the term refers to "groupings beneath the national level that on the basis of different factors (such as social structure, material interests, socialization, confessional identity, regional origin, etc.) display consistent orientations, articulate positions, and pursue courses of action with respect to central political questions

---

1. Detlef Lehnert and Klaus Megerle, "Identitäts- und Konsensprobleme einer fragmentierten Gesellschaft. Zur Politischen Kultur der Weimarer Republik," in D. Berg-Schlosser and J. Schissler, eds., *Politische Kultur in Deutschland. Bilanz und Perspektiven der Forschung* (Opladen, 1987), 83.
2. Idem, in idem, eds., *Politische Identität und nationale Gedenktage. Zur politischen Kultur der Weimarer Republik* (Opladen, 1989), 15.

and in common social life and can thus be identified in the political sphere as a collective."[3]

This use of the term "political subculture" makes it possible to combine it with several closely related, though by no means theoretically equivalent, explanatory concepts of historical electoral research. The term "political camp," for example, can be used in conjunction with Walter Dean Burnham's theory of political confessionalism to explain the varying degrees of susceptibility that adherents of the various Weimar parties displayed toward National Socialism and to distinguish between (1) a Marxist camp consisting of the Social Democrats, the Independent Socialists, and the Communists, (2) a Catholic camp consisting of the Bavarian People's Party (BVP) and the Center, (3) the camp of nonvoters, and (4) the ideologically fragmented bourgeois-Protestant camp with its plethora of individual political parties.[4] Whereas the Marxist and Catholic camps are both characterized by comprehensive world views that shape the behavior of their adherents and by the effective social integration of their members into a wide range of voluntary associations in the prepolitical sphere, this cannot be said, according to Burnham, of the liberal, conservative, and interest-oriented bourgeois-Protestant parties. Like all attempts at historical typology, however, this approach forces the living and ideologically variegated kaleidoscope of Weimar party politics into a procrustean bed of fixed, oversimplified categories that can be justified only because they supposedly lead to a better understanding of the Nazis' rise to power.

These camps – with the exception of that of the nonvoters, which was a conglomerate of the most diverse social groups – were organized along sociopolitical cleavages of profound secular importance. Borrowing from Seymour Martin Lipset and Stein Rokkan, Franz Urban Pappi explains this as "the persistent potentials for conflict between the social-structural groupings of a society which, on account of its politicization, find expression in the electoral behavior of these groupings."[5] In this respect, it is possible to distinguish between two fundamental types of conflict that arose in connection

3. Ibid., 25.
4. See Walter Dean Burnham, "Political Immunization and Political Confessionalism: The United States and Weimar Germany," *Journal of Interdisciplinary History* 3 (1972): 1–30.
5. Franz Urban Pappi, "Die konfessionell-religiöse Konfliktlinie in der deutschen Wählerschaft: Entstehung, Stabilität und Wandel," in Dieter Oberndörfer, Hans Rattinger, and Karl Schmitt, eds., *Wirtschaftlicher Wandel, religiöser Wandel und Wertwandel. Folgen für das politische Verhalten in der Bundesrepublik Deutschland* (Berlin, 1985), 264.

with the national and industrial revolutions. The first of these expresses itself in conflicts over ethnic, territorial, and cultural questions; the second in conflicts of a social-economic and structural nature. Among the former are conflicts between established churches and the government or between dominant and subordinate cultures, whereas the latter types of conflict include those between the agricultural and industrial economic sectors or between workers and employers.[6]

During the Second Empire, when the sociopolitically defined conflicts took place primarily at the local or regional level, these cleavages appear to have established themselves first and foremost, though not exclusively, in what M. Rainer Lepsius has called a "social-moral milieu." To Lepsius, the term "socio-moral milieu" refers to locally or regionally limited social entities "that are formed by the convergence of several structural dimensions such as religion, regional tradition, economic situation, cultural orientation, or stratum-specific composition of the intermediary groups."[7] According to this view, parties constitute themselves as the political action committees of the different milieus. For the Second Empire and the Weimar Republic, Lepsius distinguishes between (1) the socialist worker and artisan milieu that was characterized, at least during the Second Empire, by the "negative integration of the working-class into a subculture" and that was "tied to specific class interests"; (2) the Catholic social milieu, which also constituted itself as a "political-social entity" according to the principle of negative integration; (3) the conservative milieu, with two distinct dimensions – the feudal-agrarian and the governmental-bourgeois – united by Protestantism; and (4) the bourgeois-Protestant milieu, which during the course of the Second Empire found itself reduced more and more "to a *Mittelstand* with a specific petty-bourgeois social morality." For the most part, the four politically dominant social milieus were sharply separated from one another "by symbolically dramatized moral cleavages."[8]

How do these three theoretical concepts relate to one another? And

---

6. See Franz Urban Pappi, "Sozialstruktur und politische Konflikte in der Bundesrepublik. Individual- und Kontextanalysen der Wahlentscheidung" (unpub. Habilitation thesis, University of Cologne, 1976), 85ff.
7. M. Rainer Lepsius, "Parteiensystem und Sozialstruktur. Zum Problem der Demokratisierung der deutschen Gesellschaft," in W. Abel et al., eds., *Wirtschaft, Geschichte und Wirtschaftsgeschichte. Festschrift zum 65. Geburtstag von F. Lütge* (Stuttgart, 1966), 383.
8. See M. Rainer Lepsius, *Extremer Nationalismus. Strukturbedingungen vor der nationalsozialistischen Machtergreifung* (Stuttgart, 1966), 27ff.

what sort of contribution do they have to make to the solution of our research problem? All of them share the analysis of the relationship between social structure and party system as a common point of departure. Burnham's notion of political camps and electoral coalitions, Lipset and Rokkan's theory of political cleavages, and Lepsius's concept of the social-moral milieu are all based upon what Pappi has called a "politicized social structure." But although neither the notion of the political camp nor that of political cleavage necessarily includes a territorial element in its definition – these can appear and function at the local as well as the national level – the concept of milieu implies the existence of a "great density of informal social relationships capable of providing the respective social group with a sense of common identity" that, for the most part, can be found only in a local or, at best, regional context.[9] The norms of the milieu are thus reproduced through direct social interaction, and the behavioral uniformity of political camps and cleavage groups may result from individual identification with the political goals and behavioral norms of specific reference groups in a way that, due to the absence of an existing opportunity structure, does not automatically entail the individual's daily, informal interaction with other members of that group. Using Burnham's notion of the political camp or the Lipset–Rokkan theory of political cleavage, it is thus possible to argue that the voting propensities of "diaspora Catholics" or workers living outside the typical proletarian milieu, will, in turn, resemble those of the men and women residing in Catholic strongholds or working-class neighborhoods.[10]

The concept of a social-moral milieu represents a theoretical improvement upon those two conceptions only in the event that the adherents of a particular milieu either possess an above-average, across-the-board probability of voting for the party of that specific milieu or at least manifest a distinctive and persistent pattern of voting behavior, such as a lesser tendency to switch parties. From a statistical point of view, the first of these two requirements means that the postulated effect of the milieu works not only cumulatively – that is, it does not reflect the accumulation of behavioral characteristics associated with membership in the milieu – but also involves

9. Pappi, "Sozialstruktur und politische Konflikte," 617.
10. A quotation may elucidate this point: "Persons who find themselves in the same class situation can choose the same party on the basis of individual interests without the existence of grouping influence." See Pappi, "Sozialstruktur und politische Konflikte," 500.

a supplementary contextual and therefore multiplicatory factor.[11] Otherwise, the concept of the social-moral milieu would, from the perspective of electoral history, be no more than a label for the local concentration of certain social characteristics that one could no doubt identify but that are inconsequential as determinants of electoral behavior. These concepts contribute to determining the strength and persistence of political subcultures in two ways. First, they offer different concept-specific perspectives of classification for the categorization of political subcultures. Second, they explicitly incorporate the sociostructural and sociocultural basis of subcultures into the analysis of political and electoral behavior.

The following empirical investigation focuses upon (1) the socialist labor movement in its two principal manifestations, (2) the Catholic camp, (3) the bourgeois voter coalition identified here as "liberal-minded" that was important at least at the beginning of the Weimar Republic, and (4) the initially predominantly rural but later increasingly urban German Nationalist electoral bloc, as well as (5) the National Socialists, whose growth after 1928 came, in the opinion of most observers, at the expense of the latter two electoral groups.[12] In this connection, the term "camp," or *Lager*, refers exclusively to political constellations on the party and voter levels, without explicit reference to the underlying sociostructural and sociocultural voter coalitions. This essay employs ecological regression analysis to investigate fluctuations both between and within the individual subcultures in spite of possible stability on the part of the blocs themselves. Relying in large part upon the typology proposed by Burnham, this essay then addresses the structural cleavages – or, better said, the sociostructural correlates of the various political subcultures – whose social composition is determined with the help of ecological regression analysis.

CONTINUITIES AND DISCONTINUITIES AT THE NATIONAL LEVEL

During the Weimar Republic, there was a striking discrepancy between the proliferation of political parties and voter volatility, on the

---

11. The operational consequences of the second requirement are obvious.
12. The introduction of additional concepts such as electoral groups or electoral blocs comes about not through compulsive originality but rather in order not to assume theoretical definitions that should not be addressed here.

one hand, and a remarkable stability of individual electoral blocs, on the other. This stability could be seen as early as 1919, when these electoral blocs emerged relatively intact from military defeat, revolution, the humiliation of Versailles, and profound changes in both the franchise and the electoral system. What this suggests is that the Weimar electorate, in spite of the enormous volatility of electoral behavior, oriented itself, at least on the aggregate level, by socially and confessionally determined cleavages among the various party blocs. In the 1919 elections to the National Assembly, for example, parties belonging to the bourgeois-Protestant bloc were unable to sustain the position they had achieved in the 1912 Reichstag elections, whereas those that belonged to the political left managed to gain a substantial number of votes. This situation, however, lasted only until 1920, when the old balance of power among the three party blocs was reestablished in the first postwar Reichstag election. No substantial change in this distribution of votes was to occur prior to 1933.

Just as party blocs remained stable in the transition from the Second Empire to the Weimar Republic, so did the individual parties. The 1919 elections reflected both a shift from national liberalism to left liberalism and heavy losses for the conservative groups, which had coalesced in one right-wing catchall party, the German National People's Party (*Deutschnationale Volkspartei* or DNVP). All of this, however, proved to be more or less transitory. By 1920 political conservatism had recaptured the position it had held in 1912, as first the political left and then the bourgeois-Protestant electoral bloc began to split their votes among numerous parties in a tendency that was to become even more pronounced over the course of the next several years before making the Weimar Republic ultimately ungovernable. In the meantime, the so-called Weimar Coalition consisting of the Social Democratic Party (*Sozialdemokratische Partei Deutschlands* or SPD), the left-liberal German Democratic Party (*Deutsche Demokratische Partei* or DDP), and the Catholic Center Party (*Deutsche Zentrumspartei*) had lost its electoral and parliamentary majority, whereas the political groups that opposed the Weimar Republic had already gained a slight majority. After July 1932, the extremist parties of the left and right, which were not merely opponents but bitter enemies of the Weimar Republic, possessed a majority in terms of both the popular vote and the seats they held in the Reichstag. This development left the parties of the Weimar Coalition with no alternative but to form extremely weak minority cabinets or to coalesce with groups that were not loyal supporters of the Weimar Republic for the entire period from the middle of 1920 to the collapse of parliamentary government at the beginning of the 1930s.

The development of the bourgeois-Protestant bloc was characterized by the steady decline of the two liberal parties until they virtually disappeared on the electoral level, first through the emergence and temporary success of diverse special interest parties that also played a major role in the decline of the DNVP and then, after 1928, through the meteoric rise of the NSDAP. On the left, extremist parties established themselves as serious rivals to the more moderate Social Democrats very early in the history of the Weimar Republic. In 1920 the extremist forces on the left were represented by the Independent Social Democratic Party (*Unabhängige Sozialdemokratische Partei Deutschlands* or USPD) and in 1932 by the Communist Party (*Kommunistische Partei Deutschlands* or KPD), which at different points in the Weimar Republic succeeded in mobilizing nearly half of the leftist electorate. This, in turn, severely limited the political maneuverability of the Social Democrats throughout the Weimar Republic. Of the major electoral blocs that existed in the Weimar Republic, only the Catholic bloc experienced almost no significant shifts in power between the two main parties that formed it – the Center and the Bavarian People's Party (*Bayerische Volkspartei* or BVP) – in spite of occasional efforts on the part of dissident Catholic groups to break off and form their own parties (Table 1). For all intents and purposes, the changes in party affiliation were much stronger within the bourgeois-Protestant bloc than within the left or the Catholic bloc.

In light of these shifts of strength within the bourgeois-Protestant bloc, most contemporary observers were convinced that the NSDAP's dramatic gains at the polls came both from predominantly middle-class adherents of the bourgeois-Protestant parties and from persons who had previously not voted or had just become eligible to vote for the first time. Followers of the two socialist parties and the Catholic bloc, on the other hand, were thought to be almost totally immune to Nazi electoral propaganda. In our discussion of Table 2, we will see that these conclusions may be valid as far as general tendencies are concerned but have to be modified considerably in the light of more recent empirical research.

In the aggregate, the socialist and Catholic blocs remained remark-

378   Jürgen W. Falter

Table 1. *The electorate of the Weimar parties, 1919–33*
(percentage of eligible voters)

	Jan. 1919	June 1920	May 1924	Dec. 1924	May 1928	Sept. 1930	July 1932	Nov. 1932	March 1933
KPD	-	1.6	9.6	7.0	7.9	11.5	12.2	13.5	10.8
USPD	6.3	14.0	0.6	0.3	0.1	0.0	-	-	-
SPD	31.3	17.0	15.7	20.2	22.2	20.0	18.0	16.3	16.1
DDP	15.5	6.5	4.3	4.9	3.7	3.1	0.8	0.8	0.8
CENTER	13.2	10.7	10.2	10.6	9.0	9.6	10.4	9.5	9.9
BVP	3.1	3.3	2.5	2.9	2.3	2.5	3.1	2.7	2.4
DVP	3.7	10.9	7.0	7.8	6.5	3.9	1.0	1.5	1.0
DNVP	8.5	11.8	14.8	15.9	10.9	5.7	5.2	7.1	7.0
NSDAP	-	-	5.0	2.3	2.0	14.9	31.2	26.5	38.7
OTHER	1.3	2.6	6.6	5.8	10.4	11.1	1.7	2.1	1.4
Turnout	83.0	79.2	77.4	78.8	75.6	82.0	84.1	80.6	88.8

KPD	**Communist Party**
USPD	**Independent Socialist Party**
SPD	**Social Democratic Party**
DDP	**German Democratic Party (left liberal)**
CENTER	**Catholic Center Party**
BVP	**Bavarian People's Party (Catholic)**
DVP	**German People's Party (national liberal)**
DNVP	**German National People's Party (right wing, nationalistic)**
OTHER	**All other parties combined**

ably stable between 1920 and 1933. Throughout the history of the Weimar Republic, the SPD mobilized between 16 and 23 percent of the German electorate, and the Center and BVP received between 11 and 14 percent of the popular vote. By contrast, the fluctuations in the level of support for the KPD – and here, for purposes of simplicity, we are including the USPD – were much greater, ranging from 7 to 15 percent. The same was true for the DNVP, which showed fluctuation between 5 and 16 percent, and most markedly for the two liberal parties, which fell from 17 to 2 percent.

RECONSTRUCTING THE "REAL" GAINS AND LOSSES OF THE POLITICAL BLOCS BETWEEN 1920 AND 1933

The preceding section outlined the net fluctuations between the different political camps. These fluctuations reveal a general swing behind which significantly greater subterranean shifts in voting behavior are sometimes concealed. Since each election result reflects the gains and losses of the various parties within each bloc, it might in an extreme case be possible for two equally strong parties to exchange their electorates completely without this ever showing up in the final vote. Survey data show that even in the case of sharp electoral shifts the fluctuations between two parties are often reciprocal, though occasionally strongly asymmetric. This suggests not only a flow of voters from the losing to the winning party but also a much smaller flow in the opposite direction. It is extremely improbable that voter fluctuations were different during the Weimar Republic. Unfortunately, this aspect of voter fluctuations has been overlooked by most historical accounts of Weimar elections.

The following analysis therefore attempts, as a first step, to reconstruct the real voter movement between the different political subcultures. This reconstruction is based on estimates obtained by a method known as "ecological regression analysis." If and only if the relatively strict assumptions of this technique are met by the data will the estimates represent a true measure of the voter movement that actually occurred. If the data cannot satisfy these assumptions, they may still be regarded as the statistically best indicators of the voter exchange that took place between the individual subcultures and parties.[13]

Table 2a reports the retention rate of the different political subcultures. This retention rate is the percentage of those in each political camp or subculture who voted in any two consecutive elections

---

13. To my knowledge, the statistical technique of ecological regression analysis was first developed by the German statistician F. Bernstein as early as 1932, but his work has escaped the attention of most empirical researchers. The instrument was subsequently rediscovered by Leo Goodman in his article "Ecological Regressions and Behavior of Individuals," *American Sociological Review* 43 (1953): 557–72. The results or estimates displayed in Table 2 were calculated on the basis of a certain modification of this technique developed by Jan-Bernd Lohmöller that tries to cope with the effect of so-called contextual variables. See Jan-Bernd Lohmöller, Jürgen W. Falter, Andreas Link, and Johann de Rijke, "Unemployment and the Rise of National Socialism: Contradicting Results from Different Regional Aggregations," in Peter Nijkamp, ed., *Measuring the Unmeasurable* (Dordrecht, Boston, and Lancaster, 1985), 357–70. Unfortunately we are not able to determine from the available data if all the conditions of ecological regression analysis have been adequately satisfied. Furthermore, this technique is very sensitive to differing model specifications. Its results, therefore, should be interpreted quite cautiously and restricted to differences of magnitude, not to small percentage variations. Even then, the results should approximate what actually happened, since different model specifications and various multiple ecological regression analyses based on different aggregations produce approximately the same results, which in turn closely coincide in magnitude with normal multiple regression analyses using so-called change variables.

Table 2. *Voter fluctuations between political subcultures and parties*

Reichstag Election	1920-24A	24A-B	24B-28	28-30	30-32A	32A-B	32B-33	$\bar{X}$
(a) Stability Rates for each Pair of Elections[a]								
SPD/KPD	40	66	72	65	61	67	71	63
CENTER/BVP	50	70	55	66	65	63	74	63
DDP/DVP	30	66	45	31	6	15	12	29
DNVP	48	70	51	27	20	49	49	45
OTHER[b]	13	40	29	47	9	22	11	24
Bourgeois[c]	25	60	44	35	11	34	33	35
(b) Between-Camp Voter Fluctuations[a]								
Socialist Camp	39	19	18	22	22	18	19	22
Catholic Camp	33	20	32	30	30	28	20	28
Bourgeois-Protest.	34	17	25	41	66	37	51	39
Bourgeois[d]	34	16	23	19	19	17	9	20
Nonvoters	42	43	22	50	43	19	59	40

either for the same party or for another party belonging to the same bloc. It is no surprise that the socialist and Catholic blocs reflect the highest retention rates. From one election to the next, they managed to retain an average of two-thirds of their voters, a figure that is somewhat lower than that for the major parties of the Federal Republic. In contrast, the bourgeois-Protestant bloc had a relatively low retention rate for the period after 1924. On average, only about one-third of those who belonged to the bourgeois-Protestant bloc voted for parties that represented this bloc in consecutive elections. As early as 1924, there was a clear decline in the retention rate within this bloc, with a second wave of defections discernible between September 1930 and July 1932. Within this group, the retention rates were especially low for the liberal parties and for the various special interest and regional parties. Despite noticeable fluctuations, the DNVP was able to retain a significantly larger share of its electorate

*(c) Voter Fluctuations to and from the NSDAP*ᵃ
Column 1: From other Party to NSDAP; Column 2: From NSDAP to other Party)

SPD/KPD	13:0	4:20	3:22	15:21	21:4	10:8	15:3	16:9
CENTER/BVP	1:0	2:18	2:12	9:9	10:4	6:4	3:1	7:5
DDP/DVP	7:0	3:9	3:11	26:5	36:1	4:1	23:1	22:2
DNVP	8:0	2:29	1:10	31:3	33:5	0:3	34:3	25:4
OTHERᵇ	7:0	3:7	3:18	11:13	49:0	11:1	33:0	26:4
Nonvoters	3:0	1:7	2:22	14:11	19:0	2:6	42:2	19:5
Bourgeois-Protestant Camp					23:7	41:2	4:2	32:3

(d) Net Fluctuations to the NSDAP (in percentage of total electorate)

								(Σ)
SPD/KPD	.71	-.65	-.10	2.18	3.10	-.92	1.32	5.64
CENTER/BVP	.60	-.19	-.02	.90	.70	-.40	.12	1.71
DDP/DVP	1.26	-.44	.12	2.50	2.37	-.25	.19	5.75
DNVP	1.00	-.96	.02	3.35	1.23	-.93	1.57	5.28
OTHERᵇ	.90	-.22	-.12	.96	5.40	.02	.99	7.93
Nonvoters	.53	-.14	.06	3.42	3.36	-1.52	7.86	13.57

Transition probabilities estimated by means of multiple ecological regression analysis; community-level data (1920-1930); county-level data (1930-1933). The data is from Jürgen W. Falter and Reinhard Zintl, "The Economic Crisis of the 1930's and the Nazi Vote," *Journal of Interdisciplinary History* 19 (1987/88):55-85.

ᵃ Percentage of first election voters of respective party.

ᵇ Without NSDAP.

ᶜ DDP, DVP, DNVP and OTHER (without NSDAP).

ᵈ With NSDAP.

between 1928 and July 1932 than the other parties of the bourgeois-Protestant bloc.

Table 2b displays the complementary phenomenon of shifts from one bloc to another. The socialist bloc showed the lowest rate of voter movement to other political blocs, followed closely by the Catholic bloc. If the NSDAP, however, is included in the bourgeois-Protestant bloc, as Burnham has suggested, the rate of voter movement away from this bloc is the lowest. In fact, Table 2c indicates that voter shifts between the liberals and the conservatives as well as other political blocs, on the one hand, and the NSDAP, on the other, are clear and indisputable. In July 1932, for example, over 40 percent of the voters who had supported bourgeois-Protestant parties in 1930 switched to the NSDAP, whereas only 2 percent of those who had voted for the NSDAP in 1930 supported other bourgeois-Protestant parties in July 1932.

Voter movement to the NSDAP, however, was not restricted to supporters of the bourgeois-Protestant bloc. There were also other strongly asymmetrical voter shifts between the other political blocs and the NSDAP after 1928. An analysis of net fluctuations to the NSDAP is provided in Table 2d. This table reveals not merely the relative but, more important, the absolute contributions of the individual subcultures to the electoral surge of the NSDAP. In looking at all consecutive elections in the Weimar Republic, it becomes clear that nonvoters, or those who had not taken part in the previous election, contributed by far the largest share of votes flowing to the Hitler movement, with almost 14 percent of the Nazi vote coming from this source. This phenomenon can be explained in large part as a consequence of the enormous mobilization of prior nonvoters for the NSDAP in the election of March 1933, the first after Hitler became chancellor. Former voters for the various special-interest and regional parties in the bourgeois-Protestant bloc were another particularly important source of Nazi electoral support. Even more surprising, however, is the fact that net voter fluctuation from the socialist bloc to the NSDAP was virtually as high in absolute numbers as that from the two liberal parties or the DNVP. Of course, this is attributable to the fact that the KPD and SPD together attracted many more voters than the two Catholic parties, the two liberal parties, or the Nationalists. Elsewhere I have shown that it was primarily former SPD voters who flocked from the socialist bloc to the NSDAP after 1928.[14] By far the smallest net voter fluctuation to the NSDAP was manifested by the Catholic bloc.

For the most part, then, voters tended to switch parties within a given political bloc rather than move from one bloc to another. For the socialist and Catholic blocs, shifts within these blocs were about

---

14. Jürgen W. Falter and Dirk Hänisch, "Die Anfälligkeit von Arbeitern gegenüber der NSDAP bei den Reichstagswahlen 1928 und 1933," *Archiv für Sozialgeschichte* 26 (1986): 179–216.

three times more prevalent than shifts from one bloc to another. One must, however, consider that, for Catholic voters, moving from one party to another implied a true change of political ideology or affiliation, whereas socialist voters could switch to ideologically neighboring or related parties with much greater ease. If one includes the NSDAP with the bourgeois-Protestant bloc, the same pattern holds true for this political bloc, namely, that switches within the bloc were much more frequent than moves from it to another bloc. If, however, one excludes the NSDAP from this bloc, as some historians have done, the evidence then shows that shortly after 1924 the two liberal parties had been almost totally decimated and the nationalist-conservative party, the DNVP, partly so by the defection of their supporters to the new catchall party of the bourgeois-Protestant bloc, the NSDAP. From the purely electoral perspective, it was the fragmentation of the bourgeois-Protestant bloc and the lack of an explicit, socially sanctioned voting norm that promoted the rise of National Socialism. In this regard, Burnham's theory of "political confessionalism" can be empirically verified by our data.

THE SOCIAL FOUNDATIONS OF THE WEIMAR PARTY SYSTEM

The political parties of the Weimar Republic were organized along cleavages that had been inherited from the Second Empire, if not earlier. These cleavages can best be described, as Arthur Stinchcombe has suggested, as lines of tension separating the different coalitions between party elites and specific social groups.[15] The existence of such cleavages can be established only if four conditions are met: first, the persistence of party organizations, particularly at the local level; second, recruitment of the same core electorate over an extended period of time; third, the existence of party-specific social value orientations within the electorate; and last, continuity over time as far as the programs of the various political parties are concerned.[16]

For the Weimar Republic, it can be established that conditions one

---

15. Arthur Stinchcombe, "Social Structure and Politics," in Fred I. Greenstein and Nelson W. Polsby, eds., *Handbook of Political Science*, vol. 3, *Macropolitics* (Reading, Mass., 1975), 557–620.
16. See Franz Urban Pappi, "Sozialstruktur, Gesellschaftliche Wertorientierungen und Wahlabsicht. Ergebnisse eines Zeitvergleichs des Deutschen Elektorats 1953 und 1976," *Politische Vierteljahresschrift* 18 (1977): 196ff.

and four were met in spite of the fact that during the last years before 1933 almost all bourgeois-Protestant parties made significant changes in their party programs. Condition three cannot be analyzed by means of quantitative electoral analysis. Hence, this section concentrates on the issue of whether the political blocs in question were always able to mobilize the same core of voters or whether there were any important changes in the social composition of party electorates during the Weimar Republic.

In measuring the stability of political divisions, this section takes a close look at the stability of the denominational and class composition of party electorates between 1920 and 1933. Because of the inherent limitations of analyses based upon aggregate data, a two-step procedure is employed. First, we examine the social correlates of the political parties over time (Table 3). Then we utilize ecological regression analyses to determine the voting behavior of specific social classes and religious denominations (Tables 4 and 5). Although there are certain dramatic changes of magnitude, this analysis reveals almost no significant shifts in the sociostructural bases of the various political parties and blocs between 1920 and 1933.

SOCIAL CORRELATES AND THE MAIN POLITICAL PARTIES

Table 3 presents the statistical association between selected social characteristics and the voting results of the various parties in the form of correlation coefficients. These coefficients range from +1.0 (which indicates a perfectly positive linear relationship between two variables) to −1.0 (which represents a perfectly negative linear relationship between two variables). A relatively high coefficient, such as that between the share of blue-collar workers in the electorate and the KPD vote share after 1920, represents a strong statistical relationship between the two variables. This relationship must then be interpreted in the following way: During the Weimar Republic, on average, the percentage of the KPD vote tended to be higher when the share of blue-collar workers in the counties and cities was larger; conversely, the lower the percentage of blue-collar workers, the smaller the electoral chances of the KPD. An example of a negative correlation coefficient, on the other hand, is the fact that where the percentage of Catholics is higher, the SPD's share of the popular vote is correspondingly lower. Coefficients close to zero – all coefficients between +/−0.10 are considered close to zero – should be interpreted as

Table 3. *Some social correlates of the Weimar Parties (Pearson's r × 100)*[a]

	1920	1928	1930	1932A	1933
SPD % Catholic.	-48	-66	-66	-66	-62
% Blue-Collar	11	22	18	13	15
% Self Employed	-18	-44	-35	-41	-42
% White Collar	6	23	23	31	31
% Agrarian	-14	-39	-36	-44	-48
KPD % Catholic	-07	-25	-21	-17	-26
% Blue-Collar	29	59	66	71	69
% Self Employed	-26	-63	-68	-70	-69
% White Collar	8	29	30	27	32
% Agrarian	-19	-57	-62	-63	-68
Z/BVP % Catholic	92	92	93	93	93
% Blue-Collar	-16	-18	-24	-20	-14
% Self Employed	23	24	30	25	17
% White Collar	-20	-22	-25	-21	-16
% Agrarian	23	24	29	23	16
DDP % Catholic	-46	-47	-32	-35	-34
% Blue-Collar	-16	-15	-17	-15	-13
% Self Employed	8	-12	-1	±00	-11
% White Collar	22	46	35	29	43
% Agrarian	-16	-39	-27	-22	-36
DVP % Catholic	-56	-50	-40	-28	-32
% Blue-Collar	-3	8	9	-5	20
% Self Employed	-26	-32	-35	-14	-23
% White Collar	39	41	39	35	40
% Agrarian	-37	-47	-45	-34	-44
DNVP % Catholic	-59	-43	-36	-47	-55
% Blue-Collar	-24	-22	-13	-21	-17
% Self Employed	39	12	-3	3	±00
% White Collar	-37	-14	-2	2	7
% Agrarian	55	38	26	23	17
NSDAP % Catholic	-	-09	-53	-71	-55
% Blue-Collar	-	-13	-15	-36	-46
% Self Employed	-	11	9	46	59
% White Collar	-	5	-12	-42	-52
% Agrarian	-	-6	8	47	63

[a]Values from Jürgen W. Falter, Thomas Lindenberger, and Siegfried Schumann, *Wahlen und Abstimmungen in der Weimarer Republik* (Munich, 1986), 163–70. For the rubric "Catholics," bivariate correlation coefficient; all other rubrics, share of Catholics partialed out, that is, statistically controlled.

statistical nonassociations. This is the case, for example, for the relationship between the percentage of blue-collar workers and the DVP vote. Even correlation coefficients ranging from +/−0.10 to +/−0.20 represent at best very small, substantially insignificant statistical associations. They should, therefore, be interpreted with great caution.

Table 3 displays two different types of correlation coefficients: normal bivariate coefficients without controls for third variables and partial correlation coefficients with a control for potentially disturbing factors such as the percentage of Catholics. Partial correlation coefficients should be interpreted as if the units of analysis, such as cities and counties, were more or less denominationally the same. This method controls for the factor of "religious denomination" when analyzing the influence of other social variables. Controlling the denominational factor in this manner is necessary because the confessional cleavage was the by far the most important factor influencing Weimar voting behavior. Its influence was so important that the effect of other variables correlating with religious denomination are often virtually suppressed by it. Since in Weimar Germany the percentages of Catholics and Protestants were nearly perfectly negatively correlated – that is, a high percentage of Catholics always implied a low percentage of Protestants, and vice versa – one should not use partial correlation coefficients with controls for confession to determine the effect of religious denomination. In the case of the denominational variable, other potential influence factors are not statistically controlled. In the case of all other social variables, Table 3 deals with partial correlations with controls for the factor "Catholics."

Table 3 reflects social characteristics that are of particular importance for the analysis of sociopolitical cleavages.[17] It clearly shows the influence of at least three political cleavages acting upon the Weimar party system. In the first place, religious denomination undoubtedly separates the two Catholic parties from the other four parties. Only in the case of the KPD is the relationship very weak. A second line of cleavage is represented by the two variables "blue-collar" and "self-employed." In districts with more blue-collar workers and fewer self-employed persons than average, the share of the KPD vote and, to a somewhat lesser degree, that of the SPD are higher than average, whereas the shares of the other parties fall below

---

17. For further social correlates of the party vote in Weimar Germany, see ibid.

their national mean. A third line of cleavage is represented at its positive pole by the percentage of the population working in the agrarian sector of the economy and at its negative pole by the percentage of white-collar workers and civil servants. In general, the DNVP in Protestant areas and the Center Party and BVP to a significantly lesser extent in Catholic areas were much more successful in mobilizing voters between 1928 and 1933 wherever the percentage of those employed in the agrarian sector was higher than the national average. On the other hand, both the two socialist and the two liberal parties were significantly weaker than in the rest of the country in those areas that were predominantly agrarian in terms of their social and economic structures. Last, there was a fourth cleavage representing regional and ethnic conflicts, but this was of only minor importance in the Weimar Republic and is not discussed here.

It is clear that the confessional cleavage remained of major importance for the two Catholic parties until the very end of the Weimar Republic. The same is true in substance for the two socialist parties, especially for the SPD, and for the DNVP, all of which were clearly rooted in Protestant regions. Only for the two liberal parties, which virtually disappeared from the political stage between 1928 and 1932, did the confessional cleavage seem to lose importance after 1928. The same is true of the second cleavage, which was represented by the share of blue-collar workers in the general population. During the course of the Great Depression, however, a further line of division demarcated by the unemployment rate arose within the blue-collar sector. According to the correlation coefficients in Table 3, this new division promoted the growth of the KPD, which more and more became the party of the unemployed.[18] Finally, with regard to the third cleavage based upon the percentage of people employed in the agricultural sector, there was only a relatively minor change as far as most parties were concerned. Only the DNVP seems to have lost its strong social basis in the rural Protestant regions of Germany. The principal beneficiary of the DNVP's decline after 1930 seems to have been the NSDAP, whose electoral success in 1932 and 1933 was higher on average in those areas where the share of the Protestant rural population was high.

18. See Jürgen W. Falter, "Unemployment and the Radicalisation of the German Electorate 1928–1933: An Aggregate Data Analysis with Special Emphasis on the Rise of National Socialism," in Peter Stachura, ed., *Unemployment and the Great Depression in Weimar Germany* (Basingstoke and London, 1986), 187–208.

PARTY AFFILIATION OF SOCIAL GROUPS

The coefficients in Table 3, as well as the interpretations based upon them, are not only derived from aggregate data but are restricted to the aggregate level. That is to say, the preceding section discusses only relationships between variables that existed at the level of the thousand or so counties throughout Germany in the Weimar Republic. The hypotheses in question, however, relate to the level of the individual. Such questions can only be answered on the basis of individual data, that is, information that is not collected at the level of the counties or cities but at the level of the individual voters. Once again, evidence restricts analysis to the extrapolation about individual voting behavior through the interpretation of aggregate data by means of multiple ecological regression analysis. Table 4 depicts the results of two such ecological regression analyses for three Reichstag elections. The starting point is the May 1924 election, because this was the first time that the NSDAP competed at the national level as a junior partner of a *völkisch* coalition. Furthermore, the bipolar competition on the left between the SDP and the KPD took shape in this election. The second election under consideration is the Reichstag election of 1928, which may be regarded as the last normal election before the start of the Great Depression and the subsequent sudden rise of National Socialism from a right-wing extremist splinter group to the strongest party in Germany. Finally, the July 1932 Reichstag election was chosen because in this election the NSDAP managed to win the highest share of the popular vote in a truly free election and emerged as by far the strongest party in the Reichstag.

The percentages reported in Table 4 depict the probabilities of a Catholic and a non-Catholic or a member of the three social classes voting for one of the indicated parties at the three elections. Again, interpretation should be restricted to global orders of magnitude and should avoid overinterpreting small percentage differences.[19] Even then, the confessional cleavage proves to have been extraordinarily durable, with Catholicism being a positive predictor for support for

19. According to the formal characteristics of our statistical estimators, the results for the variable "confession" are probably better than those for the variable "social class." Thus there are no estimators for the confessional variables that are negative or higher than 100. On the other hand, some estimators for social class are negative in sign. They were smoothed by means of proportional fitting. For technical details, see Jan-Bernd Lohmöller, et al., "Unemployment and the Rise of National Socialism," in Peter Nijkamp, ed., *Measuring the Unmeasurable* (Dordrecht, 1985), 357–70.

Table 4. *The party vote of major social groups*

	CONFESSION		SOCIAL CLASS		
	CATHOLIC	OTHER	BLUE COLL	WHITE COLL.	SELF-EMPL.
SPD					
1924A	5	21	21	16	7
1928	9	28	31	24	7
1932A	6	23	22	24	7
KPD					
1924A	9	10	19	5	0
1928	5	9	14	5	0
1932A	10	13	23	6	0
Z/BVP					
1924A	43	2	9	9	27
1928	37	0	10	8	17
1932A	42	0	11	10	20
DDP/DVP					
1924A	3	15	8	18	12
1928	4	13	6	17	11
1932A	1	2	1	3	2
DNVP					
1924A	3	21	13	14	18
1928	4	14	9	10	13
1932A	2	6	4	6	6
NSDAP					
1924A	3	6	4	7	6
1928	2	2	2	2	2
1932A	16	38	25	29	42

Column percentages estimated by means of multiple ecological regression analysis. The empirical basis were the election results in 865 county units. See Jürgen W. Falter and Reinhard Zintl, "The Economic Crisis of the 1930's and the Nazi Vote," *Journal of Interdisciplinary History* 19 (1987/88):55-85.

Reading example: In May 1924, about 5 percent of the eligible Catholics and 21 percent of the non-Catholic population voted SPD.

the Center Party and the BVP and negative for the SPD, the liberals, and the DNVP. Only for the KPD electorate does Catholic confessional identity seem to have been of minor importance.[20] After 1928, the NSDAP was also a predominantly Protestant party that received disproportionately fewer Catholic votes. The data show that about 40 percent of all eligible Catholic voters opted for one of the two Catholic parties. Non-Catholics, on the other hand, gave almost no support to the Center Party and the BVP.[21] In contrast, only 10 percent of the Catholics, but almost 30 percent of the non-Catholics voted in 1928 for parties of the bourgeois-Protestant bloc.

The blue-collar vote also proved rather stable. About 40 to 45 percent of the eligible blue-collar workers seem to have voted in 1924 and 1932 for one of the two socialist parties; about 10 percent for the two Catholic parties; and between 20 and 30 percent for one of the bourgeois parties, by far mostly for the NSDAP after 1930.[22] According to the data and the statistical results, blue-collar support for the NSDAP came not from the electoral supporters of the two parties of the labor movement but mainly from former voters for the bourgeois-Protestant bloc and from nonvoters.

The two socialist parties attracted relatively few votes from the old middle class, self-employed artisans and shopkeepers, and the farming population. A relatively high percentage of the self-employed seemed to have voted for the Center or the BVP, whereas the Protestant members of the old middle class spread their vote among the various parties of the bourgeois-Protestant bloc. After 1930, the old middle class switched heavily to the NSDAP. From the perspective of the political blocs, the voting behavior of the old middle class followed traditional political cleavages more closely than that of blue-collar workers.

20. Here it is important to bear in mind that being a member of the Catholic church did not, at least in Germany, imply being a practicing Catholic.
21. The figure of 40 percent is quite a high mobilization rate, since the social characteristic "Catholic" contains both practicing and nominal Catholics. Furthermore, we are reporting as dependent variables the party vote as well as nonvoting. For analogous estimates, see the contemporary source Johannes Schauff, *Die deutschen Katholiken und die Zentrumspartei. Eine politisch-statistische Untersuchung der Reichstagswahlen seit 1871* (Cologne, 1928).
22. In interpreting these estimates, one should take into consideration the fact that the blue-collar category of the official Weimar statistics comprised not only industrial laborers but also workers from the agrarian and tertiary sectors who, as I have shown elsewhere, showed a much lower affinity for the socialist parties but seem to have voted more strongly in favor of National Socialism than the true blue-collar workers. See Jürgen W. Falter, *Hitlers Wähler* (Munich, 1991), ch. 7.

In contrast to the old middle class, the voting behavior of the new middle class of white-collar employees and civil servants was much more differentiated and less directed by historical political divisions. Between 20 and 30 percent of those voters who belonged to the so-called new middle class opted regularly for one of the two left parties. After 1928 the SPD seems to have received more support from this stratum of society than from the blue-collar electorate. About 40 percent of civil servants and white-collar employees voted for the parties of the bourgeois-Protestant bloc. After July 1932, the NSDAP collected the splinters of this group, although support from the new middle class remained much lower than that from the old middle class.

To summarize, the evidence of individual voter preferences shows that basic historical divisions of the German electorate characterized the electoral behavior of the various social strata and religious groups right up to the end of the Weimar Republic. The changes that took place occurred mainly within the bourgeois-Protestant bloc. It is important to note that no single political bloc was able to mobilize all or even an absolute majority of the members of one social class or confession for its own purposes. Only within the old middle class did a majority vote for one of the parties of the bourgeois-Protestant bloc after 1930. The NSDAP succeeded in winning more partisans from this social stratum or class than from any other social group.

THE SOCIAL COMPOSITION OF PARTY ELECTORATES

By examining the social composition of the voters for the various political parties rather than the tendency of the members of various social groups to identify themselves with those parties, it is possible once again to address the effect of the confessional cleavage: The Center party and its Bavarian counterpart recruited almost all of their voters from the Catholic sector of the population. In the other political blocs, with the exception first of the Communists and later of the National Socialists, Catholic voters represented an insignificant minority of the party electorates (Table 5). This pattern changed very little during the Weimar Republic. On the other hand, the division between blue-collar workers and self-employed persons is clearly visible. Particularly the KPD seems to have been a clearly class-based blue-collar party, despite having a small white-collar following. The SPD constituency, however, was much more mixed: More than a third – and after 1930 more than 40 percent – of those who voted for

Table 5. *The social composition of the Weimar party electorates*

	CONFESSION		SOCIAL CLASS		
	CATHOLIC	OTHER	BLUE COLL.	WHITE COLL.	SELF-EMPL.
SPD					
1924A	9	91	65	21	14
1928	13	87	65	21	13
1932A	12	88	57	28	15
KPD					
1924A	29	71	85	12	3
1928	21	79	76	16	8
1932A	28	72	81	13	6
Z/BVP					
1924A	93	7	30	16	54
1928	100	0	40	18	41
1932A	99	1	38	18	43
DDP/DVP					
1924A	10	90	34	34	33
1928	13	87	33	33	33
1932A	12	88	33	30	37
DNVP					
1924A	6	94	41	19	39
1928	11	89	41	20	39
1932A	14	86	38	27	35
NSDAP					
1924A	20	80	39	27	35
1928	30	70	40	22	37
1932A	17	83	39	19	42

Row percentages estimated by means of multiple ecological regression analysis. Basis: 865 county units.

Reading example: In May 1924, about 90 percent of the SPD voters were non-Catholic, approximately two third were blue-collar workers, 20 percent white-collar workers, etc.

the Social Democrats seem to have come from a middle-class background, analogous to the social composition of the SPD members. The other parties, especially the two liberal groups, recruited their voters from astonishingly equal proportions of blue-collar, white-collar, and self-employed voters. Both the DNVP and the NSDAP, on the other hand, had a surprisingly high share of blue-collar voters among their followers. Even here, however, the changes between 1924 and 1932 were of only minor importance. We may therefore concur with the thesis of Seymour Martin Lipset and Stein Rokkan that the political landscape of the Weimar Republic is characterized by the pronounced persistence of recruitment of voters from the same core clientele.

CONCLUSION

The goal of the preceding analysis has been to reconstruct through ecological regression analysis and aggregate data analysis the movement of voters between parties and political blocs during the Weimar Republic and to gain new insights into the political affiliations of the important social groups and, from a complementary perspective, into the social composition of the electorates of Weimar parties. The pronounced stability of electoral blocs at the national level is confirmed by a corresponding pattern of individual voter fluctuations. A strong majority of all voter shifts during the Weimar Republic were movements within specific electoral blocs. If one considers the NSDAP as part of the bourgeois-Protestant bloc, then the average shift from one camp to another between elections amounted only to 20 to 30 percent, a figure rather close to modern fluctuation rates in the former Federal Republic of Germany. Fluctuations were significantly higher only among nonvoters, many of whom were in the process of switching parties and electoral blocs, and for the liberal and conservative parties, which in the first case was almost totally and in the second partially wiped out by the National Socialists.

Despite a high rate of stability for the various electoral blocs that existed in the Weimar Republic, a significant shift of voters from the different blocs to the NSDAP could be detected during the last Reichstag elections. Both relatively and absolutely, the parties of the bourgeois-Protestant bloc lost the most voters to the NSDAP, followed by the nonvoters and the socialist bloc. Almost half of the NSDAP electorate of March 1933 had voted for one of the various parties of the bourgeois-Protestant bloc, one-third came from nonvoters, and about 7 out of 100 came from the socialist bloc.

Similarly, the cleavage of the Weimar Republic proved to be rather stable. This was especially true for the confessional cleavage, which showed no significant variation at either the aggregate or the individual level between 1920 and 1933. The effect of the second cleavage, between blue-collar workers and the self-employed, was similar. Almost none of the self-employed seem to have voted for the two socialist parties, which in turn recruited their support mainly from the blue-collar sector. On the other hand, all other political parties won an astonishingly high degree of blue-collar support. This is particularly striking with regard to the NSDAP electorate. It was socially much more heterogeneous than most contemporary sociologists and modern historians have thought. Contrary to many expectations, the SPD also seems to have been socially heterogeneous. In this respect, the social composition of its electorate more or less mirrored that of its party membership. At the end of the Weimar Republic, the KPD was the only proletarian party with strong backing from unemployed voters.

In contrast to the old middle class, the electoral behavior of the new middle class was quite differentiated and less clear-cut than has been presumed by many contemporaries and historians. Within the NSDAP electorate, the new middle class did not form a majority. It might even have been underrepresented. The non-Catholic self-employed, mostly from an agrarian background, voted largely for the National Socialists from 1930 on. Within the bourgeois-Protestant bloc, the NSDAP constituted a kind of functional equivalent as the representative of the formerly liberal, conservative, and special interest–oriented groups. More than any other party of its time, it was a force that transcended the cleavages that had become so deeply embedded in the German electorate, a factor that helps to explain its enormous surge at the electoral level between 1928 and 1932.

METHODOLOGICAL APPENDIX: DATA BASE AND STATISTICAL TECHNIQUES

Data Base: The empirical analysis in this essay is based on two data sets. The first was originally derived from the Inter-University Consortium for Political and Social Research (ICPSR) Weimar Election File.[23] The second data set, containing fewer variables but a greater

---

23. Since the ICPR Weimar Election File Data Set contains virtually thousands of minor and

number of cases, carries information on the 4,000 to 5,000 German communities with more than 2,000 inhabitants. It contains about 200 variables, mainly electoral data for all Reichstag elections between 1920 and 1933 (with the unfortunate exception of the two 1932 elections) and some valuable social, economic, and sociocultural information on the community level.[24]

Both data sets can be used for analytical purposes only if one adjusts the units for boundary changes, which occurred in Weimar Germany with considerable frequency. Since these boundary changes did not follow a random pattern but took place mainly in the more urbanized and economically active regions of the nation, serious distortions result if one does not neutralize their effect when creating county or community units that are stable over time. This restriction is often overlooked or treated in a rather cavalier fashion in the existing literature on the Nazi vote.[25] But without such adjustments, it is inadvisable to combine census and election data from different years. After the necessary adjustments, the number of cases in the county data set shrank by over 25 percent, from about 1,200 to 865. Problems created by boundary changes are even more serious for community data files if one does not restrict the adjustment procedure to pairs of elections.[26]

Research Techniques: Most hypotheses on the Nazi electorate imply individual-level relations. This kind of information is not available for the Weimar period. The only data existing are aggregate data. As

---

major errors, in the course of a large research project on the NSDAP voters we had to reconstruct our own county data set from scratch. For this purpose we used the relevant volumes of *Statistik des Deutschen Reiches* (Berlin, 1920–34) plus a multitude of other printed sources, such as unemployment statistics, fiscal reports, and so forth. The county data set now contains about 700 variables, among them some 200 to 300 containing information on all Weimar Reichstag and presidential elections plus the referenda on the expropriation of the former ruling princes (*Fürstenenteignung*) and on the Young Plan concerning the payment of reparations. The rest of the variables are social, economic, and cultural indicators of the 1,200 counties of the Weimar Republic.

24. The community data set is distributed by the Zentralarchiv für empirische Sozialforschung, Bachemerstrasse 40, W-5000 Cologne 40, Germany.
25. Some examples are discussed in Jürgen Falter and Wolf D. Gruner, "Minor and Major Flaws of a Widely Used Data Set: The ICPSR 'German Weimar Republik Data 1919–1933' under Scrutiny," *Historical Social Research* 20 (1981): 4–26.
26. For the same reason, the ecological regression analysis reported in Table 4 is based on such pairs of elections. The community data set, which in its raw form contains about 6,000 communities (all communities with 2,000 inhabitants or more plus the county-based means for all communities with fewer than 2,000 inhabitants), is thus reduced to about 4,000 community units.

a result, we must rely on percentages of parties or social indicators that are available only on a county or community level. Using this information, we are able to specify, for example, that the NSDAP fared much better between 1930 and 1933 in Protestant than in Catholic counties, that there is a negative correlation between unemployment figures and the Nazi share of the vote, and that there is a strong association between the losses of the middle-class parties and the National Socialist vote gains. What we would like to know, however, is information such as the percentage of Catholics and non-Catholics voting NSDAP in 1930 and the share of unemployed blue-collar workers voting for Adolf Hitler between 1928 and 1933. The most common yet seldom applied statistical technique to infer individual-level data from aggregate data is ecological regression analysis.[27]

Our analysis, as far as the individual level is concerned, is based on this technique. Unfortunately, ecological regression analysis works only if the data meet some rather strong statistical assumptions. Some of these assumptions (the standard assumptions of regression analysis such as linearity) can be tested by means of aggregate data. Other assumptions, including those that permit inference from aggregate to individual-level relations, cannot be tested by aggregate data alone or can be tested only under very special circumstances. The most important of these special assumptions of ecological regression analysis is that the slope of the regression line of each pair of variables under consideration is the same between the individual units as it is between the aggregate units; that is, no systematic contextual effects are permitted. Only random variation around the regression line is acceptable. From empirical evidence, we know that the assumption of noncontextuality is unrealistic in many instances. Therefore, it seemed reasonable to control our regression equations for potentially disturbing factors such as confession or urbanization. We thus might be able to neutralize, at least in part, unwelcome nonlinearities. Our findings are based on such an extension of the classic ecological regression technique. Furthermore, we weighted each county unit by its number of eligible voters in order to control for extreme variations in population. Finally, we applied a proportional fitting procedure to any negative estimators that arose since negative percentages do not exist in reality.[28] There is, however, no

---

27. See Jan-Bernd Lohmöller and Jürgen Falter, "Some Further Aspects of Ecological Regression Analysis," *Quality and Quantity* 20 (1986): 109–25.
28. Although the transition probabilities for the elections between 1920 and 1928 were calcu-

guarantee of the total elimination of bias from our findings. Our statistical approach is rational in that it is based on an explicitly statistical model and not simply on hindsight or on the straightforward inference from simple bivariate ecological correlations or aggregate-level regressions to individual-level relations. This differentiates it from much of the existing research on the Nazi electorate.[29]

> lated on the basis of our Weimar Community Data Set without the use of control variables, the 1928 to 1933 transition probabilities, as well as the voting propensities of the two confessions and the different social strata, were calculated on the basis of the 865 county units of our Weimar Republic County Data Set, using urbanization and religious denominations as control variables in order to neutralize possible contextual effects. For details, see Jan-Bernd Lohmöller et al., "Unemployment and the Rise of National Socialism: Contradicting Results from Different Regional Aggregations," in Peter Nijkamp, ed., *Measuring the Unmeasurable* (Boston, 1985), 357–70. Negative estimators or values above 100 were squeezed into the 0–100 percent interval by an iterative proportional fitting procedure.
>
> 29. For those who feel uncomfortable with this methodology, some aggregate correlations and regression coefficients are reported in Jürgen Falter, "The National Socialist Mobilization of New Voters," in Thomas Childers, ed., *The Formation of the Nazi Constituency, 1919–1933* (London, 1986), 202–31; idem, "Der Aufstieg der NSDAP in Franken bei den Reichstagswahlen 1924–1933," *German Studies Review* 9 (1986): 293–318; and, most recently, idem, *Hitlers Wähler* (Munich, 1991).

16

The Formation and Dissolution of a German National Electorate from Kaiserreich to Third Reich

RICHARD BESSEL

"Electoral politics is rarely a force of national integration."[1]

THE PROBLEM

The collapse of the Weimar Republic presents some of the most disconcerting problems facing not only historians of modern Germany but anyone concerned about and committed to the health and viability of political democracy. How are we to explain the willingness of millions of Germans in free elections to cast their votes for a political party advocating the destruction of democracy and racialist and aggressive values that must be utterly reprehensible to any thinking human being? It is not adequate to dismiss the problem by claiming simply that these millions of people somehow were hoodwinked, tricked into voting for Hitler against their own true interests.[2] For those of us accustomed to put our faith in democracy and the rightness of government by popular consent, the electoral success of the Nazi movement must be profoundly disturbing.

The problem is made more disturbing by the fact that the German Empire, as Stanley Suval demonstrated so well, saw the formation of

---

This is a revised version of a paper prepared for the German History Society Conference on "Elections, Mass Politics and Social Change in Germany, 1890–1939" in Toronto, 20–2 April 1990. It was, and remains, very much a discussion paper – an attempt to delineate a problem rather than to insist stridently upon particular theses – and I hope it will be read as such. I wish to thank participants in the conference for their helpful comments. I also want especially to thank Larry Eugene Jones, whose careful reading of my draft and thoughtful suggestions for revision have helped me clarify many points.

1. Stanley Suval, *Electoral Politics in Wilhelmine Germany* (Chapel Hill, N.C., and London, 1985), 58.
2. For an attempt to develop this argument, see Richard Bessel, "The Rise of the NSDAP and the Myth of Nazi Propaganda," *Wiener Library Bulletin,* vol. 33, nos. 51–2 (1980): 20–9. For a thoughtful critique of my article, see Ian Kershaw, "Ideology, Propaganda, and Rise of the Nazi Party," in Peter D. Stachura, ed., *The Nazi Machtergreifung* (London, 1983), esp. 170–8.

a viable electoral system. Thus, historians are faced with a fundamental and fascinating paradox: namely, that although the German electorate took shape within a political system that lent it very little power, it dissolved once it could vote for a real parliament; or, as Stanley Suval has put it, "the most positive citizenship roles were fulfilled in an authoritarian state and diminished in a democratic one."[3] Once they actually were able to vote to form governments, German electors advanced into a morass of destructive interest-group politics in which the general good was disregarded, responsible leadership punished, and demagogy rewarded at the ballot box. This abandonment of responsibility and disregard of an overarching national – as opposed to sectional – interest reflected the dissolution of the German national electorate and, in particular, of the bourgeois middle. In the process the main prop of a viable representative democracy was destroyed, thus creating an essential precondition for the rise of the Nazi movement and subsequent erection of the Third Reich. Once voting actually could change things, it was abolished as a meaningful exercise – first de facto by the voters themselves, and then de jure by Germany's Nazi masters.

Before examining the paradox presented by the collapse of electoral politics in Weimar Germany, we should be clear about what is and is not meant by a "German national electorate." It is meant neither to suggest an electorate united in its concept of the nation and its political relationship to the state, nor to imply that at some point around the turn of the century Germans could rally round the ballot box in a way no longer possible after 1918. The electorate in Germany, both before and after the First World War, was characterized by deep cleavages – of religion, class, regional allegiance, an urban–rural divide, wealth, language, and nationality. The only major new cleavage introduced in the Weimar period was sex, and, although women were granted the right to vote, no one yet has ascribed the collapse of the Weimar political system to the extension of the franchise to women. By national electorate is meant an electorate that, in increasing numbers, was prepared to accept the value and legitimacy of voting and, on the whole, to vote in a manner constructive to the existing political system. That is to say, even where people voted for opposition parties, their voting was an affirmation of the national political system – not necessarily as something desirable but never-

---

3. Suval, *Electoral Politics*, 257.

theless as something within which one functioned as a member of the polity.

Such tacit affirmation of the political system during the Wilhelmine period dissolved during the Weimar Republic. Germans still went to the polls – during the early 1930s, a greater proportion went to the polls than in most democracies before or since – but for most, voting no longer represented an affirmation of the national political system. Instead, voting increasingly reflected a widespread wish for the destruction of that system. During the first third of the twentieth century German voters finally were given responsibility for electing governments, and thereupon the national electorate disintegrated. The problem, as outlined by Suval, did not arise from an alleged depoliticization under the Kaiser or an alleged authoritarian inheritance that left German voters unsuited for real democracy; it lay in the failure of a mature electorate to apply that maturity constructively when they had the chance after 1918. This essay is a speculative attempt to explore why.

CONTINUITY AND CHANGE

It has been customary to stress the continuities in the German party system that stretched over the 1918 divide. In his 1932 study of the political parties of the Weimar Republic, Sigmund Neumann observed that "the outward picture of the parties altered practically not at all between the pre-war and post-war periods," and Karl Dietrich Bracher has spoken of the "astonishing degree of continuity which bound it [the Weimar party system] with the pre-republican constellation."[4] In a similar vein, Heino Kaack, in his handbook on the history and structure of the German party system, speaks of the "nearly unchanged party system in the Weimar Republic,"[5] and Gerhard A. Ritter opens his essay on the German party system immediately after the war by stating that "the overall shape of the German party system was relatively little changed with the transition from monarchy to republic and remained essentially stable until the rise of the National Socialist German Workers Party [*National-*

---

4. Sigmund Neumann, *Die Parteien der Weimarer Republik* (Stuttgart, 1973). This was first published in Berlin in 1932 under the title *Die politischen Parteien in Deutschland*. The quote from Neumann comes from page 27 of the 1973 edition; the quote from Bracher comes from his introduction to the 1973 volume, 11.
5. Heino Kaack, *Geschichte und Struktur des deutschen Parteiensystems* (Opladen, 1971), 62.

sozialistische Deutsche Arbeiterpartei, or NSDAP] into a mass party at the end of the 1920s."[6] Even Suval, who underlined the discontinuities after 1918, claimed that the Wilhelmine electoral system "remained recognizably alive until 1930" and that "only the victory of National Socialism . . . meant the end of the Wilhelmine electoral system."[7]

Certainly there seems a solid basis for such generalizations. Voting patterns among clearly defined social and religious groups appear to have differed little before and after the upheaval of 1918. The only unmistakable change stemmed from the fact that there were far fewer Danes and Poles in Weimar Germany and that Alsace and Lorraine had been lost to France, a factor that accounted for the decline in the importance of minority parties, which altogether had received about 5 percent of the vote in 1912. Although most of the names that graced German ballot papers during the Weimar period were new (with the exceptions of the Social Democrats and the Center), most of the parties that contested the elections in 1919 and 1920 were successors to the parties that had taken part in the elections of 1907 and 1912. Furthermore, if we exclude the elections for the National Assembly in January 1919, which took place in rather exceptional circumstances immediately after the November Revolution when the left was riding high, the aggregate support for the various parties in the early 1920s appears not to have differed radically from the support for their prewar predecessors. In 1912 the Conservative Party and the Reich Party together received 12.2 percent of the vote nationally, the National Liberals 13.6 percent, the left-liberal Progressive People's Party 12.3 percent, the Center 16.8 percent, and the Social Democratic Party 34.8 percent; in 1920 the German National People's Party (*Deutschnationale Volkspartei* or DNVP) received 15.1 percent, the German People's Party (*Deutsche Volkspartei* or DVP) 13.9 percent, the German Democratic Party (*Deutsche Demokratische Partei* or DDP) 8.3 percent, the Center and the Bavarian People's Party (*Bayerische Volkspartei* or BVP) together 17.8 percent, and the Social Democratic Party (*Sozialdemokratische Partei Deutschlands* or

6. This article has been printed, with slight modifications, a number of times. See Gerhard A. Ritter, "Kontinuität und Umformierung von Parteiensystem und Wahlergebnissen in Deutschland 1918 bis 1920," in Otto Büsch, Monika Wölk, and Wolfgang Wölk, eds., *Wählerbewegung in der deutschen Geschichte. Analysen und Berichte zu den Reichstagswahlen 1871–1933* (Berlin, 1978), 362.
7. Suval, *Electoral Politics,* 250.

SPD) and the Independent Social Democratic Party (*Unabhängige Sozialdemokratische Partei Deutschlands* or USPD) together 39.6 percent.[8] The voting patterns that developed between 1871 and 1912, as the proportion of the electorate going to the polls rose from 51.0 to 84.9 percent, did not alter fundamentally until the NSDAP became a mass party. Despite war, defeat, and revolution, voter identification with particular parties or political groupings appears to have remained quite strong, as has been the case in most countries. Indeed, after the upheavals of war, revolution, and demobilization, the attractions of maintaining a political allegiance may have been enhanced, particularly for people who felt resentful about and threatened by the unnerving changes foisted upon them.

Nevertheless, it is obvious that profound changes had occurred in the German electorate by the early 1930s. The rapid growth of the NSDAP from a fringe party on the racialist right to a mass movement capable of attracting more votes that any party had done before and from almost all sections of German society, was a development that is unique in the history of electoral politics in developed countries. Neither before nor since has a new political party whose leaders came from outside the circles of established elites managed to attract millions of voters from its established rivals, break down long-established patterns of party identification among voters, and become the most popular party in a major industrial country within the space of a few years. The question is where to locate the origins of the shift from the relative stability established during the Empire and apparently carried over the 1918 divide, on the one hand, and the electoral earthquake of the Nazis' success in the early 1930s, on the other. Although the initial temptation has been to focus upon the Nazis' electoral success after 1928, the most convincing recent studies have stressed the earlier origins of the collapse of the democratic party system. In particular, Thomas Childers and Larry Eugene Jones have demonstrated how the rise of the Nazi movement was more the consequence than the cause of the collapse of the bourgeois middle and have pointed to the problems created during the inflation – problems that poisoned German politics and prepared the ground for

---

8. See the tables in Gerhard A. Ritter (with Merith Niehuss), *Wahlgeschichtliches Arbeitsbuch. Materialien zur Statistik des Kaiserreichs 1871–1918* (Munich, 1980), 42; Jürgen Falter, Thomas Lindenberger, and Siegfried Schumann, *Wahlen und Abstimmungen in der Weimarer Republik. Materialien zum Wahlverhalten 1918–1933* (Munich, 1986), 68.

the Nazis' success.[9] During the relatively quiet years of the mid-1920s, the growth of support for single-issue, special-interest parties and the continuing difficulties of the established bourgeois parties in maintaining their support suggested that something was already rotten in the state of the German national electorate. The crises of the early Weimar years and, in particular, the bitter conflicts and divisions that arose out of the inflation led to what Childers has described as a "fundamental breakdown of voter identification with the established parties of both the bourgeois center and right."[10] This fundamental breakdown formed an essential precondition for the electoral victories of the NSDAP.

There are four main areas in which to search for reasons why this breakdown occurred, all of which revolve around the fact that although the Weimar party system constituted itself quite quickly after 1918 along the lines of Wilhelmine parties, it did so in radically different circumstances. The first such area, which has been most frequently discussed, is the economic sphere. The relative stability and increasing prosperity of the Empire were replaced by profound economic insecurity and inflation in a war-impoverished country, where bitter distributional struggles eventually tore the electorate apart – themes that will be examined at various points later.

The second area in which to search for reasons for the breakdown of German electoral politics is one that has attracted rather less attention: the altered relationship of the various parties toward government and state after the 1918 revolution. Almost overnight, the "enemies of the Reich" – most notably the Social Democrats – became pillars of government and supporters of the new political system. At the same time, the former supporters of the old authoritarian Imperial state – most notably the conservatives, but also in a less well-defined sense the National Liberals – became enemies of the Republic. For the Social Democrats the transition was relatively easy, even if many still felt more comfortable in the role of opposition.

9. Thomas Childers, "Inflation, Stabilization and Political Realignment in Germany 1919–1928," in Gerald D. Feldman, Carl-Ludwig Holtfrerich, Gerhard A. Ritter, and Peter-Christian Witt, eds., *Die deutsche Inflation. Eine Zwischenbilanz* (Berlin and New York, 1982), 409–31; Thomas Childers, *The Nazi Voter. The Social Foundations of Fascism in Germany, 1919–1933* (Chapel Hill, N.C., and London, 1983); Larry Eugene Jones, "Inflation, Revaluation and the Crisis of Middle-Class Politics. A Study of the Dissolution of the German Party System 1923–28," *Central European History* 12 (1979): 143–69; Larry Eugene Jones, *German Liberalism and the Dissolution of the Weimar Party System, 1918–1933* (Chapel Hill, N.C., and London, 1988).
10. Childers, "Inflation and Political Realignment," 430.

With the growth of electoral support for the SPD in the Empire and the rise of the socialist trade union movement, it was only natural for Social Democrats to look forward to the day when they would play a constructive role in government. Then with the changes that came about during the war – in particular the negotiations that led to the Auxiliary Service Law of 1916 and its subsequent operation – the SPD was well on its way toward accepting the transition from enemy of the Reich to supporter of the Republic. For the conservative right and the bourgeois liberal "middle," things were more difficult. These elite groups, which had regarded themselves as the natural pillars of the political order, found themselves suddenly cast out into the cold. With the collapse of a political system that had underpinned their privileged position, the conservatives in particular suddenly became outsiders, bitterly resentful of and openly hostile to the new order. The right-wing liberals were caught in the middle, and their dilemma was neatly encapsulated in the ambivalent manner with which Gustav Stresemann and his DVP colleagues greeted the new republican order during its first two years.[11] Of course, neither conservatives nor liberals had been without their doubts about the way things had been moving under the Empire,[12] but the new constitutional and political constellation of Weimar Germany left them in a particularly unfamiliar and uncomfortable position – something made all the more traumatic by the exceptional nature of the elections of January 1919, which saw an extraordinary if short-lived shift of the German electorate to the left. As a result, they lost their bearings in the new Republic and never fully found them again.

The problems of adapting to the new political system and adjusting to a fundamentally different relationship within that system no doubt were compounded greatly by the crisis-ridden nature of politics in Weimar Germany. The pressures created by the enormous economic and social costs of defeat in the First World War, the hostility with which a large proportion of the German population greeted the advent of the new democratic political system, and the economically divisive and socially corrosive effects of the inflation left little room for an easy adaptation to the new relationships between parties and state. The successive and overlapping crises that ushered

---

11. See Jones, *German Liberalism*, 15–66.
12. On the "siege mentality" of the Conservatives during the final years before the war, see James N. Retallack, *Notables of the Right. The Conservative Party and Political Mobilization in Germany, 1876–1918* (Boston and London, 1988), esp. 179–92.

in the Weimar Republic intensified the pressures and divisions within and between parties as their supporters became increasingly desperate and intolerant of interests other than their own. It was a political context in which old elites would have had the greatest difficulty finding a constructive role in the new political system even had they possessed the best will in the world – something of which few people would accuse the likes of Alfred Hugenberg, the DNVP national party chairman from 1928 to 1933.

A third area that affected the breakdown of the bourgeois electorate was the broadening of the franchise brought about by the new constitutional order of 1918 and 1919. The greatest change, at least in the size of the electorate, occurred in 1919 when women – the majority of the German adult population – were given the vote. At a stroke the size of the electorate roughly doubled, through the addition of a group whose interests often differed from those of men.[13] At the same time, the lowering of the voting age from twenty-five to twenty years gave the franchise to millions of Germans whose experience of the Empire had been as children and who had come of age during the war. Whereas in 1912 only men born before 1888 could vote, in 1920 all adults born before the turn of the century could cast their ballots. The inclusion of women, combined with the reduction in the voting age, increased the size of the electorate from roughly 14.4 million voters (22.2 percent of the total population) in 1912 to 35.9 million (60.7 percent of the population) in 1920.[14] In 1919 almost one-quarter of the male voters had never voted before the war, and by 1930 this figure had risen to slightly more than one-half.[15] The majority of voters in Weimar Germany had not voted under the Kaiserreich, and by the beginning of the 1930s the voters who had been eligible to vote in 1912 comprised only about one-quarter of the electorate. It seems hardly coincidental that the point at which the Wilhelmine electoral system finally broke down, with the rise of the NSDAP in 1930, was also the point at which more than one-half of the electorate was comprised of voters who had come of age not during the Empire but during the war or in the Weimar period. It

13. For example, during the Weimar period, questions of fertility control proved a remarkably effective means of attracting women to Social Democratic and Communist political meetings. See Cornelie Usborne, *The Politics of the Body in Weimar Germany: Reproductive Rights and Duties* (London, 1992), 156–66.
14. Figures taken from Ritter and Niehuss, *Wahlgeschichtliches Arbeitsbuch*, 42; Falter et al., *Wahlen und Abstimmungen,* 41.
15. See Monika Neugebauer-Wölk, *Wählergenerationen in Preussen zwischen Kaiserreich und Republik. Versuch zu einem Kontinuitätsproblem des protestantischen Preu en in seinen Kernprovinzen* (Berlin, 1987), 111.

would appear, therefore, that the voters who rejected the Weimar Republic were in large measure the voters who had been educated and politicized in the Weimar Republic. The generation shaped by democracy dug the grave of democracy.

Fourth, and perhaps even more important, was the fact that the electoral system itself was changed fundamentally. Whereas in Imperial Germany Reichstag deputies were elected when they received a majority in a constituency – if not in the first election, then in a runoff usually held between ten and fourteen days later – and constituency boundaries fixed in 1867 and 1871 had remained unchanged, the Reichstag of the Weimar Republic was elected by a system of proportional representation. The effects of this change were enormous and varied. To begin with, German voters were voting for something very different under the Weimar Republic than they had done under the Kaiser: namely, party lists rather than individual candidates. On the one hand, this meant that under the Weimar system almost every vote counted, a very different situation from that which had prevailed, for example, in East Elbian constituencies dominated by the conservatives or in Catholic constituencies dominated by the Center and in which votes for other parties therefore previously had been wasted. On the other hand, however, it meant that votes, and voters, were further removed from those for whom they were voting. Deputies in Weimar Germany were elected essentially according to their place on party lists. Voters no longer really needed to calculate the possible direct effects of their vote, as they had done under the Imperial system, since their political preference would count regardless of the local balance of forces. Thus the Weimar system largely dissolved the links between a deputy and his constituency. Finally, it meant that in Weimar Germany, unlike in the Empire, voting more directly reflected political preferences. Since calculations about which party's candidate actually might be elected to represent a particular constituency no longer needed to be made, voters could vote their preference with little fear that their votes would not count. This makes comparisons between elections before and after 1918 more complex and means that apparently similar aggregate voting figures often mask considerable differences revealed in local and regional election results.[16]

16. This was true especially for the liberal parties, almost all of whose Reichstag deputies were elected in runoff elections toward the end of the Kaiserreich, and can be seen clearly from the detailed comparisons of local and regional voting patterns in Prussia for the 1912 and 1924 Reichstag elections, tabulated in Horst Nöcker, *Der preussische Reichstagswähler in Kaiserreich und Republik* (Berlin, 1987), 176–537.

The introduction of proportional representation also did away with the distortions caused by the failure to alter constituency boundaries during the Kaiserreich. Before the First World War, rural districts had been privileged increasingly at the expense of the rapidly growing industrial cities, where many more votes were needed in order to elect a single deputy.[17] The shifts in the German population during the Empire – the flight from the land, the east-to-west migration, the rapid urbanization – were not reflected in the pre-1919 electoral system. Although the Reichstag (unlike the Prussian Landtag) was elected on the basis of one man/one vote, it had become increasingly unrepresentative of the German electorate and gave an increasing advantage to the Center and the conservatives at the expense of the Social Democrats. These imbalances were canceled out at a stroke after the war.

The replacement of the Imperial system of elections in increasingly unequal constituencies by a system of proportional representation in the Weimar Republic led to something of an equalization of support for the parties around the country.[18] It also led to a corresponding erosion of support for parties in areas that they had dominated previously. For example, the conservatives, resurrected in the DNVP, suffered particularly heavy losses after the war precisely in those areas where they had been most dominant before 1914: in the Junker fiefdoms of East Prussia and Pomerania. Similarly, the Center suffered its sharpest declines in the Catholic strongholds of Bavaria. At the same time, the left was able to register sizable gains in rural eastern Germany, where progress had been largely blocked during the Kaiserreich.[19] Thus, rather small changes in the aggregate percentage voting results between 1912 and the 1920s could conceal considerable changes in voter preferences, with the result that the advent of political democracy and of a new voting system led to a temporary triumph for political pluralism.

This would appear at first sight to have helped to consolidate a

---

17. For example, whereas in 1871 there had been relatively little difference in the average numbers of electors in Reichstag election districts in East Prussia, Berlin, or the Ruhr, by 1912 things had changed markedly: By then the average number of electors in the *Regierungsbezirk* Königsberg was 20,000 (only slightly higher than in 1871), and the comparable figure was 52,440 for the *Regierungsbezirk* Münster, 87,660 for Hamburg, and 84,660 for Berlin (and the 1912 figure for the largely proletarian district of Berlin north-northwest was 219,782). Figures in Johannes Schauff, *Die deutschen Katholiken und die Zentrumspartei. Eine politisch-statistische Untersuchung der Reichstagswahlen seit 1871* (Cologne, 1928), 24–5.
18. See Neugebauer-Wölk, *Wählergenerationen,* 135–8, 158.
19. See Ritter, "Kontinuität und Umformung," 368–9, 383–8.

national electorate. After all, it strengthened the hand of central party organizations that determined the party lists; it made electoral campaigns less local and more national in their focus; and it helped to even out electoral results across the country, undercutting to some extent the grip of the conservatives in rural eastern Prussia and of the Center in rural Catholic areas. Yet although the German electorate may have become more "national" in many respects, it simultaneously became more alienated from integrative national politics. A main reason for this juxtaposition was that the assumption of responsibility for the shape of governments was accompanied by a shedding of responsibility for the direct effect of a vote. That is to say, after 1919 Germans voted for a parliament to which the Reich government was responsible, but the deputies for whom they voted were no longer directly responsible to the electors. Voting became an expression of concern, protest, interest, or anger rather than careful calculation as to who actually might be elected to represent a particular district. Whether or not candidates gained seats in the Reichstag had more to do with their position on party lists – a factor that left the bourgeois parties particularly vulnerable to pressure to allot safe places on the lists to interest-group spokesmen in return for financial support – than with their relation to the electorate of their districts. Two glimpses of political life in Weimar Germany may serve to illustrate this: first, the characteristic brutality with which Hugo Stinnes responded to pleas from Gustav Stresemann for support for the hard-pressed DVP in the summer of 1923, when the industrialist replied that his firm did not need additional advertising at the time;[20] and second, the shock and amazement with which Heinrich Brüning registered the hostile reception he received while touring eastern Germany in January 1931, thus revealing his ignorance of opinion in his own constituency (Breslau, where he had been greeted with a violent mass demonstration and that he had represented in the Reichstag since the mid-1920s).[21]

Of course, it was not simply the electoral system that eroded a sense of responsibility and increased alienation among German voters. Germany's predicament after the First World War reinforced

20. Jones, *German Liberalism*, 191.
21. Brüning's confession in his memoirs of ignorance about conditions in his own constituency is as amazing as it is revealing: "Although by this time I had represented an eastern election district for six years, I nevertheless had been unable to imagine how great was the difference between the East and the West with regard to political maturity." See Heinrich Brüning, *Memoiren 1918–1934* (Stuttgart, 1970), 242.

and rewarded the politics of irresponsibility, and this made the weaknesses inherent in the electoral system more damaging. The Weimar Republic was burdened with enormous economic handicaps, not the least of which were those left behind by the war.[22] The costs of the war were huge and cast a shadow over government finance throughout the Weimar period. These problems were not simply fiscal; they were also deeply political. In essence, the costs of the war and the postwar economic transition were met through inflation, through an evasion of fiscal responsibility. The massive public expenditure that the demobilization, economic restructuring, postwar wage settlements, and social programs required were met by continued and massive deficit spending. Certainly this course had its benefits, including a reduction of unemployment during the immediate postwar years, and one can ask whether postwar German governments had any real alternative. According to one estimate, gathering sufficient revenue to meet the costs of reparations, postwar social welfare programs, and the normal running of government would have involved the trebling of prewar tax levels relative to national income – at a time when living standards were considerably below those of 1913. Such a course, it was argued, could have been pursued only by "a strong government that had the entire population behind it and was thus in a position to demand great sacrifices."[23] However, such a government was precisely what was lacking after 1918. Weimar governments lacked the popular support and legitimacy needed to push through painful but economically necessary measures on the basis of democratic parliamentary politics.

What, then, was the function of electoral politics? Although constitutionally the German electorate had become responsible for shaping the government, psychologically and practically most German voters were in no mood and no position to exercise that responsibility. During the Empire, they had lacked responsibility but wanted it; during the Republic, they had gained responsibility but were incapable of exercising it. The stakes were too high, the alternatives too unpalatable. Brave attempts to engage in the politics of priorities and

---

22. For a fuller version of this argument, see Richard Bessel, "Why Did the Weimar Republic Collapse?", in Ian Kershaw, ed., *Weimar: Why Did German Democracy Fail?* (London, 1990), 123–8.
23. Heinz Haller, "Die Rolle der Staatsfinanzen für den Inflationsprozess," in Deutsche Bundesbank, ed., *Währung und Wirtschaft in Deutschland 1876–1975* (Frankfurt a.M., 1976), 140–1, quoted in Carl-Ludwig Holtfrerich, *The German Inflation 1914–1923. Causes and Effects in International Perspective* (Berlin and New York, 1986), 137.

responsibility were the exception rather than the rule and were hardly conspicuous by their success at the ballot box. It was far easier to retreat from exercising responsibility and to take flight into either special-interest pleading[24] or socialist or nationalist rhetoric that had little to do with the limited and painful choices that responsible Weimar politicians had to make. Electioneering was largely decoupled from the politics of government, priorities, and policymaking, but within a constitutional framework that had cemented the link between electoral politics and the shape of government. Democratic politics in Weimar Germany thus became profoundly irresponsible and dangerous; against the background of economic crisis, the German electorate was attracted not to the politics of priorities but, increasingly, to the politics of demagogy.

This line of argument suggests that in order to explain the dissolution of a democratic electorate in interwar Germany, it is necessary to focus not only on the final Weimar years or the nasty residue of the inflation and "stabilization" of 1923–4, but also on the transition of 1918–19 and the profound consequences of the First World War. The war left Germany much poorer than it had been before 1914. The problem, however, was not just that the German economy had suffered a body blow, but that few Germans fully appreciated how much poorer their country had become. Paradoxically, part of the difficulty may have stemmed from the apparent success of the demobilization, especially in making jobs available for the millions of ex-soldiers, despite the fears of calamity and ruin that had been rife in 1918 and 1919. During the Weimar period, Germans tended to measure their situation against (a largely mythical image of) conditions before the war, a process that essentially bracketed out the unavoidable negative effects of the war and the 1918–19 transition.[25] The failure to appreciate the true impact of the war reinforced politically dangerous illusions: namely, that it was possible to return to healthy prewar conditions and that the war had not fundamentally circumscribed the

---

24. A revealing example of this is the history of those political groupings representing creditors harmed by the inflation. See the recent study of Michael L. Hughes, *Paying for the German Inflation* (Chapel Hill, N.C., and London, 1988).
25. On this theme, see Richard Bessel, "The Great War in German Memory: The Soldiers of the First World War, Demobilization and Weimar Political Culture," *German History* 6 (1988): 20–34, esp. 28–34; and Richard Bessel, "Kriegserfahrungen und Kriegserinnerungen: Nachwirkungen des Ersten Weltkrieges auf das politische und soziale Leben der Weimarer Republik," in Marcel van der Linden, Herman de Lange, and Gottfried Mergner, eds., *Kriegsbegeisterung und mentale Kriegsvorbereitung. Interdisziplinäre Studien* (Berlin, 1991), 125–40.

possibilities for German power politics or economic development. The incessant bitter complaints about the injustices heaped upon a defeated Germany, allegedly undefeated on the battlefield but stabbed in the back at home, in effect served to reinforce the idea that things would be normal if only the external burdens, imposed by the Allies, could be lifted. Thus politics in Weimar Germany became hostage to irresponsible illusions. Politicians who attempted to speak a language of reason and to recognize the limits within which German policy had to be formulated – as Stresemann did during the latter half of 1923, when his government ended passive resistance in the Ruhr and opened the way to a stabilization of the currency – were attacked savagely, lost popular support, and found that the policies they promoted could be pursued only by means of emergency measures that effectively bypassed parliamentary government. Instead of signifying a triumph of democratic politics, the Weimar Republic provided a stage for the triumph of irresponsible politics, which was both cause and effect of the dissolution of the German national electorate.

EXPLANATIONS

Suval rightly observed that "electoral mobilization or the politicization that ensues from voting . . . cannot serve to articulate national goals; rather, they are based on asserting differences."[26] Voting behavior is not necessarily motivated by careful calculation about the national good, but more often involves the attempt to gain representation for sectional interests. As Suval pointed out, it was the cleavages between interests – what separated Germans rather than what united them – that drew voters to the polls. When millions of Germans finally abandoned sectional interest-group politics as a dead end during the final Weimar years, they did so not as the result of any sudden conversion to political responsibility. Instead they flocked to a movement that papered over sectional interests with demagogy about the mission of the German nation and the "people's community" (*Volksgemeinschaft*) and that seemed a suitable vehicle for pursuing sectional interests under the cover of a "fanatic" belief in a charismatic *Führer* who supposedly was above the mealy-mouthed, corrupt,

26. Suval, *Electoral Politics*, 58.

and blatantly unsuccessful interest-group representation that had characterized Weimar politics.[27]

The dissolution of a responsible national electorate paralleled the collapse of German liberalism. Although the decline of German liberalism during the Weimar period stemmed in large part from the particular difficulties facing the DDP and the DVP during the 1920s and the failure of their leaders to chart a course that could integrate the various strands of their support, it also reflected two longer-term underlying processes. The first was the prior fragmentation of what Suval described as the "old majority" "based on local elites and their interests."[28] This may be seen as the corollary to the formation of a national electorate. The advent of mass, national electoral politics toward the end of the nineteenth century spelled the end of the local dominance of liberal elites. They now had nowhere to turn. Greater democratization posed a fundamental threat to liberal political elites in a country with a fast-growing industrial proletariat and a fast-growing socialist movement. The defense and consolidation of an authoritarian state structure that remained insulated from the potentially dangerous will of the people likewise left old liberal elites out in the cold. With the advent of political democracy after 1918, liberal claims to represent a higher common good soon were dragged down into a mire of interest-group representation[29] that eventually destroyed liberal elite politics in Weimar Germany. Thus, the dissolution of the national electorate – the disintegration of a foundation for politics based upon an idea of the common or national good rather than upon sectional interest – could not rescue the political movements that the creation of a national electorate had undermined.

The second of these underlying processes was a decline in concern with individual as opposed to collective interests. One expression of this was the growth of the Social Democrats and, during the Weimar period, of the Communists (*Kommunistiche Partei Deutschlands* or KPD). Another was the growth of economic interest organizations, which had begun to organize and articulate their positions effectively

27. For a good example of the way in which interest groups looked to the Nazi movement to further sectional interests, see Frank Domurad, "The Politics of Corporatism: Hamburg Handicraft in the Late Weimar Republic, 1927–1933," in Richard Bessel and E. J. Feuchtwanger, eds., *Social Change and Political Development in Weimar Germany* (London, 1981), 175–206.
28. Suval, *Electoral Politics*, 120. See also James J. Sheehan, *German Liberalism in the Nineteenth Century* (London, 1982), 221–71.
29. For one revealing example of this, see Andreas Kunz, *Civil Servants and the Politics of Inflation in Germany 1914–1924* (Berlin and New York, 1986).

in a national political marketplace during the final decades of the Empire and really came into their own with the ramshackle corporatism that began to form within the framework of the Weimar Republic. During the Weimar period, there was little room for the politics of individual rights as opposed to the pursuit of collective interests. The individualistic but universalist political ideology of liberalism had been able to find a comfortable home only with the "old majority." It had not been able to thrive in the harsh climate of the new mass politics, either in the pseudoparliamentary system of the Empire or in the democratic system of the Weimar Republic. This was a particularly bitter irony in view of the fact that the Weimar Constitution had been framed not by Social Democrats but by liberals and in many respects was a ringing declaration of an individualistic and universalist political ideology.

Although the doctrine of natural rights never played as important a role in Germany as in France or the United States, one thing that Germans shared, whether they recognized it or not, was a stake in individual rights. Under the Empire the vast majority of voters, whether supporters of the Social Democrats or the Center, of the Polish Nationalists or the left liberals, had been effectively disenfranchised by the three-class voting systems of Prussia and (from 1896 until 1909) Saxony, and by the limited role of the Reichstag in the Imperial governing structure. Once individual political rights and parliamentary democracy had been anchored in the Weimar Constitution, however, the shared interest in establishing and extending individual rights dissolved. Once individual rights had been secured, politics became an arena increasingly reserved for struggles over collective interests. In this regard, of course, the Weimar Republic was hardly unique; the same may be said for just about any representative democracy in a developed industrial country. However, the extreme economic and social pressures facing Germany during the 1920s made these struggles profoundly damaging not merely for the interest groups involved but also for the political system as a whole. What Germans held in common during the Weimar period – the often desperate need to defend sectional collective interests – also fundamentally divided them, and this had a deeply corrosive effect upon the national electorate. Before 1914 almost all German voters had been in the same boat, even if they might have had little influence on the captain and little voice about the course of the ship; after 1918 they divided into different crews of different vessels moving in different directions and often on a collision course with one another.

Another way to approach the breakdown of the German national electorate is to focus on the changed relationship between the German voter and the German state. The fact that in the Kaiserreich election results did not determine directly the composition of the government made it easier to maintain that the state existed separately from and above the various sectional interests. Of course, this was an ideal type, and of course, the state in Imperial Germany could be extremely partisan. Nevertheless, the fact that the Imperial German government was not constitutionally the expression of sectional interests, as expressed through the ballot box and represented in parliament, meant that in a sense the voters were insulated from the effects of the interest-group politics they promoted. This, in turn, reinforced the notion that the state and government existed apart from the cleavages that elections reflected. From a purely theoretical perspective, therefore, there existed in the Kaiserreich a "Germany" other than the one for which people voted. After 1918 this was no longer the case. A democratic state that was, constitutionally, the representative of interests expressed at the ballot box could be seen much less easily as an expression of some unnamed and ill-defined national interest that transcended the cleavages of German society reflected in grubby everyday politics. When the democratic state, penetrated by sectional interests, failed to meet Germans' increasingly desperate demands for economic security and political stability, the call for a dictatorial state that would transcend sectional interests and the cleavages of German society became irresistible.

In his study of the Center Party in Württemberg, David Blackbourn has stressed the development of modern political mobilization and the importance of local grievances and aspirations in shaping national politics in Wilhelmine Germany: "If there was a growing sense of national politics at the local level, then in an important sense national politics became at the same time parish-pump politics writ large."[30] This was true, but only in a limited sense. Perhaps parish-pump politics came to determine the themes and tenor of political debate and electioneering at a national level, but under the Imperial constitution the new mass politics could not directly affect the com-

---

30. David Blackbourn, *Class, Religion and Local Politics in Wilhelmine Germany. The Centre Party in Württemberg before 1914* (New Haven, Conn., and London, 1980), 18.

position of government or the conduct of the state. This is a key to understanding the difference between German politics before and after 1918. For all the understandable concern to find the roots of the political disasters of the 1930s in the peculiarities of the Empire, the crucial differences must not be overlooked. Introducing his essay on the politics of demagogy in Imperial Germany, Blackbourn notes that "it is the potentially explosive interplay between new right and old, between populists and patricians, that provides an important part to the background of German politics both on the eve of the First World War and on the eve of the Nazi seizure of power."[31] The key word here is "potentially." As Blackbourn observes, the peculiar juxtaposition within the Imperial political system of universal male suffrage with a lack of parliamentary government or ministerial responsibility "encouraged political leaders to promise anything" and "also made it more difficult to redeem the promises."[32] Certainly the demagogic politics that flourished during the quarter century before the outbreak of the First World War and that was a consequence of the increasing participation of the German people in German politics made it more difficult for the political elites to manage the political stage during the Wilhelmine period. Yet deep down, people recognized that the promises could not be redeemed within the Wilhelmine constitutional framework. The crucial difference after 1918 was not that democracy, real parliamentary government, and ministerial responsibility made politicians less prone "to promise anything" or German electors less insistent that they should. The crucial difference was that people now expected the promises to be redeemed – but in a context defined by economic and political constraints that effectively made the redemption of these promises impossible. This is what turned the potential to which Blackbourn alludes – describing a phenomenon in Imperial Germany that may have been unpleasant and disturbing but that remained relatively harmless – into a reality that helped destroy German democracy.

For this reason, it may be misleading to lump together, as Blackbourn has done, "the background of German politics both on the eve of the First World War and on the eve of the Nazi seizure of power." This emphasizes continuity where discontinuity is more significant. The demagogic language of politics may have been the same, and the

---

31. See also David Blackbourn, "The Politics of Demagogy in Imperial Germany," in David Blackbourn, *Populists and Patricians. Essays in Modern German History* (London, 1986), 217.
32. Blackbourn, "The Politics of Demagogy," 234.

vicious political vocabulary of the Weimar Republic may have been learned in large measure during the Wilhelmine period. However, this only became truly dangerous once Germans actually could vote governments in and out of office, once the elites no longer were able to manage the show, once the politics of demagogy could become the politics of government. In this sense, it is with the Weimar Republic rather than with the Kaiserreich that Blackbourn's description of German politics as the politics of demagogy and "parish-pump politics writ large" is apposite. The politics of demagogy during the Empire remained a game; after 1918 it became deadly earnest, as the responsibility for government came to rest upon the irresponsibility of the demagogue. Before 1918, the demagogue neither could nor had to redeem his promises; in 1933 the demagogic promises could be and were redeemed. Against the economic and social pressures of the Weimar period, there was in the final analysis no political basis for anything but irresponsible demagogic politics; finally given responsibility for government, the German national electorate disintegrated.

Where does this leave us? The sad history of German electoral politics to 1933 suggests that a functioning national electorate perhaps can exist only if voting remains to some extent an illusory activity – an opportunity to express one's opinions in a fairly harmless way, that is, without fundamentally affecting important political decisions. Perhaps the success of Wilhelmine electoral politics, outlined so well by Suval, occurred not in spite of, but rather because of, the distance between the ballot box and government. Perhaps the failure of Weimar electoral politics was a result of the breaking down of barriers between voters and political decision making at a time when the political options were extremely painful and voters were unprepared to recognize the constraints within which policy had to be formulated. Indeed, the most successful electoral systems may be those within political frameworks that more or less ensure that elections are not going to lead to great change: in the United States, where the structure of government seems particularly impervious to change, where the differences between Republican and Democrat are often difficult to discern, and where only about one-half of the electorate bothers to vote in any event; in France, where a technocratic elite drawn from the *grandes ecoles* runs the ministries almost regardless of who wins elections; in Britain, where the election results in a majority of parliamentary constituencies are foregone conclusions; in the Federal Republic of Germany, where the Free Democratic Party (*Freie Demokratische Partei* or FDP) remains in government no matter who becomes chancellor and where the *Wende* of 1982 left largely untouched a rather broad consensus about foreign and economic policy. However, today's United States, France, United Kingdom, and Federal Republic of Germany are profoundly different from pre-1933 Germany in other respects as well. They face no economic crises of the awesome magnitude that afflicted Germany after 1918 and again after 1929; they have generated traditions that help make a democratic language of politics the one to which voters naturally turn; and they do not have to deal with the crippling social, political, and economic costs of a lost world war.[33] Pre-1933 Germany had none of these advantages, and its voters were cast adrift in a stormy sea, with little to serve as sail, compass, or rudder. The history of Germany during the first third of the twentieth century suggests that there may be some burdens that democracy simply cannot bear. This suggestion, no less than the suggestion that the success of democratic electoral politics may be inversely related to its impact upon the real politics of priorities and government, is extremely disturbing. But these are suggestions that we, while maintaining a firm commitment to peaceful democratic politics, should not be afraid to consider.

33. When the Federal Republic did have to pay the costs of a lost world war, it did so while its domestic and foreign political options were severely constrained by limited sovereignty and the Cold War and against the background of worldwide economic growth.

Index

Aachen, 109
Abendroth, Wolfgang, 142–3
Abortion, 230, 235; legislation, 153, 154, 157–8; National Socialist policy on, 237
Agrarian League, 32, 37, 38, 41, 76
Agrarians, 25, 28, 36–9
Albert, King of Saxony, 82, 88
Allen, William Sheridan, 307
Alsace-Lorraine: elections in, 23
Antifascist Young Guard, 276n
Anti-Jewish Congress: First, Second, 66
Anti-Revolution Bill of 1894–5, 82
Anti-Semitism, 4, 25, 28, 37–8, 50, 141, 304; electoral strategy, 46; and franchise reform, 79–80, 86, 90; political, 50; and Saxon franchise reform, 84; Saxony, 55, 56, 65, 66–7, 70–5, 79. *See also* German Reform Party; German Social Party
Antisocialism, 40–1, 42, 49–50, 82, 94, 141; Bavaria, 55; Prussia, 55; Saxony, 55, 66–70, 73–9
Arbeiter–Illustrierte–Zeitung, 164, 168
Arbeitsgemeinschaft der Katholischen deutschen Studentenverbände, see Coalition of Catholic German Student Associations
Army: as election issue, 32
Artisans: and politics, 290
Association of Independent Democrats, 366
Association for the Training of Women in Crafts and Specialized Skills, 184–5
Associations for the Achievement of Popular Elections, 108
Augsburg, 110
Austria, 224; and Weimar constitution, 259
Auxiliary Service Law of 1916, 405

Baden, 39, 98, 104, 109–10, 183
Baden, Max von, Prince, 10; becomes chancellor, 337
Ballot, secret, 137, 138
Barmen, 112
Barraclough, Geoffrey, 331, 341
Barth, Theodor, 35
Baum, Marie, 185
Bäumer, Gertrud, 220
Bavaria, 39; antisocialism, 55; citizenship requirements, 105; school attendance, 183; voter participation, 110
Bavarian People's Party, 372, 377, 378, 387, 390, 391, 402
Bayerische Volkspartei (BVP), *see* Bavarian People's Party
Bayreuth, 106
Beard, Charles, 262
Bebel, August, 53, 66–7, 152, 256
Benjamin, Walter, 172
Berlin: city council, 108; National Socialist club, 319; voter participation, 110; and Weimar constitution, 259
Berliner Börsen–Zeitung, 268, 278–9
Bernays, Marie, 190
Bernstein, Eduard, 8; *Evolutionary Socialism,* 254–5, 256
Bethmann Hollweg, Theobald von, 100, 332, 333, 342
Bettman, C. A., Company, 189n
Beyes, Fritz, 267–8, 274–5
Birnbaum, 29
Birthrate: decline of, 234
Bismarck, Herbert von, 81
Bismarck, Otto von, 3, 67, 94, 144, 259; and constitution, 341, 342; and German unification, 132, 134, 136, 137; and Kar-

419

tell, 23, 95n; and *Kreistage* franchise, 114, 115; and National Liberal Party, 94; and national politics, 141; public opinion, use of, 138–9; and universal franchise, 5, 25, 85–6, 122–3, 130–1, 132–8, 140
Bismarck Youth of the German National People's Party, 354
Black Reichswehr, 341
Blackbourn, David, 139, 142, 167
Blumenthal, Werner von, 81
Brandts, Franz, 189
Braubach, Max, 142–3
Breslau, 29, 112, 409
Broch, Hermann, 307
Brooks, Peter, 166
Brüning, Heinrich, 409
Brunt, René, 261, 262
Bülow, Bernhard von, 40–1, 115, 116
Bund der Landwirte (BdL), see Agrarian League
Bund Deutscher Frauenvereine (BDF), see Federation of German Women's Associations
Bündische Jugend, see Youth: organizations
Bürgerliches Gesetzbuch (BGB), see Civil Code (1900)
Burghers, see Middle class
Burnham, Walter Dean: theory of political confessionalism, 372, 374, 375
Business and Trade Association of 1840, 289, 290
Business Party, 290

Canning, Kathleen, 158, 159
Capitalism, 225
Caprivi, Leo von, 69, 76
Catholic Action (1928), 155
Catholic Young Men's Association of Germany, 350
Catholics: discrimination against, 25, 55; in politics, 98; party preference, 111; social milieu, 373. *See also* Center Party, *Kulturkampf*
Center Party, 4, 10, 28, 44, 45, 97, 144, 290, 358, 372, 376, 377, 391, 402, 407, 408, 415; and agrarians, 38; in Baden, 98–9; characteristics of members, 111–12, 290; in Düsseldorf, 102; electoral strategy, 46–7; and fleet issue, 33, 35; and franchise issue, 39, 107–8; in local politics, 100, 103, 104, 108, 110; mobilization of women, 155, 161; nomination of candidates, 28; Reichstag elections (1898), 18; and Reichstag electoral system, 408; Reichstag majority coalition (1917), 333–5, 338; and reproductive politics, 155, 157–8; rise of influence, 115; and role of women, 234; Weimar coalition, 343; Weimar period, 378, 387; and WWI peace proposal, 332; and youth, 347–8, 350–1, 354, 355, 368. *See also* Weimar Coalition
Central Federation of Catholic Young Women's Associations, 204, 350–1
Charlottenburg, 110
Chemnitz, 53, 79; anti-Semitism in, 66; franchise laws, 80
Childers, Thomas, 123
Christian Democrats: and reproductive politics, 158
Christian textile union, 176n, 186n
Cities, growth of, 111
Citizenship, 104–7; and Weimar constitution, 261–3, 264
Civil Code (1900), 152, 223, 251, 252
Class, lower: and propaganda, 169
Class, social: consciousness, 176, 177–8, 187; formation of, 175; study of, 160
Clemenceau, Georges: and Treaty of Versailles, 339
Clubs, German, 309–11; role in German society, 320
Coalition of Catholic German Student Associations, 351
Cockburn, Cynthia, 158, 159
Cologne: textile industry, 191–2
Committee for the Distribution of Bourgeois Culture, 108
Communist Party, 267, 324, 377, 382, 413; and birth control, 406n; blue-collar membership, 384–6, 391; and Catholic electorate, 390; and fascism, 121; and feminist movement, 233; interwar period, 268–9; language and symbols, 269–70, 277–8, 285; Neukölln, 273–4; propaganda, 168–9; songs, 271, 282; and Social Democratic Party, 285, 388; Weimar period, 378; and working class, 269, 394
Communist Youth League of Germany, 267–8, 279
Conflict, sociopolitical, 373
Congress of Councils, 339
Conservative groups, 373, 376, 404, 405; in local politics, 112; and Reichstag elec-

toral system, 408; Wilhelmine period, 93–4. *See also* Conservative Party, Free Conservative Party
Conservative Party, German Conservative Party: and anti-Semitism, 70–3, 74, 75; anti-socialism, 40, 73–5, 81; Committee of Fifty, 64; and franchise reform, 51, 79, 80, 83, 84, 85, 89; and *Kreisordnung*, 114; and party reform, 80–1; Saxony, 56, 63–8, 70–3, 74, 75, 76, 77, 78–9; and Tivoli party congress (1892), 71–2, 81; Weimar period, 405; Wilhelmine period, 27, 29, 42, 47, 402
Conservative People's Party, 363–4, 365–6, 367
Council of Cities, 100
Criminal Code: Paragraph 218, 153, 154
Culture, popular: and deconstruction, 169–70; genre criticism, 164, 165; and women, 171

Dahrendorf, Ralf, 225, 247
Deconstruction, 169–70
Delbrück, Clemens von, 255–6
Delbrück, Hans, 89, 117
Delius, C. A., silk mill, 186
Demagogy, growth of, 416–17
Democracy, German, 247; failure of, 400–1; and localism, 256, 258
Depression, 235
Deutsche Demokratische Partei (DDP), *see* German Democratic Party
Deutsche Freischar (DF), *see* German Corps
Deutsche Freisinnige Partei, see German Radical Party
Deutsche Staatspartei (DStP), *see* German State Party
Deutsche Städtetag, see German Council of Cities
Deutsche Volkspartei (DVP), *see* German People's Party
Deutsche Wacht, 86
Deutsche Zentrumspartei, see Center Party
Deutsch-konservative Partei (DKP), *see* Conservative Party
Deutscher Herrenklub, see German Lords' Club
Deutscher Jugendbund, see German Youth League
Deutscher Mädchen-Wanderbund (DMWB), *see* German Girls' Hiking League

Deutscher Staatsbürgerinnen-Verband (DStV), *see* German Women Citizens' League
Deutschnationale Volkspartei (DNVP), *see* German National People's Party
Deutschnationaler Handlungsgehilfen-Verband (DHV), *see* German National Union of Commercial Employees
Deutschnationaler Jugendbund (DNJ), *see* German National Youth League
Deutschvölkischer Schutz-und Trutzbund, see German-Racist Protective and Resistance League
Diergardt foundation, Viersen, 195–6
Dillingen, 314–15
Dingeldey, Eduard, 366
Dönhoff, Carl, von, 1, 52, 62, 68, 69–70, 74, 76–7, 78, 79, 81, 82, 85
Dresden, 53, 79, 112; anti-Semitism in, 66–7; Conservative Party in, 63; franchise laws, 80; National Liberal Party in, 63
Dresdner Nachrichten, 66, 87
Dresdner Zeitung, 85
Dupeux, George, 127
Düsseldorf, 102, 182

Ebert, Friedrich: and reform program, 338; postwar aims, 339–40, 343
Ecological regression analysis, 379, 396–7
Education: adult, 264; gender differences, 184–6; gender differences, Third Reich, 239–40
Elections: methods of analysis, 17–22; Wilhelmine period, issues, 19, 25, 27, 29, 30–41; Wilhelmine period, participation, 25–6
Electoral blocs, 400–1; blue-collar, 384–7, 390, 393, 394; bourgeois-Protestant, 11, 376, 377, 380–2, 383, 384, 391, 393; Catholic, 377–8, 380, 381, 382–3, 387, 388, 390, 391; and religious denominations, 386–7, 394; socialist, 377–8, 380, 381, 382–3, 387, 390, 394; and socioeconomic factors, 386–7, 391–3, 374; Weimar period, 376; Wilhelmine period, 45–7
Electoral research, 119–24, 145–6; ecological, 128–9; geographical, 126–8; and historians, 123–4, 142–3, 145; methodology, 124–9; and modernization theory, 129, 145–6; and political history, 124, 145; statistics, 126

Electoral system, 407–9, 415; Weimar period, 12; Wilhelmine period, 42, 43–4
Eley, Geoff, 139, 142, 308
Elites, 4, 9; and political mobilization, 130–1; Saxony, and franchise laws, 52; and universal franchise, 123; Wilhelmine period, 49–50
Employment: Prussia, 53; Reich, 53; Saxony, 53
Erzberger, Matthais, 295; and reform and peace program, 333, 336
Eugenics, 236–7
Europe: prewar politics, 96; revolutions of 1830, 1848, 132
Evangelical churches: and birth control, 234–5
Evangelischer Reichsverband weiblicher Jugend, see Protestant National Federation of Female Youth
Evolutionary Socialism (Bernstein), 254–5

Falkenhayn, Erich von, 342
Fallada, Hans: *Little Man, What Now?*, 287
Falter, Jürgen W., 123, 124, 125, 129
February Club, 359, 364
Federation of German Women's Associations, 152, 208, 209
Feminist movement: generational aspects, 219–21; Weimar period, 204, 206–16, 232–4, 234. See also Women
Filmmaking: and women, 163, 170–71; German approach to, 167–8
Fischer, Fritz, 247
Fleet, German: as election issue, 30–1, 32–3, 35
Fortschrittliche Volkspartei, see Progressive People's Party, Progressives
France, 224
Franchise, 103–8; constitutional order of 1918, 1919, 406–7; reform (1919), 12; research on, 145–6; universal, 5, 39, 96, 97; universal, effects of, 130–1, 138, 139–40; universal, movement for, 131–8. See also Prussia: franchise; Saxony; Women: franchise
Free Conservative Party, Imperial Party, 33, 42, 114, 402
Free Democratic Party, 418
Free German Youth, 349, 353
Freideutsche Jugend, see Free German Youth
Freikorps, 303, 341
Freischar junger Nation (FjN), *see* Young Nation Corps

Freisinnige Volkspartei, see Radical People's Party
Friesen, Richard von, 55
Friesen-Rötha, Heinrich von, 63–4, 67, 71, 72, 73, 74, 75–6
Fritsch, Theodor, 66
"Front 1929," 359, 364
Fuhr, Werner, 270
Fürth, 105, 110

Geiger, Theodor, 293
Gender: and division of labor, 180–3, 193–4; history and theory of, 159–60; and language, 160–4; and workplace morality, 189–91. *See also* Textile industry: discipline and gender
Generational conflict: Weimar period, 348–9, 355
German Corps, 210, 216, 218
German Council of Cities, 260
German Democratic Party, 11, 290, 358, 376, 402, 413; and youth, 347–8, 351–2, 355, 358–9, 363–5. *See also* Weimar Coalition
German Democratic Republic: elections (1990), 1
German Girls' Hiking League, 207–8, 212
German Lords' Club, 356–7
German National People's Party, 11, 290, 294, 299, 352, 358, 361, 376, 377, 378, 382, 383, 387, 402, 408; and Catholic electorate, 390; and middle class, 292; Protestant membership, 387; retention of members, 380–1; and role of women, 234; supporters, social characteristics, 393; and youth, 353, 354, 359, 362, 367–8
German National Union of Commercial Employees, 353
German National Youth League, 352, 353, 354
German People's Party, 11, 290, 299, 358, 359, 402, 405, 409, 413; blue-collar membership, 386; and middle class, 292, 338; National Student Committee of, 353; and youth, 352–3, 361, 362–3, 365, 366–7
German-Racist Protective and Resistance League, 303, 312–13
German Radical Party, 59, 61, 62. *See also* Left liberals
German Reform Party, 73, 75, 77–8, 78. *See also* Anti-Semites

Index

German Social Party, 73, 76. See also Anti-Semites
German Society of Nobles, 63
German State Party, 363–5, 366, 367
German Women Citizens' League, 208–9
German Workers' Party, 310–12. See also National Socialist German Workers' Party
German Youth League, 367–8
Germany: and Depression, 288; economic problems, 404, 405–6, 410; history of, and electoral research, 121–2; history of, historiography, 9–10, 139–40, 142, 149, 150–1, 247–8, 287–8, 331–2, 341; history of, and women, 149–52; modernization, 226; November Revolution, 291; Revolution of 1848, 132, 250; territorial issues, 259, 260–1; and Treaty of Versailles, 339; unification, 132, 134, 136, 137; Weimar period, 340–1, 343–5; Weimar period, constitution, 8, 258–64, 414; Wilhelmine and Weimar periods compared, 130–1. See also Citizenship: Weimar constitution
Gessler, Otto, 341
Gewerbe- und Handelsverein von 1840, see Business and Trade Association of 1840
Gierke, Otto von, 251–3
Glatzel, Frank, 353, 361, 364, 367
Gneist, Rudolf von, 113–14
Goebbels, Joseph, 316, 318, 325
Golke, Arthur, 281
Gothein, Georg, 335; and Spring 1918 offensive, 335–6
Government, local: in cities, 102; Wilhelmine period, 100–2, 255–6
Grossdeutscher Jugendbund (GDJ), see Youth League for a Greater Germany
Grossmann, Atina, 205

Hagelweide, Gert, 270
Hagen, 29
Hahn, Kurt, 334
Hamburg, 84, 106–7; National Socialism in, 317, 318–19
Handbook for Social Democratic Voters, 36
Hannover: elections, 23; franchise, 104
Hard-Labor Bill (1899), 82
Hardt, Josef, 361
Hartwig, Gustav, 67, 76
Haussmann, Conrad, 333; reform and peace program, 334–5, 336; and Spring 1918 offensive, 335–6

Heberle, Rudolf, 128, 129
Heffter, Heinrich, 247
Hertling, Georg von, 334; asked to resign, 336–7
Hess, Rudolf, 321
Hesse, 38, 104
Heuss, Theodor, 355–6
Himmler, Heinrich, 237, 315, 323
Hindenburg League – Youth Group of the German People's Party, 363, 366–7
Hindenburg, Paul von, 341; agrees to appeal for cease-fire, 337; military strategy, 342
Hintzmann, Ernst, 367–8
Historiography, German, see Germany: history of, historiography
Hitler, Adolf, 163, 225, 276, 279n; and local organizations, 313–14, 319, 320–1, 322; *Mein Kampf*, and club life, 309–10, 314, 320; *Mein Kampf*, and "Germanic democracy," 321, 325; *Mein Kampf*, third edition, 325; and National Socialist German Workers' Party, 310–12
Hitler Youth, 367
Hohenlohe-Schillingsfürst, Chlodwig zu, 36, 82
Honoratiorenpolitik, 28, 29, 66, 102, 103, 106, 108, 110, 111
House-Owners Association (Dresden), 67
Hugenburg, Alfred, 293, 359, 361, 368, 406

Imperial Party, see Free Conservative Party.
Imperialism, social, 30, 35
Independent Socialists, 334, 372, 377, 403
Individual rights: decline of concern for, 413–14
Industry: growth of, 175, 226; women in production, 158
Inflation, 342, 403–4, 405, 410
Ingolstadt, 316, 317
International Alliance of Women for Suffrage and Equal Citizenship (1929), 209
Inter-University Consortium for Political and Social Research (ICPSR) Weimar Election File, 394

Jews: discrimination against, see Anti-Semitism
Jugendgruppen der Deutschen Volkspartei, see Youth Cadre of the German People's Party
Jung, Edgar, 357, 367, 368

Jung Spartakusbund (JS), *see* Young Spartacus League, 267
Jungakademiker Klub, *see* Young Academic Club
Jungdeutsche Schwesternschaft, *see* Young German Sisterhood
Jungdeutscher Bund, *see* Young German League
Jungdeutscher Orden, *see* Young German Order
Junge Garde, 278
Jungnationaler Bund (JNB), *see* Young National League
Jungzentrumsvereine, *see* Young Center Clubs

Kaase, Max, 129
Kapp Putsch, 341
Karl Liebknecht House, 269
Kartell, 23, 25, 36, 42–4, 94, 95*n*, 139
Kartell, Saxon, 63, 67, 72; and franchise reform, 83–4
Katholischer Jungmännerverband Deutschlands, *see* Catholic Young Men's Association of Germany
Kautsky, Karl Johann, 256
Kelly, Joan, 151
Ketteler Leagues, 350
Koch-Weser, Erich, 293
Kommunistische Partei Deutschlands (KPD), *see* Communist Party
Kommunistischer Jugendverband Deutschlands (KJVD), *see* Communist Youth League of Germany
Konservative Volkspartei (KVP), *see* Conservative People's Party
Koshar, Rudy, 256, 298, 308
Kracauer, Siegfried: "Die kleinen Ladenmädchen gehen ins Kino," 163, 172
Krebs, Albert, 317, 318–19
Kreise, 113–15
Kreisordnung (1872), 114
Kulmbach, 106
Kulturkampf, 22, 23, 41, 112, 139, 141, 144

Labor: history, and gender, 175–6, 198–9; history, historiography, 176–7
Labor code (1891), 189; paragraph, 137, 179
Lagarde, Paul de, 349
Lambach, Walther, 359
Land ownership, 252
Landesverein, Saxon Conservative, 64, 65, 71, 72, 73, 81. *See also* Conservative Party, in Saxony

Landmann, Ludwig, 265
Landvolk protests, 292, 293
Langbehn, Julius, 349
Language: gender aspects, and politics, 160–4
Lassalle, Ferdinand, 134
Law for the Defense of the Republic (1922), 295–6
Lederer, Emil, 290
Left liberals, 27, 28, 32, 35, 44, 94, 98, 105, 141; and franchise reform, 88, 102–3, 107–8; and *Kreisordnung*, 114; and National Liberals, 98, 376; press, 37; Saxony, 56, 62, 65. *See also* Liberalism
Left, political, 3–4; electoral losses, 23; police treatment of, 279*n*. *See also* Liberalism
Leipzig, 53; anti-Semitism in, 66; Conservative Party in, 63; franchise laws, 80; National Liberal Party in, 63
Leipziger Tageblatt, 87, 88
Lemmer, Ernst, 358–9
Lepsius, M. Rainer, 125, 129; social–moral milieu concept, 373–5
Liberalism, 4, 56, 225; and Catholic vote, 111–12; decline, 93–4, 96, 97–9, 116, 413–14; and franchise, 114; in local government, 95, 96–7, 99–102, 107, 108, 110, 111, 113, 115–17; post-World War I, 340, 405; in Prussia, 97; youth groups, 359–60
Lichtenberg district (Berlin): epidemic, 268, 273, 275
Lidtke, Vernon, 271
Liebknecht, Karl, 109, 277
Liebknecht, Wilhelm, 53, 86
Lipset, Seymour Martin, 372, 374, 393
Lloyd George, David: and Treaty of Versailles, 339
Localism, 7, 248, 252–3, 254; decline, 265; and democracy, 256, 258; and National Socialism, 265–6. *See also* Nationalism: and localism
London Conference (1864), 135
Löwenthal, Fritz, 283
Lübeck, 25
Ludendorff, Erich, 332, 341; annexationist ambitions, 335; military strategy, 342; nervous breakdown, 336–7; 1918 offensive, 335–6; "stab in the back" account, 342–3
Luther, Hans, 353
Luxemburg, Rosa, 277

Mahraun, Artur, 360, 361–2
Maitland, F. W., 252
Majority Socialists, 10; and World War I peace proposal, 332, 334; Reichstag majority coalition (1917), 333, 334, 335, 338; and Weimar coalition, 343
Manteuffel, Otto von, 133
Masculinity: in political study, 159–60
Max, Prince, see Baden, Max von, Prince
McWhorter-Schade, Rosemarie, 203–4, 206, 213–14
Mecklenburg, 25
Mehnert, Paul, 64, 67, 72, 73, 76, 81, 83
Melodrama, 164–8
Men: and modernization, 228; role of, 228–9
Merkl, Peter, 307–8
Meseritz-Bomst, 29
Metzsch-Reichenbach, Georg von, 69, 73, 74, 75, 76; and franchise reform, 82, 84, 87, 89, 90
Michaelis, Georg: and Erzberger Peace Resolution, 333; forced out as chancellor, 333–4
Middle class, 344–5; fears of working class, 295–6; and German People's Party, 338; interest groups, 299–300, 301, 302, 310; *Landvolk* protests, 292; mobilization, 8–9, 301–2; politics of, 289–91, 292–4, 299–301; and National Socialists, 294, 303–4, 305–6, 327, 390–1, 394, 403; and Protestants, 373, 377; and public demonstrations, 296–7; and special interests, 404
Mill, John Stuart, 252
Miquel, Johannes von, 36, 104, 115
Modernization, 223, 224–5, 234; and birth rate, 234; characteristics, 225–6, 227; in Germany, 226; and women, 226–9, 230, 241, 243
Munich, 110; and National Socialism, 312
Music: and working class movement, 8, 270–1

Nachrichten für Stadt und Land, 296
Napoleon III, 134, 135
National Association of National Liberal Youth, 351
National Committee of University groups of the German People's Party, 353
National League of German Democratic Students, 352, 355
National League of German Democratic Youth Clubs, 352, 355

National League of German Windthorst Leagues, 350, 351
National League of Lutheran Young Men's Associations of Germany, 354
National League of State Party Youth, 367
National League of Youth Groups of the German National People's Party, 354
National Liberal Party, 351, 404; and Center Party, 41; anti-Semitic challenge to, 38; and fleet issue, 33, 36; and franchise reform, 39, 102–3, 104, 107–8; and *Kreisordnung*, 114–15; and left liberals, 98; movement, and politics, 156–7; population policies, 238, 242; and Reichstag majority coalition (1917), 333–5; repudiation of anti-Semitism, 75; and Saxon franchise reform, 83, 84, 85, 88, 89; Saxony, 56, 62–3, 65–6, 72, 74–5, 76, 78–9; Wilhelmine period, 27, 29, 32, 35, 42, 46, 47, 98, 105, 402; youth cadre, 352
National Socialist German Workers' Party, 11, 293, 396, 406; abortion policy, 237; and alcohol consumption, 317–18; and associational life, 9, 313–16, 319–20; and birth control, 235, 237; blue-collar support, 390, 393, 394; and compulsory year of service, 239–40, 243; early success of, 312–13; electoral success, 324–5, 381–2, 393, 403; and employment, 238–9, 242–3; eugenics policies, 236–7, 241–2; girls' associations, 213; historical treatment of, 287–8, 307–8; leaders, oratorical skill, 315–16; local clubs, and national organization, 321–3, 325–6; at local level, 314–24, 326–7; and localism, 265–6; membership, 314–15, 324, 327; and middle class, 294, 303–4, 305–6, 327, 377, 390, 394, 403; mobilization of voters, 382; and modernization, 225; and paramilitary groups, 313; population policies, 238, 239, 242; principles of, 237–8; propaganda, 168, 322, 325–6, 328, 377; Protestant support, 387, 390, 391; and Reichstag elections (1930), 324, 365; rise of, 288, 307, 377, 403; and traditional political culture, 308–9; and violence, 318, 326; and women, 155, 161, 205–6, 224, 226, 230–2, 235–6, 237, 242–3; youth organizations, 216, 368
Nationalism, 18, 31–2, 298, 299, 302, 304–5, 340, 369; and localism, 248–55, 265

Nationalliberale Partei (NLP), *see* National Liberal Party
Nationalsozialistische Deutsche Arbeiterpartei (NSDAP) *see* National Socialist German Workers' Party
Naturgeschichte des deutschen Volkes (Riehl), 250–1, 252–3
Naumann, Friedrich, 35, 97, 117
Navy League, 31–2
Nazi Party, *see* National Socialist German Workers' Party
Neukölln district (Berlin): "Bloody Mary" incident, 273; disease in, 268, 273, 274–5; living conditions, 272–3; protest march (1930), 267–8, 275–8, 280; protest march, and police, 280–1; protest march, and press, 278–81; unemployment, 273; "Zille House," 271–2
North German Confederation, 132, 137–8
Northwest German League of Artisans, 290
Noske, Gustav, 276–7
Nuffield Group studies, 125–6, 127
Nuremberg, 105, 110

Oldenburg, 8, 25, 30*n*; demonstration (1928), 291–2; economic conditions, 292; Hindenburg birthday celebration, 296; politics, 289–90, 292–3; Rathenau memorial service, 295, 297
Osterroth, Nikolaus, 37
Outram, Dorinda, 159, 160

Pan-German League, 31, 297
Papal Peace Note, 332, 333
Pappi, Franz Urban, 372–3, 374
Payer, Friedrich von, 333, 334
People's Conservative Association, 362
People's National Action, 360
People's National Reich Association, 362, 363, 364
Peters, Wilhelm, and Company, 189*n*
Petro, Patrice, 172
Pinkert, Alexander, 66
Plauen, 53
Poles: in Germany, discrimination against, 25, 32
Political culture: Wilhelmine period, 144
Political mobilization, 96, 130–1, 143, 155–6
Political parties: electoral shifts, 11, 379–83, 393, 402–3; fragmentation, 293–4; in Reichstag, 44–6; local organizations, 103; and middle class, 292–3; and regionalism, 140–1; and special interests, 404, 406, 409; supporters, social characteristics, 391, 393; Weimar period, 383–91, 401–3; Wilhelmine period, development of, 94–5; and youth, 348, 354–69. *See also* Electoral blocs
Politics: historical study of, 150; women, role of in, 150–1
Politics, local, 4, 99–102, 256; and clubs, 311; issues, 111; and social groups, 373; voter participation, 109–10; Weimar period, 288–9
Politics, mass, 1, 23, 177, 413, 415–16; emergence of, 23, 138, 141–2, 143, 292; and language, 161–4; and Social Democratic Party, 27–8, 29–30; and women, 162–4, 171–2
Politics, national, 143, 144, 256; growth of, 298, 304–5
Politics of notables, see *Honoratiorenpolitik*
Popp, Adelheid, 165, 171
Population shifts, 408
Populism, 18, 302–3, 304–5
Posadowsky-Wehner, Arthur, 40
Press: and Neukölln demonstration, 278–80
Preuss, Hugo, 8, 253, 256; "Draft of a Future Constitution of the Reich," 258–60
Preussische Jahrbücher, 89
Principle of differentiation, 260–1
Progressives, 97; and franchise reform, 83, 84, 107–8; and National Liberals, 105; post-World War I, 340; Reichstag majority coalition (1917), 333–5, 338; and Spring 1918 offensive, 335; Weimar coalition, 343; and World War I peace proposal, 332, 334. *See also* Left liberals, Progressive People's Party, Saxon Progressive Party
Progressive People's Party, 10, 79, 97; and franchise reform, 107. *See also* Progressives
Protestant National Federation of Female Youth, 204
Prussia: agrarian movement, 38; anti-Semitism, 38; antisocialism, 55; city councillor requirements, 109; division of, proposed, 259, 260; elections, 23; franchise, 39, 104, 107, 113, 134, 138, 334, 414; and German unification, 132, 134; Junkers, predominance of, 94; liberal

Index

parties in, 98, 116; school attendance, 183; voter participation, 110; and Weimar constitution, 259–60
Public opinion: influences on, 143

Quadragesimo Anno, 238

Radical Democratic Party, 366
Radical People's Party, 35–6, 46; in Saxony, 59, 61, 62, 79. *See also* Left liberals
Rathenau, Walther, 100–1, 294
Rationalism, 225
Red Young Front, 276*n*
Reformvereine, 66, 71. *See also* German Reform Party
Reich Association of Young Populists, 361, 364, 366–7
Reich Center for Homeland Services, 263
Reichsausschuss der Hochschulgruppen der Deutschen Volkspartei, see National Committee of University Groups of the German People's Party
Reichsbote, 268, 279–80
Reichsbund Deutscher Demokraitischer Jugendvereine, see National League of German Democratic Youth Clubs
Reichsbund Deutscher Demokratischer Studenten, see National League of German Democratic Students
Reichsbund staatsparteilicher Jugend, see National League of State Party Youth
Reichsgemeinschaft junger Volksparteiler (RjV), *see* Reich Association of Young Populists, 361
Reichstag: elections, 77–8; (1874), 22; elections (1878–1907), 22–25; elections (1887), 23; elections (1893), 72–3; elections (1898), 18, 30–41, 47; elections (1903), 30–41, 47; elections (1930), 324; political parties in, 44–6, 408
Reichsverband der deutschen Windthorstbünde, see National League of German Windthorst Leagues
Reichsverband der evangelischen Jungmännerbünde Deutschlands, see National League of Lutheran Young Men's Associations of Germany
Reichsverband der Jugendgruppen der Deutschnationalen Volkspartei, see National League of Youth Groups of the German National People's Party

Reichsverband der nationalliberalen Jugend, see National Association of National Liberal Youth
Reichs- und Freikonservative Partei, see Free Conservative Party
Reinhardt, Fritz: speakers' school, 322–4
Rheinbaben, Rochus von, 359–60
Rhineland: textile industry, 177, 180, 181, 188, 189, 195
Richter, Eugen, 35, 62
Riehl, Wilhelm Heinrich, 7–8, 136; *Naturgeschichte des deutschen Volkes*, 250–1, 252–3
Right, political, 3; and antisocialism, 51; electoral gains, 23; and party politics, 212–13; police treatment of, 279*n*; and youth, 356–8. *See also* Conservative Party
Ritter, Gerhard A., 125
Rohe, Karl, 124–5
Rokkan, Stein, 123, 129, 372, 374, 393
Roman Catholic Church: on birth control, 234–5. *See also* Catholics
Rosenberg, Hans, 145
Rostock, 104
Rote Fahne, 271–2, 274–5, 281
Ruhr: National Socialism in, 318
Rural population: and National Socialism, 240–1; and universal franchise, 133–4, 137
Rust, Bernhard, 239

Sächsische Fortschrittspartei, see Saxon Progressive Party
Sammlungspolitik, 30–1, 36, 38, 42
Saxon Progressive Party, 62
Saxony, 50; antisocialism in, 55, 66–70, 72, 74, 76; Reichstag by-election (1892), 72; (1895), 77–8 city councillor requirements, 109; elections (1891), 1; industry, 53; Landtag, Conservative caucus, 64, 98; Landtag elections, 1, 56, 58–62, 63, 65, 68–9, 74–5, 78–9; Landtag franchise law, 39, 68–9, 76, 79–80, 83–90, 414; Landtag franchise reform, effects, 90; liberal parties in, 62–3, 98; politics of, 4; Reichstag elections (1893), 72–3; socialism in, 52–5, 68–70
Scheidt, Johann, 190–1
Schieder, Theodor, 130
Schleswig: elections, 23
Schleswig-Holstein, 104, 135

Schmoller, Gustav von, 249
Schoenbaum, David, 225
Scholz, Ernst, 362-3
Schönefeld, 109
Schulthess' Europäischer Geschichtskalender, 18
Schwäbische Tageszeitung, 39
Scott, Joan, 159
Secularism, 225
Seeck, Hans von, 341
Severing, Carl, 234, 276
Sheehan, James, 250
Siegfried, André, 126-7
Singer, Paul, 109
Social Democratic Party of Germany, 4, 27-8, 32, 166, 168, 302, 372, 376, 377, 382, 402, 413; and birth control, 406n; and Catholic electorate, 384-6, 390; and Communist Party, 285, 388; electoral strategy, 46; and fascism, 121; and fleet issue, 32, 35; and franchise issue, 39, 75, 86-7, 108; and German Reform Party, 77; in local government, politics, 100, 103, 105, 108-9, 110, 112-13; and middle class, 338; Neukölln, 273; party structure, 95; Protestant membership, 387; Reichstag elections, 18, 23, 36-7, 38-9, 48, 55, 77, 408; rise of influence, 115; and role of women, 234; in Saxony, 50, 53-5, 65, 68, 69-70, 72, 73, 75, 78-9; songs, 271; supporters, social characteristics, 391, 393, 394; and tariff issue, 38-9; Weimar period, 378, 402-3, 404-5; Wilhelmine period, 19-20, 25, 27, 28, 29-30, 97, 98-9, 402; working class membership, 177, 269, 299; World War I, effects of, 340. *See also* Weimar Coalition
Social Democratic Textile Workers' Union, 179n
Socialism: and democracy, 254-5; Oldenburg, 289; Saxony, 52-5
Socialist Workers Party of Germany, 53
Socialists: discrimination against, 25, 45-6
Society for the Eastern Marches, 32
Songs: Neukölln demonstration, 276-7, 278; and politics, 275; prohibited, and police, 280, 281, 282-4
Soviet Union, 224, 277
Sozialdemokratische Partei Deutschlands (SPD), *see* Social Democratic Party
Sozialistische Arbeiterpartei Deutschlands, *see* Socialist Workers Party of Germany
Spartacists, 277; suppression of, 340

Special interests, *see* Middle class: special interests; Political parties: special interests
Spengler, Oswald, 343
"Stab in the back" legend, 342-3, 412
Städtetag, *see* Council of Cities
Staewen-Ordemann, Gertrud, 219-20
Stahlhelm, 297, 298, 299, 300, 303, 355, 369
Stapel, Wilhelm, 353
State, theory of the, 253
Stegewald, Hermann, 336
Stein, Freiherr vom, 101-2, 113
Stinnes, Hugo, 409
Stöcker, Adolf, 66-7, 72, 81
Strasser, Gregor, 316, 322, 325
Streicher, Julius, 316
Stresemann, Gustav, 63, 293, 297, 340, 359, 361, 369, 405, 409, 412; and compromise peace, 333
Stübel, Paul Alfred, 67
Stumm-Halberg, Karl Ferdinand von, Baron, 152
Stürmer, Michael, 131
Suval, Stanley, 119-24, 145, 399
Swabia, 25

Täglicher Anzeiger, 301
Tantzen, Theodor, 295
Tariffs: protective, 32, 36, 36-9, 41
Textile industry: discipline and gender, 187-94; division of labor, 180-3; employment of women, 177, 178-9; job longevity, 195-6; job training, 184-7; regulation of morality, 189-91; welfare activities, 191-3
Thun, Alfons, 189-90
Trade union movement, 94
Treaty of Brest-Litovsk, 335
Treaty of Versailles, 339
Treviranus, G. R., 362
Trier, 112

Ulich-Beil, Else, 209
Union of Independent Democrats, 364
United German Silk Weaving Mills, 185-6
Upper Franconia, 106
Urban population: and National Socialism, 240-1
Urbanization, 225-6, 253-4

Vaterland, 73, 76, 87
Verband für handwerksmässige und fachgewerbliche Ausbildung der Frau, *see* Asso-

ciation for the Training of Women in Crafts and Specialized Skills
Vereine, see Clubs, German
Vereinigten deutscher Seidenwebereien, see United German Silk Weaving Mills
Vereinigung Unabhängiger Demokraten, see Union of Independent Democrats, 364
Vienna: and Weimar constitution, 259
Völkerndorff, Otto von, 135
Volkskonservative Vereinigung (VKV), see People's Conservative Association
Volksnationale Reichsvereinigung (VNR), see People's National Reich Association
Volkszeitung, 119
Voluntary labor service, 217, 218
Vorwärts, 38
Voters: alienation of, Weimar period, 409–11, 413, 414–15; influences on, 126; participation, Wilhelmine period, 25–6, 109–10; and special interests, 412–13

Wagener, Hermann, 134
Wages: industrial, and gender, 179–80
Walker, Mack, 250
Watzdorf, Werner von, 74, 78
Weber, Max, 249, 258n
Wedding: "Bloody Mary" incident, 273
Weida, 317
Weimar, 109
Weimar Coalition (February 1919), 338–9, 343, 376–7
Weissner, Max, 352
Westarp, Kuno von, 293
Westphalia: textile industry, 177, 180, 188, 195
Wettstein-Adelt, Minna, 190
Wetzlar, 317
Wilhelm I, Kaiser, 134
Wilhelm II, Kaiser, 82, 144; abdication, 337
Wilson, Woodrow, 337, 339
Windthorst Leagues, 350, 354, 367, 368
Wirsitz-Schubin, 29
Wirtschaftspartei des deutschen Mittelstandes, see Business Party
Wirth, Joseph, 294–5
Women: and abortion legislation, 153, 154; admitted to legal profession, 233; associational life, 156; Catholic, mobilization, 155; discrimination, 227, 228–9; dormitories, textile mill, 191–2; economic opportunity, 228–9; education, Third Reich, 239–40; elected to office (1920), 153; exclusion, 158, 159, 223; fertility, control of, 223, 224, 229–30, 233–5, 237, 406n; franchise, 161, 162, 207, 223–4, 233, 400; impact of Depression on, 235–6; in historical accounts, 149–52; in industrial production, 158, 178–80, 185–7; influence on Civil Code (1900), 152; and job identification, 176–7, 194–7, 196–7; job longevity, 196; and mass culture, 171, 172; and mass politics, 5, 162–4; and melodrama, 166, 168; mobilization, 155–6, 160–2, 169, 231–2; and modernization, 226–9, 230; and National Socialism, 7, 155, 161, 205–6, 213, 224, 230–2, 235–6, 237, 242 3; political awareness, 204–5, 207; progress, role of in politics, 150–1, 171, 201–3, 211–16, 217–19, 220, 223; in rural areas, 227, 240–1; in textile industry, 180–1, 183–4, 185; in textile industry, discipline, 188–94; in textile industry, job training, 183–7, 192–3; Third Reich, 238–9; Weimar period, 6, 152–3; in youth organizations, 203–4, 217–18. See also Feminist movement; Gender
Work camp movement, 217
Work cultures, 197–8; female, 194–8
Worker's Sport Club Köpenick, 283
Working class, 5, 253–4, 373; associational life, 299; and Communist Party, 269; and job identification, 176–7; and Social Democratic Party, 269. See also Music: and working class movement
World War I, 344; armistice appeal, 337; German military strategy, 342; German offensive (1918), 335–6; German setbacks, 336–7; impact of, 411–12; peace proposals, 332
Württemberg, 39, 183
Würzburg, 112

Young Academic Club, 357
Young Center Clubs, 350
Young German League, 353
Young German Order, 215, 335, 359–62, 364, 366, 369
Young German Sisterhood, 215
Young German Youth, 355
Young Nation Corps, 209, 213, 216
Young National League, 209, 213, 353–4
Young Spartacus League, 267, 279
Youth: in politics, 201–2; organizations, 203; organizations, and politics, 206,

212, 216–17; political fragmentation, 220; and paramilitary right, 356–8
Youth Cadre of the German People's Party, 352–3
Youth League for a Greater Germany, 209, 214, 215
Youth movement, 10; Wilhelmine period, 347–8, 349–50, 361

Zabern Coalition, 332, 341
Zentralverband der katholischen Jungfrauenvereinigungen Deutschlands, see Central Federation of Catholic Young Women's Associations
Zille, Heinrich, 271–2n
Zwiespruch, Der, 209